EDUCATIONAL
RENEWAL

EDUCATIONAL RENEWAL

BETTER TEACHERS, BETTER SCHOOLS

JOHN I. GOODLAD

Jossey-Bass Publishers · San Francisco

The epigraph on p. 96 is from the book *Immortality* by Milan Kundera, Copyright © 1991 Grove Press. Used with permission of Grove/Atlantic Monthly Press.

The quotation from Kenneth Sirotnik's article reprinted on pp. 109–113 is from K. A. Sirotnik, "Making School-University Partnerships Work," *Metropolitan Universities,* 1991, *2*(1), 19–23. Reprinted with permission. Copyright © Metropolitan Universities.

For sales outside the United States, contact Maxwell Macmillan International Publishing Group, 866 Third Avenue, New York, New York 10022.

Manufactured in the United States of America. Nearly all Jossey-Bass books and jackets are printed on recycled paper that contains at least 50 percent recycled waste, including 10 percent postconsumer waste. Many of our materials are also printed with vegetable-based ink; during the printing process these inks emit fewer volatile organic compounds (VOCs) than petroleum-based inks. VOCs contribute to the formation of smog.

Library of Congress Cataloging-in-Publication Data

Goodlad, John I.
   Educational renewal : better teachers, better schools / John I. Goodlad.
      p.   cm.
   "A joint publication in the Jossey-Bass education series and the Jossey-Bass higher and adult education series."
   Includes bibliographical references and index.
   ISBN 1-55542-631-X
   1. Teachers—Training of—United States.   2. Education—Study and teaching (Higher)—United States.   3. Education—Study and teaching (Higher)—United States—Curricula.   I. Title.   II. Series: Jossey-Bass education series.   III. Series: Jossey-Bass higher and adult education series.
LB1715.G52   1994
370.71'0973—dc20   93-40695
                                                                        CIP

FIRST EDITION
HB Printing   10 9 8 7 6 5 4 3 2 1   *Code 9428*

A joint publication in

The Jossey-Bass
Education Series
and
The Jossey-Bass
Higher and Adult Education Series

Contents

Preface

Book manuscripts have a way of taking on a life of their own, often departing markedly from the authors' initial intentions as they progress. My long-time good friend and professional colleague the late Larry Cremin once remarked that only a fool eschews the preparation of an outline, but only a greater fool sticks with it. The question of how far one dare depart from that outline before entering the domain of foolhardiness remains, however.

I *did* prepare an outline — one that faded increasingly into fuzziness after the fourth chapter. There were several major changes in the titles and contents of the later chapters early on, and the number of chapters jumped around from nine to eleven, back to nine, and later to eight. But I was well into Chapter Seven before the nature of Chapter Eight began to take shape in my mind. Halfway through Chapter Seven, I realized how much the orientation of the book had changed — enough, in fact, to require scrapping the title and making appropriate revisions earlier on in the manuscript.

Purpose

The book started with a relatively simple purpose: to answer the questions most often raised about the trilogy published in 1990 based on the rather comprehensive inquiry into the education of educators that several colleagues and I had conducted over several immediately preceding years — *Places Where Teachers Are Taught, The Moral Dimensions of Teaching,* and *Teachers for Our*

Nation's Schools. The first two of these, edited by Roger Soder, Kenneth A. Sirotnik, and me, brought together a fine group of authors to expound essentially historical and philosophical aspects. The third represented my effort to make sense out of the enormous body of data assembled by staff members of the Center for Educational Renewal at the University of Washington. Without the technical reports prepared by these colleagues, which collated data gleaned from documents, questionnaires, and interviews pertaining to a representative sample of teacher-preparing institutions, my task would have been impossible.

As it was, the need to include and document the very large array of findings to the degree possible curtailed analysis and discussion. Readers were left with questions for which they wanted expanded responses. Among these were many addressed to my treatment of centers of pedagogy, fleshed out considerably (but apparently not enough) in Chapter Nine of *Teachers for Our Nation's Schools.* Consequently, I focused on these and so titled the anticipated book *Centers of Pedagogy*—until halfway through Chapter Seven. How far I strayed from (and expanded beyond) that theme becomes apparent: it is not even the subtitle of this book.

The large body of data and the concept of a natural connection between good teachers and good schools that drove the writing of *Teachers for Our Nations' Schools* tended to push aside the larger context that must come into play if we are to have significant educational renewal. The discussion of this larger context was the part of the whole requiring expansion—the part, I realized in retrospect, that so many of the questions addressed. For example, What must go on in schools for them to participate productively in teacher education? What goes on in the rest of a large school or college of education when part of it is carved out to become part of a center of pedagogy? In your emphasis on the importance of the arts and sciences departments, surely you do not mean for the whole of undergraduate education to be directed specifically to what teaching in schools requires? Are you suggesting a role for teachers as professionals similar to that of lawyers and doctors? Where do parents and the home get into the act? How do your recommendations connect with licensing, certifying, and accrediting? And what is simultaneous educational renewal anyway?

Of course, there were many questions directed specifically to the concept of a center of pedagogy, too. Why have one? What is it, and what is it for? Who participates as its faculty? Just how protected are its borders to be? What are to be the rewards for those who participate? How do partner or professional development schools fit into the scheme? These are the kinds of questions I set out initially to answer.

Contents

My original intent carried me well into Chapter Four, as I said. This was the chapter that brought me specifically into multiple contextual relationships. Up to this point, the work had not been much fun (though there should be a strong element of fun in all work). I had worked and reworked, in my mind and in writing, much of the contents. There was not enough new to be stimulating, and this showed through in the writing. (I have something to say shortly about the substantial revision that came later.)

The first four chapters, then, stayed quite close to the original intent: to respond to questions such as those above directed to the nature and design of centers of pedagogy. These questions represent a natural extension and expansion of the connecting of teacher education and schools to which a substantial part of *Teachers for Our Nation's Schools* is devoted. Chapter Four, on school-university partnerships and partner schools (a recurring theme for me) delved into territory mentioned but scarcely touched in *Teachers for Our Nation's Schools*. It was also a significant turning point in determining what Chapter Seven, in particular, was to become. Chapters Five and Six turned inward again to the curriculum issues that centers of pedagogy inevitably face and must resolve in program development.

Chapters One through Six appeared to me, upon my completion of a draft, to have a certain integrity in themselves in constituting a package dealing with most of the questions about centers of pedagogy that we had been asked and several going beyond. And so I distributed them to my colleagues in the Center for Educational Renewal and the Institute for Educational Inquiry and to several other individuals, with an invitation to present criticism in general and to respond to several questions. I went on to the writing of Chapter Seven, experiencing four incredibly frustrating starts.

The volume and nature of the responses from colleagues turned the manuscript around and took me from my frustrations with Chapter Seven to a substantial revision of Chapters One through Six. Only about half of the first draft survived. And the resulting rethinking and rewriting revealed to me what Chapter Seven should be.

The first six chapters still stand as an exposition of centers of pedagogy in their role of effecting the simultaneous renewal of schools and the preparation programs of those who are their primary stewards. But what the writing of these chapters so clearly revealed to me is the fact that what the best teachers can do is limited by the context in which and by which much of the culture of schools is shaped — circumstances that lie largely beyond their making and remedying. And so, in Chapter Seven, I addressed the inquiry processes of schools through which teachers can make them good. But for schools to become *very* good, collaboration among agencies and reasoned discourse must become characteristic of communities. After all, we have traditions that speak to the dependence of our democracy on an educated citizenry.

The scope of the book clearly had expanded beyond my initial intent. The title then changed from *Centers of Pedagogy* to the present one, *Educational Renewal: Better Teachers, Better Schools*. Nonetheless, the center of pedagogy still serves as a major organizing theme of the book.

I use Chapter Eight as a forum for illustrating that the major sets of conditions embraced by the postulates (explicated in Chapter Three) are not unrealistic and unattainable. The fifteen settings currently constituting the National Network for Educational Renewal (NNER), coordinated by the Center for Educational Renewal, are several years into the process of establishing them. Progress to date is very encouraging. I draw from the NNER settings examples of this progress as a way of revisiting the themes of the preceding chapters: from steps toward creating new settings, to heartening examples of commitment and leadership, to exemplary curriculum development, to the establishment of school-university partnerships, to the transformation of school and university cultures, to collaboration involving agencies beyond schools and universities, to influences on state policies. Chapter Eight, then, is a summary of the whole that takes us from conceptualization to implementation.

Some Matters of Style

I have taken steps to make what follows user-friendly. First, I have endeavored to write in as straightforward a style as possible, eschewing professional jargon. Second, I have refrained from the scholarly custom of supporting generalizations with extensive footnoting of references, even when such references are readily available. Third, I have not cited bibliographic information when a reference is virtually in the public domain (for example, *Walden Two*). Fourth, in referring to several articles or books bearing together on a topic, I have clustered these in a single citation. And fifth, I have placed all the reference notes at the end of the book, clustered by chapters. My intent is to reach a broad audience interested in educational improvement that includes professional practitioners and researchers.

Seattle, Washington John I. Goodlad
December 1993

Acknowledgments

Two sources of support for the writing of this book warrant very special recognition. The launching of the work of the Institute for Educational Inquiry in 1992, referred to quite often in what follows, was made possible by grants from philanthropic foundations. One of these, the Merck Family Fund, recognized the importance of accompanying an initiative in educational renewal with solid conceptual underpinnings. Consequently, the Institute has been able to look beyond the recommendations for the improvement of teacher education emerging from the research of the Center for Educational Renewal. The grant from the Merck Family Fund has supported, for example, the Work in Progress series of papers, which endeavors to advance understanding of the moral educative mission to which both the Center and the Institute are committed. Similarly, the grant from the Fund made it possible to deploy resources in such a way that I could find the discretionary time the writing of this book has required. My colleagues and I extend thanks and appreciation to the trustees of the Merck Family Fund.

Just as I was beginning to think seriously about writing this book, I received an invitation that resulted in a period of residency at the Hoover Institution as a Distinguished Visiting Scholar in Educational Policy. The seclusion and support services there provided the opportunity to write first drafts of four of the eight chapters. I am grateful to Lewis B. Stuart of the Four Square Foundation for making this possible.

In the Preface, I referred to sending the initial six chapters to colleagues for comment. The responses, some of them quite detailed, were very helpful, and my thanks go to everyone who responded. All but Hal Lawson, a professor at Miami University in Oxford, Ohio, are connected with the Center or the Institute in research or consulting capacities. Hal was, during 1992–93, a leadership associate in the Institute. He looked at the manuscript from the perspective of a "user" in a member setting of the National Network for Educational Renewal. His suggestions resulted in substantial changes in Chapter One, in particular.

Senior associate Richard Clark's critique produced revisions in all six chapters and sent me back to the writing table to clarify distinctions among centers of pedagogy, school-university partnerships, and partner schools. Senior associate Phyllis Edmundson (of Boise State University) had been a member of the earlier teacher education research team. Her suggestions were particularly helpful in clarifying the implications of some of our research findings for implementing the recommendations. Senior associate Robert Egbert (of the University of Nebraska) bored into the two curriculum chapters (Five and Six), offering suggestions that helped to clear up ambiguities in the initial draft. Senior associate Calvin Frazier (then of the University of Denver) raised questions that caused me to do some rewriting with the interests of policymakers in mind. Senior associate Wilma Smith made suggestions directed particularly to the practical problems being confronted in settings of the National Network for Educational Renewal and the fundamental concepts being developed in the Institute's Leadership Program, which she directs. Research assistants Judy Ellsworth (of the University of Wyoming) and Jianping Shen (of the Center for Educational Renewal) provided a joint critique that helped me clarify for the reader some writing that otherwise would have had only in-house meaning. Researcher Tim McMannon (of the Institute for Educational Inquiry) proved to be a reliable check on the historical perspective and details that almost always enter into my work.

I always count on Roger Soder (associate director of the

Center and vice president of the Institute) for picking up unintended nuances and obscure meanings. This he did, one more time. And my long-time colleague and senior associate of the institute, Kenneth Sirotnik, was always there when needed for sage advice. David Imig, executive director of the American Association of Colleges for Teacher Education, aware of what I was trying to do, sent helpful suggestions and materials. Colleagues in the settings of the National Network for Educational Renewal responded quickly to our request for any additional documents that might help me with the contents of Chapter Eight. Thanks go to Center staff member Joan Waiss for sorting through these and arranging selections to ease my task of choosing examples to illustrate progress with the agenda of renewal.

Paula McMannon of the Center and the Institute was "chief worrier" for this manuscript throughout. This involved much more than can be summarized here—especially since a good deal of what she did is undoubtedly unknown to me! Regarding the manuscript itself, her questions produced changes, and she probably made some changes on her own to save me from embarrassment over my silliest mistakes.

The able people at Jossey-Bass Publishers were as helpful and friendly as usual. Once again, I was blessed with incredibly good editing. It is a pleasure to work with them.

Thank you all, good friends and colleagues. Paying attention to your many suggestions was a bit of a pain, but the manuscript is better for them. I should say that I take full responsibility for what I did with them, but you are not off the hook entirely.

My wife, Len (known to our friends as Lynn), provided, as always, the support that sustained bouts of writing require. And as usual, the writing messed up some of those precious Northwest summer days that might have been well spent doing other things. However, the timeline for this book was shorter and the inconveniences somewhat less than normal. For this small mercy, we are both grateful.

J.I.G.

The Author

JOHN I. GOODLAD is professor emeritus of the University of California, Los Angeles, and the University of Washington. Currently, he is director of the Center for Educational Renewal at the latter institution and president of the Institute for Educational Inquiry in Seattle. His B.A. and M.A. degrees are from the University of British Columbia, and his Ph.D. is from the University of Chicago, where he was a professor for some years. He holds honorary degrees from fourteen colleges and universities in Canada and the United States.

Much of what Goodlad has learned over more than fifty years of involvement with schooling and higher education is expressed in some twenty-five books and hundreds of chapters and articles. Several of his books have been translated into languages such as French, Hebrew, Italian, and Japanese, and several have received outstanding-book-of-the-year awards from professional organizations. In 1993, he received the American Educational Research Association Award for Outstanding Contributions to Educational Research.

At present, Goodlad directs through the National Network for Educational Renewal a nationwide initiative in the simultaneous renewal of schooling and the education of educators based on previous research. The research on schools and teacher education is reported in his *A Place Called School* (1984) and the trilogy published in 1990: *The Moral Dimensions of Teaching* and *Places Where Teachers Are Taught* (both edited by J. I. Goodlad,

R. Soder, and K. A. Sirotnik) and his *Teachers for Our Nation's Schools*. This book, *Educational Renewal: Better Teachers, Better Schools,* extends some of the ideas regarding educational improvement contained in the earlier publications and reports ongoing progress with these ideas in the settings constituting the National Network for Educational Renewal.

EDUCATIONAL
RENEWAL

1

New Settings

Creating a setting is one of man's most absorbing experiences,
compounded as it is of dreams, hopes, effort and thought.[1]
— Seymour B. Sarason

A remarkable thing happened on the way to the 1990s. An era of national attention to the system of schooling in the United States of America was sustained over three presidencies into a second decade. This longevity defied predictions and the odds.

During this period, hundreds of commission reports and dozens of books were directed to school reform, but only a few to teacher education. Over successive eras of educational reform throughout the twentieth century, the reform of schools and the reform of teacher education have rarely been connected. The sharp break with the past that occurred in the early years of the 1990s was the growing realization of the need for close connectedness. We are not likely to have good schools without a continuing supply of excellent teachers. Nor are we likely to have excellent teachers unless they are immersed in exemplary schools for significant portions of their induction into teaching.

Herein lies a dilemma. What comes first, good schools or good teacher education programs? The answer is that both must come together. There are not now the thousands of good schools needed for the internships of tens of thousands of future teachers. The long-term solution — unfortunately, there is no quick one — is to renew the two together. There must be a

1

continuous process of educational renewal in which colleges and universities, the traditional producers of teachers, join schools, the recipients of the products, as equal partners in the simultaneous renewal of schooling and the education of educators. The sooner the process begins, the sooner we will have good schools.

This book is about such beginnings. They involve the creation and nurturing of new settings. These new settings may take a variety of forms, but all require certain essential conditions. I have chosen in what follows to describe a prototype and have named it a *center of pedagogy*. It necessarily embraces the renewal of both schools and university programs for the education of educators. But I have chosen deliberately to emphasize the more neglected, higher education ingredient and do not get seriously to the partnership with schools until Chapter Four. This is in part because, up to now, the schools have been the primary focus in educational renewal and in part because I believe the higher education partner to be the one requiring the most coaxing and nurturing. The schools are more accustomed to being called upon to change.

It is necessary to remind the reader here (and several times subsequently) that my use of the words "teacher education" involves a unique twist away from convention. The conventional interpretation involves something performed on college and university campuses with a stint of student teaching tacked on. But I use "teacher education" to convey something done together by schools and colleges or universities. Unlike the traditional college or school of education, a center of pedagogy embraces elementary and secondary schools, much as a school of medicine embraces a teaching hospital (or several). Without partner or teaching schools, teacher education programs are deficient and disabled. Unless renewal is built into the functioning of all of the parts, the whole will inevitably malfunction.

A center of pedagogy is intended to bring to the fore the centrality and the clarity of the teacher education mission in a democratic society. It is a setting that brings together and blends harmoniously and coherently the three essential ingredients of a teacher's education: general, liberal education; the study of educational practices; and the guided exercise of the art, science, and skill of teaching. This chapter addresses two questions in tandem: What is a center of pedagogy, and why have one?

Context and General Rationale

John Dewey, who carried the title "head professor of philosophy and pedagogy," argued passionately a century ago for a department of pedagogy at the University of Chicago. He viewed the very foundations of our entire primary and secondary educational system as "being left unduly to the mercy of accident, caprice, routine or useless experiment from lack of scientific training" (of the teachers). "The first University to undertake this work will, in my judgment, secure the recognition, and, indeed, the leadership of the educational forces of the country."[2]

Although Dewey emphasized the theoretical grounding of such a department, the "nerve of the whole scheme" was to be the extension of the laboratory school from its then primary years to embrace all the years up to college. Without such, he wrote, "the theoretical work partakes of a farce and imposture — it is like professing to give thorough training in a science and then neglecting to provide a laboratory for faculty and students to work in." The ultimate mission was to provide children with "as nearly as possible an ideal education."[3]

In the Preface, I state that this book picks up where *Teachers for Our Nation's Schools* (particularly Chapter Nine) left off. The research on which that book is based revealed no university achieving national recognition because of its department of pedagogy (in fact, *no* departments of pedagogy); it found that the few remaining laboratory schools were only loosely linked to schools, colleges, and departments of education (SCDEs); and it discovered little to no mission of a teacher education enterprise tied to the role of schools in a democratic society. Were John Dewey to awake from his several decades of slumber, he might well ponder the nonfulfillment of his vision. And so might we all.

Teachers for Our Nation's Schools and one of its two companion volumes in particular, *The Moral Dimensions of Teaching,* attempted to move to the forefront of educational reform nationwide attention to these and other omissions. The most critically important omission is a vision that encompasses a good and just society, the centrality of education to the renewal of that society, the role of schools bringing this education equitably to all, and the kind of preparation teachers require for their stewardship of the nation's schools. This is the vision that provides the moral grounding of the teacher education mission and gives direction to those teachers of teachers responsible for designing coherent programs for the education of educators.

Prior to studying a representative sample of teacher-preparing settings, my colleagues and I perused reports advocating reform in either schooling or teacher education from just before the years of Dewey's appeal for a department of pedagogy to the present, and we examined documents describing extant teacher education programs in colleges and universities. In the latter group, we found no compelling missions for teacher education; indeed, except in the instances of a few church-related institutions, we found no compelling missions for higher education. And in the reform reports, we found little to no joining of schooling and teacher education, whether in mission or programmatic connecting.[4]

We found ourselves pushed toward inquiry not anticipated—the formulation of a mission for teacher education. Guided by a desire to be both comprehensive and minimalistic, we came up with four major curricular themes, each transfused with and transcended by moral dimensions and implications. Two of these components—enculturating the young in a social and political democracy and providing access to the knowledge effective humans require—arise out of the educational functions assigned to our schools. The other two—teaching in a nurturing way and exercising moral stewardship of schools—are what teachers must do exceedingly well. Moral considerations give dimensionality and coherence to the whole (see Figure 1.1); they are the substance of teacher education programs and the basis of a teaching profession.

Little in the documents we studied in 1985 and later encouraged us to believe that ongoing teacher education in the United States reflected our vision of what should be. We feared

Figure 1.1. The Mission of Teacher Education in a Center of Pedagogy
Geared to the Mission of Schooling in a Democratic Society.

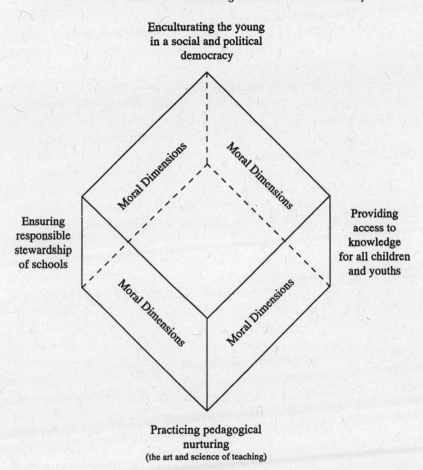

Enculturating the young
in a social and political
democracy

Moral Dimensions

Moral Dimensions

Ensuring
responsible
stewardship
of schools

Providing
access to
knowledge
for all children
and youths

Moral Dimensions

Moral Dimensions

Practicing pedagogical
nurturing
(the art and science of teaching)

the general nonexistence of the mission (or an equally comprehensive alternative) and the conditions necessary to its fulfillment. Our intensive inquiry into places where teachers are
taught during 1987 and 1988 confirmed these fears. Awaken-
ing today and inquiring as we did, Dewey probably would conclude what he concluded a century ago: the foundations of our
primary and secondary educational system are being left unduly

to the mercy of accident, caprice, routine, and experiment (both useful and not).

The conceptual work that preceded data gathering added extensive detail to the mission model of Figure 1.1. We addressed conditions we believed would characterize serious efforts to move toward that model with tangible success. These ranged from institutional commitment, to financial resources, to the nature of the student body and faculty, to laboratory or "teaching" schools, to curricular designs, to supportive state policies. This line of reasoning produced twenty-two interrelated sets of conditions, which we ultimately refined into nineteen postulates. From these, we deduced most of the questions that guided our research—the examination of the many documents provided by the settings studied, the preparation of questionnaires for students and faculty members, and the conduct of approximately 1,800 hours of interviews.

Again, the findings paralleled those with respect to mission. Only bits and pieces of the coherent totality we deemed essential were in place. Just as Abraham Flexner had found missing the optimal conditions of medical education in 1910,[5] we found missing those conditions our several years of inquiry had pushed to the forefront as sensible, reasonable, and basic to the health of settings committed to the education of educators. A few sites showcased for us pieces of the whole that smacked of solid philosophical grounding. But only rarely did we find evidence of close connections between the piece controlled by the SCDE and the necessary subject concentrations controlled by the arts and sciences. And the linkages to the schools for student teaching, which most of the people in our research sample (and almost everyone else who has studied teacher education) ranked very high in importance, ranged from casual to dissonant. The dissonance took the form primarily of contradictions in both the intent and the conduct of university-based and school-based practices. We are not, my colleagues and I concluded, producing in anything close to adequate numbers the well-prepared teachers our children deserve.

Our recommendations, in the form of the nineteen postulates espousing necessary conditions to be put in place, did not at first hit a responsive note. That kind of advocacy is common neither to the field of education nor to educational reform. Some critics looked for empirical "proof" of what are essentially normative statements, argued as one argues truth, beauty, and justice. Our data gathering was not to test postulates but to weigh evidence as to the presence or absence of the conditions embedded in them. We looked for well-designed, well-constructed houses of teacher education and found roofs missing, doors hanging loose, and windows broken. What bothered us most was that teacher educators were insufficiently aware of things amiss and devoted insufficient energy to making them right. There was a considerable degree of weariness and wariness about launching one more round of curriculum reform likely to be aborted by commission reports and legislative action to change licensure requirements in the state.

Some critics viewed the postulates as a clutch of discrete recommendations, each to be weighed on its individual merits. There is nothing unusual about this reaction. Most reform reports come out with recommendations of different kinds and at various levels of generality. Some catch attention; some do not. We sought, however, to provide a comprehensive set of interrelated conditions that, taken together, address the array of circumstances that define both the supportive context and the nature of a healthy teacher education enterprise. The removal of any one would leave missing a necessary component and weaken the whole.

One question goes to the very heart of our work: Are the conditions embedded in the postulates *necessary*? Or, stated differently, how reasonable is the line of argument in the postulates? In pondering that issue, it is useful to turn to Margret Buchmann's discussion of what she refers to as "authorized" convictions: "In convictions, the measure of authority is reasonableness. Reasonableness involves more than marshalling the facts. Where they are relevant and available, data constitute part of an array of good reasons, while concepts, norms and the other (substantive and formal) characteristics of what people consider a good case account for the rest."[6] My colleagues and I believe that the inquiry producing the postulates makes of them authorized convictions. And the care that went into the subsequent research gives strong support to our conclusions regarding widespread absence of the conditions prescribed by the postulates as necessary to the good health of teacher education and, as a consequence, the schools.

Faced with trying to respond to the above issues and to not unexpected misunderstandings, we were delighted to discover an effective answer in the comments of a charismatic panelist at a statewide conference in South Carolina. Using the postulates as his reference points, he simply described in precisely opposite statements what he called the existing paradigm of teacher education: the lack of mission, the absence of faculty rewards for preparing teachers, unprotected budgets, misguided regulatory intrusions, and more.[7] His message struck home. Teacher education has been a neglected, often maligned, endeavor; positives must replace the negatives.

Since then, my colleague Roger Soder has refined this response. In *Teachers for Our Nation's Schools,* Postulate One is stated as follows: *Programs for the education of the nation's educators must be viewed by institutions offering them as a major responsibility to society and be adequately supported and promoted and vigorously advanced by the institution's top leadership.* Roger Soder rewords the statement to say that it does not matter whether the institution and its top leadership value the teacher education program and then, warming to his subject, goes on to say, "In fact, it doesn't matter whether the president states a personal desire to get rid of it." By the time he has savaged a few of the postulates in this manner, most people comprehend the message we are endeavoring to convey.

The question that now arises pertains to the kind of structure required to address the mission and advance the educational renewal embedded in the postulates. In *Teachers for Our Nation's Schools,* I proposed a center of pedagogy; in Chapter Nine, I posed the beginnings of one such center at the mythical Northern State University. I chose to make it part of the college of education there, but there are other defensible alternatives. In choosing to name it the Smith Center of Pedagogy, I sought to recognize the contribution in this area of the late

B. Othanel Smith. Like Dewey, he sought to integrate theory and practice and so paid much attention to schools as the laboratories in which the two would be productively joined.[8] It is the general neglect of the school-based component that led Seymour Sarason and his colleagues to label teacher education an unstudied problem.[9]

In the postulates and in that brief sketch of Northern State, the collaboration and integration of the arts and sciences, SCDEs, and schools as equal partners are a necessary condition. Figure 1.2 shows the intersection of all three in the shaded square. All three perform other functions and have other business to attend to. But when we come to consider the good health of teacher education, the ecosystem is comprised of all three components. There is no one model for the coming together; but come together they must.

Most of what follows employs the center of pedagogy as a vehicle for moving forward with the concepts and logistics of this tripartite collaboration. The intent is not to derive *the* model but to provoke creativity and action in moving from old to new paradigms. I have chosen to begin with and focus on what is still the general route producing most of our teachers: the four-

Figure 1.2. Major Collaborators in a Center of Pedagogy.

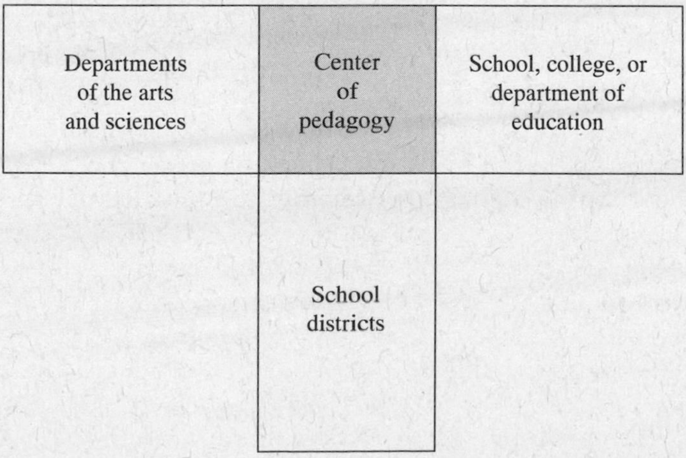

Departments of the arts and sciences	Center of pedagogy	School, college, or department of education
	School districts	

year undergraduate curriculum of general and special studies
interspersed with essentially required courses in education and
student teaching. However, because our research revealed so
many problems with the actual conduct of this pattern, I use
it merely as a base from which to diverge markedly (one of
several major departures being to add a fifth year composed
primarily of internships and reflective seminars).

By choosing this common pattern, I am virtually pushed
into considering most of the problems and issues that efforts to
mount alternative routes with equal attention to quality would
confront. I have chosen postbaccalaureate programs for persons
leaving other careers as a secondary focus. Much of what follows has been motivated by questions commonly asked by educators joined with us or otherwise interested in our work.

The Concept

A center of pedagogy is both a concept and a setting. As a concept, it brings together simultaneously and integratively the commonly scattered pieces of the teacher education enterprise and
embeds them in reflective attention to the art and science of
teaching. A center of pedagogy *could* be named a center of teacher
education, of course. But then the concept's implementation
might (and probably would) embrace only what the name implies — the conduct of teacher education programs devoid of or
apart from inquiry into pedagogy. The common neglect of such
inquiry has contributed to the low status of teacher education
and, to a considerable degree, of teaching itself. Thus I choose
to align with what John Dewey and B. Othanel Smith were seeking in their stress on pedagogy. The term *center of pedagogy* con-
notes for me an inquiring setting for the education of educators
that embraces schools and universities.

Unfortunately, teacher education has come to be associated only with training and the mechanistic ways we teach dogs,
horses, and humans to perform certain routinized tasks. This
is largely because we have reduced our view of education to such.
But teaching the young in schools *must not* be perceived this way.
The education teachers receive should cause them to reject out

of hand the intellectual isolation in school settings so tellingly described by Dan Lortie in *Schoolteacher*. Philip Jackson's *Life in Classrooms* reminds us of the hundreds of decisions affecting the lives of children that each teacher makes each day.[10] There is no way for *training* alone to prepare for these, let alone for the moral perspective that teaching in schools requires. But there are very fundamental ways to educate teachers so that they do more than cope with school and classroom exigencies — so that, cumulatively, their daily decisions shape the character, sensitivities, and lifelong effectiveness of their students. Yes, teachers require training, but they also need *education,* in the very best sense of the word.

How humans learn and how they can best be taught are subjects of great importance and profound complexity. For teacher education programs not to be connected with ongoing inquiry into these domains is to guarantee their mediocrity and inadequacy. The best assurance of this connection is for teacher education to be conducted in centers of inquiry focused on this learning and teaching — that is, in centers of pedagogy where the art and science of teaching are brought to bear on the education of educators and where the *whole* is the subject of continuous inquiry. Only then will professional programs avoid stagnation and be renewed. In concept, then, a center of pedagogy is both systemic and dynamic. It envisions faculty members representing the necessary components of coherent teacher education programs coming together in informed dialogue to sustain renewal — their own and their programs'. In so doing, they demonstrate to their students (and ideally involve them in) the very processes of reflective renewal desired in individual teachers and schools. Without this modeling, teachers of teachers run the danger of conveying that tiresome message, Do as I say, not as I do.

But why centers of pedagogy at all? My colleagues and I have been told that we do not need them; we already have the equivalent in schools and colleges of education. We are not locked into the notion that what we propose for centers of pedagogy cannot be achieved in some other organizational context, including SCDEs. After all, schools and colleges of education

emerged out of a teacher education commitment and function
in the first place. But what has transpired since, especially in
the large, multipurpose schools of education and their university context, has served the cause of teacher education poorly.
To serve it well calls for profound shifts in the orientation and
conduct of these schools.

We did not study SCDEs as our central focus. However,
we learned a good deal about them in the course of inquiring
into their role in the education of educators. This inquiry,
together with decades of close association with them, leads me
to the conclusion that something equivalent to a center of pedagogy is essential to the well-being of teacher education. It may
well be essential to the future health of any given school or college of education, too, but this is another issue and brings with
it other kinds of problems. Important things go on in schools
and colleges of education that have little or nothing to do with
teacher education. Many of the people involved in these other
things have more power and more to say regarding whether and
how teacher education shall be conducted than people with much
greater involvement and a greater stake in the enterprise have.
Professors not accountable for teacher education vote and make
policy regarding its conduct. With few exceptions, this situation is not a healthy one for teacher education.

The concept of a center of pedagogy depicted in Figure 1.2
transcends the long-standing convention of responsibility for
teacher education centered in SCDEs. Yet broad acceptance of
the convention inhibits our thinking regarding other alternatives. In Chapter Nine of *Teachers for Our Nation's Schools,* I chose
to stay close to convention and so placed the Smith Center of
Pedagogy squarely in the College of Education under Dean
Harriet Bryan's administration. To do otherwise, I reasoned,
called for more argument and detail than the concluding chapter of an already long manuscript warranted. Even situated
within the norm, however, the concept of a center of pedagogy
proved controversial and aroused some resistance.

The conceptualization breaking most with convention
places the center of pedagogy in some intermediate position between university and school district—part of both but creature

of neither. Robert M. Hutchins pushed the professional schools to the periphery of the campus in his conception of the ideal university, because he viewed so much of their work as vocational and technical rather than fundamentally intellectual.[11] Although he had the health of the university more in mind than that of professional schools, his proposal might have favored the latter in any case — and indeed, the strong professional schools have effected considerable separation. Flexner, on the other hand, strongly persuaded by the low educational level of prospective doctors and their shoddy training, sought to bring medical education, including "educational control" of the teaching hospitals, centrally into the university. The degree to which the research professor has risen in status and the clinical professor/ practitioner has fallen bespeaks the power of socialization into the university. This shift is not quite what Flexner had in mind. He probably would have joined in the several major efforts of later reformers in medical education to seek a balance.

I have chosen in what follows to conceive of a center of pedagogy that encompasses within its borders faculty members from the three entities portrayed in Figure 1.2. These borders provide an organizational identity that is essential to the well-being of all institutions. But they are necessarily permeable, in that this entity requires more resources, especially intellectual, than are included within its borders — resources that come primarily from the collaborating host university and school districts. I view this organizational identity as evolutionary, beginning close to the conventional university context and reaching out, but moving over the years to the intermediate position between university and school district mentioned earlier.

Although I took what appeared to be the easier of the two most obvious alternative routes in placing the Smith Center in Northern State's College of Education, this may not be in the long run either the easier or the better. Difficult problems and difficult decisions clutter both routes. If I were a president or provost confronting the decision and deeply committed to the health of teacher education, I would want to examine an array of considerations. If I were an education dean or chair, it would be difficult for me not to favor keeping the center within the existing school or department, but I would like to be objective enough to consider other possibilities. The proper criterion is not the welfare of existing organizational arrangements but the future vitality of teacher education. The mission and necessary conditions embedded in the postulates remain the same, regardless of structural differences and variations in lines of authority.

Does a center of pedagogy include programs for the preparation of school administrators? Not necessarily. I believe that programs for the preparation of teachers and principals, both responsible for the stewardship of individual schools, should have both common elements and separate identities, and they should be closely linked. Consequently, I recommend that both be lodged in a center of pedagogy and discuss possibilities for this later. In concept, I include the preparation of school superintendents, *but not at the outset*. There are enough problems peculiar to this area to warrant separate renewal efforts initially. However, once this field gets beyond its fascination with the corporate world and large-scale management issues and begins to focus on the role of school superintendents in creating educative communities, closer integration will come to make sense and perhaps be natural rather than forced. Indeed, if schools of education, in the restructuring now being contemplated and in some settings already begun, should decide to organize themselves around the function of educating educators, with all else connected to and supportive of professional preparation programs, they could become over time centers of pedagogy writ large and still carry the designation "school or college of education."

Currently, there is commendable interest among deans of education and members of their faculties in rethinking the mission, functions, and programs of their schools and colleges. In the mid 1980s, the initial small group of deans and provosts who came together as the Holmes Group raised important questions about the proper role of these schools, and indeed their universities, in the ongoing school reform movement. Greater attention to teacher education tied closely to professional development schools emerged as a priority. The momentum generated has led to introspection regarding schools and colleges of education in toto. The result should be a clearer perspective regarding the place of teacher education both in and outside of them.

This is a worthy effort. In the long run, it could be highly beneficial to teacher education, but there is no way of predicting the extent of the effect. If the recommendations emerging are modest, they will benefit teacher education very little. If they are sweeping and radical, they will take a long time to implement in practice; consequently, changes in teacher education will be slow in coming. The reform of teacher education is already piggybacking on the reform of schooling, however, and need not await the redesign of schools of education. Indeed, the attention by schools of education to the renewal of teacher education may be one of the most promising avenues to their own renewal.

There will be readers who believe passionately that the right and proper journey is to redesign SCDEs with accompanying high attention to righting the neglect of teacher education. I respect such a belief and commend the accompanying commitment. I trust that we shall come to share a conviction: the malaise this nation is beginning to sense is a correlate of shameful neglect of the educational ecology of which teacher education and schools are critically important parts.

In concept, a center of pedagogy is both old and new. It is old in the sense that the normal schools in Massachusetts were created for the purpose of providing teachers for the rapidly expanding need for schools in the mid 1840s. It quickly became apparent that the minimally schooled candidates who showed up required education in the fundamentals of writing, speaking, spelling, and arithmetic that were taught in the lower schools. With more and more students coming for general education and showing little or no interest in becoming teachers, the teacher education function steadily lost its identity. As Jurgen Herbst points out, the normal schools may have contributed as much as the early land-grant universities to educating our people through the college level.[12] The passage of normal schools to teachers colleges to state colleges to state universities not only further obfuscated the identity of teacher education but contributed to its prestige deprivation.

The concept of a center of pedagogy is new in the sense that the three essential ingredients have traditionally been more separated than integrated; the turf they share scarcely overlaps.

It is new also in the sense that it is something other than a school, college, or department of education (even when lodged in one of these) and rejects the assumption that SCDEs and centers of pedagogy are one and the same.

The concept is both old and new in that it seeks to resurrect at least the ideal of the normal school in the context of the modern university. In the present four-year sweep of time (to which I add an additional year), the future teacher prepares for practice while immersed in general and pedagogical studies basic to practice. The one-year normal school sought more to remedy shortcomings in subject matter in the context of preparing to teach. Just as Flexner kept to the forefront the ideal of a well-educated person becoming a physician, I have in mind the dual concept of inquiry into the canons of knowledge to know for oneself and simultaneously to know for educating others. The concept of the normal school is updated to take advantage of the richness of American higher education and the schools as partners in educational renewal.

Implementation of the concept necessitates the creation of a setting. Attention to and involvement of all the necessary ingredients at once solves few problems of logistics but may move the participants somewhat quickly beyond wrangling over turf — whose it is and who shall be allowed to walk on it — that usually delays productive dialogue and action. Thus the game in a center of pedagogy proceeds best with all the relevant players in uniform from the beginning. This does not put an end to disputes over who owns the terrain, but much time is saved by having the rightful participants engaged from the outset. The concept of a center of pedagogy embraces all the necessary components and even desirable relationships among them but solves by itself none of the logistics of creating and renewing educational settings.

The Creation and Renewal of Settings

Paul Lazarsfeld saw the need for organizational arrangements to advance neglected, inadequately recognized, or currently impotent areas of human interest and concern. He advocated the

creation of centers to bring the social sciences into a more powerful scholarly and societal role through focused research. Seymour Sarason has written insightfully about the creation of settings as an unformulated problem: the paucity of inquiry
regarding commonalities in the genealogy of many different types
of settings, descriptions that tend to omit the before-the-
beginning phases so crucial to helping others get off to a good
start, the oversimplification in explanations of success and
failure, and so on.[13]

What conditions are essential to robust settings? William
Pfaff's analysis of nationhood suggests some basics: a confident
political identity, cultural autonomy, homogeneity of population, and clear and secure borders.[14] The importance of these
for a center of pedagogy comes to the fore in Chapter Two.

What internal conditions are essential to continued vitality? Clearly, renewal is among them. There is a comprehensive literature on the renewal of individual human beings—
from psychiatry, psychology, psychoanalysis, biology, kinesiol-
ogy, the health sciences, various genres of spirituality, and
more—but relatively little on the renewal of settings. B. F. Skin-
ner's *Walden Two* is one man's vision of the necessary interplay
between human adaptation and contingencies in a social setting designed to advance human well-being.

Individual and institutional renewal are closely inter-
twined. The setting provides a context for inquiry. The mission and problems of pursuing this mission provide subject matter and require of the setting's stewards not just dialogue but
reflection, reading, inventing, and rethinking. Regrettably, people in schools do little of this, and people in universities do much
less of this than is commonly assumed. Robert Schaefer, in *The
School as a Center for Inquiry,* envisioned a quite different ethos
for schools; Louis Smith and William Geoffrey described the
classroom nucleus of a renewing school in the image of the
Schaefer vision.[15] The literature is not devoid of conceptuali-
zations and illustrations, but it is sparse.[16]

One need turn only to teacher education to see that there
is little or no expectation of or provision for teachers to be critically inquiring stewards of schools. Their training prepares them

to view and to accept the regularities of schools as givens, particularly those governing the organization and conduct of classrooms. But the attention of future teachers is directed scarcely at all to settings; the units of attention in their courses are individuals and groups of individuals and the control and management of individuals and groups in the classroom. It is unrealistic to expect teachers to create schools for inquiry when the settings in which they are prepared are rarely reflective, introspective, or self-critical.

Can settings be simultaneously vital and morally silent or neutral? No. Is there such a thing as institutional morality? Yes. Again, there is an impressive literature on individual morality. The part that touches on institutional morality tends toward a concept of collective morality that is the sum of individual morality. The resulting impression is one of sustained institutional neutrality: like clay, inanimate settings await shaping by human heads and hands. There is an element of truth in this; clearly, individuals and clusters of individuals do shape settings. But the clay they work has embedded in it the collective shaping of those who were here before. Embedded in settings, then, are the views — the moral positions — of those who shaped them. These artifacts, whether ignored or dealt with, legitimate the notion of settings as being moral or immoral.[17] Institutions are significant historical artifacts with stories to tell.

Since institutions embody the values that shaped them, they are made up of moral and immoral characteristics. They are not morally neutral. These characteristics are as real as the materials that give institutional settings physical shape. There can be no renewal and no institutional vitality without consideration of these moral dimensions.

The foregoing is intended to remind us that the creation and nurturing of settings has a long history from which at least some guidelines for renewal can be derived. What emerges by way of a general answer out of probes into the experience and reflection of others is the realization that the stewardship of healthy settings involves a great deal of reflective conversation on the part of those charged with worrying about them. The progressive ill health, decline, and death of settings appear to be in large part the result of this conversation fading, frequently because key actors withdraw from it. This malaise endangers the future of settings about as much as another: the prolongation of conversation to the point where it becomes confused with or substitutes for making decisions and taking actions. Fascination with dialogue must never obscure its purpose: the transformation of institutional functions. Nor should it obscure the importance of leaders—the chief worriers—who see to it that decisions are made and actions taken.

Functions of the Center of Pedagogy

Like other settings, centers of pedagogy take on their identity from the clarity and precision of their functions and how well they perform them. First, they prepare educators for early-childhood educational settings, elementary schools, and secondary schools of various types. Consequently, they have a mission outside of themselves, embedded deeply in a public context. There is no surrounding, protective moat, no walls to protect from the slings and arrows that come from general and special public interest.

Second, centers of pedagogy engage in at least three kinds of inquiry. The first is into the needs and characteristics of this public context—a context that includes the educational institutions for which teachers are being prepared. This inquiry goes far beyond determination of the present nature of this context. It is, rather, historical, philosophical, and—yes—judgmental. A center of pedagogy can no more be neutral in its relationship to the public context than a school of public health can stand above the health of its community. The inquiry function is designed to achieve the kind of understanding basic to participating in improvement.

The second kind of inquiry addresses the preparation program. What do its alumni need to know and be able to do in order to perform effectively as educators and mentors to children and youths? There is now a voluminous body of relevant literature, some of it organized in encyclopedic fashion, on human development, brain functioning, learning, teaching, and even directly on what beginning teachers should know.[18] One would expect there to be a productive tension between the production and use of this knowledge, but the connection is exceedingly loose. It will be many years, if ever, before there are taxonomies that connect this knowledge base with the diverse, complex requirements of teaching in schools. But this does not relieve centers of pedagogy from the tasks of selecting carefully and organizing into a coherent program the knowledge, skills, and values that appear necessary to fulfilling the chosen mission.

The third kind of inquiry is into the effectiveness of a setting's own specific program. Given the array of choices regarding the themes around which curricular modules could be organized, have we made the best ones? Do individual professors have too much freedom in the choice of field experiences for their students? Not enough? What are we doing to get feedback from graduates, and what are we doing about those data that we acquire? Is the central core of faculty members contracting in number, with resulting fragmentation of programs? These and more are the questions for continuing inquiry guiding renewal.

Another function of centers of pedagogy is research and scholarship pertaining to teaching. I usually prefer to substitute *inquiry* for *research* in the hope of broadening the image to include more than some people are willing to include under the research umbrella. But the preceding discussion of inquiry could be interpreted as omitting research that appears to be only loosely linked to understanding for improvement. A center of pedagogy should be continuously studying elements indigenous to pedagogy. Lee Shulman's work on content-specific method is illustrative because of its focus simultaneously on subject matter and its teaching — an area of long-time controversy and little enlightenment.[19] But, as we shall see, there is much more to pedagogy than method. Unlike the follow-your-nose character of much research in academe, I am proposing center-determined and center-organized research of the kind championed by Paul Lazarsfeld to advance an area of understanding. Not all centers of pedagogy will be capable of mounting such research; it is best for some to concentrate on evaluative research directed to the teacher education program under way. But all must be capable of adapting the work of others.

Focus on the art and science of teaching will create for some centers of pedagogy an additional function: a service role regarding the improvement of teaching generally. They could become, for example, sources of information and guidance for college and university departments seeking to improve their own teaching—a need increasingly coming to the forefront. Centers of pedagogy might come to play a significant role in addressing the interests that teaching assistants and professors have in regard to their own teaching, just as they undoubtedly will for teachers in the partner schools.

In this regard, I am reminded of the friendly but pointed jibes of Charles Colwell, himself a creative teacher, when he was dean of faculties at Emory University and I headed the division of teacher education there. "John," he would say, always with a smile, "are students increasingly flocking to your division's classes simply for the pure joy of experiencing good teaching? The word must be getting around." I always wished—and wish still—that I could have looked him squarely in the eye and said honestly, "Of course."

Components of the Center of Pedagogy

Earlier, I listed three essential ingredients of a teacher's education: general, liberal education; praxis (the whole of practice); and praxeology (the study of practice). Our research showed these to be divided among three distinct faculty groups, with very little communication among the three: faculty drawn from the liberal arts departments, the SCDE, and the schools. In addition, there are divisions of a more specific nature within each of these.

There is little thought given to the education of teachers among arts and sciences professors planning the curriculum for and teaching in the first two years of college. What is good lower-division education for all students is good education for teachers, it is claimed. Yet it is common for schools of medicine and of engineering, for example, to have strong voices regarding lower-division courses to be offered as prerequisites to admission. In the upper division, professors are often somewhat closer to teacher education, serving on committees to determine subject-

matter concentrations in fields taught also in high schools and
sometimes teaching the "methods" courses in mathematics, English, and so on. Sometimes they serve on university-wide councils and committees responsible for various matters pertaining
to teacher education. Yet most of the committees with which
we met appeared to be functioning below the levels of authority and responsibility defined for them on paper. We found few
professors in the arts and sciences for whom a teacher education agenda was compelling; few had their hands on this plow.

     With respect to the education of pre-service teachers, vari-
ations in faculty involvement appeared to increase with increased size of the SCDE. Most members of departments of education in the smaller colleges were involved; very little of the
basic course sequence was delegated to non–tenure-line faculty
members prior to the student-teaching phase. In large schools
and colleges of education, most tenure-line faculty members had
little to do with conducting the teacher education program,
although they had great authority over it. A few professors, especially those in such fields as science or social studies or mathematics education, taught regularly in the pre-service program.
In schools and colleges of education with large graduate and
research programs, there was almost invariably a group of non–
tenure-line faculty members, usually on year-to-year appoint-
ments, employed exclusively for both teaching some of the required courses and supervising student teachers. All involved
in the part of the total program based in a school or college of
education constituted something less than a well-knit, responsible, clearly identifiable faculty group.

     Once future teachers were placed in schools for their stu-
dent teaching, their connection to the university campus and
their former professors dropped off quickly. The final shaping
and socializing of these neophytes was in the hands of cooperating teachers in the schools—usually on a one-to-one basis.
Commonly, these beginners had only casual connections with
any other teachers in their school of placement. Their new mentors, for the most part, had similarly casual connections with
the university-based faculty members providing the teacher education program up to the student-teaching portion. Authority

and responsibility for assigning the final grade for student teaching was often a matter of considerable controversy.

A major purpose of a center of pedagogy is to tighten up this array of loose connections. This entails encompassing within clear boundaries responsible persons representing the three major program components, charging these persons with authority and responsibility for developing and renewing a teacher education program that includes within it renewing schools, and providing all the human and financial resources, materials, facilities, and laboratories necessary to educate for elementary and secondary schools a number of future teachers proportionate to this commitment of resources. There are other necessary conditions.

Earlier, Figure 1.2 depicted the three entities to be represented in a center of pedagogy: departments of the arts and sciences, SCDEs, and schools. Where the three overlap, such a center begins to define its borders and take shape. The departments in the arts and sciences do much more than prepare teachers, of course. So do the schools, colleges, and departments of education. And so do the school districts. But all three consider teacher education to be one of their appropriate functions; all three contribute resources, each set of resources being unique to that part of the whole. All three look to their own and the others' renewal. Later in this book we will see an expanded configuration that embraces additional collaborators. But for now (and for almost all that follows), this three-way collaboration is sufficient to keep in mind and implement.

Figure 1.3 is designed to show more clearly the unique and particular contribution of school districts to the simultaneous renewal of schools and teacher education. (For clarity, the twofold collaboration inside the university — that is, the collaboration between the departments of arts and sciences and the SCDE — is assumed rather than explicitly depicted.) The involvement of three school districts, each helping to sustain "partner schools," is depicted here. Now we see the central ellipse to be the center of pedagogy in which the university and the school district join. Inside this ellipse are three smaller ones containing the partner schools that are to be an *integral component* of the center.

Figure 1.3. Simultaneous Renewal of Schools and the Education of Educators.

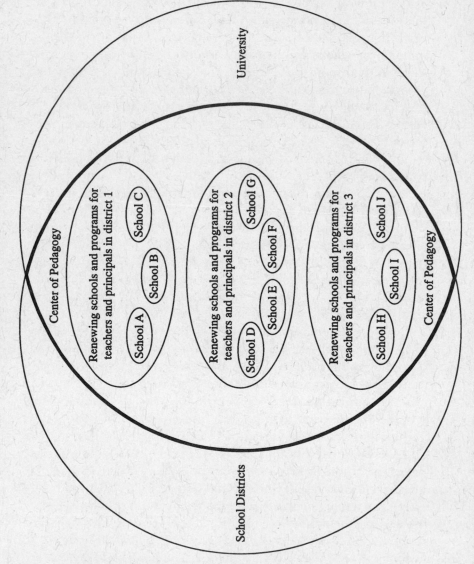

University

Center of Pedagogy

Renewing schools and programs for teachers and principals in district 1

School A   School B   School C

Renewing schools and programs for teachers and principals in district 2

School D   School E   School F   School G

Renewing schools and programs for teachers and principals in district 3

School H   School I   School J

Center of Pedagogy

School Districts

This concept of partner schools shared by school districts and universities and integral to the conception and operation of a center of pedagogy is one of the most difficult to comprehend. There has been much talk and much writing recently about professional development schools, but much of this discussion envisions a cooperating school "out there" being used for the placement of student teachers, the research of faculty members, and a host of school-university collaborative activities. The new model is not a cooperating teacher but a cooperating school for teacher education. This is not my view, as we shall see in Chapter Four.

Some of this talk and writing shares my perception of schools in which professors from the university and teachers in these schools are closely joined in a common mission embracing simultaneously both school renewal and the education of educators. Please note the caption for Figure 1.3: "Simultaneous Renewal of Schools and the Education of Educators." Again, these partner schools are not outside the center of pedagogy; they are an integral part of it. This is an exceedingly important condition.

Alternatives to Collaborative Reform

The foregoing broad conception of a center of pedagogy raises a host of problems and issues for each of the three groups of collaborators—issues regarding both their respective roles and the collaborative entity itself. When these three groups function separately—the common condition identified in our research—their work conspires to produce incoherent programs. Not only does the whole lack coherence but, with surprising frequency, the pieces lack vitality. And unfortunately, no matter how hard and creatively the separate groups work on their respective pieces, the results are disappointing. Even if they were to come together to assemble the parts of the vehicle each has created, the composite result would not function well.

The proposed coming together will not be accomplished easily. For more than a dozen years, colleagues and I have been advocating and assisting in the development of school-university

partnerships. We began with SCDEs and school districts because there has been a historic (albeit weak) tie between the two.
From the beginning, we stressed the intent that the partnership
involve sectors of universities in addition to SCDEs. But years
later, very few professors in the arts and sciences, let alone whole
departments, have become involved. Education faculty members simply are not accustomed to inviting these supposed colleagues to join them. (The reverse is equally true, of course.)

But even in school-university partnerships involving only
schools and colleges of education on the university side, communication and trust among the partners cannot be taken for
granted even years after the establishment of formal agreements.
There is no history of symbiosis to draw upon; there has been
little recognition and satisfaction of mutual needs. School-based
people have turned to the university for studies designed to advance their careers; professors of education have frequently
served the schools as speakers and consultants. There has been
little collaboration on a common agenda such as teacher education. What appears to be a natural connection is not.[20]

To recommend, then, the three-way collaboration called
for in the foregoing conception of a center of pedagogy is to call
for what has not yet been and will not easily be. Yet to reject
it because of the unfamiliarity of the concept and the obvious
difficulty of implementing it is simply to postpone indefinitely
the renewal of teacher education. Worse, it is to invite alternatives likely to take teacher education almost entirely out of the
university. This would have been a disaster for medical education; it would be a disaster for teacher education.

Take teacher education out of the university? My Scot-
tish mother might have asked, "Are ye daft?" And the artifact
still hanging on the wall of her grandson's former bedroom might
well be regarded as the right answer: "But Mom, everybody
smokes pot." No, it is a question that must be taken seriously.

David Imig, executive director of the American Association of Colleges for Teacher Education, has provided a stun-
ning summary of developments that lead or could lead the preparation of teachers toward an assortment of alternatives that are
far afield of the rigorous professional preparation commonly ac-

knowledged as necessary for nursing, engineering, public health services, dentistry, law, medicine, and an array of occupations that are much less risk-laden than that of teaching our children.[21] These appeal to a variety of groups for varied reasons: most are inexpensive; some appeal to the notion of getting "the best and the brightest" into teaching, if only for a couple of years; others touch a nerve regarding distaste for schools of education and their "Mickey Mouse" courses; more than a few reward in some way the special-interest groups promoting them; others attract because they appear to entail good old American entrepreneurship. Missing in expressions of enthusiasm for whatever appeals are hard questions regarding the educational mission to be sought; the degree to which academic credentials acquired twenty years ago are valid for effective teaching today; whether a major in biology and a six-week workshop prepares one to cope with, let alone teach, classes of today's student diversity; or whether a teaching cadre widely regarded as not doing an adequate job is up to the demands of mentoring a markedly more effective cadre.

Unfortunately, even if one is highly critical of traditional modes of preparing teachers but is perceived to be attached in some manner to them, one's attack on ill-conceived alternatives — however measured in tone and substance — is rejected as self-serving. Undoubtedly, Imig's careful analysis is so perceived in many quarters, even though he is regarded in many of these same quarters as rational, thoughtful, and fair. It is difficult to imagine the emergence of even a limited array of alternative routes to licensing in the other professions. And one can readily imagine the outcry from those now attached to the conventional route should such alternatives be proposed (and the comparative paucity of charges that their protest is merely self-serving). What would be the response of medical and law deans and professors to the sudden appearance of alternative routes to their professions on their own campuses? The quite different circumstances surrounding the teacher education enterprise are as puzzling as they are disturbing.

What I find to be particularly puzzling and disturbing stems from the tranquility of the higher education community regarding teacher education, especially at a time when universities are coming under sharp criticism for their aloofness from elementary and secondary education and school reform. In recent months, I have listened to business executives, foundation officials, policymakers, and education writers express their frustration over the dearth of leadership in this area among university presidents. Professors of education in research-oriented universities debate the issue of whether their schools of education should make major commitments to teacher education — as though the prevailing attitude among legislators debating the need for schools of education were full of understanding of and support for whatever else schools of education do. And some thoughtful deans of education have been virtually pilloried by faculty groups for suggesting a possible link between involvement in schools and teacher education and the prospect of protected future budgets. There is something unreal about this suicidal denial.

Professors in the arts and sciences generally are ill-informed about or not aware of what David Imig describes as "an extraordinary number of conditions that threaten campus-based teacher education." Given the historic place of teacher education in liberal arts colleges and the awareness of many professors in them that persons enrolled in teacher education programs make up a proportion — sometimes a significant one — of their classes, it is difficult to believe that increased awareness would fail to produce disquietude. I believe that there is at least as significant a contingent of arts and sciences professors committed to and engaged in teacher education as there is a contingent of education professors. And I believe that the long overdue renaissance of teacher education is as appropriate and as promising for the university setting as the Flexner-inspired renaissance in medical education in the 1920s and 1930s.

The center of pedagogy I envision brings into combination these two groups of critically important actors and the higher education culture they represent with their equally essential counterparts in the schools and the culture they represent. The general failure of these three groups of actors to come together symbiotically in the past around a common teacher education mission provides the major reason why even a sympathetic critic cannot endorse continuation of traditional programs. This failure also helps to fuel endorsements of many alternatives that cannot stand up to critical examination. As one of my mentors, James B. Conant, was wont to say, "A plague on both these houses."

Remedying what ails conventional programs through a necessary collaboration among essential partners appears to be the most promising, if not the easiest, route to the comprehensive redesign of teacher education. In fact, given the degree to which each represents an essential component and all three together represent virtually all commonly recognized components, this probably is the only route to what the National Board for Professional Teaching Standards recognizes as the strongest guarantee of professional competence:

> The combination of a rigorous assessment, an extended course of professional study and a well-supervised practicum provides the strongest warrant of competence. Such a requirement assures not only that certain studies have been completed, but that certificate holders have been socialized in college and university settings where there is extended time for interaction and reflection with peers and faculty on matters of professional practice, ethics, and tradition. Similarly, engagement in professional training on a full-time basis enhances the character of study, the quality of inquiry and the commitment to scholarship of the entering novice.[22]

Needed for this combination to be fully effective are the conditions described in Chapter Two.

2

Essential Conditions

Education . . . is the provision of means to fellow human beings enabling them to continually enlarge their knowledge, understanding, authenticity, virtue, and sense of place in the past, present and future of the human race.[1]

— Gary D Fenstermacher

Little by little . . . we have been giving up the *old* for the *new* faith. Near eighty years ago we began by declaring that all men are created equal, but now from that beginning we have run down to the other declaration, that for *some* men to enslave *others* is a "sacred right of self-government." These principles can not stand together. . . . [2]

— Abraham Lincoln

In Chapter One, I cited William Pfaff's conditions for strong nationhood: a confident political identity, cultural autonomy, homogeneity of population, and clear and secure borders. Although these are equally important for strong institutions and professional programs, teacher education has enjoyed none of them. Centers of pedagogy are intended to ensure the identity and cohesiveness that teacher education programs now lack. Chapter Two addresses the requisite conditions.

A caveat regarding these conditions is in order. There are many ways to fulfill them, but the domains they occupy cannot be dismissed. These domains might well be termed "commonplaces" — elements in common. All houses have in common roofs, walls, floors, and support systems, for example, although the specifics of each commonplace differ enormously. Floors can be of wood, tile, plastic, concrete, soil, and so on, but floors remain common to houses.

There are things common to all teacher education programs as well — mission, students, and resources, for example. Each omission of one of these lessens the aptness of the descriptor "teacher education program," and the ill-defined nature of any of these lessens the credibility of the claim "*good* teacher education program."

I argue that these commonplaces are essential. I do not argue that their expression and implementation must be everywhere the same; nor do I argue that the ways and results of their fulfillment are equally good, just, and beautiful.

I urge caution on the part of those who, seeking to renew a teacher education program, shop among my proposals for fulfilling the commonplaces, adopting some and rejecting others according to perceived validity and usefulness. My choices are guided by a set of values that produces certain relationships among all the decisions I make and a resulting symmetry and coherence in the recommended program. Another set of values would produce something different, with its coherence and symmetry dependent on the worth and strength of the value system.

Let me illustrate. Mission is a commonplace — an element essential to good teacher education programs — but it does not stand alone. The mission drives and binds the constituent elements of the entire program. If those responsible for the program omit or eschew mission, there can be no claims to programmatic coherence. For automobiles to serve their intended function, they require wheels; automobiles that work have wheels. Teacher education programs that work have a mission to which all else is connected.

Once having settled on this commonplace, one seeks the nature of the mission. If I am addressing the mission of education for teachers of elementary and secondary schools — as I am in almost all that follows — I look to schooling for part of the definition of that mission. Others might not, and so we disagree — not on mission as the commonplace but on the K-12 system of schools as a domain in which to seek it. Still other readers might agree on the K-12 system as the domain of search but see the function of that system to be one of processing raw materials (students) to satisfy the nation's needs for workers. With such a conception as the source of the mission for teacher education, those readers come up with a quite different teacher education program than the one that adheres to my mission.

And so we turn now to the commonplaces — those elements that may not be dismissed. Then on to their fulfillment, where there is ample room for variability and creativity. Nonetheless, the process of critical thinking that goes into consideration of each commonplace must be grounded in values and rigorously self-disciplined, or the resulting program will be incoherent and ineffective.

Mission

The mission of a center of pedagogy is, of course, to prepare teachers well. But that leaves us still with the task of defining that mission. Such a mission arises out of two belief contexts. The first is the nature of education; the second is the *proper* role of schools in a democratic society. Since schools are expected to perform an educative function while serving one of day care, the two contexts are connected. The word "proper" in the second directs the mission-seeker to the same kinds of philosophical and epistemological considerations involved in the first.

Universities readily accept this first context as an appropriate domain for inquiry. Epistemological matters are regarded as virtually their prerogative. A few decades ago, one could assume in the teacher education curriculum at least a course on the aims of education and the major philosophical perspectives that might be brought to bear on their definition. Today it is common to encounter recent graduates who know nothing about the relevant contributions of such seminal thinkers as Alfred North Whitehead and John Dewey. Further, there is no agreement among their former professors regarding what they should read. The historical and philosophical underpinnings once common to the education of teachers have almost faded away.[3]

In their place are less challenging matters that scarcely warrant their university context. The introductory course that once was historical or philosophical or both has been replaced quite commonly with a potpourri of topics, many of them mandated by the states. Inquiry into the nature and aims of education has largely been replaced by a kind of reductionism: the derivation of proficiencies or competencies from the assumed tasks of teachers translated into behavioral objectives or outcomes. Only occasionally does one find in the teacher education classroom a professor and future teachers immersed in discourse about education as conceived by Gary Fenstermacher (see introductory quote for this chapter) or Israel Scheffler, who spoke of "the formation of habits of judgment and the development of character, the elevation of standards, the facilitation of understanding, the development of taste and discrimination, the stimulation of curiosity and wonder, the fostering of style and a sense of beauty, the growth of a thirst for new ideas and visions of the yet unknown."[4]

Beyond the ken of young adults? I think not. To argue yes is to argue against courses in ethics, epistemology, aesthetics, comparative religion, and the like in the general education of freshmen and sophomores. Some of the professors we interviewed expressed the point of view that disciplined conversations about matters such as these were outside of the interest and intellectual maturity of undergraduates. Most—as well as many of the students we interviewed—thought quite the opposite: that their programs were not marked by such discourse but should be.

The three groups of faculty members who make up a center of pedagogy not only must begin a continuing dialogue over the nature and aims of education but must create a design for the curriculum that ensures that such issues are a recurring theme for students: not just an introductory course to be done with but a fostering of the most significant and critical issues of education throughout their programs. Just as Abraham Flexner saw universities as the proper milieu for medical education, so must they be for teacher education.[5] But those responsible for teacher education must be constantly vigilant regarding the education future teachers are receiving, because the technical and vocational have taken over undergraduate education to a considerable degree.

The schooling context of mission has contributed significantly to corruption in the transformation of education from intellectual substance to near-trivia, because that context is a public one. A mission for teacher education arising out of it brings public expectations and accountability. There is a public of individuals and groups with highly personalized and special interests that are understandably parochial. Their elected officials in government are caught up in the struggle among conflicting interests and considerations of the common weal. One result is a kind of policy gridlock — in educational as well as virtually all other matters of public interest. Another is gross oversimplification of the meaning of education and the role of our schools.

Public schools, in turn, find themselves dealing with two sets of unclear messages. Since parents and the community want it all — a rather vague vision involving the intellectual, social, vocational, and personal development of the young — there are always individuals and groups who perceive one or more of these to be neglected or not appropriate. Although the rhetoric of interest is loosely educative, the focus is more likely on how the school conducts its (custodial) business: attention to *my* child, student safety, drug and alcohol use, student misbehavior, reference to a middle school rather than a junior high, and more. The lack of resources and a poor curriculum rank lower than these topics among parental and even student concerns.[6] Rearranging the weekly schedule to provide time for total faculty planning often causes more of a community ruckus than making a rather major change in the curriculum of a subject field. And serious efforts to promote independent thinking in students inflame some special-interest groups from coast to coast.

Just as parents watch closely and react to changes in what Seymour Sarason refers to as the *regularities* of schools, the states mandate many of what Gary Fenstermacher calls the *systemics:* texts, tests, Carnegie units, graduation requirements, and so on. And increasingly in recent years, the federal and state message to schools calls for their instrumental role in regard to better jobs and a competitive economy. This is not the message that brings teachers early to school each day. But it most certainly is part of the cacophony that rings in their ears as they seek to teach our children. Linda McNeil has tellingly described how difficult it is for teachers to respond to their own inner voices or any other voices that might help them define and carry out the educative role that is obscured by relentless political and bureaucratic attention to the systemics of schooling.[7]

It makes no sense for those engaged in the education of teachers for elementary and secondary schools not to look to the public context for part of their mission. They have done and still do so. But our research reveals that contextual attention to the systemics of schooling and the mechanics of teaching have dominated in the process and overwhelmed the curriculum to the detriment of the educative role of schools.

Three forces in particular have been at work. The first pertains to the systemics of universities. The arts and sciences dominate in the undergraduate curriculum and properly play a major role in the education of teachers. But this obvious relevance of the arts and sciences, coupled with the low status of the teaching profession and teacher education, has deprived the preparation component of a clear identity. It belongs to everyone but not specifically to anyone. The so-called professional sequence is no sequence at all. It is a fragmented journey: students navigate the curricular requirements of the arts and sciences departments, interspersing courses required for certification. The conditions for programmatic coherence are missing.

This academic journey is shaped considerably by the regulatory public context. It is not uncommon for states not only to cap the number of hours of teacher education devoted to the so-called professional components but also to specify some of the content that is to go into them. In responding to these requirements—almost invariably addressed to the systemics and mechanics of schools and teaching rather than the educative function—the intellectual character of the program declines and the school, college, or department of education comes under increased fire from professors in the arts and sciences who lament what they perceive to be a nonintellectual or even anti-intellectual curriculum. Yet they commonly fail to support their education colleagues in resisting dysfunctional curricular intrusions.

The third force is the tyranny of ongoing practice—much of it bureaucratically determined, as Linda McNeil points out.

As future teachers engage in student teaching, entering individually into schools and the supervision of a cooperating teacher there, they become overwhelmed with and sometimes frightened by the sheer mechanics of surviving each day with an incredibly diverse class of young people. Groups of prospective teachers at this stage in their preparation told me that they just could not get enough of courses directed to classroom management and ways to teach—the very courses that academicians decry and many policymakers would do away with entirely. In addition, a dissonance between what they had learned to do and what district systemics required them to do raised in their minds even more worry about being on their own very soon in the classroom. No wonder they rated field experiences, methods courses, and student teaching as those parts of their preparation programs that had the most impact—and the parts most influencing their values and beliefs, for better or for worse.

There is a profound irony in all of this. Clearly, the three forces briefly described above create an enormous pull on teacher education toward an axis of immediate practicality—not the long-term practicality of fundamental, relevant principles and theories but the immediate practicality of survival in circumstances largely ordered by noneducative considerations. Schools are no longer tubs on their own bottoms, doing educationally for young people those things that most homes are less well equipped to do or prefer not to do, in a system serving primarily to ensure the distribution of human and material resources required for schools to do their job. The highly politicized bureaucracies that have emerged over the past four to five decades, particularly in the larger cities, have made it increasingly difficult for teachers to exercise what properly is called professional judgment.[8] Indeed, their freedom to make decisions is sharply curtailed. At the same time, there has been more pomp and circumstance over making teaching a profession than at any time in our history. Those of us who went into teaching years ago and the many teachers with whom I associate have thought all along that we are in a profession and that we need all the support and encouragement we can get in order to be able to behave professionally.

We begin to see the great potential significance of centers of pedagogy, so clear and determined of educative mission, so coherent in programs tied to that mission, that they provide the necessary pull toward another axis — a properly educative one. There is widespread rhetorical agreement that teaching is a profession. There is widespread agreement within the strongest professions that the best assurance of professional competence is the careful selection of candidates on relevant criteria, an extended period of studies and practice, and a carefully planned and conducted socialization process throughout this period that provides for interaction and reflection among both faculty and students on matters of professional practice, ethics, and tradition. What is strongly recommended for the strongest professions is what must be assured for teachers.

My colleagues and I defined a four-part professional mission for teacher education, each part characterized by moral dimensions. The first two parts are derived from the proper, educative mission of schools: the education of citizens to uphold and strive toward the nation's democratic ideals and the education of individuals to transcend narcissism and ignorance. No other institution is assigned this two-part responsibility. Becoming educated and ensuring education for all is both the moral and the political responsibility of citizens individually and collectively.

Clearly, to carry out the educative function of elementary and secondary schools, teachers must be deeply steeped in democratic ideals and understandings, as well as in the disciplined systems of knowledge and knowing derived from sustained study of human experience and its context. Centers of pedagogy should withhold certificates of program completion from individuals considered ill-prepared in these domains, and states should bar from licensing candidates unable to present such certificates.

The first two parts of the teacher education mission are endangered mostly by omission. It is commonly and erroneously assumed that graduation from a four-year college provides the necessary preparation even when such graduation took place twenty or more years ago. This is a dangerous assumption. The second two parts, nurturing pedagogy and the stewardship of schools, are endangered by both omission and commission. Many people view the art and science of teaching as unnecessary, unwarranted pedantry; knowledge of one's subject is sufficient. For them, I recommend the taking over — just for a few weeks — of a first-grade class or from five to seven periods a day of their favorite subject at the junior or senior high school level. Their no-need-for-courses-in-pedagogy bias would be rudely shaken. The danger from commission is derived primarily from that force of immediate practicality for survival in the classroom described above. Attention to the stewardship of schools is largely missing in teacher education. We found almost the whole of practice-directed preparation to embrace individual pupils, groups of pupils, and classes, not whole schools.

The three-part faculty of a center of pedagogy is advised to emphasize, prior to getting into the details of curriculum, the reflective way instruction and stewardship are to be addressed throughout the program. The mission is not just to prepare teachers for the mechanics of their occupation, although this too must be done, but to develop in them the intellectual habits of reflection on their calling and daily work that are the mark of a professional continuously engaged in self-improvement. There may be little difference in the *initial* performance of one teacher trained only in the how-to-do-its of generic methods of teaching and another guided by basic principles versed reflectively in a half-dozen fundamentally different applications of these principles and morally grounded in what it means to nurture and develop all the students in one's educative care. But fundamental differences will become apparent over time. The lifelong demonstration of these qualities by this second teacher will provide verifying testimony to the success of a center of pedagogy. It is folly to seek to assess these professional qualities in the first year of teaching. But they are the distinguishing marks of the professional three to five years out of the preparation program.[9] The professional tends not to repeat mistakes commonly made when just beginning.

Getting Started

The syndicated column of Tom Peters appears regularly on the financial pages of newspapers across the country. One of his admonitions is, "Don't stand there; do something." This advice is much needed in the academic community.

Many of my colleagues in higher education refer jokingly but pointedly to the glacierlike pace of making decisions and taking action on campus. Dialogue about modest changes in a given curriculum often goes on for years. My experiences with schools suggest that matters move a little more rapidly there, but not much. Both groups have trouble reaching the necessary "working consensus" in which there is not full agreement but there appear to be no serious objections. And even when decisions representing this consensus are reached, firm actions do not always follow and there are always people who seem to forget the nature of the decisions. Robust centers of pedagogy are unlikely to emerge from this all-too-common way of conducting academic business.

During the 1987–88 academic year, I had the good fortune to participate in a quite different kind of academic process. Several of us in the University of Washington became so disenchanted with our program for preparing school principals—in spite of the fact that the College of Education had just been cited for the high quality of its work in preparing educational administrators—that we decided to do something about it. By late winter, a group of us from both the university and nearby schools had determined to have in place by the coming summer both a redesigned program and the first cohort group of candidates. We were vastly aided in this undertaking by joint membership and participation in a school-university partnership created several years earlier and by an analytical memorandum prepared by two colleagues which provided a sense of direction.

To reach our goal in a matter of months, we had to abandon our usual way of doing faculty business in the university—that is, in monthly meetings. Instead, we roughed out the scope of anticipated work, drawing from the memorandum referred to above, and the hours it might take to accomplish it. We then announced the meeting dates and times, being careful to stagger meetings over different days of the week, and invited those who initially had expressed an interest (and some others) to attend as frequently as possible. A small group of chief worriers assumed certain continuing leadership responsibilities. Most of us attended most of the time; the chief worriers attended all of the time. Some people volunteered for between-meeting tasks. By June 1988, a new program had been designed; a cohort group of fifteen individuals had been selected; the first activities were begun.

Below are some key learnings from this experience that might be useful for faculty members coming together with the commitment to redesign teacher education.

- First, "business as usual" will not suffice.
- Second, a few initial sessions of brainstorming over a provocative mission-oriented document can be powerfully productive. It is unproductive at this stage to challenge on epistemological or other grounds the convictions of colleagues. Ask them to illustrate, to say it differently, or to write a short position piece. But do not confront and discredit contributions out of hand. The rough edges and even the individual sources of ideas will be smoothed out and will disappear as the mission takes shape. There will be ample time and opportunity for rethinking and revision later.
- Third, declare no present assumptions and regularities of program to be sacred. The needed reform of teacher education cannot be accommodated within existing systemics. In planning the program briefly referred to above, we simply rejected the notions that principal preparation programs must be adapted to the after-school schedules of candidates, that instruction must be adapted to courses, that internships and reflective seminars can be productively conducted apart, that a cohort group coming through the program together is optional, and more. The initial document had already savaged a number of rarely questioned traditional practices.
- Fourth, once having agreed on some essential themes of the mission, see to it that they become organizing elements of the curriculum, to be developed continuously over time, with theory and practice integrated as one. We agreed on such central themes as the school curriculum, organizational development and renewal, and the moral dimensions of leadership. They are dealt with in cumulative fashion over the entire year of the program's duration.

- Fifth, determine the essential mechanics that the scope of a teacher's work requires and set aside programmatic time for them. Do not let the inescapable demands of these on students' growing apprehensions about the job (in contrast to the work) of teaching block the central core of reflection on practice. Daily survival, daily management of a class, and a host of related worries are overwhelming. Left to float freely in the curriculum, they will loom larger and larger, crowding out all else in students' minds. In the principal preparation program, we determined the major "skill" areas and set aside a series of all-day sessions throughout the year for purposes of addressing them. This did not mean the abandonment of principles, theory, and reflection. Quite the reverse. The sequence of these sessions was designed, to the degree possible, to parallel the several central themes of the whole for purposes of integration.
- Sixth, do not hold back from launching the new program until all the specifics are in the plan. Otherwise, it will be years and years in the making. Those in the first cohort group in our redesigned principal preparation program knew that they were in the pilot year and that there were many wrinkles to be smoothed out. They enjoyed being called upon to evaluate and suggest changes. The process of formative evaluation and subsequent revision that began that first year continues and always will. It is as much a part of the total experience as the reflective seminars. Indeed, it is part of the reflective process.[10]

In considering all these observations about getting started, remember that the beginnings of renewal are vitally significant in determining all that follows. All processes of individual and institutional renewal create and sanctify certain traditions and artifacts that tend to be carried forward, for better or for worse. The care taken at the outset contributes enormously to the determination of whether these will prove themselves to be useful or a hindrance to creativity in the future. Let us then be especially prescient in what we create early on in the renewal process.

Because the process of getting group agreement on a mission is so difficult, it is often useful to begin with something representing the work of others that is already on paper. Participants are able to voice their agreements and disagreements without attacking the ideas of colleagues and yet get on the table the different views represented. Face-to-face challenges will come eventually, of course, but they will be handled more constructively if group members have already had some opportunity to comprehend where others stand on issues and to assess for themselves the nature and degree of agreement and disagreement.

My colleagues and I have discovered that the four-part mission put forward in the three books reporting our work (see the Preface) serves as a useful stimulant to group discourse on the mission of teacher education. As I noted in Chapter One, two parts of this mission arise out of the mission of schools and two out of an analysis of what is required of teachers to address productively the mission of schools. All four parts are characterized by moral dimensions and implications.

After having put forward this mission and become quite comfortable with it, we turned our attention to the conditions necessary to fulfilling the mission. These ultimately were expressed in nineteen postulates. Later, with our research on existing circumstances pertaining to teacher education completed, we found ourselves caught up in a process of helping others understand them. We came to refer to this process as "unpacking the postulates" — that is, extracting for careful examination each of the necessary conditions embedded in them. Most of the postulates contain two or three; some contain as many as five or six. I seek to carry the reader through this process in Chapter Three.

Those of us connected with the Center for Educational Renewal discovered in our sessions with others that this process of unpacking was aided enormously by first clustering several closely related postulates around the larger ideas they collectively represent and seek to advance. Several of the postulates advance the importance of commitment and leadership; others address the necessity of clear and protected borders for the teacher education entity; others state conditions pertaining to faculty members and students; some have to do with formal and informal socialization processes (the formal and informal curriculum); a couple focus on laboratories and field stations (partner schools); and several address connections with alumni, the profession, and the regulatory context.

To these clusters we now turn. I strongly recommend that groups coming together for purposes of understanding the full meaning of the postulates begin with a discussion of the larger essentials that the postulates seek to describe in somewhat greater detail. This appears to be a productive way to get beyond the interpersonal differences that so often get in the way of the doing that Peters and many others view as necessary to productive beginnings.

Commitment and Leadership

The circumstances of schools and of those who work in them today are such that there must be no fuzziness in the commitment of colleges and universities involved in educating teachers. The critical importance of good teachers to good schools is such that there is no place for institutional waffling. Those colleges and universities that engage in teacher education halfheartedly should be nudged out of the business.

The proper commitment is essentially a moral one. Schooling or its equivalent is compulsory in our nation, but many of those young people required to be in the classroom fail to grasp the significance of education to their own future; large numbers have little notion about their responsibilities as citizens and the role education plays in effective citizenship, parenting, working, and living. Some people of color see schools as not intended for them. Some of our young who must attend bring with them characteristics that do not mesh with the schools' expectations for them. Schools do not now provide equality of educational opportunity. They do not yet reflect the ideal to which Lincoln referred in his Peoria address of 1854 (quoted at the beginning of this chapter). Teachers are not well equipped with the attitudes, knowledge, and skills needed to provide excellent education for all. The moral commitment arises out of belief that a system of higher education praised throughout the world has the power and the responsibility, at a minimum, to provide teachers capable of doing more than merely coping with the circumstances of the lower schools.

Documents of the early normal schools and liberal arts colleges portrayed their commitment to the cultivation of character and basic literacy in the young; the preparation of teachers and ministers was at the heart of their mission. They counted heavily on homes, religious institutions, and schools to lay the foundation. Today the uncertainty of a strong interinstitutional partnership increases the urgency of a commitment to quality and equality in the education of teachers for elementary and secondary schools.

There is growing evidence of a raised consciousness of this need in the higher education community. The initial question of the Holmes Group of education deans regarding responsibility of their universities to schools has led to increased attention to their teacher education programs and to reflection on the mission of the units they head. The idea of a school of education as an active player in the educational health of communities was clearly seen in the early 1980s by President Kennedy of Stanford University and Chancellor Heyman of the University of California, Berkeley. Since then, hundreds of college and university presidents have expressed their support of a stronger commitment to teacher education in what has come to be known as "The Letter," ultimately signed by more than two hundred and distributed under the auspices of the American Association for Higher Education and through meetings and publications of the American Association of Colleges for Teacher Education and the Renaissance Group.[11]

This rhetoric preceded a generally unanticipated downturn in state budgets and sharp cuts in allocations to public colleges and universities. At the same time, tuition and other costs were hitting high levels among private institutions and markedly increasing in public ones. The best that those in charge of teacher education could hope for was that the moral language of the late 1980s would carry over into somewhat charitable restraint on the part of those in the central office seeking to make ends meet. They could have little hope of the infusion of dollars that the tying together of reforming schools and reforming teacher education had briefly promised (and sorely needed).

The history of teacher education — and, to a considerable degree, schooling as well — has been very much like this. It takes years for concern over the quality of our educational system to reach the point of driving concerted action, and that point seems almost invariably to coincide with a period of fiscal recession. The problem, clearly, is that we either value schooling less than we say we do or we assume that there always will be enough caring people to hold the system together, through good times and bad. Either way, the message is that we do not value children very much, our frequent protestations to the contrary notwithstanding.

There is an unmistakable message here for educators: they have had and will continue to have among their members a substantial number who perceive themselves, rightly, to be the primary advocates for and stewards of our schools. Whether or not this should be is beside the point; this condition simply goes with the territory. There is a corollary message for teacher educators: there is on some college and university campuses a longstanding, continuing commitment to the education of educators because a succession of education deans, chairs, and directors made it so and sustained it. When presidents express support, the explanation is more likely to be the good work of these individuals than natural inclination on the part of the chief executive officer of each campus.

The head of the center of pedagogy must be a "presence" in the offices of the provost (or academic vice president) and president. Because of the rapid turnover in both of these positions, this head cannot afford to have teacher education on the agenda of only one or the other. Just as the president is constantly reminded by the dean of medicine that producing the class of 80 physicians in 2002 requires budgetary provisions for hospital facilities, he or she must be reminded that producing 250 qualified teachers that year requires the use of and entails expenses for 20 or more partner schools. This is an awareness that comes from deliberate intentions fulfilled by the head of the center: he or she keeps teacher education on the institution's agenda.

If the head of a center of pedagogy is doing the job well, he or she will have made sure that all members of the staff are allies in building the center's work into the permanent fabric of the institution as a whole. For example, ensuring that campuswide promotion and merit committees are fully aware that the criteria for reviewing teacher educators both add to and differ from those designed for professors in the arts and sciences requires constant vigilance. There is a never-ending job to be done in reminding arts and sciences professors that those academic deficiencies among incoming freshmen are due in some considerable degree to their failure to contribute adequately to the education of the teachers who taught these young people.

If teacher education is to enjoy a campus commitment that is more than rhetorical, those connected with it — especially its designated leader — must assume the risks of the proverbial messengers who are first to be shot. They must argue continuously and effectively that ratios of thirty or forty future teachers to each faculty member are unacceptable, that there is no place for large lecture classes, that the part of the undergraduate curriculum specifically designed for teachers must not take second place to the schedule of arts and sciences classes, that a considerable part of the program is best carried out through seminars closely tied to field experiences, that sustained teaching with accompanying reflection constitutes the bulk of the fifth year of preparation, and more. A teacher education program cannot function effectively within the conventional regularities of classes and credits geared to sitting and listening. The conditions necessary to exemplary teacher education programs can be very annoying to those in administrative offices who prefer rigid conformity and consistency to fluidity, flexibility, and change. Yet the center of pedagogy must make its needs known and be prepared to push vigorously for their fulfillment.

One of the obstacles to institutional commitment that a center of pedagogy must overcome, whatever its organizational identity within the university, is the institution's uneasiness with the close connection of teacher education to the public context and the accountability that comes with it. This connection invites and legitimates regulatory intrusion far beyond anything experienced by the arts and sciences departments, which are far more attuned to parental than to policymakers' expectations.

Perhaps Robert Hutchins had the potential of these intrusions more in mind than the relevance of professional schools to the central intellectual role of the university when, in *The Higher Learning in America,* he relegated them to the periphery as institutes loosely linked to the campus core.[12]

In *Teachers for Our Nation's Schools,* I described the very close relationship that once characterized the connection between deans of education and the states' regulatory activity in teacher education. The deans and their heads of teacher education sat regularly with those responsible for advising on and administering state requirements. There was self-serving, of course, but the moral framework of protecting the public and a degree of institutional autonomy served as a moderating backdrop. In probing this relationship, James B. Conant rejected critics' charges of conspiracy. University administrators complained of intrusion even under these circumstances, but, on balance, they had less reason for uneasiness than they have today.

The evolution of universities and the related evolution of schools and colleges of education toward greater emphasis on research turned the attention of education deans inward, on one hand, outward to funding sources, on the other, and away from continued vigilance over the autonomy of their teacher education programs and the increasing incoherence produced by regulation. If the model set by the "beacon" schools described by Geraldine Clifford and James Guthrie prevails, education deans will continue to be preoccupied with matters other than teacher education and its connection to the state.[13] If, however, the introspection now under way in many schools leads to a reorganization in which professional programs dominate, massaging the state connection will be high on the agendas of education deans.

But teacher education is too important to await the results of introspection that will take years. At least the scaffolding of a center of pedagogy can be put together in a matter of months, with the requisite conditions to follow. The processes of deliberating, making decisions, evaluating, and revising will continue indefinitely, of course. Because there never will be the "right" time, there are some good arguments for beginning now.

First, there is still considerable momentum for school reform, and the education of educators is now tied to it, at least rhetorically. Second, there is considerable interest both within and outside of higher education for greater attention to and improvement in college teaching. The idea of a center of pedagogy benefits from this interest. Indeed, teacher education benefits whenever teaching is taken more seriously. Third, a greater commitment to teacher education by colleges and universities now resonates well with legislators, especially when its conduct is to be tied more closely to schools, as is so frequently recommended. There are clear messages here for university trustees and administrators, who always must keep a keen eye on their sources of funds.

It would be comforting to believe that the most powerful driving force for strong commitment to teacher education is increased sensitivity to the moral responsibility of higher education to the educational health of a university's host community. Even if the possibility of some financial return is more motivating, however, leaders in teacher education should remember that strong statements from university presidents are out there that can be used to good advantage. And they must remember that, for their leadership to succeed, it is the moral imperative that is most likely to carry the day — with students planning to teach, with faculty members, and with the public.

Clear and Secure Borders

Clear and secure borders have little to do with the moral dimensions of the teacher education enterprise, but they have much to do with its vitality. They are essential to the fulfillment of moral commitment. The greater the distance or the slack between the teacher education program and the boundaries of the unit that encompasses it, the greater the likelihood that activities irrelevant to it or disruptive of it will fill in the space. These activities not only will compete for recognition and resources from the outside but also will compete on the inside, even for funds already designated for teacher education. In the past, teacher education has tended to lose.

Vaguely demarcated entities are weak if only for this lack of definition. They are more vulnerable to pillage from without than are clearly defined, well-articulated, and widely recognized settings. Over the years, schools of education have commonly been the depositories for marginal entities no longer welcome elsewhere in the university — a mark of their fuzzy identity and weakness. Part of the orphanlike status of teacher education within some schools and colleges of education is due to a lack of a clear identity within these units.

A cloak of virtue provides little protection. The best protection is an organizational identity that bespeaks internal coherence to a clearly articulated public mission enthusiastically embraced by the host institution. Schools and colleges of education might have become such — and might still — were they to have embraced a mission such as that put forward here for centers of pedagogy. These centers are professionally oriented settings continuously renewing themselves through inquiry and accompanying action. Each has its own designated budget, leader, faculty, students, laboratories, field stations, and operating procedures.

This kind of specificity runs counter to certain conventions rarely challenged in the academic teacher education community and in accrediting criteria. Almost sacred is the notion of teacher education as a university-wide responsibility, for example. But this criterion has spawned more form than substance. During the course of our research, I met with a couple dozen campuswide committees on teacher education. Few were able to articulate a clear function. Some had not met for many months. None lived up in execution to its written descriptions of authority and responsibility. They all appeared to be particularly lax in regard to two of their more important functions: keeping the gates to program admission and monitoring students' progress thereafter. What is so routinely referred to as campuswide responsibility apparently licensed casual stewardship.

Ambiguities surrounding the role of these campuswide committees, coupled with the loose connections of many of their members to ongoing programs, serve to obfuscate the authority and responsibility of the primary actors in, for example, the preparation program for prospective elementary school teachers. Important questions arise and go unanswered: How did these students get admitted? What is my responsibility in regard to students about whom I have reservations? Who is seeing to it that students follow the stated sequence? In time, with no answers forthcoming, nobody cares.

Creation of a center of pedagogy does not automatically answer these or any other questions. But designation of the faculty embraced by this center pinpoints responsibility. Full recognition of authority must follow. The center will fail and teacher education will be the loser one more time if authority is held, for example, by professors outside of it. Currently, many professors of education who play no part in teacher education programs in the school or college of education vote on virtually all of the major matters pertaining to these programs.

Nowhere is this violation of borders clearer than in regard to budget. Teacher education has always struggled for financial survival. In our visits to campuses, evidence of the modest to marginal support usually surfaced quickly. In large, multipurpose schools of education, the frequent use of part-time or nontenured instructors produced disproportionately large numbers of courses for dollars spent on teacher education compared to most other programs. Neil Theobald's probe into this issue suggests that teacher education may very well be a cash-cow in the very unit of the campus that is charged with its nourishment.[14] But bringing such information to the surface can be very threatening. Shifts toward equity without the infusion of additional funds into the overall budget of such schools of education would place teacher education in competition with activities closer to the interests of faculty members who exert much more clout in policy decisions than do many of those engaged primarily or exclusively in teacher education. Clearly, raising the status of and support for teacher education on university campuses is fraught with complications, some of them of sufficient internal political importance to endanger the administrative careers of individuals such as deans who make the attempt. Presidents and provosts need to be acutely aware of what is at stake and where and when to provide strong support.

Faculty interests come sharply to bear in the recruitment

of colleagues—a matter shared rather delicately with administrators but widely regarded as primarily a faculty prerogative. On several occasions in my former role as a dean, I found myself having to make special appeals to the central administration for faculty positions in order to shore up a teacher education enterprise eroding as faculty members gained tenure and research grants enabled them to reduce their teaching loads by "buying up" some of their own time. The instructions to the search committees were to submit up to six candidates, ranked according to preference if they so wished. By the time the process was completed, criteria other than service to teacher education had taken over. The teacher education mission of the school was subverted to the graduate research mission. On one occasion, the leading candidate told me in the final interview that she knew nothing about teacher education and was not interested in it but that she would participate if that was the only way she could get the appointment. Situations of this sort would not arise were recruitment specifically for a center of pedagogy.

The choice before a dean of education in such situations— not unfamiliar to many deans in large multipurpose schools— becomes one of choosing the top-ranked candidate and disregarding the integrity of the initial, justifying criteria or of choosing a lower-ranked candidate and incurring the wrath of the search committee. One makes the latter choice only so many times before using up the small bank of chips held by deans at the time of their appointment.

Nowhere are the boundaries and resources of teacher education more ill-defined than with respect to the disputed turf of methods courses in the subject fields of secondary school teachers. This perennial dispute was being waged on the campuses visited by the Conant team (of which I was a member) in the early 1960s. The dispute and its arguments had changed little when my colleagues and I visited campuses—a few of the same ones included—more than a quarter of a century later. Sometimes the turf is ruled by the school of education; sometimes it is ruled by the relevant academic department; sometimes it is a standoff; almost always it is disputed; almost always, too, programs and students are the losers.

The debate will not necessarily abate with the creation of a center of pedagogy. But the debate itself is not the problem. The problem grows out of the conventional practice of requiring, sometimes because of state regulations, courses in methods of teaching such subjects as English, mathematics, biology, the individual or collective social sciences, and more. Often the security of the course, wherever taught in the university context, depends on the tenure of a specific professor. With this professor's departure, a struggle ensues. The search now is for another professor of English or mathematics, not a professor in the pedagogy of the subject. The English department not uncommonly disavows any responsibility for staffing the methods course while simultaneously renouncing either the right or the ability of the education department to offer it. The old debate flares again. The sensible answer—rarely offered or available—is for a clearly designated unit in teacher education to possess the financial resources to jolly well employ a qualified person for the job. Can any professional program be of stable health if dependent for its constituent elements on the goodwill of departments whose primary interests lie elsewhere? Of course not, and yet this has been and still is characteristic of teacher education in the United States—a situation that most deans of education have allowed to continue.

Ironically, it is a characteristic to which both schools of education and departments in the arts and sciences have contributed both separately and jointly. It is a situation that I believe will continue virtually unchecked so long as teacher education continues to be denied clear and protected borders within which are designated budgets, leaders, faculty members, students, laboratories, field stations, governance structures, and basic operating procedures. The creation of a center of pedagogy embracing these several necessary conditions, whether within or outside of a school or college of education, is a major step in the right direction.

Faculty

As I stated in Chapter One, a center of pedagogy is intended to bring together the three essential ingredients of a future teacher's curriculum: general education, practice, and the study of practice (praxeology). Its creation and development proceed best when all the relevant players are involved from the beginning—especially since they must be eventually, in any case. Figures 1.2 and 1.3 depict the general nature of the three-way involvement.

Traditionally, schools of education have been regarded as guardians of the teacher education enterprise. Involvement of people beyond this unit has tended to be token, as with the campuswide committees we found to be marginal in functioning and impact. The fact that written charges to these committees often are all-encompassing notwithstanding, the power and the critical decisions lie elsewhere. If not, would the guardians be a party to drafting such sweeping statements of authority and responsibility? It must be remembered that the existence of these committees serves political purposes—for example, impressing visiting accreditation teams.

The irony is, of course, that the actual campus guardians of teacher education are sharply curtailed in their authority by regulatory agencies. And because the arts and sciences departments and neighboring schools are pro forma members of committees that usually function in desultory fashion, they are not vigorous defenders of the greater autonomy that teacher education requires to be robust. Indeed, their frequent stance is worse than neutral in that both these groups frequently offer criticism that feeds the imposition of external controls and alternative programs only marginally or not at all associated with universities.

There is growing recognition of the need for close collaboration of the three groups—arts and sciences departments, the SCDE, and local schools—in selecting and building the faculty of a center of pedagogy. But such a direction places deans of education in a hard place, particularly if they preside over multipurpose schools. Many faculty members in education rightly perceive themselves as having sustained programs through the ups and downs of the rather troubled history of teacher education. They have doubts about the degree to which colleagues in the arts and sciences will exhibit equal devotion over the long haul.

   Some professors of education not involved in teacher education like the present situation: they hold considerable power
in such vital matters as the attention and resources to be allocated to teacher education, yet they need not get more directly
involved. Some no doubt are aware of the disproportionately
low fraction of the total budget committed to teacher education.
Yet the achievement of equity without additions to the overall
budget of the school implies losses in their areas of greatest interest and commitment. A combination of increased general interest in teacher education and a broader participation in its
conduct beyond the school of education is at once threatening
and troublesome to argue against. Consequently, deans of education who push for both of these constitute personification of
this threat.

   Such deans find themselves in a catch-22 situation. To
push teacher education to the forefront, especially in the context of collaboration that growing numbers of policymakers and
others appear to understand and appreciate, is to incur the wrath
of many faculty members. Yet because not to do so is likely to
ensure decline in funding for their schools, even contentment
with the status quo endangers their future. Many deans understand this dilemma very well, while faculty members are either
much less clear on it or are gambling on the likelihood of its
dissipation over time. They sometimes view the dean's early disappearance as a good beginning.

   It is not surprising that some deans of education are wary
of carrying the dialogue regarding the renewal of teacher education beyond the borders of their own schools or colleges, even
though they expect to do this eventually. They believe that
faculty concerns can be resolved through rational processes and
that strong disagreements are best kept within the family. Understandably, they perceive stewardship of their entire school
as their primary responsibility. The redesign of teacher education thus becomes a schoolwide enterprise.

   This stance may work for deans in relatively small schools
where most faculty members are involved in several major sets
of activities, including teacher education, none of which is far
from the deans' attention. But it is the route of short tenure for

deans in large schools, especially if full faculty participation in the dialogue is to determine the future of teacher education. In the first place, there simply are too many potentially (or currently) conflicting agendas. Second, the opportunities for extended total faculty participation are too few for these agendas to be reconciled for the common good. Third, the sheer load of management is too great for any dean to devote the time necessary to assuage all the unease, complaints, and dissonances left uncared for in scheduled meetings or even two-day retreats. Fourth, even if resolution of major differences is feasible, that end lies years, not months, in the future. And then it will be necessary to begin a large part of the dialogue anew with the two groups of actors — those from the arts and sciences and the schools — not included at the outset.

As was stated in Chapter One, I believe that the route described above is antithetical to the best interests of teacher education. I further believe what I only hinted at in Chapter One: that in the long run, schools of education will be better served by vigorously promoting at the outset a clearly defined, protected setting for teacher education that embraces the three faculty groups already identified. This is more rather than less likely to build understanding of and appreciation for schools of education that are now widely viewed as having botched the job of preparing educators for the K-12 system (and doing little else of much public worth). By coming out of their considerable isolation, schools of education gain the opportunity to demonstrate their vital role in teacher education and the considerable capability for research and development they have cultivated over the past quarter-century. In so doing, they avoid waiting for years to garner for teacher education the attention and resources it needs now.

Those who make policy for and otherwise "frame" the conduct of teacher education must be those who are to carry it out. These are individuals in several departments of the arts and sciences, in a portion of the school or college of education, and in several elementary and secondary schools who must come together as equals in the new setting constituting a center of pedagogy. Establishing criteria for those who will qualify and designating them as the responsible faculty is a task of great import that must be undertaken carefully and seriously in each setting charged with the stewardship of teacher education. Unfortunately, there appear to be no exemplary models in existence.

Students

Our research revealed at least five rather major shortcomings in regard to extant conditions related directly to students in teacher education. First, efforts to broaden and deepen the pool of candidates, especially to reflect the diversity of school populations, appear to range from sporadic to nonexistent. Second, students drift into programs, beginning at different times and entry points. Third, the admissions process is casual and limited. Fourth, there is no clearly identifiable student body — the class of '98, as in law or medicine — prior to student teaching. Fifth, the formal and informal socialization process through which future teachers identify with their profession lacks continuity and coherence. (I leave discussion of this fifth weakness to the next section.)

We found enough examples of promising efforts in all of these areas to suggest the elements of an exemplary composite. To address the first shortcoming, each setting must reach down into the junior and senior high schools with well-planned, well-conducted efforts to acquaint young people with the potential career possibilities and satisfactions in teaching. Future-teacher clubs are an obvious vehicle. In addition, centers must join with other agencies in reaching out to individuals employed elsewhere. One valuable resource is Recruiting New Teachers, with headquarters in Belmont, Massachusetts. This organization works nationwide through attractive literature and films; people who respond by calling in are directed to teacher-preparing institutions geographically close to them.[15] In Seattle, Washington, a nonprofit effort, Teachers Recruiting Future Teachers, is supported by grants from the business community. To give a financial incentive in recruiting, local firms often provide scholarships in their name to aspiring teachers.

The most serious need is the recruitment of diversity in

the teaching force paralleling diversity in the school population, a condition that hangs far out in the future. We found an average of only 8 percent people of color enrolled in the programs we studied (a figure close to the national norm), compared to nearly 40 percent of the school population. June Gordon, of our Center for Educational Renewal, has documented significant elements of the problem, discovering reasons for nonentry of minority students not previously considered and articulating recommendations for alleviating the situation.[16] She found, for example, that many individuals of minority groups do not view institutions of higher education as nurturing places for them and are cautious of repeating there the prejudice already experienced in schools. Teacher-preparing settings constituting the National Network for Educational Renewal are joined in our commitment to work aggressively toward student bodies in teacher education reflecting the mix in the student bodies of nearby schools.

Next, I make it clear in *Teachers for Our Nation's Schools* and here (especially in Chapter Six) that there must be a marked gate for which aspirants prepare their case for admission (although the institution should provide opportunities prior to this admissions point for freshmen and sophomores to confront expectations for teachers and their own suitability for teaching). Part of the interview process at the gate of a center of pedagogy points out the degree to which the program is oriented toward teaching as a moral endeavor and clarifies what this requires of the candidate. There are no second entry gates in the undergraduate program, and once through the entry gates, students enter a planned programmatic sequence. They may not circumvent part of it or subvert the sequence, although they will encounter alternative learning opportunities. Similar expectations and conditions mark the postbaccalaureate alternative. There is a class of '98, and its student membership is different from the class of '99.

Throughout the three years beyond the undergraduate admissions gate, there is a continuing process of formative evaluation focused on both the program and the student. Passing grades in foundations and methods courses are no longer sufficient. Instead, faculty members responsible for cohort groups and for mentoring individuals are frequently asking themselves, "Is this person living up to our expectations of what is necessary progress to date?" and asking the student, "How do you feel about your present state of readiness to become a teacher?" These questions and the answers are shared by all members of the faculty, whether primarily university-based or school-based.

As we shall see in Chapter Eight, the Center for Educational Renewal and its affiliated settings are working on the complex issues associated with such formative evaluation. There is growing awareness in the educational scholarly community of the need to develop far better, more comprehensive systems for selecting future teachers and monitoring their progress.[17] There is an equally urgent need to engage in continuously evaluating the program.

Socialization into Teaching

There is a paradox in the gap between rhetoric that places students at the heart of the educational process and programs that do not. The gap in teacher education no doubt contributes to the gap in many of our schools. Every now and then, as the mammoth federal, state, and local educational enterprise grinds on, we pause to say, "It's all for the kids." Why must we deliberately remind ourselves of this?

I addressed part of the reason earlier: the relegation of education and schooling to a secondary, instrumental status, usually economic or "military." This relegation concomitantly assigns instrumental value to schoolteachers, students, and the parents who produce the needed "instruments"—children. There is evidence everywhere of this utilitarian perspective aborting or corrupting the educational process.

There is little doubt that the instrumental axis will always dominate educational policy and pull the conduct of education toward it. The antidote is for educators and parents to join in maintaining a tension between this axis and a caring, nurturing, educational axis that pulls children and youths to the center of teaching and learning. The fact that this axis is currently weak does not negate the argument that parents and teachers could collaborate to make it strong.

We were deeply troubled over three sets of conditions in many of the teacher education settings we visited: the absence of institutional welcome to students, the weak to nonexistent informal process of socialization, and the absence of mission-oriented coherence in the formal program. The few exceptions drew attention to the common omissions. My student host at an institution that exhibited a good deal of caring had visited five others, each of which expressed little or no interest in his career plans, before settling on one that did. At another that cared, students were given the home phone numbers of faculty members and told to call when in need. Faculty members routinely visited sick students to wish them well and bring them up to date on class activity.

Teacher education settings are commonly marked and thrive by the efforts of individual professors to provide for students a sense of identity as aspiring teachers and of identification with place and colleagues. The wonderful Agnes Snyder of Adelphi College (when it was not yet a university) on Long Island, New York, comes to mind as exemplary. She was a role model of great personal power, primarily because she so obviously cared. But the informal socialization process must be deliberately planned and conducted if it is to have broad impact in nurturing students and developing in them the expectations and competencies that go with the moral responsibilities of teachers. Socialization into teaching is too important to leave to the chance that the preparation program will include on the faculty roster at least one great teacher.

Nor can the preparation program's focus on mission be left to chance. Yet there was little in our findings to give us confidence regarding, for example, ongoing processes designed to prepare teachers for the moral stewardship of schools.[18] Their vision and accompanying preparation had more to do with the management of classrooms and the mechanics of teaching. Such preparation falls short of producing teachers to provide the nurturing kind of teaching our children never needed more than they do now and schools that are moral places. The program defined in Chapter Six endeavors to provide at least a framework for both informal and formal processes of socialization to function effectively.

Laboratories and Field Stations

In the first chapter of *Teachers for Our Nation's Schools,* I argue from a historical perspective that teacher education has been, from its beginnings in the 1840s, a neglected enterprise. Much of its current neglect arises from its educational context; in particular, the prevailing, defective view of teaching, learning, and the teacher-student relationship. In this high-tech age of worker-friendly facilities and support systems in the corporate world, the prevailing image of teachers and students only modestly expands that of Mark Hopkins seated at one end of the log and students at the other (though Hopkins would be more bureaucratically controlled today). Much as we admonish teachers at all levels to depart from "frontal teaching," we provide a context that not only encourages it but inhibits efforts to change. Indeed, the requirements specified for teachers in some states guide them toward a heavy emphasis on didactics.

I could write impassioned pages about my efforts over more than half a century to get students' desks unscrewed from the floor or slats; a hallway fan (air-conditioning being out of the question) to reduce the morning temperature of offices and classrooms in our noninsulated, temporary building (it still houses the teacher education program forty years later); some sort of common room for faculty and students in several different settings; an elementary school with a measure of flexible, discretionary space; just one classroom with that sort of space in a major university; and on and on. The common context of teaching and learning in higher education — especially in the arts and sciences — is an ill-equipped office for the professor and a boxlike classroom for his or her teaching and students' learning. Unfortunately, whether or not teacher education is housed in a "professional" school or college of education, the contextual expectation is much like that for the social sciences and humanities; no other amenities are needed.

The argument here is not that teacher education needs *more;* it is simply that it needs what is appropriate for this particular enterprise. It is for this reason that I have reworked the wording of Postulate Two (see Chapter Three for all nineteen) to read as follows: *Programs for the education of educators must enjoy parity with other professional education programs, full legitimacy and institutional commitment, and rewards for faculty geared to the nature of the field.* The previous wording called for parity with other campus programs, but identification with the professions is more accurate and, in the long run, more promising in regard to changing the condition of neglect. My purpose here is to get for teacher education what the enterprise, the schools, the children, and the nation must have.

In envisioning the necessary conditions, this postulate must be aligned with Postulate Fifteen: *Programs for the education of educators must assure for each candidate the availability of a wide array of settings for simulation, observation, hands-on experiences, and exemplary schools for internships and residencies; they must admit no more students to their programs than can be assured these quality experiences.* (*Simulation* was added to the original.) I tie several of the material needs to the curriculum in Chapter Six and to the settings for observation, internships, and residencies in Chapter Four.

The point to be made here is that teacher education will continue to be a dangerously neglected enterprise, no matter what the resolve and commitment of the faculty, if it continues to be framed by conventional visions of frontal teaching (the lecturing, telling, and questioning of a class) and seat-based learning. Moving from neglect involves reexamining the nature of exemplary professional preparation, faculty loads in relationship to programmatic requirements, and the necessary laboratory-type components that must be put in place.

It is my very rough estimate that most settings will require average budgetary increases in the neighborhood of 25 to 30 percent, exclusive of physical plant and equipment requirements in both universities and partner schools. We have abandoned long ago in higher education the notion of a simple yardstick in determining the allocation of resources. The differing allocations currently prevailing are the result of recognizing different needs for differing academic enterprises, with need usually massaged to the point of recognition by enterprising deans and department chairs. So must it be in teacher education.

But before a dean of education seeks differential recognition for teacher education (should teacher education be housed in the school or college of education), he or she would be well advised to develop the case carefully, preparing a critical analysis of current priorities and budgetary allocations. Academic vice presidents and provosts should be acutely aware of the fact that teacher education on many campuses is sacrificed to other programs and is characterized by comparatively high course output in relation to dollar input. Because changing this could be suicidal for deans, higher administrative officials may need to step in by earmarking funds for purposes that are not negotiable after these funds are allocated.

Continuing Connections

One area of additional cost involves putting in place conditions to serve two purposes pertaining to teacher education students' entry into full-time teaching. The first is to derive from graduates information of potential use in renewing programs. The second is to provide support during the early months and years. I address both in Chapter Six; there is need for very little more here.

But one point must be made over and over with respect to the transition of aspiring teachers coming through a planned program into life as teachers. The education of educators suffers from one of its distinctive characteristics: the way in which continuing education and degrees overlap, roll into one another, and relate to career and income advantages. Many teacher education programs are built on the proposition that they provide only beginning preparation; many of their shortcomings are similarly defended. Perhaps I am off-base in seeing here the seeds of precisely what should *not* be the intellectual and professional orientation of educators.

The concept of being a lifelong learner should be part of the socialization process from the outset. Aspiring teachers should be guided into the journals they should read and the organizations in which they should hold membership. Inquiry and reflection should become habitual.

We found little in teacher education programs to fuel our

confidence that this kind of intellectual orientation was being fostered. We found less to suggest that teachers were going out as confident, reflective practitioners with continuing connections to the college or university of which they had been a part. And we know from our earlier research that the in-service or staff development activities into which they move are topical in nature, of very short episodic duration, and heavily slanted toward what appears to be immediately practical.[19] There appears to be little coherence in the course-getting that can add up to a master's degree, and the process of pursuing this advanced degree is crammed into a demanding schedule of school and family responsibilities. A schedule of reading for personal and professional growth seems not to be the norm for educators in the schools. Reading and accompanying discussion with colleagues is not the norm of daily life in the workplace, but it should be in schools.

Changing all this will not be easy. It must begin with preservice socialization into intellectual life as a teacher and continue in the partner schools in which future teachers become part of the faculty — schools in which, as a reasonable outgrowth of a school-university partnership, reading and discussion would be the norm of daily life. In several settings across the country, programs for the preparation of school principals are being designed so as to develop an intellectual orientation among candidates and both awareness of and ability to fulfill the leadership role involved in making schools centers of inquiry. We have found that school-university partnerships offer promising mechanisms for building into the lives of all involved increased attention to reflection and the importance of continuing intellectual growth.

A center of pedagogy is incomplete if those responsible for it see their work done when their teacher graduates walk out the door. It is essential that graduate programs for master teachers, specialists, principals, and superintendents be equally clear in mission and coherence. I envision a time when centers of pedagogy will either contribute significantly to (or operate as part of their outreach) professional development centers offering a wide range of educational opportunities for those who contribute to the making of educative communities.

The Regulatory Context

In seeking to exercise their constitutional rights and responsibilities in education, states have been overly intrusive in regard to specifications that drive teacher education programs. There have been at least three negative consequences. First, this intrusiveness has caused some strong universities to be wary about continued or new involvement with an enterprise so closely monitored by the state. Second, it has added to the academic attractiveness for professors of education to move out of curricular prescriptions for teacher education programs to less controlled graduate teaching. Third, the fact of curricular prescriptions accompanied by the vagaries of change in requirements has discouraged professors from devoting time and energy to fundamental change. These combined consequences conspire to drive quality down, and they have been exacerbated by the extent to which the need for an adequate supply of teachers, together with the never-ending interest in preparing them cheaply, opens the door to low-quality alternatives.

To rectify all of this, attention must be addressed to three critical focal points. The first is to put in place the conditions necessary to exemplary programs presented here and further elaborated in what follows. Completion of these programs leads to degrees and certificates of completion but does not carry with it a license to teach. The licensing process, our second focal point, is a state prerogative. At one time, the certificate of completion and receipt of a license were virtually one and the same — hence emergence of the convention "state certification." Unfortunately, the reason that the two were so often joined was that much of the curriculum completed was prescribed by the state.

The danger today is that the state may not be willing to give up its role in curricular prescription, instead adding still more to control by requiring, for example, some measure of outcomes. To the degree that states move in the direction of outcome measures while retaining curricular control, they add to the consequences listed above; state prescription of teacher education curricula is a dead-end street. So how *should* the states be involved? They have the right to use licensing measures designed to protect the public, certainly. Checking for criminal records, for example, is entirely appropriate. In law and medicine, the states control licensing examinations, and there is no good reason that they could not do something similar in regard to teaching in schools. However, developing valid measures of teaching ability is more complicated than most policymakers believe; maintaining and revising them requires a considerable bureaucracy and can be costly.

States might be on higher ground in seeking to ensure adequate commitment, resources, and processes of renewal in each approved setting and then accepting certificates of completion as a prerequisite for seeking to meet the states' licensing requirements. This turns attention to the third focal point— namely, accreditation. There is much to be gained by attending to accreditation procedures through which the interests of the public, teacher candidates, teacher education settings, and the teaching profession are represented and protected. States should not relinquish their role, however—a role best fulfilled by being an active player in accreditation and the major authority in seeing to it that teacher education programs have the conditions in place that give one confidence in certificates of completion.

Postulates

My colleagues and I have translated the foregoing conditions thought necessary to exemplary programs for the education of educators into nineteen postulates, each arguing for one or more of the essential elements. There are many different paths to their attainment. But, we argue, each omission and each misguided or bungled effort to attain a given condition reduces the prospect of attaining high quality.

The postulates can be highly serviceable for faculty groups coming together in a center of pedagogy for purposes of redesigning and renewing programs for the education of educators— programs that require the simultaneous renewal of the partner schools embraced by the center. First, they provide a set of specifications for a structure to be created. Second, they suggest questions to be asked and answered in seeking to assess attainments to date. Third, they enable the responsible parties to set finite agendas — finite in the sense that what is to be attained is tangible and consequently subject to verification. In other words, they do not work endlessly toward general goals but work rather on the planks of the bridge agreed on at the outset as most likely to span the river dependably.

Getting insight into the precise intent of each postulate and its potential utility involves a process of unpacking the postulates. Let us go to this now.

3

Unpacking
the Postulates

There is no need now of recriminations over what has been, or
of apologies by way of defending a regime practically obsolete.
Let us address ourselves resolutely to the task of reconstructing
the American medical school on the lines of the highest modern
ideals of efficiency and in accordance with the finest conceptions
of public service.[1]

— Henry S. Pritchett

The challenge above, presented for medical education in
1910 by Henry S. Pritchett, the president of the Carnegie Foundation for the Advancement of Teaching, is very
similar to the challenge we face in teacher education as the century draws to a close. Pritchett saw a very large portion of that
challenge as moral, calling for "an educational patriotism on
the part of the institutions of learning and a medical patriotism
on the part of the physician." He saw no way for any university
to maintain its respect while retaining a low-grade professional
school for the sake of its own completeness and no way for the
profession to maintain its respect while diluting itself with people from weak medical schools with low ideals of both education and professional honor. He raised far-reaching economic
questions to which society had as yet given little attention.[2]

Pritchett's scope of moral responsibility was inclusive: the

Note: Most of the content of this chapter derives from work in progress by colleagues in the Center for Educational Renewal. I am grateful especially to Judith
Ellsworth, Jianping Shen, Kenneth Sirotnik, and Roger Soder.

physician, the medical school, the university, and the nation. So must it be for the education of educators.

The contribution of Abraham Flexner's report, for which Pritchett wrote the introduction, was definition of the conditions necessary to fulfillment of this responsibility. The purpose of the nineteen postulates referred to in preceding chapters is to posit for careful perusal and potential wide approval and adoption a similar set of equally encompassing conditions related to teacher education. Before this adoption can occur, however, both the postulates and their implications must be understood.

My colleagues and I are encouraged by the degree to which the postulates and other aspects of our work have served as bases for dialogue regarding the renewal of teacher education in the United States. Many settings have sent us documents prepared for or growing out of discussions of the postulates involving a wide range of participants.[3] In addition, those committed to fulfilling the postulates and affiliated with us in the National Network for Educational Renewal have analyzed and debated their merits. Nonetheless, we believe that their potential for both giving direction to renewal and evaluating progress has been only moderately tapped. Using the postulates productively requires an intellectual orientation somewhat uncommon in an enterprise much more accustomed to setting educational goals and objectives as the end, and frequently also as the means, of educational improvement.

Genesis of the Postulates

In conceptualizing our research into the conduct of the education of educators, my colleagues and I did not set out by posing postulates; nor did we come upon them under a rock in the woods. We did what comes rather naturally to academicians: we read selectively and quite a lot; we studied the histories of education in other professions; we talked with knowledgeable others about how they would try to get a handle on what we hoped to do; we probed into the question of current agreement on existing good teacher education programs (though we found little); we looked at some descriptions of existing programs; and we exchanged and discussed various position papers each of us was moved at times to write.

Throughout all of this preparatory period, and indeed beyond, I was much influenced by my own experiences as director of teacher education and teacher education projects in four rather different institutions of higher learning. My several years of participating in the conduct and aftermath of the study by James B. Conant in the first half of the 1960s also shaped my thinking considerably. At one stage in our planning, I wrote a long list of questions that one might consider asking about any teacher education program in considering its quality and context. They covered a broad range of issues, from institutional commitment and support, to the state regulatory structure, to details about the program.

What was missing, as in any list of open-ended questions, was a tilt toward value premises on the basis of which the adequacy and virtue of answers might be judged—what Ralph Tyler refers to in his curriculum rationale as a *philosophical screen*.[4] We agreed firmly on the proposition that not all values are equally sound. For example, a totalitarian value screen for determining the desired nature of programs designed to educate the young for participation in a social and political democracy is unacceptable. We have at no time disagreed about or wavered in this position. Consequently, we proceeded to rewrite the questions as affirmations of what we believed the answers would be if just, good, and beautiful. More than twenty such affirmations resulted; subsequently, they were reduced to nineteen. In setting out to write *Teachers for Our Nation's Schools*, I had to find a rubric by which to identify them. The word *postulate* drifted into my mind from a rather lively discussion with several colleagues at the University of Chicago years earlier. That word, meaning a carefully reasoned argument or set of presuppositions, seemed to fit our intent admirably. My colleagues agreed.

We had before us, then, not only a conceptualization of the major components of and surrounding programs for the education of educators but also affirmations describing their healthy state. Strong support from the top leadership of a teacher-preparing institution is an indicator of good health; diffidence is a sign of ill-health. Programmatic coherence around a mission is a sign of good health; lack of mission and coherence of program suggest poor health. An identifiable faculty group at work on program renewal is a sign of healthy teacher education; a faculty engaged primarily in other matters and simply teaching courses required for certification gives one pause.

Our decisions with respect to good health did not arise out of empirical research. As I have noted, they are affirmations as to what is *good*. (As I stated in Chapter One, we recommend that persons uncomfortable with norms so formulated rewrite each of the postulates so as to affirm the opposite. They will not like the results.) The challenge in the empirical research that followed the hard work of conceptualization was to employ as many techniques as possible in probing into the health of each setting in our representative sample. These techniques are described in detail elsewhere.[5]

This research produced a picture of the degree to which each setting that we studied approached (and fell short of) good health as posed in each postulate. It enabled us also to create a composite picture—the picture presented in *Teachers for Our Nation's Schools*. The perceived gap reported between the conditions we found and those favored in the postulates provides an agenda, the particulars of which differ for each individual setting. The settings constituting the National Network for Educational Renewal currently are at work on the agendas that emerged from their own self-analysis. Some are endeavoring to work across the board on all or most fronts at once. Most are concentrating on just a few selected as having top priority. All are committed to the ultimate implementation of the conditions embedded in all nineteen.

Using the Postulates

There are many ways to use the postulates for program review and renewal. The unpacking of them that has gone on in the Center for Educational Renewal serves primarily the purpose of determining progress in the settings with which we are affiliated and productive employment of the Center's resources in providing assistance. A teacher education setting might use what follows in getting started or for evaluating progress periodically.

It is important to note that each postulate devotes attention to several elements or conditions to be taken into account simultaneously. Each of these essential elements should be identified in the overall context provided by the postulate and singled out for attention. The questions I raise in what follows suggest the kind of evidence to be sought in attempting to determine the degree of attention being given in the setting to the several components of that specific postulate. The list of questions is not intended to be all-inclusive; circumstances in a given setting may suggest different or additional questions. It is important in proceeding to keep in mind the interconnectedness of the entire group of postulates.

Almost half of the postulates have been reworded since their initial appearance in *Teachers for Our Nation's Schools*. I note as I come to them changes in Postulates Two, Four, Six, Twelve, Fifteen, Sixteen, Eighteen, and Nineteen — changes that do not alter the intended meaning but help to clarify. The desirability of making these modest revisions emerged out of discussions with many different groups of teacher educators.

Early in these discussions, it became apparent that the orientation of the postulates is toward the college or university side of what my colleagues and I recommend be a joint endeavor with school districts and schools. This is probably the almost inevitable result of two significant factors. First, higher education has so dominated the conduct of teacher education over the years that responsibility, let alone authority, on the part of the schools has never been seriously assumed. Second, our conceptualization and related research focused primarily on the traditionally responsible higher education side.

We recognize now the need to include in unpacking the present postulates questions that clearly encompass the school-university partnership in addressing such matters as the commitment, rewards, and resources that must come from the school side if the relationship is to be robust and the program exemplary. Some of the postulates imply the partnership, but additional explication is required. As steps in this direction, I draw attention to the role of schools and school personnel in some of what follows and then address further implications in the discussion of school-university partnerships and partner schools in Chapter Four. It is essential to keep in mind that the centers of pedagogy referred to frequently below include in their composition personnel from both schools and institutions of higher education. Ensuring a responsible role for schools is essential to the health of centers of pedagogy and carries us into much relatively unexplored terrain.

Postulate One. Programs for the education of the nation's educators must be viewed by institutions offering them as a major responsibility to society and be adequately supported and promoted and vigorously advanced by the institution's top leadership.

The key concepts here are "major responsibility to society," "adequately supported and promoted," and "top leadership." In following the overall intent of this postulate, one would want to look for the identification and treatment of teacher education in whatever long-range planning documents are available for the institution as a whole. Is there anything that suggests a sense of moral stewardship in the way top leadership views the fact that the institution prepares educators for the schools? If so, it would be appropriate and expedient for the person primarily responsible for teacher education — the dean or chair of the SCDE or the director of teacher education — to send to the president a note of commendation and appreciation. If not, this person should watch for opportunities to point out the omission repeatedly. Parallel relationships are to be developed with the superintendents of collaborating school districts.

Clearly, it is important that the president and academic vice president of the university and the several superintendents of the connected school districts be keenly aware of who this person is and whether or not he or she is providing aggressive leadership. The head of teacher education must go knocking on the doors of key administrators who do not already possess a sense of responsibility for advancing teacher education.

The faculty group constituting (or soon to constitute) a center of pedagogy and seeking to determine the degree to which the institutional setting reflects attention to Postulate One would want to seek answers to such questions as the following:

1. What is the nature of references to the teacher education program in university or college documents such as the general catalogue, alumni magazines, newsletters of the board of trustees, major addresses of the president and provost, and so on? How frequent are such references?

2. Does the top leadership have a plan for the positive future of the teacher education program in the most recent long-range planning documents?

3. Has there been in recent years any unusual material support (that is, support in the form of human and monetary resources) as part of a demonstration of commitment to preserve or enhance teacher education?

4. During budget cuts, is the teacher education program cut proportionally, or is it cut more or less than other programs?

5. Assuming that the president and provost selectively attend important functions of the various campus units, does it appear that they attend proportionally such major activities of the SCDE as the annual alumni gathering, important lectures by leading educators, and critical meetings of the faculty? When was the most recent such attendance, by whom, and for what?

6. Does the institution's top leadership express clearly both the delegation of authority to those responsible for teacher education and full support to that delegated authority?

7. Have there been any instances in the past two years when the president or academic vice president was called upon to assist the teacher education program with a problem or crisis? What was the nature of the response?

8. Have there been in the past two years any accomplishments in the program or by professors connected with it that are of the sort commonly used by the institution in its public relations effort?

9. What policies with respect to school districts' participation have been formulated by their respective boards? What evidences of implementation are there—for example, in administrative procedures or collective bargaining contracts?

As answers to questions such as these get assembled and collated, certain trends with respect to the component parts of the postulate will begin to emerge. This information must not simply be kept available for use at some possible later time. Instead, the director of a center of pedagogy, for example, must use this information in every way possible to draw the attention of the president, the academic vice president, and school officials to the importance and needs of the teacher education enterprise.

Postulate Two. Programs for the education of educators must enjoy parity with other professional education programs, full legitimacy and institutional commitment, and rewards for faculty geared to the nature of the field. (Wording is changed from the original.)

The full implications of this postulate do not quickly settle in one's mind and one's image of the possible. What is the prevailing institutional perception of the nature of the teacher education enterprise and of the kinds of activities to be rewarded and adequately supported? The formula commonly governing the allocation of resources to undergraduate departments will not suffice, and prospects for the formula governing the medical school may be out of sight. But a high level of attention to individual students and involvement with them in field-based activities necessitate a lower student-teacher ratio than currently prevails in most settings. And it requires resources long ignored.

The key components here pertain to what constitutes "parity with other professional programs," bases of "rewards," and the relevance of these "to the nature of the field." Relevant questions include the following:

1. What is the current basis for determining budgetary allocations to the teacher education program? Is there any evidence from the faculty to suggest satisfaction or dissatisfaction with the student load? Are all component parts of the teacher education enterprise encompassed by the annual budget, or must certain parts be defended separately from year to year?

2. What does evidence regarding the allocation of their individual time by the president and provost suggest with respect to parity of treatment of the teacher education program? Do they pay attention only when asked, for example, or do they

sometimes take the initiative in seeking out information regarding the welfare of teacher education? Is parity demonstrated in the public relations efforts of the institution?

3. Does the institutional commitment to recruitment provide parity in resources for and treatment of teacher education? To what extent has the institution supported rhetorically and with resources an effort to recruit both faculty and students representing the diverse nature of the school population of the United States?

4. To what extent do the institutional criteria for promotion and merit recognition include consideration of the particular nature of the demands in teacher education? Do other professional fields receive rewards that are not similarly provided for accomplishment in teacher education?

5. Has the SCDE or the center of pedagogy made any serious, sustained effort to revise its merit, promotion, and tenure system in order to attract and reward faculty for significantly increased involvement in the teacher education program? Are there any differences in the criteria used for faculty involved or not involved in the teacher education program, and if so, what is the nature of these differences? What is the present degree of satisfaction or dissatisfaction with these criteria and their use on the part of faculty generally and in teacher education specifically? Are there now criteria that give recognition to involvement in developing school-university partnerships and community service? To what degree do the criteria used in evaluating research productivity give recognition to research on educational phenomena calling for qualitative methods or the use of a relatively wide range of research methods?

6. Are members of the faculty of the center of pedagogy (or the teacher education program) given adequate recognition by their home bases for participating in teacher education? Specifically, is the work of teachers in partner schools and faculty members in the arts and sciences recognized in their home settings or departments?

7. To what degree does there appear to be parity for those involved in teacher education in regard to salary levels, leaves and sabbaticals, amenities of the workplace, and respect?

Postulate Three. Programs for the education of educators must be autonomous and secure in their borders, with clear organizational identity, constancy of budget and personnel, and decision-making authority similar to that enjoyed by the major professional schools.

The key concepts here are "autonomous and secure . . . borders," "clear organizational identity," "constancy of budget and personnel," and "decision-making authority" commensurate with the assigned responsibility — all these at levels "enjoyed by the major professional schools." Surely this is not asking too much for the unit charged with providing teachers for our young people. If it is, then our claims regarding the role and value of education in a democratic society are largely empty rhetoric.

In searching for good news in answers to questions such as the following, faculties in settings all across the United States are likely to come up short. Borders such as those proposed around clearly identifiable entities are far from the existing pattern in teacher education.

1. Who participates in existing teacher education programs? Are the arts and sciences, the schools, and the SCDE proportionately represented? Where are the participants physically located? When and in what kind of configurations do they come together to plan and conduct the teacher education enterprise? How do they identify themselves when asked what they do? Is there a physical facility or significant part of a facility marked for and used by an identifiable faculty and student body?

2. Under what rubrics is the teacher education budget identified and classified? Is it handled separately, as an autonomous unit or program? As a line item in the budget of the SCDE? As part of the budget of a department or division in the SCDE, such as curriculum and instruction? Not at all?

3. How are budgetary resources in teacher education obtained? Once obtained, are the resources used solely for teacher education? Who is in charge of this budget? How is the budget put together and subsequently monitored?

4. Are there faculty positions specifically designated for teacher education, and are budgetary resources tied to these posi-

tions? When someone significantly involved in teacher education leaves or resigns, is the position subsequently protected for teacher education? Is there a discrete teacher education faculty, or are faculty members essentially "borrowed" from schools, departments in the SCDE, and the rest of the university? Is the budget developed and utilized in such a way as to guarantee continuity of school personnel in all planning, decision making, and ongoing programs?

5. Who participates in decisions regarding teacher education, from recruitment and use of faculty members, to budget allocations, to program development? Are any individuals who participate regularly in such decisions connected only minimally or not at all to teacher education? Are there individuals who participate regularly in teacher education but do not have the right to vote on any of the decisions pertaining to personnel, budget, and program? How many layers of individuals in higher authority are there between the director of teacher education and the provost or academic vice president?

6. In what ways is the teacher education program autonomous with respect to organization, program development and approval, faculty promotion, and like matters? How does the program's degree of autonomy compare with that of schools of engineering, business, and architecture?

7. If teacher education is conducted as part of an SCDE, how does it compare with other divisions or units with respect to the ratio between financial resources put in (especially in connection with faculty members) and courses generated?

8. How comprehensive and available are data that show the relative standing of campus units with respect to budget allocations, faculty salaries, faculty authority over programs, and so on? If the data are available, how do comparisons that include teacher education shape up? If the data are not available, how important are they and how can they be obtained?

Postulate Four. There must exist a clearly identifiable group of academic and clinical faculty members for whom teacher education is the top priority; the group must be responsible and accountable for selecting

diverse groups of students and monitoring their progress, planning and main-
taining the full scope and sequence of the curriculum, continuously evalu-
ating and improving programs, and facilitating the entry of graduates into
teaching careers. (There is a slight addition to the original wording.)

This postulate spells out major characteristics of the center, unit, or program of Postulate Three that is to have secure boundaries. Specifically, there is "a clearly identifiable group of academic and clinical faculty members" who are "responsible and accountable" for recruiting and "selecting students and monitoring their progress," for "planning and maintaining the full scope and sequence of the curriculum," for "continuously evaluating and improving programs," and for "facilitating the entry of graduates into teaching careers." These faculty members are drawn from the schools, the arts and sciences, and the SCDE. They join in all aspects of the renewal process.

If there is to be renewal, this is the group that will do it. Rarely is the group now presumably responsible either in existence as specified or engaged in renewing the campus program, let alone partner schools and campus components simultaneously. There are many questions to ask and answers to ponder.

1. What is the representation of the current faculty group responsible for planning and conducting the teacher education program? How are members distributed with respect to affiliation with the SCDE, departments outside of the SCDE, and schools? How are they distributed with respect to rank and eligibility to vote on all relevant matters? Do any members participate actively but not vote — for example, those not on the tenure track? Who should be involved but is not?

2. How is this faculty group distributed with respect to percentage of time committed to and involved with teacher education, whether on a college or university campus or in partner schools?

3. To whom on the college and university campus and in the cooperating school districts is this faculty group accountable? How do those to whom the group is accountable monitor the exercise of authority and responsibility on the part of the faculty group?

4. How is this group involved in recruitment, and what attention does it give to the recruitment of a diverse array of faculty and students? What mechanisms have been established to bring this group together for planning, conducting, evaluating, and renewing programs? Are there any other bodies on the campus or in the cooperating school districts that regard themselves (or are regarded by others) as also having responsibility for some significant part of the teacher education program?

5. What procedures are in place for evaluating ongoing programs? To what extent do current students or graduates participate in or provide data relevant to this process?

6. What evidence is there to show that open exchange of views is taking place among all responsible faculty? What evidence is there to suggest that there is true collaboration among faculty members devoting differing proportions of their time to differing components of the total program?

7. What ongoing processes exist for monitoring and evaluating the success of individual students? How many students are dropping out, and why? How many are being deliberately eliminated, and why? What procedures are in place for ensuring that students are ready for placement as interns in school settings? Is there any evidence to suggest that there are marked differences among differing groups of students (by sex, race, ethnicity, and so on) in regard to dropouts?

8. What attention is being given to such constructs as scope, continuity, sequence, integration, and organizing elements in the development of the curriculum? How are basic curricular changes effected?

9. What continuing thought is being given to questions of evaluation? Have any outside evaluations been conducted in recent years, and with what results? How is evidence gathered as to the evolution of each individual student's self-perception from student to teacher?

10. What is the nature of conscious efforts, if any, to keep the teacher education program connected both to programs elsewhere and to the changing nature of the larger educational context to which teacher education should relate?

Postulate Five. The responsible group of academic and clinical faculty members described above must have a comprehensive understanding of the aims of education and the role of schools in our society and be fully committed to selecting and preparing teachers to assume the full range of educational responsibilities required.

Postulate Five is the first in a series of several devoted almost exclusively to curricular considerations ranging from orientation, to the role of schools in a democratic society, to moral and ethical dimensions, to preparing teachers to be inquirers, to the necessary components of coherent programs. These matters are discussed in such detail in Chapters Five and Six that I shall say no more here. The unpacking process from here on, with just a few exceptions, is confined to some of the important questions that should be raised by those seeking to determine the present conditions of programs and areas in need of urgent attention.

1. Is there now, or is the faculty now working on, a set of basic agreements regarding the aims of public schooling in a pluralistic democratic society? If not, what are the prospects of creating dialogue among the responsible faculty members with respect to the mission for the education of educators?
2. To what degree is there a comprehensive statement embracing the full range of educational responsibilities teachers are to assume?
3. To what extent do the recruitment and selection of students for teacher education include orientation to the mission and responsibilities assumed in the previous two questions? How does the program convey to prospective teachers the responsibilities they are expected to take on in their later careers?
4. To what degree are faculty members in all three of the participating groups currently engaged in scholarly work focused on a better understanding of the aims of education and the role of schools in a democracy?
5. How broadly does the current faculty represent in its educational background and diversity the interests and understandings basic to the implications inherent in this postulate?

Postulate Six. The responsible group of academic and clinical faculty members must seek out and select for a predetermined number of student places in the program those candidates who reveal an initial commitment to the moral, ethical, and enculturating responsibilities to be assumed, and make clear to them that preparing for these responsibilities is central to this program. (This statement includes an addition to the original.)

Again, the questions are intended to direct attention to critical aspects of a given institutional setting's program.

1. What is being done to actively recruit teacher candidates? Do faculty members visit schools to talk with prospective students, for example, or place ads in particular newspapers?

2. Are there specific ways by which minority teacher candidates are recruited? Why have minority students been actively recruited? Are a certain number of student places reserved for minority students? Why or why not? Is there a timetable for increasing the proportion of minority teacher candidates to match that proportion of the public school population?

3. How are applicants selected? What are the criteria for selection? What are the reasons for the criteria?

4. What does the whole application package look like? For example, is it strongly weighted toward test scores and GPAs, or does it include assessment through such measures as portfolios and interviews?

5. Are there any criteria to ensure that teacher candidates manifest an initial commitment to moral, ethical, and enculturating responsibilities?

6. How is the ideal candidate for the program defined? What are the major differences between the applicants who are chosen and not chosen?

7. How is the number of student places determined? Does the program take in as many qualified applicants as possible, or does it have a predetermined number of places? Why? Is the teacher education program perceived as a cash-cow?

8. How are conflicts dealt with over the enrollment proposed by the administration of the university or college and the enrollment perceived as ideal by the responsible faculty?

9. How are moral, ethical, and enculturating responsibilities defined? Can examples be given to illustrate teacher candidates' moral commitment?

10.   What specific actions suggest that teacher candidates will
      be moral stewards? For example, are there experiences,
      such as volunteer work with children, described on their
      applications that give such evidence?

*Postulate Seven. Programs for the education of educators, whether
elementary or secondary, must carry the responsibility to ensure that all
candidates progressing through them possess or acquire the literacy and
critical-thinking abilities associated with the concept of an educated person.*

1.   What is the program's conception of an "educated person"?
2.   What are the general curriculum requirements for admis-
     sion into the teacher education program? Are applicants
     required to pass tests on general knowledge and skills? Are
     there specific curriculum requirements that every applicant
     must meet? For students who show promise as future teach-
     ers but lack proficiency in a basic knowledge or skill area,
     is there a conditional admission policy?
3.   Are there remedial programs for students who need help
     in improving such basic skills as reading, writing, mathe-
     matical computing, and reasoning?
4.   Do future teachers demonstrate skills in critical thinking
     and social reasoning? Do future high school teachers demon-
     strate competency in their chosen disciplines? Do future
     elementary teachers have the necessary breadth and depth
     of knowledge? What is the evidence?
5.   Do students have the habit of reading and thinking about
     contemporary educational issues? Do they subscribe to,
     read, and comment on the significant periodicals in edu-
     cation and their subject area? Are the occasional significant
     books that appear on the educational scene immediately in-
     corporated into the curriculum?

*Postulate Eight. Programs for the education of educators must
provide extensive opportunities for future teachers to move beyond being
students of organized knowledge to become teachers who inquire into both
knowledge and its teaching.*

1.   Which foundations courses does the program offer? Do
     foundations courses and related seminars help future teach-

ers inquire into the nature of education and schooling? Do
the courses and seminars include the development of American education and the evolution of educational thought?
Are themes that are introduced early on picked up and developed later?

2. Are child development courses available to help future
   teachers become familiar with the basic theories of learning and teaching and understand the mental, emotional,
   and physical development of children and adolescents?

3. Does the program offer courses in both general pedagogical knowledge and subject-specific pedagogical knowledge?
   Are both emphasized? How is undue duplication avoided?

4. Are teacher candidates introduced to major modes of knowing? How is their knowledge of these determined and
   deepened?

5. Are future teachers familiar with the theories of learning
   and teaching? Do they know the implications of differing
   theories of teaching and learning?

6. How does the teacher education program help future teachers form their philosophy of teaching and their belief about
   what good teaching is and is not?

7. How are field experiences coordinated with courses and
   seminars? How are theory and practice deliberately linked?

8. Are teacher candidates introduced to journals in their disciplines and in general curriculum fields? How and when?

*Postulate Nine. Programs for the education of educators must
be characterized by a socialization process through which candidates transcend their self-oriented student preoccupations to become more other-oriented
in identifying with a culture of teaching.*

1. What evidence suggests that the attention given to socializing students and the quality of this effort together have contributed to a reputation for the teacher education program
   that attracts students even when more conveniently located
   and perhaps easier alternatives are available?

2. What evidence is there of deliberate attention to a socialization process that builds deliberately on initial experiences
   to include an increasingly broad and deep orientation to

the demands and expectations of teaching? What are these activities, who is responsible for them, and how are faculty members from both the university and the schools rewarded for their efforts? How do teacher candidates become familiar with the availability of these orienting activities?

3.   Are groups of students admitted together as cohorts with a specific year of completion in mind, so that there is a class of '98 or '99? How are these groups put together and maintained? To what degree do students identify themselves with a peer cohort?

4.   To what extent do both formal and informal socialization processes combine to introduce future teachers to a relatively wide range of theories and practices, the principles and assumptions underlying them, and the nature of ongoing debates regarding their validity? How are conflicts such as those between some of the teachings on campus and some of the practices to be found in schools dealt with as they arise throughout the teacher education program?

5.   How are students encouraged to become conscious of teaching as a profession—its demands, responsibilities, and opportunities? To what extent are they made aware of various efforts to establish professional standards for the field, for programs, and for practitioners? In what ways are the existence, nature, and role of teacher unions brought into the preparation program?

6.   Are there seminars deliberately designed to help students reflect on their total array of experiences in the teacher education program? What is the nature of these seminars?

Postulate Ten. *Programs for the education of educators must be characterized in all respects by the conditions for learning that future teachers are to establish in their own schools and classrooms.*

1.   What is the ongoing programmatic effort to raise consciousness among the faculty regarding the need to demonstrate excellence in teaching, quality content throughout, use of a wide range of instructional materials, attention to the nature of the physical environment, the nature of the student-teacher relationship, and so on? In other words, what is

the responsible faculty group doing to ensure that what it does on a daily basis is exemplary in all respects?

2. What efforts are made to see through the eyes of teacher candidates what they see in their teachers and in the programs provided? What conclusions can be drawn from the information available? What efforts need to be made to secure more information on this perspective?

3. Are future teachers being encouraged at all times to evaluate what is being done to them and happening to them in the program and to relate their perceptions to their own self-expectations?

4. What appears to be the general relationship between the faculty and the students throughout the length and breadth of the program? What aspects of this relationship are worthy of satisfaction and self-commendation? What aspects are worrisome and in need of careful attention and remediation?

5. What processes exist for eliminating from the teacher education program practices that should not be emulated and for taking more drastic action when these processes fail to produce results?

Postulate Eleven. Programs for the education of educators must be conducted in such a way that future teachers inquire into the nature of teaching and schooling and assume that they will do so as a natural aspect of their careers.

1. Does the teacher education program intentionally reveal its own structure, conditions, processes, curriculum, and outcomes in a way that clearly models this practice for students?

2. What courses are offered to help students reflect on the nature of teaching and learning? What is the content of these courses?

3. How is the idea of "reflective practice" talked about, encouraged, and formally incorporated as a rigorous part of the program? Do students keep reflective journals? How are these journals used? Are they shared with faculty and peers?

4. Are future teachers formally initiated into habits of reading, thinking, and talking about contemporary educational issues? Are they encouraged to read major educational periodicals through classes and seminars? Are new books, reports, and other publications brought to their attention and, where appropriate, incorporated into classrooms?
5. Do future teachers have the opportunity to engage in intelligent, informed discussion and debate on educational issues throughout their preparation program, including student teaching and internships?

Postulate Twelve. Programs for the education of educators must involve future teachers in the issues and dilemmas that emerge out of the never-ending tension between the rights and interests of individual parents and interest groups and the role of schools in transcending parochialism and advancing community in a democratic society. (This postulate has been slightly revised and expanded.)

This postulate gets to the heart of the role of schools in a democratic society. Schools must act in the best interests of all equitably. But they must also relate to the particular needs of all children. Schools are never free of the tension between functioning for the common weal, on one hand, and satisfying (but not overly catering to) a wide array of individual and small-group interests on the other. Teachers must understand that this tension is not something that affects only administrators. As moral stewards of the schools, they are inescapably a part of it.

Those responsible for teacher education must ponder the implications of this societal tension for their programs. Questions to be asked include the following:

1. Do foundations courses address these fundamental educational tensions and dilemmas? Are future teachers engaged in critical discourse about them? Do they see the discourse as relevant to their work rather than "just philosophy"?
2. As future teachers progress through the program, do they revisit the major tensions, dilemmas, and underlying issues in public education both nationally and regionally?

3. Does the teacher education program involve future teachers in issues of tracking, equal access to knowledge, socioeconomic obstacles to access, and so on? Are these issues developed as thematic strands through the curriculum rather than packaged into an introductory foundations course?

4. What evidence is there that students actively participate in rigorous critical discourse about fundamental educational tensions and dilemmas?

5. How do students and faculty talk about what is in the public interest; about how schooling should address conflicts among family, community, state, and national interests; about the proper role of public schooling in a pluralistic society? What are students and faculty reading on these matters?

6. Do future teachers become actively engaged in issues such as those raised above in field experiences (especially their internships)? Do they actually get involved with current educational issues confronting the schools in which they are placed, or are their experiences confined to talking and reading about them?

Postulate Thirteen. Programs for the education of educators must be infused with understanding of and commitment to the moral obligation of teachers to ensure equitable access to and engagement in the best possible K-12 education for all *children and youths.*

In the mission for teacher education, we identify a moral dimension to each of the four major components. In Chapter Six, I address the foundations for those dimensions as they should be encountered in general education. However, teaching in the schools of a compulsory education system is a special case of teaching that compounds the moral stewardship of educators. Consequently, special attention must be paid in preparation programs to the infusion of the whole with the special moral considerations that arise out of this stewardship. The moral and ethical issues should be continuing themes, introduced in the selection process, continued in courses in educational foundations, and then addressed as part of all subsequent educational experiences. These questions assume this perspective:

1. Is the moral dimension of teaching a thematic strand running through the program? How is the moral dimension of teaching reflected in the courses and field experiences?

2. Does the teacher education program emphasize the following aspects: enculturation, equitable access to knowledge, effective teacher-student connections, and good stewardship? Does it address the moral, ethical, and legal aspects of the teacher-student relationship?

3. Are teacher candidates able to illustrate that "teaching is a moral endeavor"? What evidence is there to suggest that future teachers understand that education is a moral endeavor? Do student teachers reveal their commitment to the moral obligation of teachers in their student teaching? What is the evidence?

4. Are students familiar with the issues surrounding and the literature on equitable access to education and knowledge? What materials have they read on this, and what are they reading now? Are students familiar with the research on enrollment, retention, and academic achievements of different economic, ethnic, and racial groups?

5. What direct experiences do students have with exemplary schools? What conceptions of the ideal school underlie the program? What are the conceptions of the ideal school held by present faculty and students?

6. How do students and faculty talk about quality versus quantity, universalization versus elevation, and meritocracy versus mediocrity? What are students and faculty reading on these matters?

Postulate Fourteen. Programs for the education of educators must involve future teachers not only in understanding schools as they are but in alternatives, the assumptions underlying alternatives, and how to effect needed changes in school organization, pupil grouping, curriculum, and more.

1. Does the teacher education program provide a comprehensive introduction to schools as cultural entities? Are students reading about and discussing educational reform efforts and the alternatives being proposed?

2. What evidence is there that aspiring teachers are being en-
    culturated into the idea that schools must not remain un-
    changed in a changing society (even though they must offer
    considerable stability to students now enrolled)? To what
    extent does the curriculum prepare teachers to retain things
    the way they are instead of to question, inquire, and make
    changes based on this inquiry?

3. To what extent does the program include specific attention
    to theory and research on change, with particular atten-
    tion to the teacher's role as steward of schools? Is the focus
    almost exclusively on the classroom, or is the experience
    of teacher candidates broadened to include the whole school
    and the nature of its component elements?

4. To what degree does the introduction to schooling include
    specific attention to alternative ways of organizing class-
    rooms and grades, alternative ways of evaluating student
    progress, and ways of organizing the curriculum other than
    into a series of specific, subject-centered periods of the day?
    Are future teachers coming to understand their appropri-
    ate role in site-based management and school renewal?

5. What provision is there in the program for experiences out-
    side of individual classrooms that focus attention on prob-
    lems of the school as a whole?

6. What opportunities are there, if any, for students to work
    together in developing new ideas and exploring how these
    might be implemented in schools? In general, are students
    learning to work in collegial groups, as is necessary for prin-
    cipals and teachers in renewing schools?

*Postulate Fifteen. Programs for the education of educators must
assure for each candidate the availability of a wide array of laboratory
settings for simulation, observation, hands-on experiences, and exemplary
schools for internships and residencies; they must admit no more students
to their programs than can be assured these quality experiences.* (The word
simulation has been added to the original to include an important characteristic of forward-looking programs.)

A critical element of this postulate is the degree to which
the intake of students is geared to the available laboratory settings, especially partner schools. It is now common to admit

candidates with little or no thought to the institution's ability to provide the full array of resources necessary to quality. I am proposing an almost unheard of proposition: no more students are to be admitted than can be accommodated comfortably. This means an adequate supply of able faculty members, delivery of the entire curriculum, and placement of every candidate in first-rate field settings. Those hastily put together, last-minute adjustments to accommodate the casual intake of too many candidates must go.

1. How many partner schools are there? Is there a sufficient number for the placement of each group of interns?

2. Does every future teacher have access to laboratory settings for observation and hands-on experience and exemplary schools for internships? Do any of your graduates get certified without any field experiences other than student teaching?

3. Is there a planned sequence for teacher candidates to have field experiences? What is the sequence? Does this sequence move students steadily forward to take up the full responsibilities of being teachers?

4. Are there enough urban, racially heterogeneous sites to accommodate at least one internship experience for each student at such sites? If not, how is the need for experiences with diverse student populations being met? Are students required to do at least one internship? Are clinical experiences arranged to ensure that future teachers have experiences in a variety of school settings—urban, suburban, and rural?

5. Do student teaching experiences include both classroom teaching and whole-school involvement? Do student teachers essentially serve as junior members of each partner school's faculty?

6. Are the partner schools renewing? How do you know? Do faculty members in education and the arts and sciences participate in the renewal process? How?

7. Are all members of the teacher education faculty involved in supervising student teachers in these settings? What roles

do they play in the schools? How is evaluation of teacher candidates conducted?

Postulate Sixteen. Programs for the education of educators must engage future teachers in the problems and dilemmas arising out of the inevitable conflicts and incongruities between what is perceived to work in practice and the research and theory supporting other options. (Wording is changed slightly from the original.)

1. How do faculty members take into account the dilemma of the practical versus the theoretical when developing the teacher education program? How are students made conscious of the disparity between the practical and the theoretical? Is course time devoted to this issue? How about a reflective seminar? When this issue is raised in student teaching, how is it resolved?
2. What is the relationship between faculty members and student teachers? Is it reflective and focused on teaching and learning, or is it based on checklists and feedback?
3. Are there procedures by which undesirable teaching practices in the identified laboratory settings come to light and are officially dealt with in the center of pedagogy? What mechanisms are available for working with and improving problematic members of the responsible faculty?
4. What dual programmatic use is made of both university settings and school settings? How are decisions made with respect to the appropriate settings for instruction? How do the different groups of faculty members differentiate their responsibilities and collaborate?

Postulate Seventeen. Programs for the education of educators must establish linkages with graduates for purposes of both evaluating and revising these programs and easing the critical early years of transition into teaching.

1. Are there any mechanisms to maintain continued contact with program graduates? What are these mechanisms? How do they work? Is there an informal network by which to contact and get feedback from program graduates? What is it, and how does it work?

2.   Are there any activities or events for alumni of the program? What are they, and who is responsible for them?

3.   Who is involved in evaluating and revising the teacher education program? Does the evaluation system make provision for and actually include and use follow-up data from program graduates? Are there some good examples? How often is the program evaluated and revised? How is information regarding program revision and improvement disseminated?

4.   How is the effectiveness of partner schools working with teacher candidates evaluated? What criteria are used to determine the effectiveness of a partner school's program? Who defines the criteria?

5.   Does the program have anything resembling a "residency" experience for students in their first year (or more) of employment? How is the residency experience organized? What are the roles of the faculty and site-based educators?

6.   Is there a follow-up evaluation system for teachers in their first few years of teaching? What is the system, and who is involved? What is the role of those involved? What information is sought through this evaluation? For example, does it address strengths and weaknesses of the teacher education program, strengths and weaknesses of partner schools, common needs of beginning teachers, identification of useful seminars and workshops?

7.   If there is a procedure by which to contact recent program graduates, is there also a mechanism to help them if they have difficulties? Is there a network among recent program graduates so that they can help each other in their early years of professional life?

Postulate Eighteen. Programs for the education of educators require a regulatory context with respect to licensing, certifying, and accrediting that ensures at all times the presence of the necessary conditions embraced by the seventeen preceding postulates. (This postulate has been substantially revised.)

The most critical implication of this postulate is that there needs to be in each state a shared understanding of the role of and differences among licensing, certifying, and accrediting.

Currently, this entire area is an intellectual swamp; understandings and respective responsibilities are not well sorted out.

1. What mechanisms now exist in the state to ensure continuing dialogue about licensing, certifying, and accrediting among the various interested parties: the state, the profession, and the institution? Is there some kind of statewide council or association that brings together at least annually all the relevant parties to develop both understanding and clear-cut differentiation of licensing, certifying, and accrediting?
2. What is the present state of program autonomy with respect to the larger institutional as well as state context? How clearly defined are the limits of this autonomy?
3. What is the role of the state in specifying the components of the teacher education curriculum? What curricular flexibility now exists? To what degree is state intrusion inhibiting program renewal? To what degree is there mutual understanding and close collaboration between the state and accrediting agencies in regard to program approval and improvement? To what degree does the accreditation process enhance or inhibit renewal? To what degree do current trends in licensing, specification of curricular requirements, and accreditation policies and procedures need to be redirected? How does the institution exert influence in regard to necessary redirection? To what extent is the setting as a whole—especially its top leadership—aware of and involved in the clarification and maintenance of institutional autonomy with respect to teacher education?

Postulate Nineteen. Programs for the education of educators must compete in an arena that rewards efforts to continuously improve on the conditions embedded in all of the postulates and tolerates no shortcuts intended to ensure a supply of teachers. (This postulate has been revised to be as constructive as possible in its implications.)

1. How does the teacher education program compare with and differ from other programs in the state and community? Does it change requirements in order to attract students?

Does it alter requirements and admit more students than the program can handle so as to cut costs?

2. What is the general climate in the state toward teacher education? Do the governor, the state legislature, and citizens tend to support or reject teacher education reform? Do the state legislature and the state board of education recognize and seek to ensure the time and resources required for fundamental change to occur?

3. What is the climate of the community in which partner schools have been established? Does the community support the philosophy and practice of partner schools? How?

4. Is there pressure from the state on the teacher education program to admit more students than it can accommodate well? In the case of some pressure, does the program turn down the demand?

5. Does the state allow back-door emergency programs and/or temporary teaching licenses when there is a shortage of schoolteachers or pressure to cut costs? Under what circumstances and in what ways does the institution modify the length and breadth of programs in order to meet demands for quantity? Why?

6. Are there problems in the teacher preparation program over the tension between quality and quantity? What are some of these? Do they inhibit renewal?

Concluding Observations

There are dangers in the process of reflecting as a faculty group on the degree to which the conditions uncovered by questions such as these match the group's understanding of the postulates. One is the danger of a superficial, non–data-based perusal leading to the conclusion that all is well. At the other extreme is the danger of prolonged self-analysis leading to a detailed, comprehensive report divorced from action. We have seen both in the several years since our research findings and recommendations were published.

I have in my files letters from administrators, in particular, rejoicing over a faculty meeting or retreat that led to the general conclusion that most of the conditions embraced by the postulates were in place in their programs; only minor revisions were required, they reported. Given the consistency of our findings regarding the absence (or near-absence) of many of these conditions in the settings we visited, we are forced to conclude that those reports represent self-delusion. The cause of that self-delusion, I believe, is a superficial understanding of what is embedded in each postulate. In too many settings, faculty members go about their business individually, coming together in faculty meetings primarily to discuss and act on short-term matters. Serious dialogue, decision making, and action are far removed from common practice. This hypothesis tends to be confirmed by discussions I have had with colleagues in relatively strong settings who report considerable depth of inquiry into the meaning and implications of a single postulate.

The second problem is somewhat endemic to our calling. We got ourselves into a process of self-study that knows neither boundaries of inquiry nor plateaus of attainment. Ultimately, we wear out without having taken action as part of the deliberative process, and another impressive report goes on the shelf.

I urge an inquiry that carries through in each instance from raising a significant question, to getting hard data to help in answering it, to determining alternative actions, to taking one or more actions, and then, at some future time, to reviewing actions taken. This kind of process proceeds with some speed when the work to be done is parceled out, when progress reports are shared by the entire group from time to time, and when it is agreed that a new policy or new activity is to stand until experience with it warrants reexamination.

Our experiences with the use of the postulates to date suggest that they serve well the need to get early focus on the issues and problems most participants believe must be addressed. And for those already down the road in the change process, they provide tangible criteria for the formative evaluation of progress. The process of unpacking the postulates should not be one of checking them off as conditions met or unmet. It is, rather, a process of inquiry directed to the solid substance of what now exists and what should exist. And this process is as continuous as the teacher education program itself, rising and falling and rising again in intensity over time.

4

Partnerships and
Partner Schools

The wheels of imagology turn without having any effect upon
history. . . . Imagology organizes peaceful alternation of its systems in lively seasonal rhythms.[1]
—Milan Kundera

A center of pedagogy brings together in a single faculty three
different groups of actors from three different settings:
the schools, the arts and sciences, and the schools, colleges, or departments of education. Two of these groups share
the same college or university house and many of the same
values, though they live largely apart in separate wings. Those
from the schools occupy quite different houses. Many of their
values and preoccupations differ in both kind and degree from
those of professors who abide in colleges and universities. Over
the years, they have rarely come together to share the total
conduct of a teacher education program. Rather, they have contributed separately, eschewing the conversation and actions
necessary to making such a program coherent.

Several of the postulates call explicitly for close connection among these actors and their organizational settings in a
new setting with clearly defined borders. But working together
closely will not come easily. Until it becomes a way of life,
teacher education programs will continue to lack coherence.

Contributing to the center of pedagogy is not all that these
people and their institutions do and will do. A professor of biology attached to the center, for example, will teach biology

courses in which future teachers happen to be enrolled. (So will that professor's colleagues in the department of biology.) But a portion of his time is budgeted in the center, not the biology department, for team teaching a seminar in biology-specific pedagogy with a professor of educational psychology (also employed part-time by the center). Part of this center-budgeted time is spent in partner schools (more description later), where the two professors work as a team with a teacher of science.

This science teacher is well known to both of the others, because she is counselor to a cohort group of eleven future science teachers and has been with these students and the two professors since the former were admitted to the program. Further, this teacher has served throughout as a role model to which these future teachers aspire. Discussion of her teaching and that of the students is frequently the focus of their biology-specific seminar. (Incidentally, there are nineteen, not eleven, students enrolled in this seminar, because it serves double duty for future science teachers enrolled in the two-year postbaccalaureate teacher education program.)

This brief example of collaboration and team teaching serves to illustrate not only the considerable autonomy of the center with respect to resources but also the way the center uses this autonomy in bringing into a single faculty the diverse array of people required for the coherence and conduct of the programs. But the borders and activities of this center of pedagogy are not coterminous with the borders of the organized units from which these resources are drawn. The university from which come the various professors and the school districts from which come the teachers do many other things, some of them jointly but not under the auspices of the center. Formal agreements between the college or university and the cooperating school districts spell out what each is to contribute to ensure the center's stability and health over time. These conditions are embedded in the postulates and are protected by contracts agreed to and signed by the chief administrative officers of the institutions involved. These contracts guarantee, for example, the continued availability of partner or professional development schools.

Both sets of institutions have many such contractual arrangements, with each other and with other institutions and agencies. For example, although universities frequently operate their own teaching hospitals for medical education, many have contractual arrangements with private and city or county hospitals in order to secure the necessary clinical facilities.

A center of pedagogy may require twenty or thirty partner or "teaching" schools to accommodate its future-teacher student body. The university involved could contract directly with private schools, of course, but there would not be enough of them available and they would not provide the circumstances for which teachers for the public schools must be prepared. But the schools required are part of a larger organizational structure: the school district. Consequently, there must be a formal agreement between the parent university and the parent district (or districts) to secure for the center of pedagogy the needed partner schools. The idea of charter schools — schools specifically chartered for the simultaneous renewal of schooling and the education of educators and freed to considerable degree from district control — offers interesting possibilities for the future. For the immediate present, however, it is necessary to move ahead with school-university partnerships that provide the essential resources, including partner schools, for the centers of pedagogy under discussion here.

The necessary joining would be complex even if there were not the rather troubled history of conflict between the two university groups — those from the arts and sciences, on one hand, and those from the SCDE, on the other. The central problems and issues to be addressed in developing teacher education programs tend to be pushed aside by the micro-management priorities arising out of disagreement over the control of turf claimed but disputed. The rhetoric of moral persuasion often serves to bring parties to the table, but it is no guarantee of programmatic agreement. There is thus something to be gained by shifting the locus of proposed collaboration to a neutral site: a partner school. Although philosophical disagreements are not muted in this neutral setting (nor should they be), university participants are given the opportunity to separate relevant conversation from some of the baggage that has burdened on-campus discourse over the years.

The schools are not new settings for those who work in them, of course, but the infusion of new colleagues from a college or university and the adoption of a new mission create a new mix and fresh possibilities. Instability and insecurity are tempered to some degree by a stable physical environment — at least until changing it becomes a deliberate part of the agenda. One of the deterrents in the creation of entirely new settings is the degree to which the initial absence of physical amenities, coupled with the immediate need for them, overwhelms the agenda, so sapping human energy that models from past experience sneak in to become the paradigms of the present. Little changes but the appearance of change.

It is critically important to remember the extent to which the threat of uncertainty accompanies and can obliterate the promise of new challenges. Becoming involved with rather than just observing or studying schools is threatening to many university-based people. They should not be coerced or embarrassed into partnership; there are other worthy tasks for them to pursue in their present departmental affiliations. On the other hand, deans and directors of teacher education should work diligently at creating opportunities for involvement that cater at first to the strengths of individual professors while offering some promise of subsequent, perhaps more vital, initiatives.

There is threat on the school side as well. A considerable body of research leads not only to the conclusion that teachers work in considerable isolation but also to the finding that many prefer to, and to the hypothesis that some choose teaching because it offers a degree of reclusiveness. A collaboration designed to bring college and university professors into schools and classrooms is obviously very threatening to this genre of teachers and even to others who welcome collegiality up to a point — as, for example, in periodic meetings — but are nervous about having professors (some of them previous mentors) in their classrooms. District or state mandates that *direct* schools to become professional development schools for teacher education programs threaten the healthy development of a promising concept.[2]

The greatest danger to solid, lasting collaboration of university and school personnel in partner schools is *imagology*—the transformation of both reality and ideology into various images of them. There occurs just enough progress to create the image of close connections when, in actuality, there exists as yet little more than symbols. (One is reminded of the two-dimensional film props of old saloons and stables used in low-budget Westerns.) For example, in the foregoing I have described some of the collaboration that I hope will become commonplace in centers of pedagogy. But to create in doing so an impression of this being reality today is to engage in imagology.

Imagology ultimately convinces even the imagologues that the imagery they create is the genuine article, superior even to the models they sought initially to emulate. Unfortunately, this belief is usually accompanied by an expanding self-confidence that often intimidates laborers in other vineyards, causing them to believe that the difficulties inevitably encountered arise out of their own incompetence. And so they are open to counsel from these new "experts," who are often less accomplished than they. Imagology is a major industry that increasingly characterizes our times; education has not been left unscathed.

In the early stages of redesigning settings or creating new ones, it is not wise to go forth seeking models elsewhere. There should first be a great deal of inquiry into and conversation about what needs to be changed and why, and into alternative possibilities. Armed with the fruits of such inquiry, those who go out to view the efforts of like-minded others have in mind the questions they need to answer and criteria for judging the value and usefulness of what they see and hear. Often the most useful field trips are to settings that only recently worked their way through some of the major problems now confronting the visitors. If the area of common interest is relatively new to everyone, as the development of school-university partnerships and partner schools will continue to be for some years, beware the self-proclaimed expert. He or she may turn out to be little more than an imagologue.

This chapter addresses partnerships between school districts and universities and then turns to the partner schools constituting long-term components of firmly established centers of pedagogy. (The reader is advised to revisit Figure 1.3 in Chapter One.) My colleagues and I have had more questions directed to us about these issues than about any other of the conditions we propose as necessary to healthy programs for the education of educators. I seek to answer in what follows those questions that tap most directly into our experience and that of others with whom we have worked over a period of years. Implicit is my strong orientation toward the view that launching early into the essential school-university collaboration, relatively uncharted though it is, pays dividends in regard to effecting simultaneously the conversation between professors of education and the arts and sciences essential to programmatic health. The conversation of both with their partners in the schools is, by comparison, easy.

I remind the reader that the terms "teacher education program" and "program for the education of educators" are inclusive of the partner schools embraced by the center of pedagogy. Similarly, "the renewal of teacher education" assumes the inclusion of renewing schools. I refer quite frequently to "the simultaneous renewal of schools and the education of educators," but in addressing the redesign of teacher education, the first half of this clutch of words is a redundancy. There cannot be renewal in teacher education without there being simultaneously both schools and their renewal. We are dealing with an ecosystem within the larger ecosystem of communities. Educational initiatives from without contribute to improvement when they become an integral part of the ongoing interactions within ecosystems engaged in renewal.

School-University Partnerships

Until only a couple of decades ago, the relationship between universities and schools was akin to a one-way street. Schoolteachers and administrators flocked to nearby universities for courses leading first to bachelor's degrees and then to advanced degrees. Their salary schedules were tied primarily to course credits and degrees. Their in-service education activities com-

monly were made up of short institutes and workshops, where
they heard once again from college and university professors.

Then came a dramatic shift. With the bachelor's degree
now a prerequisite for getting a teaching job, with rapidly increasing numbers of teachers already holding master's degrees,
and with school districts and professional associations becoming the prime providers of in-service education,[3] the need for
those treks to university campuses diminished. (And that decline
will continue.) With discretionary funds increasingly available
to directors of staff development, it became fashionable for school
districts to compete for the services of outside consultants tied
to or conversant in innovative ideas and practices: teaching to
behavioral objectives, team teaching, nongrading, quality circles, mastery learning, cooperative learning, whole-language approaches to teaching reading, learning outcomes, and more.
Those on the consulting circuit were not necessarily the crea-
tors of the ideas, but they were articulate advocates. For the
most part, what they advocated and what teachers did about
it were outside of the mainstream of degree-oriented university
curricula. Indeed, when *A Nation at Risk* broke its bad news about
American schooling in 1983, and in the immediate aftermath
of reform hype and activity, university professors were conspic-
uously absent.

Studying teacher education programs a half-dozen years
later, my colleagues and I were startled by the innocence of
prospective teachers (and to only a slightly lesser degree their
professors) regarding the reform rhetoric—specifically, the several research-based books being widely cited in the hundreds
of national and state commission reports that followed quickly
on the heels of *A Nation at Risk.* For these neophytes, the waves
of indictments and recommendations for change that had been
washing for several years over the schools in which they soon
would teach were too far away to be more than an irritant or,
for some, a soothing lullaby.[4] In going out into these schools
to become student teachers, they left behind most of the professors who had presided over their earlier curriculum. They were
now in a milieu quite detached from universities and quite
detached from educational reform directed to the lower schools.

It is critically important for us to understand these twin detachments several years later in the context of a remarkable rhetorical sea change. Today advocacy of school-university partnerships is de rigeur; not to have one or be part of one could be dangerous to your educational health. Perhaps more dangerous, however, is the "trophy mentality" described by my colleague Nathalie Gehrke, which drives us to have a partnership quickly (and immaculately, if possible).[5] The one-way relationship between universities and schools that prevailed for years and the near-separation that followed should tell us that the necessary joining will not come easily and that we must work at it intensively and with great care. And we should be attuned to the probability that most of those reports on school-university partnerships that blossomed so soon after the first seeds of the concept were planted were largely the smoke and mirrors of imagology.[6] Wherever we come upon coherent ideology and sustained efforts to test it, there is much to be learned from mistakes as well as successes.

Symbiosis

Because teaching hospitals and laboratory schools have lives of their own with their patients and students, the best potential for good health is a symbiotic rather than utilitarian or instrumental relationship with the professional school of which they are a part. Indeed, the tensions between these units and their parent bodies grow primarily out of the perception of the former that their parents are inattentive to their needs and of the latter that their progeny are negligent in their familial duties. These tensions are exacerbated in the marriage relationship represented by a school-university partnership. The potential for success rests on effecting symbiosis and, ultimately, near-organic fusion.

Powerfully productive symbioses depend on the following:

1. *Distinctive differences between the courting parties.* We hear over and over the lament that schools and universities are poles apart and have too little in common to warrant joining.

Nonsense. The greater the similarities, the less there is to gain from sharing. The distinct cultural differences between schools and universities are an asset, not a liability.

2. *The complementarity of these differences — that is, the degree to which each side contributes to the other's lack.* The growing apart of schools and universities described above was accompanied by considerable separation of practitioners from the university research intended for them. The inattention of a school-based audience massaged the general tendency of researchers to write for one another, compounding the inaccessibility of their work to this audience. And the decline of this audience reduced the motivation for trying to reach it. The potential for an about-face through the medium of a school-university partnership is obvious.

3. *The degree to which the courting parties first envision and then comprehend through experience the extent to which this complementarity depends on commitment and effort fully shared.* One eager partner cannot effect productive symbiosis by seeking to pick up the slack left by a diffident one. The bonds may remain, but the marriage will be hollow.

4. *Powerful contextual contingencies.* These include the promise or the reality of additional resources, higher status, or even being in fashion — rewards sufficient to offset the inevitable burdens of a sustained relationship. But these contingencies will not suffice if those most actively involved fail to derive deep satisfaction from the relationship or to have clear reasons for continuing. There are few good substitutes for internal motivation arising out of continuing progress toward a shared mission.

Phillip Schlechty and Betty Lou Whitford argue that collaborative efforts must move from symbiotic to organic relationships.[7] Schlechty and Whitford perceive a necessary progression to a shared vision and shared problems. Without that, nothing of substance will be accomplished. The four sets of circumstances described above are necessary conditions. Given these, the partners shape an agenda directed to the simultaneous renewal of schooling and the education of educators in partner schools, which are vital body organs of this agenda.

Genesis of an Idea

Colleagues and I entered seriously into promoting and developing school-university partnerships soon after creating the Center for Educational Renewal in 1985. We brought to this effort a substantial history of experiences and research leading up to creating in 1986 the National Network (of school-university partnerships) for Educational Renewal.[8] Our comprehensive study of schooling, beginning in the late 1970s, resulted in a conclusion that is key to this issue: that the renewal of schools and of the education of those who work in them had to go hand in hand for there to be significant educational improvement. The Southern California School-University Partnership, an attempt to join symbiotically the Laboratory in School and Community Education of UCLA and over a dozen school districts in the region, grew out of this conclusion and proved to be a profound learning experience in understanding and designing school-university partnerships.[9] Subsequently, I had the opportunity not only to use this learning productively in helping to create the BYU–Public School Partnership but also to learn more from this connection and over a dozen more during the second half of the 1980s and into the 1990s.

In particular, I learned how important it is to have the prospective partner settings represented from the beginning, seated at the table as equals, under circumstances that bespeak this equality. This theme is laced through every chapter of this book. *The right beginning is critical.*

We came close to making the wrong first move in creating the BYU–Public School Partnership, simply by following convention. Dean Curtis van Alfen of Brigham Young University and a copy of *A Nation at Risk* showed up in my office at UCLA at about the same time (but separately) in the spring of 1983. He was aware that we had created the Laboratory for School and Community Education and that we had joined it with nearby school districts in the Southern California Partnership. He and some colleagues had resonated to the concepts of mutual collaboration that we had employed at UCLA. Van Alfen saw them as having profound implications for the mission and activities of the college of education over which he presided.

His hopes for the use of some of my time and my plans to leave the deanship in a few months coincided nicely.

During the following year, I engaged in extensive conversation with faculty members of BYU and educators in five nearby districts enrolling about 30 percent of the elementary and secondary student body in Utah. In planning for my final visit of that academic year, Dean van Alfen proposed that we secure closure by formally creating a partnership between the university and these school districts. The agenda awaiting my arrival was not to my liking. On Monday and Tuesday, I was to meet with deans and department heads; on Tuesday, with a large segment of the College of Education faculty; and on Wednesday, with college administrators and the five superintendents, presumably to cement agreements. In retrospect, I realize how delinquent I was during that year in not insisting on extensive involvement of faculty from the arts and sciences (although I did meet with central administrators, some of the other deans, and some of the faculty members participating in teacher education). It was too late to seek this inclusion for the week at hand.

What I was able to do, however, was to reconstruct the week's agenda. We kept to the plans for Monday and Tuesday. But arrangements were made for me to meet on Wednesday in the board room of the Provo school district with the five superintendents. The proposed joint meeting was then postponed to Thursday and the place changed from the BYU campus to a downtown hotel. These changes represented more than subtleties.

The experiences of that week impressed on me the importance of being sure at the outset that the conditions necessary to a symbiotic relationship are present. Because education is essentially a helping profession, the tendency in seeking a partnership is to seek to do good. Yet relationships built on benign intentions tend to be fleeting. There is greater potential in first seeing in the other partner a source of satisfying one's own needs. If there is a touch of cynicism here, so be it; but it is more a recognition of realities. And there is another important reality closely related: if in seeking satisfaction of one's own needs, the needs of the partners are ignored, the partnership will soon dissolve.

To BYU personnel early on in our meetings, I posed the question, "What might you have to gain from a close partnership with the schools?" About a dozen major areas of potential benefit emerged. On Wednesday, at the meeting on their turf, I asked the five superintendents the same question. Again, about a dozen major topics emerged. There was overlap in about half of the topics agreed upon by each group. On Thursday of that week, on the neutral turf of the hotel, I presented six topics identified commonly by the two groups as a possible agenda for collaboration. With incredible speed and unanimity, the combined groups agreed to form a school-university partnership to address this agenda of overlapping self-interests, which included such themes as teacher education, the preparation of school principals, curriculum development, and research on critical problem areas. The partnership is still in place, as is the agenda. The remarkable thing is that now, a decade later, only one of the initial superintendents remains and the deanship has turned over three times. To have survived that turnover, this relationship must be symbiotic and perhaps even organic.

I cite these events in some detail for three reasons. First, I believe that the careful recognition of the sensitivities of prospective partners with respect to turf and the symbolism of turf was significant to the relatively successful outcomes. University-based personnel tend to have an insensitive noblesse oblige attitude toward people in the schools. School superintendents, in turn, often have less than flattering views of their academic colleagues in universities. How they are brought together initially greatly affects the seriousness and permanence of what the two groups forge.

Second, even though I have described these events in public gatherings and endorsed strongly the importance of recognizing the interests of both groups, I know of few attempts to replicate the process. Indeed, more often than not it appears that little care was taken to anticipate and provide for sensitivities that later engendered or even aborted collaboration.

Third, I believe that school-university partnerships will be successful only to the degree that they are forged early on and address consciously a common agenda. A loosely constructed

umbrella of collaboration based only on mutual goodwill, with
no sense of symbiosis, is bound to collapse in the face of relatively common exigencies: changes in leadership, declining
resources, or the emergence of even relatively minor value
conflicts. School-university partnerships that fail to mature to
the point of recognizing and welcoming the need for each other
are bound to wither and die.

The BYU–Public School Partnership was the second of
more than a dozen in which the Center for Educational Renewal
became involved between 1985 and today. The core of the mission, not clearly articulated initially, was the mutual involvement of school-based and university-based people in simultaneously renewing schools and the education of educators.

There is no doubt that the formal creation of these school-
university partnerships, each with a budget and a full- or part-
time executive director (and all joined in the National Network
for Educational Renewal), promoted an array of collaborative
endeavors that probably would not have occurred otherwise.
But it is also true that many of these endeavors involved the
coming together of professors and teachers in projects that did
not require major adjustments in the ownership of institutional
turf. The symbiotic and organic joining of institutions that
Richard Clark found to be missing in earlier unions and networks continued to elude most of the partnerships.[10] The sudden outpouring of reports on school-university partnerships at
professional meetings represented hope and promise rather than
solid accomplishment.[11]

The seemingly natural connection between universities
and schools, particularly in the joint endeavor of renewing
schools for the renewal of teacher education, is far from natural
in execution. Myriad factors conspire to delay, frustrate, and
sometimes scuttle progress. Our research on teacher education,
culminating with publication of the three books in 1990, has
led us, nonetheless, even more surely than did our previous research on schools, to the firm conclusion that we will not have
markedly better teachers and schools until school-university collaboration succeeds in ensuring under its broad umbrella units
for teacher education—centers of pedagogy—that include as a

fixed, permanent part of their structure enough renewing partner schools to embrace each successive cohort of student teachers.

This research, built on top of the earlier research on
schools, led us to a much clearer and more commanding conceptualization of schools as integral components of the three-
way partnership among teachers joined with professors in education and the arts and sciences for the education of educators.
The necessity of that collaboration is embedded in several of
the postulates. The designation and development of renewing
partner schools is a major part of the agenda taken on by the
present members of the National Network for Educational
Renewal. But there is no easy road to the attainment and stabili-
zation of this necessary condition. We believe, however, that
the prior existence of a school-university partnership eases the
journey along this road to the creation of centers of pedagogy.

Our experiences with school-university partnerships since
1980 have provided some lessons that might be of use to those
making that journey. My colleague Kenneth Sirotnik has brought
together a list of ten lessons worth heeding.[12] If there are any
shortcuts, my guess is that a share of them lie in comprehending and closely following what these lessons might imply for planning and acting.

> *Lesson 1: Dealing with Cultural Clash.* School systems
> and universities are not cut from the same cul-
> tural cloth. The norms, roles, and expectations
> of educators in each of these educational realms
> could not be more different — e.g., the regimen
> of time and space in the schools vs. the relative
> freedom of these precious commodities in the
> university setting; an ethic of inquiry in the uni-
> versity vs. an ethic of action and meeting im-
> mediate needs in the schools; a merit system with
> promotion and tenure in the university vs. an
> egalitarian work ethic in the schools. . . .
>
> These two cultures are quite different, and
> it is hard to fit them together in productive, long-
> term, useful ways. . . .

Lesson 2: Dealing with Schools of Education. [Of the
two sides of the partnership fence], the university side, usually the school (college or department) of education, is the more intractable. . . .
The primary culprit is a misguided reward system that is an outgrowth of misplaced values,
status deprivation, and identity crisis. . . .

Lesson 3: Sustaining Leadership and Commitment. One
of the more consistent and enduring findings in
the research on complex organizations has to do
with the importance of leadership at the top, and
the ability to clearly, authentically, and consistently communicate mission, vision, a sense of
what the organization can and must be about.
This appears to be essential to maintaining
school-university partnerships of the type I have
been describing. University presidents and deans,
school superintendents, executive directors—
these leaders need to be visible and clearly supportive of the partnership concept and effort.

Lesson 4: Providing Adequate Resources. Much of leadership is symbolic. But symbols, ceremony, and
celebration will not go far unless they are backed
up by resources. . . .

Lesson 5: Modeling Authentic Collaboration. An ethic
of collaboration and collaborative inquiry and action, more than anything else, characterizes (or
ought to characterize) the processes that go on
in a school-university partnership. What it means
to collaborate needs to be modeled every step of
the way. Since building partnerships is mostly
a two-steps-forward/one-step-backward kind of
activity, inappropriate, unilateral decisions can
destroy the process. . . .

*Lesson 6: Living with Goal-Free Planning, Action, and
Evaluation.* . . . Often, in fact, it is precisely *as a
result* of activity that we become clearer about
what we are doing and why we are doing it. Con-

sequently, the world of human activity in and between educational organizations does not lend itself well to concrete, sequential models of planning and evaluation.

The subtitle of this lesson is "living with ambiguity," and our mentor is the organizational theorist, James March. For March, ambiguity is not a dirty word. Not only does he tolerate it, he embraces it. Closure *is* a dirty word. Rarely is it ever achieved. In fact, if it is achieved, it is a good sign that either the issues are trivial or people are jumping to conclusions too quickly. . . .

Lesson 7: Avoiding the Quick-Fix Syndrome. The "quick-fix" syndrome and its kissing cousin, the "let's get something up on the scoreboard" syndrome, are extremely hazardous to the health of school-university partnerships, especially early in their formative stages. . . .

There often is a perceived press to get something up on the scoreboard so that various publics believe something actually is going on. . . . Yet, if it is a serious partnership effort, a lot *is* going on: structures are being built, lines of communication are being established, working relationships and collaborative processes are being nurtured, and some activities are being explored by pockets of work groups here and there. Unfortunately, structures and processes do not happen overnight, and they cannot be hung on the evaluative hooks the public has grown accustomed to for education and schooling — standardized test score averages, for example.

Lesson 8: Winning the Process/Substance Debate. . . . The debate apparently revolves around this question: What work is of most value — making things happen or the happening of things?

The only way to win this debate is to render it a nonissue; it is, indeed, a false dichotomy to

be put alongside a number of other classic prob-
lematical dualities (qualitative/quantitative;
theory/practice; talk/action; etc.). There is great
substance in process and great process in substance. Developing new ways for educators to
communicate with one another and engage in
work to solve problems of common concern is
highly substantive. Developing and evaluating
new programs (e.g., for the education of educators) demands much attention to process. . . .

Lesson 9: Avoiding Over- and Understructuring. Organizing and governance structures are important for
developing and sustaining school-university partnerships, but they take different forms depending upon local contexts. The Puget Sound Educational Consortium is highly structured. . . . The
Southern Maine Partnership is organized very
informally. . . .

Both of these partnerships appear to be
working well. But watch out for both over- and
understructuring; either may interfere with the
work most important to partnership efforts. Ultimately, the crucial points of coordination are
at the levels where real work is taking place, with
the rest of the coordination and structure being
in place to *support* that work.

Lesson 10: Translating Leadership as Empowerment and
Shared Responsibility. The partnership ethic must
be enculturated at all individual levels and organizational levels. The power to lead cannot re-
side in just one or several charismatic figures.
The more leadership is spread around, the better off the partnership will be.

This should not be seen as contradictory
to Lesson 3 and the importance of leadership at
the top, of communicating and sustaining vision
and mission, and of backing it all up with resources. Power, however, is not a finite concept.

The more it is shared, the more there seems to be. And with power comes responsibility; responsible leadership entails creating the opportunities for responsible leadership in others. A viable school-university partnership cannot depend on the presence or absence of one or several human beings. Certainly, being an "idea champion" is important for leadership, but charisma is not the foundation of partnership. . . .

The creation and refinement of partner schools is a special case of school-university collaboration and symbiosis, involving all the problems and issues identified in Sirotnik's analysis. To this special case we now turn.

Partner Schools

This probably is a good place to pause for a brief summary of several different but closely related concepts—centers of pedagogy, school-university partnerships, and partner schools—and their organizational representations.

The central focus of this book is on centers of pedagogy: essentially new settings designed to provide a more precise identity for the education of educators than commonly exists. Its intent is to bring together into a single faculty a sufficient number of the three groups of actors requisite to developing coherent preparation programs. A center of pedagogy, whether located organizationally inside or outside of an SCDE, is characterized by all the conditions necessary to its healthy functioning—conditions comparable to those in professional schools or institutes. Most of the faculty members divide their time between the needs of such a center and their home departments or, in the case of personnel from the schools, in their home schools or organized units within their schools. Each center has a core group of faculty members who devote all or more than half of their time to it. There are clear guidelines with respect to voting privileges, criteria for advancement and merit awards, and the like.

A school-university partnership represents a formal agree-

ment between a college or university (or one or more of its constituent parts) and one or more school districts to collaborate
on programs and projects in which both have a common interest. This agreement includes designation of a governing body,
commitment of resources (usually varying in nature and amount
over time), an executive officer, a secretariat (usually modest,
in our experience), and an approved budget. The agenda in
robust partnerships is made up of activities that require for their
vigorous pursuit joint planning and action. Partnerships serve
little or no purpose if one partner could carry on the activities
just as well without the inevitable demands of collaboration.

     A productive partnership could proceed for years with only
some of the people employed in the collaborating institutions being involved. All institutions will conduct many activities, some
of them together, without involving or being involved in an existing school-university partnership. In other words, a school-
university partnership represents only a part of what universities and school districts do, whether separately or together. A
school-university partnership is an arrangement through which
the two sets of institutions address selected overlapping self-
interests.

     To be whole, a center of pedagogy requires teaching
schools in the same way most medical education units and programs require teaching hospitals. Because most such centers
require several teaching schools, the cost of "owning" them is
prohibitive. Further, owning makes little sense when already
existing schools — not designated as teaching schools — are nearby.
The sensible course is to select some of these schools for purposes of fulfilling the center's mission and then to engage with
them in the process that readies them for their role in renewing
programs for the education of educators. Such schools become
central, not adjunct, to the simultaneous renewal of schooling
and the education of educators in a center of pedagogy.

     These schools are variously referred to in educational liter-
ature and practice as professional development, clinical, and
practice schools. The term "professional development school"
surfaced in the 1986 reports of the Carnegie Forum on Education and the Economy and the Holmes Group.[13] We introduced

the term "partner school" in launching the renewal initiative of
the Center for Educational Renewal in 1985 and have chosen
to stay with it in our subsequent emphasis on exemplary sites
in pre-service teacher education—sites "in which novices may
learn to practice under the guidance of expert practitioners"
joined by university colleagues in a center of pedagogy.[14]

The term "partner school" carries special meaning for us
in the context of the lessons learned over the years from experiences with school-university partnerships. The establishment
of such partnerships is not a necessary prerequisite to seeking
partner schools as integral components of centers of pedagogy—
but it helps enormously. As Kenneth Sirotnik writes in Lesson 5
of the preceding section, "building partnerships is mostly a two-
steps-forward/one-step-backward kind of activity." With a good
deal of this activity out of the way in a mature partnership, subsequent movement to the selection of partner schools for a center
of pedagogy requiring the close connecting of school and university personnel proceeds more quickly. The partner school becomes just another collaborative endeavor—albeit one to be
entered into very deliberately and carefully, since its success
depends on fine-tuned human connections.

Concept and Context

Many teacher educators now resonate to the concept of professional development or partner schools simultaneously modeling new practices and immersing prospective teachers in them.
Likewise, many policymakers find the idea to be attractive. Some
like it so much that they endorse the equitable principle of opening the opportunity to every school in the state and giving each
a turn.

This is the kind of uncomprehending thinking that ruins
many good ideas in schooling and education. They are smoth-
ered in the cradle by clumsy loving.

Although schools as "clinical" sites for practice now exist
under a variety of names in a good many settings, few would
stand scrutiny as exemplars of the many virtues envisioned for
them. While those school and university personnel with the best

track record to date continue to struggle with the difficulties involved (and candidly confessed), the rhetorical picture of virtues to be realized expands. These schools are to be demographically representative exemplars of good practice—a condition some critics deem impossible within the existing structure of public education. They are to be builders of knowledge through the collaborative research of school and university educators. They are to be part of the redesign of teacher education and places where experienced teachers will gain renewal. A few thoughtful analysts raise important questions about the role of unions, the degree to which some organized groups of parents oppose change, what to do about teachers who do not want to participate but do not intend to leave the school, and the difficulty of focusing on institutions as units of change when traditional paradigms have focused on individuals. And then, of course, there are the dangers of a murky journey through unmapped territory to be undertaken by travelers not accustomed to talking let alone working together.

Neither the lofty goals nor the potential problems offer sufficient argument for turning back, however. My purpose in citing some of the major obstacles is to put a damper on the rhapsodic twiddle that confuses paradise envisioned with paradise gained. Our experience with school-university collaboration has revealed the significance of problems so commonplace as to be readily passed over: from that of school and university personnel so pleased with their planning conversations that the urgency to do something fades, to that of professors (particularly nontenured ones) having their newly found satisfaction in school-based activities muted by fear that those activities will not lead to promotion.

The Center for Educational Renewal and associated settings in the National Network for Educational Renewal are unequivocally committed to the organic involvement of partner schools in renewing programs for the education of educators as specified or implied in several of the postulates. We share in many of the visions of their potential. But our attention is on the seemingly modest but very difficult steps that must be taken now toward the realization of realities that lie years in the future.

And so we have narrowed the scope of the initial agenda. The goal is that stated earlier: to establish within clear borders all of the conditions necessary to healthy, robust, renewing programs for the education of educators. (*Educators* refers to the team of people preparing to become stewards of a school unit — classroom teachers, various specialists, and the principal. Clearly, district personnel also must be steeped in what it means to support this stewardship, but their education is not yet at the forefront of this agenda.) The borders encompass a center of pedagogy. Partner schools are an integral component of the center. The faculty is a blend of people from the university and the partner schools who serve as equal partners in the renewal of these schools and the professional preparation programs of which they are a part.

Initially, these schools might not be exemplary. They must be committed to renewal, however, and have in place at the outset a principal and a core group of teachers who understand the major demands of this commitment and who have demonstrated some of what it will take to fulfill it. The purposes and process of renewal must be shared by the responsible faculty group of the center. Preliminary research by Jianping Shen suggests that school-based and university-based personnel working in the same partner schools are not necessarily together in their understanding and commitment to this purpose several years into the process.[15]

Some advocates of professional development schools cite their potential for ground-breaking innovation. Such innovation probably will occur ultimately (as well as, from time to time, serendipitously). But I am skeptical about setting it as a goal. In *A Place Called School*, I introduced the idea of schools of choice in the public sector deliberately intended to be forerunners in testing and developing new practices and designated them "key" schools (to avoid equating them with other special-purpose, alternative schools). I then explored the prospects for these schools also serving as demonstration schools in pre-service and in-service education. This led me into questions regarding their additional use as an integral part of educator preparation programs — as professional development or partner schools.

My conclusions were significantly influenced by years of experience with the laboratory school at UCLA. There it became apparent to me, as it had to both external and internal committees charged with evaluating the school, that it was burdened with not only too many expectations but expectations that were not entirely compatible: research, innovation, teacher education, demonstration to a diverse host of visitors, and excellence for its students. The way out was a narrowing and ranking of priorities. I believe that a similar sorting out is essential to both the concept of and the charge to partner schools. In *A Place Called School,* I recommended two sets of special-purpose schools: key schools as ground-breakers in the development and testing of promising new practices and teacher education schools employing the best of tested practice to provide exemplary settings for the learning of their long-term student body and their relatively short-term students learning to teach.

I realize that there are strong advocates for professional development schools committed primarily to research, experimentation and innovation, or in-service staff development. I have no quarrel with such priorities. But none of these is the primary purpose of the partner schools I have in mind. Presumably, then, a partner school is a special type within the genre of professional development schools.

From Crawling to Walking

To have in mind a partner school in which will culminate in practice what has gone on previously in the curriculum (see Chapter Six) is to envision a setting peopled by teachers in this school, professors of education, and professors in the arts and sciences departments—all members of the center of pedagogy faculty. To have in this center faculty members—whether school-based or university-based—innocent of the purposes of this school is to court turbulence, at best, and disaster, at worst. We see once more why it is so important to establish early on the makeup of this faculty and to initiate conversation among all its members. Let us assume the accomplishment of this condition—no easy task.

Given the years of work it undoubtedly will take to have up and running a renewing school functioning effectively in pursuit of the center's mission, there must be at the outset some firm contractual agreements designed to guarantee continuity. For example, there must be protection against the ill-conceived egalitarian notion that every school in the district should be in line for a three-year stint as a partner school. Various philanthropic foundations already have granted hundreds of thousands of dollars to get some schools started down the road to becoming partner schools. It is now time to ensure that this will not be a wasted investment. States must get together with collaboratives (such as school-university partnerships) in devising funding formulas that guarantee partner schools as long-term components of centers of pedagogy.

Policymakers, union leaders, and interested educators must come to grips with the fact that a partner school is not a freestanding entity, appropriately groomed and ready for the overtures of a university suitor. It is not an adjunct, an appendage, to the core business of teacher education traditionally assumed to be the prerogative of higher education. It is, rather, an organic part of the whole, connected to the other parts of the corpus by bones, joints, arteries, and tissue. The full grasp of this understanding represents a fundamental sea change from an almost unbroken tradition of school-university separation.

The necessary contractual agreements occur beyond the center of pedagogy. They are institutional agreements signed off by the chief executive officers of the participating institutions. They provide an essential element in the clear borders and secure resources necessary to the continuing, confident existence of the center of pedagogy and its responsible stewardship in producing teachers for the nation's schools.

Most of what follows lies within the purview of the center. A first step is to secure agreement within (and without, with those still exercising authority) to phase out another convention: the placement of student teachers individually with cooperating teachers scattered about in schools. Our study of a sample of teacher-preparing settings produced no argument for continuing that present practice. The gaps and shortcomings

are too many. We came up with a new design—a design that
reinforces recommendations that have surfaced from many quarters in recent years: immerse future teachers in the whole of
schooling and schools, not merely in single classrooms with individual teachers willing to provide some mentoring. We con-
cur in those added recommendations for cohort groups of beginners to serve as junior faculty members for months at a time.
Recommendations for building prospective teachers into teaching teams with experienced colleagues and some financial remu-
neration have been on the books for years.

Decisions paralleling the sunsetting of outmoded patterns
of student teaching involve two critical choices. The first choice
is of levels of preparation to offer: early childhood, elementary,
secondary. The second is of numbers, broken down into special-
ties. The commitment need not be comprehensive. Some of the
best programs, largely of the past, have emerged from institutional commitment in a narrow realm—for example, early childhood or elementary education only. Attempting to cover too
broad a spectrum endangers excellence: an institution's willing-
ness to patch together a program for one future teacher of French
may be good for institutional public relations but not for that
same teacher's future students.

Postulates Six and Fifteen link student admissions to places
available in the program and those places to the availability of
exemplary schools—both partner schools and schools selected
with particular programmatic purposes in mind. In the past,
very little consideration has been given to this relationship. The
criteria of admission have been almost exclusively academic
records or demonstrations and an often loosely observed ratio
of students to faculty. The professional education programs that
have achieved major status, however—those in law and medicine, for example—stick to a specified number of admissions
and move that figure up or down in response to its addition or
loss of resources, whether in faculty, laboratories, or clinical facilities. Their admissions policies embrace more than considerations pertaining only to students in seeking to ensure quality
programs for them. In recommending similar considerations for
teacher education programs, my colleagues and I did not an-

ticipate the disbelief that ensued. We have grown accustomed in teacher preparation to low expectations and the accompanying inadequate provision of programmatic conditions necessary to quality.

Early in the process of building partner schools into a center of pedagogy, criteria pertaining primarily to the quality of the renewing process already under way and the general readiness of school personnel to participate may be sufficient. But as the number of additional schools required dwindles, it will become increasingly necessary to match decisions regarding the nature of the future-teacher student body desired to more finely tuned criteria regarding the selection of settings. For example, the intention to have a strong program in the production of teachers in the arts must be accompanied by a successful search for both artistically and pedagogically strong school-based teachers and programs in potential partner schools.

The process of developing a center of pedagogy that is virtually complete in its faculty, partner schools, and other necessities requires years, not months. Consequently, I stress this caveat: in sunsetting existing programs with the intention of phasing in the new, with partner schools sufficient for all cohort groups in place, estimate very carefully the time needed for the full transition. If the relevant data suggest greater ease in selecting elementary schools, the wise decision probably is to stagger the sunsetting process so that the transition at the secondary level lags behind by a year or two.

Let us assume a fast-track timeline of three years (probably in settings quite far along at the outset in the collaborations required) and a norm of five years for the complete transition. At "completion," the center will have clear borders and all components: specific time allocations (subject to annual revision) and accompanying criteria for the reward of the three-part faculty; a student body predetermined with respect to total size and specializations; and the requisite kind and number of laboratory settings, including partner schools. This resulting identity is not something to be messed with. It involves contracts, guarantees, allocation of resources, and more. There is in the teacher education business a certain expectation of and pride in dealing with flux and crisis: "We're egalitarian, flexible, and people-oriented here. Tell us what you need, and we'll work it out." But the education of our teachers is too important to leave to the exigencies of well-intentioned but often makeshift accommodations.

Clear borders and stable interiors should not block out exploration and experimentation, however. It will be necessary from time to time to phase out and replace partner schools and to find additions to accommodate new or expanded programs. There will be need for identifying special programs in schools not currently within the center's borders. There may be strong arguments for placing a cohort of future teachers in a particular nonpartner school during an interesting time in that school's history. When centers of pedagogy function within the context of a school-university partnership of the kind described earlier, the prospect of knowing about and using such opportunities expands enormously. The caution, once again, is to avoid slipping into exigencies geared to convenience and casual accommodation.

Walking Before Running

The crawling stage with respect to partner schools involves building them into the fabric of the center of pedagogy. The walking stage is blending them into habit and custom. In this stage, professors of education and from the departments of the arts and sciences are "on location" as a matter of course. Interns, because of the school-based experiences they have had earlier in their programs, are accustomed to taking over elementary or secondary school classes while the regular teachers — designated members of the center's faculty — are on the university campus team teaching a seminar with colleagues commonly on location in the school. The partner school has an additional assistant principal who is in the internship phase of the newly designed principal preparation program of the center of pedagogy. All of the partner schools devote space in the regular building or in portables to accommodate the needs of prospective teachers and their teachers. The school-based members of the center's faculty have designated facilities on the university campus.

The road to this stage will have been marked by operational, organizational, and interpersonal decisions, problems, and crises too many and too varied to predict. Although these will decline in frequency and crises will tend to be less monumental over time, they will continue. Some teaching hospitals appear to the uninitiated to be incredibly ordered places. The non-stop calls for Doctor X, Doctor Y, and Doctor Z sounding out in elevators and corridors convey the correct impression of professional personnel engaged in varied tasks throughout the building. They do not convey, however, the continuing clash of values that arise out of the effort to blend patient care, medical education, and research. The presence of a school of nursing sharing the hospital facility usually raises considerably the decibels of the cacophony.

To anticipate only sweetness and light in the blending of university and school culture in a center of pedagogy is to dream. To delay seeking this blending just because it is certain to be difficult is to postpone the opportunity for teacher education to be first-rate. There are, too, some strong arguments for believing that bringing into a coherent whole the straggling trails of teacher education will be easier than that effort in medical education. A decade should suffice for what transpired over two or three decades in medical education.

Running

There is much to overcome in seeking to get beyond unimaginative conventional practice in schooling and teacher education. The first obstacle is the legacy of viewing and treating them separately, largely because of the identification of teacher education with higher education — an identification that persists despite the downplaying that the former received in the progression of teachers colleges to universities.

When the Center for Educational Renewal launched in 1985 its initiative in the "*simultaneous* renewal of schooling and the education of educators," hardly anyone noticed the words after *and,* given the concentration then on school reform. Even most of the members of the National Network for Educational

Renewal failed to resonate to the call for change on the higher
education side. Then, after completing its research on teacher
education, the Center was perceived to be focused on only the
higher education component, its continuing initiative in simultaneous renewal disregarded.

Indeed, the various directories of reform initiatives neatly
categorized the Center for Educational Renewal as engaged in
teacher education, ignoring the fact that this was simply a long-
overdue effort on our part to include attention to a major, missing ingredient in educational reform and to link it through the
notion of "simultaneous." We found ourselves working as hard
to keep schools in the design of educator preparation programs
as we had worked a few years earlier to draw attention to the
need for renewal on the higher education side. One is inclined
to be a little skeptical about exuberant expectations for "systemic"
reform in a nation that so sharply separates its thinking, policies, and practices in higher education from those of its system
of elementary and secondary schooling.

Largely because of this sharp split, attention to needed
improvement in teacher education that includes some conception of professional development schools tends to address the
need to get future teachers "out there" without working out what
"out there" must provide for effectiveness. A major goal of our
work is to effect this linkage conceptually and operationally. The
logistics of making the transition from placing student teachers
individually with cooperating teachers to immersing cohort
groups in whole schools is grist for the discussion mill in meetings of education deans, as are the logistics of relating to such
schools. But it is much more difficult to get them involved in
anything to do with the design and redesign of these schools.
This, presumably, is a task for school-based educators. But
Shen's exploratory research, cited earlier, suggests that much
conversation between university-based and school-based faculty
members, even when formally joined in a center of pedagogy,
will be required for partner schools to be simultaneously renewing and serving as vital components of coherent teacher education programs.

The potential for creative solutions to several major logjams in effecting fundamental educational improvement is enormous. Much of this potential becomes apparent when we envision a center of pedagogy operating at a level of considerable comfort and satisfaction for members of the three groups of faculty members who, in the past, have contributed separately and often dysfunctionally to incoherence in the teacher education program they share. For example, faculty members in SCDEs produce thousands of research papers on such highly important topics as the learning of mathematical and linguistic concepts and processes while their students in teacher education settle rather comfortably into the way things are done in schools. Surely the tension between theory, research, and practice can be tightened up productively by placing these faculty members in residence in partner schools as a regular part of their role in centers of pedagogy. Similarly, professors in departments that supposedly build on the education provided in departments of the same name in secondary schools have the opportunity to shift from complaining about to working with teachers in partner schools to improve both curricular continuity and the preparation of high school teachers. In the process, it is reasonable to expect them to see the need for improving the quality of their own departments.

Intriguing ideas for redesigning the educational delivery system in schools have emerged and disappeared, reemerged and redisappeared, several times over the past several decades. Through the hard work of advocates and believers, a few find hospitable lodging for a few years before relentless forces push them back once more, to be replaced by conventional practice. Jill Andrews describes what it took by way of advocacy, district support, leadership, and hard work for an elementary school to become nongraded and then continue to deviate somewhat from the mainstream of practice over a quarter-century.[16] The concept of nongradedness is old and not particularly complex, yet its implementation in practice is sparse. Colleagues and I worked intensively and rather productively with eighteen schools — the League of Cooperating Schools in southern California — from 1966 to 1972. We managed to break with the conventions of grades and individual teachers allocated to egg-crate classrooms, but such changes fall far short of what should be. The idea of giving teachers more authority for decision making — a reform initiative popular today — is exceedingly important, but unfettered teachers whose entire preparation programs focus on individual classrooms and a teacher assigned to each will not bring us redesigned schools for the twenty-first century. They simply do not have control of enough of the variables or the resources to effect fundamental reconstruction of the educational delivery system. Centers of pedagogy, constructed as recommended here, have the potential to do so.

Foregoing descriptions present an entity in which the production of new teachers is joined with the settings of their future employment. These settings — partner schools — already are staffed. The teacher education program likewise is staffed up to and including the practice phase in partner schools. We now have two sets of staffs coming together in a center of pedagogy to be jointly responsible for the whole of the program. What needs to happen, once this amalgam is functioning smoothly, is to break the mold with respect to the allocation of all available resources. It is difficult to envision this and even more difficult to effect it when the schools receiving future teachers and the university sending them into the schools operate separately, as is the convention.

The joining of the two in the center of pedagogy creates an opportunity to envision the two as one. Once again, I repeat the point that faculty members of the center are drawn from three sources: the arts and sciences, the field of education, and the partner schools. The opportunity now is to convert this entire faculty roster into FTEs — full-time equivalents. Within this total there need to be divisions, of course, into the number required to support each programmatic component. The need in the arts and sciences may be 2.5 FTEs in mathematics, .5 in Spanish, 4.0 in English, and so on; in the field of education, a total of 22.5; and in partner schools, an average of 6.0 per school. It should be remembered that, although not all teachers in a partner school are participating at all times in the center of pedagogy, the school always is. (And *all* the teachers are involved in the school renewal process, of course.) The allocation of FTEs for use of the partner school covers the time of those teachers currently active in the teacher education program. Again, there are many alternatives for their potential involvement.

But now let us return to the issue of roadblocks to fundamental redesign of the educational delivery systems in schools and use a specific example. In *A Place Called School,* I recommended the reconstruction of elementary and secondary schooling into a 4-4-4 plan, beginning at age four and concluding as early as sixteen. Surely we can provide effectively over these years the general education that the Swiss provide effectively by the age of fifteen. In a single piece of restructuring, the much-recommended attention to the earlier educational needs of the young and the opening up of two postsecondary years for a variety of educational purposes (again, much-recommended, especially today) would be effected.

Most of the resulting criticism addressed the upper end of this proposed restructuring. I do not recall a letter or telephone call that challenged my educational arguments, however. There was concern, rather, for such things as the future of inter–high school competitive athletics (with the older students now elsewhere) and for "dumping" sixteen-year-olds on the streets ill-prepared for the job market. Today these recommendations for earlier childhood education and educational alternatives after the age of sixteen would be much more favorably viewed, I suspect.

Since in *A Place Called School* I provided most detail in discussing the first of these three phases of schooling, it may be useful to carry the possibilities a little further in the present context of the educational delivery system facilitated by a center of pedagogy. Envision a self-standing school or a school within a school of eighty children, age four through seven, and the allocation of 5.0 FTEs for their teaching. Twenty new pupils enter each year (on their fourth birthday), twenty leave at about the age of eight, and there are the usual additions and losses at various age levels between the entry and departure dates.

I recommended that the teachers work as a team with the entire student group over the four-year period. The conventional delivery system, even with this structural redesign, would be five certified, licensed teachers. But with this school a partner school in a center of pedagogy, other alternatives become readily apparent — if we keep in mind the allocation of 5.0 FTEs but not necessarily the five teachers.

Here is just one of several possibilities. There is a head teacher, currently occupying .7 FTE of the 5.0 FTEs available to the unit. There are two fully certified career teachers, currently occupying 2.0 FTEs. The head teacher holds a doctorate in pedagogy, with specialization in the language arts and reading, and has been credentialed by virtue of experience, education, and selection to hold a head teacher position. Four trainees, three in the five-year program and one in the two-year post-baccalaureate program, occupy a total of 1.3 FTEs. Currently, the remaining 1.0 FTE is divided between two licensed teachers whose family responsibilities preclude full-time teaching. All of the licensed teachers are on the salary schedule of their district, with the head teacher higher on the scale. The trainees are on the bottom rung of the prevailing scale and have slightly varying FTE allocations because of differences in their schedules of study and teaching.

Currently, then, a total of nine teachers spend varying amounts of time with and share responsibility for eighty children. During some previous years, a portion of the 5.0 FTEs went to enrich the supply of multimedia programs and materials available to the group, but these have been built up enough that they will not require such expenditures for a few years. Parents were brought into the schools as partners from the time their children's birthdays qualified attendance; many are active in the school's program. It is not uncommon on a given day for five for six parents to be part of a team directed by one of the teachers. Present policy calls for the school always to ensure a *minimum* of one head teacher and two full-time certified teachers. Beyond this requirement, the team is free to make annual changes in the allocation of resources and to meet emergencies as they arise.

It will be noted that the head teacher occupies only .7 FTE. The remaining .3 FTE is allocated to the school from the center of pedagogy (to be used as most needed), in return for the .3 FTE remainder of the head teacher's time. This remainder covers the regular teaching of a portion of the teacher education curriculum in the teaching of reading and the language arts and a role in supervising the trainees, shared with the counselors of the cohort groups of which these trainees are a part.

The above description is, of course, fiction seeking to explore new territory. It is guided here only by some previous personal experience in loosening up the convention of translating FTEs into full-time teachers exclusively. Thirty positions can be used to employ thirty, forty, or fifty people, some of whom are necessarily on part-time salaries, whether or not voluntarily serving full-time. With the convention broken for staffing schools and the additional resources of a center of pedagogy brought into the picture, the potential for creative patterns of utilization expands enormously. An essential criterion, however, is the provision of a sufficient core of full-time people to ensure continuity and stability.

The reader is perhaps reminded of several relevant earlier observations. First, a school becoming a partner school in a center of pedagogy requires some additional resources. Because of the parsimonious treatment of teacher education in higher education, these resources cannot be acquired solely through trade-offs with the university-based parts of the center of pedagogy. It will be necessary for states to add resources to settings committed to the joining and sharing implied here.

Second, the experimentation in staff utilization described above does not run counter to my earlier caveat not to burden professional development schools with too many different expectations. Teacher education must not be neatly separated from matters of the educational delivery system. The way teaching resources are to be deployed must be closely connected to the education of educators. In the past, monolithic patterns of use have driven monolithic patterns of preparation.

Third, there is little point in going to the literature or on the road in search of models. To my knowledge, none exists. There is a small body of useful writing with which to begin. But the future requires creativity and the sharing of ideas, successes, and failures.

Postulates from the School Perspective

This chapter has looked more to the school than to the higher education side of the collaboration called for in centers of pedagogy. Consequently, it has raised implicitly the relevance of the postulates for directing attention to the conditions for effective teacher education to which schools and school districts must contribute.

My initial intent was to conclude the chapter with some rewriting of the postulates to reflect the schools' perspective and responsibilities. The process of getting to this point has caused me to conclude that such rewriting is not necessary. The unpacking in Chapter Three produced a good many questions directed to schools seeking to investigate the conditions of a given postulate.

The need, I have decided, is not one of restating the postulates. Rather, it is one of keeping always in mind the mission and the implications of simultaneously renewing schools and the education of educators and of eschewing separation of the two. Because teacher education has been regarded for so long as the prerogative of higher education — in spite of the obvious role of schools — analysis of the postulates almost invariably proceeds from the perspective of higher education.

Analysts and discussants simply must discipline themselves to be inclusive of both perspectives. There are commitments to be made and leadership to be provided by chief executives in school districts, just as there are for those in universities. The identifiable, responsible faculty must include school personnel, and there must be appropriate rewards for their services. There cannot be coherent programs without involvement of school-based personnel in all of their planning and conduct. There must be school-based laboratory facilities within the clearly defined borders of the center of pedagogy. And each state's policies must ensure the support requisite to the inclusion and high quality of these resources. The need is to develop the habit of thinking of the school and the university roles simultaneously in all efforts intended for the better education of the nation's educators.

5

Curriculum, Curricula

Fish in troubled waters.[1]
—Stratagem 20 of Ancient China

This chapter and the next address the major ingredients of a coherent, comprehensive teacher education program. They pick up where *Teachers for Our Nation's Schools* left off, using and fleshing out to considerable degree the major elements of the curriculum briefly sketched in that volume's Chapter Nine.

The issue of detail looms once again. Several of the reviews of *Teachers for Our Nation's Schools* were critical of the lack of curricular detail there. In subsequent responses to this criticism, I have cited three reasons for the omission. First, I think that presentation of a rather specific curriculum would have directed attention away from my general message regarding the absence of and need for conditions that support and encourage solid curriculum planning in each teacher-preparing setting. Second, I question the usefulness of a curriculum dreamed up out of one head intended for all settings. Third (and closely related), curriculum development is a continuous process that has great value for those responsible for the results and for the quality of what results. There are no surrogates for this process; at best, there can be only helpful guidelines.

And so, once again, I eschew the presentation of a detailed curriculum. I do so against the advice of several thoughtful readers of this manuscript who urged me to provide more detail.

What I have endeavored to provide instead is a broad framework that stresses attention to the arts and sciences, pedagogy and the educational content that supports it, enough time for fundamental themes to appear and reappear, the integration of theory and practice throughout the length and breadth of the whole, modeling on the part of the responsible faculty of the practices they hope their students will emulate as teachers, the availability of an array of exemplary field settings, and much more. Within this house of teacher education there are many possible mansions to be planned and built by the responsible faculty of a center of pedagogy. Let the voices of John Dewey, Jean Piaget, Max Black, Jerome Bruner, Maria Montessori, William James, Edward L. Thorndike, Alfred North Whitehead, Maxine Greene, Gerald Edelman, Howard Gardner, and many others echo throughout this house as faculty groups from the arts and sciences, the schools, and the SCDE argue their positions and build curricula.

This is a fortuitous time for serious engagement in the planning of curricula for future educators. The process necessarily bridges the two traditionally separated cultures of the so-called lower schools and higher education. The very words of definition betray the chasm. It is a chasm of much more than physical and organizational separation; it is also one of attitudinal separation, with a history and condition of low status but high instrumental expectations for elementary and secondary schools on one side and near-regal status and comparatively low accountability on the other. For teacher education, however, there have been neither high expectations nor regal status.

All this is undergoing fresh scrutiny and some change. The turbulence that characterized schooling in the 1980s continues; the relative tranquility of higher education is being disturbed by an unprecedented cacophony of questions from both without and within. Questions having to do with teaching, undergraduate and professional curricula, what universities are doing about the schools, and reward structures favor fresh initiatives. Questions addressing the simultaneous renewal of schooling and the education of educators are among these.

Several reviewers of *Teachers for Our Nation's Schools,* although not critical of the findings and conclusions, viewed some of the major recommendations as unrealistically idealistic. Those reviewers were much less optimistic than I regarding the prospects that teacher education would gain significantly in prestige and in freedom from external controls, for example. I believe, however, that people tend to become inured to the familiar—so inured that they come not to see the warts and blemishes and therefore fail to see the need, let alone the possibility, for improvement. In periods of rapidly changing, even confusing, circumstances, the comforting stability of the familiar erodes. Disorientation begins to replace orientation to what previously was a given. And this creates opportunities for change.

It is in this context that alternatives previously seen as unnecessary, troublesome, or unrealistically ideal often are tolerated and sometimes welcomed. Hence one of the classic 36 Stratagems of Ancient China: fish in troubled waters. At the time of this writing, it is difficult to find placid waters, whether one looks out over education and schooling or surveys the larger social, political, and economic scene. Hence, according to this argument regarding the opportunities inherent in disequilibrium, the times are ripe for change and innovation.

Curricular Waters

The cynic might respond that there are enough difficulties with curriculum planning itself and with the unique circumstances of higher education to daunt the most determined, agile fisherman on the shores of curricular waters in teacher education; there is no need to further roil these waters. This is, of course, to miss the point of the above argument. Nonetheless, recognizing and taking into account difficulties likely to be encountered helps us benefit from rather than stumble over opportunity. Let us now turn to some of the difficulties that come with the territory.

The Ubiquitous Curriculum

Recently, several consecutive issues of a local weekly newspaper chronicled a rather bizarre curricular tale. A gratifying period of parent-teacher dialogue regarding an elementary school had climaxed in the appointment of a respected teacher as principal. Then a small group of parents, presumably representing more, wrote a long letter to the newspaper praising the school's nurturing but lamenting (in carefully chosen, constructive language) a near-nonexistent curriculum. This was read by many to suggest that the school was a warm, caring place that lacked a curriculum. The response was predictable. Letters announcing the existence of a curriculum and resenting the implication that there was none poured in — many of them from the teachers, of course. Some took the trouble to describe parts of it. Letters of explanation and counterexplanation followed, week after week.

It is difficult to understand so much misunderstanding over an obvious fact: *all* schools have curricula. The trouble is that they have many — from those experienced by students to those in the minds of teachers and parents. The lack of information regarding what a given parent has in mind may lead that parent to conclude that a curriculum scarcely exists. The curriculum of a teacher's intentions may be so engraved in his mind as to blind him to the only curriculum that really matters — the curriculum experienced by students. Regrettably, this is the one that people with curriculum in mind are least likely to consider. Ask a principal to describe the curriculum of her school, and chances are she will list curricular offerings, probably in categories constituting graduation requirements. Even probe as you choose, answers about students' curricular "takings" are hard to come by.

Curriculum, in the sense of a definable entity, is elusive. One is reminded of Gertrude Stein's oft-quoted words, "There is no there there." Yet in educational institutions, especially elementary and secondary schools, "the curriculum" is a powerful, even ghostlike presence. Whether it is Sylvia Ashton-Warner's remembrances of teaching the Maori children (in her book *Teacher*[2]) or an autobiographer chronicling his or her experiences as the lone teacher in a small school, the curriculum ghost haunts the classroom, a constant reminder of things to be taught.

The problem with the many faces of curriculum carries over into serious scholarly work in what now defines itself as

a field of study. Its literature is vast enough to warrant encyclopedic attention.[3] Yet swarming cadres of curriculum theorists
and specialists have difficulty agreeing on what the curriculum
thing is. Differing definitions abound.

A good deal of this disagreement is, unfortunately, of the
either-or variety. A curriculum is a course of studies, laid out
more or less as a track to be run. Or it is none of this; rather,
it is what students experience. Need it be simply one or the other?
Can it not be both? There are other disagreements, but most
appear ultimately to settle on two genres: curricula of intentions and curricula experienced. Both are real and legitimate.

In most countries, ministries of education specify what
they think students in the schools should encounter in the curriculum, sometimes in daily detail. Many expect teachers to follow these stated intentions very closely. In the United States,
state and school district courses of study are intended to be guidelines for teachers to follow. Commonly, textbooks geared rather
closely to these play a major role in implementing intentions.
Almost invariably, though, there is tension between teachers'
perceptions of these guidelines and their own curricular intentions. There is an even greater tension between intentions getting
through to students and what they make of them.

But students' curricular perceptions and experiences rank
relatively low on the agendas of curriculum development and
philosophical justification. In scholarly curriculum circles, it is
difficult to move forward without stepping on philosophical land
mines. The debate over subject-centered versus child-centered
curricula, how curricula reflect dominant social values, recon-
ceptualism versus linear rationality, who controls school curricula versus who should, and more appears to have sapped energies to the point that little of practical use to practitioners emerges.
Bits and pieces of curricular thought and product are picked
up and used in various settings, but systemic use is rare. And
the scholarly debate goes on and on.

Meanwhile, a rather simplistic framework prevails for
presenting the various curricula of intentions, whether of a state,
a school district, or a school. First, there are goals encompassing academic, social, vocational, and personal educational expec-

tations for students. These often are followed by reminders that teachers have considerable freedom in regard to selecting means of attainment. Domains of knowledge and knowing are presented as well, in varying degrees of generality. At some point, the meat of the intended curriculum emerges. Familiar school subjects are listed, usually arranged in hierarchical fashion for the grades: kindergarten or first grade through twelfth.

Much less simplistic and, in my judgment, of much greater educational value are those few guides that maximize fundamental concepts or principles serving to organize a field of study and use specific topics only as illustrative examples for developing these organizing elements. These curriculum guides are more likely to remind teachers of broad expectations for schools and point out that the subjects are a means to their attainment. They emphasize the importance of teachers' being professionally prepared to exercise judgment in deciding what and how to teach.

In general, the ubiquitous curriculum makes subject-matter content the end. Students will be tested in it many times, by both teacher-made and standardized tests. Subject matter is what teachers are expected to deliver. This is what teacher education is to prepare teachers for. So it has been, and so it is. But this is not what could and should be.

Consequently, the nature of disequilibrium in the schools has much to do with the potential for vitality in teacher education programs. If the debate over school reform fastens narrowly on the need for mechanistic, rote attention to subject-matter specifics and eschews inquiry, questioning, curiosity, and a thirst for new ideas—the concept of education put forward in Chapter Two—then hope for renewal in teacher education fades. Teacher education sentences itself to a dreary fate if it cuts itself off from opportunities to roil the waters of curriculum renewal in the schools. The renewal of schools and of teacher education programs must go hand in hand to ensure teachers who see curriculum content as means, not ends, and who are prepared as educators, not trainers. Teacher educators must not be unwitting accomplices in the advocacy of unexamined ideologies in the schools.

Unfortunately, our research revealed all too clearly the

degree to which teacher education is geared to placid waters, to accepting the familiar as both the norm and the possible. When, for example, students in teacher education programs experienced dissonance between what they had encountered in their early teacher-training curriculum and conventional ways of doing things encountered later in the classrooms of their student teaching, their professors commonly told them to conform to the latter. We had hoped to find prospective teachers and their teachers crying out, "Curriculum, curricula!" with respect to curricula on both sides of the chasm and busily fishing together in troubled waters for a gratifying catch. Unfortunately, university-based and school-based individuals involved in the same teacher education programs rarely got close enough to one another to cut bait together, let alone fish and talk. A center of pedagogy seeks to remedy situations of this kind by bringing together all of the groups of actors required to develop coherent, renewing teacher education programs.

The Higher Waters of Academe

The late Beardsley Ruml, when with the Ford Foundation, was reported to have said that the faculty in higher education is incapable of planning a coherent curriculum. Whether or not it *can* is a moot question. It is fair to say, however, that it rarely *does*. And when faculty groups come close — as they have from time to time, especially in creating and operating small colleges within larger undergraduate colleges in the arts and sciences — the resulting publicity supports the proposition that such occurs rarely.

Curriculum planning appears to have kinship with military logistics. There is an end in view, and a route must ultimately be chosen. But the similarities are only superficial. Military objectives tend to be clear-cut, even if their underlying foreign policy is not; curriculum planners, on the other hand, have great difficulty agreeing on the battle to be fought and on what constitutes winning. Much more than in the military, there is a changing array of players, many of whom are not (and do not perceive themselves to be) readily accountable, yet they do not hesitate to get into the act. And curriculum development, like the devil's work, is never finished. It is always there, differently perceived by the various players (or not seen at all), waiting to engage heads and hands, watched over by ghosts of curricula past and present.

Much more than in the schools, shot through as they are with all manner of intrusions, curricular dilemmas in higher education *appear* to be of a simpler genre: the faculty sets the curriculum, and the students partake of it. Comparatively free of state mandates and administrative fiats, the faculty sets some requirements for all, recommendations for some, and electives as benign recognition of students' individual interests. The array of players changes slowly and in rather orderly fashion. Accountability is equitably distributed; some faculty members are more equal than others, but uncertainties are clarified by designations of rank.

But the appearance of simplicity soon fades into finely textured complexity — layers of it. There is agreement on ends only at a most general level, and it tends to be unwritten and tacit. There is agreement on the concept of general education for all, but again at a general level; further elaboration usually results in disagreement. Formal curricular documents express courses as means. However, parsimony in regard to institutional mission (except in church-related institutions, in particular) and philosophical context raises the specter of courses as ends rather than means. Here, at least, emerges a kinship with the lower schools, whether or not we wish to acknowledge the family connection.

The courses-become-ends are determined and controlled by relatively autonomous fiefdoms. Although each enjoys the rhetoric of being part of a community of scholars, each functions most of the time according to the particulars of an intellectual ghetto. Years ago, Charles Colwell, once a key academic administrator at the University of Chicago, described to me both the hopes for and the extant reality of the Quadrangle Club there: "The intent was to create interdisciplinary communication over lunch. But, almost from the first day, there emerged a history table, a biology table, a philosophy table, and so on."

Since the total curricular acreage controlled by each college or university is relatively finite, each fiefdom expands its turf at the expense of another. As part of a community of scholars, fiefdoms engage in open warfare only at great risk and very rarely. And since the areas open to internecine struggle are few in number and sharply limited in available turf, tactics must be and are exceedingly subtle. One of the more obvious, of course, is to find ways to keep entire fields off the turf entirely. Teacher education has served over the years as a near-willing victim of this tactic.

Academic departments, not unlike other human entities, often equate expansion or growth with progress and improvement. As I stated above, progress so defined is exceedingly difficult when the acreage shared with others is finite. The available avenues are few—though somewhat more in universities than in colleges—and sharply watched. One of the least subtle is to claim ground in the freshman and sophomore years on the basis of the relevance of one's particular field to general education. An equally obvious avenue is to seek expansion of the courses required of a major in that field by making a good case for the rapid growth of knowledge in it. A third is to seek recognition of certain courses in that field as basic to various professions and hence appropriate as prerequisites. A common fourth avenue is to get that department's courses listed as electives in as many subcurricula as possible.

Given the small number and obvious nature of the several avenues to growth, department chairs would be well advised to immerse themselves in the subtleties of the 36 Stratagems of Ancient China. Several in particular come to mind. Stratagem 6 is employed in many human pursuits: "Make a feint to the east while attacking in the west." More subtle is Stratagem 11: "Sacrifice the plum tree for the peach tree." Then there is that venerable Stratagem 16: "Snag the enemy by letting him off the hook." Stratagem 4 smacks of gentility: "Relax while the enemy exhausts himself." Many of us who are or have been academic administrators have made frequent use of Stratagem 7: "Create something out of nothing." These ancient stratagems help us to remember that curriculum development is in large part a political process, usually played out with considerable subtlety in academic settings. Perhaps it is the use of these and other stratagems that gave rise to this oft-repeated sentence: The reason that academic politics are so vicious is that the stakes are so small.

But the cumulative effect is not at all small. We found that intrusion of departments into the freshman and sophomore years had chewed dangerously close to and sometimes into the integrity of a two-year general education curriculum. On one hand, some courses finding their way there appeared to be geared more to serving as prerequisites to a given major than to fulfilling the concept of general, liberal education. On the other, increased alternatives in a given domain of knowledge served to confound student choice. Faculty failure to make tough choices passed responsibility to students. I am not alone in believing that students at this age need considerable curricular guidance.

Many faculty members in the arts and sciences argue that courses in vocational or professional preparation should be kept out of the undergraduate curriculum. I empathize with this position. But in multipurpose universities, the undergraduate major commonly is directed first toward graduate studies and ultimately toward employment in this or a related field. In other words, the orientation is one of professional or vocational preparation, regardless of the contrary rhetoric. More than a few entrepreneuring departments have increased course requirements to the extent that graduation with the standard, widely publicized 120 semester or 180 quarter hours is the norm of the past. As stated earlier, there are some institutions of higher education, particularly four-year colleges with few or no graduate programs, that have assiduously avoided such excess. But this inflated graduation was the reality in most of the universities we studied, and students deplored the lack of truth in advertising.

This and other departures from some of the curricular regularities higher education tends to support rhetorically create troublesome dilemmas for sound curriculum development in teacher education. But again, increased roiling of the previously more placid higher education waters creates opportunities. Today there are lively debates over what history, what cultures, what languages, and what literature students should study. There are strong expressions of concern from within and without regarding the quality of university teaching. Dangers lurk in turbulence, of course. Recognizing them is important but will not still the waters. Lively times create opportunities for enticing proposals and determined action.

There are two steps that people deeply committed to quality in teacher education should take in these opportune times: review and redesign the general undergraduate curriculum and formulate a pre–teacher education component. The first is for the common good; the second nicely blends self-serving and the common good. We address these now.

The General Undergraduate Curriculum

Institutional evolution from normal school to teachers college to state college to state university has largely disenfranchised faculty members commonly held accountable for teacher education from the undergraduate curriculum. They have little or no voice in it. Undergraduate programs in teacher education must weave their way around what other faculty members have put in place. There is strong opposition both within universities and from outside to undergraduate majors in education. Ironically, there is no comparable magnitude of opposition to undergraduate concentrations in business and engineering, for example, in spite of the degree of vocationalism in the curricula. Indeed, many academic administrators in the universities we studied highlighted the growth of their business schools in listing institutional strengths. Schools and colleges of education have exacerbated their undergraduate disenfranchisement by moving toward primarily or exclusively graduate preparation of teachers, thus effectively removing themselves from the curriculum that undergirds their work.

No faculty members engaged in professional preparation have as legitimate an interest in the undergraduate curriculum as do those involved in teacher education. Teachers enculturate the young by drawing upon organized bodies of knowledge — the academic disciplines being continuously revised through inquiry. They must learn their fields as students and continue to learn them as teachers.

The professional lore of doctors, lawyers, engineers, and others who "practice a profession" is to some degree built on these subject matters, but those professionals are not engaged in using them to educate others. Yet schools of medicine, law, and engineering exercise far more influence over the so-called general education of undergraduates than do schools and colleges of education. Add to this irony that of public blame going to schools and colleges of education for perceived subject-matter deficiencies among teachers.

No group of academicians should be more concerned about the nature and quality of undergraduate education than those who prepare teachers. Consequently, teacher educators do society and teachers a disservice by withdrawing from or allowing themselves to be isolated from the process of planning first-rate undergraduate curricula for all students, among whom are many prospective teachers.

I am not arguing for an undergraduate major in education. At this point, I am not even arguing for including preparation programs designated for prospective teachers in undergraduate curricula. What I am arguing for is a general education undergraduate curriculum that has not been savaged by the aggrandizement of entrepreneurial departments and professional schools—an undergraduate program deliberately designed to produce broadly educated citizens. At a minimum, that is the necessary grounding for teachers.

I am arguing also that teacher educators are morally obliged to assist in the planning of this curriculum. To stand aside is reprehensible, however bumpy the road to enfranchisement. The times are unlikely to be more opportune.

I have argued elsewhere many times that determination of the general education required of an elementary school teacher is as likely a route as any for arriving at an exemplary undergraduate curriculum—again, on the grounds that such a person engages daily in enculturating the young through drawing upon all of our major knowledge systems. What might evolve from this perspective on the essential undergraduate curriculum?

All students would have intellectual encounters with major concepts, principles, and ideas in six knowledge domains: the nature of the human species; social, political, and economic systems (the global village); the world as a physical system; the world as a biological system; evaluative and belief systems; and communicative and expressive systems. These are depicted in Figure 5.1.[4] Within each of these domains are listed the conventional rubrics under which academic studies are conducted and understandings gained. The individual learner is at the heart of the curriculum. Obviously, no individual undergraduate student can hope for more than a few months of engagement with relevant areas of studies in each domain.

The challenge of designing such a curriculum is, of course, a daunting one. It tests the necessary resolve of the faculty to ensure in each domain choices agreed upon as having approximately equal potential for the desired intellectual encounters. It tests over time the ability of these responsible parties to guard against intrusions of less appropriate curricular options. Then, in addition to the demands of design and renewal, there is the need to guide and monitor student selections. Individual students' curricula must be reviewed periodically to ensure balance. These and related faculty responsibilities are likely to be fulfilled well only if sustained attention to curricular matters ranks high in the reward structure.

The question arises as to how long in the four years of undergraduate education each student's curriculum is to mirror this design. One answer is the first two years, during which time each student would devote the equivalent of fifteen credit hours per quarter and fifteen hours per domain for a total of ninety quarter hours. This leaves ninety quarter hours over the last two years for the customary majors, minors, and electives of the undergraduate program.

I would argue, however, for a period of turbulence accompanied by inquiry into these regularities, to which we may have become too inured. We tend to argue the virtues of majors as now presented as indisputable givens. Yes, they prepare students for advanced, graduate studies in the field. Yes, what is good for majors is also good for nonmajors taking courses as

Figure 5.1. The World's Systems and
the Scope of an Undergraduate Curriculum.

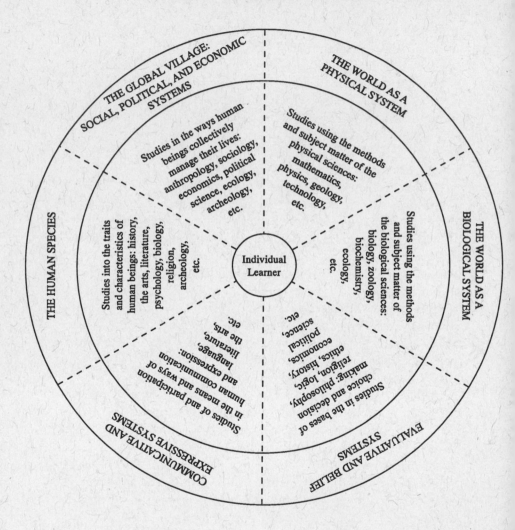

THE GLOBAL VILLAGE:
SOCIAL, POLITICAL, AND ECONOMIC
SYSTEMS

THE WORLD AS A
PHYSICAL SYSTEM

THE HUMAN SPECIES

THE WORLD AS A
BIOLOGICAL SYSTEM

COMMUNICATIVE AND
EXPRESSIVE SYSTEMS

EVALUATIVE AND BELIEF
SYSTEMS

Studies in the ways human
beings collectively
manage their lives:
anthropology, sociology,
economics, political
science, ecology,
archeology,
etc.

Studies using the methods
and subject matter of the
physical sciences:
mathematics,
physics, geology,
technology,
etc.

Studies into the traits
and characteristics of
human beings: history,
the arts, literature,
psychology, biology,
religion,
archeology,
etc.

Studies using the methods
and subject matter of
the biological sciences:
biology, zoology,
biochemistry,
ecology,
etc.

Individual
Learner

Studies of and participation
in the means and ways of
human communication
and expression:
language,
literature,
the arts,
etc.

Studies in the bases of
choice and decision
making: philosophy,
religion, logic,
ethics, history,
economics,
political
science,
etc.

Source: From John I. Goodlad, "The Learner at the World's Center," *Social
Education, 50,* no. 6 (October 1986): 431. Reprinted by permission.
    Adapted from Kenneth E. Boulding, *The World as a Total System* (Newbury
Park, Calif.: Sage, 1985).

electives. The arguments often sound more like cant than solid substance.

Years ago, when director of the Center for Teacher Education at the University of Chicago, I had occasion to confer with professors in many departments about a then-popular topic among curricular theorists: the structure of academic disciplines. Teachers require, I believed then and believe still, a rigorous intellectual grasp of the basic elements one brings to bear in order to understand and explain phenomena that a given discipline purports to unravel. Jerome Bruner was soon to captivate readers and audiences with his views on the structure of knowledge as a curricular device and the power of intuition as a pedagogical one.[5] I wanted to derive from my interviews whether, how, and when these professors sought and sensed in their students a growing awareness of this structure. It usually required quite a few minutes of each conversation to convey a reasonably clear notion of what I was after.

Two kinds of responses dismayed me and contributed significantly to my skepticism regarding the near-sacred claims to virtue for the upper-division major, *as commonly organized and taught*. The first was the frequently expressed doubt that more than a few undergraduates had an intellectual grasp, intuitive or otherwise, of something that might be termed the structure of the discipline and the belief that those who did achieved it by dint of their own acuity rather than deliberate curricular or instructional intent. Most perceived this grasp of the subject being shaped in doctoral seminars. (I am shaken to the core once again by thoughts of all those policymakers who view possession of a bachelor's degree with a major in history as virtually a license to enculturate high school students through exposure to the social sciences.)

The second type of response will always remain in my mind. Several of these professors said to me in all seriousness that they would just as soon — one said *rather* — begin with graduate students fresh: that is, with individuals having no more than an introductory acquaintance with the subject as part of their general education. Otherwise, they said, there are too many fixations to undo. Are we forever doomed to each successively higher level in our organized educational system viewing the one immediately below as seriously flawed?

There was a time when reexamination of the undergraduate curriculum was de rigueur. And still there are always some individuals and institutions engaged in the process. We found recent or ongoing revision most often in the liberal arts colleges. We also found more coherence there and greater acceptance of curriculum work as a normal part of the professorial expectation. There were not on these campuses, of course, intrusion of the interests of graduate departments and professional schools. There were not often large, generously funded research projects relentlessly demanding faculty commitment of time. Nonetheless, the powerful regularities of the four-year college curriculum were in place and little questioned. But the rhetoric of what is good and beautiful and the curriculum actually in place tended to be more closely matched than in most of the other kinds of institutions in our sample.

Inquiry is the hallmark of academe. The time may be just right for serious inquiry into the design of undergraduate curricula. It would be refreshing and useful to critique the arguments presumably supporting what currently exists.

Several decades ago, carefully planned options leading to the single-subject major were not uncommon. When I joined UCLA in 1960, there existed a composite major in the social sciences that many of my colleagues regarded as ideal preparation in the content fields for elementary school teachers. It came to an end several years later, eliminated on the grounds that there were too many introductory courses. One wonders whether the hierarchical numbering of courses accurately reflects a hierarchy in the subject matter that precludes learning if the sequence is not followed. Studies of student transcripts reveal patterns that seem to deny the implied assumption. There are fields, presumably, where skipping around in the recommended course sequence is dysfunctional. As a history major, however, I rarely found myself handicapped by the order in which I took courses. The professors at the University of Chicago who would just as readily accept into graduate studies students who had not majored in the field clearly had intellectual qualities in mind that were not dependent upon assumed hierarchies of subject matter.

I am not arguing against depth in subject fields as an intellectual virtue. Rather, I am concerned about habitual curricular assumptions. Specialists in academic fields who demonstrate some expertise in general curriculum development do so primarily by accident. There is little in their own education that prepares them for so complex a task, either substantively or politically. The complexity is compounded when curricula that combine or blend subjects are considered. The predictable disintegration of composite curricula, built with great care and hard work over a period of years, probably has much less to do with their educational invalidity than with the professional comfort that comes from dealing exclusively with one's chosen subject and the general curriculum as though cut from the same piece of cloth. Specialization leads professors to graduate programs and away from the complexities of planning undergraduate curricula.

The Pre–Teacher Education Component

Abraham Flexner argued strongly for a general education curriculum to ensure that the physician would be a well-educated citizen. He also argued strongly for what he considered to be the scientific underpinnings of the professional curriculum to follow. Definitions of these underpinnings have become known as the pre-med curriculum. Some medical educators have argued that this pre-med curriculum has expanded too much, eating too far into nonscience general education. They recommend more attention to the humanities, in particular, lamenting the degree to which applicants to medical school are narrowly educated.

It will be a long time, if ever, before most institutions preparing teachers commonly produce students with the balanced general education curriculum recommended earlier. Curriculum development in higher education moves slowly, free of a sense of urgency. The need for excellent teachers in our schools, and therefore for exemplary teacher education programs, is too great to await this slow, deliberative process. But some specific steps toward improving the general education of future teachers can be taken while we await the results of more comprehensive renewal.

Although teacher educators are urged to participate continuously in the redesign of undergraduate curricula, it is essential that they take advantage of present circumstances to address the matter of the pre-ed, as in pre-med, curriculum. This is not a call to the entrepreneurial game of getting one's own courses into the first two years of college. Rather, it is an admonition to teacher educators regarding their need to pay attention to curricular offerings in these two years: what prospective teachers are taking and — with the mission of teacher education in mind — what they should. I am not at all sanguine regarding the wisdom exercised by young men and women as they select courses early in their college years. They need guidance.

The guidance I have in mind is the counseling of students declaring an interest in becoming teachers regarding areas of study likely to prepare them for their later responsibilities. Even if the curriculum recommended earlier were in place, there are studies that are more or less relevant. The mission depicted in Figure 1.1 points rather directly to studies in civics, government, ethics, and religion — all commonly included as acceptable choices in areas specified as required for general education. The design of the undergraduate curriculum as a whole will determine whether there are likely to be critically important omissions in other areas, such as literature, multicultural education, communications, aesthetics, logic, and technology. None of these is "professional" preparation in education. None is inappropriate as part of a general, liberal education. But they constitute highly relevant underpinnings for individuals seeking to become teachers. In fact, they are appropriate for any educated person, whether or not he or she becomes a teacher (as are all studies defined as pre-ed).

The process of determining this pre-ed curriculum serves a dual purpose — that of guiding the curriculum of the sizable number of individuals who come to college intending to prepare to teach, and that of providing a basis for scrutinizing the transcripts of those who make this decision later. In *Teachers for Our Nation's Schools,* I set the final quarter or semester of the sophomore year as the latest decision-making point for the undergraduate. The next opportunity comes after graduation, if postbaccalaureate programs are available. If teacher educators, after careful deliberation, come to view studies in ethics, for example, to be an essential ingredient of a teacher education program, provision for inclusion is essential, whatever the point of a candidate's entry.

As we shall see in the next chapter, there are essential curricular themes for teachers that arise out of the general education underpinnings, such as studies in ethics. But these become part of the professional curriculum, with attention focused on classroom, school, and the interplay of interests among teachers, principals, parents, and students. It became clear as our inquiry into the education of educators progressed that the several different kinds of curricular demands on prospective teachers produced a hurried, inadequately reflective passage into the myriad responsibilities of teaching. Even with the expansion of four-year programs into five that we recommend, there will not be any discretionary time. Consequently, the formal and informal processes of socialization into teaching are enormously enhanced when students select out of the options in general education those of particular relevance to the mission that they ultimately will take on.

Curricular Reflections

On General Education Courses for Teachers

Preceding pages have taken us into topics that deserve some further attention. Subsequent discussion serves to flesh out several topics so as to bring them from peripheral to more central attention. This chapter addresses that large part of a teacher's education that is either ignored or assumed not to require serious corrective attention — the liberal, general education that graduation from college presumably provides. Indeed, the equating of graduation and a liberal education is so widespread that many people think that a college degree warrants a license to teach in elementary and secondary schools. I have serious reservations about that assumption.

In holding these reservations, I am not alone. There has been in recent years an unprecedented rash of books criticizing the undergraduate curriculum, the nature and quality of teaching, and faculty inattention to students. One of the most vigorous of these attacks comes from George H. Douglas, professor of English at the University of Illinois, who argues that rampant specialization has virtually destroyed liberal learning in the university.[6] He has the temerity to suggest that undergraduates would be better served by closer allegiance of universities to the English than the German model of higher education. This would be a major shift, indeed.

The little I have written about the general education of teachers, and especially what I referred to in *Teachers for Our Nation's Schools* as their pre-ed curriculum, has created some misunderstandings. I am charged, I am told, with proposing content courses—even watered-down content courses—for future teachers. Nothing could be further from what I am endeavoring to recommend on preceding pages; few proposals could be more abhorrent to me.

My argument regarding the general education of teachers embraces essentially two strands of thought. First, teacher educators—whether in schools, the arts and sciences, or SCDEs—should be active participants in promoting and advancing undergraduate curricular reform, and not just for the improved education of teachers but for all students. A quarter-century ago, teacher educators were somewhat more active in this arena than they are today, but the movement of teacher education to the graduate level on some campuses has resulted in many from this group simply disenfranchising themselves as participants in the renewal of general education.

The second part of my argument notes that curriculum development in higher education works in wondrously circuitous ways, characterized particularly by a sluggish pace. The need for better-educated teachers is sufficiently urgent to commend for teacher educators the use of curricular strategies of a more expedient sort, such as those employed by some professional schools in making demands on the general education offerings of academic departments. Many of the lower-division courses from which students select in meeting their general education requirements are there because the schools of engineering, law, and medicine arranged for them to be there. Teacher educators have a responsibility to ensure comparable opportunities for future teachers and to provide guidance in course selection. Presumably, the courses proposed for general education with future teachers in mind are at least as legitimate as those proposed with future engineers, lawyers, and doctors in mind. I go so far as to write that those proposed with future teachers in mind are likely to meet very well the criteria of good general education for *all* students. Indeed, they must.

What I am proposing is a far cry from developing special content courses for teachers (and certainly not courses that have been watered down). Courses in ethics, comparative religion, multiculturalism, government, and aesthetics surely cannot be described as specialized. I would prefer to eschew the entrepreneurial curricular logistics of some of the professional schools, but to do so is naive. So long as believing in the inherent virtue of general education as now commonly provided in the undergraduate college continues to be naive, it will be naive also to continue to believe that the best interests of teacher education are being taken care of in the normal business of higher education.

On External Curricular Controls

As I have noted, the troubled waters of schooling, together with the increasingly troubled waters of higher education, create unique opportunities for bringing the education of educators to the forefront of attention. One of the major obstacles to significant improvement in this education, however, is the degree to which the loosely connected enterprises of lower and higher education are restrained by both the specifics and the fact of state control.

Practitioners in both domains are chronically restive because of the degree and specificity of intervention, particularly into the curriculum. Consequently, they often turn eagerly to proposals appearing to ease restraints, sometimes without examining them with sufficient care. These proposals are sometimes couched in wording that appears completely rational and above objection. (Consider, for example, goals stated as outcomes for students and teachers.)

A classic example that I have cited elsewhere bears repeating.[7] Some years ago, a state we shall name Fanciful passed a bill requiring school districts to define the proficiencies students were to acquire at successive stages of progression to graduation. This directive meshed with an earlier one specifying that teacher education programs should prepare teachers in the competencies presumed to be needed to ensure the development of students' proficiencies. How clever and how exquisitely rational! Just match teacher competencies A, B, and C with student proficiencies X, Y, and Z and we have, at long last, a closely coupled educational system. Just like hard-wiring neurons A, B, and C to neurons X, Y, and Z to produce the connections we want in a computerized simulation of the brain. Except that the human brain is extraordinarily more complicated than this; there are about one million billion connections in the cortical sheet.[8] There may be fewer potential combinations and permutations in the matching of students' proficiencies in learning with teachers' competencies in teaching, but not many. No matter. The prospects remain enticing and are so easily mandated as expectations for those who will be held accountable that they emerge again and again as a simple, commonsense answer to educational reform.

The current version of the familiar, linear, rational model is couched in language that tends to soften criticism of the kind presented above. The outcomes desired for students and teachers are stated (or are to be stated) in very general terms. "Assessments" are to take the place of tests, and these are to be "authentic" in that they consist of evidences of accomplishments accurately reflecting the intended outcomes. Some state agencies are getting into the silliness domain by proposing to translate legislated policies into procedures for approving teacher education programs based on the degree to which graduates produce stated outcomes in students of the K-12 system.

There is something very curious about the way in which these weak models of anticipated synaptic connections appear and reappear on the education scene. The phenomenon takes on the character of ceremonial rain dances. Having little or no control over the forces at work and understanding them hardly at all, we order them into systemic rigor. The fact that very little happens as a result (and that many good things that might have happened are stifled by regulation) is no deterrent to dashing off once again in pursuit of the rational specter when it comes dancing across the stage.

The current wave of interest appeals to many educators and policymakers, but for quite different reasons. The latter group wants order; "systemic" reform is the current "in" word. Outcomes will generate a more orderly curriculum, be it for schoolchildren or future teachers, and assessments will provide evidence of progress in this curriculum toward outcomes to be stated ultimately as standards. For educators, the appeal lies elsewhere. The means of attainment will be left to local authorities and the educators. There is a ring of greater freedom here that fills a long-standing hunger on the part of many educators. And there is a professional appeal in the assumption that they will play a greater role in determining what and how to teach.

Yes, that *does* sound enticing, but I am skeptical. First, the model of accountability built into the system provides an easy way out for those policymakers unwilling to face up to the costs of putting in place the conditions essential to a first-class educational system. Second, such plans leave the marketplace uncontrolled in regard to moral issues pertaining to such matters as access to educational opportunity. With outcomes the measure of success, the expedient route is to select at the outset only candidates who appear most likely to be able to achieve them. Those who will require more help and will take longer become a burden to be eased aside as soon as possible. A free market in the education of children and their teachers and a free market in oil and soybeans are quite different things. Third, not messing with the details of curricula for the K-12 system and teacher education simply is not in the lexicon of policymakers. With the specification of outcomes and assessment measures, there will continue to be the steady creep, creep, creep of this or that legislated curricular nightcrawler.

Curriculum Development the Old-Fashioned Way

Serious curriculum development requires very hard work. Whatever the rhetoric of freeing teachers to determine what to teach, the employment year provides no time for rethinking the school curriculum. Ruml was provocative but not quite accurate in saying that faculty members are incapable of planning coherent curricula. The task simply is very difficult and demanding and offers few tangible rewards. Indeed, extensive involvement is dangerous to one's career.

Pronouncements from on high regarding standards to be met and outcomes to be attained do nothing to alleviate these built-in difficulties. The record of educational reform is revealing: relatively complex, interwoven designs of a systemic nature tend to fall of their own weight; specific requirements find their niche but do not change fundamental ways of doing business. Given the weak fabric of the infrastructure between state policy and educational settings (and the internal contradiction of state agencies' having the dual role of requiring compliance and providing assistance), mandates lose their power and often their intent in the journey from statehouse to schoolhouse. As Seymour Sarason pointed out years ago, institutional culture then takes care of whatever is left of initial intentions.[9]

One of the understandable problems with national and state reform agendas is that they must attract the time and support of educational leaders: heads of professional organizations and unions, superintendents of schools, presidents and deans of universities, and, if possible, some of the gurus who have an educational following in their own right. Consequently, such agendas pull a great many workers, especially the designated leaders, out of the setting where change ultimately must occur. The challenge to these leaders is to remain plugged in to the external agenda while engaged in the arduous, necessarily long-range tasks of effecting improvement back on the ranch. One solution is to share the load with a co-leader whose job requirements keep him or her on the ranch most of the time. Universities have achieved a modicum of success by rather sharply dividing the roles of president and provost or academic vice president, for example.

But the problem remains a critical one for the old-fashioned responsibilities of sustaining in the home setting processes of renewal and a measure of attention to reform initiatives, so often billed as being in the nation's or the people's best interests. Failure to be responsive is commonly viewed as resistance to change. But immersion in the external agenda can be so all-consuming that the home front suffers. The vacuum in leadership in some settings is the direct result of the designated leader's making a career out of attendance at meetings and membership on state and national committees. The mark of an effective leadership style is either learning to balance the external and internal responsibilities personally or making sure that the authority and responsibility delegated to another are widely understood.

A robust center of pedagogy depends on the sensitive orchestration of several different groups of players necessary to comprehensive, coherent curricula. It requires a director whose talents lie in blending diverse strengths. The misleading stereotypes of school-based people being interested only in the immediately practical, of professors in the arts and sciences being fixed on the virtues of their subjects, and of professors of education being caught up in educational theory bring a unique urgency to the curriculum development process. The group in charge must be aware of the larger context of proposals affecting their work, but to be highly responsive to them is self-defeating. The interlocking competencies-proficiencies reform mandates of Fanciful State referred to earlier, heralded in the relatively recent past as the driving mechanism for unprecedented statewide reform, are so far beyond memory that most people enamored with the new versions fail to connect them with those now filling educational garbage cans.

There are no substitutes, however sensible and enticing they appear to be, for the institution-based curriculum development process of setting and holding to a mission, determining the nature and needs of the student body, sorting out the most fundamental curricular themes, projecting the necessary array of organizing centers for developing these themes, sorting out faculty commitments and responsibilities, and engaging in formative evaluations and revision of the whole. I have proposed throughout this manuscript organization of the whole into a semiautonomous center of pedagogy representing three groups of critical actors who work to ensure the conditions essential to its good health.

Such a center requires a full-time, stay-at-home (most of the time) leader who reports to the dean of education (if the center is within the SCDE) or the provost (if the center is independent of the SCDE). I have argued that this center of pedagogy must be a force not simply to design the segment of teacher education curriculum usually designated "professional" but the whole of it. Such a center has a legitimate claim on the design of general education in the college or university and a moral obligation to exercise that claim.

I have argued, also, that there is now sufficient unrest and uncertainty both within and beyond the institutional setting to facilitate the easy entry of countervailing ideas likely to be rejected out of hand during more settled times. It is an opportune time for deans and chairs of SCDEs and directors of centers of pedagogy to lead. But I must remind them of John Steinbeck's admonition in *East of Eden:* Take a long look at your destination and then concentrate on your feet, lest ye stumble.

6

The Teacher Education Program

> The practitioner must choose. Shall he remain on the high ground
> where he can solve relatively unimportant problems according
> to prevailing standards of rigor, or shall he descend to the swamp
> of important problems and nonrigorous inquiry?[1]
>   —Donald A. Schön

For decades, there have been essentially two authorized routes to licensed teaching in the public schools of the United States. The longest standing of the two, producing the most teachers, is a four-year program embracing two years of general studies (the lower division of the undergraduate college) and two years (the upper division) of more specialized studies, including specific courses and teaching experiences designed to meet state requirements. The second is a postbaccalaureate program, usually focused almost exclusively on state licensing specifications but offering the option of adding courses to meet requirements for the institution's master's degree (commonly the M.A.T. or the M.Ed.). The master of arts in teaching degree, pioneered by President James B. Conant of Harvard and administered by a joint board of arts and sciences and education professors there, took off under the leadership of Dean Francis Keppel following World War II. At many universities, it became the route favored by faculty members in the arts and sciences departments.

But both of these routes have been fuzzy around the edges in many settings. On most of the campuses we studied, the so-

157

called four-year course required additional time for students to meet both graduation and teacher education requirements. Some students extended their time as undergraduates; some graduated in the institution's modal time and then continued beyond to complete certain licensing requirements — commonly, student teaching. There were also students who picked up just a few education courses as electives during their undergraduate years and then, after graduating, continued directly into a postbaccalaureate teacher education program. Campuses varied in the credits required of students wanting to qualify for both a master's degree and a teaching certificate. Some of the older postbaccalaureate students coming out of other occupations were already teaching with temporary certificates; they shopped for institutions offering the courses they needed at times that fit their schedules. In short, future teachers had a variety of routes to choose from. Not all the routes enjoyed untarnished reputations, however: many students who were enrolled from beginning to end in complete programs thought that some of the alternatives available downgraded teaching as a profession.

Clearly, the gates to teaching are unlatched, this one requiring less of a push than that. And in the resulting tension between quality and quantity, quality loses out. The state is culpable, but there seem always to be institutions of higher education ready to provide what is minimally required. Our research suggested that the more specific the state curricular mandates, the greater the likelihood of mechanistic, minimalistic institutional responses serving to drive quality down.

Clearing up these shoddy conditions will take determination, commitment, time, and unprecedented collaboration among states, institutions, and the teaching profession. Tension among the interests of the major players there must be. But it should be a tension that maintains a taut line between clear visions of quality teachers for our schools and the quality of programs preparing them. Just as there must not be simultaneously high standards for physicians and routes to the medical profession that ignore them, so also must the routes to teaching respect the high standards set for teachers.

It is argued in many quarters that entry into teaching is artificially and arbitrarily controlled by a self-serving educational establishment. Often the argument is supported by a case of one: the physics professor's wife who graduated cum laude in English before raising a family and now wants to teach; the legislator's niece who does not want to take "those silly education courses"; the retired colonel who taught military logistics in the marines and now wants to ease the shortage of mathematics teachers. There are gates loosely latched for all three. Not uncommonly, though, these backdoor teachers want something more than the chance to teach: an authorization certificate from a given flagship university, preferably carrying the signature of the dean of its school of education. They would not expect the same were their intentions to become lawyers, dentists, or engineers.

A large part of the expectation grows out of two related misconceptions. The first is that teaching is a *right*—at least for me. The second is a limited, often single-factor conception of teaching. I recall the relevant anecdote in *Teachers for Our Nation's Schools:* the professors who offered their services to the university's laboratory school but told the principal at the end of a grueling day that they would not come back unless she kept the regular teacher in the classroom to control the children. They seemed to want to inject their subject into the minds of children, not educate them.

I make no excuses and offer no defenses for the present conduct of authorized teacher education programs. Our report from studying a representative sample is highly critical—in many ways, more so than that of James B. Conant in the early 1960s, and more radical and sweeping in its recommendations. I am open to alternative routes (though not so widely varying in quality as those now available), but I am not willing to waive for any reason the conditions that have high potential for ensuring quality. Simplistic views of what teaching is and good teaching requires lead to casual attention to who passes through the gates and how they got to them.

What I am particularly concerned about here is the necessity of clearing up the lack of definition in authorized routes that creates much of the current slack between the expectations we should have for our teachers and the casualness with which we allow many to gain entry. What follows is written with this clarification in mind.

The Traditional Four-Year Model

Even though many people enter teaching through some kind of postbaccalaureate route, the majority have come and continue to come through a four-year undergraduate curriculum, as I have noted. This route, on which state policy and approval tends to focus most attention, has become increasingly ill-defined and longer over the years. The intent here is to unveil the deficiencies in the existing model and pose in its stead a more coherent, less hurried, five-year alternative. This then provides criteria for planning and judging postbaccalaureate models of supposed equal validity and rigor.

Four-year programs seek to account for four sets of curricular intentions: general education, specialized subject matter thought relevant to what teachers must teach, foundational studies in the field of education, and both observation of and participation in teaching. Generally, each is conducted by different groups of faculty members, with some overlap but not much communication between and among them. There is rarely any evidence to suggest that each group is guided by a shared vision among its members regarding what their students are to be and do as teachers. The center of pedagogy described in earlier chapters is intended to bring the several groups together around a shared vision and a coherent program.

The Program for Prospective Secondary School Teachers

There has been and is considerable interinstitutional similarity in the contours of programs for prospective high school teachers. The two-year lower-division chunk usually requires general education in the humanities, social sciences, physical and biological sciences, and mathematics, with varying degrees of choice among courses listed. The upper division requires a minimum of a third of the total credit hours in the so-called professional education sequence, with up to half of these in student teaching. This leaves up to two-thirds of the upper division for a major in a high school teaching field, courses related to this field, and electives. Unless the student plans very carefully from the first quarter on, selection of electives is sharply limited. Usually, the exigencies of the schedule of required courses in the major necessitate taking one or more during the student-teaching phase; this in turn necessitates placement in a nearby school, some commuting between college and school, and frequent breaks in the daily teaching schedule.

The general pattern of such a program is depicted in Figure 6.1. It would be difficult to differentiate either the general education curriculum or the left side of the upper-division portion from the curriculum of students as a whole. The prospective teacher simply forgoes the luxury of discretionary choices of electives. The arrows in the upper-right-hand chunk of both the junior and senior years suggest possible intrusion into the upper-left-hand chunk, because some students' majors leave a little room for an additional course in education as an elective, and completion of the major often intrudes into the time schedule for student teaching. The foundations courses depicted were once educational philosophy, educational history, and educational

Figure 6.1. Common Curricular Configuration of Traditional Four-Year Programs for the Preparation of Secondary School Teachers.

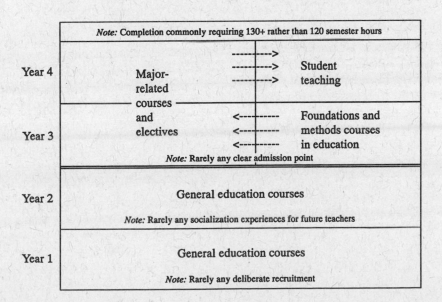

psychology, commonly followed by a generic or a content-specific methods course (and sometimes both). The first two foundational courses have been largely replaced by a potpourri that includes a smattering of state-mandated topics and some drawn from the two foundational disciplines. The courses in educational psychology and methods remain. Student teaching frequently involves two placements, each at a different secondary school grade level.

This depiction rather accurately reflects practice in regard to preparing teachers for high school mathematics, English, science, social studies, and foreign language teaching. The variations increase somewhat for vocational education, health and physical education, and the arts, but not enough to produce a different configuration. Some of these other programs commonly require more courses in the field of specialization and more time for completion.

The Program for Prospective Elementary School Teachers

Although programs for the preparation of elementary school teachers change the model in several major ways, the deviations are more in balance than in major curricular components. We found programs that pushed more teacher-specific courses into the general education component, for example. (I have shaded in a small slice of the sophomore year in Figure 6.2 to indicate that trend—although intrusion might just as well have resulted from an education course taken in the *freshman* year.) The big change is in the upper division, with courses specifically designed for teacher education now taking up a larger chunk. Commonly, these are courses covering both content thought desirable for teachers required to teach many subjects and suggested methods for teaching mathematics, science, language arts, the arts, social studies, and so on. In colleges offering a major in elementary education, the proportion of the upper division devoted to such courses invariably is greater than is the case in colleges requiring prospective elementary teachers to offer for graduation subject-matter concentrations like those for students generally. The almost inevitable consequence of this requirement is

Figure 6.2. Common Curricular Configuration of Traditional Four-Year Programs for the Preparation of Elementary School Teachers.

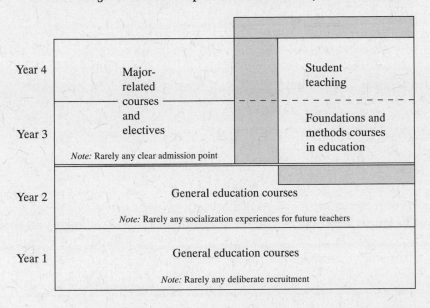

Year 4

Major-related courses and electives

Student teaching

Foundations and methods courses in education

Note: Rarely any clear admission point

Year 3

Year 2

General education courses

Note: Rarely any socialization experiences for future teachers

Year 1

General education courses

Note: Rarely any deliberate recruitment

Note: Frequent extensions from the basic block of studies are depicted in shaded sectors.

extension of the student's time and credits substantially beyond four years and 120 semester or 180 quarter hours. This common extension is usually greater for elementary than for secondary candidates.

The minimal sector of the total undergraduate curriculum given over to education courses and student teaching in the preparation of elementary school teachers is depicted as the unshaded upper-right-hand portion of Figure 6.2. This rectangle represents a little less than a quarter of the whole. We found this degree of "containment" rarely. Where we did encounter it, courses in specific content and methods of teaching in the school subjects were usually combined into some kind of "block" curriculum arrangement: a block encompassing mathematics, science, language arts, and social studies or two blocks combining the first two and then the last two subjects. Sometimes the teaching of reading and the language arts were brought into the block; more often, they appeared as discrete courses.

A much more common pattern, however, is curricular push into one or more—sometimes all—of the shaded areas: a course depicted in the upper-right-hand rectangle taken in the lower division, for example; a major in elementary education pushing into the major depicted in the upper-left-hand sector (years three and four); continuation of internships into a fifth year (130 to 140 semester hours or up to and beyond 200 quarter hours). Not infrequently, these additional credits are acquired by adding a course each quarter or semester to the normal load.

It is this nibbling into the general education requirements of the lower division (not commonly found in our studies) and into the academic majors of the upper division (a much more common finding) that has led to both justified and exaggerated charges against "all those methods courses taken at the expense of academic studies." These charges have led to elimination in many colleges and universities of all undergraduate majors in education. Yet many people who make such charges go beyond reason in proposing programs solely in the academic disciplines for all teachers. As I noted in an earlier chapter, they have no answer to (or do not consider) the question of how to prepare an elementary school teacher; their image almost invariably is of high school teachers teaching history, mathematics, or English.

Our studies did nothing to make us sanguine about the current preparation of high school teachers. Our earlier research[2] and that of others reveals much uneasiness and frustration on the part of high school teachers regarding their ability to interest students in their fields and to handle students' behavioral problems, a growing array of learning disabilities, and the teaching of higher-order thinking. Our more recent research on preparation programs confirmed (and left us very dissatisfied with) the common model depicted in Figure 6.1.[3] The waters of reform in this area are much too placid; the questions about curriculum planning in higher education raised in the preceding chapter are relevant, as are most of the recommendations of this chapter.

But it is the situation in the preparation of elementary school teachers that sharpens the urgency of the need at both levels. Increasingly, teacher educators have recognized and attempted to provide for the perplexing demands that confront teachers of the young daily. Policymakers have muddied teacher education curricula with specific requirements while criticizing the intrusion of these curricula into what they view as the academic domain. The net effect is a curricular racetrack along which future teachers scurry, looking always for opportunities to shorten the distance to the finish line. They have little time for sustained reflection; that they will become reflective practitioners appears exceedingly doubtful.

Nearly all of the future teachers we interviewed were seeking the high ground of certainty; they hoped to be able to solve problems by reaching into pockets and handbags for ready-made answers. The closer they were to taking over their own classrooms, the more they wanted what could be used next week. Given their curricular circumstances, the interviewer leans more readily to empathy than criticism. But continuing to tinker with four-year models will do little to change these circumstances.

Toward a Five-Year Model

In earlier chapters, I discussed specifically some of the organizational arrangements necessary to the creation of centers of pedagogy and the design of new programs for the education of educators. I stress again two organizational recommendations. The first is that the three-part faculty necessary to the conduct of teacher education be brought simultaneously into the renewal process. The second is that the group begin by sunsetting the existing program or programs. The dates of both sunsetting, in the sense of not admitting any more students, and grandfathering, in the sense of fulfilling commitments to those already admitted, are critical. They must be determined carefully to ensure sufficient time to plan and launch the new program. I shall not repeat here the schedule for Northern State University put forward in Chapter Nine of *Teachers for Our Nation's Schools,* which spread out over more than half the decade of the 1990s. That schedule had the virtue of producing from the institution nearly the same number of teachers each year over the period of complete transition from the old to the new — a condition of some importance politically. At no time was there a period of obvious letdown in the number of students being accommodated and of professors teaching.

There is one matter presented earlier that I do need to repeat: the figure depicting the mission of teacher education. This mission, which we propose for all teacher education programs mounted by a center of pedagogy (whatever the model), is shown again in Figure 6.3.

Figure 6.3. The Mission of Teacher Education in a Center of Pedagogy Geared to the Mission of Schooling in a Democratic Society.

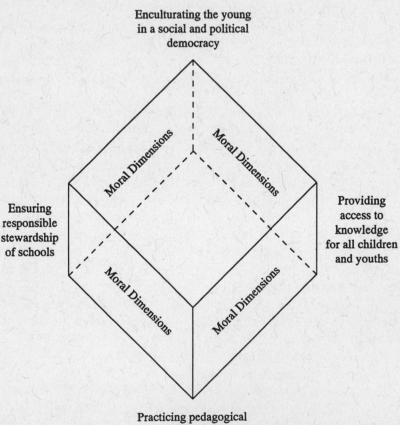

The postulates having most to do with programmatic arrangements for fulfilling this mission are Six through Seventeen. Each stipulates several program components that, taken together, guide students from the time they express an interest in becoming teachers (as long as this occurs during the first two undergraduate years) through at least their first year of teaching. Admission occurs during the concluding semester or quarter of the sophomore year. To those readers who say, "Yes, but what about those who decide in their junior year?" my answer is, "Sorry, they may seek entry, following graduation from college, to the two-year postbaccalaureate program" (described briefly later in this chapter). There is no way to provide an exemplary, coherent program if students are permitted to enter when they please.

The major components of this program, addressed briefly in Chapter Eight of *Teachers for Our Nation's Schools* and subsequently built into the renewal process at Northern State University in Chapter Nine of that book, are summarized below. Subsequently, they are depicted in Figure 6.4.

- *Recruitment.* First, there is a deliberate recruitment program that seeks diversity and extends down into junior and senior high schools.
- *General studies.* Second, all future teachers engage in two years of general studies designed to meet the institution's graduation requirements in academic breadth. From the perspective of teacher education, these contribute to the fulfillment of Postulate Seven: acquiring the literacy and critical-thinking abilities associated with the concept of an educated person. The faculty of the center of pedagogy recommends inclusion of courses such as those listed in Chapter Five, with an eye to what is appropriate to a pre-education curriculum, in the same spirit that schools of medicine recommend pre-med courses.
- *Socialization.* Third, running through these two years is a small but continuous stream of socializing experiences involving visits to schools and various human service agencies, lectures and seminars on the nature of teaching and the teaching profession, informal gatherings of various kinds, and hands-on experiences with individuals and groups of

students. These experiences reflect the intent of Postulate Six: introduction to the moral, ethical, and enculturating responsibilities to be assumed. They begin the socialization process described in Postulate Nine, through which candidates come to identify with a culture of teaching. Readers are reminded of some of the relevant organizational arrangements accompanying the first two years of general studies: establishment of cohort groups, continuing access to an adviser, the voluntary nature of participation, and its possible relevance to the admissions process that occurs in the fourth semester or sixth quarter. One of the important purposes of this component is to help students decide if teaching is likely to be appropriate for and satisfying to them. In order to make this decision wisely, they need to experience interactions with children and youths, not merely talk about teaching and the teaching profession. (Of course, some candidates — those who decide about teaching in the sophomore year — will come to the entry gate without this background of orientation and socialization.)

- *Subject-matter specialization.* Fourth, there are upper-division studies in the academic disciplines. These add to fulfillment of Postulates Seven (above) and Eight (dealing with the transition from being students of organized knowledge to scholar-teachers who inquire into this knowledge and its teaching). In Chapter Five, I argued strongly for critical inquiry on the part of the faculty into assumptions now underlying long-standing curricular regularities regarding breadth and depth; majors, minors, and electives; and the degree to which departmental offerings contribute to vocational rather than general education in the field. The arguments for breadth in several related fields of a knowledge domain appear to be about as strong as arguments for depth in just one. When we consider the nature and realities of secondary school teaching, serious participation in dialogue regarding the issues involved becomes an imperative for the entire teacher education faculty.

- *Professional sequence.* The fifth area of the curriculum represents turf already conceded to teacher preparation, albeit begrudgingly. It is that portion of the upper-division years usually referred to as the professional sequence and designated in the upper-right-hand rectangle of Figures 6.1 and 6.2—larger for future elementary than for future high school teachers. Clearly, this is the segment most completely controlled by the faculty of the center of pedagogy. It requires *comprehensive* rethinking. There is ample room for innovation and creativity.

Unlike the status quo depictions in Figures 6.1 and 6.2, however, this segment in a center of pedagogy is not necessarily confined to the upper-division years of college (whether or not extended into extra course credits). It is part of a professional sequence that begins formally in the junior year and extends through a fifth year. This combination of undergraduate and postbaccalaureate studies both parallels and links up with studies in academic disciplines central to the K-12 schools, the whole constituting a three-year curriculum. (This three-year sequence is discussed in greater detail later in the chapter.)

There are at least three arguments against pushing all of this to the postbaccalaureate level. The most important of these—one that I have put forward several times—is that teaching in the schools, unlike other occupations and professions, requires the use of the organized disciplines as tools. Consequently, future teachers should be contemplating the pedagogical use of the subjects they are studying as undergraduates. The second argument, an outgrowth of the first, is that this subject matter needs to be a significant curricular component of the three years; it is not something to be deferred to a postbaccalaureate curriculum. The third is simply that a postbaccalaureate three-year curriculum for teachers cannot be politically and economically justified. Perhaps it can and will be years from now.

There is some curricular clarity to be gained by viewing that upper-right-hand segment of Figures 6.1 and 6.2 as the fifth component—the so-called professional sequence—and the postbaccalaureate year as the sixth component (discussed below) of the proposed new program. Although the former invokes field experiences, the orientation is primarily to the college or university campus, whereas the latter is mostly school-oriented. The former seeks to illustrate and confirm theory in practice; the latter seeks to justify and verify practice in theory. Both seek this continuing weaving of the two.[4] I would hope, however, that there would be a very natural progression from the fourth to the fifth year.

- *Internship.* The sixth curricular component, embracing a two-semester or three-quarter postbaccalaureate year, immerses each candidate for extended periods in two rather different partner schools in quite different settings. In cohort groups, aspiring teachers become essentially junior members of the faculty. In both of these settings, they should be able to relieve regular staff members so that the latter may fulfill their responsibilities as teacher educators. These junior teachers should receive some modest pay, just as interns do in medical education.

    The various combinations of technology, interns, teacher aides, career teachers, head teachers, and university personnel working together in partner schools have scarcely been explored conceptually. This is a rich area for inquiry, research, and creative practice. There clearly are important implications for the economical use of resources, some of which were suggested in Chapter Four.

- *Feedback and follow-up.* The seventh component is curricular primarily in the sense of providing feedback into the effectiveness of the preparation program. We were surprised in our visits to campuses to find so little evidence of formative evaluation of ongoing programs. There is much to be gained by securing the views of students as they progress and of graduates in their early months and years of teaching. Postulate Seventeen is put forward with both this evaluation and support to beginning teachers in mind. For those going out into nearby districts (more common than not), partner schools and other kinds of professional development centers offer opportunities for continuing communication. For students going elsewhere, reciprocity with other teacher-preparing settings is necessary. The teaching occupation in the United States remains primitive in regard to the availability to all of support centers, although regional centers serving teachers in several districts offer promise. The flurry of interest in teacher centers that arose in the 1970s, in part out of the widely heralded English experience, appears to be one more good idea cultivated for a time but not sustained.

Figure 6.4 attempts a pictorial composite of these seven

Figure 6.4. A Five-Year Teacher Education Program Leading to Both a Bachelor's Degree in General Studies After Four Years and a Professional Bachelor's Degree in Pedagogy or Education and a Certificate of Completion at the End of Five Years.

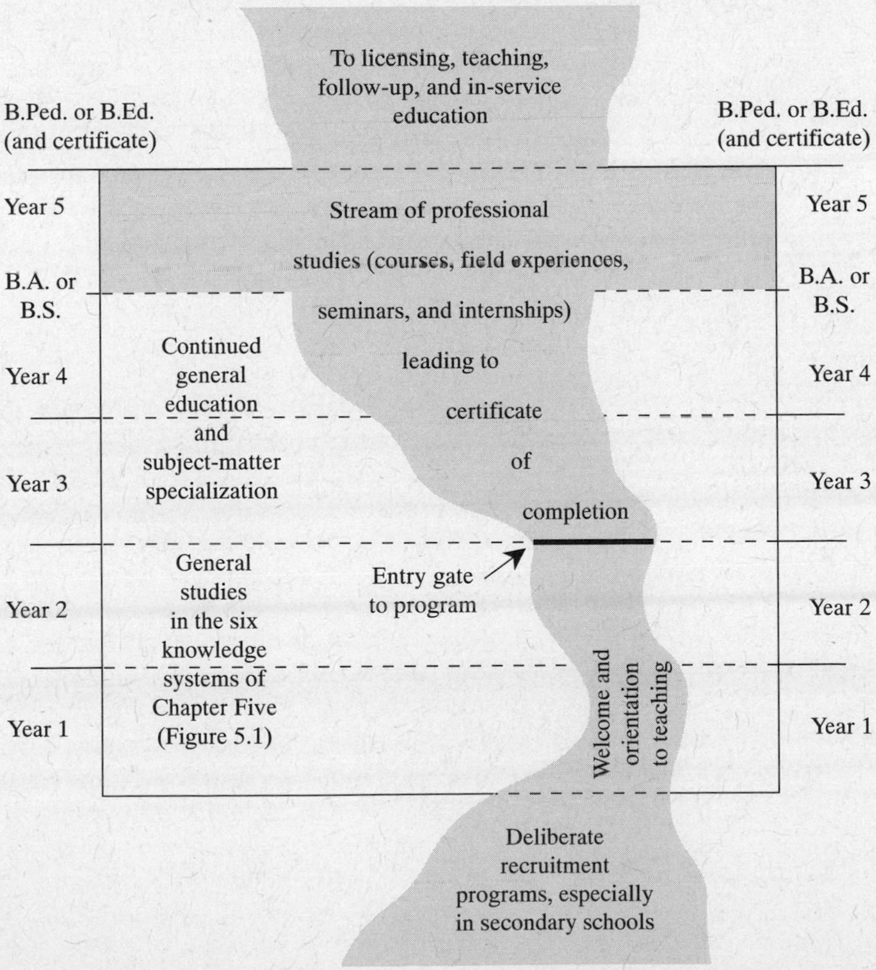

B.Ped. or B.Ed. (and certificate)

To licensing, teaching, follow-up, and in-service education

B.Ped. or B.Ed. (and certificate)

Year 5

Stream of professional studies (courses, field experiences, seminars, and internships) leading to certificate of completion

Year 5

B.A. or B.S.

B.A. or B.S.

Year 4

Continued general education and subject-matter specialization

Year 4

Year 3

Year 3

General studies in the six knowledge systems of Chapter Five (Figure 5.1)

Entry gate to program

Year 2

Year 2

Year 1

Welcome and orientation to teaching

Year 1

Deliberate recruitment programs, especially in secondary schools

program components and is intended to suggest a broadening
river of professional preparation over the years. The program
is renewed continuously, with the processes of formulative evaluation fed by data from both the students and the faculty engaged
in it.

Some Programmatic Characteristics and Caveats

In the Preface, I noted that most of this manuscript was widely
circulated among colleagues and that it benefited enormously
from their comments and suggestions. Not surprisingly, some
of the most fundamental questions were addressed to this chapter. And, again not surprisingly, the views of its contents ranged
widely and were sometimes contradictory. The widest disagreement pertained to specificity. Some thought I went too far; they
were concerned that, in spite of my caveats that there are many
ways to fulfill the conditions, readers would view what follows
as *the* way. Others thought that more specificity would be helpful.
        My reading of the many comments and suggestions in
the margins of that earlier draft convinced me of the need for
a preamble to the discussion of the professional sequence. Four
topics surfaced as requiring further clarification and elaboration. The comments bringing them to my attention persuaded
me to make many small changes in that draft and to add the
new four-part section below.

Pedagogy

In conventional parlance, it is common to talk about teaching
as a series of overt acts. Thus the word *pedagogy* is used as a
synonym for *teaching,* not as a differing view of it, even when
defined as the art and science of teaching. Within this conventional view, a center of pedagogy would be merely a unit or
place where these acts are studied and perfected.
        I take a much more comprehensive view of pedagogy,
especially in thinking about a center of pedagogy devoted to
the art and science of teaching in the context of educating the

nation's teachers — the context that grounds the mission. But, as several of my colleagues — all familiar with and committed to this broad conception — noted, it is not easily sustained in the difficult work of developing coherent teacher education curricula. That is why I repeated in Figure 6.3 the depiction of the mission for teacher education that appeared early on in Chapter One.

But, as I am reminded repeatedly, the tendency to narrow and simplify prevails. It is essential to keep emphasizing the necessity for continuing faculty and student attention to the role of schools in a social and political democracy — the first mission component. To the historical and philosophical perspective must be added experiences in school settings where both individual and group rights are being argued. The public school context makes of teaching a very special case of pedagogy, unlike any other. Similarly, the second component of the mission — providing all children and youths with equal opportunities for access to knowledge — places unique demands on both schoolteachers and those who educate them. These first two components relate to and interact with the second two: cultivating the art and science of teaching and preparing for the moral stewardship of schools.

The above are givens in the agenda of our Center for Educational Renewal. The necessary conditions for a center of pedagogy and its work on the art and science of teaching and in educating educators derive from this mission. But the roads to the mission and the alternative ways of putting the conditions in place are many and varied.

Curricular Specificity

The issue of curricular specification versus options comes to a head when we attempt to determine and organize the components of a teacher education curriculum. In much of what follows in this chapter, I refer to the necessity of agreeing upon themes but then leaving to individual faculty members or groups of faculty members freedom to exercise their creativity in developing these themes. Whether any or all of the curriculum should be fixed or predetermined is a question that has fueled controversy everywhere. It always will.

My position on this issue, explicated in Chapter Five, is not fleeting; I did not come to it easily. In that explication, I state that general education for all students in the first two years of college should be balanced among the domains of the world's systems of knowledge and knowing. In regard to both secondary and higher education, I stop short of Mortimer Adler's specifications for commonality recommended in *The Paideia Proposal,* addressed to the former level of schooling, while agreeing with its thrust toward a common core.[5]

The distinction I wish to make between what shall be common and what shall be optional or discretionary in any curriculum has to do with the difference between *organizing elements* and *organizing centers.* Organizing elements are, from my perspective, the major themes, concepts, principles, or "big ideas" constituting the essential nature or substance of a field of study or domain of human experience and action. These change over time, as new knowledge and insights accumulate. These organizing elements are agreed upon by responsible persons whose own experience and credentials give authority to their opinions. These organizing elements are sufficiently fundamental to serve as bases for a curriculum over a period of time — at least a year but usually several years. They are revised and updated periodically by the group of responsible parties, members of which agree to revisions. In this chapter, I also refer to these organizing elements of the teacher education curriculum as *themes.*

In seeking to develop these organizing elements, those teaching in the curriculum are free to select *organizing centers* that they believe to have promise for achieving this purpose effectively. The center on which attention is focused could be a student's anecdotal account of a riveting field experience, a film, an article in a professional journal, a novel, a case study. The central criterion is the degree to which what is chosen is likely to engage all those individuals for whom it is intended in advancing the theme already decided upon as the organizing element. Attention to the organizing element is *not* optional; choice of the organizing centers *is* optional and is a continuing challenge to the creative mind.

Let us consider an example. Most faculty groups in a contemporary center of pedagogy probably would agree on a multicultural theme for all prospective teachers as an organizing element of their curriculum. They probably would disagree on how best to advance it. Variation in viewpoint will range from specifying a course or two to the recommendation that faculty members should strive for a multicultural perspective throughout. Although the latter position has much going for it conceptually, it tends not to square with reality. A theme not deliberately built into the curriculum, with time provided for it and the requirement that faculty members provide evidence of provision for it, tends to slip to the periphery. This danger with respect to multicultural education is perceived by my colleague James Banks to be so great that he insists on the inclusion of a required course or two. For this and all other organizing elements, there are defensible alternatives. These must be characterized by agreement on the portion of the total curriculum to be allocated to each theme, designation of a responsible faculty member or group of faculty members for each, periodic formative evaluation of how things are going (in which students participate), and the use of review teams from the outside preparatory to effecting revisions.

In the mission for teacher education programs depicted in Figure 1.1 (and reproduced in Figure 6.3), there are four major components (to be translated into curricula), each having moral dimensions. In developing any curriculum, I would not be content with the decision to settle, in general terms, for a moral perspective throughout, with no other provision designed to ensure sensitivity to and ability to address the moral issues that are, in the words of Christopher Clark, "intrinsic to and ubiquitous in teaching."[6] Yes, I want the entire program to be characterized by a moral perspective throughout. But I also want there to be deliberate, disciplined inquiry into teaching as a fundamentally moral enterprise, the specifics of which carry one into territory not commonly included in a course in ethics. Clark states well the need and the responsibility of teacher education programs in this area: "No one essay or set of exhortations and object lessons can make the moral complexities of teaching simple, straightforward, and unerringly good. My hope is to raise questions in the minds of educators about honesty, respect, selflessness, and moral scrutiny of means and ends. . . . After that between parent and child, the most profoundly moral relationship our children experience is that between the teacher and the taught."[7]

Active, Reflective Learning

Much of the attack on schools in the context of proposals for reform has focused on "seat time" and the need for evidence that there is some positive connection between time spent and the amount and quality of learning. The passages in my book *A Place Called School* that cited the percentage of time devoted to frontal teaching (lecturing, telling, questioning the total class) and the passivity of students presumably listening have been referred to in hundreds of reports—far more than anything else on its pages. Similar reports and criticisms are now being directed to undergraduate education in colleges and universities.

In *Teachers for Our Nation's Schools,* I referred to John Dewey's 1904 admonition to schools and colleges of education: seek lessons from the "matured experience" of other professional callings. They did not. Instead, they sought largely to model and be approved by the arts and sciences departments. Today, in the reward system of universities, there is less attention to the unique demands on professors engaged in the education of educators than is the case with respect to those preparing lawyers and architects. The criteria for promotion of the former group are essentially those established by and for the arts and sciences.

There is nothing inherently wrong in this mimicry. Were teaching in the arts and sciences favored more highly than it is, were it based on sound theories of learning, and were it (as a consequence) the envy and sought-after model of others, the professional schools would benefit by seeking to emulate it. The major irony is that the part of higher education most valued rhetorically—the years devoted to "general, liberal education"—is probably the part least characterized by conditions conducive to learning. We may recoil at the description of the commonly large freshman and sophomore classes in universities given by

George Douglas, but the flash of recognition hurts: "Mainly, . . . when one is a professor looking out into the sea of faces, what one sees is a huge horde of human blanks being processed in the name of liberal education. . . . Seldom do students enjoy the opportunity to question what they are being taught. They are passive receivers. They may on rare occasions get a chance to ask a question, but it is likely to be something they need to know to survive and pass the professor's examination. The subject matter itself and its place in the broader picture of science or human culture are never brought into question."[8]

The blame must be widely shared. We are not disposed, particularly in regard to taxing ourselves, to cover the costs of what good education requires. Nor are we disposed to lowering the magical power of college degrees in the marketplace. And so the demand increases along with the conveyer-belt delivery system. Higher education, at least in the universities, has adapted by developing formulas for the allocation of resources to specializations and graduate studies that drastically reduce the costs of providing "general" education.

Undergraduate teacher education, lacking the clear identity and boundaries of professional schools, has suffered from its inability to transcend some of these circumstances and to profit from the considerable gains of the more mature professions. The determination of teacher-student ratios tends to follow the formula for allocating resources to the arts and sciences, assuming that many of the same cost-saving exigencies will prevail. But large classes taught by inexperienced teaching assistants have no place in the education of teachers in a nation that claims for schooling powerful leverage in maintaining the image and the reality of its leadership role, nor do the didactics and the passivity that characterize such a large part of undergraduate teaching and learning.

I assume in the professional sequence described below a faculty-student ratio throughout that is never too large for interactions of the kind that characterize serious human conversation. I have difficulty envisioning groups of more than twenty future teachers for any part of the program — with the exception of guest speakers addressing an entire class from time to time. Yet I can readily envision a role for graduate students planning to become teacher educators—for example, in guiding a cohort group of ten candidates serving as teacher aides during the orientation and socializing phase of the program. Two groups of ten then come together as the larger cohort of twenty assigned as advisees to a professor over the two years of this sequence of experiences. Six, ten, twenty, or more of such cohorts—in various combinations over the years—might well constitute the entire cohort known as the class of '99.

One learns a great deal about teaching by observing someone teaching and then analyzing the reasons for and the problems with what one has observed. Some of this observation and discussion can be productively focused on films of classrooms in action. But observing and talking do not a teacher make. One must teach—individuals, groups, whole classes—under observation, observe one's own teaching via videotape, reflect on and discuss with peers and mentors that teaching, and teach some more. Actual experience in teaching must serve as an organizing element of the curriculum—an element to be developed over time through a series of deliberately planned field experiences in a variety of settings, culminating in the internships of the fifth year. Hands-on experiences, observations of many kinds, role-playing, introspection, reflection, and critical conversation characterize the entire program.[9]

Distinctions Between Elementary and Secondary Preparation

A point of dissonance for some readers of the initial draft was a misleading statement—now eliminated—pertaining to a lack of differentiation in the preparation of elementary and secondary school teachers. In recommending a lack of differentiation, I meant to refer only to time allocated to the professional sequence, not to possible differences in the educational use of this time. I argue here for both considerable similarity—much more than currently is the case—and some characteristics unique to each.

In the best of worlds, we would devote far more time to

the education of teachers of the young than to teachers of advanced levels of our educational system. We are victims of an upside-down value system that provides casually for educating the young and their teachers and lavishes attention on graduate specialization, with ample provision for one-on-one professor-student ratios at the doctoral level. The Swiss are not similarly afflicted.[10]

Here again, we suffer the continuing effects of an unfortunate legacy. First, we need go back only a few generations to the time when the saying "Children are to be seen and not heard" was taken quite literally[11] and a brood of children was viewed as instrumental to family survival. Even now, children are still widely seen as incomplete human creatures being groomed to become adults. Women, too, have been valued more for their services to men than as humans in their own right. The early Dame Schools, then, combined these twin instrumentalities in a concept of "civilizing" the young in the care of women now beyond in age their traditional usefulness. Not surprisingly, preparing to teach in a normal school and teaching children (not youths) was a nineteenth-century female occupation of low status, requiring only modest credentials. Throughout the twentieth century, movies of pioneering days and the great, wide West have portrayed the schoolmarm "looking after the kids" while the men valiantly take care of everything important (and glamorous).

The emergence of a body of knowledge about children's learning, the degree to which the early years are mother and father to the adult, and the possible implications of this for those who teach or aspire to teach the young is a relatively recent development. One needs only modest familiarity with the scientific underpinnings of modern pedagogy to realize the degree to which we shortchange our children by shortchanging the education of their teachers. Largely because of the anti-intellectual legacy that still surrounds teaching in the lower grades, just a smidgen of all this is encapsulated in a few courses begrudgingly allocated to the teacher education curriculum — courses vulnerable at all times to the capricious actions of those among the legislators who do not recognize their own ignorance.

Given my own views on the critical importance of the early years in the education of human beings and the potential for bringing to bear on the process an incredibly rich array of knowledge and insight, I believe I could argue convincingly for a six- or seven-year rather than a five-year teacher education program. But, in the light of readiness on the part of policymakers for much shorter and cheaper routes to teaching than exist in the conventional programs of today, such a recommendation would only precipitate even more folly than already prevails. And so my argument for what follows in the next section represents a compromise.

Given the fact, then, that the proposed professional sequence already represents a compromise with respect to the preparation of elementary school teachers, I am not about to settle for even less for prospective secondary school teachers. Their preparation has suffered from a different kind of legacy — the twofold misguided pedagogical myth that adolescents require for their learning only two disciplines: the discipline of the subject matter and the discipline of the schoolmaster. Until quite recently, movies portrayed the male high school teacher, often at a chalkboard covered with algebraic equations, with pointer in hand for purposes presumably of pointing out and striking out.

Circumstances have engulfed this stereotype. Telling and pointing are dull routines for a generation transfixed by television before it could talk and now entering the new age of virtual reality. But methods of teaching and assessing students' knowledge have changed scarcely at all. David Berliner observes, "One might properly ask why we do not test our children on decoding information from complex audiovisual displays, or on remembering information presented in auditory or visual forms, on comprehending extremely fast-changing video arrays of information, and so forth."[12]

Striking out with the pointer could readily result in a retaliating gunshot or knife wound in today's classroom. In our earlier research on schools, very few high school teachers reported inadequacies in their subject-matter knowledge as a source of difficulty in teaching. Their major difficulty was dealing with difficult students. Our later research on future teachers revealed their concern over perceived inadequate preparation to deal both with the diversity of the student population and with parents. Future secondary school teachers, like future elementary school teachers, deserve and require more than their currently parsimonious introduction to human development, cognition, learning disabilities, multiculturalism, social organization and disorganization, and counseling.

The common inability of secondary school teachers, particularly of mathematics, social studies, science, and English (as compared with the arts, physical education, and vocational education) to interest students in their subjects is well documented. The fact that few teachers in our research cited their lack of knowledge of the subject as a problem suggests, unfortunately, their innocence with respect to knowing their subjects from a pedagogical perspective. In the 1960s, there was a flurry of educational excitement over Jerome Bruner's persuasive conception of teaching that employed understanding of the structure of the discipline to bring into play students' powerful "intuitive" ability to grasp connections. Teaching enlightened by depth in this dual understanding would bring to reality Bruner's heuristic: "We begin with the proposition that any subject can be taught effectively in some intellectually honest form to any child at any stage of development."[13]

The brief era of subject-centered school reform that followed in the 1960s into the 1970s was to some degree influenced by the Bruner hypothesis. Comprehensive reform of the secondary biological sciences curriculum profited from the influence of Joseph Schwab, who added depth to the curricular and pedagogical implications of the structural thesis.[14] But the influence of Bruner, Schwab, and others was insufficient to stem the tide of simplistic behavioristic impulses that sought to specify myriad objectives for children and youths to be taught by teachers steeped in the competencies geared to their attainment. The place of subject matter in pedagogy failed to bubble up from its brief popularity in school curriculum reform to a legitimate place in the renewal of teacher education. The place of pedagogy in the education of secondary school teachers continued to be almost wholly represented by a course on generic methods of teaching. And there it stayed until the work of Lee Shulman and his students brought the idea of pedagogical content knowledge firmly into the conversation and research of teacher educators.[15]

Pamela Grossman's research probe into the topic is provocative in several important ways. First, her comparison of three bright teachers with subject-specific pedagogy and three without, all with strong credentials in the same general subject field, advances the Shulman hypothesis. Second, her findings raise serious questions about competence in the subject serving as adequate readiness to teach. Third, attention to subject-specific pedagogy in teacher education appears to unveil for future teachers some of the ways their students are likely to be derailed in the learning process and to prepare them for what otherwise would go unrecognized and ignored. In her concluding comments, Grossman warns against shortcuts in preparing teachers that would rule out attention to subject-specific pedagogy.[16]

The earlier work on the structure of the disciplines and the new work on subject-specific pedagogy, together with the demands and the complexities of guiding all our young people through secondary schooling, renders specious for thoughtful people the tired argument that high school teachers need be versed in only their chosen subjects. Add to our expectations for elementary school teachers competency in subject-specific pedagogy in all the subjects they are required to teach, and the charge to them and to their preparation programs becomes overwhelming. But it would be dysfunctional, given the challenge to both groups and the limited prospects of gaining more years for the education in pedagogy (as broadly defined earlier) that both groups require, to cut shorter the time for prospective secondary school teachers in deference to the obvious needs of elementary school teachers. The professional education of both requires attention far beyond what currently prevails. It is disgraceful to realize how much even this minimal attention is so begrudgingly given by its critics.

This has been a rather long digression from a narrative intended to explicate, major piece by major piece, the components of five-year teacher education programs for prospective elementary and secondary school teachers. But my experience with the reaction of colleagues to the earlier version convinced me that this discussion would add perspective and understanding to what follows. I suggest that the reader now turn back for a quick review of Figure 6.4 before reading on.

The Professional Sequence

In contrast to the professional components of conventional four-year programs depicted in Figures 6.1 and 6.2, the professional sequence of Figure 6.4 shows no arrows of intrusion or shaded intrusions downward, upward, or sideways. I propose, rather, that the professional sequence within both secondary and elementary school preparation not exceed half of the upper-division curriculum—that is, thirty semester or forty-five quarter hours. The fifth year is proposed in part to relieve the pressures this sequence has exerted on the arts and sciences, as well as to provide more time for integrating theory and practice.

There should be sufficient flexibility in the curricular specifications for this half of the upper division to include a course or two in the arts and sciences deemed by a student's adviser to be highly relevant to that student's needs. For example, he or she might have been admitted to the program with the understanding that the course in ethics not taken in the lower division would be included later. In *Teachers for Our Nation's Schools,* I recommended several courses for future elementary school teachers that should be made available—courses sometimes included in the general education curriculum that add breadth relevant to the demands of teaching across a broad spectrum of knowledge. The faculty of a center of pedagogy must be creative in designing the three-year sequence so as to ensure considerable breadth and depth in subject matter, ways to teach, field experiences, and the range of problems and issues accompanying the stewardship of schools.

Prospective secondary school teachers usually are at least modestly prepared in one of the major cornerstones of the teaching mission: knowledge in academic subjects. But they commonly fall short in their understanding of what equal access to that knowledge means and how to ensure it. They need much more preparation in the role of schools in a democratic society, human cognition and development, both general and content-specific pedagogy, their responsibilities as moral stewards of schools, and curricular and organizational alternatives in schooling.

A major in elementary education is not the answer to vexing dilemmas in preparing elementary school teachers. Rather, the answer lies in rethinking the scope and sequence made possible by the postbaccalaureate year in particular and by the role of partner schools and teachers in providing some of what teacher educators currently seek to accomplish in courses taken prior to student teaching. The notion that prospective elementary teachers must encounter, for example, a smattering of ways to teach each of the school subjects prior to student teaching warrants reexamination, particularly in light of the preceding discussion of subject-specific pedagogy.

I suggest as one possible alternative for both the elementary and the secondary level a closely linked series of hands-on experiences extended over the junior and senior years, with accompanying analyses on the part of both students and faculty. In Chapter Four, I introduced along with partner schools the concept of broader school-university partnerships within which strong teachers not necessarily connected with partner schools are identified for participation in teacher education. Some would be engaging lecturers, others expert in cooperative learning techniques, others skilled in developing higher-order thinking, some competent in weaving field experiences or projects into their courses, and still others talented at promoting creativity or intellectual risk taking. All prospective teachers would observe and discuss exemplary teaching at both levels; all would teach and be aided in critiques of their teaching. This series of experiences would both replace and supplement much of what now goes into generic methods classes, with careful attention in the curriculum planning to the elimination of repetition.

Educational Foundations

In his report on teacher education early in the 1960s, James B. Conant was very much caught up in practice as both preparation to teach and the basis of evidence for admission into teaching. He saw little use for courses in pedagogy, not because he rejected the art and science of teaching as unimportant but because he doubted that it could be taught—modeled, yes, but taught didactically? Probably not. Consequently, he recommended a major role for clinical professors—competent practitioners who would introduce neophytes into practice. He saw some usefulness in the teaching of philosophy, history, and sociology by professors in these fields who turned their attention to problems of American education. He was highly critical of education courses in these fields, however—particularly of eclectic foundations courses that touched on a wide array of topics and bits and pieces of a diverse literature.[17] Yet these latter courses were far more common more than a quarter-century later than they were at the time of Conant's research.[18]

In the Conant study, many of the students interviewed also expressed negative views of these introductory courses. As a member of the research team, I pushed hard on the nature of their discontent. It usually turned out not to be the intellectual inferiority of the courses compared to somewhat parallel courses in the academic disciplines but their lack of perceived relevance. In the later study conducted by my colleagues and me, students ranked foundations courses—whatever their nature— low with respect to their contribution to one's future success as a teacher. Their professors ranked them only a little higher. The rankings of both groups were more favorable for methods courses, field experiences, and student teaching, with the student quest for what works in the classroom increasing as students progressed toward graduation.

We must exercise great care in interpreting these findings, especially when others are added to them. Many of the students we interviewed, whether undergraduate or postbaccalaureate, were ill-prepared to discuss issues pertaining to the larger political, economic, and social context of schooling. They had limited vocabulary and intellectual tools for addressing education as a moral endeavor—and yet most educational decisions are ultimately moral in nature. In a few settings, they were able to recall sustained discussion of major educational issues and viewpoints, but they remembered little or no follow-up in subsequent courses. More commonly, they recalled only a class session or two on purposes of schools in a democracy, a specific educational philosophy, a historical epoch, or an issue such as educational equity. Yet there appeared to be among these students no lack of interest in the major moral, ethical, and value-oriented themes we introduced. The professors we interviewed recognized these themes as important but noted that they were largely absent in preparation programs; a few saw them as beyond the maturity level of undergraduates.

Is the major problem one of overconcession to immediate practicality? By allowing foundations courses to erode into an eclectic potpourri, by giving way to changing pressures for this or that contemporary preoccupation, by not planning coherent curricula around major themes introduced early and deepened over time, have we created a kind of self-fulfilling prophecy? Do future teachers get the idea that there are — somewhere — answers to everyday problems and ultimately come to judge both their pre-service and their in-service education by the degree to which they appear to deliver answers? If so, we do them a great disservice.

The intensity with which many prospective teachers expressed a desire for all the courses they could get that provided classroom applications may have been in part the result of being generally deprived of systemic, sustained exposure to practice. They found themselves in or facing student teaching after having had only a little exposure to and hardly any experience in the daily demands of the classroom.

What the tripartite faculty of a center of pedagogy must do early on is to determine a small number of themes of such fundamental importance that they become the organizing elements of the teacher education curriculum. Agreement will not come easily;[19] there will be change over time. It is imperative that each responsible group come to a working agreement; otherwise, they will lack the level of understanding required for an operational curriculum to be coherent, and implementation will fail. The mission presented in Figure 6.3 provides a basis for themes pertaining to the nature and meaning of democracy, the role of schools in a democratic society, the nature of knowledge and its teaching, major pedagogical alternatives, various ways to view and develop each of the major commonplaces of schooling, and the ethical and moral dimensions of teaching and schooling. With themes determined, the faculty of the center has both direction and the freedom to engage in the creative tasks of selecting case studies, developing multimedia simulations of practice, selecting field experiences, and so on — to put meat on the bones of the curricular skeleton.

I agree with Conant's statement: "Under the best conditions, it seems to me a course in the philosophy of education would legitimately presuppose that the students had been exposed to the basic issues of epistemology, ontology, and ethics in an introductory philosophy course required of all teachers as part of their general requirements."[20] This is part of what I had in mind earlier in recommending that there be specific pre–teacher education courses in general education for persons planning to teach. Such courses would make it much easier for a foundations course in educational philosophy to address "the problems, the language, the assumptions, and the value premises that enter into educational theory and practice."[21]

Theory and Practice

Conventional programs, as depicted in Figures 6.1 and 6.2, tend to comprise a series of discrete courses, sometimes including within them some field experiences, followed by a rather abrupt transition into student teaching. Because I see courses and field experiences blending into one and flowing into dominantly school-based activity accompanied by reflection, I find it easiest to discuss the whole under the rubric of theory and practice. In order to symbolize this synthesis of the two, in Figure 6.4 the orientation-to-teaching stream that runs through the lower division is shown to broaden into a river that flows through the upper division into a veritable ocean of postbaccalaureate practice accompanied by seminars. This suggests fluidity, integration, and potential for change.

It also suggests a seamlessness not readily attained. I view this seamlessness as an ideal to strive toward, not a criterion for judging adequacy or inadequacy. It is easier to create a seamless curriculum out of just a few clearly related elements than to weave into a pattern a diverse array of scattered pieces. Consequently, it may be advantageous to seek first the most relevant pieces and relationships among them, leaving open the design of quilts. In a delightful essay, "Coherence, the Rebel Angel," Margret Buchmann and Robert Floden exult in the degree to which coherence, unlike consistency, is hospitable to change and imagination.[22]

Early on in planning, then, a faculty group would be well advised to pull together into several themes the various pieces pertaining to the development of schooling in the United States, moral issues, and dilemmas dealing with access, human development, cultural diversity, and the like. Each exploration of a theme would include field experiences, case studies, and analysis of videotapes; these would be aimed at developing better understanding of the theme, not at some other purpose (such as learning to manage a classroom). In other words, the concrete experiences in the field would be in the spirit of sound teaching and learning in any field: the demonstration in a college course of the principles that future teachers are to establish in their own schools and classrooms (Postulate Ten).

Some of the content of these historical, philosophical, and psychological themes would arise out of observation in schools and classrooms. Students would inquire into settings observed, seeking from the teachers reasons for what they do and then into their own classes for validation and possible disagreement (Postulate Eleven). Some of their field experiences would be designed to encounter issues of parental rights and responsibilities with respect to their children's education and schools (Postulate Twelve). Class discussions and related reading would grow out of analysis of school district policies with respect to attending kindergarten, promotion and nonpromotion, classes for the gifted, mainstreaming, tracking, and graduation requirements (Postulates Thirteen and Fourteen). Field experiences would include opportunities to be with teachers and principals dealing with controversy.

Certain themes would appear and reappear, whether the perspective were historical, philosophical, sociological, or psychological, or whether in reading, observations of ongoing practice, classroom discourse, or actual teaching. A given segment might consist of more time in schools than in the college classroom; a later segment might reverse that distribution. In any case, the credit hours would attempt to mirror the basis for credit hours generally. The entire set of educational experiences could well show up simply as a rectangle occupying up to 20 percent of the upper division; students' records might show credit for twelve semester hours.

Although what I have described in preceding paragraphs would be part of the required professional sequence for teachers, I would not rule out its availability to students generally, *given adequate provision of resources.* Most college graduates are ignorant about educational matters beyond their own personal experiences, and yet educational reform will emerge several times in their lives as a national concern; many must make important decisions about the education of their children; all will pay taxes that go to support elementary and secondary schools; nearly all will teach in some kind of circumstance. The fact that part of each course involves observation and hands-on experiences in educational settings need not restrict courses to teacher education. Rather, it simply demonstrates the good teaching and learning conditions that should prevail generally. The reader may recall my chagrin in Chapter Two over the admonition of Charles Colwell: presumably students from all over the campus are flocking to classes in the division of education just to experience superb teaching. I wish I could have said yes.

A second major cluster of pieces pertains to pedagogy. Once again, the somewhat indeterminate banks of the professional-orientation stream of Figure 6.4 are deliberate — for the reasons already given and one other. This other pertains to the degree that there is some fusion of what lies within the professional sequence and the general and specialized studies surrounding it. For both prospective elementary and secondary teachers, greater fusion than presently exists is highly desirable but not easily obtained. As I stated earlier, students should be guided in thinking about teaching subject matter while engaged in its study (Postulate Eight). In addition, all should engage deliberately in inquiry into content-specific pedagogy and experience practice of the kind so well described by Pamela Grossman. One of my major reasons for proposing the three-part faculty of centers of pedagogy is to increase the likelihood that programmatic attention to pedagogy will go beyond generic teaching.

Breaking down the barriers that currently exist between the conduct of studies in the academic disciplines and preparing to teach in elementary schools offers unique opportunities in the curriculum segment defined as "methods." We have seen how requirements in this area push downward, sideways, and upward to endanger general studies and crowd students' programs. In my judgment, a stronger, more economical curriculum would result from attempting to use some of the academic courses already in place to involve students in subject-specific pedagogical inquiry, to be accompanied or followed by subject-specific teaching experiences.

I recommend that faculty members in the center of pedagogy identify also the several relatively discrete generic methods of teaching with which all future teachers (elementary and secondary) should be familiar and, in time, competent. At the beginning of this section on the professional sequence, I addressed the obvious: involving exemplary teachers in the schools as a source of experience and analysis. Less obvious but equally important are opportunities in the college or university to study systematically various instructional procedures being deliberately undertaken and refined by exemplary teachers. Over time, these would not only benefit the teacher education program but would also contribute significantly to increased campuswide interest in teaching. The center of pedagogy might well become, as it should, a major force for and contributor to the improvement of teaching generally.

The Fifth Year

Although the fifth year of the proposed teacher education program represents an extension of the theory-practice relationship sought in the preceding years, it also entails a definitive shift. The primary setting is no longer a university or college campus, marked by many planned extensions to schools and communities. Prospective teachers are now, in every respect, an integral part of school life. They are essentially junior members of the faculty of a partner school (enjoying some payment for their work) — in fact, two partner schools over the course of the year. They will have visited one or more partner schools before, and teachers from these schools will have been their teachers, commonly team teaching with their university professors. Prospective teachers will now encounter in partner schools some of the professors of education and of the arts and sciences encountered earlier. They will come in cohort groups, the members of which will be their colleagues in ongoing informal conversations and seminars. During the year, they will get extensive hands-on experience in all of the instructional procedures that they both observed and practiced earlier. Because the transition from college campus to school campus will have been anticipated and ensured from the time of entry into the program (Postulate Fifteen), it will proceed smoothly.

Institutions will differ in their full implementation of the fifth year. Presumably, there will be carefully planned seminars supplementing the time spent in each partner school for each cohort group, as well as individual help from relevant faculty members. Some settings may choose to concentrate teaching in partner schools in the first and third quarters to ensure experience with both the opening and closing of school. The middle quarter could provide for further studies in academic fields or special problems of teaching, depending on individual need.

Consideration of the fifth year provides a convenient opportunity to address solely postbaccalaureate programs — the two-year alternative introduced briefly early on in this chapter. Some settings may choose to offer only this alternative; some may opt for both. Earlier, I assumed for two-year programs at the postbaccalaureate level student completion of the general education and specialized studies required for graduation. But I do not assume that these studies will have provided what a five-year program planned by the faculty of a center of pedagogy would seek. Further, many of the candidates will be coming from years spent in other occupations and will present transcripts dating back a decade or two. (They should be required to demonstrate through satisfactory performance on tests their competence in general education and appropriate content fields and make up any deficiencies revealed.) Perhaps most important, they will not have experienced the recommended professional sequence.

Despite the handicap that these students face, I believe that progression through a carefully planned two-year program — certainly no shorter! — can be the equivalent of the five-year program and is a reasonable alternative for strongly motivated individuals who decide to seek entry to teaching at some time after leaving college. The degree obtained at time of completion is the same as that for graduates of the five-year program — bachelor's degree in teaching or pedagogy. Various kinds of specialization leading to the master's degree lie beyond.

Additional Programmatic Considerations

As I stated at the outset, the preceding discussion of the curriculum in teacher education must be juxtaposed with much of the content of other chapters. Earlier, I mentioned team teaching. This should be, in my judgment, more the mode than a casual occurrence. Each group of faculty members brought together in a center of pedagogy represents a major curricular component. A few serve full-time in the center and constitute a core. Most have a home base elsewhere — in a department of education, a department in the arts and sciences, or a partner school — and a second home in the center. What each brings into the professional sequence is related in some way to what others bring; the pieces must come together in a coherent (but not a fixed, consistent) whole. Team teaching facilitates progress toward this ideal.

Faculty members from their differing home bases come together in teams to facilitate curricular coherence and integration by both students and faculty members. Early on, faculty members from partner schools and appropriate university departments responsible for the foundations block come together not only to join theory and practice but also to promote later attention to themes already introduced. Later, various combinations of faculty members familiar with these themes seek to deepen them in field experiences and seminars devoted to pedagogy and the stewardship of schools. Still later, during the postbaccalaureate year, when dominant responsibility shifts to partner schools, the teachers who taught as a team on the college campus extend still further the concepts introduced earlier. The dissonance between campus courses, as now conducted, and students' experiences in cooperating schools may not disappear entirely, but it is reasonable to assume that it will be markedly reduced. Indeed, addressing that dissonance is readily envisioned as a significant learning experience for all.

Students within any given cohort will have come together in various and evolving subcohorts throughout their lower-division years. When they are given their fifth-year teaching assignments at partner schools, the membership of those subgroups will often change again. To ensure ongoing socialization, perhaps something akin to the orientation-to-teaching stream should have a life of its own during the upper-division years. There are good arguments for this, and many interesting alternative patterns. Doctoral candidates in teacher education might make themselves available to students on a voluntary basis, for example, or upper-division students might be assigned in clusters to mentors. One promising alternative brings into cohort groups students with similar career goals (for example, secondary school teaching); these students would be socialized together as part of the upper-division curriculum. Of course, assignment to partner schools in cohort groups is, in my judgment, an essential part of the internship year, completely replacing present practice.

I have said nothing in the foregoing about technology — a topic that must at least be touched on. I see the need for rapid progress on several fronts. First and foremost — and most difficult — the educational delivery systems of schools must be redesigned into configurations of head teachers, career teachers, interns, aides, and multimedia modules, as recommended in

Chapter Four. Participating in the design of such configurations should be part of each aspiring teacher's preparatory experience. Second, the use of technology in delivering the curriculum should be explored throughout the entire five-year program. Of particular promise are case studies developed around rather persistent teaching situations and presented in multimedia format. Third, there are many topics of practical value for teachers that need not be part of courses and seminars. These can be presented in multimedia modules to be used voluntarily by students during periods of discretionary time.

There are, of course, formidable obstacles to achieving what has been described. Some derive from sheer logistical difficulties; some grow out of the fact that significant change invariably requires human adjustments of considerable magnitude. The main obstacle, however, is the view that what I propose is so idealistic as to be out of reach. Yet by lowering expectations, one learns to be comfortable with less.

The irony in this possible reaction to what I have written is that there are, here and there, exemplary versions of almost every component described, be it recruitment, socialization, or integration of some theory with practice, with exemplary partner or professional development schools just on the horizon. The challenge now is to put that Rebel Angel, coherence, to work in creating whole programs.

7

Tomorrow's Schools
and Communities

The new model of school reform must seek to develop communities of learning grounded in communities of democratic discourse.[1]
— Linda Darling-Hammond

The redesign of the education of educators proposed throughout these pages is grounded in a vital component of the mission of our schools: enculturating the young in a social and political democracy. This enculturation has two fundamental components. The first is a deep understanding of and commitment to the democratic ideals underlying the nation's founding and the rights and responsibilities embedded in its Constitution. The second is the ability to participate widely and deeply in simultaneously enjoying and extending to all the individual and collective freedoms implied in *e pluribus unum*.

This redesign is to take place in what is essentially a new setting — a center of pedagogy — that brings schools and universities together in a close renewing relationship. Our concentration on this agenda has brought forward questions regarding the role of the home and other agencies. Clearly, the well-defined borders necessary to a robust center of pedagogy must not — and, for that matter, cannot — block out discourse and commerce with the larger social context. To seek to enculturate the young and to educate their teachers to do so and then ignore this context would be contradictory and self-defeating. I have said earlier that the public interest in schooling and teacher education is a condition to be fostered and massaged.

195

The creation and nurturing of a center of pedagogy focused on educational renewal is demanding under the best of circumstances. The problems of turf, time, and interpersonal relations common to educational reform are exacerbated in the effort to blend two quite different cultures. I have chosen up to now not to complicate this agenda further by pulling into it the exigencies of the larger context. But the time has come to take a hard look at surrounding circumstances that have profound implications for school improvement and the ways teacher educators must view and conduct their business.[2]

The biggest mistake we could make in viewing this context is to assume that the challenge is to prepare teachers to do the usual things better. In the recent past, public concern over schools tended to focus on teachers and teaching. Johnny couldn't read because teachers were not taught properly how to teach him to read. But today the prime focus is the school as an institution and the degree to which it is caught up almost irreparably in an unresponsive bureaucratic system. Many reform proposals call for dismantling the system. As my colleague Roger Soder states it, there is under way a struggle for the soul of the public school system.

The second mistake is to assume that dismantling the system will produce, through some form of near-immaculate conception, good schools. The surge of anticipation would soon founder on shoals of disagreement over the nature of good schools and how to have one. The heady stuff of creating "free schools" in the 1960s and 1970s turned sour in the face of unanticipated parental disagreements. The number in existence peaked rather quickly because those closing down in the face of unreconciled differences in viewpoint equaled and then exceeded in number those just coming into existence. The visions of sugarplum schools now in the heads of some who would do away with what we have might be tempered by a little look into this informative history.

Teacher educators must be acutely aware of the fact that producing teachers who are individually good teachers is not sufficient; they must also be stewards of good schools. This means that these teachers must join with colleagues in creating and renewing schools that fulfill their educative mission in the face of conflicting expectations. But fulfillment will be impeded by the degree to which other agencies in the community, particularly the home, fail in the performance of their functions. Consequently, the continued existence of a good school depends heavily on the nature of its connections with the rest of the community ecosystem. And for a school to be *very* good, the component parts of this ecosystem must be attentive to their role in an educational system of which schools are an important, but not the only, part.

I share the view that we need a new model of schools and of school reform. To help create and implement that new model, future educators must be prepared with the expectations, knowledge, and skills to participate effectively in the renewing process. Even though expertise will develop over time, it is essential that their pre-service education include extensive immersion in the partner schools of centers of pedagogy, themselves engaged in the renewal process.

I view this new model as one that recognizes the diverse array of expectations that make up our democratic society, not one in which each school is dependent upon the satisfaction of expectations geared to various genres of homogeneity. To conform to narrow expectations is to endanger the making of a democratic public and, consequently, democracy itself. This is part of the moral dimension of schooling that even beginning teachers must understand. This is the essence of the "public" in schooling.

We must not beguile ourselves into believing, however, that the new schools will solve all the problems now erroneously attached to the assumed instrumentality of schooling. To be educative in the personal, caring sense conveyed in the definitions of Fenstermacher and Scheffler (Chapter Two) would be quite enough, if attained. But to expect of schools what today's economic, social, and political context exhorts for them is to make the coming of the new school virtually impossible. Worse, it takes our attention from the larger issues of community disarray, human engineering, and public policy that must be addressed if our society is to be robust.

This chapter is about dilemmas in seeking to have good

schools, the nature of good schools, and the community infrastructure required for *very* good schools. The implications for
the education of educators are far-reaching.

The Tyranny of Mixed Signals

Today's clash of mixed expectations makes it difficult for schools
to set and stay with a clear mission. To do so, they must be
educationally self-conscious — acutely so — in a context of contradictory expectations, many of which are only marginally
educative.

There was little internal contradiction in expectations for
our earliest schools. Householders of the colonies chose to tax
themselves to provide schools for the immigrant commoners who
could not provide privately for their children's education. Teaching children to read and write and simultaneously acquire the
values and beliefs embedded in the laws of the land and religious principles were the primary expectations for schools into
the nineteenth century. The requirements for this basic literacy expanded but were only loosely attached to jobs. The former appears not to have been regarded as a requirement for
gaining access to the latter.

Indeed, some writing of the time suggests the responsibility of government to provide jointly for both. Consider these
words from 1831: "To conceive of a *popular government* devoid
of a system of *popular education,* is as difficult as to conceive of
a civilized society destitute of a *system of industry.*"[3] In its plat-
form of 1830, the Boston Working Man's Party put forward as
a discrete plank "the establishment of a liberal system of education, attainable by all," along with its several planks addressed
to the right to productive industry, including the remarkable
twelfth plank: "That we are resolved to advocate, as one of our
leading objects, the entire abrogation of all laws authorizing the
imprisonment of the body for debt — at least until poverty shall
be rendered criminal by law."[4] There were to be, in the views
cited above, two systems, neither instrumental to the other.

This conceptual separation appears to have prevailed right
up into and beyond the rapid expansion of schooling in the sec-

ond half of the nineteenth century to ensure what many families were unable to provide. Courses deliberately geared to vocational opportunities appeared in the curriculum, as did courses thought necessary for meeting increasingly complex expectations for effective citizenship. A third curricular expansion occurred in the first half of the twentieth century to meet growing expectations for a school role in educating for the wise use of leisure time and "self-realization." Mortimer Adler stated in the late 1980s a mission that nicely balanced all three: "Preparation for duties of citizenship is one of the three objectives of any sound system of public schooling in our society. Preparation for earning a living is another, and the third is preparation for discharging everyone's moral obligation to lead a good life and make as much of one's self as possible."[5]

Two major shifts, both accelerating over the last several decades, have occurred in the role perceived for our public schools. First, schools have been asked to do more and more until our education system and our system of schooling are seen virtually as one. In addressing the degree to which there is substantial support in some major segment of our society for each of the possible goals for schooling—academic, social, vocational, and personal—Ernest Boyer (1983) and I (1984), working quite separately from one another, entitled the relevant chapter in our respective books "We Want It All."[6] As a consequence of this melding of all educational possibilities into schools, any perceived shortcoming in individual or collective behavior or circumstances is attributed to schools. We feel good about ourselves as a nation, and our schools are great; we feel down as a nation, and our schools are terrible. The rhetoric "Good schools make good societies" appears to be upside-down. A more accurate depiction would be "Good societies have good schools."

The second shift in perception in the role of schools involves one of Adler's objectives—preparation for earning a living. It is now front and center in the argument for better schools, whether for individual or the nation's economic well-being. Adler's other two objectives have become little more than afterthoughts in the rhetoric of reform. "Better schools mean better jobs" is the rallying cry, not better schools for better citizenship and richer, more caring lives.

Adler concluded the paragraph quoted above with this sentence: "Our present system of compulsory basic schooling, kindergarten through the twelfth grade, does not serve any of these objectives well."[7] His particular concern was with the first of the three objectives. He documented the extent of illiteracy in regard to the ideas and ideals of the Constitution, taking aim first at high school graduates. But he found similar deficiencies among graduates of our best colleges: individuals having reached positions of eminence in industry, journalism, the professions, and government. In our research, we found precious little to suggest that today's teachers are being educated in such a way as to correct this neglect even a little. To assume that simply growing up in our culture and attending schools that prepare one for the workplace will provide this enculturation is dangerously naive.

As a result of the pair of changed perceptions described above, school improvement finds itself in a virtually no-win situation. In equating education with schooling, we push the educative role of other agencies aside. Indeed, in some settings, these agencies have become adversarial, blaming the schools for shortcomings for which home and church, for example, should share some responsibility. Yet the home remains protective of its turf in regard to the teaching of values and civility — while often doing little about either — and remains suspicious of proposals for schools to step into the breach. And so the school gets blamed for not doing or not doing well what it is clearly asked to do, what it probably should do, and what it never has been told clearly to do.

The larger social context compounds this dilemma. The school's traditional role has been to provide access to knowledge and skills not readily acquired elsewhere — knowledge and skills assumed in the three goals stated above (usually broken down into a dozen or so statements, not three). The subjects adapted by the school were taken on with more in mind than preparation for earning a living. They were intended for a much broader conception of enculturation. Yet in spite of the increased emphasis on the economic instrumentality of schooling (with the other goals pushed more and more to the periphery), there have been no profound accompanying curricular changes. From six to eight subjects continue to show up in the course "takings" of secondary school students, regardless of recent stress on the importance of mathematics and the sciences over some others.

There is no evidence to show that the subjects entering into the curriculum over the years to provide for expanding expectations in the arenas of social, vocational, academic, and personal development are significantly instrumental to economic goals, whether personal or national. (Nor, for that matter, is there convincing evidence of their instrumentality to the goals of virtue, civility, and good citizenship for which these subjects presumably were selected.) Yet the emerging standard for judging the quality of our schools is the degree to which students' performance on tests of such subjects qualify them for the job market and advancement of the nation's economy. The whole of educating in schools is narrowed to this limited, utilitarian conception of what education is for.

It is the contradiction between what it takes to be a good and satisfying school and this instrumental conception of the societal role of schools that makes school improvement virtually impossible. In their demands for a rigorous academic curriculum, employers have in mind a broad set of traits in prospective employees: good work habits, company loyalty, dependability, honesty, teamwork, and the like. Although the correlation between these traits and tests presumably measuring curricular attainments is low, the galvanic response to a continued shortfall in the desired characteristics of employees is nonetheless a cry for more rigor in the school subjects.

To these expectations of employers must be added all those others put forward by various sectors of the population. The schools coming closest to satisfying this diverse array of community expectations are characterized by unique human connections on the inside and with their patrons — connections built up through very hard work over time.[8] The correlation between the presence of these connections and test scores is low.

A further complication: to be a good and satisfying school in the eyes of diverse beholders is not necessarily to be a good school as reflected in high achievement on standardized tests. Indeed, given the degree to which the former condition is viewed as "soft" and of little consequence on the standards by which schooling is judged, it is not to be a good school at all. Many critics of schools cite the fact that parents rate their local schools quite high and schooling in general much lower as an indicator of lethargy in the populace regarding the need for reform. These critics appear to be unaware of the degree to which polls create and not just measure public opinion. The parents know their school and view it as moderately satisfactory or good. But there is so much bashing of schools that they rate general schooling much lower. Ironically, many of the critics argue for schools of choice. Their position would take on greater credibility if they had more faith in parents' ability to judge the quality of schools.

During a decade of school reform initiatives following publication of *A Nation at Risk* (1983), there were many exhortations to get on this or that bandwagon. That of Education Secretary Alexander, "America 2000," during the presidency of George Bush, made good use of the train metaphor. We were to get on the train bound for a vague destination through unknown territory. Once on board, we would talk. Failure to get on board would leave us out of the loop. What is both remarkable and frightening is that something so lacking in substance could attract so much attention — and even hope — and so many passengers. By the end of the decade and inauguration of a new president, there was no sign of the train, let alone the tracks on which it supposedly was running.[9]

However, whenever education and schooling move to the front of national concern, with or without an agenda, there invariably is a grass roots response. This usually takes the form of segments of schools or whole schools latching on to curricular, instructional, or organizational ideas that promise improved learning or a more pleasant, productive work environment. Often these are not new ideas but old ones back in new dress. Many of those being explored in the 1960s were revisited in the 1980s, for example.

By the early 1990s, some policymakers were becoming aware that there were now schools — quite a few of them scattered across the country—that had quietly become rather good places for boys and girls to be. Some of them suddenly were in the spotlight, visited and featured at educational conferences to a degree that may have endangered their health. Most of them appear to have found their way around the quandary of contradicting criteria of goodness. They did this primarily by paying close attention to their own educational business and largely ignoring the changing exhortations of a national reform crusade. Strangely, most reports about these schools say little or nothing about their percentile rank on standardized test scores.

At first glance, these schools appear to be one-of-a-kind mavericks. A closer look reveals some general characteristics in common, however. Almost invariably, they have strong, determined principals, quietly charismatic and able to articulate an agenda that resonates in a very personal way with both students and their parents. The principal and teachers have engaged over the years in a great deal of planning, most of it in clusters closely attached to groups of students. The conversation is about teaching and learning, using the language of education, not rewards and punishments. A concern for quality work shows through, but not in the trappings of test scores. Theodore Sizer's Coalition of Essential Schools, for example, has pushed to the forefront the concept of *exhibition:* award of the high school diploma on the basis of a successful final demonstration of the student's grasp of the central skills and knowledge of the school's program.[10]

Schools becoming good respond, it seems, to appealing educational ideas that, on careful examination, offer to replace something not now working well or to improve on practices that have demonstrated their usefulness. Good teachers are driven in their daily work by neither the goal of improving the nation's economic competitiveness nor that of enhancing the school's test scores. Instead, they are driven by a desire to teach satisfyingly, to have all their students excited about learning, to have their daily work square with their conception of what this work should be and do. Yet a strong thread running through everything they do is the expectation that each child or youth will do his or her best and receive unflagging support toward that end.

A not-surprising early reaction of policymakers who begin to become aware of the existence of such schools is the familiar, "Bottle it!" This response is not the province solely of lay leaders, however. Educators, too, look for simple solutions that can be easily implemented. Much of the so-called effective schools movement that grew out of some solid research on factors characteristic of good schools foundered on efforts to reduce complexity to a few simple concepts. So long as we choose not to look deeply into the conditions characterizing schools that appear to be working, there will be a brisk industry in elixirs that promise much but deliver little. The market in palliatives for the common cold thrives on our ignorance of how to prevent it.

Commerce in the characteristics of good schools far exceeds the availability of functioning examples, simply because implementing new concepts is so labor-intensive. The constructive desire to make these examples the norm founders on the rock of conventional practices of school reform. At the time of writing, the favored language in state policy discourse about the road to good schools is "systemic reform." There is a refreshing hint of nonlinearity here, but it is quickly overwhelmed by the almost unquestioned recourse to target-directed, linear approaches to change that traditional rationality dictates. Almost immediately, systemic reform is transformed into a necessary tightening up of the ends-means connections among outcomes, a curriculum to deliver these, and tests to measure them.

Linda Darling-Hammond addresses the dilemma of two very different and often contradictory theories of school reform: one focused on tightening these connections; the other, on increasing the capacity of teachers to develop schools as inquiring, collaborative organizations. This second model of educational improvement struggles for recognition, understanding, and support. But the contingencies of the context are inhospitable to it and in harmony with the first. "Practitioners are well aware that there is an unresolved tension between the policy framework that currently exists and the policy desires that are being voiced in the rhetoric of school-based reform. Until the new vision is more fully enacted, practitioners, parents, and students will live in a state of policy conflict."[11]

Enactment of the new vision depends on the production of teachers who understand and are committed to it and who possess the knowledge and skills to implement it. This dependence is on a very fragile thread so long as teachers are viewed merely as stewards of established classroom norms and are simply cloned by teachers already in place. Virtually every good educational idea embraced and fostered by a handful of enterprising schools has gone little further because there were not in more schools the cadres of teachers required for them to flourish.

The tyranny over school improvement exercised by conflicting expectations and models will not be overcome solely through the more comprehensive preparation programs for educators recommended for centers of pedagogy, however. We have seen how important it is for policymakers to grasp the new vision and enact their part of its implementation. Likewise, parents must understand the nature of good schools — schools that provide broadly for the academic, vocational, personal, and social education of all children. Although there always will be disagreement regarding what the balance among these components should be, providing for the *whole* is something that good schools can do. But schools never will become good, even when diverse parental expectations are being satisfied, when the standard by which they are judged bears little or no relationship to the educational mission they strive to attain.

It is easier to eliminate illness and disease in communities that are health-conscious and attuned to medical science than in those that are not. But physicians are able to make solid progress toward healthy communities even when these understandings are primitive. Not so with communities and their schools. Superb, balanced progress toward all the major goal areas for which there is a considerable community constituency secures for no school a seal of approval unless there is widespread perception of compatibility between the ongoing effort and the prevailing standard of excellence. Unfortunately, the picture beginning to emerge regarding the nature of good schools is at odds with the standard of excellence that has been vigorously promoted within the policy framework of reform.

The route out of this dilemma is community discourse that produces a core of shared understandings about the nature of education and good schools and grows over time to reach an increasingly larger public. This will not occur if teachers wrap themselves in a professional mantle in such a way as to communicate the view that they know best. Rather, the schoolhouse must become a center of inquiry and a forum in which both educational ideas and what this particular school is trying to do (and why) are regularly discussed.

The time is propitious for this. (Of course, I am one who believes that the exercise of will makes *all* times propitious.) It is becoming increasingly clear that little to celebrate has emerged from hundreds of school reform initiatives launched with impressive displays of fireworks. It is difficult to remember even the names of all those enthusiasts who just a few years ago haughtily rebuked us for raising questions about the claims of success for projects just begun. If interest in school improvement can be sustained while faith in linear, top-down rationality as a change model subsides, there is hope for alternative models. Unfortunately, in the late 1960s, the promising alternatives becoming visible faded with policymakers' disillusionment with a school reform movement remarkably similar to that pursued with such enthusiasm for nearly a decade after *A Nation at Risk* was published.

This time around, however, there is a glimmer of hope in the fact that many of those enthusiasts have been replaced by individuals who were not the original proponents of the reappearing alternatives and consequently do not need to exhaust their energies in defending them. They are in a position to take a new look. This look should include attention to the schools referred to above that quietly have become good and the research that increasingly supports the conditions appearing rather consistently to characterize them. The essence of these schools lies in their internal functioning and their responsive connectedness to the larger community ecosystem of which they are a part. They are not unaware of exhortations to excellence that come and go, but care is taken not to let the culture of the school be driven by these changing themes of reform.

This new look must be broad-based and include policymakers, educators, parents, and a cross section of the citizenry. It must put orthodoxy, recrimination, and villain theories aside.

The outcome, over a decade, could be many good schools in communities that are becoming healthy.

Good Schools

Much of this section is devoted to a summary of conditions that appear to characterize good schools and that lie within a school's power to shape. There can be only frustration in the charge to be good if the prerequisites to goodness are not within a school's span of control—compounding the frustration that most schools already feel over the *conflict* in standards of goodness discussed above.

Criteria of Excellence

The attainment of excellence for most schools is impossible, because the conditions contributing most to the usual criteria of excellence are outside of their control. The most common yardstick is comparative academic achievement as measured by standardized tests. But what of the Coleman thesis that the most significant contributor to a child's success in school is what he brings there from home and encounters there from other homes? In other words, a child of parents who are both college graduates who attends school with other children whose parents are college graduates is likely to do well there, especially if this child and most of his or her classmates come from unbroken homes and have parents who read to them and otherwise attend to their education.

There is no more dependable predictor of success in school and of high scores on academic measures than the level of schooling attained by one's parents. Similarly, there is no better predictor of continued wealth than several generations of wealth in one's family. This does not mean that schools and individual diligence cannot and do not make a significant difference. But the presence of these conditions vastly reduces the grade of the slope to be climbed by schools seeking to be excellent or individuals seeking to be or remain wealthy.

The schools of the wealthy ghetto, whether public or private, do not have to try very hard to be regarded as excellent on the criteria of test scores and admission of graduates to elite colleges and universities. Although we can and do ask whether these schools are doing as well as they should, they are not pressed to answer. Meanwhile, however, the daily papers cite statistics to show that schools less favored with the predictors of success have many students performing below grade level. Data regarding how hard and well both groups of schools are working with conditions *under their control* are missing.

We are back into the dilemma of making all of our schools good when the standard of judgment allows only a few to be good. To question the standard is to be accused of misguided egalitarianism. Yet in a democratic society, we *must* question a standard that inequitably distributes awards so that inherited attributes count for more than do diligence and effort. Ironically, such a system can be devastatingly evenhanded as well as selective in its ill-effects. Clearly, the schools least advantaged with the predictors of student success are further disadvantaged. But I am convinced that the quality of education provided in many of our "best" schools shortchanges both individuals and the nation in regard to the traits embedded in the balanced set of goals we set for our schools and our leaders.

Schools perceived to be excellent (on the criterion of percentile rank on standardized tests) are not necessarily characterized by conditions of educational goodness. Indeed, some are rather vicious places for boys and girls to be. Earlier, I commented on the low correlation between success in school and an array of characteristics of human goodness. Surely our best schools should be those most committed to and productive of human goodness. But in recent years in particular, we have witnessed a surge of corruption in high places on the part of many much-schooled individuals. We should give serious consideration to the hypothesis that we have got it all wrong with respect to the criteria of excellence most commonly used to judge the quality of our schools.

Then what might be a reasonable alternative? I return to the observation that quite a few schools across the country have quietly become good — a sufficient number to raise in the minds of policymakers the prospect of cloning these. Unfortunately, there is then a propensity to do this "systemically" through connecting standards, tests, and curricula, and so the slide toward traditional views of excellence continues. Might it not make more sense to try to get a handle on the conditions seemingly characterizing these good schools and then endeavor to provide support for these conditions in all schools?

But what shall be the standard to look for in seeking these schools? They have come to our attention because of the good things said about them (in the same way that a good restaurant comes to our attention). We do not necessarily agree at first glance, but as we get closer to the school or the restaurant and talk with the patrons, the percentage of agreement rapidly increases. What we are encountering is the oldest and most powerful of all standards of judgment — that composite of many things known as *satisfaction*.

The degree to which we shy away from the criterion of satisfaction in regard to judging the quality of schools — particularly in educational research — is extraordinary. We rely primarily on satisfaction in virtually everything else: choosing a mate, a car, a house, a vacation spot. But when parents think their school is good, critics often interpret this to be a sign of indifference. When teachers think their school is good, critics are inclined to view them as self-serving. And when students appear to be enjoying their school, we conclude that it must be too undemanding.

The use of satisfaction as a standard is quite often soft, but it need not be so. My colleagues and I used it in our comprehensive study of schooling several years ago and endeavored to make it rigorous in two ways. First, we used a standard of satisfaction that combined the views of all three groups closely connected to the school: parents, students, and teachers. Second, we eschewed questions directed specifically to satisfaction and instead built a composite out of many questions directed to the three groups: questions pertaining to school climate, class climate, principal-teacher relationships, curricula, teaching, teacher-teacher relationships, school-community relationships, parent-teacher relationships, and more. We were then able to produce a quantitative index for each school. An index of .27, for example, showed very low satisfaction on the part of all three raters and placed a school near the bottom of the group on the standard of satisfaction. An index of .73 reflected high satisfaction among the groups and placed the school in the top group. Analysis of an index of .52 might reveal rather low student satisfaction, greater parent satisfaction, and still higher teacher satisfaction.

Of course, we had no data by which to compare our group of schools with schools nationwide, but this was not our interest. With data on our sample of schools to guide us in examining schools of relatively high and relatively low indexes of satisfaction, we were able to make considerable progress in ferreting out characteristics appearing to differentiate schools high and low in satisfaction. Again and again, we discovered a close relationship between these characteristics and concepts or principles commonly referred to in the literature as educationally sound. Our total body of data — thousands of data points pertaining to the commonplaces of each school — revealed schools with a very low satisfaction index to be almost literally coming apart and schools with a high index to be taking care of their business very well.

Application of the criterion of satisfaction in judging the quality of schools requires analysis far beyond that which would be appropriate here. First, the index used must be as encompassing as the one described above. Second, it must be combined with other indexes derived from independent observation of the elements of schooling from which satisfaction is or is not being derived. We had in our possession a great deal of data from which we made judgments to be checked against the satisfaction index of a given school. Third, we need a great deal of research and integration of research conclusions regarding the qualities of the elements of schooling that warrant the description "good." It appears to me that the criterion of satisfaction, with all of its limitations, promises much more for the creation of good schools than the standards conventionally used and the exhortations to excellence employed for purposes of motivation.

The most dangerous potential excess in employing the criterion of satisfaction lies in the opportunity it offers for homo-

geneous groups to create little enclaves of schooling with precon-
ditions of satisfaction based on shared values and prejudices.
But we have such ghetto schools now. This is a blemish on our
democratic way of life that transcends the power of educators
to ensure good schools.

Characteristics of Good Schools

The emergence of schools enjoying reputations of goodness derived from their industry is not a new phenomenon. It is the
growing numbers that carry our thoughts beyond explanations
of happy accidents. Yes, the name of a particular leader or school
tends to be attached to schools of the past and to some in the
present. But there are now too many for this precise identification to be attached to each. Often there is a patron—a James
Comer, Howard Gardner, Henry Levin, Theodore Sizer, or
philanthropic foundation. Often, too, there is a network—perhaps one sponsored by the patron, or Carl Glickman's League
of Professional Schools,[12] or the network of I.G.E. (Individually Guided Education) schools growing out of the work of the
Institute for Development of Educational Activities (/I/D/E/A/)
when it was the education arm of the Kettering Foundation,
or the network of the Research and Development Center at the
University of Wisconsin. And these individual schools are being heard from and about. An interesting surge in the past
several years has been the number of mini-case studies appearing
in professional journals or reported at conferences. These probably would not have appeared a decade ago, because they did
not fit the canons of legitimate research. But today, doing something about educational ideas has become fashionable.

When we were pulling out of our findings several years
ago some heuristics regarding the nature of good schools, we
found ourselves nodding over the degree to which these conclusions squared with much of what already was in a kind of
collective experience regarding such schools: our own, our ex-
changes of anecdotes with others, novels, case studies, biogra-
phies, and the literature of educational inquiry (particularly the
growing body of qualitative research).[13] None of the schools in

the representative sample we studied possessed anything close to a composite of what were emerging as desired characteristics, nor did any we heard about. But many were struggling with a kind of vision of what might be. Reality fell far short, but each piece being worked on fit into a conception of the whole.

My guess, given what has transpired in regard to the emergence of good schools since then (circa 1982), is that we would today nod far more vigorously on seeing each of our heuristics line up with accumulating insight into the nature of good schools. Without going into detail, I endeavor to summarize below some of the generalizations about good schools that appear to be standing up over time.

- First, a good school is a good school in virtually all respects. The converse is equally true for a poor school. A school is a kind of organic thing—a system of organs and connections. It appears that neither a good school nor a bad school is a creature made up of both good and poor organs and connections. Most school reform tends to be narrowly focused on a part, in ignorance and neglect of the ecosystem. Consequently, the results often are akin to putting more pressure on frozen pipes.
- Second, where elementary schools feed into middle or junior high schools that, in turn, feed into senior high schools in a unified school district, the level of goodness tends to persist (while simultaneously fading with progress upward). This suggests that conditions of the school district itself impinge upon the quality of individual schools. Good schools tend to enjoy district support. The question is, Is it this support that helps to make them better, or do good schools manage to shape a kind of protective peace with the district? The degree of consistency in the levels of goodness maintained by schools connected as described above suggests some power to influence in the district itself.
- Third, a good school is self-conscious of its culture. A poor school virtually trips over itself each day, seemingly unaware of the nature and magnitude of its malaise. This usually means that the good school frequently resorts to principle

in discussing students not doing well and relations with parents, for example. The poor school uses up human energies in coping with problems; there is no time for reflection.

- Fourth, a good school takes care of its business. There are orderly ways of handling routines that most people appear to understand, accept, and follow. Processes of dialogue, making decisions, taking actions, and following up evaluatively regarding these actions are built into the culture of the school. Bad schools, on the other hand, appear to run on an ad hoc basis. It is interesting to note that the range of faculty participation in decision making from good school to bad school appears to be quite consistent. It is lack of ambiguity in regard to the authority of the principal and the teachers, respectively, that is a vital factor in a school's being good. In poor schools, there appears to be considerable ambiguity with respect to who does what — and a good deal of unhappiness with whatever way responsibility comes down.
- Fifth, a good school seems to have come to terms with external standards by developing an internal sense of its educational role and the importance of academic work. "Smart kids" are not looked down upon; indeed, they often are elected by their peers to leadership positions. Teachers in good schools are conscious of the importance of quality learning time; they get more instructional time out of the school week than do teachers in poor schools. Students in good schools appear to be much more in harmony with teachers' efforts to have them learn than are students in poor schools. Interestingly, many students in poor schools — those who appear to be part of, if not the whole of, the cause of poor student performance — are resentful of the fact that their school appears not to be providing them with a good education.
- Sixth, a good school is characterized by an array of positive human connections. Teachers are viewed by students as not having favorites and not using sarcasm. In poor schools, that is much less likely to be true. Teachers in good schools view their peers as professionals who know what they are doing. Teachers in poor schools are not so positive in their views,

tending more to question the professionalism of their peers. Principals in good schools take a positive view of the teachers, viewing them as professionals who perform well in their classrooms. Principals in poor schools frequently perceive the teachers as the major problem.

- Seventh, the good school appears to be connected to homes and parents in positive ways. Parents report knowing their children's teachers and meeting with them. They claim to know what the school is doing, in part because of school efforts to keep them informed. Parents in poor schools are more likely to report not knowing or talking to their children's teachers. They claim not to know much about the school their children attend and complain that the school does little to keep them informed.

This list of seven macro-characteristics of good schools is sufficient for my purposes here (although there are many more, including a host pertaining to organizational, curricular, and instructional matters). There are two major observations I wish to draw from them that have major implications for the education of educators and school improvement efforts.

First, there is a connectedness here that would become even more apparent with the addition of more generalizations and further development, with examples, of each characteristic on the list. This connectedness is made up particularly of two general factors. There is ongoing discourse regarding all of the components of schooling by the people most affected by them on a daily basis: the responsible educators (principal and teachers), the students, and the parents. Further, this discourse is marked by civility. Not just civility in the sense of politeness but civility as an outward manifestation of deep moral respect for self and others: teachers and students, students and students, teachers and teachers, parents and teachers, and so on. This is at the heart of any healthy ecosystem or culture. A good school is a healthy ecosystem marked by these manifestations of moral connectedness.

The second observation is that the conditions marking a good school — a *truly* good school, not just a school that achieves high test scores—are those within the power of those people closely associated with it to shape. Nowhere in any state mandates are there requirements that these conditions be met. Nowhere, until recently, have there been school accrediting criteria requiring that these conditions be put in place. I say "until recently" because in the mid 1980s, a small team of leaders in the Southern Association of Colleges and Schools reflected on my observations and conclusions in *A Place Called School* and pondered the relationship between these and extant criteria used by the association in accrediting schools. They drew from the book some fifty-five criteria of good schools and chose two dozen of these as representing processes of renewal to be encouraged in pilot schools interested in pursuing an alternative route to accreditation. Whether this kind of approach to school improvement and accreditation becomes standard remains to be seen.[14]

There were clear differences in the way the schools in the top and bottom quartiles on the criterion of satisfaction in our sample took care of their business and in the quality of daily school life exhibited. We were unable to identify demographic factors that might have accounted in large part for these differences. It is significant, I think, that the smallest schools in the sample were in the top quartile, the largest in the bottom. It is not impossible for a large school to be satisfying, but it seems to require greater effort. In a small school, it is easier to cultivate the properties of human connectedness productive of satisfaction.

Careful examination of the seven generalizations regarding schools with high and low levels of satisfaction reveals no mention of the very heart of schools as educational institutions: curriculum and instruction. The heavy reliance on frontal teaching—lecturing, telling, and questioning—in secondary schools and the heavily textbook-oriented curriculum reported in *A Place Called School* characterized our sample generally. Variations from this pattern appeared in some classrooms scattered across the entire sample, and there was more variability in the primary than in the higher grades. But no such variations differentiated the top quartile of schools from the bottom.

Several different explanatory hypotheses emerge. There may be some power in all of them together. One having appeal

for me is that there are no impositions from outside in regard
to the quality of life to be created inside a school. A determined
principal can make a good deal of headway in shaping the way
students, teachers, and parents work together in eliminating
abrasive factors and conducting business in an orderly, sensitive manner. Districts that move principals around in the hope
of "shaking things up" probably convey the wrong message and
inhibit the desired leadership.

But why did not the able principals in the top quartile
of our sample effect the curricular and instructional changes that
would have marked their schools as different in these areas from
those in the bottom quartile? One possible explanation is that
external forces tend to regulate the curriculum. Our data showed
a heavy dependence of teachers on textbooks and district (more
than state) curriculum guides. Teachers also reported their own
experience as a source of the curriculum they delivered; they
tended to pass on what they had received. And so it tends to
be with their methods of teaching: teachers teach the ways they
were taught in schools and colleges; these were the ways we
documented consistently in all but a few classrooms.

There also appears to be some of the taboo in the K-12
system that prevails in higher education regarding administrative tampering with teaching. Most of the principals in the most
satisfying schools in our sample credited the teachers with knowing what they were doing in the classroom and said that *they
left them alone* to do it. This view does not augur well for taking
teaching out from behind the classroom door to make it an
agenda item for school improvement. It is of interest to note
that the theme of "the principal as instructional leader" found
its most hospitable context in elementary schools, where teachers
traditionally have had less autonomy than in secondary schools
and universities.

In preceding chapters, I have written a good deal about
the mission of schooling and the mission for the education of
educators that emerges from it. Let us now consider the relationship between mission and function. *Mission* pertains to goals
and directions—what is desired and to be sought. *Function* pertains to actual use. If a watch could be energized by a mission,

it would be to provide an accurate portrayal of time, within the extant convention of time, under all circumstances. Improvement would generally be seen as enhancements in its ability to do this. Its quality would be determined on its precision in performing this time-telling *function*. But what if other criteria enter in (as they do)? Many watches are now purchased with little regard to the time-telling mission. What is dominant in the mind of the buyer is an aesthetic function. A watch could cease functioning as a timepiece on a wrist and still be valued for the function of dazzling with the shape, color, and brilliance of its decorative diamonds. What does this tell us about education? For schools to become very good, the relationship between mission and function must be considerably closer than it currently is.

An Ecological Perspective

The mission of schooling bespeaks an educative function. But the primary function now being performed by schools is child care. The many tantalizing proposals for school reform designed to fundamentally change our schools — for restructuring them, if you will — that go nowhere founder largely because of their failure to address this function. The redesign of schooling proposed in Chapter Four has gone nowhere and will go somewhere only when there are satisfying answers to the questions of child care that this and other reforms invariably provoke.

The significance of the child-care function is evident at the level of the school itself. The decision of a faculty to dismiss the students an hour earlier once a month to facilitate longer staff meetings brings forth such a cacophony of complaint from parents that it is rescinded. It would be easier to make a significant change in a portion of the social studies curriculum than to alter the school day. Our data showed satisfaction with the curriculum and teaching to be high when satisfaction with such things as students' safety, attention to individual children, students' behavior, and control of alcohol and drug use was high — in other words, when the function of child care was being taken care of quite well.

Schools, it appears, can be quite highly regarded by those closely connected to them even when they are only moderately successful in improving their educative function. We should not take lightly the functioning of a school that gains a good reputation for providing a setting of safety and joy for students there. Large numbers of schools cannot be so described, and large numbers of these perform their educative function poorly as well. The challenge is to create and renew schools that are simultaneously places of joy and places of learning.[15]

Our findings suggest that creating a school that is a good and satisfying place for students, teachers, and parents is an enormously challenging enterprise. Even the schools we found to be best on this criterion were not nearly as far along as one might hope. When we add to this goal the charge to be simultaneously powerfully educative, we come to realize how puny and narrowly focused have been our efforts to have an excellent system of schools. The conventional model of improvement and strategies of implementation simply do not accommodate the nature and circumstances of schools.

Schools are cultures seeking to maintain a state of equilibrium within that allows them to function in the face of perturbations from without. They are ecosystems within larger ecosystems. The organism that is a school is a system in which individuals interact with one another and with the whole, within an often ill-defined environmental matrix. I have argued on preceding pages that the "goodness" of a school depends on the quality of the interactions within and with this matrix. In a good school, these interactions are healthy, enabling the school both to conduct its daily business effectively and to cope with exigencies. In a poor school, these interactions are unhealthy, making the conduct of business difficult. Bad schools are in a constant state of crisis and near-crisis.

To attain and maintain this healthy state of functioning requires a considerable daily expenditure of energy on the part of the principal and teachers. There is precious little time and energy for the tilting of equilibrium that significant change from the existing regularities and systemics of schooling requires. The rhetoric of restructuring, of creating a school for the twenty-first century, may appeal to us, but at best it stimulates talk rather than concerted action. Consequently, as I have noted, reports of success tend to be of paradise envisioned, not gained.

The "good-enough" school rarely gets beyond a state of equilibrium that is satisfying to students, teachers, and parents. We should not knock this considerable accomplishment, particularly in the demanding, changing times of today. I argue that schools cannot become *very* good until they are good enough on the criteria of ecological health introduced here. I argue, further, that they cannot and will not become very good, even if ecologically healthy, unless these good-enough schools are provided with the conditions that make it easier to sustain equilibrium and dissonance simultaneously. This combination of equilibrium and dissonance is the essence of renewal, whether we are speaking of individuals or institutions.

The long-standing model of school reform runs counter to this ecological perspective. First of all, it is derived from psychological theories focused on individuals, not institutions. Second, it is linear, not circular and pervasive, reflecting the industrial age in which it is rooted. Third, it addresses inputs and outputs, favoring economic models over the more appropriately descriptive and explanatory models of political science, sociology, anthropology, and ecology. Consequently, the conventional model eschews context. Fourth, the methods of implementing reform stemming from this model are necessarily singular or at least sharply restricted in number. Otherwise, there is no way of quantifying inputs and outputs and attributing cause and effect.

These characteristics suggest low predictability of success for the model that has dominated virtually every school reform era of the twentieth century. The model has been employed again and again in seeking to inject or manipulate a given variable for purposes of increasing students' academic achievement. And again and again, research has revealed neither consistent nor significant effects. By controlling a dozen or so variables, significant results might be achieved. But which to select and how to control them confounds the conduct of such experiments. Increasingly, we are learning that there is more potential in educating teachers to recognize and maximize the factors in their school and classroom environments that have the most potential for enhancing students' learning. Likewise, they need to be able to recognize and minimize the effects of those that interfere. Needed is a kind of connoisseurship that enables "fine-grained discriminations among complex and subtle qualities" constituting the environmental matrix — what Elliot Eisner refers to as the enlightened eye.[16]

The findings from our studies of schools reported earlier in this chapter suggest that the elements that good-enough schools fail to address creatively are curriculum and instruction. Until they do, they will not be fully exemplary. Since even the most satisfying schools in our sample stopped short of renewal in these two critical components, the ecological perspective on change directs us to seek possible explanations and solutions in the cultural circumstances. Let us consider two potential approaches — one based in the ecosystem of the school, the other in the larger environmental matrix.

In most states, the systemics of schools call for them to function with their students 180 days a year, with a few days tagged on at the outset for the staff to get ready for the student onslaught and a day or two at the end to clean up odds and ends of business. Good schools take care of the 185 days or so in an orderly fashion. But no expectations and time for redesigning the regularities are built into these systemics, whatever the rhetoric of school reform. By being good stewards, principals and teachers make conventional schools rather satisfying places for young people to be, for parents who send them, and for the teachers there. This is good enough. Many schools do not attain this level of goodness; until they do, they have no readiness for anything new. The lances of reform splinter on school and classroom doors.

Poor schools require a great deal of district support just to take care of regular business. To move beyond that, staff development resources must be decentralized to the local school, along with a strong consultant who can work toward improving all of the internal human connections. The principal must be charged with and helped in developing (with teachers, students, and parents) a plan of attack on the malaise interfering each day with the health of the school's ecosystem. If it becomes apparent that he or she is incapable of doing this, even with strong support and assistance, the principal must be replaced.

Three years of concentrated attention on the school's functioning should be quite enough to establish the connections with
parents necessary to get students to school regularly and on time,
establish and achieve internal behavioral expectations, set up
regular monitoring of the hours spent on instruction in a given
week, and so on. Another two years should be sufficient for a
school to become truly good.

The school on the road to excellence must tackle a different kind of problem in that additional two years: it must go beyond taking care of daily business to create a far more interesting, challenging curriculum and ensure teachers' use of three
or four instructional techniques that go far beyond today's dependence on frontal teaching. For today's teachers, these new
ways are best acquired at the school site through provisions for
staff development during the regular school year and beyond.
No successful corporation would enter into significantly different ways of conducting its business without providing in-service
training prior to implementation. For tomorrow's teachers,
centers of pedagogy must provide hands-on experiences with
the necessary range of instructional practices in partner schools
that are in the process of going beyond the stewardship of conventional practices.

It is the curriculum problem, in particular, that takes us
beyond the culture of the school into the larger environmental
matrix. Many years will pass before teachers are provided with
the time and tools for even modest renewal of the extant curriculum. Fundamental renewal will elude them. A more promising approach is to provide them with curricular alternatives to
the mundane ones that have dominated. Instructional materials
have been restrained by a straitjacket that has virtually ensured
conformity and mediocrity.

Since World War II, dozens of small companies and a
few large ones have failed in their creative efforts to provide
materials beyond textbooks and workbooks. These new products
have been marketed as supplements to the generally accepted
standard of textbook series in virtually every subject. Ironically,
not until 1992 did California approve for adoption (and approve
the use of state funds to purchase) comprehensive, stand-alone

multimedia programs. Among these was FOSS, the full-option junior high science program developed and marketed by Encyclopaedia Britannica Educational Corporation on the basis of years of research by scholars and curriculum developers of the Lawrence Hall of Science, University of California, Berkeley.

Similarly, the Edunetics Corporation is working with districts across the United States to introduce into their schools computer-based multimedia programs in mathematics and science. Years and years of research and development by a competent staff of curriculum generalists and specialists lie behind these programs. Particularly appealing is the instructional management system that facilitates students' transcending the individuality of most computer-based instruction to join in creating and solving problems together and enabling teachers to incorporate and manage the whole as an integral part of the total curriculum. This is the kind of curricular support system teachers need in order to break out of the curricular and instructional conventions that simultaneously dominate and intimidate, effectively blocking change even in good schools.

It is most unfortunate that a large part of the private sector's curricular concern has focused almost exclusively on the schools' supposed intransigence with respect to change, with much of the blame directed at districts. Clearly, the bureaucratic functioning of many districts, particularly large urban and suburban ones, is *part* of the problem. But this considerable tunnel vision blinds many people to the fact that the standard model of change proposed for schools ignores their culture and is almost consistently ineffective.

Dismantling the public school system and resorting to schools of choice in no way solves the problems of changing school cultures — problems that the work of Seymour Sarason, the RAND studies, and other extensive inquiries have laid bare. How much more productive and beneficial to the nation it would be if the business and corporate world were to turn its attention aggressively to the production of curricular and instructional materials, since that production lies well beyond the capabilities of teachers and schools. This is the kind of competition American business knows something about and from which it could derive both pride and profit.

I have argued in the foregoing that schools have the power to shape most, but not all, of the conditions characterizing good schools. I have argued, further, that the linear, ends-means model dominating school reform efforts is dysfunctional, in that it both ignores and interferes with the systemic functioning of schools, endangering school health by consuming energy and causing distress. I proposed and briefly described an alternative, ecological perspective that squares with the nature of schools and fosters improvement approaches more likely to support school renewal. Then I described some of the conditions and support a school needs to become and remain good.

But sustained attention to all of the above is likely to leave us short of the very good or excellent schools we want. The barriers to this next level are formidable, and their removal seems to lie beyond the capability of individual schools. They have to do with time, the present nature of pre-service and in-service teacher education, and instructional materials. In seeking support as they dismantle these barriers, schools also face the formidable problem of district and union bureaucracies. They must look for support from without as well: the productive joining of educators, philanthropy, and business is essential to the richness of curricular and instructional resources required for schools to go beyond being good enough.

The drive of this nation toward an excellent system of education requires parallel attention to more than schools. Equating education and schooling has led us astray. Today homes and religious institutions no longer buttress schools as they once did; many are negligent in the performance of their educative roles. Most communities lack coordination of their services. Many agencies either fall short or are counterproductive, from the schools' perspective, in fulfilling their educational functions. Malaise and shortcomings in the community infrastructure place burdens of day care on schools that compound their efforts to be educationally good.

The Community Context of Educational Renewal

The educational historian Lawrence Cremin, in a little book published just before his death, wrote that it is folly to talk about excellence in American education without including, in addition to schooling, the education proffered by families, day-care centers, peer groups, television broadcasters, and workplaces.[17] Cremin contributed significantly to the idea that our educational history embraces much more than chronicles of our system of schooling. To think systemically about educating is to think of a system of education that includes much more than schools. At the core of this system are educative communities of which schools are an important part.

Toward a Collaborative Community Infrastructure

By focusing on schools to solve all our problems, we look right past troublesome matters that not only need to be addressed directly, for their own sake, but also contribute to the shortcomings of schools. Simultaneously, teachers' energies are diverted from school renewal and we are distracted from the necessary business of taking care of other sectors of the community: not to worry about today's impoverished and homeless; our schools will make it right tomorrow.

Traditional models of education that focus only on the nature of learning and child development simply do not encompass children's community context. According to Urie Bronfenbrenner, dominant theories

> seldom include the adjacent or encompassing systems which may in fact determine what can or cannot occur in the more immediate context. Such encompassing systems include the nature and requirements of the parents' work, characteristics of the neighborhood, transportation facilities, the relation between school and community, the role of television . . . and a host of other ecological circumstances and changes which determine with whom and how the child spends his time: for example, the fragmentation of the extended family, the separation of residential and business areas, the disappearance of neighborhoods, zoning ordinances, geographic and social

mobility, growth of single parent families, the abo-
lition of the apprentice system, consolidated schools,
commuting, the working mother, the delegation
of child care to specialists and others outside the
home, urban renewal, or the existence and character of an explicit national policy on children and
families.[18]

There is a growing realization all across the United States,
especially in urban settings, of these changed community circumstances and of disrepair. Not only is there little sense of community, but the entities that make it up are often in poor shape.
It is unreasonable to expect the schools to pick up the slack when
families fall apart, religious institutions no longer attract the
young, children are malnourished, drug addiction is rampant,
prime-time television programs are vacuous and educationally
bankrupt, and gang members, athletes, and narcissistic celebri-
ties are the admired adolescent role models. A few schools have
succeeded in rising educationally above all this, but the frequency
of their mention conveys the fact that the number, although
growing, is small.

Some of the models of community schools developed decades ago with support from philanthropic foundations such as
Mott and Kellogg are being dusted off and updated to address
the problem. And once again, philanthropy is funding collaborative projects. Some school-based leaders are vigorously facilitating collaborations among all those health and other human service agencies that focus on children and families. These are
unlikely to be successful if coordinated in and by schools unless
the domain of schooling is expanded to a 24-hour day, a 7-day
week, and a 365-day year. The needs of the community will
be ill taken care of if the collaborating infrastructure is governed
by the systemics and regularities of schools. Entirely new patterns of organization and governance must be devised.

Needed are healthy collaborative relationships among all
the agencies and institutions serving young people and the rest
of the community. The collaboration required will not remove
child care from the school; nor will it call for the school to take

over. The school is not alone in being staffed by college graduates with professional preparation. Most of the individuals employed in these other agencies are well educated and well trained;
many are as well as or better versed than their school-based collaborators in the educational literature; many are as morally
sensitive to their nurturing role. The primary task is for each
group to do its particular job well and to align its work with
that of others so that children and families are well served, and
for all the groups together to figure out what can be done to
fill in the gaps in regard to services needed but not yet being
rendered. There is plenty of demanding work to be accomplished
and a great deal of additional learning to be acquired if it is
to be done well. There is much that teacher educators must do
to prepare those who work in schools for the realities of today's
communities, many of which have few of the characteristics
described in the relevant literature just a short time ago.

There is ample room for the play of creativity in designing models of effective communication around children and
youths and the new circumstances of home and community life.
I would like to believe that the obvious need and the virtue it
conjures up in my mind would be sufficient to inspire equally
virtuous means. Realistically, however, we must anticipate and
endeavor to plan for the human frailties of well-intentioned individuals required to play new roles whose present leadership
will be threatened and who will be required to share turf long
considered to be their own. Getting school-based people and
university-based people to work together as equals in redesigning teacher education is already bringing out all the inherent
difficulties discussed in the extensive literature on change. The
problems will be magnified when the scope is enlarged to embrace whole communities and a clutch of professions that have
worked more in parallel than in unison even when focused on
the same clientele.

As I have noted, educators in schools and teacher educators must divest themselves of any naive notions that interinstitutional collaboration will relieve schools of their child-caring
function.[19] Although scenarios that do away with school build-
ings in favor of some kind of multimedia shopping mall with

an electronic smorgasbord of educational goodies are intriguing, they butt up against the pervasiveness of the day-care function that some institutions must provide. Such scenarios also tend to slight the part of the educational function that schools are uniquely charged to provide: instilling civility and citizenship. Undoubtedly, schools of the future will be characterized in part by features of these scenarios, but it is equally possible that they will embrace features akin to yesterday's best homes and yesterday's schools, which served as surrogates of homes.

Jane Roland Martin, drawing particularly from the work of Maria Montessori, argues convincingly for the idea of a "schoolhome" that combines educating with caring in a nurturing context, beginning in the early years.[20] There has been for some years, of course, the model of the Israeli kibbutz nursery school-home, where the children are nourished, socialized, and educated in a setting that relieves parents of some burdens of child rearing and yet provides readily for a full range of family activities.[21]

Many specialists in early childhood development and education have resisted my inclusion of four-year-olds in a unit of schooling that embraces the years of nursery school, kindergarten, and the first grade or two. They fear domination of what is now a child-centered concept of early education by a systemics-oriented reality of schooling. They and others are coming around to the position, however, that the school is to a considerable degree now and to a greater degree potentially among the most stable institutions in the community. Consequently, new models of community-wide institutional collaboration might be built around modifications of existing schools resembling the school-home ideas of Martin and others proposed and tried over the years.

Despite the attacks leveled on schools in the 1980s and 1990s, most schools may be working better than many other parts of the community, particularly if we add to whatever educational functions they still provide some credit for the functions they have picked up because of changing circumstances. But this is an argument that deserves only passing attention. The point to be made and acted upon is that the host of circumstances to which Bronfenbrenner referred some years ago and the changes that have occurred since require comprehensive overhaul of the community infrastructure. No institution can or will remain unchanged, and the collaborative arrangements required are as yet uncharted. There is much to be done.[22]

Educative Communities

To ask schools to develop the best of human traits in each young person and to do this by providing compelling encounters with sound knowledge and thought is to expect of them a great deal — especially when circumstances press for processing students like raw materials to serve utilitarian ends. To ask schools to join with other agencies and those agencies to join with schools in order to ensure a strong network of support services seems to run against the grain of the independent, self-reliant individuality seen to characterize the nation's past strength. But the challenge now is to deal with new frontiers that have to do with human relationships, multicultural understanding and appreciation, collaborative enterprise, and the making of a self-renewing polity. The most demanding political responsibility is to be a good citizen. The individuality likely to be most valued in the future will be marked by the successful blending of personal maturity and a continuing contribution to the public context that shapes personality. Education is at the heart of it all. Schools, however good, are not sufficient.

There is no question that schools could and should be much better. And there is no question that schools would do their appropriate work better if home, place of worship, health and social services, and other agencies would do their job better and in concert. But even if our schools *were* better, they could not ensure either the individual maturity or the polity necessary to a just, robust, renewing, democratic state.

We are so fixed on schools as the source of our enlightenment and well-being that when we contemplate becoming a better nation or stronger individually, we turn first to schools. We prod and poke them and, even while proclaiming that they do their job poorly, ask them to do it longer. And even as we point to Japan and other countries as models of the longer schooling we would emulate, they are engaged in shortening the school week. We ignore the strong, supportive family of the Japanese child and the delightful art, music, crafts, science, and recreational after-school programs of the Chinese (designed to compensate for the absence of working parents until late in the afternoon). Until we apply ourselves to using the present hours of schooling in more educationally productive ways, the only excuse for a longer day, week, or year is to extend the babysitting function to accommodate the changing patterns of family life. But there are other ways to engage the time of children and youths usefully than to add minutes to the time of present classes or provide three or four replicas of today's classes on Saturday mornings.

If all the contingencies in the environment provided educational encounters related to their ongoing functions, we would have educative communities. There are villages in India and Africa where the first duty of all adults is to raise the young successfully in the culture. When a child approaches the blacksmith at work, for example, it is the latter's unhesitating responsibility to introduce the child to what he is doing. The villagers raise not only their own children but all the children within their daily scope of activities. This process of enculturation is truly education through *paideia* (that is, by virtue of the educative community).

While this casual approach to education may be sufficient for people at the margins of technological advancement and world markets, it is clearly insufficient for most of the countries of the world, including our own. But there is a powerful message for us: we should assign to our schools only the cultivation of traits that require for their development years of cumulative attention in carefully designed, systemic curricula. Here is where Theodore Sizer is right on target in proposing that less is more: curricula organized around key concepts and themes that are deepened over the years by coming at them through varied instructional procedures. The required pedagogy recognizes and seeks to bring into play those multiple intelligences of which Howard Gardner writes so convincingly.[23] Students are intensively engaged in making meanings rather than in picking through the textbook garbage for clues to the tests they are about to take.

The surge in good health and longevity seen particularly within the upper middle class of this country is due, in part, to people's financial wherewithal to seek medical help. In addition, though, many people have taken advantage of educational opportunities beyond schools to learn about what to eat and not eat, the benefits of certain kinds of exercise, and the dangers of drugs, alcohol, and tobacco. And much of this learning has taken place in the face of vested interests promoting precisely the opposite of what these people have chosen to do. But large numbers of people — many with the necessary financial resources — have not learned to sort out the messages around them or have failed to develop the necessary habits of self-discipline. Many more have access neither to good education nor to the dollars necessary to sustaining personal well-being.

Parents and children attached over a period of years to the University Elementary School at the University of California, Los Angeles, profited from the relentless message of Doctor Wagner — "Martie," as he was affectionately known to most of us. You must learn to take care of your own health, he said over and over. This is an educational process that should characterize the whole of our living. It is aided enormously when not just schools but all the related agencies and institutions take on as naturally as the villagers referred to above their appropriate part of the cacophony of teaching to which Lawrence Cremin referred. Martie Wagner saw little of this sort of health-consciousness in his profession. He spoke nostalgically of his periodic visits to Denmark, where education for good health in the whole of living was built into the ecology of all communities. (My most recent visit with him was during a brief visit to the United States; he and his family had settled in Denmark.)

The concept of the educative community encompasses much more than schools doing their educative job more easily and better because all other agencies are doing theirs so well that the schools need pay only modest attention to the health and social service tasks that now occupy so much of their time. There is the expectation that these other agencies will be appropriately educative, too — and certainly not *mis*educative. This is asking a great deal—indeed, so much that the concept not only is virtually missing from public discourse but often invites disdain when introduced.

It is difficult for many and impossible for some groups and enterprises to align their self-interests with the public good, and that is what an educative role in the positive sense invariably requires. It is equally difficult for a public educated much more for individual development and competition than for personal responsibility and community welfare to sort out the degree to which adversaries are indeed locked in struggles that affect us all when one side claims to be for the common good. We are aware that the Bill of Rights and the Declaration of Independence had some things to say about individual rights and the common weal, but we have not found it necessary to derive personal meanings. Such matters are not part of the human conversation for most of us.

Do television producers and broadcasters, for example, have any responsibility for educating in Scheffler's meaning of the word (see quote in Chapter Two)? Should they be more conscious of the public good and choose good role models of diction and grammar over good-looking people to anchor the morning wake-up programs? An unexpected change in schedule put my wife, Lynn, and me in London for a welcome longer visit than usual, and drizzle attached us longer than usual to the delights of the BBC. The early-evening newscaster—no beauty—presented the news with exemplary diction and language structure and then took the concluding five minutes to define and employ in other contexts some of the least familiar words she had used. Surely this responsibility for educating makes the work of schools a little easier, yet it was not intended as a service to schools. It is evidence of responsible awareness of the public good inherent in education.

Given the shortcomings of schools and the considerable ill health in the ecosystem of our communities, inserting the chimeric idea of educative communities into the conversation may appear to be dysfunctional. To the contrary, however, the concept appears to possess practical potential for hastening school improvement and educational reform more broadly conceived.

Once we get beyond the myopic notion that education is

something to be assigned to schools primarily or exclusively, we are on the way to a far more realistic comprehension of what has taken place relatively recently in our society and on a potentially productive road to restoring the health of our communities. We begin to look around to perceive where else education occurs. It takes only a little looking to develop awareness of the incredible learning taking place during the preschool years and the role of the home in this process—from inflicting life-long damage to creating a supportive educative environment that virtually ensures life-long learning. It takes even less effort to accept the probability that television, more than schools, is now shaping the character, beliefs, and worldviews of young people and their parents. Yet few of those who make the major decisions about the contents of this medium claim to be *educating;* we entertain and provide information, they say. And consider the long-standing, cumulative body of research into the educative power of the peer group—much of that power characterized by elements that are disturbing, especially when we realize the degree to which they mirror things that have gone wrong in the adult world.

The message coming through from any reasonably thoughtful scanning of informal and nonformal education in the community is the degree to which it eludes critical attention and action. The potential good in paying serious attention to this education boggles the mind. We begin to envision education for parenting, one of the most neglected and most significant human enterprises. We see the urgent need for constructive ways to use the out-of-school time of those adolescents turned loose on streets and in malls, who should not for long be out of the sight of caring adults. And it would not require drastic change in network policies to answer responsibly one question about all television programs: Is this program likely to be more constructive than destructive in its impact on the values and beliefs of viewers? (Of course, the visual media have the opportunity to be *deliberately* educative as well, opening up the world's wonders and beauties as they are so wondrously capable of doing.) If education is as critical to the future lives of our people and to the nation's well-being as a diverse array of political and business leaders are telling us, dare we continue to ignore the haphazard education engulfing us — education that commonly undermines rather than enhances the work of schools?

A second potential benefit in perceiving the education taking place beyond schools is the prospect of being more realistic in our expectations for schools. We may come to see that schools are limited in their ability to compensate for parental abuse and neglect of children, educationally impoverished home environments, nutritional deprivation of children, and more. Schools are not the powerful equalizers we sometimes imagine them to be. For example, the inherited advantages some children bring to school remain potent for years after many of them have graduated from elite schools of law and medicine.[24] Ensuring a better and more educative start for all children will not eliminate a wide range in readiness to learn at school, but it would place the school in more advantageous circumstances for educating. There is considerable likelihood that, as we become more conscious of and more disposed to improve upon the informal and nonformal education that is now pervasive, we will look more to schools for the educative function they should perform and less for all the instrumental functions they cannot.

For the long run, the greatest potential benefit in comprehending and developing the educative potential of agencies and institutions beyond schools is the emergence of educative communities. Judging, discriminating, wondering, testing, creating, and the like become a way of life whether the setting or situation is one of living together as a family, providing basic services, renewing a school, refining a system of governance, maintaining a successful business, or eliminating homelessness. If a family is stumbling, one looks for explanations in the erosion of the conditions that make a family, not to the school the parents once attended. If a school is no longer renewing, one looks to the omission of conditions that make renewal possible. If a business is failing, one looks to the conditions that contributed to success or failure. One does not place blame on how the local school fared last year on standardized tests. Human enterprises that fail or succeed almost invariably do so because of the decisions made by those who run them on the inside or by those who prey upon them from the outside, many of whom are much-schooled.

We have come around full cycle to the ecological perspective on education and communities introduced early on in this chapter. This is a perspective that forces inspection of the system — each of its working parts and the relationships among all parts essential to the healthy functioning of the whole. It is a perspective that requires the formulation of norms or standards of good health. In seeking to understand the present malfunctioning, we create a mental picture of an ecosystem functioning to perfection against which to appraise both the parts and the whole. We need have little interest in whether one system is functioning better than another. Such a comparison tends to lead to misplaced satisfaction with the one working better even when it, too, is functioning poorly.

There are no good operating models of the educative community. Consequently, there are no apprenticeships through which tomorrow's community builders can learn simply by observing today's. An attempt at such mimicry would be akin to the traditional custom of yesterday's physicians passing along to neophytes the practice of letting blood. Although apprenticing will not suffice, it is equally apparent that business as usual on the part of our university-based professional schools will not suffice either. Much of what goes on in them appears better suited to the well-being of the incumbents than to the health of the community beyond.

I have been using the word *community* in two senses: first, to convey the conventional notion of the geographic entity, such as a section of a city, with which dwellers identify, and second, as a metaphor for an institution, such as a school, or for something as comprehensively embracing as a nation — or even the present whole of civilization. We need to understand and learn to live productive, satisfying lives in communities as small as the family and as large as the universe. The educative process required is one of self-understanding and self-transcendence.[25] In this, it helps a great deal to have understanding, caring, well-educated teachers who have successfully navigated several of life's significant rites of passage.

8

Toward Centers
of Pedagogy

Outcomes are not simply reducible to the billiard-ball interaction
of individuals. . . . Institutions . . . embody historical trajectories
and turning points. History matters because it is path dependent:
what comes first . . . conditions what comes later. Individuals may
"choose" their institutions, but they do not choose them under
circumstances of their own making. . . .[1]

　　　　　　　　　　　　　　　　　—Robert D. Putnam

This book is primarily about the teacher education side
of educational renewal. (Remember that "teacher education" is convenient shorthand for "the education of educators." The terms are used interchangeably.) Until recently,
educational reform eras have focused narrowly on schools; they
have ignored other agencies in the educational ecology, referring only occasionally to the importance of teachers and even
more rarely to their education. Similarly, the less frequent attention to the reform of teacher education has referred only ob-
liquely to schools, if at all, and ignored the larger community
ecosystem.

　　　As I stated earlier, my colleagues and I came out of a
project directed to school improvement in the League of Cooperating Schools (1966–1972) and a comprehensive study of schooling (1975–1983) convinced of both a natural connection between the condition of schools and that of the education of
educators and its absence. Our study of the education of educators (1985–1990) strengthened the dual elements of that conviction. But the conviction was already strong enough in 1985

235

to motivate our launching, through the Center for Educational Renewal, a long-term initiative directed to the simultaneous renewal of schooling and the education of educators.

Our perceptions were agreeably reinforced by two significant reports appearing in 1986, referred to in Chapter Four—that of the Carnegie Forum on Education and the Economy and that of the Holmes Group. Both effectively joined the reform of schooling and of teacher education in looking toward tomorrow's schools and tomorrow's teachers. Nonetheless, the concept of simultaneous renewal took hold slowly. Policymakers continued to be caught up in reform focused exclusively on schools; teacher education remained at the periphery. Teacher educators continued to address their programs as though suspended somewhat above and aloof from the furor over schools. The many future teachers we interviewed, all far along in their preparation programs, were only dimly aware of national and state initiatives and leaders in school reform.

From our new Center for Educational Renewal at the University of Washington, we sought simultaneous renewal through the encouragement of school-university partnerships. In Chapter Four, I described the genesis of this program. By April 1986, ten such partnerships in ten states constituted the new National Network for Educational Renewal (NNER).

Although the mission statement to which all ten presumably were committed emphasized rather repeatedly the simultaneous involvement of schools and universities in the intended renewal process, the lens of collective vision focused on the school side. It was assumed that the universities would participate in school renewal, but few minds grasped the intended duality, particularly with respect to the education of educators. Once again, the noblesse oblige view of university responsibility to the schools, especially in regard to the research knowledge to be carried to their problems, came to the surface. In fact, the school administrators actively involved in the creation and subsequent support of a given partnership saw this as the only role likely to be both of interest to the university and within its capability — and were critical of what they perceived. On the university side, there was little recognition of a possible role for school personnel in the preparation of teachers and principals beyond the giving of some practical advice. Certainly, they were not to participate in any final decisions. The "simultaneous renewal of schooling and the education of educators" was catchy rhetoric in the mission of the NNER, but implementation largely omitted the university partner.

From Research to Development

Completion of our study of the education of educators, the trilogy of books reporting this inquiry, and the major components of a renewal agenda in 1990 injected new substance into the mission of the NNER rather abruptly. Whereas previously there had existed a state of "open season" with respect to school reform, there had been no equally visible catch-hold points for the reform of teacher education. The nineteen postulates provided these; most drew attention to the need not only for simultaneous renewal but also for the necessary involvement of the arts and sciences. There was now an agenda that embraced the major components of the "simultaneous renewal" initiative.

There is a powerful lesson here for educational improvement. General exhortations to change, restructure, reform, redesign, or whatever do not produce much in the form of concerted, cumulative accomplishment. The several networks of schools referred to in Chapter Seven have improvement agendas, some of them quite precise. Absent an agenda, the outcomes of initiatives begun are shaped by the legacies of institutional history and the politics brought into play when present states of equilibrium are threatened. But institutional commitment to an agenda begins to shape the new identities, roles, and activities of at least some of the key actors in line with their perception of the mission. That is no guarantee of successful outcomes, of course. But without the agenda, institutional legacies and politics will block any outcomes beyond perhaps a slightly altered state of equilibrium (minor adjustment being the price of compromise).

Some of the partnerships in the NNER had made some progress toward the mission of simultaneous renewal prior to

238   Educational Renewal

1990. Most had not. Given particularly the omnipresence of the postulates in the expectations then perceived by and for members as new or in a new light, it was now very difficult to ignore the dual intentionality of renewal. Those who saw the duality of the mission as new had not perceived it, apparently, in the initial mission to which they had made a commitment. Some of the members who saw it in a new light were prepared to move ahead; others either did not have a university commitment to their partnership sufficient to address the renewal of teacher education or had already committed a good deal of attention to their teacher education programs independent of the partnership (and did not wish to tackle the education of educators anew). In effect, ambiguity in the earlier agenda of simultaneous renewal had been cleared up sufficiently to trigger reappraisal on the part of most members of the NNER with respect to relevance of the agenda to them. I consider this to be healthy and further evidence of the importance of a rather clearly defined agenda when individuals and institutions are considering commitment to educational improvement initiatives of considerable magnitude.

My colleagues and I in the Center for Educational Renewal were anxious to move from our research into a phase of development that would build into school-university collaborations the conditions we believed necessary to robust programs for the education of educators—in other words, the conditions set forth in the postulates. Prior discussion with executive directors of the members of the NNER had revealed the interest and readiness of some of the partnerships to participate in the development phase; but because most of the universities in these partnerships were flagship research institutions, that sample was rather limited. Although the capability of doing research on educational improvement had been a major criterion in the initial application and selection process, our research had been into six different types of institutions of higher education that prepare teachers. We thought it important to seek a similarly representative sample for the next phase of the simultaneous renewal initiative.

Actually, the desirability of broad representation had been perceived more than a year before we published the results of our research. We had joined in creating a committee representing the American Association of Colleges for Teacher Education (AACTE) and the Education Commission of the States (ECS) to develop a plan of action. The intent that emerged was to invite a small cadre of from six to eight settings to work with us on the agenda of renewal. This proved to be unnecessary.

Jointly, we announced this plan at a press conference in November 1990 without revealing the identity of the short list from which we planned to invite an initial group of pilot sites. But to our surprise and delight, serious inquiries about joining this proposed venture began to trickle and then to pour in. We found ourselves having to develop criteria for screening the formal applications we subsequently received, even though the timeline for providing information and answering questions pertaining to commitment and ability to produce was very short. We chose eight settings. Adequate representation of research-oriented universities came from several of the most mature school-university partnerships in the existing NNER.

The committee referred to above was interested in a much broader attempt at the renewal of teacher education than was offered by this pilot effort. Its members saw the need to promote a greater sense of urgency in regard to the teacher education component of school improvement and to the joining of the K-12 system and higher education in collaborative efforts. In addition, it sought to work toward the development of supportive state policies, as emphasized by the postulates. The Agenda for Teacher Education in a Democracy was born, led by the Education Commission of the States and supported by a grant from the Southwestern Bell Foundation.

Three important sets of activities characterized the first eighteen months of this Agenda. First, about half the states were successful in receiving mini-grants for purposes of holding conversations on simultaneous renewal among all the major groups of players.[2] Second, in the eight states where Agenda pilot sites are located, there was an extended period of dialogue among state officials, presidents and deans of the pilot settings, and others. This had very positive effects on the troublesome issues surrounding congruence and incongruence between state regula-

tions and institutional efforts to redesign programs. At the end
of the first phase of this important work, each of the eight sites
received $25,000 from the Southwestern Bell grant. Third, the
Agenda has been built into the annual meetings of both the
AACTE and the ECS in such a way as to provide a continuing
forum, once again involving representation from most of the
key groups of players.

Meanwhile, the Center for Educational Renewal was concentrating its resources and energies primarily on the changing, expanding National Network for Educational Renewal.
Seven additional settings were brought in, expanding the total
to fifteen, with about half of these from the original network
of school-university partnerships. At the time of this writing,
negotiations with several additional sites are ongoing. Given the
degree to which the intent of representing the diverse array of
teacher-preparing settings in the United States will have been
met by adding these potential members, there are no current
plans for further expanding the NNER, although expansion is
not ruled out. Rather, and to the extent that resources permit,
energy will be devoted to a number of settings that have expressed interest in some kind of affiliation and to the continuing relationship with the AACTE and the ECS in the Agenda
for Teacher Education in a Democracy.

Centers of Pedagogy

The story of the Smith Center of Pedagogy, which is the core
of Chapter Nine in *Teachers for Our Nation's Schools,* is a fable in
two senses. First, it is a fable because the institutions and their
people are fictitious. (However, although I tried very hard to
come up with a somewhat generic fictitious name for the university involved, I learned later, to my chagrin, that there is a
Northern State.) The geographic setting and the key actors are
composites of places and people I know or have known. And
although I had no specific person or composite of persons in
mind when creating Dean Harriet Bryan, nearly all of her experiences in seeking to effect change are real. I had them or know
well others whose experiences were similar to hers.

The second sense in which the Smith Center narrative is a fable is that major changes in the ways things are done in teacher education occurred with uncommon speed in its pages. There was much conversation, to be sure — but not endless talk without action. The seven-year time span during which Northern State moved from sunsetting the existing programs to graduating its first class from the new may seem long, but it would be nearly impossible to shorten it (and few settings would be able to proceed this quickly).

In retrospect, I have some regrets about having added the words "A Fable" to the title of that chapter — "Renewal at Northern State University: A Fable." They caused some readers — quite a few, I have learned — to more or less write off the possibility of doing what Dean Bryan and her colleagues in the university and the schools accomplished. Some wrote off Superintendent Peter Junger as unreal and President Rosemary Scott's support and suggestions as unlikely. Although I was endeavoring to highlight desired expectations for individuals in these leadership roles, I did not intend for their behavior to be seen as unreal or unlikely — as "fabulous." I have had the good fortune to know a few individuals for whom Peter Junger and Rosemary Scott are the prototypes.

I do not know how much labeling the chapter a fable contributed to the almost complete initial omission of the renewing scenario and Harriet Bryan's role in the discussions of our agenda, both within and beyond the NNER. I had intended the chapter to be a sort of mapping of the territory to be encountered in simultaneously renewing schooling and the education of educators. Harriet was the intended medium for portraying actions to be taken, debris likely to be encountered, and pitfalls to be anticipated (and, if possible, avoided).

My many ensuing conversations with deans of education and other leaders in the member settings of the NNER suggest two major explanations for what appeared at first to be a kind of rejection or denial. First, the agenda of simultaneous renewal is daunting, as many people told me at the outset. There was considerable skepticism about our being able to bring it off, with criticism directed particularly to the university side and to deans of education. The conception of a center of pedagogy, or something similar, as a vehicle for bringing together partner schools and elements of the arts and sciences and SCDEs presents a formidable challenge. A trajectory of change is called for that runs counter to a long history of separation and considerable hostility among the three major components of teacher education programs.

The second explanation pertains to the ecology of institutions discussed in Chapter Seven. Universities and the units within them are no less protective of their equilibrium than are schools. Indeed, the closer attachment of schools to their communities, their more open borders, and the degree to which criticism of schools is so often in fashion conspire to make these institutions somewhat less threatened by and more resilient in the face of major proposals for change. But the decade of the 1990s stirred winds of change and troubled waters in higher education. A turning inward defensively against attacks on undergraduate teaching, a "publish or perish" syndrome run amok, and the indifference of universities to the lower schools were followed by a turn of the wheel and a shift in direction of the huge academic tanker. Not a major shift, mind you, but a few degrees on the compass.

For SCDEs, however, the storm warnings were much stronger. The route to be taken was not at all clear, but the words "teacher education" and "schools" appeared often on the muddied pages of directives. What had become apparent to us in our research and was confirmed repeatedly in our associations with members of the NNER is the magnitude of the differences among teacher-preparing institutions. Though differences in institutional type are quite apparent, these are compounded by unique histories and contexts within and across types. As Robert Putnam points out, "Individuals may 'choose' their institutions, but they do not choose them under circumstances of their own making."[3]

It should not surprise us, then, that deans of education reading Chapter Nine of *Teachers for Our Nation's Schools* and committed to the NNER agenda would turn not to Harriet Bryan but to their own contexts for clues as to where to begin. The dean of a college of education in a major research-oriented university, with perhaps half of the budget largely in the hands of professors with grants, is in a situation quite different from that of the head of an SCDE with a primary commitment to teacher education and a budget to match. Although threats to the existing state of equilibrium will bring forth a predictable pull and tug of political struggle in each, the circumstances and nature of this struggle will be unique. The wise leader pays much attention to this context. The fictitious experiences of Dean Harriet Bryan may offer both encouragement and commiseration down the road a piece, but they provide no map at the outset.

We have seen from the opening pages of this book and throughout that a center of pedagogy, whether a metaphor or an entity, involves three rather distinct groups of players equally, and I have recommended the representation of all three from the start. But there must be a beginning somewhere—the launching of an initiative. Although SCDEs provide only one of the three player groups, they are commonly seen as the major one—indeed, when it comes to blame, the only one. Given my background as a professor and dean of education and the network of associations such experience has provided, looking to heads of SCDEs as catalysts in creating the National Network for Educational Renewal came naturally. It was directly from these heads or at their instigation, with a few exceptions, that initial inquiries and subsequent applications derived. And it was they and their immediate associates, such as associate deans or directors of teacher education, who took the initiative in the home settings.

When representatives of another group were included near the beginning of the conversation, these almost invariably were from the schools, not the arts and sciences. An SCDE engaged in teacher education always has connections with schools, if only in regard to the placement of student teachers, while direct connections with the arts and sciences departments can be, and often are, almost nonexistent. We found the so-called all-campus councils or committees on teacher education to be almost always rather weak, nonpenetrating symbols rather than vehicles of genuine collaboration.

The required evidence of commitment to this tripartite alliance for simultaneous renewal of schools and all segments of university-based teacher education was a condition of admission to the NNER. Even so, when serious discussion of the meaning of the postulates got under way, for example, it rarely involved more than the faculty of the SCDE. Only in a few settings were the other partners involved, and again, the other participants were almost exclusively from the schools. (This broadening to include schools was most likely to occur when the setting was one of the school-university partnerships launched during the 1985–1990 phase of development.)

Although something closer to full-scale three-partner conversation would have been gratifying, what occurred is predictable and understandable. Anything markedly different would have run counter to history, custom, and context. Even within their own houses, the three groups of players are not that accustomed to sustained inquiry, potentially involving philosophical disagreement and self-criticism. Though each of the three "families" may be contentious within itself, serious conversation about how each runs its business (and how it *should* do so) is less threatening "in private" than when strangers are present. It is not at all surprising that the heads of the SCDEs — with more knowledge than most of their colleagues about the demands of the agenda, largely because they had been meeting regularly as a group — would seek first of all to get their own houses in order. Although I still hold to the hypothesis that there would be faster progress in the long run if all three groups were fully involved almost from the beginning, I fully appreciate the perspective of these leaders.

What became evident early on, however, was a very uneven level of understanding, within and among settings, regarding the substance of the agenda. The Center for Educational Renewal enjoyed grants to strengthen the school-university connection, but none focused on the connection of the arts and sciences to the whole — a connection that was particularly weak. Compounding the problem, severe budget restrictions at participating institutions cut into resources for conferences at those sites and for travel to activities that the Center would have provided if participants had been able to get to them. The Center sought to compensate for this unfortunate development by increasing services from its senior associates to the settings. But it was evident that something further needed to be done to increase the number of well-informed individuals in leadership roles at the sites.

We sought to address this problem by creating in 1992 a new independent, nonprofit entity, the Institute for Educational Inquiry, that would be lean, flexible, and capable of quick action. We did not want to complicate the agenda of the Center for Educational Renewal, growing in stability and recognition, by adding to it. We had in mind for the Institute two major purposes: inquiry into the nature of tomorrow's schools, communities, and teacher education (the subject matter of Chapter Seven of this book), and the immersion of leaders and potential leaders from all three of the groups necessary to centers of pedagogy in such a way as to increase their competence in advancing the agenda. A grant from the Philip Morris Companies Inc. launched the Leadership Program, enabling the recruitment of three successive cohorts of Institute associates (nominated by their respective settings), each participating in four week-long sessions and other activities spread over an entire year. The result is a small cadre of very knowledgeable individuals from the three critical partner groups in most of the settings constituting the NNER. This program, highly acclaimed by those closely connected with it (whether or not participants), may prove to be one of the most powerful contributors to full tripartite participation in the agenda to which each site is committed.

The creation of a new setting — a center of pedagogy — embracing a responsible faculty from three traditionally separated entities of schooling and higher education, threatens established structures and customs. The Center for Educational Renewal has not pushed for such a setting at participating sites but uses the concept frequently in the metaphorical sense described in Chapter One. More and more, however, the problem of ill-defined borders confounds — and is being *seen* as confounding — cumulative conversation. In setting up a meeting, it is difficult to know who should be invited, for example. Participants disappear; new ones appear. Increasingly, there are productive attempts to identify and keep together the same group of players.

The most significant progress being made on the campuses with which we are working is in the area of identifying and bringing into teacher education clusters of partner schools. It is becoming clear to participants that, due to the investment, there simply must not be a changing array. We have seen how difficult it is to renew schools. Simultaneous renewal of partner schools and teacher education is even more difficult. At the time of this writing, it is fair to say that a two-way collaboration is coming along rather nicely, with settings spread out on a continuum in regard to both the number of partner schools involved and the depth of penetration in the joining.

As suggested above, a strong force in bringing the arts and sciences into the three-part relationship is the leadership program described above. An increasing number of professors in these departments, some in administrative roles, are deeply steeped in the concepts. The presence of several of these at a recent conference deliberately designed to involve all three groups was a considerable asset in moving the dialogue forward.

Although the arts and sciences departments are so widely recognized for their role in teacher education that some critics see little need for anything else in a teacher's preparation, it is the school side of the collaboration that attracts financial support. The Center for Educational Renewal has received more funds to support attention to partner schools than for anything else. Similarly, several settings in the NNER have been successful in securing grants for moving ahead in this area. Some have had part of their budgets protected for this purpose during the cutting process generally suffered. I have had to go into detail in seeking funding of the arts and sciences component, but mere mention of the partner school component virtually carries the day when I am seeking support for it. Clearly, we still have a considerable distance to go in advancing the cause of simultaneous renewal in educational improvement.

Several of the settings are quite far down the road in accepting the idea of a center of pedagogy and probably would move quite quickly to implement such a center if there were funds sufficient to ease the strain of simultaneously designing the tripartite venture and sunsetting existing teacher education programs. The severity of budget cuts has virtually ruled out the tactic of "borrowing on retirements": hiring assistant professors a few years prior to retiring full professors so as to provide overlap during the bulge created by a period of conducting both sets of programs simultaneously — a tactic that Dean Bryan was able to employ at Northern State. Here lies a strategically significant opportunity for private philanthropy — the provision of at least partial support until new programs are phased into existing budgets.

No single setting in the National Network for Educational Renewal has as yet put all parts of the agenda into an integrated whole. All are exemplary in some component or components. Several, increasingly aware of the need to establish clear borders in regard to who (and what) is involved and potentially involved, are well on the road toward establishing a center of pedagogy. They would have been further along had not the rounds of institutional budget cuts occurred.

Ohio's Miami University, for example, has gone beyond metaphor in creating the Institute for Educational Renewal. Within its compass, the university and twelve schools and their surrounding communities are joined as equal partners. Although each of these "school communities" is regarded as a village with its own context, characteristics, and challenges, all are joined with the thirteenth partner, the university, in a shared vision. The twelve are in eight communities — four within Cincinnati. The university side includes the school of education and allied professions, the college of arts and sciences, and the school of fine arts. The Institute's member villages are engaged selectively in a variety of interrelated areas, including pre-service and continuing education of human service professionals, school curricula, assessment and evaluation, and research and dissemination. The overall mission is akin to that described for educative communities in Chapter Seven.

Each NNER setting is pushing forward with a particular part of the agenda while endeavoring to keep the whole in view and the other major components moving—to combine equilibrium and a tolerable degree of disequilibrium. In the next section of this chapter, I revisit the essential conditions of robust programs that join university and school efforts in simultaneous renewal. This time, however, I refer selectively to NNER settings to illustrate progress with the agenda.

There are three kinds of risks here. First, in being illustrative rather than comprehensive, I single out a setting while simultaneously ignoring other settings equally far along. Some excellent examples are necessarily omitted. Second, I freeze in time situations that are necessarily fluid and changing. Third, in drawing attention to a setting, I may prompt a rash of inquiries and visits. I referred earlier to the publicity that can endanger the health of an institution and to visits that are premature for both the visited and the visitor. For the former, there are cycles of equilibrium and disequilibrium that can be affected by (and baffle) the visitor. For the latter, there is the need for much inquiry prior to visiting at all.

It is essential to remember in what follows that I probably could have used any one of several settings as illustration. I extend my apologies to those left out. Succeeding pages are intended to depict challenges and progress, not provide an inventory of all the good things going on in the settings constituting the National Network for Educational Renewal.

Putting the Conditions in Place

At the time of this writing, there are fifteen settings in thirteen states in the National Network for Educational Renewal; seven of these were in the original NNER configuration. By the time this book is published, there probably will be two or three more. The seven school-university partnerships have had a much longer time to establish this part of the necessary tripartite collaboration. Most of the other eight had established a variety of connections with schools and school districts but the agenda of simultaneous renewal was essentially new. Each setting now consists of a college or university (a consortium setting consists of five institutions of higher education) and a clutch of schools in various stages of becoming partner schools. We will see in what follows that most progress during the year or two since all fifteen committed to the agenda has been in the arena of school-university linkages.

The Center for Educational Renewal seeks to advance the whole by making its staff available to the sites for conferences with groups and individuals, hosting quarterly meetings of site directors, and sponsoring a variety of meetings for representatives of the three groups of players in each setting. It publishes and distributes a newsletter, a bulletin devoted to analyses and reports of progress, and an Occasional Paper series in which major topics, many of them research-based, are discussed at some length.

The Institute for Educational Inquiry seeks to leverage the NNER agenda in two major ways: inquiry into what the future holds for schools, communities, and the education of educators and the leadership training program already described. It publishes a Work in Progress series of papers devoted primarily to the fundamental concepts underlying the initiative in educational renewal to which the Center, the Institute, and the National Network are committed.

Although the array of settings constituting the NNER is very diverse, with each setting unique in its history and context, the conceptual underpinnings are transcendental. There is at times a strong desire for deans of education or executive directors of school-university partnerships, for example, to meet with their job-alike colleagues. But the prevailing norm is recognition of the benefits to be obtained from the diversity represented in the whole. The commonness of mission and grounding principles overshadows uniqueness of applicability from setting to setting. It is the sharing of these and the continued unfolding of a common agenda that drive the initiative and shape reflection, conversation, and action.

Conceptual Underpinnings

The educational arena is not devoid of ideas. Indeed, there is a glut. Perhaps it is the overload that makes it so difficult for ideas to penetrate sufficiently to make a difference in educational practice. Or perhaps the time and energy required to translate potentially useful ideas into practice create a lack of confidence in them so that other ideas become a kind of distraction. At any rate, the odds appear to be against long-term, cumulative improvement efforts guided by close adherence to a set of educational concepts or principles.

Educational renewal suffers also from the degree to which individualism characterizes the workplace in both schools and higher education. In some settings, cooperation in learning among students is regarded as borderline cheating. In higher education, there is more certain reward for individual research and publication than for group efforts. In teacher education programs, the socialization process favors individualism. Ironically, the literature of educational improvement favors group processes. But groups have a terrible time bringing intellectual rigor to these processes.

Years of studying and seeking to effect educational change were behind us when the Center for Educational Renewal launched the initiative described here. Consequently, we were acutely aware that its conceptual underpinnings would be competing for attention in a crowded forum, particularly in an era of reform still ongoing. We were also aware that serious faculty discussion of the mission of teacher education and the postulates put forward in *Teachers for Our Nation's Schools* and the normative arguments put forward in *The Moral Dimensions of Teaching* could not be anticipated as the norm in either formal meetings or coffee shop conversations. It would be necessary to promote the desired discussion as part of the ongoing strategy.

Consequently, one of the conditions to be met by those applying for membership in the NNER was evidence of institutional self-analysis of the degree to which the conditions built into the postulates were or were not being met. Demonstrated commitment of key actors from all three groups of players was also a requirement. Needless to say, there was wide variation among the applications in regard to such matters as involvement and time spent in the conversations we endeavored to encourage dealing with these and other criteria. But the conversations *did* begin, and once begun, they spread. The efforts of the Center and the Institute to promote and extend discussion have already been mentioned. It has been gratifying not only to participate in sustained conversations in many different kinds of settings but also to learn that groups in institutions beyond the NNER were in various ways unpacking the postulates.

Earlier in this chapter, I referred to the importance of institutional history and context in the initiation of change and the distinctive differences among members of the NNER. It should not surprise us that the Montclair State College context was fertile ground for the kinds of conversations we hoped would occur early on. For more than a decade before Montclair State became a member, it had pioneered work in the area of critical thinking as a means of organizing curricula and delivering instruction in teacher education. The existence of a Clinical Schools Network at Montclair State facilitated the inclusion of personnel from the schools in the initial dialogue. Support from the central administration expanded involvement to include all five of the schools that constitute the college. To further enhance knowledge and advancement of the agenda, Montclair State took immediate and subsequent steps to nominate associates for the leadership program of the Institute for Educational Inquiry.

The benefits of this good leadership and readiness to inquire into the ideas driving the agenda have gone beyond Montclair State. They have enhanced the dialogue at meetings of representatives of the fifteen settings and made the institution a visible source of information for other settings in the region. The clear and sustained enunciation of beliefs guiding the work has played a key role in statewide discussions regarding the role of policy for teacher education in New Jersey.[4]

Another familiar obstacle to sustained educational renewal is the degree to which value-based statements of mission are seen as abstractions that have little to do with practicality. On the contrary, there is something very wrong with conceptual underpinnings, however couched in mission or principle, that cannot readily be translated into decisions, action, and evaluation.

The breakdown of the postulates in Chapter Three is deliberately oriented toward gathering evaluative information about ongoing programs, the results of which have implications for decisions and actions to be taken. In the Center for Educational Renewal, we make much use of this approach in estimating where we are at a given time in regard to the overall agenda: What is going well and what is not? On the basis of information gathered and analyzed, we make decisions regarding the allocation of resources and the actions to be taken by designated staff members. Without this guiding framework and its use in formative evaluation, we would be indecisive and our actions would be random.

We have evidence of similar use of the postulates in individual NNER settings. One of the most ambitious and comprehensive efforts was initiated by the dean of the college of education at Texas A&M University and carried out by a member of the faculty. He first identified the groups of actors within the university most likely to have influence on or be influenced by the necessary conditions for effective teacher education embedded in each of the postulates. He then identified key questions to be asked of relevant administrators, professors, and students. The relatively large number of individuals interviewed and the range of these interviews produced extraordinarily useful information regarding understanding of the postulates, progress in implementing them, and prospects for the future.[5]

The report pointed very clearly to matters well worth celebrating, but it also pinpointed conditions requiring corrective action over both the short and the long haul. Most of these troubling conditions surfaced because of interview questions centered on the postulates. But the unique experience of being asked for their views in itself elicited responses from students becoming teachers that should be invaluable to those responsible for planning and conducting the programs. All institutions preparing teachers should have such information; surprisingly, few do. One of the nice touches in the report is the reminder that it is moral deliberation and attention to moral principle that provide the most solid footing in journeys of educational renewal.

Institutional Commitment

Applications to the NNER brought with them letters of commitment and support from relevant officials in the institutions and agencies that play a part in the complex business of educating those who staff our schools. Many of these officials are so accustomed to writing letters of support for this or that endeavor that the process is routine. No doubt some knew little about the substance of the letter signed, but subsequent experience has led me to believe that such cursory reflexes were rare.

The kind of information requested in the twelve questions to be answered and documented in the application called for involvement of a variety of individuals and groups. Earlier association with and field visits to the various settings by Center personnel reinforced the validity of claims to commitment. The statewide dialogues referred to earlier — those sponsored by the Education Commission of the States — created awareness beyond the norm among busy people. The kinds of conversations in which colleagues and I participated on our visits to the settings revealed considerable knowledge about the simultaneous reform initiative among university presidents, superintendents of schools, provosts, deans, and state officials. Teacher education has a long way to go before it attains the parity with the education of other professionals that the postulates pinpoint as necessary. But there is no doubt in my mind about the steady growth in recognition and support that most of the settings in the NNER have enjoyed.

The University of Wyoming and the school-university partnership to which it belongs constituted one of the initial group of eight settings. The governor of the state and the president of the university joined the dean of education at the invitational forum in Washington, D.C., that launched our present initiative in November 1990. The newly elected state superintendent of schools gave her strong support from the time of assuming office. The university substantially expanded its relationship with schools by playing a key role in establishing centers for teaching and learning by the fall of 1992 in five partner districts. This was to become a model for joining school and university personnel in the education of cohort groups of students gaining field experiences in these centers and, subsequently, for connecting pre-service education and the continuing education of educators.[6]

Although this powerful joining of the university and the schools in educational renewal could not escape the growing fiscal problems of the state and university, it fared relatively well. In fact, a longer and therefore more costly teacher preparation program was launched as part of this expanded school-university collaboration. The departure of the energetic dean of education who had been a catalyst for innovation and renewal brought forth from superintendents a strong appeal for continuing what was well begun and assurance from the university's president that continuation would play a large part in the context of the search for his successor.

Far to the east of Wyoming, Maine provides another ongoing example of strong commitment and testimony to the critical role of institutional leaders in sustaining long-term programs in educational renewal. I have argued that universities should either take the education of educators for our schools very seriously or get out of the business. The University of Southern Maine and surrounding school districts took the former path, launching the Southern Maine Partnership in 1985. This partnership was one of the original members of the NNER in its first configuration. Today the Extended Teacher Education Program (ETEP) is embedded, in part, in five partnership districts, each an ETEP site for the fifth (or professional) year. Each site has a university and school-based coordinator (a teacher released half-time to do teacher education work) and is governed by a steering committee composed of university and school faculty, the latter serving as adjunct members of the college of education. Behind what exists now are years of working with the concept of partner schools and the restructuring of teacher education within the university. The outward manifestations of success mask the degree to which the familiar tensions of school-university collaboration were here, too, and are perhaps never fully resolved.[7]

The importance of the years of work that went into development of this school-university partnership as a context for dealing with tensions that arise in redesigning teacher education in a renewing mode cannot be overestimated. Nor can be the significance of commitment and support from leaders. The president of the University of Southern Maine walked into a situation that was not of his own making with a background, he frankly admits, that did not prepare him for the role he knew he would have to play in this generally neglected area. He chose to represent his institution (with others) at the orientation conference for the first eight sites in the reconstructed NNER in August 1991. He listened; he asked; he reflected; he contributed to the conversation.

Since then, his attention to the appointment of new deans in the arts and sciences and education has reflected keen interest in and awareness of the Southern Maine Partnership, the ETEP, and the NNER. And he is not working alone. Growing recognition of the role played (and to be played) by teacher education statewide led the chancellor of the University of Southern Maine system to target teacher education as the topic for a major conference that brought together administrators and professors from all campuses. Both he and the president of the Southern Maine campus revealed understanding and keen insight in reporting on the university's commitment to teacher education and the schools at the 1993 summer conference of the Education Commission of the States. As the chancellor said, it required something of great importance to take him from his vacation on the beach during the short Maine summer.

Clear and Protected Borders

The most elusive part of our agenda pertains to what and who are encompassed by a teacher education initiative embracing partner schools, all or portions of an SCDE, and selected professors in the arts and sciences. The issues, possibilities, and potential logistics are ongoing topics in the settings and in the conferences held under the auspices of the NNER. Renewal within each of the major parts is demanding; the agenda of *simultaneous* renewal is particularly daunting. As Lynne Miller, who served for a time as director of both the Southern Maine Partnership and the Extended Teacher Education Program, points out, simultaneous renewal "implies that the two components of the agenda are reciprocal and interdependent, that they are woven from the same cloth. In many ways, the two agendas are connected. And in many ways, they are not. . . . We are challenging deeply held assumptions, long-standing modes of behavior and interaction, and traditional organizational arrangements as they have never been challenged before. We have to learn to live with the tensions that our work provokes and to give up on the notion that they can and should be resolved."[8]

It probably is wise that most of the settings continue to circle the terrain, looking for ways to move forward in a reasonably organized fashion without closing down the options. Most of the efforts to date have concentrated on the school-university relationship and the need to integrate this into the SCDE. For the most part, close SCDE–arts and sciences linkages have not occurred. At the time of this writing, emphasis on connecting all three of the major components has moved to the top of the NNER agenda.

We have already seen something of the degree to which Miami University has sought to effect a composite of schools and their communities, the school of education and allied professions, and both the college of arts and sciences and the school of fine arts in its Institute for Educational Renewal. The whole represents an incredible array of partners within and connections without.[9] Miami University's effort attempts to bring together under one organizational roof the agencies and programs, including the preparation of school teachers and principals, necessary to community health in a broad ecological sense.

The configuration emerging in the BYU–Public School Partnership, described earlier, is quite different. This long-standing and well-established partnership has demonstrated the elements of a new setting by transcending transitions in top leadership, even though the role of superintendents and deans of education is major and critical. Administrators of the university took advantage of the need to appoint a new dean of education—the fourth since the founding of the partnership in 1984—to engage in formative reevaluation of the direction they had followed for several years. This resulted in strong reaffirmation of and subsequent steps to strengthen the university's capacity in the education of educators. The job definition of the new dean placed him in a position of coordinating the planning and utilization of all contributing elements. Instead of having to go hat-in-hand for resources in the arts and sciences, this education dean has direct access to the key administrators who are members of the planning and decision-making group he chairs. The organizational structure recognizes the importance of this dean's having direct access to both the central administrators who determine the place of educator preparation in the institution's mission and the resources for it.

Within the college of education at BYU, the authority and responsibility of each coordinating council and of each associate dean assigned to it and the functions it represents are clear. A breakdown of the postulates provided the conceptual framework: the buck stops with the dean in seeing to it that the education of professionals in education flies on the institutional mast of commitment (Postulates One, Two, and Three); Postulates Eight, Eleven, and Sixteen are the particular responsibility of an associate dean and a coordinating council; Postulates Four, Five, Six, Seven, Thirteen, and Seventeen fall to another associate dean and council; Postulates Nine, Ten, Twelve, Fourteen, Fifteen, Eighteen, and Nineteen connect closely to the schools and state policies; ultimate responsibility lies with the director of the BYU–Public School Partnership and its governing board.

This is an elaborate structure, but Brigham Young University is a major producer of teachers and administrators for the schools, and the five districts of the partnership embrace over 30 percent of the students enrolled in the elementary and secondary schools of Utah. The various parts of the whole and the relationships among them have been sorted out in a way that surely is enlightening to individuals who otherwise would know little of the whole house beyond the cubicles in which they work each day. That the postulates proved useful in the process of identifying and sorting out the pieces is exceedingly gratifying.

As our research revealed, there is considerable murkiness inside schools and colleges of education regarding the identity of teacher education. Many SCDEs want to tackle the considerable task of sorting that identity out in their own minds before broadening the effort to include the necessary linkages with the arts and sciences and the schools. The direction in most of the

sites is toward creating some kind of unit that will first cluster
the relevant ingredients within and then reach outward to embrace the contributing elements of the arts and sciences and partner schools — more or less within the image of a center of pedagogy or teacher education. Currently, reaching out to the schools
runs ahead of creating this new entity, as I have noted.

Students

Finding students is not a problem for teacher-preparing settings,
whether within or beyond the NNER. Creating a diverse student population is; I turn to that issue very soon. Another formidable problem is finding ways to sustain quality in the face
of large numbers. Although academic requirements for entering a program and staying there have increased nationwide in
recent years, the numbers have increased, too. One of the conditions not accurately figured into enrollment productions is the
state of the economy. A depressed economy attracts individuals
seeking security of employment; it brings former teachers back
into the market.

The premium placed on quality in the postulates of the
NNER agenda forces partnerships to pay serious attention to
problems of quantity. The guidance to be provided to cohort
groups in the first two years of the program proposed in Chapter Six draws on faculty resources usually reserved for the later,
more formal socialization. Similarly, the establishment of broad-
ened criteria of admissions and a gate adds to the costs. And
for settings with several hundred student teachers scattered about
with cooperating teachers in schools over a large area, pulling
the internship phase into a much smaller network of partner
schools is a challenge. Clearly, the postulates put quality above
quantity, injecting into teacher education the almost unheard
of notions of careful student selection, the involvement throughout of a substantial proportion of professors in addition to other
instructional personnel, a much closer teacher-student relationship than customarily prevails, and enrollment geared to the
availability of necessary resources. Are we ready for this?

The quantity-quality issue is being confronted in one form

or another in nearly all of the NNER settings. The issues are not only those pertaining to state policy and the public purse. Colleges and universities have had little or no experience dealing with the maintenance of quality in teacher education as a top priority. The relatively low cost of producing teachers has helped to offset the high cost of doctoral programs in some institutions. In cutting student numbers, will budgets be trimmed back to adjust to old norms, or will they be retained at present levels (with a higher cost per future teacher)? Will colleagues teaching large classes in general education courses be pleased to see teacher education included among the few programs to get a better deal? What adjustments are the organized teaching profession willing to make if the production of well-qualified teachers should decline in the face of increased attention to high quality? And what of the unions? There will be need for a unique combination of instructional resources of the kind suggested earlier in this book — a development that teacher unions have tended to resist. Will the unions recognize that as long as we continue to place the quantity of supply first, there will continue to be limited opportunities for well-educated, competent teachers? Issues such as these increase the challenges and the tensions for those who engage seriously in educational renewal.

Recruiting more future teachers is not a pressing problem, but recruiting individuals of great promise always will be. Included in a pool scarcely reached are many of promise for whom teaching as a career has received, at most, only passing consideration. Teaching continues to be disproportionately a choice of the middle-class white population. There is a severe (and growing) shortage of black male teacher role models. Efforts across the nation to recruit prospective first-generation college students who might become teachers have been inadequate and relatively unproductive. Many of those who are enrolled cannot afford the extra years it will take to overcome inadequacies in their earlier education. Some men and women from minority groups who have at one time or another considered becoming teachers do not look forward to repeating their school experiences with prejudice in college settings. June Gordon, a former staff member of the Center for Educational Renewal, has documented a litany of deterrents, some of them overlooked in efforts to recruit people of color into teaching (as I noted in Chapter Two).[10]

Chapter Nine of *Teachers for Our Nation's Schools* puts forward the obligation to recruit at each setting a diversity of future teachers comparable to the diversity of the elementary and secondary school student population in the surrounding area. The program put forward here in Chapter Six calls also for field experiences and internships in schools of diverse student bodies for all future teachers. We have put forward both sets of conditions among those to which the NNER settings are committed.

California Polytechnic State University in San Luis Obispo has made valiant efforts in both areas. Recently, it has added to its field resources schools of diverse populations in a district with which it was not formerly engaged. Other settings have found it necessary to make similar moves, replacing the criterion of proximity of schools with the principle of aligning practice with commitment.

California Polytechnic has contributed doubly to the overall effort to recruit more minorities into teaching by developing an exceedingly useful videocassette on diversity in the teaching profession. It is used in this institution's efforts and distributed to the other NNER settings. The video addresses virtually all of the blocks to minority entry into teacher education programs identified in Gordon's research. It is low-key — no impassioned romanticizing of the joys of teaching — in its reliance on the statements of satisfaction coming from teachers who are black or Latino and of other role models who provide serious commentary on the importance of teaching to society.[11]

One of the serious problems we identified in our research is the degree to which students coming to college intending to become teachers are ignored during their freshman and sophomore years and then admitted casually to programs. Benedict College, one of the five colleges and universities constituting the setting commonly referred to as the South Carolina Collaborative, has chosen to celebrate the occasion of students' acceptance into the teacher education program. These students are honored in a special ceremony recognizing their successful achievement of admission, their commitment, and the moral mission of teaching. On an occasion in April 1993, when one of the Center's senior associates visited, the recognition ceremony was attended by students from future-teacher clubs in twelve high schools; most were African-American. If we are to reverse the decline in the diversity of the teaching force, the possible interest of students must be tapped in junior and senior high schools and potential candidates must be carefully nurtured into and through preparation programs.

Program Renewal

It would be silly to think that the new settings envisioned here and referred to as centers of pedagogy would be rising visibly out of educational renewal processes that have been under way for just a few years. Visitors who anticipate such celerity are fantasizing. As Robert Putnam reminds us, we must keep our heads straight regarding the pace of institutional change: "Examined week by week, or month by month, or sometimes even year by year, development in any institution is hard to chart. The rhythms of institutional change are slow. Often several generations must pass through a new institution before its distinctive effects on culture and behavior become clear. Evanescent fads and the vagaries of individual participants obscure deeper trends."[12]

Yet my colleagues and I are at times startled by what we learn about developments in the settings. To have in mind a grand house that will take shape systematically, from foundation to girders to siding to roof and then glorious colors in paint or stain would be a mistake. That is not the way educational renewal takes place. The rhythms are not just slow; they are uneven. At times, during periods of concentration on just one component, it looks as though pieces of the whole have been forgotten entirely.

What follows is a potpourri of developments in some of the settings. If all were combined into one, we would be close to having the house we have envisioned. What startles us most of all is that we often find out in roundabout ways about accomplishments worth celebrating. They tend not to be announced to the sound of bugles; rather, they slip out when a site director is reporting to colleagues at a meeting, appear somewhat casually in a newsletter, or are stumbled over by a member of the Center staff during a visit. Sometimes, when we are about to conclude that part of the agenda is being ignored, reports of progress start coming at us from all sides.

The NNER initiative in the simultaneous renewal of schooling and the education of educators inherited some pluses at the outset, if only because there were criteria embedded in the postulates that interested partnerships had to meet in the selection process. Wheelock College, for example, is now almost alone nationally as an institution with a teacher education mission. Yet the college is deeply committed to the liberal arts and the concept of the teacher as a well-educated member of the community. We are reminded of Abraham Flexner's admonition that "the physician's function is fast becoming social and preventive, rather than individual and curative. Upon him society relies to ascertain and, through measures essentially educational, to enforce the conditions that prevent disease and make positively for physical and moral well-being. It goes without saying that this type of doctor is first of all an educated man."[13]

When Wheelock College turns to curriculum development, the focus is on the educated person who will be a teacher. A full-scale revision of the undergraduate curriculum just prior to the NNER application was regarded by the selection committee as a major asset. I have referred several times to the arts and sciences involvement as the least developed component of the initiative in educational renewal. Not so at Wheelock — and not so in most of the liberal arts colleges we studied, even though, unlike Wheelock, teacher education is not their central mission.

Research-oriented universities, such as the University of Washington, present a quite different situation. Teacher education, now being reexamined on that campus, has been primarily a postbaccalaureate enterprise for years. As a result, the needs of future teachers enter hardly at all into undergraduate curricular considerations. Yet professional schools other than the college of education assert strong claims on general education; they tug and pull on the lower-division years in particular.

Earlier, I put forward the view that many of the young people entering large universities do not choose wisely from the array of course offerings in the major domains of knowledge. The college of arts and sciences at the University of Washington has done several significant things to help. It has established the Freshman Interest Group (FIG) Program, within which groups of twenty to twenty-four freshmen provide mutual support and are guided by advisers in choices about courses, majors, and careers. To further assist this process, the general-studies areas are broken down into divisions (for example, humanities and fine arts), and within each of these, the courses that satisfy general education requirements are described so as to sharpen choice. For example, the title of English 205, "Method, Imagination, and Inquiry," conjures up many possibilities, but the description narrows the focus: "A critical examination of texts ranging from Plato to Faulkner and including works of philosophy, literature, and the history and philosophy of science. The central concept is that collective intellectual life is organized by the notion of inquiry and that all inquiries depend on method and imagination."[14]

The results of this kind of service contribute immensely to the task of developing a recommended pre-education general-studies program for future teachers of the kind suggested in Chapter Six. In addition, the college of education has initiated plans for finding and providing guidance and socializing experiences for students entering the University of Washington with an interest in becoming teachers. This will provide teacher educators the opportunity to be close to these students while they are making choices from among the courses described for the freshman and sophomore years and to provide an orientation to teaching as a career.

Both Metropolitan State College of Denver and Wright State University in Dayton, Ohio, provide the NNER not only urban contexts (not the only ones, of course) but also great potential because of their orientation to context. The former has a history of not merely sending student teachers out into schools but sending faculty members with them. The Colorado Partnership for Educational Renewal included Metropolitan State from the beginning and was one of the initial school-university partnerships in the NNER. Thus the concept of partner schools as an integral part of simultaneous educational renewal was not at all new. The president viewed the teacher education initiative represented by affiliation with the NNER as very much in Metropolitan's character and the best interests of the institution, while a new dean perceived the whole to be in concert with his plans for the school of professional studies. The expansion of the Colorado Partnership over the past several years to include several institutions of higher education appears to be paying off in the development of a consortium (somewhat like the one in South Carolina, mentioned earlier) and the prospect of a reconfigured setting in the NNER that would include these as well as Metropolitan State.

Wright State has been a leader in defining for universities of this type a distinctive metropolitan role that departs from the traditional separation of town and gown. It also endeavors to raise the importance of both teaching and research but directs its research toward metropolitan problems and issues. The campus is home to a new journal, *Metropolitan Universities,* which is oriented to this mission (as are a couple of educational journals produced on campus). Instead of a school or college of education, there is a college of education and human services, in which both halves of this appellation together bespeak a mission increasingly approaching that of educative communities described in Chapter Seven.

An incredibly comprehensive planning effort embracing representatives of all three major components of the NNER initiative preceded Wright State's membership application. Once again, we saw the strong hands of both the president and the provost pushing forward—sometimes to the point of wanting the already energetic dean to bring the planning process to a head even more quickly. Wright State's effort to embrace schools has been particularly encompassing.

If there is anything approximating exemplary status across many of the sites of the NNER, it is a virtual renaissance in dialogue with school districts and schools. And this is the arena where both the Center and the Institute have been able to provide the most help and expertise, ranging from the work of senior staff members at sites, to regional conferences, to part of the curriculum of the workshops for Institute associates, to publications. I could use almost any setting to illustrate this dialogue, whether it is Texas A&M reaching far out to include urban school connections or Brigham Young University literally building itself into the infrastructure of the five surrounding school districts.

The Hawaii School/University Partnership is unique in several significant ways. The state itself is unusual in its centralization of educational authority into a single school board, accompanied by considerable decentralization through the local role of administrators and specialists assigned by the department of education to individual districts. Consequently, both the state and the districts are now partners in a collaboration that embraces not only the University of Hawaii but also the highly influential Kamehameha Schools of the Bishop Estate. From the time of his appointment, the dean of the college of education has exerted strong leadership not only in the creation of this unusual, complex partnership but also in aligning his view of the college to the partnership's mission: "To solve collaboratively the major problems related to the education of school-age youth in Hawaii. Special attention is to be given to the educationally disadvantaged who include at-risk and/or minority students."[15]

Dean Dolly of the University of Hawaii is one of that small cadre of education deans prescient enough to see in the early 1980s that the future viability of SCDEs was dependent upon their ability to connect to the schools and the profession. Most were still fixed upon the model of those beacon schools of education becoming research institutes that had set the pace from the mid 1960s through the 1970s and into the 1980s. Dean Patricia Graham of the Harvard Graduate School of Education was one of these, too. She later wrote, "Any professional school must be in a state of tension with its profession. That tension requires that the professional school be both knowledgeable and concerned about the profession's problems, and that these problems form the heart of the school's agenda. . . . A first vitally important way schools of education can help the schools is to improve the training of teachers."[16]

John Dolly was well on the way to building the foundations of a school-university partnership out of his University of
Wyoming base when he accepted the Hawaii appointment and
began the building there. (His successors at the University of
Wyoming went on to create what has been partially described
earlier.) He recognized both the assets and the liabilities embedded in the Hawaiian context, as did others who were drawn into
the collaboration that steadily took shape over a period of six
years, until the simultaneous renewal of schooling and the education of educators became a functioning reality in both language and deed. There were the kinds of changes in leadership
that threaten not only continuity but the very existence of the
complex initiatives in educational change that are so much political at heart. The relatively long tenure of John Dolly and
several other key leaders, some in changing roles, together with
a mission which so many people understood and internalized,
proved to be of critical importance during times of near-crisis.

The State Context

The National Network for Educational Renewal, in its original
configuration, was focused almost exclusively on the substance
and processes of joining symbiotically two quite different educational cultures—that of the schools and that of institutions of
higher education.[17] Later, the Agenda for Teacher Education
in a Democracy, bringing the American Association of Colleges
for Teacher Education, the Center for Educational Renewal,
and the Education Commission of the States into collaboration,
recognized the importance of the state context. There is no doubt
that the joining of schools and universities and their working
together in simultaneously renewing schools and the education
of educators is the major area of progress to date.[18] In second
place is improvement in the state context, although many aspects
of the relationship to the state with respect to certification, licensure, and accreditation remain unresolved. There is danger,
however, that because the expectations in this area remain low,
a little progress may too easily be exaggerated.

I have already written about the role being played by
Montclair State in helping to clarify state policy in New Jersey,

a state with several years of prior experience in the advocacy of alternative routes to teacher and principal licensing. Recent conversations there between the university and the state have served to broaden the perspective. The Colorado setting has been closely connected to relevant educational developments in that state and is in a good position to influence implementation of the Educators' Licensing Act. Calvin Frazier, a Center senior associate, has represented the Agenda for Teacher Education in a Democracy in dozens of interviews and conferences designed to sort out the characteristics of state policies that would simultaneously encourage creativity in teacher education and satisfy the state's responsibility to the citizens in regard to ensuring quality.

The dual and sometimes internally conflicting role of the state loomed large in the minds of those in settings contemplating membership in the NNER in the early 1990s — a concern that continues. The South Carolina consortium, through its coordinating mechanism, the Center for the Advancement of Teaching and School Leadership, was able to gain not only financial support from the state but also a five-year exemption from mandated program requirements. As part of that agreement, the state sponsors an annual conference on teacher education, with a major part of the agenda devoted to programs in the several settings constituting the consortium.

Relationships with the state are improving elsewhere as well. After devoting many months to the redesign of teacher education at the University of Southern Maine, the group representing both the university and the schools learned that graduates from the new program could not be licensed under existing regulations. A two-year reprieve was granted by the state, however. By the end of this period, the president reported brightly at a conference, the regulations will conform to the university's new model.

Each of the happenings described is in itself cause for celebration — and periodic celebration lubricates renewal. But more important, they are tangible evidences of growing support for collaborative models that bring together traditional protagonists in an atmosphere of seeking what is best for the common weal.

Cultural Transformation

The idea of universities reaching out to schools in order to engage with them in renewing both, rather than merely using them for purposes of teacher education, appeared to catch on slowly after it surfaced in the second half of the 1980s. But then the curve in both conversation and action accelerated sharply. With that acceleration came an increased awareness of how blithely difficulties and complexities are tossed aside by individuals beginning to get on the rhetorical bandwagon but not yet initiated. One needs a few years of experience to become a veteran. Lynne Miller's earlier comments about the tensions created within and between the two cultures reveal the difference between the experienced veteran and the starry-eyed neophyte.

A story that began inside the school of education at the University of Connecticut provides the "real stuff" of cultures collaborating and cultures transforming. On that campus, analysis of the larger context of change in the surrounding society led to a complete redesign of professional educator preparation across all grade levels and teaching disciplines. Central to the restructuring were strong partnerships with school districts representing the diverse, multicultural population of the state. A set of agreements on the necessary conditions of professional preparation was hammered out, translated into program components, and pilot-tested over a period of several years.[19]

Out of the collaboration with school districts emerged professional development centers (PDCs), each unique in location and local culture. Although school personnel and university faculty members join in other program components, it is in these particularly that they work together in shaping new cultures — and in the process contribute to changes in the larger context of higher education and schooling. This shaping occurs through discourse; a culture of inquiry begins to develop. (We have seen in Chapter Seven the degree to which good schools are characterized by dialogue that involves inquiry into their educational business, decisions, actions, and evaluation.) The Connecticut group describes talk focused on such topics as mainstreaming, the development of curricula for global education, alternative teaching methods, and classroom research efforts.[20]

This culture of inquiry increasingly becomes pervasive, not only among teachers, administrators, faculty, and students in each PDC but within the larger context of participating institutions.

There is now an extensive body of literature addressing the absence of what has been described above — most of it focused on schools, but some targeted at universities and teacher education programs. There are now also the results of decades of research and inquiry leading up to strong heuristics and toward a theory of educational improvement in which the development of an inquiring culture is seen to be central to renewal. The Connecticut setting is adding new evidence.

The uniqueness of location and culture sought in the PDCs of the Connecticut collaboration was obtained in the configuration of settings constituting the NNER. This is apparent, of course, in the foregoing descriptions of aspects of what is transpiring in these settings as they engage in simultaneous renewal. A volume edited by Russell Osguthorpe and Carl Harris of Brigham Young University adds to the picture of differing settings taking on quite differently a common element of the NNER agenda — namely, partner schools.[21]

The setting that embraces the University of Texas and its El Paso context added significantly to variability among members of the NNER. The El Paso Center for Professional Development and Technology (El Paso CPDT) took on a very precise educational mission — increasing academic achievement among the region's diverse student populations — and then surrounded it with proposed attention to components of the educational ecosystem most relevant to success (and failure). The CPDT is in itself a unique partnership that joins three school districts, the university, the regional education service center, the El Paso Collaborative for Academic Excellence, and various community agencies. In essence, the CPDT represents both a radical departure from traditional teacher preparation and a broadening of the customarily rather narrow agenda and range of players involved. Because the CPDT is connecting with, rather than merely adding to, the infrastructure already in existence, the serendipity inherent in renewal and innovation is more likely to occur.

In spite of the fact that success will depend heavily on a pulling together of many agencies in a large urban metropolitan area, there is a sharpness to the mission and clarity to the agenda. The goals are not intangibles in future time. They are of the present and speak of putting in place, with the first word in each directing actions to be taken: establish, implement, initiate, disseminate, align, and so on.

Lined up (or being lined up) behind mission are other necessary conditions embedded in the postulates: strong support from the president (who initiated the move to join the NNER), a philosopher dean of the college of education who understands that he must lead (and who enjoys the advantage of having been a vice president) an organizational entity with rather clear borders and a collaborative governance structure, widely shared philosophical underpinnings, attention to upgrading and redesigning instruction through the addition of technology, heavy emphasis on collaborative field-based components in educator preparation, the establishment of strong connections with the state for purposes of influencing regulatory policies, and so on.[22] Financial support from national foundations has been sought and received. All of this has increased the confidence of state policymakers whose actions toward teacher education in the recent past have often been punitive. This positive change in attitude is reflected in the addition of state resources to those coming from the private sector.

Clearly, institutional cultural transformation is taking place in El Paso. It is too early to say what the distinctive effects on the metropolitan and regional culture are likely to be. There is much poverty and low educational attainment among large sectors of the population. There is no doubt, however, that major shifts are occurring in the way the critical core of key actors views the role of educational institutions in the community and perceives what is required in the larger culture for their success. Institutions thrive in healthy communities; healthy communities have healthy institutions.

Reprise

From one perspective, this is still another book in the continuing saga of school reform. But it seeks to broaden the relatively

narrow concentration on schools alone in several significant
ways. First, it adds to growing awareness that better teachers
shape better schools and that schools and programs for the education of educators must be renewed together. Second, preceding chapters put forward the argument that even better teachers
will encounter grave difficulties in fulfilling the educational mission of schools if other agencies, especially the home, fail in their
nurturing, educative role. Consequently, to be successful, initiatives in educational improvement must address, much more
than past initiatives have, the community ecosystem of human
service agencies. And finally, to sustain a robust, renewing, democratic society, communities must become increasingly educative in ways extending beyond schools.

The central thesis is that schools must be centers or cultures of inquiry, renewing themselves continuously by addressing
self-consciously the total array of circumstances constituting their
business — and in this way become good. To become *very* good,
schools must place education at the heart of renewal, vastly
broadening their instructional practices and rejuvenating their
curricula. This necessitates far more effective, comprehensive
educator preparation programs than we now have. And these
are possible only by closely linking schools and universities in
the simultaneous process of renewal described throughout these
pages.

I have proposed for this huge task a center of pedagogy
characterized by the necessary conditions embedded in nineteen
propositions referred to as *postulates*. In this volume, I carry on
from Center for Educational Renewal research on teacher education and from the several reports that emerged from it, merg-
ing the findings with those of earlier research on the nature of
schools. This merger also resulted in the initiative in the simultaneous renewal of schools and the education of educators being advanced by a clutch of settings constituting the National
Network for Educational Renewal. This concluding chapter
summarizes some of the progress to date in the fifteen current
members of the NNER.

The concept of the center of pedagogy has served as a
vehicle to carry us through the terrain of joining the elements
with the greatest potential for making schools powerfully educa-

tional: the principals and teachers who are the moral stewards and custodians of schools, the professors whose interests and studies focus on educational institutions and processes, and the professors whose careers are directed to understanding and advancing humankind's domains of knowledge and knowing. Members of this group must take responsibility for the necessary process of renewal within their own institutions and in the development of cultures of inquiry that derive from a symbiotic and then an organic joining. With this group as the core, educational renewal broadens to include homes, places of worship, health and human service agencies, and workplaces in the creation of educative communities.

I began with a quote from a Seymour Sarason book — one that appears not to be well known to educators: *The Creation of Settings and the Future Societies* (1972). No body of writing is more relevant to what I have written here than that of Sarason. I could pluck from the shelves in my study any one of the nine or ten of his books lined up there (and these constitute only a small part of the corpus of his seminal work) and quote from it to embellish my narrative.

Seymour Sarason and his two coauthors were far ahead of their times in 1962 when they addressed a book largely to the irrelevance of teacher education to the tasks of teaching in schools. [23] In the revised 1986 edition, they began the preface with the following comment on the 1962 version:

> In 1962 we knew that a book with the major thesis that teacher education was, at best, irrelevant to classroom life and the culture of the school and, at worst, harmful to the future teacher, would not sit well with many people in the educational community. Furthermore, our assertion that the preparation of teachers was an *unstudied* problem — in the sense of systematic study of the relationship between preparation and the realities of the classroom *and* the school system — seemed both unkind and unfair to generations of theorists and researchers, let alone to those who were responsible for preparing others for a teaching career. [24]

In the years following publication of the first edition, the situation deteriorated. Teacher education remained not only remote from school and classroom and aloof from growing concern over the quality of schooling; it also fell further from grace in the major research universities. The second edition turned out to be among the several major reports of that year addressing at long last the hiatus between teacher education and the schools documented by Sarason and his associates a quarter of a century earlier. They concluded this revised edition with a call for the kind of research that would help shift the controversy over teacher education from the realm of opinion to that of scientific inquiry.

Sarason turned once again to this theme in a book published in 1993. Even more directly than before, he connects conceptually teacher education and the schools, describing the latter in the context of severe social problems to be addressed. He warns against indulging in fantasy of the kind represented by "America 2000" and concludes with a call for radically changing teacher education programs so that educators "will be better prepared to cope with and prevent some of the untoward consequences of . . . present realities."[25]

Seymour, good friend, it's been a long haul through rough terrain, much of it mapped by you. In pages of your book, I sense a note of cautious optimism. The writing of this book has brought me to a similar point, largely because of what our colleagues are doing in the fifteen settings constituting the National Network for Educational Renewal. Dare we be more than *cautiously* optimistic?

Notes

Chapter One

1. S. B. Sarason, *The Creation of Settings and the Future Societies* (San Francisco: Jossey-Bass, 1972), p. 272.
2. J. Dewey, letter to the Board of Trustees of the University of Chicago, 1896.
3. Dewey, letter to the Board of Trustees.
4. Z. Su, "Teacher Education Reform in the United States (1890–1986)," Occasional Paper no. 3 (Seattle: Center for Educational Renewal, College of Education, University of Washington, 1986).
5. A. Flexner, *Medical Education in the United States and Canada* (New York: Carnegie Foundation for the Advancement of Teaching, 1910).
6. M. Buchmann, "Reporting and Using Educational Research: Conviction or Persuasion?" in J. I. Goodlad (ed.), *The Ecology of School Renewal*, Eighty-Sixth Yearbook of the National Society for the Study of Education, part 1 (Chicago: University of Chicago Press, 1987), p. 173.
7. M. William Youngblood, a senior attorney in the McNair Law firm in Charleston, South Carolina, sent me what follows. After summarizing our findings from the Center's study of the education of educators, he adroitly shifts to a picture of what teacher education should and could be characterized by, combining into a single paragraph some of the necessary conditions embedded in our postulates.

275

I have shortened his statement only slightly (by dropping some specific references to South Carolina).

My first response, as a layman, to John Goodlad's most recent book, *Teachers for America's* [sic] *Schools,* is that the prescriptions contained in it are a purist's prescription for a very impure world.

The Existing Paradigm

- If, because of the restrained status of women in the 19th Century, moving to the rapid growth and bureaucratization of schools in the second half of the 20th Century, teaching is not yet "valued" as a profession in our society; and
- If, nobody (apparently) is demanding successive crops of fresh, professionally trained teachers to enter and renew our schools; and
- If, few of our teacher preparation efforts are pursuing any mission clearly linking teacher preparation to a conception of what teachers could do, at their best; and
- If, the political volatility of education reform prevents a serious and informed inquiry into the simultaneous renewal of schools and education of educators; and
- If, the rewards for faculty members interested in teacher education are for studying teachers, not preparing them; and
- If, research and publication continue to play ever-increasing roles in tenure and promotion decisions; and
- If, prospective teachers, as students, can only assume that distinguished professors of education exist but enjoy no daily association with them; and
- If, teacher education programs rarely have protected budgets; and
- If, our universities have been transformed from teaching enterprises to knowledge producing, research driven enterprises; and
- If, there is not a clear beginning point for students to be welcomed into teacher preparation; and
- If, there is no informal socialization process to transform eager student into reflective practitioner; and
- If, there is no well designed gateway for admission to student teaching; and
- If, the whole system is constrained by misguided regulatory intrusions . . . which constantly change; and
- If, there is a current disjuncture between what happens on university campuses and what happens in collaborating schools, with theory and practice rarely meeting; and
- If, policy makers, opinion makers and the society at large do not understand any of this;

Then, what is it about the existing paradigm that we wish to save?
    In every successful public policy initiative, leaders turn problems into a positive vision and use that vision statement to

raise the public's consciousness of a vital opportunity which we cannot afford to let pass us by.

Doing this we would see South Carolina, in the year 2000, as a state in which teaching is "valued" as a profession and policy makers at all levels are demanding successive crops of fresh, professionally trained teachers prepared to lead the renewal of our schools. All of our teacher education programs have clearly defined mission statements linking teacher preparation to a conception of what teachers can do, at their best; policy makers at all levels engage in a continuing, serious and informed inquiry into ways in which to renew our schools and prepare our teachers simultaneously. The reward structure for faculty members values those who prepare teachers. Our universities are both teaching enterprises and knowledge producing, research driven enterprises. Tenure and promotion decisions reflect this change. The teacher education programs have protected budgets. There is a clear beginning point for students to be welcomed into the teacher preparation programs and a clear socialization process to transform eager student into reflective practitioner. There is a well-designed gateway for admission to student teaching. There is a marked absence of regulatory intrusion and there is a workable system of on-going, meaningful collaboration between the colleges and the schools which is practice based.

The Product

As an economic developer, I see our "product" as children prepared for a responsible participation as citizens and for critical dialogue in the human condition and I would begin shaping a new paradigm with the following points:

1. We cannot compete in world-class competition with a second-rate workforce.
2. We will not produce that workforce unless we revitalize the teaching and learning enterprise simultaneously.
3. It is not education's problem alone, we all have a stake in this one.

Jean Monnet, the father of the European community, once suggested that no change is possible without individual leaders and no change is lasting without institutions. We must craft a vision of teacher education programs which are healthy institutions. . . . These leaders, together, can be transforming leaders who help shape that new vision.

In closing, I am reminded of the warning of the *Old Testament* writer: "Where there is no vision, the people perish." Reflect for a moment on the converse of that: Where the vision is clear (and widely shared) and the will is strong, the people will surely prosper.

M. William Youngblood
McNair Law Firm
Charleston, South Carolina

8. B. O. Smith, *A Design for a School of Pedagogy* (Washington, D.C.: U.S. Department of Education, 1980).

9. S. B. Sarason, K. S. Davidson, and B. Blatt, *The Preparation of Teachers: An Unstudied Problem in Education* (New York: Wiley, 1962; Cambridge, Mass.: Brookline Books, 1986 [rev.]).

10. D. C. Lortie, *Schoolteacher: A Sociological Study* (Chicago: University of Chicago Press, 1975); P. W. Jackson, *Life in Classrooms* (Troy, Mo.: Holt, Rinehart & Winston, 1968). These two books are cited frequently because of the degree to which they illuminate the school (Lortie) and classroom (Jackson) environments that appear to control significantly the daily lives of teachers. To fail to prepare teachers to question and change many of the regularities of schooling is to doom them and their schools to mediocrity. Most teachers are prepared to fit into, not challenge, the norms of schooling. Analyses such as theirs and that of L. M. Smith and W. Geoffrey, *The Complexities of an Urban Classroom* (New York: Holt, Rinehart & Winston, 1968) mark an overdue transition in educational research to include both new methodologies and especially units of selection for study beyond the convention of focusing experimentally on individuals. A good many inquiries have since helped to blaze and open up this important trail.

11. See in particular R. M. Hutchins, *The Higher Learning in America* (New Haven, Conn.: Yale University Press, 1936), p. 114.

12. The reader seeking to understand the historical context of teaching and teacher education in the United States would go well beyond a beginning by reading four of many books available (the first out of print but available in good university libraries): M. L. Borrowman, *The Liberal and Technical in Teacher Education* (New York: Teachers College Press, 1956); G. J. Clifford and J. W. Guthrie, *Ed School* (Chicago: University of Chicago Press, 1988); J. Herbst, *And Sadly Teach* (Madison: University of Wisconsin Press, 1989); and D. Warren (ed.), *American Teachers: Histories of a Profession at Work* (New York: Macmillan, 1989).

13. In his *Organizing Educational Research* (Englewood Cliffs, N.J.: Prentice-Hall, 1964), P. F. Lazarsfeld was most interested in advancing emerging areas of research in the social sciences. But he, like S. B. Sarason in *The Creation of Settings and the Future Societies,* sought understanding of what makes settings function effectively. Lazarsfeld and his students looked particularly to the nature of leadership; Sarason to a core group of continuing worriers.

14. W. Pfaff, *Barbarian Sentiments* (New York: Hill & Wang, 1989), p. 132. Of course, educational settings, like nations, possess such characteristics only to a degree. But both are in trouble if these are only modestly present — and in even deeper trouble if those whose fate is tied up with them perceive these characteristics to be virtually absent.

15. R. J. Schaefer, *The School as a Center for Inquiry* (New York: Harper & Row, 1967); Smith and Geoffrey, *The Complexities of an Urban Classroom.*

16. Two books by Bellah and his colleagues are exceedingly useful in considering the renewing individual, the renewing society, and the interplay between the two: R. N. Bellah and others, *Habits of the Heart* (Berkeley: University of California Press, 1985), and *The Good Society* (New York: Knopf, 1991). Their emphases are essentially moral in nature, whether addressing individuality or commonality. The renewal of schools depends heavily on viewing schools as cultures, but this appears to be an idea whose time is not yet come. Teacher education continues to focus on individuals, paying little attention to the school cultures in which student teachers soon will teach.

17. Lawrence Kohlberg's name is closely associated with his conception of individual morality, but he increasingly turned toward issues of institutional morality as a consequence of human morality; see J. I. Goodlad, "The Moral Dimensions of Schooling and Teacher Education" (fourth annual Kohlberg Memorial Lecture), *Journal of Moral Education,* 1992, *21,* 87–97.

18. Regarding this encyclopedic body of work addressed specifically to teacher education, readers are directed particularly to M. C. Reynolds (ed.), *Knowledge Base for the*

Beginning Teacher (Elmsford, N.Y.: Pergamon Press, 1989); and W. R. Houston (ed.), *Handbook of Research on Teacher Education* (New York: Macmillan, 1990).

19.   L. S. Shulman, "Knowledge and Teaching: Foundations of the New Reform," *Harvard Educational Review*, 1987, *57*, 1–22.

20.   Years of working with school-university partnerships have convinced several colleagues and me that the symbiotic joining of the two cultures, however difficult, is essential to the renewal of both schools and the education of educators, and that the two processes are best undertaken simultaneously. Our experiences have produced a substantial body of writing. See, in particular, K. A. Sirotnik and J. I. Goodlad (eds.), *School-University Partnerships in Action* (New York: Teachers College Press, 1988); J. I. Goodlad, "Linking Schools and Universities: Symbiotic Partnerships," Occasional Paper no. 1 (Seattle: Center for Educational Renewal, College of Education, University of Washington, 1986 [rev. 1987]); R. W. Clark, "School/University Relations: Partnerships and Networks," Occasional Paper no. 2 (1986); C. M. Frazier, "An Analysis of a Social Experiment: School-University Partnerships in 1988," Occasional Paper no. 6 (1988); J. I. Goodlad, "The National Network for Educational Renewal: Past, Present, Future," Occasional Paper no. 7 (1988); C. Wilson, R. Clark, P. Heckman, "Breaking New Ground: Reflections on School-University Partnerships in the NNER," Occasional Paper no. 8 (1989); Z. Su, "School-University Partnerships: Ideas and Experiments, 1986–1990," Occasional Paper no. 12 (1990); J. I. Goodlad and R. Soder, "School-University Partnerships: An Appraisal of an Idea," Occasional Paper no. 15 (1992); and R. W. Clark, P. Heckman, C. Wilson, and R. Soder, "Summary Reports of Site Visits: National Network for Educational Renewal School-University Partnerships, 1989–1990," Technical Report no. 12 (Seattle: Center for Educational Renewal, College of Education, University of Washington, 1991). The place and development of partner schools in this collab-

oration are discussed in J. I. Goodlad, "School-University Partnerships and Partner Schools," *Educational Policy,* 1993, *7,* 24–39.

21. D. G. Imig, memorandum to the Board of Directors, American Association of Colleges for Teacher Education, Feb. 22, 1993.

22. National Board for Professional Teaching Standards, *Toward High and Rigorous Standards for the Teaching Profession* (Detroit and Washington, D.C.: National Board for Professional Teaching Standards, 1989), p. 49.

Chapter Two

1. G. D Fenstermacher, "Where Are We Going? Who Will Lead Us?" Presidential Address at the annual meeting of the American Association of Colleges for Teacher Education, San Antonio, Tex., Feb. 25, 1992.

2. Abraham Lincoln in his Peoria speech of 1854 on the Kansas-Nebraska Act legalizing the expansion of slavery. See R. P. Basler (ed.), *The Collected Works of Abraham Lincoln,* vol. 2 (New Brunswick, N.J.: Rutgers University Press, 1953), p. 275.

3. When I visited teacher education programs early in the 1960s with James B. Conant and his team, one could predict with more confidence than is warranted today that courses in the history and philosophy of education (either singly or separately) would be quite common. Conant recommended — partly at the urging of team members — their continuance. See J. B. Conant, *The Education of American Teachers* (New York: McGraw-Hill, 1963). When my colleagues and I visited a representative sample about twenty-seven years later, we found much less consistency. See K. A. Sirotnik, "On the Eroding Foundations of Teacher Education," *Phi Delta Kappan,* 1990, *71,* 710–716.

4. I. Scheffler, "Basic Mathematical Skills: Some Philosophical and Practical Remarks," *Teachers College Record,* 1976, *78*(2), 205–212.

5. We are at a critical juncture today in teacher education,

not unlike that in medical education at the beginning of this century. A. Flexner, in his pivotal report, *Medical Education in the United States and Canada* (New York: Carnegie Foundation for the Advancement of Teaching, 1910), placed medical education squarely in the university context of research and scholarship. The practice of medicine would not have advanced to where it is today had he endorsed the route popular with and lucrative for many physicians of the time: the mentoring of new doctors with those now practicing without accompanying immersion in the basic sciences and exemplary clinical practice. The fact that universities currently provide less than exemplary teacher education programs does not warrant adopting the popular notion of mentoring tomorrow's teachers by today's in school settings divorced from universities. I have more to say later regarding the observation that drawing on the medical education experience in this way should not lead readers to the conclusion that medical education provides an appropriate model for teacher education; it does not.

6. In our research on schools, we found that large percentages of parents wanted their local school to pay more, not less, attention to the personal development of their children. Inadequate attention to academics had to become quite apparent before personal development slipped as a strongly perceived parental concern. See J. I. Goodlad, *A Place Called School* (New York: McGraw-Hill, 1984), chaps. 2 and 3.

7. Seymour Sarason and Gary Fenstermacher, respectively, describe the degree to which regularities and systemics characterize the culture of schools and resist change. See S. B. Sarason, *The Culture of the School and the Problem of Change* (Newton, Mass.: Allyn & Bacon, 1971 [rev. 1982]); and Fenstermacher, "Where Are We Going? Who Will Lead Us?" Linda M. McNeil, in turn, portrays a picture of teachers yielding to systemics imposed on them by district and state fiat when they want to exercise their professional judgment. See L. M. McNeil, *Contradictions of Control: School Structure and School Knowledge* (New York: Routledge Kegan Paul, 1986).

8. Teaching is quite unlike such professions as medicine, law, and dentistry in regard to the relationship to clients and to the public in general. It does not have and must not have the same kind of detached autonomy of these other professions. For an exceedingly useful, if complex, analysis of this difference and the need for the teaching profession not to become autonomous and semidetached, see B. L. Bull, "The Limits of Teacher Professionalism," in J. I. Goodlad, R. Soder, and K. A. Sirotnik (eds.), *The Moral Dimensions of Teaching* (San Francisco: Jossey-Bass, 1990), pp. 87–129.

9. Much of what I have written in this section on mission has been influenced by the recent writing of Gary D Fenstermacher and sustained conversation with him regarding it. I am grateful and indebted to him for the influence he has had on my views of teachers, teaching, and the teaching profession.

10. For a quite detailed description and analysis of this principal preparation program, see K. A. Sirotnik and K. Mueller, "Challenging the Wisdom of Conventional Principal Preparation Programs and Getting Away with It (So Far)," in J. Murphy (ed.), *Preparing Tomorrow's School Leaders: Alternative Designs* (University Park: University Council for Educational Administration and Pennsylvania State University College of Education, 1993).

11. Relevant publications regarding these several initiatives include Holmes Group, *Tomorrow's Teachers: A Report of the Holmes Group* (East Lansing, Mich.: Holmes Group, 1986); "The Letter: 37 Presidents Write . . . ," American Association for Higher Education *Bulletin*, 1989, *40*(3), 10–13; J. S. Johnston, Jr., and Associates, *Those Who Can: Undergraduate Programs to Prepare Arts and Sciences Majors for Teaching* (Washington, D.C.: American Association of Colleges, 1989); T. Warren (ed.), *A View from the Top* (Lanham, Md.: University Press of America, 1990); The Renaissance Group, *Educating the New American Student* (Cedar Falls: University of Northern Iowa, 1993).

12.   R. M. Hutchins, *The Higher Learning in America* (New Haven, Conn.: Yale University Press, 1936).

13.   G. J. Clifford and J. W. Guthrie, *Ed School* (Chicago: University of Chicago Press, 1988).

14.   N. Theobald, "Allocating Resources to Renew Teacher Education," Occasional Paper no. 14 (Seattle: Center for Educational Renewal, College of Education, University of Washington, 1992).

15.   Recruiting New Teachers, Inc., 385 Concord Ave., Suite 100, Belmont, Mass. 02178.

16.   J. Gordon, "Fundamental Issues for Minority Teachers and Multicultural Teacher Education," Occasional Paper no. 13 (Seattle: Center for Educational Renewal, College of Education, University of Washington, 1991 [rev. 1992]).

17.   For a rather detailed example, see M. Scriven, "Teacher Selection," in J. Millman and L. Darling-Hammond (eds.), *The New Handbook of Teacher Evaluation: Assessing Elementary and Secondary School Teachers* (Newbury Park, Calif.: Sage, 1990), pp. 76–103.

18.   Z. Su, "Exploring the Moral Socialization of Teachers: Factors Related to the Development of Beliefs, Attitudes, and Values in Teacher Candidates," Technical Report no. 7 (Seattle: Center for Educational Renewal, College of Education, University of Washington, 1989).

19.   K. A. Tye, "Changing Our Schools: The Realities," Technical Report no. 30 (Los Angeles: A Study of Schooling, Laboratory in School and Community Education, University of California, 1981).

Chapter Three

1.   H. S. Pritchett, "Introduction," in A. Flexner, *Medical Education in the United States and Canada* (New York: Carnegie Foundation for the Advancement of Teaching, 1910), p. xvi.

2.   Pritchett, "Introduction," pp. xi, xiii, and xiv. It is not useful to carry the comparison of medical education and teacher education much beyond a few broad generalities.

Much of what has occurred in medicine and medical education is not well suited to the nature and needs of teaching in and preparing teachers for the schools.

3. Those from the University of Northern Iowa and Texas A&M University, for example, are impressive; see Institute for Educational Leadership, *A Dialogue on Teacher Education Reform* (Cedar Falls: University of Northern Iowa, 1992); and P. Theobald, "The Texas A&M Teacher Preparation Program and the Goodlad Educational Renewal Postulates," unpublished manuscript (College Station: College of Education, Texas A&M University, 1992). Also, the postulates framed statewide discussions funded by the Southwestern Bell Foundation; see J. E. Finney, *At the Crossroads: Linking Teacher Education to School Reform* (Denver: Education Commission of the States, 1992).

4. R. W. Tyler, *Basic Principles of Curriculum and Instruction* (Chicago: University of Chicago Press, 1949).

5. K. A. Sirotnik, "Studying the Education of Educators: Methodology," Technical Report no. 2 (Seattle: Center for Educational Renewal, College of Education, University of Washington, 1989).

Chapter Four

1. M. Kundera, *Immortality* (New York: Grove Press, 1991), pp. 115–116.

2. We get considerable insight into why teachers in schools might be uneasy about the intrusion of university professors into their midst by the research that depicts their isolation from one another, on one hand, and the degree to which expectations from outside loom large, on the other. Daily collaboration with university-based personnel adds another major ingredient to be coped with. See D. C. Lortie, *Schoolteacher: A Sociological Study* (Chicago: University of Chicago Press, 1975); M. M. Cohn and R. B. Kottkamp, *Teachers: The Missing Voice in Education* (Albany: State University of New York Press, 1993); and L. M. McNeil,

Contradictions of Control: School Structure and School Knowledge
(New York: Routledge Kegan Paul, 1986).

3. For a revealing report on the sources of in-service education
    for teachers at the end of the 1970s, see chap. 9 in K. A.
    Tye, *The Junior High: School in Search of a Mission* (Lanham,
    Md.: University Press of America, 1985). The trend toward
    domination of in-service education by districts, school per-
    sonnel, and itinerant consultants was clearly evident.

4. Readers who may have forgotten the unrelenting intensity
    of this rhetoric throughout the second half of the 1980s and
    into the 1990s will be vividly reminded by T. Toch, *In the
    Name of Excellence* (New York: Oxford University Press,
    1991).

5. N. J. Gehrke, "Simultaneous Improvement of Schooling
    and the Education of Teachers: Creating a Collaborative
    Consciousness," *Metropolitan Universities,* 1991, *2*(1), 43–50.

6. For several years, the Center for Educational Renewal has
    reported in its Occasional Paper series the results of its
    efforts to track progress across the nation in regard to the
    development of school-university partnerships. The popu-
    lar image is of many in existence; the reality is that there
    are few. See J. I. Goodlad and R. Soder, "School-University
    Partnerships: An Appraisal of an Idea," Occasional Paper
    no. 15 (Seattle: Center for Educational Renewal, College
    of Education, University of Washington, 1992).

7. P. C. Schlechty and B. L. Whitford, "Shared Problems and
    Shared Vision: Organic Collaboration," in K. A. Sirotnik
    and J. I. Goodlad (eds.), *School-University Partnerships in Ac-
    tion* (New York: Teachers College Press, 1988), pp. 191–
    204.

8. A substantial part of this history is described in J. I. Good-
    lad, "School-University Partnerships for Educational
    Renewal: Rationale and Concepts," in Sirotnik and Goodlad
    (eds.), *School-University Partnerships in Action,* pp. 3–31; and
    J. I. Goodlad, "School-University Partnerships and Part-
    ner Schools," *Educational Policy,* 1993, *7,* 24–39.

9. See P. E. Heckman, "The Southern California Partnership:

A Retrospective Analysis," in Sirotnik and Goodlad (eds.), *School-University Partnerships in Action,* pp. 106–123.

10. R. W. Clark, "School/University Relations: Partnerships and Networks," Occasional Paper no. 2 (Seattle: Center for Educational Renewal, College of Education, University of Washington, 1986).

11. Z. Su, "School-University Partnerships: Ideas and Experiments (1986–1990)", Occasional Paper no. 12 (Seattle: Center for Educational Renewal, College of Education, University of Washington, 1990).

12. K. A. Sirotnik, "Making School-University Partnerships Work," *Metropolitan Universities,* 1991, *2*(1), 19–23.

13. Carnegie Forum on Education and the Economy, *A Nation Prepared: Teachers for the 21st Century* (Washington, D.C.: Carnegie Forum on Education and the Economy, 1986); and Holmes Group, *Tomorrow's Teachers: A Report of the Holmes Group* (East Lansing, Mich.: Holmes Group, 1986).

14. L. Darling-Hammond, "Developing Professional Development Schools: Early Lessons, Challenge, and Promise," in L. Darling-Hammond (ed.), *Professional Development Schools: Schools for Developing a Profession* (New York: Teachers College Press, 1994).

15. Jianping Shen's research probe into a professional development school representing four years of school-university collaboration sharpens the importance of working continuously toward mutual understanding of the central mission and fundamental concepts involved. See J. Shen, "Views from the Field: School-based Faculty Members' Vision of Preservice Teacher Education in the Context of a Professional Development School," Occasional Paper no. 16 (Seattle: Center for Educational Renewal, College of Education, University of Washington, 1993).

16. J. B. Andrews, "Braeburn Elementary School, 1967–1990: An Innovation That Survived," unpublished doctoral dissertation, College of Education, University of Washington, 1993.

Chapter Five

1. See G. Yuan, *Lure the Tiger Out of the Mountains* (New York: Simon & Schuster, 1991), for a list and discussion of the 36 Stratagems of Ancient China.

2. S. Ashton-Warner, *Teacher* (New York: Simon & Schuster, 1963).

3. See, for example, P. W. Jackson (ed.), *Handbook of Research on Curriculum* (New York: Macmillan, 1992); and sections on curriculum in T. Husén and T. N. Postlethwaite (eds.), *International Encyclopedia of Education* (Oxford, England: Pergamon Press, 1985).

4. The systems of knowledge and knowing illustrated in Figure 5.1 are adapted from K. E. Boulding, *The World as a Total System* (Newbury Park, Calif.: Sage, 1985).

5. J. S. Bruner, *The Process of Education* (New York: Vintage Books, 1960).

6. G. H. Douglas, *Education Without Impact* (New York: Birch Lane Press, 1992).

7. J. I. Goodlad, "Structure, Process, and an Agenda," in J. I. Goodlad (ed.), *The Ecology of School Renewal,* Eighty-Sixth Yearbook of the National Society for the Study of Education, part 1 (Chicago: University of Chicago Press, 1987), pp. 1–2.

8. G. M. Edelman, *Bright Air, Brilliant Fire: On the Matter of the Mind* (New York: Basic Books, 1992), p. 17.

9. S. B. Sarason, *The Culture of the School and the Problem of Change* (Newton, Mass.: Allyn & Bacon, 1971).

Chapter Six

1. D. A. Schön, *Educating the Reflective Practitioner: Toward a New Design for Teaching and Learning in the Professions* (San Francisco: Jossey-Bass, 1987), p. 3.

2. J. I. Goodlad, *A Place Called School* (New York: McGraw-Hill, 1984).

3. For further elaboration of our findings, see P. J. Edmundson, "The Curriculum in Teacher Education," Technical

Report no. 6 (Seattle: Center for Educational Renewal, College of Education, University of Washington, 1989).

4. This continuous linking of theory and practice is central to the entire curriculum design. For useful insights, see particularly J. Dewey, *The Sources of a Science of Education* (New York: Horace Liveright, 1929); and R. J. Schaefer, *The School as a Center of Inquiry* (New York: Harper & Row, 1967).

5. M. J. Adler, *The Paideia Proposal* (New York: Macmillan, 1982).

6. C. M. Clark, "The Teacher and the Taught: Moral Transactions in the Classroom," in J. I. Goodlad, R. Soder, and K. A. Sirotnik (eds.), *The Moral Dimensions of Teaching* (San Francisco: Jossey-Bass, 1990), p. 263.

7. Clark, "The Teacher and the Taught," pp. 264–265.

8. G. H. Douglas, *Education Without Impact* (New York: Birch Lane Press, 1992), pp. 120–121.

9. Much of the essence of becoming a teacher is nicely captured by N. J. Gehrke, *On Being a Teacher* (West Lafayette, Ind.: Kappa Delta Pi, 1987). Chap. 2 on learning is particularly relevant to the preceding discussion.

10. J. Bugnion, "Overhauling American Education—The Swiss Way," unpublished manuscript transmitted with private correspondence to the author, July 26, 1991.

11. There has not come to my attention any better description of children's slow progress from out of sight and sound in Western civilization than that of a book published several decades ago: P. Ariès, *Centuries of Childhood*, trans. R. Baldick (New York: Vintage Books, 1962).

12. D. C. Berliner, "Mythology and the American System of Education," *Phi Delta Kappan*, 1993, *74*, 634.

13. J. S. Bruner, *The Process of Education* (New York: Vintage Books, 1960), p. 33.

14. Schwab's views at the time are well represented in G. W. Ford and L. Pugno (eds.), *The Structure of Knowledge and the Curriculum* (Chicago: Rand McNally and Co., 1964).

15. See particularly L. S. Shulman, "Those Who Understand: Knowledge Growth in Teaching," *Educational Researcher*,

1986, *15*, 4–14; and "Blue Freeways: Traveling the Alternate Route with Big-City Teacher Trainees," *Journal of Teacher Education*, 1989, *40*, 2–8.

16. P. L. Grossman, *The Making of a Teacher* (New York: Teachers College Press, 1990).

17. J. B. Conant, *The Education of American Teachers* (New York: McGraw-Hill, 1963), pp. 126–132.

18. K. A. Sirotnik, "On the Eroding Foundations of Teacher Education," *Phi Delta Kappan*, 1990, *71*, 710–716. For a perspective on the fortunes and misfortunes of the foundations of education extending over four decades, the reader is referred to the first of three essays in a monograph by R. F. Butts, *In the First Person Singular: The Foundations of Education* (San Francisco: Caddo Gap Press, 1993), pp. v–34.

19. While writing this book, I sent a short letter to several dozen leaders in education and teacher education requesting that they send me the titles and authors of up to ten books every teacher should at some time read. The total list is almost as long as the maximum number possible if there were no repetitions in the list. It proved difficult also to group the books listed around major themes that might run through teacher education programs somewhat commonly. These findings paralleled those from the inquiry into this situation that was a small part of our research into teacher education.

20. Conant, *The Education of American Teachers*, p. 129.

21. Conant, *The Education of American Teachers*, p. 130.

22. M. Buchmann and R. E. Floden, "Coherence, the Rebel Angel," *Educational Researcher*, 1992, *21*, 4–9.

Chapter Seven

1. L. Darling-Hammond, "Reforming the School Reform Agenda," *Phi Delta Kappan*, 1993, *74*, 761.

2. Some of what follows is a revision and extension of an earlier exploration of this terrain: J. I. Goodlad, "Toward Educative Communities and Tomorrow's Teachers," *Work*

in Progress no. 1 (Seattle: Institute for Educational Inquiry, 1992). This series is supported by a grant from the Merck Family Fund to the Institute.

3. S. Simpson, "The Working Man's Party of Philadelphia Calls for Free, Equal Education for All (1831)," *The Working Man's Manual* (Philadelphia, 1831), p. 119. Cited in S. Cohen (ed.), *Education in the United States: A Documentary History* (New York: Random House, 1974), p. 1055.

4. As quoted in J. R. Commons, *A Documentary History of American Industrial Society* (Cleveland, 1910–1911), vol. 5, pp. 188–189. Cited in Cohen (ed.), *Education in the United States,* p. 1059.

5. M. J. Adler, *We Hold These Truths* (New York: Macmillan, 1987), p. 20.

6. E. L. Boyer, *High School* (New York: Harper & Row, 1983); J. I. Goodlad, *A Place Called School* (New York: McGraw-Hill, 1984).

7. Adler, *We Hold These Truths,* p. 20.

8. This is a characteristic that appears to be virtually a constant in case studies of individual schools singled out as good — "good enough," as Sara Lightfoot puts it in her analysis of six portraits of high schools: S. L. Lightfoot, *The Good High School* (New York: Basic Books, 1983). It proved also to be the major defining characteristic of the top quartile of the "goodness" criteria my colleagues and I developed out of a long list of indicators of students', teachers', and parents' satisfaction; see chap. 8 of Goodlad, *A Place Called School.*

9. For further discussion of this remarkable phenomenon, see J. I. Goodlad, "On Taking School Reform Seriously," *Phi Delta Kappan,* 1992, *74,* 232–238.

10. T. R. Sizer, *Horace's School: Redesigning the American High School* (Boston: Houghton Mifflin, 1992).

11. Darling-Hammond, "Reforming the School Reform Agenda," p. 755.

12. C. D. Glickman, *Renewing America's Schools: A Guide for School-Based Action* (San Francisco: Jossey-Bass, 1993).

13. This is the corpus of material needing to be collated now

and subsequently. To reference even part of it here would serve little purpose, because the referencing would suffer from the selectivity necessarily involved. There are some good beginning summaries, but none as yet is adequate.

14. Southern Association of Colleges and Schools, "The School Renewal Process: An Alternative Route to Regional Accreditation," Report of the Commission on Elementary Schools (Decatur, Ga.: Southern Association of Colleges and Schools, July 1993).

15. For borrowing from the lovely title of his book, I apologize to Theodore R. Sizer, *Places for Learning, Places for Joy* (Cambridge, Mass.: Harvard University Press, 1973).

16. E. W. Eisner, *The Enlightened Eye* (New York: Macmillan, 1991).

17. L. A. Cremin, *Popular Education and Its Discontents* (New York: Harper & Row, 1990), pp. 17–18.

18. U. Bronfenbrenner, "Ecological Experiments in Socialization Research," Presidential Address, Division of Personality and Social Psychology, at the annual meeting of the American Psychological Association, New Orleans, La., 1974, p. 7.

19. For further elaboration of the caring theme in our society, see D. Kerr, "Beyond Education: In Search of Nurture," Work in Progress no. 2 (Seattle: Institute for Educational Inquiry, 1993); and H. A. Lawson, "Toward Healthy Learners, Schools, and Communities: Footprints in a Continuing Journey," Work in Progress no. 3 (Seattle: Institute for Educational Inquiry, 1993).

20. J. R. Martin, *The Schoolhome* (Cambridge, Mass.: Harvard University Press, 1992).

21. For one account, see B. Bettelheim, *Children of the Dream* (New York: Macmillan, 1969). See also A. Lombard, "Early Schooling in Israel," in N. B. Feshback, J. I. Goodlad, and A. Lombard, *Early Schooling in England and Israel* (New York: McGraw-Hill, 1973), pp. 76–78.

22. For an excellent discussion of parallel circumstances in Europe, see T. Husén, A. Tuijnman, and W. D. Halls, *Schooling in Modern European Society* (Oxford, England: Pergamon Press, 1992).

23. H. E. Gardner, *Frames of Mind: The Theory of Multiple Intelligences* (New York: Basic Books, 1983).

24. N. Lemann, "Ruling by Degree," *Washington Monthly* (Jan./Feb. 1993), pp. 41–46.

25. R. Ulich, *The Human Career: A Philosophy of Self-Transcendence* (New York: Harper and Brothers, 1955).

Chapter Eight

1. R. D. Putnam, *Making Democracy Work: Civic Traditions in Modern Italy* (Princeton, N.J.: Princeton University Press, 1993), p. 9.

2. For a summary and analysis of this activity, see J. E. Finney, *At the Crossroads: Linking Teacher Education to School Reform* (Denver: Education Commission of the States, 1992).

3. Putnam, *Making Democracy Work,* p. 9.

4. For further information, see School of Professional Studies, "The Agenda for Teacher Education in a Democracy Project," Summary of New Jersey Policy Recommendations (Upper Montclair, N.J.: Office of the Dean, School of Professional Studies, Montclair State College, 1993).

5. P. Theobald, "The Texas A&M Teacher Education Program and the Goodlad Educational Renewal Postulates," unpublished manuscript (College Station: College of Education, Texas A&M University, 1992).

6. For further information, see the newsletters of the Wyoming School-University Partnership emanating from the University of Wyoming's College of Education in Laramie, Wyoming.

7. For more information and a candid discussion of these, see L. Miller, "Spotlight on Sites: University of Southern Maine," *Center Correspondent,* June 1993 (6), pp. 2–9.

8. Miller, "Spotlight on Sites," p. 9.

9. See, for example, Figure 2 in "Institute for Educational Renewal at Miami University," Draft Document no. 2 (Oxford, Ohio: School of Education and Allied Professions, Miami University, 1993), p. 13.

10. J. Gordon, "Fundamental Issues for Minority Teachers and Multicultural Teacher Education," Occasional Paper

no. 13 (Seattle: Center for Educational Renewal, College of Education, University of Washington, 1991 [rev. 1992]).

11. California Polytechnic State University, "Teacher Diversity Video" (San Luis Obispo: California Polytechnic State University, 1991).

12. Putnam, *Making Democracy Work,* p. 60.

13. A. Flexner, *Medical Education in the United States and Canada* (New York: Carnegie Foundation for the Advancement of Teaching, 1910), p. 26.

14. There are bulletins describing both the FIG Program and these options in general education: "FIGS" and "College Studies Program" (Seattle: University of Washington, 1992 [and periodically updated]).

15. Hawaii School/University Partnership, "Exemplary Sites for the Education of Educators and School Renewal," Task Force Report (Honolulu: Hawaii School/University Partnership, March 1990), p. 2. Another useful report of the partnership is entitled "Systemic Strategies for School Success" (1990). In addition, there are exceedingly helpful unpublished reports of the College of Education, University of Hawaii, Manoa, that emanated from the comprehensive programmatic revisions in teacher education that accompanied the university's role in the partnership.

16. P. A. Graham, *S. O. S.: Sustain Our Schools* (New York: Hill & Wang, 1992), p. 125.

17. J. I. Goodlad, "Linking Schools and Universities: Symbiotic Partnerships," Occasional Paper no. 1 (Seattle: Center for Educational Renewal, College of Education, University of Washington, 1986 [rev. 1987]).

18. At the time of this writing, representatives of most of the settings, with Center senior associate Richard Clark, are well along with the preparation of a document defining partner schools and their place in the educational renewal process.

19. For a short summary, see K. A. Norlander, C. W. Case, J. A. Meagher, and T. G. Reagan, "Teacher Preparation at the University of Connecticut" (Storrs: School of Education, University of Connecticut, 1992).

20. C. W. Case, K. A. Norlander, and T. G. Reagan, "Cultural Transformation in an Urban Professional Development Center: Policy Implications for School-University Collaboration," *Educational Policy,* 1993, *7,* 40–60.

21. R. T. Osguthorpe, R. C. Harris, and M. F. Harris (eds.), *Partner Schools: Centers for Educational Renewal* (San Francisco: Jossey-Bass, 1995).

22. For a detailed description, see College of Education, "Center for Professional Development and Technology, Phase 4" (El Paso: College of Education, University of Texas, 1993).

23. S. B. Sarason, K. S. Davidson, and B. Blatt, *The Preparation of Teachers: An Unstudied Problem* (New York: Wiley, 1962).

24. S. B. Sarason, K. S. Davidson, and B. Blatt, *The Preparation of Teachers: An Unstudied Problem,* rev. ed. (Cambridge, Mass.: Brookline Books, 1986), p. i.

25. S. B. Sarason, *The Case for Change: Rethinking the Preparation of Educators* (San Francisco: Jossey-Bass, 1993), p. 282.

Index

297

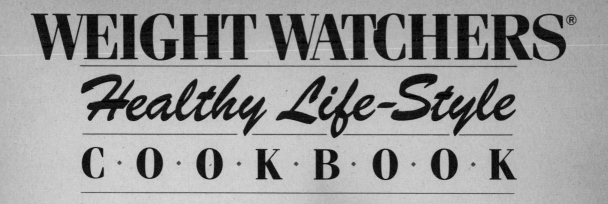

WEIGHT WATCHERS®
Healthy Life-Style
C·O·O·K·B·O·O·K

Over 250 Recipes Based on the
Personal Choice® Program

Set design and photography by Gus Francisco

A PLUME BOOK

WEIGHT WATCHERS is a registered trademark of
Weight Watchers International, Inc.

PLUME
Published by the Penguin Group
Penguin Books USA Inc., 375 Hudson Street,
New York, New York 10014, U.S.A.
Penguin Books Ltd, 27 Wrights Lane,
London W8 5TZ, England
Penguin Books Australia Ltd, Ringwood,
Victoria, Australia
Penguin Books Canada Ltd, 10 Alcorn Ave.,
Toronto, Ontario, Canada M4V 3B2
Penguin Books (N.Z.) Ltd, 182–190 Wairau Road,
Auckland 10, New Zealand

Penguin Books Ltd, Registered Offices:
Harmondsworth, Middlesex, England

First published by Plume,
an imprint of New American Library,
a division of Penguin Books USA Inc.
Previously published in an NAL Books edition.

First Plume Printing, February, 1992
10 9 8 7 6 5 4 3 2 1

We would like to thank the following for kindly lending us
serving pieces and other props or for supplying us with
settings for the photo insert: Laura Ashley, New York, N.Y.;
Richard Bennett Pottery, Housatonic, Mass.; Brandywine
Restaurant, New York, N.Y.; Paul Chaleff Pottery, Pine
Plains, N.Y.; James Madden, Bayshore, N.Y.; Judy Milne,
New York, N.Y.; Queens Botanical Gardens, Flushing, N.Y.;
Barbara Zitz Antiques, Rhinebeck, N.Y.

Ⓟ REGISTERED TRADEMARK—MARCA REGISTRADA

LIBRARY OF CONGRESS CATALOGING-IN-PUBLICATION DATA
Weight Watchers healthy life-style cookbook / photography by
   Gus Francisco.
      p.   cm.
   ISBN 0-452-26755-2
   1. Salt-free diet—Recipes.   2. Low-cholesterol diet—Recipes.
3. Low-fat diet—Recipes.   4. Low-calorie diet—Recipes.
I. Weight Watchers International.
RM237.8.W45   1991
641.5'63—dc20   90-13817
                                                 CIP

Printed in the United States of America
Set in ITC Goudy Sans Book
Designed by Julian Hamer
Food stylist: Nina Procaccini
Prop stylist: Laurie Beck
Illustrations by Dolores R. Santoliquido
Introductions by Anne Hosansky
Nutrition analysis by Hill Nutrition Associates, Inc.

Acknowledgments

A dish doesn't prepare itself, neither does a cookbook. Both require proficient and caring hands. Weight Watchers International is fortunate to have those dedicated hands on board. We pay well-deserved tribute to our Publications Management Department, with a special bow to General Manager Eileen Pregosin for her vigilant and perceptive guidance.

In the busy test kitchen at Weight Watchers International, an inspired corps of chefs worked for nearly a year developing and testing more than 250 recipes, as well as creating the food styling for the mouth-watering photographs you'll find in these pages. Our admiring thanks to chefs Nina Procaccini, Susan Astre, Christy Foley-McHale, and Judi Rettmer, as well as test kitchen assistant Jacqueline Hines.

Recipes have to be translated, not only into savory dishes but also into easy-to-follow language. We are grateful for the unflagging efforts of our editorial staff—Patricia Barnett, Isabel Fleisher, Elizabeth Resnick-Healy, Melonie Rothman, and April Rozea—who researched, edited, and proofread this manuscript through countless revisions, abetted by the secretarial expertise of Nancy Biordi.

Last, but far from least (like dessert!)—our appreciation to Barbara Warmflash, General Manager, Products and Licensing, who deftly managed the myriad other details involved in steering this cookbook from our kitchen to yours.

—Weight Watchers International

Contents

Introduction

With today's busy life-styles, having the best foods with the least fuss is every cook's dream. That's why the more than 250 recipes in this book are all geared to getting you in and out of the kitchen quickly—while still providing some of the most delectable, nutritious dishes you've ever tasted. And our recipes, which are based on the Weight Watchers food plan, help make it a pleasure to control your weight.

Every recipe can be prepared within an hour—many in just half that time. More than 50 recipes take advantage of the jet speed of the microwave oven, and every recipe is headed by a note telling you the approximate total time needed for preparation.

But speed is never obtained at the expense of good nutrition. A savvy life-style for the nineties is one that focuses on healthful eating and an awareness of proper nutrition. Our recipes are based on the most up-to-date nutritional information available and we share that data with you. Each recipe contains analyses for calories, protein, fat, carbohydrate, calcium, sodium, cholesterol, and dietary fiber. In addition, many recipes are highlighted by a symbol indicating that we've controlled the sodium, fat, and/or cholesterol levels. A special section provides information on the thinking underlying the current nutritional guidelines.

To help you with your weight-control efforts, each recipe provides Selection Information, explaining how the dish fits into the Weight Watchers food plan. To make it even easier, there are 14 recipe-keyed one-day menu planners that do a lot of your thinking for you. And there is a handy additional index that enables you to find in a flash the recipes that will meet your particular needs.

You'll also find a wealth of helpful cooking tips, such as how to enhance flavors without adding sodium, fat, or cholesterol, as well as a convenient spice chart that gives a quick view of which seasonings "marry" well with different foods. And if you're shy about admitting that you don't understand various cooking directions, you'll be delighted to see that we've included a glossary of cooking terms.

The recipes (which are mostly for two servings) take you through the day from breakfasts and brunches to suppers and snacks. There are *taste*-ful recipes for appetizers, soups, and dips; poultry, meat, fish, and shellfish; legumes; egg substitutes and cheese; side dishes; desserts and beverages.

Every recipe has been prepared and tested in the test kitchen of Weight Watchers International. That's your best guarantee of high quality, for Weight Watchers is staffed by the most qualified nutritionists, home economists, and chefs, all of whom understand *your* life-style needs.

The Weight Watchers organization has been an acknowledged leader in the weight-control field for more than 27 years. In that time, Weight Watchers has grown from a handful of people to millions of enrollments. People of all ages, from children to senior citizens, attend weekly meetings virtually around the globe. In addition, the popular expanding line of convenience foods, best-selling cookbooks and engagement calendars, and exercise audio cassettes are all dedicated to the continuing concept of a healthy life-style. You can be confident that this cookbook provides not only an express trip through the kitchen but a delicious route to nutritious eating.

Recipes That Fit Your Life-Style

Does a delicious, nutritious dish, prepared in just about the time it takes you to read this chapter, seem too good to be true? If so, this is the cookbook for you—all of these recipes can be prepared within an hour and many in even less time.

To get the most from our recipes, read the guidelines on the following pages. They'll help you create appetizing dishes faster and more effortlessly than you ever dreamed possible.

First, however, let's take a look at the most important ingredient in our recipes: *good nutrition*.

What Is "Good Nutrition"?

Never cut corners on nutrition. The key to healthy eating—and to a safe and healthy weight loss—is to eat a *variety of nutritious foods in moderation*.

A healthful menu plan should provide your body with basic nutrients while staying within caloric limits. The reason variety is so important is that no single food can supply all the essential nutrients in the amounts needed. Cutting out one type of food isn't the answer to weight loss, since it's the *amount* of protein, fat, and carbohydrate that determines its caloric content. The more you vary your choices, the less likely you are to develop either a deficiency or an excess of any nutrient. Variety also helps avoid the pitfall of boredom, which can lead to detours from the Food Plan.

To stay healthy your body needs approximately 40 different nutrients, including protein, fat, carbohydrate, fiber, vitamins, minerals, and water. These nutrients have a lot of work to do in your body.

Protein builds and maintains body tissue and is an excellent source of iron and B vitamins. The best sources of protein are poultry, lean meats, fish, eggs, milk, cheese, legumes, and peanut butter.

Carbohydrate is the body's primary energy source and also provides fiber and B vitamins. Fruits, vegetables, cereals, breads, legumes, and whole grains are excellent sources of carbohydrate.

Dietary fiber—so prominent in the news these days—is found in two forms: soluble and insoluble. *Insoluble fiber* helps maintain regularity and is found in bran products, whole grains, legumes, fruits, and vegetables. *Soluble fiber* may help to lower blood cholesterol levels and to control levels of blood sugar. Some good sources of this type of fiber are oats, barley, beans, and fruits, especially apples.

Vitamins and *minerals* are also essential for proper body functioning and each has its own role to play. For instance, vitamin B_1 helps cells convert carbohydrates into energy, vitamin C helps strengthen body tissues, and vitamin A is important for good vision.

Iron, so vital for the formation of red blood cells, is one of the most difficult minerals to get in adequate supply, especially for women. Some good sources are lean meats, poultry, shellfish, liver, legumes, and whole or enriched grains.

Calcium builds and maintains strong bones and teeth. Without adequate calcium your body has to take what it needs from your bones, which may cause them to become weak and brittle and to fracture more easily. The most well-known sources of calcium are, of course, milk and other dairy products. In addition, calcium is found in canned sardines and salmon (with bones), tofu, cooked soybeans, and oranges and in such vegetables as cooked collards, turnips, mustard greens, broccoli, and spinach.

The Trio to Be Wary Of

Sodium—Cholesterol—Fat—The red flag goes up in any nutrition-conscious mind at those words. However, these "villains" have their useful sides, too.

Sodium

Sodium is an important regulator of the fluid balance in your body. By attracting water into the blood vessels, sodium helps maintain normal blood volume and pressure—making small amounts of sodium a necessity. However, too much may contribute to high blood pressure which can, in turn, lead to heart and kidney diseases and strokes. Sodium may also be a problem in weight loss, since it can mask the actual loss and even send the scale up because of water retention (caused by sodium's effect on the body's water balance).

Sodium occurs naturally in certain foods, and overzealous cooks may add additional amounts in the form of table salt. In addition, sodium is often added in the processing of prepared foods such as canned vegetables, meats, and poultry; prepared salad dressings; cured, smoked, canned, and dried fish; cheese and processed cheese products, foods, and spreads; baking soda and baking powder; and food preservatives such as monosodium glutamate (MSG).

The guideline to remember is that your daily intake of sodium *should not exceed 3 grams (3000 milligrams)*. (Did you know that just ¼ teaspoon of salt contains a whopping 533 milligrams of sodium?)

Here are some ways to avoid excess sodium:

- Ignore the salt shaker when cooking pasta, vegetables, rice, soups, and cereals. (Let each person add her/his own salt at the table.)

- Use reduced-sodium versions of soy sauce and broth in your favorite recipes or season with herbs and spices.

- When cooking canned legumes, drain and rinse with cold water before using, to remove some of the excess sodium.

- Do a balancing act: reduce or eliminate the amount of salt called for in a recipe containing a high-sodium item (for example, pickles, celery, olives, sauerkraut, and canned or frozen vegetables with added salt).

- Take advantage of the popular new reduced-sodium products currently on the market, such as reduced-sodium tomato sauce and cheese. (Some of our recipes call for reduced-fat cheese, which is often lower in sodium as well.)

Cholesterol

"LDL" . . . "HDL" . . . Those initials are on everyone's cholesterol-counting lips these days. But what do these terms really mean? Put quite simply, LDLs are low-density lipoproteins, while HDLs are high-density lipoproteins. Both types carry cholesterol and fats in the bloodstream.

The "bad" cholesterol is LDL, which apparently promotes the deposit of cholesterol on artery walls, increasing the risk of heart disease. On the other hand, the "good" cholesterol, HDL, is believed to carry cholesterol away from the arteries.

There are two types of cholesterol: *blood* (serum) and *dietary*. Blood cholesterol, a fat-like substance manufactured by the body, is found in every living cell and is essential for normal functioning. Dietary cholesterol is found in foods of animal origin (meats and dairy products).

Research has shown that a diet rich in saturated fat and cholesterol tends to raise blood cholesterol levels, increasing the risk of heart disease. *Therefore, we recommend that you limit your cholesterol intake to an average of 300 milligrams per day* (based on your weekly intake). This can be done by reducing your consumption of butter, hard cheeses, heavy cream, red meats, eggs, and organ meats. You should also limit foods made with coconut, palm, and palm kernel oils.

Plant foods, on the other hand, are free of dietary cholesterol. So be sure to include healthful amounts of complex carbohydrates and high-fiber foods such as whole grain breads and cereals, legumes, and fresh fruits and vegetables.

Don't make the mistake of thinking that eliminating a particular food or eating just one type will solve the cholesterol problem. Your best remedy is to get into the habit of making nutritious low-fat menu choices.

Fat

The plus side of fat is that it's a major source of energy. It also cushions body organs, acts as an insulator, enables the body to carry fat-soluble vitamins, and provides essential fatty acids. It's easy to see that small amounts of fat are a necessary part of our daily diet. The other side of the coin is that too much fat (especially the saturated variety) has been linked to heart disease and some types of cancer.

There are three types of fat in foods: *saturated fat*, found primarily in animal foods such as meats, butter, and cream, as well as in coconut, palm, and palm kernel oils; *polyunsaturated fat*, present in most liquid vegetable oils, including corn, soy, safflower, sesame, cottonseed, soybean, and sunflower; and *monounsaturated fat*, found in olives and olive oil, avocados, and peanut and canola (rapeseed) oils.

The three types play very different roles in the cholesterol scene. Saturated fat is the villain that tends to raise blood cholesterol by increasing the LDL levels. Polyunsaturated fat is both helpful and nonhelpful. It apparently reduces the total blood cholesterol level by lowering LDLs, but seems to lower HDLs as well. The fat that gets the highest rating is monounsaturated, which seems to lower LDLs while leaving HDLs unaffected.

Regardless of whether the fat is saturated or not, it's still high in calories. Each gram contains 9 calories, more than double the calories in equivalent amounts of carbohydrates or protein.

Since a low-fat diet helps with weight control, give yourself a boost by following these fat-reducing suggestions:

- Steam or microwave vegetables without added fat, rather than sautéing them in butter, margarine, or oil.

- When preparing homemade broths, soups, and stews, refrigerate them before serving so that the fat can congeal and be easily removed.

- Use lean cuts of meat and remove any visible fat before eating.

- Use a rack when baking, roasting, or broiling beef, lamb, or pork, so that the fat will drip off. When boiling these meats, discard any fat that cooks out.

- Remove the skin from poultry (it's a source of saturated fat) before pan-broiling, sautéing, stir-frying, or stewing. When baking, broiling, or boiling poultry, remove the skin before serving.

Become knowledgeable about nutrition by making it a habit to read product labels. They provide nutrition information that will help you succeed on the Food Plan. Some products, for instance, are permissible on the Weight Watchers food plan only if they meet certain nutritional guidelines.

In addition, some of the recipes in this book call for items of specific caloric content and the label will clue you as to whether it's the appropriate product.

How to Read the Recipes

- On each recipe the approximate preparation time is given. This does *not* include marinating, freezing, cooling, or chilling time, since these tasks can be taking place while your attention is on other things. (For example, a dish can marinate in the refrigerator overnight, while a dessert can cool during the time you're enjoying the meal.)

- Following each recipe is Selection Information (e.g., Each serving provides: 1 Milk; 2 Proteins; 30 Optional Calories), explaining how one serving fits into the Weight Watchers food plan. You'll find this information helpful when preparing your menus, since it helps you keep track of your Selections. *If you make any changes in the recipe be sure to adjust the Selection Information accordingly.*

- In step with the current emphasis on nutritional awareness, each recipe also includes a per serving nutritional analysis for calories, protein, fat, carbohydrate, calcium, sodium, cholesterol, and dietary fiber. These amounts are based on the most up-to-date data available. *Be aware that these figures will be altered by any changes you make in a recipe, whether or not it affects the Selection Information.* The nutritional analysis for recipes containing cooked items (such as rice, pasta, or vegetables) assumes that no extra salt or fat is added during cooking.

- Many recipes have a symbol indicating that they are reduced in sodium, fat, and/or cholesterol. For optimum healthfulness, we've often used such foods as egg substitutes, reduced-fat cheeses, and low-sodium broths.

 on a recipe that contains 2 or more Proteins indicates that each serving has 50 milligrams or less of cholesterol. All other recipes with this symbol contain 25 milligrams or less of cholesterol per serving.

 indicates that 30% or less of the calories come from fat.

on a recipe that contains 2 or more Proteins indicates that each serving has 400 milligrams or less of sodium. All other recipes with this symbol contain 200 milligrams or less of sodium per serving.

Cooking Cues

Organize Before Starting

Before beginning to prepare a recipe, read it through so that you know exactly what you'll have to do before you begin. To save you time, we've kept ingredients to a minimum. Make sure you have everything you need within easy reach, including utensils. Proper organization saves time, too.

Have the Proper Cookware

Use nonstick cookware so that you can cook with little or no fat. If you don't own this type of cookware, spray an ordinary pan with nonstick cooking spray.

Make Use of Cooked Meats

To help speed up cooking time, many of the recipes call for cooked meat or poultry— a savory (and economical) way to use up leftovers. If you don't have any on hand, purchase precooked meats, such as barbecued chicken, roast beef, or ham, from your supermarket's take-out department.

Thaw in a Time-Saving Way

When thawed ingredients are called for, the most time-wise way is to let them thaw overnight (in the refrigerator, not out on the counter!) or let your microwave oven do a speedy thawing job.

Start with Pre-Preparation Amounts

The weights of fresh fruits and vegetables given in the recipes are the weights *before* any peeling, cutting, or other procedure. For example, if a recipe calls for one pound of apples, cored, pared, and diced, start with one pound; then proceed according to recipe directions.

Weigh and Measure Properly

Never gauge amounts by guesswork. Take time to weigh and measure carefully. It's important for the success of the recipe, as well as for accurate portion sizes.

- Foods should be weighed on a food scale.
- Liquids should be measured in a standard glass or clear plastic measuring cup. For amounts of less than $1/4$ cup, use standard measuring spoons.
- Dry ingredients should be measured in metal or plastic measuring cups that come in $1/4$-, $1/3$-, $1/2$-, and 1-cup sizes. Be sure to level the amount with a knife or spatula. To measure less than $1/4$ cup, use standard measuring spoons and level the contents the same way.
- "Dash" means approximately $1/16$ of a teaspoon ($1/2$ of a $1/8$-teaspoon measure or $1/4$ of a $1/4$-teaspoon measure).

- Weights in recipes are given in pounds and fractions of a pound. Following are the ounce equivalents:

1 pound = 16 ounces	½ pound = 8 ounces
¾ pound = 12 ounces	¼ pound = 4 ounces

Serving Sizes

When preparing a recipe for more than one serving, mix ingredients well and divide evenly so that each portion will contain equal amounts.

Multiplying or Dividing Recipes

Recipes can be doubled, tripled, etc.—or halved—but seasonings *cannot* be automatically multiplied or divided. Begin by using less than the multiplied or divided recipe would call for, then, if necessary, increase the amount according to your taste.

Marinating

It's best to marinate foods in glass or stainless-steel containers, rather than aluminum, since marinades usually contain acidic ingredients which may react adversely with the aluminum.

Tip: Marinating items in a securely fastened leakproof plastic bag eliminates having to wash a container.

Refrigerating/Freezing

- If a cooked food is to be chilled or frozen, first allow it to cool slightly. Placing a very hot food in the refrigerator or freezer may affect the efficiency of the appliance, as well as warming the other foods in it.
- The best way to refrigerate or freeze a large quantity of food is to divide it into smaller portions after cooking. They'll cool faster, reducing the chance of spoilage.
- All refrigerator items should be securely covered. To prevent freezer burn, make sure that all foods that are going to be frozen are covered or wrapped properly.

Oven Suggestions

- Remember that ovens—like cooks—aren't identical, so always check for doneness as directed.

- Keep tabs on the accuracy of your oven thermostat by checking it from time to time. Any discrepancy may affect the quality of your cooking. To determine whether the thermostat is registering correctly, place an oven thermometer on a rack centered in the oven. Set the oven temperature, wait 10 to 15 minutes, then check the thermometer. If the actual oven temperature doesn't match the temperature setting, adjust the setting higher or lower as needed to compensate for the difference until the oven can be repaired.

- To prevent heat loss, close the oven door promptly after putting food in and don't open the door unnecessarily.

- When baking, place the pan in the middle of the center oven rack so that air can circulate freely, enabling the food to bake evenly. It's best to use one oven rack at a time. If using two, position them so that they divide the oven into thirds. Stagger the pans so that they're not directly above each other.

- When broiling, the standard distance from the source of heat is four inches. This guideline should be followed unless the recipe specifies otherwise.

Tip: When using only some of the cups in a muffin pan, prevent the pan from warping or burning by partially filling the empty cups with water. When you're ready to remove the muffins from the pan, carefully drain off the boiling hot water.

Microwave Ovens

"Microwaving": this is a popular word in our current kitchen vocabulary. Not only does a microwave oven provide an express route through cooking and thawing, it does so while the kitchen stays comfortably cool. These ovens have also transformed the brown-bag scene by making it possible to bring a microwavable meal to your office (provided that it has a microwave oven) and prepare a hot lunch in minutes.

Because of this ease and popularity, we've included more than 50 microwave recipes in this cookbook. They were tested in 650- to 700-watt microwave ovens with variable power levels. These levels control the percentage of power introduced into the oven cavity and automatically cycle power on and off. Lower power levels cook more slowly; higher levels cook faster. The power levels may also vary depending on the brand of oven.

Our recipes use the following power levels:

HIGH (100%)
MEDIUM-HIGH (60–70%)
MEDIUM (50%)
LOW (10–20%)

If the levels in your microwave oven are different from these, you may need to adjust the recipe. If you own a lower-wattage oven, increase the cooking time, check it, and cook longer, if necessary. For higher-wattage ovens, decrease the cooking time slightly.

When cooking in your microwave oven, be sure to use cookware that is specifically recommended for use in the microwave oven, such as microwavable casseroles with matching covers. When food is arranged on a microwavable plate or in custard cups, an inverted microwavable pie plate or saucer can serve as a cover.

Becoming Familiar with Some Ingredients

BACON—Bacon is occasionally used because of its special taste and unbeatable aroma. Whenever possible a recipe variation has been included that does not include bacon.

BROTH—Canned ready-to-serve low-sodium broth is used in many of the recipes. This convenient product adds flavor to a dish while keeping the sodium level under control.

BUTTER—When the recipe calls for butter or whipped butter, use the lightly salted kind unless sweet butter is specified. Although most of our recipes use lower-saturated fat alternatives (such as nonstick cooking spray, margarine, vegetable oil, or olive oil), at times a small amount of butter is included because it can go a long way toward enhancing the flavor of a recipe.

CHEESE—The cheese used in our recipes is very often the *reduced-fat* variety, since other kinds can add a substantial amount of fat to your diet. This variety is often lower in sodium as well.

EGGS—Because of the danger of salmonella, certain precautions should be taken with eggs:

- Never buy cracked or dirty eggs. If you find any cracked ones in the carton, discard them immediately.
- Only purchase eggs stored in a refrigerator case.
- Refrigerate eggs as soon as possible. Store them in their carton so they won't absorb odors from the refrigerator. Don't wash them before storing or using.
- Don't eat raw eggs or foods made with raw eggs.
- Cook eggs until both the whites and the yolks are firm, not runny; "over well" is safer than "sunny-side up."
- Avoid foods that are rich in eggs that are only lightly cooked, such as soft custards and meringues.
- Don't leave eggs—either raw or hard-cooked—out of the refrigerator for longer than two hours.
- Use fresh eggs within five weeks and hard-cooked ones within one week.

- Leftover uncooked egg whites and yolks should be refrigerated immediately and discarded after four days.
- Any areas of the kitchen that come in contact with raw eggs should be washed with hot soapy water.
- Serve eggs and egg-rich foods promptly after cooking.

Tip: When using eggs, break each one individually into a cup or bowl before combining with each other or with additional ingredients. This avoids wasting other items if an egg is spoiled or a piece of shell falls into it.

EGG SUBSTITUTES are made mostly of egg white (the high-protein portion of the egg). They are cholesterol-free (some brands are also fat-free) and are usually available in the supermarket freezer section.

Keep frozen egg substitutes frozen until needed. Thaw the container in the refrigerator or speed thawing by putting the container under cold running water.

FRUITS and FRUIT JUICES (canned and frozen) should not contain added sugar (sugar substitutes are permitted). Canned fruit may be packed in its own juice or in another fruit juice, blend of juices, or water.

GELATIN—When dissolving unflavored gelatin over direct heat, keep the heat low and stir constantly since gelatin burns very easily.

LIQUEURS—If a specified liqueur is unavailable, you may substitute one of your favorites.

OILS—Vegetable oils have certain characteristics that make them appropriate for specific recipes. However, one can often be substituted for another. In recipes where no particular type is specified, you have the option of using safflower, sunflower, soybean, corn, cottonseed, or any combination of these. However, olive, walnut, and peanut oils have distinctive flavors so use when specified. When Chinese sesame oil is indicated, use the *dark* (rather than the light) kind. The light is relatively flavorless and may be used as a substitute for any other vegetable oil, whereas the dark variety, which is made from toasted sesame seeds, has a rich amber color and characteristic sesame flavor.

Nut and seed oils (such as walnut, hazelnut, peanut, almond, and sesame) should be stored in the refrigerator after they've been opened, so they won't become rancid or develop odors. Since these oils are usually more expensive, buy in small quantities and store them properly. (Other oils may be stored in the cupboard.)

SHELLFISH—*Clams* and *mussels* should be purchased live and have shells that are tightly closed. Give any slightly open shells a hard tap. They should snap shut. If they don't, discard them. Remember that shells open during cooking. (To avoid last-minute dashes to the store, buy more shellfish than the recipe requires. Any leftovers can be used as part of a meal the next day.)

VEGETABLES called for in the recipes mean *fresh* ones, unless otherwise indicated. You may substitute canned or frozen varieties, but the cooking times should be adjusted accordingly. Canned or thawed frozen vegetables would take less time; those frozen solid may take slightly longer. Be aware that canned vegetables may also increase the sodium content of the recipe.

CHILI PEPPERS contain volatile oils that can make your skin and eyes burn. When working with these hot peppers, wear rubber gloves and be careful not to touch your face or eyes. Before continuing with the recipe preparation, thoroughly wash your hands and the knife and cutting board to remove all traces of the peppers.

LETTUCE called for in the recipes assumes either iceberg or romaine. Four lettuce leaves provide one Vegetable Selection. If you use any other type of lettuce (such as Boston or Bibb), 8 lettuce leaves provide one Vegetable Selection.

WHIPPED TOPPING—This lower-calorie alternative to whipped cream is used in a few dessert recipes. As a way to cut back on saturated fat, when the topping is just a garnish, the recipe has a variation that does not include it.

NOTE: To take you on a culinary adventure, some of the recipes include exotic ingredients such as sun-dried tomatoes, shiitake mushrooms, and balsamic and raspberry vinegars. Once found only in the finest restaurants, today these elegant treats are as accessible as your neighborhood supermarket. We invite you to broaden your experiences by trying them. However, in case your tastes run to the less daring, familiar alternatives are provided in the recipes.

Seasonings

What nutritional allies herbs and spices are! They increase tastiness without compromising health since they can easily be substituted for flavorings too high in fat, sodium, or cholesterol.

We recommend using fresh herbs in many of our recipes. When appropriate, the amount of dried herb that may be substituted is also indicated. If the recipe doesn't have a dried alternative, use fresh herbs.

When substituting fresh spices for ground spices, use approximately 8 times the amount (for example, 1 teaspoon minced pared gingerroot instead of 1/8 teaspoon ground ginger).

Some Well-Seasoned Suggestions

- Dried herbs are stronger in flavor than fresh. Therefore, use less.
- For cold spreads, dips, and dressings, add herbs several hours ahead of time to allow the flavors to blend.
- When using fresh herbs, to release the most flavor cut the leaves very fine.
- Fresh herbs can easily be stored in the freezer. Simply rinse the herb in cold water and freeze in a resealable plastic freezer bag. The frozen herb can be added during cooking (thawing isn't necessary).

"Marrying" Seasonings to Compatible Foods

BEEF	Black or green peppercorns, chili powder, dill, garlic, paprika, powdered mustard, rosemary, sage
EGGS	Basil, chervil, chili powder, chives, curry powder, paprika, red or black pepper, tarragon
FISH	Basil, bay leaf, cilantro (Chinese parsley), dill, fennel, garlic, pepper, rosemary, saffron, tarragon
LAMB	Curry, garlic, ginger, mint, mustard, rosemary, saffron, sage
PORK	Cloves, coriander, garlic, ginger, lemon, rosemary
POULTRY	Dill, garlic, ginger, oregano, paprika, powdered mustard, sage, tarragon
VEAL	Garlic, ginger, marjoram, mustard, oregano, thyme
VEGETABLES	Allspice, basil, chervil, chives, cilantro (Chinese parsley), dill, garlic, marjoram, mint, nutmeg, parsley, red pepper, rosemary

Easy Garnishing

Savvy chefs know that nutritious food should be a feast for the eyes as well as the palate. We like to present attractive dishes, especially when entertaining—but not at the cost of hours of preparation. Fortunately, the simplest dishes can be dressed up in glamorous style with the aid of some very easy garnishing techniques.

DIPS can be made colorful by sprinkling them with chopped scallions (green onions) or grated carrots.

FISH dishes take on appetizing attractiveness when accompanied by lemon or lime wedges dipped in finely chopped parsley or paprika. Or try an easy citrus twist: cut into a slice of lemon or lime from the edge to the center, then twist in opposite directions.

FRUIT SALADS and **COOKED VEGETABLES** appear more savory when sprinkled with grated lemon, orange, or lime peel, while strips of orange peel or mint leaves add a cool appeal to fruit salads.

LETTUCE leaves "blush" attractively when colored by paprika.

SALADS take on a new look when garnished with carrot curls or dressed up with tomato wedges or slices that have been dipped in finely chopped parsley.

SOUPS gain visual appeal when chopped scallion (green onion), grated carrot, or the ever-popular popcorn is added (popcorn should be counted toward your Bread Selections). A bowl of steaming broth can be deliciously garnished with chopped fresh herbs such as parsley, tarragon, dill, rosemary, basil, or chives.

VEGETABLES and **SOUPS** look more elegant when sprinkled with small amounts of grated Parmesan cheese (count it toward your Optional Calories).

USING FRESH HERBS in your recipe? Garnish with a matching sprig.

FOR AN IMAGINATIVE "SERVING BOWL" for a dip or an egg or tuna salad, use a hollowed-out bell pepper (green, red, or yellow) or a small cabbage.

P.S. When garnishing isn't called for, you can still brighten the appearance of foods by arranging them creatively on a pretty dish.

Tips for Toting

"Brown-bagging" has become a way of life because it's convenient, necessary, and economical. Many of our recipes lend themselves to a portable life-style.

Here are helpful hints to keep in mind when packing meals or snacks.

Cold Foods

- Pack chilled foods in an insulated bag or lunch box.
- Use well-chilled ingredients when making sandwiches.

- Make a week's worth of sandwiches in advance and freeze them for freshness. Then just take one with you in the morning; it will be thawed by the time you're ready for lunch. Peanut butter, meat, and poultry fillings freeze well. (Do *not* freeze raw vegetables, such as lettuce or tomato, since this may affect their texture. And never freeze mayonnaise fillings.)
- When possible, keep the brown-bag meal refrigerated until time to eat. Foods such as meats, poultry, fish, and eggs may spoil if kept at room temperature longer than two hours.

Hot Foods

- When toting hot foods, keep them above 140°F (hot to the touch).
- Hot foods should be packed in an insulated vacuum container. To help keep foods hot longer, preheat the container by filling with hot water and allowing it to stand for several minutes. Then pour out the water and fill the container with hot foods.

Appetizers, Soups, and Dips

Dip into an array of dishes that get your meal off to a nutritious start. Guests will applaud your cholesterol-reduced Tofu-Tahini Dip, and no one need know it only takes a cool (no cooking) five minutes to prepare. And something Popeye never knew is that his favorite vegetable could show up at a party as Spinach Pinwheel Hors d'Oeuvres. Soups don't have to be limited to dinner; for a change-of-pace luncheon add our novel Buttermilk-Walnut Soup. Not home at lunchtime? Simply ladle soup into an insulated vacuum container for a filling pick-me-up.

P.S. Our dips make snappy snacks, too!

Spicy Deviled Eggs

4 hard-cooked eggs
2 tablespoons plus 2 teaspoons
  reduced-calorie mayonnaise
2 tablespoons *each* finely
  chopped red bell pepper, green
  bell pepper, and celery
2 teaspoons minced scallion
  (green onion)
½ teaspoon seeded and minced
  jalapeño pepper
Dash *each* chili powder, hot
  sauce, and Worcestershire
  sauce
Garnish: diced red bell pepper

Deviled eggs make an attractive hors d'oeuvre or a totable lunch.

1. Cut eggs in half lengthwise; remove egg yolks to small mixing bowl, reserving whites.

2. Add remaining ingredients except garnish to egg yolks and, using a fork, mash until combined. Spoon an equal amount of yolk mixture into each egg white half. Cover and refrigerate until ready to serve.

3. To serve, garnish with diced red bell pepper.

APPROXIMATE TOTAL TIME: 15 MINUTES

MAKES 4 SERVINGS

Each serving provides: 1 Fat; 1 Protein; ¼ Vegetable
Per serving: 107 calories; 6 g protein; 8 g fat; 2 g carbohydrate; 28 mg calcium; 123 mg sodium; 216 mg cholesterol; 0.2 g dietary fiber

Ham 'n' Cheese Biscuits ⌄C⌄

½ ounce *each* reduced-fat
   Cheddar cheese, shredded, and
   diced turkey-ham
2 teaspoons reduced-calorie
   mayonnaise
1 teaspoon *each* sweet pickle
   relish and country Dijon-style
   mustard
4 ready-to-bake refrigerated
   buttermilk flaky biscuits
   (1 ounce each)*

1. Preheat oven to 400°F. In small mixing bowl combine all ingredients except biscuits, stirring until thoroughly combined; set aside.

2. Carefully separate each biscuit into 2 thin layers, then partially separate each layer, forming a pocket. Spoon an equal amount of ham mixture into each pocket; crimp edges of each biscuit to enclose filling.

3. Arrange biscuits on nonstick baking sheet and bake until biscuits are lightly browned, 8 to 10 minutes. Serve immediately.

* Keep biscuits refrigerated until ready to use. Separate dough into layers as soon as biscuits are removed from refrigerator; they will be difficult to work with if allowed to come to room temperature.

APPROXIMATE TOTAL TIME: 20 MINUTES

MAKES 4 SERVINGS, 2 BISCUITS EACH

Each serving provides: ¼ Fat; 1 Bread; 25 Optional Calories
Per serving: 111 calories; 3 g protein; 5 g fat; 13 g carbohydrate; 32 mg calcium; 421 mg sodium; 3 mg cholesterol; dietary fiber data not available

Scallion-Cheese Filled Tomatoes Ⓒ Ⓢ

6 cherry tomatoes
¼ cup finely chopped scallions (green onions)
1 ounce chèvre (French goat cheese)

1. Cut a thin slice from stem end of each tomato. Scoop out and discard pulp, reserving shells; set aside.

2. In small bowl combine remaining ingredients, mixing well. Fill each reserved tomato shell with an equal amount of scallion-cheese mixture.

3. Preheat broiler. Set tomato shells on nonstick baking sheet and broil until cheese is bubbly, about 1 minute. Serve warm.

APPROXIMATE TOTAL TIME: 10 MINUTES

MAKES 2 SERVINGS, 3 TOMATOES EACH

Each serving provides: ½ Protein; ½ Vegetable; 10 Optional Calories
Per serving: 60 calories; 3 g protein; 4 g fat; 3 g carbohydrate; 31 mg calcium; 90 mg sodium; 13 mg cholesterol; 1 g dietary fiber

Spinach Pinwheel Hors d'Oeuvres ▽C ▽F

1 tablespoon plus 2 teaspoons
  olive *or* vegetable oil
½ cup finely chopped onion
4 garlic cloves, chopped
2 cups thawed and well-drained
  frozen chopped spinach
2 tablespoons chopped fresh
  parsley
1 teaspoon Italian seasoning
⅛ teaspoon crushed red pepper
⅓ cup less 1 teaspoon grated
  Parmesan *or* Romano cheese
1 package refrigerated ready-to-
  bake pizza crust dough (10
  ounces)
1 tablespoon thawed frozen egg
  substitute

1. In 10-inch nonstick skillet heat oil; add onion and garlic and cook over medium-high heat, stirring frequently, until onion begins to soften, about 3 minutes. Add spinach, parsley, Italian seasoning, and red pepper and cook, stirring occasionally, until spinach is heated through, about 3 minutes. Let cool slightly; add cheese and stir to combine.

2. Preheat oven to 425°F. Stretch pizza dough into a 16 x 12-inch rectangle. Spread spinach mixture evenly over dough, leaving a 1½-inch border around edge of dough. Starting from the narrow end roll dough over spinach, jelly-roll fashion, to enclose filling; pinch seam well to seal.

3. Spray nonstick baking sheet with nonstick cooking spray and arrange roll, seam side down, on sheet. Brush egg substitute over roll and bake until golden brown, about 15 minutes.

4. Cut roll into 20 equal slices.

APPROXIMATE TOTAL TIME: 30 MINUTES (includes baking time)

MAKES 10 SERVINGS, 2 SLICES EACH

Each serving provides: ½ Fat; ½ Vegetable; 1 Bread; 15 Optional Calories
Per serving with Parmesan cheese: 120 calories; 5 g protein; 4 g fat; 16 g carbohydrate; 88 mg calcium; 219 mg sodium; 2 mg cholesterol; 1 g dietary fiber (this figure does not include pizza dough; nutrition analysis not available)
With Romano cheese: 118 calories; 5 g protein; 4 g fat; 16 g carbohydrate; 80 mg calcium; 202 mg sodium; 3 mg cholesterol; 1 g dietary fiber (this figure does not include pizza dough; nutrition analysis not available)

Apple, Walnut, and Cheddar Soup �)C⟩ ⟨S⟩

1 teaspoon sweet margarine
½ pound Granny Smith apples, cored, pared, and chopped
½ cup chopped onion
½ ounce shelled walnuts
1 cup canned ready-to-serve low-sodium chicken broth
¾ ounce reduced-fat Cheddar cheese, shredded

1. In 1½-quart nonstick saucepan melt margarine; add apples, onion, and walnuts. Cover and cook over medium heat, stirring occasionally, until apples are soft, about 10 minutes. Let cool slightly.

2. Transfer mixture to blender; add broth and process until smooth. Return to saucepan; stir in cheese and cook over low heat, stirring constantly, until cheese melts, about 2 minutes.

APPROXIMATE TOTAL TIME: 25 MINUTES

MAKES 2 SERVINGS, ABOUT 1¼ CUPS EACH

Each serving provides: 1 Fat; 1 Protein; ½ Vegetable; 1 Fruit; 20 Optional Calories
Per serving: 181 calories; 6 g protein; 9 g fat; 20 g carbohydrate; 115 mg calcium; 103 mg sodium; 8 mg cholesterol; 3 g dietary fiber

Buttermilk-Walnut Soup ▽c

1½ cups low-fat buttermilk
  (1% milk fat)
1 ounce finely ground walnuts
½ teaspoon minced scallion
  (green onion)
1 garlic clove, minced
½ packet (about ½ teaspoon)
  instant chicken broth and
  seasoning mix
⅛ teaspoon salt
Dash white pepper
1½ teaspoons minced fresh dill

1. In blender combine all ingredients except dill and process until smooth; stir in dill. Cover and refrigerate until flavors blend, at least 1 hour.

APPROXIMATE TOTAL TIME: 10 MINUTES (does not include chilling time)

MAKES 2 SERVINGS, ABOUT ¾ CUP EACH

Each serving provides: ¾ Milk; 1 Fat; 1 Protein; 20 Optional Calories
Per serving: 170 calories; 8 g protein; 10 g fat; 12 g carbohydrate; 234 mg calcium; 581 mg sodium; 7 mg cholesterol; 1 g dietary fiber

Cheese and Broccoli Soup ▽C ▽F

2 teaspoons reduced-calorie margarine (tub)
2 tablespoons finely chopped onion
1 tablespoon plus 1½ teaspoons all-purpose flour
1 cup *each* skim *or* nonfat milk and broccoli florets
1 packet instant chicken broth and seasoning mix
½ teaspoon chopped fresh parsley
Dash white pepper
¾ ounce reduced-fat Cheddar *or* Monterey Jack cheese, shredded

1. In 2-quart nonstick saucepan melt margarine; add onion and sauté over medium-high heat, until softened, 1 to 2 minutes. Sprinkle flour over onion and stir quickly to combine. Continuing to stir, add *1 cup water* and the milk; add broccoli, broth mix, parsley, and pepper.

2. Reduce heat to low and cook, stirring occasionally, until broccoli is tender, 10 to 15 minutes (*do not boil*). Let cool slightly.

3. In blender process half of the soup until smooth; return to saucepan. Stir in cheese and cook over low heat until cheese is melted, about 5 minutes.

APPROXIMATE TOTAL TIME: 30 MINUTES

MAKES 2 SERVINGS, ABOUT 1¼ CUPS EACH

Each serving provides: ½ Milk; ½ Fat; ½ Protein; 1⅛ Vegetables; ¼ Bread; 5 Optional Calories
Per serving with Cheddar cheese: 142 calories; 11 g protein; 4 g fat; 16 g carbohydrate; 276 mg calcium; 690 mg sodium; 10 mg cholesterol; 0.3 g dietary fiber (this figure does not include broccoli florets; nutrition analysis not available)
With Monterey Jack cheese: 138 calories; 11 g protein; 4 g fat; 15 g carbohydrate; 276 mg calcium; 682 mg sodium; 10 mg cholesterol; 0.3 g dietary fiber (this figure does not include broccoli florets; nutrition analysis not available)

Fresh Tomato-Basil Soup ⊽c ⊽s

2 teaspoons olive *or* vegetable oil
1 cup chopped onions
½ small garlic clove, mashed
6 large plum tomatoes, blanched, peeled, seeded, and chopped
1 cup canned ready-to-serve low-sodium chicken broth
2 tablespoons chopped fresh basil
Garnish: 2 basil sprigs

1. In 1½-quart nonstick saucepan heat oil; add onions and garlic and cook over medium-high heat until tender-crisp, about 2 minutes.

2. Stir in remaining ingredients and bring mixture to a boil. Reduce heat to low and let simmer, stirring occasionally, until flavors blend, about 15 minutes.

3. Pour soup into 2 soup bowls and garnish each portion with a basil sprig.

APPROXIMATE TOTAL TIME: 30 MINUTES

MAKES 2 SERVINGS, ABOUT 1¼ CUPS EACH

Each serving provides: 1 Fat; 4 Vegetables; 20 Optional Calories
Per serving: 114 calories; 4 g protein; 6 g fat; 14 g carbohydrate; 55 mg calcium; 41 mg sodium; 0 mg cholesterol; 3 g dietary fiber

Lima Bean Soup (C) (F) (S)

½ cup chopped onion
¼ cup chopped carrot
2 teaspoons sweet margarine
1 cup *each* frozen green lima beans and canned ready-to-serve low-sodium chicken broth
Dash white pepper

1. In 1½-quart microwavable casserole combine first 3 ingredients. Microwave on High (100%) for 2 minutes until margarine is melted; add beans and broth. Cover and microwave on High for 5 minutes. Let cool slightly.

2. Transfer to blender and process until smooth. Return to casserole and microwave on High for 2 minutes, until thoroughly heated. Stir in pepper.

APPROXIMATE TOTAL TIME: 20 MINUTES

MAKES 2 SERVINGS, ABOUT 1 CUP EACH

Each serving provides: 1 Fat; 1 Bread; ¾ Vegetable; 20 Optional Calories
Per serving: 154 calories; 7 g protein; 5 g fat; 21 g carbohydrate; 34 mg calcium; 79 mg sodium; 0 mg cholesterol; 11 g dietary fiber

Microwave Vichyssoise ⬇C ⬇S

2 teaspoons margarine
1 cup thoroughly washed thinly sliced leeks (white portion only)
1 cup canned ready-to-serve low-sodium chicken broth
6 ounces finely diced pared all-purpose potato
½ cup whole milk
1 tablespoon half-and-half (blend of milk and cream)
Dash *each* white pepper and ground nutmeg
2 teaspoons minced fresh chives *or* 1 teaspoon chopped chives

1. In 1-quart microwavable casserole microwave margarine on High (100%) for 30 seconds until melted. Add leeks and microwave on High for 1½ minutes, until slightly softened.

2. Add chicken broth and potato; cover and microwave on High for 5 minutes, until potato is tender, stirring halfway through cooking. Let stand for 1 minute. Uncover and let cool slightly, about 5 minutes.

3. Transfer potato-leek mixture to food processor and process until pureed. Return mixture to casserole.

4. Using a wire whisk, stir in milk, half-and-half, pepper, and nutmeg. Cover and refrigerate until chilled, at least 1 hour.

5. Divide soup into 2 soup bowls and sprinkle each portion with an equal amount of chives.

APPROXIMATE TOTAL TIME: 25 MINUTES (does not include chilling time)

MAKES 2 SERVINGS, ABOUT 1 CUP EACH

Each serving provides: ¼ Milk; 1 Fat; 1 Vegetable; 1 Bread; 50 Optional Calories
Per serving: 196 calories; 6 g protein; 8 g fat; 27 g carbohydrate; 120 mg calcium; 120 mg sodium; 11 mg cholesterol; 2 g dietary fiber

Oriental Hot Pot ▽C ▽F

1 tablespoon *each* rice vinegar
  and reduced-sodium soy sauce
1 packet instant beef broth and
  seasoning mix
1 teaspoon minced pared
  gingerroot
½ cup sliced carrot
1 cup thinly sliced Chinese chard
  (bok choy)
½ cup *each* bean sprouts, snow
  peas (Chinese pea pods), and
  sliced shiitake mushrooms *or*
  white mushrooms
¼ cup sliced scallions (green
  onions)
2 ounces uncooked cellophane
  noodles*

In this traditional Chinese dish, guests cook a selection of ingredients in hot broth in a pot set in the center of the table. Our version is completely prepared on the range prior to serving.

1. In 3-quart saucepan combine 3 *cups water*, the vinegar, soy sauce, broth mix, and gingerroot; cover and cook over medium-high heat until mixture comes to a boil.

2. Reduce heat to low; add carrot and cook, uncovered, until tender, 8 to 10 minutes. Add remaining ingredients except noodles and stir to combine; cover and cook until vegetables are tender-crisp, about 5 minutes. Add noodles and stir to combine. Cook, uncovered, until noodles are transparent, about 3 minutes.

* Two ounces uncooked cellophane noodles yield about 1 cup cooked noodles.

APPROXIMATE TOTAL TIME: 30 MINUTES

MAKES 2 SERVINGS, ABOUT 2 CUPS EACH

Each serving provides: 3¼ Vegetables; 1 Bread; 5 Optional Calories
Per serving: 154 calories; 4 g protein; 0.4 g fat; 35 g carbohydrate; 79 mg calcium; 802 mg sodium; 0 mg cholesterol; 2 g dietary fiber (this figure does not include Chinese chard; nutrition analysis not available)

Puree of Green Bean Soup ⱽc ⱽf ⱽs

2 cups sliced trimmed green
  beans
1 cup chopped onions
2 teaspoons reduced-calorie
  margarine (tub)
1 cup low-fat milk (1% milk fat)
¼ cup canned ready-to-serve
  low-sodium chicken broth
1 teaspoon all-purpose flour
Garnish: 6 trimmed chives

1. In 1-quart microwavable casserole combine first 3 ingredients; microwave on High (100%) for 2 minutes, until margarine is melted. Add ½ cup water and microwave on High for 5 minutes, until beans are tender. Let cool slightly.

2. Transfer mixture to blender and process until smooth; add remaining ingredients and process until combined. Return to casserole and microwave on High for 1 minute, until mixture thickens slightly and is thoroughly heated.

3. Pour soup into 2 soup bowls and garnish each portion with 3 trimmed chives.

APPROXIMATE TOTAL TIME: 20 MINUTES

MAKES 2 SERVINGS, ABOUT 2 CUPS EACH

Each serving provides: ½ Milk; ½ Fat; 3 Vegetables; 20 Optional Calories
Per serving: 138 calories; 7 g protein; 4 g fat; 21 g carbohydrate; 211 mg calcium; 116 mg sodium; 5 mg cholesterol; 3 g dietary fiber

Black Bean Dip ⱽ© ⱽᶠ

**4 ounces rinsed drained canned
black (turtle) beans
I small garlic clove, chopped
I cup prepared thick and chunky
mild salsa**

*Serve this nutritious dip with vege-
table crudités or toasted tortilla
pieces.*

I. In food processor combine beans and garlic and
process, using on-off motion, until smooth (do not
puree). Transfer to bowl and stir in salsa.

APPROXIMATE TOTAL TIME: 10 MINUTES

MAKES 4 SERVINGS, ABOUT ½ CUP EACH

Each serving provides: ½ Protein; ½ Vegetable
Per serving: 49 calories; 2 g protein; 0.1 g fat; 10 g carbohydrate; 12 mg calcium; 456 mg sodium (estimated);
0 mg cholesterol; 1 g dietary fiber

Italian Herbed Dip ▽C ▽S

2 tablespoons thawed frozen egg
   substitute
1 teaspoon balsamic *or* red wine
   vinegar
1 small garlic clove
¼ cup *each* olive oil and finely
   chopped scallions (green
   onions)
1 tablespoon *each* finely chopped
   fresh basil and Italian
   (flat-leaf) parsley
¼ teaspoon oregano leaves

*This party dip is also great as a salad
dressing.*

1. In blender combine first 3 ingredients and process until combined. With motor running, gradually add oil in a steady stream until mixture thickens.

2. Transfer mixture to bowl; stir in remaining ingredients. Cover and refrigerate until chilled, at least 15 minutes.

APPROXIMATE TOTAL TIME: 10 MINUTES (does not include chilling time)

MAKES 12 SERVINGS, ABOUT 2 TEASPOONS EACH

Each serving provides: 1 Fat; 3 Optional Calories
Per serving: 42 calories; 0.3 g protein; 5 g fat; 0.3 g carbohydrate; 6 mg calcium; 5 mg sodium; 0 mg cholesterol; 0.1 g dietary fiber

Salmon Mousse ▽C

7 ounces drained canned salmon (packed in water), mashed

3 tablespoons whipped cream cheese, softened

2 tablespoons plus 2 teaspoons reduced-calorie mayonnaise

2 tablespoons *each* finely diced red onion, rinsed drained capers, and chopped fresh parsley

1 teaspoon lemon juice

1 teaspoon unflavored gelatin

½ packet (about ½ teaspoon) instant chicken broth and seasoning mix

3 egg whites

If canned salmon is too costly for your budget, substitute canned tuna.

1. Spray a 7⅜ x 3⅝ x 2¼-inch nonstick loaf pan with nonstick cooking spray. Cut a sheet of wax paper 7½ inches long and set in pan, folding excess paper over wide sides of pan; spray pan again with cooking spray. Set aside.

2. In large mixing bowl combine salmon, cream cheese, mayonnaise, onion, capers, parsley, and lemon juice; mix well and set aside.

3. In 1-quart saucepan sprinkle gelatin over ¼ *cup water*; let stand 1 minute to soften. Cook over medium heat, stirring constantly, until gelatin is completely dissolved, about 1 minute. Stir in broth mix. Remove from heat and let stand for 5 minutes.

4. Using mixer on medium-high speed, beat egg whites until stiff.

5. Add gelatin mixture to salmon mixture and stir to thoroughly combine. Add ⅓ of the egg whites to salmon-gelatin mixture and stir to combine; fold in remaining egg whites.

6. Spoon salmon mixture into prepared pan, spreading top smooth. Cover pan with plastic wrap and refrigerate until set, at least 2 hours or overnight.

7. To serve, invert pan onto serving platter and cut crosswise into 8 equal slices.

APPROXIMATE TOTAL TIME: 20 MINUTES (does not include chilling time)

MAKES 8 SERVINGS

Each serving provides: ½ Fat; 1 Protein; 15 Optional Calories
Per serving: 69 calories; 7 g protein; 4 g fat; 1 g carbohydrate; 67 mg calcium; 310 mg sodium; 15 mg cholesterol; 0.1 g dietary fiber

Spinach Dip

½ cup evaporated skimmed milk
2 teaspoons all-purpose flour
3 tablespoons whipped cream cheese
2 tablespoons sour cream
½ cup frozen chopped spinach, thawed and well drained
2 tablespoons finely chopped onion
1 small garlic clove, minced
1 teaspoon *each* grated Parmesan cheese and Worcestershire sauce
⅛ teaspoon *each* salt and pepper
Dash hot sauce

Serve with melba rounds, flatbreads, or vegetable crudités.

1. Using a wire whisk, in 1-quart shallow microwavable casserole combine milk and flour, stirring until flour is dissolved. Microwave on Medium (50%) for 1½ minutes, stirring once halfway through cooking, until mixture thickens.

2. Stir in cream cheese and sour cream; microwave on Medium for 2½ minutes, stirring once after every minute.

3. Stir in spinach, onion, and garlic and microwave on Medium for 2 minutes, stirring once halfway through cooking.

4. Stir in remaining ingredients until thoroughly combined.

5. Transfer to serving bowl and serve immediately.

APPROXIMATE TOTAL TIME: 10 MINUTES

MAKES 4 SERVINGS

Each serving provides: ¼ Milk; ¼ Vegetable; 50 Optional Calories
Per serving: 121 calories; 6 g protein; 5 g fat; 15 g carbohydrate; 146 mg calcium; 180 mg sodium; 12 mg cholesterol; 1 g dietary fiber

Tofu-Tahini Dip ▽c

2 ounces firm-style tofu
1 tablespoon *each* tahini (sesame paste) and chopped scallion (green onion)
2 teaspoons ketchup
1 teaspoon *each* lemon juice and reduced-sodium soy sauce
½ garlic clove, chopped
1 teaspoon sesame seed, toasted
2 small pitas (1 ounce each), heated and cut into quarters

1. In blender combine all ingredients except sesame seed and pitas and process until pureed, about 1 minute. Transfer to serving bowl. Sprinkle with sesame seed and serve with pitas.

APPROXIMATE TOTAL TIME: 5 MINUTES

MAKES 2 SERVINGS

Each serving provides: ½ Fat; 1 Protein; 1 Bread; 15 Optional Calories
Per serving: 191 calories; 9 g protein; 7 g fat; 24 g carbohydrate; 116 mg calcium; 355 mg sodium; 0 mg cholesterol; 1 g dietary fiber

Breakfasts
and Brunches

Breakfast is coming into its own. Nutrition-conscious people recognize that it's important to fuel up for the day with a nourishing meal. Our recipes make this easy with quickly prepared tasty dishes, many of them complete meals in themselves. How about Polenta with Blueberries in Syrup, microwaved in a nifty five minutes? Or a tasty Basil-Vegetable Quiche for brunch? Those who race off to work will find many of our items conveniently totable. (Pack an Apple-Cheddar Muffin for an energizing way to start your workday.)

Apple-Cheddar Muffins △C △S

1¾ cups all-purpose flour
½ pound apples, cored, pared, and finely chopped
½ cup rye flour
2 ounces reduced-fat Cheddar cheese, shredded
1½ ounces chopped walnuts
¼ cup granulated sugar
2 tablespoons dark raisins
2 teaspoons double-acting baking powder
¼ teaspoon ground allspice *or* ground cinnamon
½ cup skim *or* nonfat milk
⅓ cup plus 2 teaspoons reduced-calorie margarine (tub)
¼ cup thawed frozen egg substitute

These muffins are great for toting to the office when you want breakfast in a hurry. Enjoy with skim milk, yogurt, or cottage cheese.

1. Preheat oven to 375°F. In medium mixing bowl combine first 9 ingredients; stir to combine and set aside.

2. In blender combine remaining ingredients and process until smooth. Pour into dry ingredients and stir until moistened (*do not beat or overmix*).

3. Spray twelve 2½-inch nonstick muffin-pan cups with nonstick cooking spray; fill each cup with an equal amount of batter (each will be about ¾ full). Bake in middle of center oven rack for 20 minutes (until muffins are golden and a toothpick, inserted in center, comes out dry).

4. Invert muffins onto wire rack and let cool.

APPROXIMATE TOTAL TIME: 30 MINUTES (includes baking time)

MAKES 12 SERVINGS, 1 MUFFIN EACH

Each serving provides: 1 Fat; ½ Protein; 1 Bread; ¼ Fruit; 30 Optional Calories
Per serving: 181 calories; 5 g protein; 6 g fat; 26 g carbohydrate; 101 mg calcium; 180 mg sodium; 4 mg cholesterol; 2 g dietary fiber

Blueberry-Oat Bran Loaf ⑤▽

1¼ cups plus 1 tablespoon cake flour, sifted
2¼ ounces uncooked unprocessed oat bran
1½ ounces uncooked quick-cooking oats
1 teaspoon *each* ground cinnamon and baking soda
¼ teaspoon ground nutmeg
1 cup part-skim ricotta cheese
¾ cup low-fat buttermilk (1% milk fat)
2 eggs, lightly beaten
¼ cup *each* granulated sugar and vegetable oil
1½ cups fresh *or* frozen blueberries (no sugar added)

Loaf can be cut into slices and each slice individually wrapped and stored in the freezer. Thaw slices at room temperature. A slice of this nutritious loaf is delicious with a glass of skim milk for breakfast.

1. Preheat oven to 350°F. In medium mixing bowl combine flour, oat bran, oats, cinnamon, baking soda, and nutmeg, stirring to combine.

2. In separate medium mixing bowl combine remaining ingredients except blueberries and stir to combine. Add to flour mixture and stir until moistened; fold in blueberries.

3. Spray a 9 × 5 × 3-inch loaf pan with nonstick cooking spray and spread batter evenly in pan. Bake in middle of center oven rack for 55 minutes (until a cake tester, inserted in center, comes out dry). Set loaf pan on wire rack and let cool for 5 minutes; invert onto wire rack and let cool completely.

APPROXIMATE TOTAL TIME: 60 MINUTES (includes baking time; does not include cooling time)

MAKES 12 SERVINGS

Each serving provides: 1 Fat; ½ Protein; 1 Bread; ¼ Fruit; 25 Optional Calories
Per serving: 195 calories; 7 g protein; 8 g fat; 24 g carbohydrate; 89 mg calcium; 122 mg sodium; 42 mg cholesterol; 2 g dietary fiber

Cranberry-Wheat Muffins ▽C ▽F

3 tablespoons granulated sugar
2 tablespoons thawed frozen
   concentrated apple juice
   (no sugar added)
½ cup cranberries
¼ cup plus 1 tablespoon golden
   or dark raisins
¾ cup low-fat buttermilk
   (1% milk fat)
¼ cup thawed frozen egg
   substitute
2 tablespoons plus 2 teaspoons
   margarine, melted
1 cup all-purpose flour
½ cup buckwheat flour
2 teaspoons double-acting baking
   powder
½ teaspoon baking soda

Store muffins in the freezer. They taste as fresh as the day they were baked when thawed at room temperature. To make this meal complete, try a cup of reduced-calorie hot cocoa.

1. Preheat oven to 425°F. In small mixing bowl combine sugar, *2 tablespoons water*, and the apple juice concentrate, stirring to dissolve sugar. Add cranberries and raisins; stir to combine and set aside.

2. Using a fork, in separate small mixing bowl beat together buttermilk, egg substitute, and margarine; set aside.

3. In medium mixing bowl combine remaining ingredients; stir in buttermilk mixture, stirring until moistened. Stir in cranberry mixture.

4. Spray eight 2½-inch nonstick muffin-pan cups with nonstick cooking spray; fill each cup with an equal amount of batter and partially fill remaining cups with water (this will prevent pan from burning and/or warping). Bake in middle of center oven rack for 20 minutes (until muffins are lightly browned and a toothpick, inserted in center, comes out dry). Transfer muffins to wire rack and let cool.

APPROXIMATE TOTAL TIME: 30 MINUTES (includes baking time)

MAKES 8 SERVINGS, 1 MUFFIN EACH

Each serving provides: 1 Fat; 1 Bread; ½ Fruit; 40 Optional Calories
Per serving: 167 calories; 4 g protein; 4 g fat; 29 g carbohydrate; 98 mg calcium; 242 mg sodium; 1 mg cholesterol; 1 g dietary fiber (this figure does not include cranberries and buckwheat flour; nutrition analyses not available)

Applesauce-Cheese Toast ⬦C⬦ ⬦S⬦

¼ cup applesauce (no sugar added)
½ teaspoon maple syrup
¼ teaspoon ground cinnamon
¼ cup part-skim ricotta cheese
2 tablespoons whipped cream cheese
2 slices reduced-calorie raisin bread (40 calories per slice), lightly toasted
½ ounce chopped walnuts

1. In small mixing bowl combine first 3 ingredients; stir to combine and set aside.

2. In separate small mixing bowl combine cheeses, stirring to combine.

3. Onto each slice of bread spread half of the cheese mixture; top each with half of the applesauce mixture and half of the walnuts. Arrange bread slices on oven tray or baking sheet and bake at 425°F in toaster-oven or oven until applesauce mixture is heated through, 2 to 3 minutes.

APPROXIMATE TOTAL TIME: 10 MINUTES (includes baking time)

MAKES 2 SERVINGS

Each serving provides: ½ Fat; 1 Protein; ½ Bread; ¼ Fruit; 40 Optional Calories
Per serving: 178 calories; 7 g protein; 10 g fat; 17 g carbohydrate; 123 mg calcium; 170 mg sodium; 19 mg cholesterol; 1 g dietary fiber

English Muffin with Date-Nut Topping ⟨c⟩ ⟨s⟩

¼ cup part-skim ricotta cheese
2 tablespoons whipped cream
  cheese
½ ounce shelled walnuts, toasted
  and chopped
2 pitted dates, chopped
1 cinnamon-raisin English muffin
  (2 ounces), split in half and
  toasted
Dash ground cinnamon

1. In small mixing bowl combine cheeses, mixing well; stir in nuts and dates.

2. Onto each muffin half spread half of the cheese mixture; sprinkle each with cinnamon.

3. Arrange muffin halves on oven tray of toaster-oven* and broil or top brown until cheese is heated through, 1 to 2 minutes.

* Broiler may be substituted for toaster-oven.

APPROXIMATE TOTAL TIME: 10 MINUTES

MAKES 2 SERVINGS

Each serving provides: ½ Fat; 1 Protein; 1 Bread; ½ Fruit; 35 Optional Calories
Per serving: 213 calories; 8 g protein; 11 g fat; 22 g carbohydrate; 119 mg calcium; 158 mg sodium; 19 mg cholesterol; 1 g dietary fiber

Apple-Cinnamon Popovers ▽C ▽F

1 cup thawed frozen egg
  substitute
¾ cup all-purpose flour
½ cup applesauce (no sugar
  added)
⅓ cup low-fat buttermilk
  (1% milk fat)
2 tablespoons plus 2 teaspoons
  reduced-calorie margarine
  (tub), melted and cooled
1 teaspoon ground cinnamon
¾ teaspoon granulated sugar
¼ teaspoon baking soda

*Start the weekend off right with a
breakfast of warm popovers and
fruit-topped yogurt.*

1. Preheat oven to 425°F. Spray four 10-ounce custard cups with nonstick cooking spray; set aside.

2. In blender process all ingredients until smooth. Pour ¼ of batter into each prepared cup. Set cups on baking sheet and bake in middle of center oven rack for 25 minutes, until puffed and golden brown.

3. Using a knife, pierce the top of each popover to allow steam to escape; bake 5 minutes longer.

APPROXIMATE TOTAL TIME: 35 MINUTES (includes baking time)

MAKES 4 SERVINGS, 1 POPOVER EACH

Each serving provides: 1 Fat; 1 Protein; 1 Bread; ¼ Fruit; 15 Optional Calories
Per serving: 178 calories; 10 g protein; 4 g fat; 25 g carbohydrate; 62 mg calcium; 260 mg sodium; 1 mg cholesterol; 1 g dietary fiber

Hawaiian Oatmeal ▽C ▽F ▽S

¾ ounce uncooked instant oatmeal
¼ cup drained canned pineapple chunks (no sugar added)
¼ ounce macadamia nuts, sliced
½ teaspoon *each* firmly packed light brown sugar and shredded coconut
½ cup skim *or* nonfat milk

▬

Serve this island treat with skim milk or reduced-calorie hot cocoa for a complete breakfast.

1. In medium microwavable bowl combine oatmeal and ½ *cup water*, stirring to combine; microwave on High (100%) for 1 minute, stirring once halfway through cooking.

2. Add pineapple and microwave on High for 30 seconds.

3. To serve, divide cereal into 2 serving bowls and top each portion with half of the nuts, sugar, and coconut; pour half of the milk over each portion of cereal.

APPROXIMATE TOTAL TIME: 5 MINUTES

MAKES 2 SERVINGS

Each serving provides: ¼ Milk; ¼ Protein; ½ Bread; ¼ Fruit; 20 Optional Calories
Per serving: 112 calories; 4 g protein; 4 g fat; 17 g carbohydrate; 89 mg calcium; 34 mg sodium; 1 mg cholesterol; 1 g dietary fiber (this figure does not include macadamia nuts; nutrition analysis not available)

Maple-Spice Oat Bran ▽C ▽F ▽S

½ cup apple juice (no sugar added)
¾ ounce uncooked unprocessed oat bran
1 tablespoon dark raisins
¼ teaspoon apple pie spice
1 teaspoon maple syrup
¼ cup skim or nonfat milk

Hot cereal cooks in minutes in the microwave oven. Team it up with a glass of skim milk for a complete breakfast.

1. In medium microwavable mixing bowl combine apple juice, *¼ cup water*, and the oat bran, stirring to combine; microwave on High (100%) for 2 minutes, stirring once every 30 seconds. Stir in raisins and spice.

2. To serve, transfer to serving bowl and top with syrup and milk.

APPROXIMATE TOTAL TIME: 10 MINUTES

MAKES 1 SERVING

Each serving provides: ¼ Milk; 1 Bread; 1½ Fruits; 20 Optional Calories
Per serving: 206 calories; 7 g protein; 2 g fat; 42 g carbohydrate; 119 mg calcium; 38 mg sodium; 1 mg cholesterol; 4 g dietary fiber

Polenta with Blueberries in Syrup 🔻C 🔻F 🔻S

¾ ounce instant polenta (quick cooking yellow cornmeal)
½ cup blueberries
1 tablespoon reduced-calorie pancake syrup (30 calories per fluid ounce)

▬

Top off this unusual breakfast with a serving of reduced-calorie hot cocoa, yogurt, or a glass of skim milk.

1. In medium microwavable bowl microwave ¾ cup *water* on High (100%) for 3 minutes, until boiling. Stir in polenta and microwave on High for 1 minute, stirring halfway through cooking.

2. In small microwavable mixing bowl combine blueberries and syrup. Microwave on Medium (50%) for 1 minute, until hot.

3. Serve polenta topped with blueberry mixture.

APPROXIMATE TOTAL TIME: 5 MINUTES

MAKES 1 SERVING

Each serving provides: 1 Bread; 1 Fruit; 15 Optional Calories
Per serving: 131 calories; 2 g protein; 1 g fat; 31 g carbohydrate; 5 mg calcium; 5 mg sodium; 0 mg cholesterol; 3 g dietary fiber

Raisin-Nut Breakfast ▽c ▽f ▽s

1½ ounces uncooked quick-
   cooking farina
¼ cup golden raisins
Dash ground cinnamon
1 cup skim *or* nonfat milk
½ ounce sliced almonds,
   toasted

1. In 1-quart saucepan bring *1½ cups water* to a boil; gradually stir in farina. Add raisins and cinnamon and cook, stirring constantly, for 2 to 3 minutes.

2. Into each of 2 serving bowls spoon half of the farina mixture; top each with ½ cup milk and ¼ ounce almonds.

APPROXIMATE TOTAL TIME: 5 MINUTES

MAKES 2 SERVINGS

Each serving provides: ½ Milk; ½ Fat; ½ Protein; 1 Bread; 1 Fruit;
Per serving: 218 calories; 8 g protein; 4 g fat; 39 g carbohydrate; 184 mg calcium; 67 mg sodium; 2 mg cholesterol; 2 g dietary fiber (this figure does not include almonds; nutrition analysis not available)

Egg in a Nest �▽ⓒ ⽗Ⓕ

2 slices reduced-calorie wheat
  bread (40 calories per slice)
1 teaspoon reduced-calorie sweet
  margarine (tub), divided
¼ cup thawed frozen egg
  substitute, divided

1. Using a 3-inch round cookie-cutter, cut a circle in center of each bread slice. Remove circles and reserve.

2. In 9-inch nonstick skillet melt ½ teaspoon margarine; add 1 bread slice and 1 bread circle. Pour 2 tablespoons egg substitute into hole in center of bread slice. Cook until bottom of bread is lightly browned, about 1 minute. Carefully turn over bread slice and bread circle and cook until other side is browned, about 1 minute longer. Transfer bread slice to plate and top with bread circle; keep warm.

3. Repeat procedure using remaining margarine, bread slice, bread circle, and egg substitute.

APPROXIMATE TOTAL TIME: 10 MINUTES

MAKES 1 SERVING

Each serving provides: ½ Fat; 1 Protein; 1 Bread
Per serving: 121 calories; 9 g protein; 2 g fat; 19 g carbohydrate; 60 mg calcium; 270 mg sodium; 0 mg cholesterol; dietary fiber data not available

Frittata Monterey

2 teaspoons margarine, divided
½ cup *each* sliced onion, sliced red bell pepper, and sliced zucchini
2 small plum tomatoes, diced
1 tablespoon chopped fresh basil
Dash pepper
½ cup thawed frozen egg substitute
⅓ cup low-fat cottage cheese (1% milk fat)
¼ cup evaporated skimmed milk
¾ ounce reduced-fat Monterey Jack cheese, shredded

1. In 10-inch nonstick skillet melt 1 teaspoon margarine; add onion, bell pepper, and zucchini and sauté over medium-high heat, until vegetables are lightly browned, 2 to 3 minutes.

2. Add tomatoes, basil, and pepper to skillet and stir to combine. Reduce heat to medium-low and cook until flavors blend, 2 to 3 minutes. Transfer vegetables to plate and keep warm.

3. Preheat broiler. In blender combine egg substitute, cottage cheese, and milk and process until smooth, scraping down sides of container as necessary; set aside.

4. In 10-inch nonstick skillet that has a metal or removable handle melt remaining margarine; add egg mixture and cook over medium-high heat until bottom begins to brown, about 1 minute. Transfer skillet to broiler and broil until top is set, 2 to 3 minutes.

5. Spread vegetable mixture over egg mixture and then sprinkle with cheese; broil until cheese melts, 1 to 2 minutes.

APPROXIMATE TOTAL TIME: 20 MINUTES

MAKES 2 SERVINGS

Each serving provides: ¼ Milk; 1 Fat; 2 Proteins; 2 Vegetables
Per serving: 181 calories; 18 g protein; 6 g fat; 13 g carbohydrate; 268 mg calcium; 412 mg sodium; 10 mg cholesterol; 2 g dietary fiber

Spanish Omelet ▽ⓢ

1 teaspoon vegetable oil
¼ cup *each* diced green bell
    pepper and chopped onion
2 garlic cloves, minced
½ cup canned Italian tomatoes
    (reserve liquid), seeded and
    finely chopped
2 eggs
1 teaspoon margarine
1½ ounces reduced-fat Monterey
    Jack cheese, shredded

1. In small saucepan heat oil; add pepper, onion, and garlic and cook over medium heat, stirring frequently, until pepper is softened, 1 to 2 minutes.

2. Add tomatoes with reserved liquid and stir to combine. Reduce heat to low and let simmer, stirring occasionally, until mixture is reduced by half, 5 to 10 minutes.

3. While tomato mixture cooks prepare omelet. Using a fork, in small mixing bowl beat together eggs and *2 tablespoons water*.

4. Preheat broiler. In 9-inch nonstick skillet that has a metal or removable handle melt margarine; add eggs and cook over medium-high heat, tilting pan, until bottom of omelet is set and lightly browned, about 1 minute. Sprinkle cheese over omelet.

5. Transfer skillet to broiler and broil 5 inches from heat source until omelet is cooked through, 2 to 3 minutes.

6. To serve, fold omelet in half and arrange on serving platter; spoon tomato mixture over center of omelet.

APPROXIMATE TOTAL TIME: 20 MINUTES

MAKES 2 SERVINGS

Each serving provides: 1 Fat; 2 Proteins; 1 Vegetable
Per serving: 198 calories; 13 g protein; 13 g fat; 6 g carbohydrate; 239 mg calcium; 319 mg sodium; 228 mg cholesterol; 1 g dietary fiber

Western Omelet

¼ cup finely diced onion
2 tablespoons *each* finely diced
  red and green bell pepper
3 ounces diced cooked potato
1 ounce finely diced turkey-ham
¾ ounce reduced-fat Cheddar
  cheese, shredded
Dash pepper
2 teaspoons margarine
¾ cup thawed frozen egg
  substitute
1 cherry tomato, cut in half
¼ cup alfalfa sprouts

Enjoy the taste of an omelet for breakfast without a large amount of cholesterol, thanks to egg substitute, reduced-fat Cheddar cheese, and turkey-ham.

1. Spray 10-inch nonstick skillet with nonstick cooking spray and heat; add onion and bell peppers and cook over medium-high heat, stirring frequently, until onion is translucent, about 2 minutes. Add potato and turkey-ham; continuing to stir, cook until potato is heated through, about 1 minute. Remove from heat; stir in cheese and pepper. Transfer to plate; set aside and keep warm.

2. Wipe skillet clean. Melt margarine in skillet; add egg substitute and cook over medium heat, stirring occasionally, for 30 seconds. Continue cooking without stirring until egg substitute is set, about 1½ minutes.

3. Spoon potato mixture onto center of omelet; fold in half to enclose filling and transfer to serving platter. Garnish platter with tomato halves and sprouts.

APPROXIMATE TOTAL TIME: 15 MINUTES

MAKES 2 SERVINGS

Each serving provides: 1 Fat; 2½ Proteins; ¾ Vegetable; ½ Bread
Per serving: 172 calories; 14 g protein; 7 g fat; 13 g carbohydrate; 138 mg calcium; 384 mg sodium; 8 mg cholesterol; 1 g dietary fiber

Basil-Vegetable Quiche ⓋC ⓋF ⓋS

1 cup thinly sliced onions
1½ medium red bell peppers,
   seeded and cut into 6 strips
   and 12 diamonds; dice
   remaining pepper
¾ cup sliced mushrooms
1 small garlic clove, minced
1½ cups thawed frozen egg
   substitute
1½ ounces reduced-fat Swiss
   cheese, shredded
½ cup fresh basil, chopped
2 medium zucchini (about 10
   ounces), cut lengthwise into
   thin slices and steamed
Garnish: basil sprigs

1. Preheat oven to 350°F. Spray 9-inch nonstick skillet with nonstick cooking spray; add onions, all of the peppers, the mushrooms, and garlic and cook over medium heat, stirring frequently, until onions are lightly browned, 1 to 2 minutes. Add *1 tablespoon water*; cover and cook until vegetables are tender, about 1 minute longer.

2. Remove pepper strips, pepper diamonds, and ¼ cup mushrooms to plate and set aside. Transfer remaining vegetable mixture to medium mixing bowl; add egg substitute, cheese, and chopped basil and stir to combine. Carefully pour into 9-inch quiche dish or pie plate. Decoratively arrange zucchini over egg substitute mixture.

3. Bake for 15 to 20 minutes (until a knife, inserted in center, comes out dry).

4. Garnish quiche with the reserved pepper strips and diamonds, mushrooms, and the basil sprigs.

APPROXIMATE TOTAL TIME: 40 MINUTES (includes baking time; does not include cooling time)

MAKES 4 SERVINGS

Each serving provides: 2 Proteins; 2½ Vegetables
Per serving: 111 calories; 13 g protein; 2 g fat; 10 g carbohydrate; 233 mg calcium; 142 mg sodium; 8 mg cholesterol; 2 g dietary fiber

Broccoli and Cheese Stratas

2 slices white bread (I ounce
  each)
¾ ounce reduced-fat Cheddar
  cheese, shredded
I cup thawed frozen chopped
  broccoli
3 eggs
½ cup low-fat milk (1% milk fat)
¼ cup evaporated skimmed milk
½ teaspoon Dijon-style mustard
Dash white pepper

*For convenience, you can prepare
this recipe ahead (except for the baking) and store it in the refrigerator
for several hours or overnight.*

1. Preheat oven to 350°F. Using a 3-inch round biscuit-cutter, cut out a circle from the center of each slice of bread and set aside. Cut remaining bread into ½-inch cubes.

2. Into each of two 10-ounce custard cups arrange half of the bread cubes. Sprinkle each portion with half of the cheese and broccoli, then top each with a reserved bread circle. Set aside.

3. Using a wire whisk, in medium mixing bowl beat together remaining ingredients; pour half of mixture into each custard cup, making sure bread circles are moistened.

4. Bake in middle of center oven rack for 30 minutes (until a knife, inserted in center, comes out dry).

APPROXIMATE TOTAL TIME: 45 MINUTES (in-cludes baking time)

MAKES 2 SERVINGS

Each serving provides: ½ Milk; 2 Proteins; I Vegetable; I Bread; 5 Optional Calories
Per serving: 286 calories; 20 g protein; 11 g fat; 24 g carbohydrate; 347 mg calcium; 428 mg sodium; 331 mg cholesterol; I g dietary fiber

Savory Orzo Custards ▽C ▽S

1 teaspoon margarine
2 cups finely chopped onions
1 small garlic clove, minced
1½ ounces orzo (rice-shaped pasta), cooked according to package directions
½ cup *each* thawed frozen egg substitute and skim *or* nonfat milk
2 ounces Fontina cheese, shredded
1 tablespoon chopped fresh basil

This custard, made the cholesterol-reduced way, uses egg substitute rather than eggs.

1. Preheat oven to 400°F. In 9-inch nonstick skillet melt margarine; add onions and garlic and sauté over medium heat, until tender-crisp, 2 to 3 minutes.

2. Transfer onion mixture to medium mixing bowl; add remaining ingredients and stir to combine. Spray two 10-ounce custard cups with nonstick cooking spray; spoon half of the orzo-onion mixture into each cup.

3. Bake for 20 minutes (until a knife, inserted in center, comes out dry). Set aside and let cool slightly.

4. To serve, invert custards onto serving plates.

APPROXIMATE TOTAL TIME: 40 MINUTES (includes baking time)

MAKES 2 SERVINGS, 1 CUSTARD EACH

Each serving provides: ¼ Milk; ½ Fat; 2 Proteins; 2 Vegetables; 1 Bread; 25 Optional Calories
Per serving: 309 calories; 19 g protein; 12 g fat; 33 g carbohydrate; 311 mg calcium; 138 mg sodium; 34 mg cholesterol; 3 g dietary fiber

German Egg Cakes ⑤

⅓ cup plus 2 teaspoons all-purpose flour

½ teaspoon double-acting baking powder

¼ teaspoon baking soda

⅓ cup plus 2 teaspoons low-fat buttermilk (1% milk fat)

4 eggs, separated

1 teaspoon vanilla extract

¼ teaspoon cream of tartar

¼ cup reduced-calorie raspberry spread (16 calories per 2 teaspoons), melted

1 tablespoon plus 1 teaspoon sour cream

1. In large mixing bowl combine first 3 ingredients; stir in buttermilk, egg yolks, and vanilla, stirring until smooth. Set aside.

2. Using mixer on high speed, in separate large mixing bowl beat egg whites until foamy; add cream of tartar and continue beating until whites are stiff but not dry.

3. Gently fold beaten whites into flour mixture.

4. Spray nonstick griddle or 12-inch nonstick skillet with nonstick cooking spray and heat. Using ¼ of batter, drop batter on griddle, forming 4 cakes. Cook over medium-high heat until bottom is lightly browned, 3 to 4 minutes; using pancake turner, turn cakes over and cook until the other side is browned, 2 to 3 minutes longer.

5. Remove cakes to plate and keep warm. Repeat procedure 3 more times, spraying griddle with cooking spray and making 12 more cakes.

6. Serve each portion of cakes topped with 1 tablespoon spread and 1 teaspoon sour cream.

APPROXIMATE TOTAL TIME: 45 MINUTES

MAKES 4 SERVINGS, 4 CAKES EACH

Each serving provides: 1 Protein; ½ Bread; 45 Optional Calories
Per serving: 165 calories; 8 g protein; 6 g fat; 17 g carbohydrate; 85 mg calcium; 193 mg sodium; 216 mg cholesterol; 0.3 g dietary fiber

Oat-Raisin Pancakes with Sausages

3 ounces uncooked quick-cooking oats

1 cup skim *or* nonfat milk

1 egg *or* ¼ cup thawed frozen egg substitute

1 tablespoon *each* all-purpose flour and granulated sugar

¼ teaspoon *each* double-acting baking powder and baking soda

½ cup dark raisins, plumped

1 tablespoon plus 1 teaspoon vegetable oil, divided

16 mild fresh turkey breakfast sausage links (1 ounce each)*

¼ cup reduced-calorie pancake syrup (60 calories per fluid ounce)

1 small orange (about 6 ounces), cut into 8 wedges

Mint sprigs

1. In blender process oats into powder; add milk, egg, flour, sugar, baking powder, and baking soda and process until combined. Transfer to medium mixing bowl; add raisins and stir to combine. Let batter stand for 10 minutes.

2. In 12-inch nonstick skillet or griddle heat 2 teaspoons oil. Using half of batter, drop batter by scant ¼-cup measures, making 4 pancakes, each 3 inches in diameter. Cook over medium heat until bubbles appear on surface and bottom is golden brown, 2 to 3 minutes. Using pancake turner, turn pancakes over and cook until the other side is browned. Remove pancakes to plate and keep warm. Repeat procedure, using remaining oil and making 4 more pancakes.

3. Spray 9-inch nonstick skillet with nonstick cooking spray; add sausages and cook over medium heat until browned on all sides, 4 to 5 minutes.

4. To serve, on serving platter arrange pancakes and sausages and top pancakes with syrup. Decoratively arrange orange wedges and mint sprigs on platter.

* A 1-ounce turkey breakfast sausage will yield about ½ ounce cooked sausage.

APPROXIMATE TOTAL TIME: 40 MINUTES

MAKES 4 SERVINGS, 2 PANCAKES AND 4 SAUSAGES EACH

Each serving provides: ¼ Milk; 1 Fat; 2¼ Proteins; 1 Bread; 1¼ Fruits; 55 Optional Calories
Per serving with egg: 531 calories; 33 g protein; 24 g fat; 46 g carbohydrate; 151 mg calcium; 938 mg sodium; 146 mg cholesterol; 3 g dietary fiber
With egg substitute: 518 calories; 33 g protein; 23 g fat; 46 g carbohydrate; 149 mg calcium; 942 mg sodium; 93 mg cholesterol; 3 g dietary fiber

Orange-Pecan French Toast ⱽC ⱽF

½ cup thawed frozen egg
  substitute
1 teaspoon vanilla extract
¼ teaspoon *each* grated orange
  peel and ground cinnamon
2 teaspoons reduced-calorie
  margarine (tub)
4 slices reduced-calorie raisin
  bread (40 calories per slice)
½ cup orange juice (no sugar
  added)
1 tablespoon maple syrup
1½ teaspoons cornstarch
½ ounce shelled pecans, toasted
  and chopped

�▬

*This French toast is made the
cholesterol-reduced way, with egg
substitute rather than eggs.*

1. Using a fork, in medium mixing bowl beat together egg substitute, vanilla, orange peel, and cinnamon; set aside.

2. Spray 10-inch nonstick skillet with nonstick cooking spray; add margarine and melt. Dip bread slices into egg mixture, coating both sides; add to skillet and pour an equal amount of any remaining egg mixture over each slice. Cook until lightly browned, 2 to 3 minutes on each side. Cut each slice of French toast in half diagonally, making 8 triangles. Transfer to serving platter and keep warm.

3. In small saucepan combine juice, syrup, and cornstarch; cook over medium-high heat until mixture comes to a boil. Reduce heat to low, stir in pecans, and let simmer until mixture thickens slightly, 3 to 4 minutes. Pour over French toast.

APPROXIMATE TOTAL TIME: 15 MINUTES

MAKES 2 SERVINGS

Each serving provides: 1 Fat; 1½ Proteins; 1 Bread; ½ Fruit; 40 Optional Calories
Per serving: 246 calories; 12 g protein; 7 g fat; 36 g carbohydrate; 8 mg calcium; 338 mg sodium; 0 mg cholesterol; 1 g dietary fiber

Fruit and Nut Breakfast Bars $\triangledown$ $\triangledown$

1½ cups golden raisins, plumped and drained
1 tablespoon all-purpose flour
9 ounces uncooked quick *or* old-fashioned oats
5 ounces coarsely chopped almonds
½ cup *each* firmly packed light brown sugar and thawed frozen egg substitute
⅓ cup reduced-calorie magarine (tub), melted
½ teaspoon vanilla extract
⅛ teaspoon almond extract

1. Preheat oven to 350°F. Spray 13 × 9 × 2-inch nonstick baking pan with nonstick cooking spray. Line pan with a sheet of wax paper over bottom and up sides of pan; set aside.

2. In medium mixing bowl combine raisins with flour, tossing to coat. Add oats, almonds, and sugar and stir to combine; set aside.

3. In 1-cup liquid measure combine remaining ingredients; add to dry ingredients and stir until moistened.

4. Press mixture into prepared pan. Bake until golden brown, about 25 minutes. Set pan on wire rack and let cool for 30 minutes. Invert pan onto clean work surface, discarding wax paper; let cool completely.

5. Cut in half lengthwise, then cut each half into 12 equal bars, making 24 bars. Wrap each bar in plastic wrap and freeze for future use.

APPROXIMATE TOTAL TIME: 35 MINUTES (includes baking time; does not include cooling time)

MAKES 12 SERVINGS, 2 BARS EACH

Each serving provides: 1½ Fats; 1 Protein; 1 Bread; 1 Fruit; 45 Optional Calories
Per serving: 269 calories; 7 g protein; 10 g fat; 41 g carbohydrate; 63 mg calcium; 69 mg sodium; 0 mg cholesterol; 3 g dietary fiber

Egg Substitutes and Cheeses

Egg lovers look out! Now there's egg substitutes. All the flavor of eggs but usually little or no cholesterol. Keep them on hand in your freezer for added convenience. Enjoy them in our delectable puddings and cholesterol-reduced "Hollandaise" Sauce. When it comes to cheeses, select those that are reduced-fat; they're often lower in sodium as well. (Remember to read package labels.) Our cheese-topped Eggplant Pizzas keep the calorie count down even further by using eggplant slices for a unique "crust."

Blueberry-Corn Pudding ▽C ▽F

½ cup *each* low-fat milk
(1% milk fat) and thawed
frozen egg substitute

1 tablespoon plus 1 teaspoon
reduced-calorie margarine
(tub), melted and cooled

1 tablespoon *each* all-purpose
flour and granulated sugar

1 cup *each* fresh *or* frozen
blueberries and thawed frozen
whole-kernel corn

1. Preheat oven to 375°F. In medium mixing bowl combine all ingredients except blueberries and corn and stir until thoroughly blended. Gently fold in blueberries and corn.

2. Spray two 10-ounce custard cups with nonstick cooking spray and fill each cup with half of the blueberry-corn mixture. Set cups in 8 × 8 × 2-inch baking pan and fill with water to a depth of about 1 inch.

3. Bake for 20 minutes (until a knife, inserted in center, comes out dry).

APPROXIMATE TOTAL TIME: 30 MINUTES

MAKES 2 SERVINGS

Each serving provides: ¼ Milk; 1 Fat; 1 Protein; 1 Bread; 1 Fruit; 50 Optional Calories
Per serving: 243 calories; 12 g protein; 6 g fat; 41 g carbohydrate; 110 mg calcium; 224 mg sodium; 2 mg cholesterol; 3 g dietary fiber

Tomato-Bread Pudding ▽C ▽F

1½ cups drained canned stewed tomatoes (reserve ½ cup liquid), chopped
2 ounces *each* seasoned croutons and reduced-fat Swiss *or* Cheddar cheese, shredded, divided
½ cup thawed frozen egg substitute

1. In medium mixing bowl combine tomatoes with reserved liquid, the croutons, 1 ounce cheese, and the egg substitute, stirring to combine.

2. Spray four 10-ounce microwavable custard cups with nonstick cooking spray and fill each cup with ¼ of the tomato mixture. Top each with an equal amount of the remaining cheese.

3. Set cups in 8 × 8 × 2-inch baking dish and pour water into dish to a depth of about 2 inches. Cover and microwave on Medium (50%) for 8 minutes, rotating cups every 2 minutes. Let cool slightly.

APPROXIMATE TOTAL TIME: 20 MINUTES

MAKES 4 SERVINGS

Each serving provides: 1 Protein; ¾ Vegetable; 1 Bread; 10 Optional Calories
Per serving with Swiss cheese: 165 calories; 11 g protein; 6 g fat; 18 g carbohydrate; 250 mg calcium; 600 mg sodium; 10 mg cholesterol; dietary fiber data not available
With Cheddar cheese: 165 calories; 11 g protein; 6 g fat; 18 g carbohydrate; 200 mg calcium; 677 mg sodium; 10 mg cholesterol; dietary fiber data not available

"Hollandaise" Sauce ⱱC ⱱS

¼ cup thawed frozen egg
   substitute
1 tablespoon plus 1 teaspoon
   reduced-calorie margarine (tub)
1 teaspoon lemon juice
½ teaspoon Dijon-style mustard
Dash ground red pepper

▬

*This cholesterol-reduced version of
a classic sauce is made the easy way,
in the microwave oven. Serve it over
cooked vegetables, fish, chicken, or
roast beef.*

1. In 1-cup microwavable liquid measure combine first 2 ingredients; microwave on Low (20%) for 1 minute, stirring once halfway through cooking, until margarine is softened.

2. Stir juice and mustard into egg substitute mixture; microwave on Low for 3 minutes, stirring every 30 seconds, until thickened. Stir in pepper. (If mixture curdles, transfer to blender and process on low speed for 30 seconds, until smooth.)

APPROXIMATE TOTAL TIME: 10 MINUTES

MAKES 2 SERVINGS, ABOUT 3 TABLESPOONS EACH

Each serving provides: 1 Fat; ½ Protein
Per serving: 52 calories; 3 g protein; 4 g fat; 1 g carbohydrate; 14 mg calcium; 171 mg sodium; 0 mg cholesterol; dietary fiber data not available

Baked Cauliflower Casserole ▽c

4 cups cauliflower florets, blanched
½ cup tomato sauce
1½ ounces mozzarella cheese, shredded
2 tablespoons grated Parmesan cheese

It takes only four ingredients to make this sensational dish.

1. Preheat oven to 375°F. Spray 9-inch glass pie plate with nonstick cooking spray. Arrange cauliflower in pie plate and spoon tomato sauce over cauliflower.

2. In small mixing bowl combine cheeses; sprinkle over tomato sauce.

3. Bake until cauliflower is thoroughly heated, about 15 minutes.

APPROXIMATE TOTAL TIME: 30 MINUTES (includes baking time)

MAKES 4 SERVINGS

Each serving provides: ½ Protein; 2¼ Vegetables; 15 Optional Calories
Per serving: 74 calories; 5 g protein; 3 g fat; 7 g carbohydrate; 123 mg calcium; 286 mg sodium; 10 mg cholesterol; 3 g dietary fiber

Cheese Crisp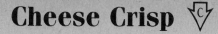

1 flour tortilla (6-inch diameter)
¼ cup chopped drained canned
   mild chili *or* jalapeño pepper
1½ ounces reduced-fat Colby *or*
   Cheddar cheese, shredded
1 tablespoon sour cream

1. Preheat broiler. Arrange tortilla directly on oven rack, 6 inches from heat source, and broil until lightly toasted, 1 to 2 minutes on each side.

2. Transfer tortilla to baking sheet; top with pepper and sprinkle with cheese. Broil until cheese is melted, 1 to 2 minutes.

3. To serve, arrange tortilla on serving plate and top with sour cream.

APPROXIMATE TOTAL TIME: 10 MINUTES

MAKES 1 SERVING

Each serving provides: 2 Proteins; ½ Vegetable; 1 Bread;
35 Optional Calories
Per serving with Colby cheese: 229 calories; 15 g protein;
13 g fat; 16 g carbohydrate; 359 mg calcium; 595 mg
sodium, 36 mg cholesterol; 1 g dietary fiber
With Cheddar cheese: 244 calories; 15 g protein; 13 g fat;
16 g carbohydrate; 434 mg calcium; 655 mg sodium; 36
mg cholesterol; 1 g dietary fiber

Eggplant Pizzas ▽C

6 ounces eggplant, cut crosswise into four ¼-inch-thick round slices
¼ teaspoon salt
¼ cup thawed frozen egg substitute
¼ teaspoon garlic powder
3 tablespoons plain dried bread crumbs
¾ ounce (2 tablespoons) uncooked yellow cornmeal
1 teaspoon olive or vegetable oil
4 slices Provolone cheese (½ ounce each)
2 tablespoons drained julienne-cut (matchstick pieces) pimiento
2 teaspoons grated Parmesan cheese

Eggplant slices provide a nutritious low-calorie crust for these tasty pizzas.

1. On paper towels arrange eggplant slices in a single layer; sprinkle both sides of each eggplant slice with salt and let stand for 10 minutes.

2. In small mixing bowl combine egg substitute, ½ *teaspoon water*, and the garlic powder and, using a fork, beat until combined. On sheet of wax paper combine bread crumbs and cornmeal.

3. Pat eggplant dry. Dip each eggplant slice in egg substitute mixture, then in crumb mixture, coating both sides and using all of egg substitute and crumb mixtures.

4. In 10-inch nonstick skillet heat oil; add eggplant slices and cook over medium-high heat, until golden, 7 minutes on each side (*being careful not to burn crumb mixture*).

5. Preheat broiler. Arrange eggplant slices on broiler pan. Top each eggplant slice with 1 slice Provolone cheese, ¼ of the pimiento, and ¼ of the Parmesan cheese. Broil until cheeses are golden, about 2 minutes.

APPROXIMATE TOTAL TIME: 30 MINUTES

MAKES 2 SERVINGS, 2 PIZZAS EACH

Each serving provides: ½ Fat; 1½ Proteins; 1¼ Vegetables; 1 Bread; 35 Optional Calories
Per serving: 241 calories; 14 g protein; 11 g fat; 23 g carbohydrate; 293 mg calcium; 665 mg sodium; 21 mg cholesterol; 2 g dietary fiber

Italian Grilled Cheese Sandwich ▽©

¾ ounce mozzarella cheese, shredded
Dash oregano leaves
2 slices reduced-calorie white bread (40 calories per slice)
2 teaspoons reduced-calorie margarine (tub), melted
3 fresh basil leaves *or* dash dried basil
½ medium tomato, cut into 3 slices

Fresh basil and mozzarella cheese add a boost of flavor to the familiar grilled cheese sandwich.

1. In small mixing bowl combine cheese and oregano; set aside.

2. Brush both sides of each slice of bread with margarine; top 1 slice of bread with cheese mixture, the basil, tomato, and remaining bread slice.

3. Spray 6-inch nonstick skillet with nonstick cooking spray and heat; add sandwich and cook over low heat, turning frequently, until cheese is melted, about 5 minutes.

APPROXIMATE TOTAL TIME: 10 MINUTES

MAKES 1 SERVING

Each serving provides: 1 Fat; 1 Protein; 1 Vegetable; 1 Bread
Per serving: 185 calories; 9 g fat; 9 g protein; 21 g carbohydrate; 157 mg calcium; 354 mg sodium; 17 mg cholesterol; 1 g dietary fiber

Vegetable Quesadillas ▽©

¼ cup *each* seeded and diced tomato and diced yellow *or* red bell pepper

2 tablespoons chopped scallion (green onion)

1 teaspoon *each* seeded and chopped hot chili pepper and chopped fresh cilantro (Chinese parsley) *or* Italian (flat-leaf) parsley

2 flour tortillas (6-inch diameter each)

1½ ounces reduced-fat Monterey Jack cheese, shredded

1 teaspoon vegetable oil

1. In small mixing bowl combine tomato, bell pepper, scallion, chili pepper, and cilantro; set aside.

2. In 10-inch nonstick skillet cook 1 tortilla over medium heat until flexible, about 1 minute on each side. Transfer tortilla to a plate.

3. Top half of tortilla with half of the cheese and then with half of the vegetable mixture; fold tortilla in half to cover filling. Repeat procedure with remaining tortilla, cheese, and vegetable mixture.

4. In same skillet heat oil; add tortillas and cook until cheese is melted, 1 to 2 minutes on each side. Cut each tortilla in half.

APPROXIMATE TOTAL TIME: 15 MINUTES

MAKES 2 SERVINGS

Each serving provides: ½ Fat; 1 Protein; ¾ Vegetable; 1 Bread
Per serving: 160 calories; 8 g protein; 8 g fat; 14 g carbohydrate; 234 mg calcium; 278 mg sodium; 15 mg cholesterol; 1 g dietary fiber

Warm Cheese-Walnut Pitas ▽C̶

2 ounces reduced-fat Swiss cheese, shredded
½ cup grated seeded pared cucumber
½ ounce chopped walnuts
1 teaspoon olive *or* vegetable oil
½ teaspoon country Dijon-style mustard
Dash *each* oregano leaves, basil leaves, and garlic powder
2 small pitas (1 ounce each); each cut in half horizontally

Here's a special brown-bag meal if your office is equipped with a toaster oven. Prepare this recipe at home but bake it at the office.

1. Preheat oven to 400°F. In small mixing bowl combine all ingredients except pitas.

2. Onto bottom half of each pita spread half of the cheese-walnut mixture; top each with remaining half of pita.

3. Arrange pitas on baking sheet and bake until cheese is melted, about 15 minutes. Cut each pita in half.

APPROXIMATE TOTAL TIME: 25 MINUTES (includes baking time)

MAKES 2 SERVINGS, 1 PITA EACH

Each serving provides: 1 Fat; 1½ Proteins; ½ Vegetable; 1 Bread; 25 Optional Calories
Per serving: 249 calories; 14 g protein; 12 g fat; 22 g carbohydrate; 369 mg calcium; 267 mg sodium; 20 mg cholesterol; 1 g dietary fiber

"Pizza" Stuffed Potato

1 baking potato (6 ounces),
  baked
1½ ounces mozzarella cheese,
  shredded, divided
¼ cup *each* tomato sauce and
  part-skim ricotta cheese
⅛ teaspoon *each* oregano leaves
  and garlic powder
2 teaspoons grated Parmesan
  cheese

---

*You'll need a baked potato for this
recipe. Do the baking in your microwave oven or plan ahead and do it
the night before.*

1. Preheat oven to 450°F. Cut potato in half lengthwise. Scoop out pulp from potato halves into a bowl,
leaving ¼-inch-thick shells; mash pulp and reserve
shells.

2 Add 1 ounce mozzarella cheese, the tomato sauce,
ricotta cheese, oregano, and garlic powder to potato
pulp and stir to combine.

3. Spoon half of potato mixture into each reserved
shell; top each with half of the remaining mozzarella
cheese and half of the Parmesan cheese. Set potato
shells in 1-quart casserole and bake until thoroughly
heated, about 10 minutes.

**APPROXIMATE TOTAL TIME: 30 MINUTES (in-
cludes baking time)**

MAKES 2 SERVINGS

Each serving provides: 1½ Proteins; ¼ Vegetable; 1 Bread;
10 Optional Calories
Per serving: 183 calories; 11 g protein; 8 g fat; 19 g carbohydrate; 233 mg calcium; 339 mg sodium; 27 mg cholesterol; 2 g dietary fiber

Cheese and Vegetable Manicotti ▽ⓒ

1 tablespoon plus 1 teaspoon olive oil, divided

½ cup *each* finely chopped onion, mushrooms, and red bell pepper

1 small garlic clove, minced

1 package (10 ounces) frozen chopped spinach *or* broccoli, thawed

1 cup part-skim ricotta cheese

¼ cup thawed frozen egg substitute

2 tablespoons chopped fresh basil *or* 1 teaspoon basil leaves

1½ ounces *each* grated Parmesan cheese and shredded mozzarella cheese

8 manicotti shells (¾ ounce each), cooked according to package directions

1 cup canned Italian tomatoes (reserve liquid), finely chopped

1. Preheat oven to 350°F. In 9-inch nonstick skillet heat 2 teaspoons oil; add onion, mushrooms, pepper, and garlic and cook over medium-high heat until pepper is softened, about 2 minutes.

2. Add spinach and cook, stirring constantly, until moisture has evaporated, about 2 minutes. Transfer to large mixing bowl; add ricotta cheese, egg substitute, and basil and stir to combine. Set aside.

3. In small mixing bowl combine Parmesan and mozzarella cheeses; add ⅔ of cheese mixture to spinach-ricotta mixture and stir to combine.

4. Spray a 13 × 9 × 2-inch baking dish with nonstick cooking spray. Fill each manicotti shell with an equal amount of spinach-cheese mixture and set shells in baking dish. Brush manicotti shells evenly with remaining oil. Cover with foil and bake for 15 minutes.

5. Spoon tomatoes with reserved liquid over top of manicotti shells and sprinkle with remaining cheese mixture. Bake, uncovered, until cheeses melt, about 5 minutes longer.

APPROXIMATE TOTAL TIME: 35 MINUTES (includes baking time)

MAKES 4 SERVINGS, 2 MANICOTTI EACH

Each serving provides: 1 Fat; 2¼ Proteins; 2¼ Vegetables; 2 Breads

Per serving: 412 calories; 24 g protein; 16 g fat; 44 g carbohydrate; 492 mg calcium; 496 mg sodium; 36 mg cholesterol; 4 g dietary fiber

Spinach and Pasta Casserole ▽C

1 tablespoon *each* reduced-calorie margarine (tub) and all-purpose flour
½ cup skim *or* nonfat milk
¼ cup canned ready-to-serve low-sodium chicken broth
2¼ ounces ditalini *or* other small tubular pasta, cooked according to package directions
½ cup *each* well-drained cooked chopped spinach and part-skim ricotta cheese
1½ ounces mozzarella cheese, shredded, divided
¼ cup thawed frozen egg substitute
2 tablespoons grated Parmesan *or* Romano cheese, divided

1. In 1-quart saucepan melt margarine over high heat; sprinkle with flour and stir quickly to combine. Continuing to stir, cook for 30 seconds. Gradually stir in milk and chicken broth. Reduce heat to medium-high and cook, stirring constantly, until mixture thickens slightly, about 3 minutes.

2. Add pasta and spinach and stir well to combine; set aside.

3. Preheat oven to 350°F. In medium mixing bowl combine ricotta cheese, 1 ounce mozzarella cheese, the egg substitute, and 1 tablespoon Parmesan cheese; add spinach mixture and stir to combine.

4. Spray 1-quart casserole with nonstick cooking spray and add spinach-cheese mixture to casserole. Sprinkle with remaining mozzarella and Parmesan cheeses and bake until cheeses are melted, about 20 minutes.

APPROXIMATE TOTAL TIME: 35 MINUTES (includes baking time)

MAKES 2 SERVINGS

Each serving provides: ¼ Milk; ¾ Fat; 2½ Proteins; ½ Vegetable; 1½ Breads; 50 Optional Calories
Per serving with Parmesan cheese: 372 calories; 24 g protein; 15 g fat; 36 g carbohydrate; 501 mg calcium; 503 mg sodium; 41 mg cholesterol; 2 g dietary fiber
With Romano cheese: 368 calories; 23 g protein; 15 g fat; 36 g carbohydrate; 485 mg calcium; 470 mg sodium; 42 mg cholesterol; 2 g dietary fiber

Beet and Feta Salad (C) (S)

2 cups watercress
½ cup *each* thinly sliced cucumber and julienne-cut (matchstick pieces) cooked beet
¼ cup thinly sliced red onion
¾ ounce feta cheese, crumbled
½ ounce chopped walnuts
1 tablespoon plus 1 teaspoon red wine vinegar
1 teaspoon *each* walnut* and olive oil
⅛ teaspoon pepper

Cook the beet for this colorful salad in your microwave oven . . . it's a real timesaver!

1. Line serving platter with watercress. Decoratively arrange cucumber, beet, and onion on watercress; top with cheese and sprinkle with walnuts.

2. In small mixing bowl combine *1 tablespoon water* and the remaining ingredients, mixing well. Pour over salad.

* Olive oil may be substituted for the walnut oil.

APPROXIMATE TOTAL TIME: 15 MINUTES

MAKES 2 SERVINGS

Each serving provides: 1½ Fats; 1 Protein; 3¼ Vegetables
Per serving: 130 calories; 4 g protein; 10 g fat; 8 g carbohydrate; 115 mg calcium; 155 mg sodium; 9 mg cholesterol; 3 g dietary fiber

Fish and Shellfish

Look to fish for good nutrition. Many species, including so-called fatty fish and shellfish, are prime sources of omega-3 fatty acids, which may help maintain cardiovascular health. Among the best sources of omega-3 fatty acids are salmon, tuna, bluefish, anchovy, catfish, bass, and trout. Salmon becomes a stand-in for clams in an innovative Salmon Chowder. Trout, a gourmet favorite, takes on easy elegance in our Pecan Trout, and the world will be your oyster when you serve Spinach Salad with Oysters.

Clams Fra Diavolo

1½ cups canned Italian tomatoes (reserve liquid), divided
¼ cup minced onion
2 teaspoons olive or vegetable oil
2 garlic cloves, minced
2 dozen littleneck clams*
1 tablespoon chopped fresh basil or 1 teaspoon basil leaves
⅛ teaspoon each crushed red pepper and black pepper

To ensure that clams are free of sand, the night before preparing this dish, place them in a large bowl and cover with uncooked cornmeal and some water; refrigerate overnight. Before preparing, discard the cornmeal mixture and thoroughly scrub the clams, rinsing them under running cold water.

1. In blender process 1 cup tomatoes with reserved liquid until pureed; set aside. Seed and chop remaining tomatoes; set aside.

2. In 10-inch round microwavable shallow baking dish combine onion, oil, and garlic and stir to combine. Microwave on High (100%) for 1 minute, until onion is translucent.

3. Set sieve over onion mixture and press pureed tomatoes through sieve into dish, discarding solids; add chopped tomatoes and stir to combine. Microwave on High for 8 minutes, stirring halfway through cooking.

4. Arrange clams over tomato mixture with hinged sides facing toward center of dish. Cover and microwave on High for 5 minutes, until clam shells open. Sprinkle with basil and peppers.

* Two dozen littleneck clams will yield about ¼ pound cooked seafood.

APPROXIMATE TOTAL TIME: 25 MINUTES

MAKES 2 SERVINGS

Each serving provides: 1 Fat; 2 Proteins; 1¾ Vegetables
Per serving: 174 calories; 17 g protein; 6 g fat; 14 g carbohydrate; 126 mg calcium; 358 mg sodium; 38 mg cholesterol; 2 g dietary fiber

Mussels with Pepper Vinaigrette ▽C ▽S

1 dozen medium mussels,*
   scrubbed
1 teaspoon Dijon-style mustard
2 teaspoons *each* white wine
   vinegar and olive oil
1 tablespoon *each* finely chopped
   red and yellow bell pepper
1 tablespoon chopped fresh
   Italian (flat-leaf) parsley
Garnish: Italian (flat-leaf) parsley
   sprigs

1. In 2-quart microwavable casserole microwave ½ *cup water* on High (100%) for 3 minutes, until boiling.

2. Add mussels to casserole; cover and microwave on High for 2 minutes, rotating casserole ½ turn halfway through cooking, until shells open. Uncover and set aside until mussels are cool enough to handle.

3. Using a wire whisk, in small mixing bowl beat together *1 tablespoon water*, the mustard, and vinegar. Gradually beat in oil, a few drops at a time. Stir in peppers and chopped parsley.

4. Remove mussels from cooking liquid, discarding liquid. Remove and discard top shell from each mussel. Loosen meat in remaining shell and arrange on serving platter. Top each mussel with an equal amount of pepper mixture (about 1 teaspoon). Garnish with parsley sprigs.

* One dozen medium mussels will yield about ¼ pound cooked seafood.

APPROXIMATE TOTAL TIME: 15 MINUTES

MAKES 2 SERVINGS

Each serving provides: 1 Fat; 2 Proteins; ⅛ Vegetable
Per serving: 143 calories; 14 g protein; 7 g fat; 5 g carbohydrate; 20 mg calcium; 285 mg sodium; 32 mg cholesterol; 0.1 g dietary fiber

Spinach Salad with Oysters ⌄ⓒ

4 cups spinach leaves, trimmed, thoroughly washed, and drained
1 teaspoon vegetable oil
½ cup *each* julienne-cut (matchstick pieces) red and yellow bell pepper
¼ cup thinly sliced onion
1 garlic clove, minced
5 ounces shucked oysters (drain and reserve liquid)
1 tablespoon *each* reduced-sodium soy sauce, balsamic vinegar, and dry sherry
1 teaspoon Worcestershire sauce

1. On serving platter arrange spinach leaves; set aside.

2. In 10-inch nonstick skillet heat oil; add peppers, onion, and garlic and cook, stirring frequently, until peppers are tender-crisp, 2 to 3 minutes. Spoon over spinach leaves; keep warm.

3. In same skillet cook oysters over high heat, turning once, until lightly browned, 1 to 2 minutes.

4. In small bowl combine reserved oyster liquid and remaining ingredients; stir into skillet and cook, stirring frequently, until liquid is reduced by half, 2 to 3 minutes.

5. Using a slotted spoon, arrange oysters over vegetables on serving platter; pour oyster liquid mixture over salad.

APPROXIMATE TOTAL TIME: 20 MINUTES

MAKES 2 SERVINGS

Each serving provides: ½ Fat; 2 Proteins; 5¼ Vegetables; 5 Optional Calories
Per serving: 135 calories, 10 g protein; 5 g fat; 14 g carbohydrate; 156 mg calcium; 498 mg sodium; 39 mg cholesterol; 4 g dietary fiber

Buttery Braised Scallops �

4 cups broccoli rabe, chopped
1 tablespoon whipped butter
¼ teaspoon salt
⅛ teaspoon pepper
2 teaspoons olive oil
2 garlic cloves, minced
½ pound sea scallops
3 tablespoons dry white
   table wine
1 slice crisp bacon, crumbled
1 tablespoon balsamic *or* red
   wine vinegar
2 teaspoons lemon juice

If you prefer, broccoli florets can be substituted for the broccoli rabe.

1. In 10-inch nonstick skillet bring ¼ *cup water* to a boil; add broccoli rabe, cover, and cook over medium-high heat, stirring occasionally, until broccoli rabe is tender-crisp, 3 to 4 minutes.

2. Remove from heat; stir in butter, salt, and pepper. Transfer to serving platter; keep warm.

3. In same skillet heat oil; add garlic and cook over medium-high heat, stirring occasionally, until lightly golden, about 1 minute. Add scallops and cook, stirring occasionally, until scallops are slightly opaque, 2 to 3 minutes.

4. Add remaining ingredients and stir to combine; cook until liquid is reduced by half, 2 to 3 minutes.

5. Using a slotted spoon, arrange scallop mixture over broccoli rabe; pour cooking liquid over broccoli rabe and scallop mixture.

APPROXIMATE TOTAL TIME: 20 MINUTES

MAKES 2 SERVINGS

Each serving provides: 1 Fat; 3 Proteins; 4 Vegetables; 65 Optional Calories
Per serving: 243 calories; 24 g protein; 10 g fat; 11 g carbohydrate; 136 mg calcium; 603 mg sodium; 48 mg cholesterol; 4 g dietary fiber

Variation: Braised Scallops—Omit whipped butter and bacon from recipe. In Serving Information decrease Optional Calories to 20.
Per serving: 199 calories; 24 g protein; 6 g fat; 11 g carbohydrate; 135 mg calcium; 524 mg sodium; 37 mg cholesterol; 4 g dietary fiber

Greek-Style Scallops ▽C ▽F ▽S

2 teaspoons olive *or* vegetable oil
1 cup chopped onions
1 small garlic clove, minced
4 large plum tomatoes, blanched, peeled, seeded, and chopped
2 tablespoons *each* chopped fresh dill and fresh basil
7 ounces bay *or* sea scallops (cut into quarters)
1½ ounces uncooked orzo (rice-shaped pasta), cooked according to package directions
2 teaspoons lemon juice
¾ ounce feta cheese, crumbled

1. In 9-inch nonstick skillet heat oil; add onions and garlic and cook over medium-high heat, stirring occasionally, until tender-crisp, about 2 minutes. Stir in tomatoes, dill, and basil and bring mixture to a boil. Reduce heat to low; add scallops and stir to combine. Cook, stirring constantly, until scallops turn opaque. Set aside.

2. Preheat broiler. Spray 2 individual flameproof casseroles with nonstick cooking spray and spread half of the orzo over bottom of each casserole. Drizzle half of the lemon juice over each portion of ozro and then top each with half of the scallop-tomato mixture. Top each portion with half of the cheese.

3. Broil until cheese melts, about 2 minutes.

APPROXIMATE TOTAL TIME: 35 MINUTES

MAKES 2 SERVINGS

Each serving provides: 1 Fat; 3 Proteins; 3 Vegetables; 1 Bread
Per serving: 288 calories; 23 g protein; 8 g fat; 31 g carbohydrate; 147 mg calcium; 293 mg sodium; 42 mg cholesterol; 3 g dietary fiber

Oven-"Fried" Scallops ▽C ▽F

15 ounces sea scallops, cut into quarters
3 tablespoons low-fat buttermilk (1% milk fat)
⅓ cup plus 2 teaspoons seasoned dried bread crumbs
½ teaspoon ground thyme

Here's a way to have crispy-coated scallops without the fat and calories associated with frying.

1. Preheat oven to 500°F. Spray baking sheet with nonstick cooking spray and set aside.

2. In medium mixing bowl combine scallops and buttermilk, turning to coat; let stand at room temperature for 15 minutes to marinate.

3. In small mixing bowl combine bread crumbs and thyme. Dredge each scallop in bread crumb mixture, coating both sides, and arrange scallops on prepared baking sheet.

4. Bake, carefully turning scallops over until browned on all sides, about 5 minutes.

APPROXIMATE TOTAL TIME: 10 MINUTES (includes baking time; does not include marinating time)

MAKES 4 SERVINGS

Each serving provides: 3 Proteins; ½ Bread; 5 Optional Calories
Per serving: 139 calories; 20 g protein; 1 g fat; 11 g carbohydrate; 52 mg calcium; 481 mg sodium; 36 mg cholesterol; 0.5 g dietary fiber

Scallops with Cucumbers ⓋC Ⓥs

1 medium cucumber (about ½
   pound), scored, cut lengthwise
   into quarters, seeded, and
   sliced
½ cup sliced scallions (green
   onions)
2 teaspoons peanut *or* vegetable
   oil
½ pound bay *or* sea scallops
   (cut into quarters)
2 tablespoons rice wine vinegar
½ teaspoon granulated sugar
1 teaspoon sesame seed, toasted

*Cucumbers are more than just for
salads. Here we've combined them
with scallops and cooked them in the
microwave oven. It's a dish well
worth a try.*

1. In 1-quart microwavable casserole combine cucumber, scallions, and oil and stir to coat; microwave on High (100%) for 2 minutes, stirring once halfway through cooking, until scallions are softened.

2. Add scallops and stir to combine; microwave on High for 2 minutes, stirring once halfway through cooking.

3. Add vinegar and sugar and stir to combine; microwave on High for 1 minute, until scallops are opaque.

4. Sprinkle with sesame seed.

APPROXIMATE TOTAL TIME: 15 MINUTES

MAKES 2 SERVINGS

Each serving provides: 1 Fat; 3 Proteins; 1½ Vegetables; 15 Optional Calories
Per serving: 174 calories; 20 g protein; 6 g fat; 9 g carbohydrate; 60 mg calcium; 189 mg sodium; 37 mg cholesterol; 2 g dietary fiber (this figure does not include sesame seed; nutrition analysis not available)

Southwest Scallops and Pasta $\triangledown$ $\triangledown$ $\triangledown$

¼ cup *each* sliced scallions (green onions), diced green bell pepper, and diced red bell pepper
2 teaspoons olive *or* vegetable oil
½ small jalapeño pepper, seeded and minced
1 small garlic clove, minced
5 ounces bay *or* sea scallops (cut into quarters)
½ cup frozen whole-kernel corn
1 cup cooked thin spaghetti
2 tablespoons *each* chopped cilantro (Chinese parsley) *or* Italian (flat-leaf) parsley and lime juice (no sugar added)
Dash hot sauce (optional)

To save time use leftover spaghetti in this colorful dish.

1. In 1-quart microwavable casserole combine scallions, bell peppers, oil, jalapeño pepper, and garlic and stir to coat with oil. Microwave on High (100%) for 2 minutes, stirring once halfway through cooking, until bell peppers are tender-crisp.

2. Add scallops and corn and stir to combine; microwave on Medium (50%) for 4 minutes, stirring once every 1½ minutes.

3. Add remaining ingredients and stir to combine. Cover and microwave on Medium for 1 minute, stirring once halfway through cooking. Let stand for 1 minute until scallops are opaque and cooking is completed.

APPROXIMATE TOTAL TIME: 20 MINUTES

MAKES 2 SERVINGS

Each serving provides: 1 Fat; 2 Proteins; ¾ Vegetable; 1½ Breads
Per serving: 252 calories; 17 g protein; 6 g fat; 34 g carbohydrate; 38 mg calcium; 120 mg sodium; 23 mg cholesterol; 3 g dietary fiber

Creamy Scallop Salad ▽C ▽F ▽S

½ cup sliced scallions (green onions), white portion and some green
¼ cup *each* diced red bell pepper and sliced celery
½ pound bay *or* sea scallops (cut into quarters)
¼ cup plain low-fat yogurt
1 tablespoon *each* chopped fresh dill and tartar sauce
2 cups torn lettuce leaves

■

For a change of pace from the usual tuna salad, try this warm scallop salad.

1. In 1-quart microwavable casserole combine scallions, pepper, and celery; microwave on High (100%) for 1 minute, until scallions are softened.

2. Add scallops and stir to combine; microwave on Medium (50%) for 3 minutes, stirring once halfway through cooking, until scallops are opaque.

3. Add remaining ingredients except lettuce and stir to combine.

4. Onto each of 2 individual serving plates arrange 1 cup lettuce; top with half of the scallop mixture.

APPROXIMATE TOTAL TIME: 15 MINUTES

MAKES 2 SERVINGS

Each serving provides: ¼ Milk; 1 Fat; 3 Proteins; 3 Vegetables
Per serving: 179 calories; 22 g protein; 6 g fat; 10 g carbohydrate; 147 mg calcium; 274 mg sodium; 43 mg cholesterol; 2 g dietary fiber

Italian Seafood Stew ▽F

2 cups sliced carrots (1-inch
  pieces)
1 cup canned Italian tomatoes
  (with liquid), pureed
3 ounces diced pared all-purpose
  potato
½ cup thoroughly washed diced
  leeks (white portion and some
  green)
¼ cup dry white table wine
2 teaspoons all-purpose flour
2 garlic cloves, minced
¼ pound *each* sea scallops and
  shelled and deveined large
  shrimp
2 bay leaves
¼ teaspoon fennel seed
⅛ teaspoon crushed red pepper

1. In 3-quart microwavable casserole combine *1½
cups water*, the carrots, tomatoes, potato, leeks, wine,
flour, and garlic, stirring to dissolve flour. Cover and
microwave on High (100%) for 10 minutes, until
carrots are tender.

2. Add scallops, shrimp, and bay leaves; cover and
microwave on High for 3 minutes until shrimp turn
pink.

3. Add fennel seed and pepper and stir to combine.
Remove and discard bay leaves.

APPROXIMATE TOTAL TIME: 25 MINUTES

MAKES 2 SERVINGS

Each serving provides: 3 Proteins; 3½ Vegetables; ½ Bread;
35 Optional Calories
Per serving: 268 calories; 25 g protein; 2 g fat; 33 g carbohydrate; 138 mg calcium; 420 mg sodium; 105 mg
cholesterol; 6 g dietary fiber

Lemon Scallops and Shrimp ▽Ⓢ

¼ pound *each* sea scallops and
  shelled and deveined large
  shrimp
1 tablespoon plus 1 teaspoon all-
  purpose flour
2 teaspoons olive *or* vegetable oil
2 garlic cloves, minced
¼ cup *each* dry white table wine
  and canned ready-to-serve low-
  sodium chicken broth
2 tablespoons lemon juice
1 teaspoon chopped fresh parsley

1. On sheet of wax paper dredge scallops and shrimp in flour, coating all sides.

2. In 10-inch nonstick skillet heat oil; add scallops and shrimp and cook over medium-high heat, turning occasionally, until shrimp begin to turn pink, 2 to 3 minutes. Transfer to plate.

3. To same skillet add garlic and cook over medium heat, stirring frequently, until golden, about 1 minute. Add wine, broth, lemon juice, and parsley; return scallops and shrimp to skillet. Cook until flavors blend, 2 to 4 minutes.

APPROXIMATE TOTAL TIME: 20 MINUTES

MAKES 2 SERVINGS

Each serving provides: 1 Fat; 3 Proteins; 50 Optional Calories
Per serving: 201 calories; 22 g protein; 6 g fat; 8 g carbohydrate; 55 mg calcium; 188 mg sodium; 105 mg cholesterol; 0.2 g dietary fiber

Russian Shrimp Cocktail

1 cup shredded iceberg lettuce
2 tablespoons thinly sliced red
  onion
1 tablespoon plus 1 teaspoon
  reduced-calorie mayonnaise
1 tablespoon ketchup
1 teaspoon red wine vinegar
1 medium tomato, blanched,
  peeled, seeded, and chopped
3 ounces shelled and deveined
  cooked medium shrimp, chilled
  and cut lengthwise into halves

1. In medium mixing bowl combine lettuce and onion, tossing to combine; arrange on serving platter.

2. Using a wire whisk, in small mixing bowl beat together mayonnaise, ketchup, and vinegar; add tomato and stir to coat. Spoon tomato mixture onto center of lettuce-onion mixture; top with shrimp.

APPROXIMATE TOTAL TIME: 15 MINUTES

MAKES 2 SERVINGS

Each serving provides: 1 Fat; 1½ Proteins; 2⅛ Vegetables; 10 Optional Calories
Per serving: 98 calories; 10 g protein; 3 g fat; 7 g carbohydrate; 46 mg calcium; 268 mg sodium; 86 mg cholesterol; 1 g dietary fiber

Cinnamon-Pepper Shrimp ▽Ⓢ

2 teaspoons olive *or* vegetable oil
½ pound shelled and deveined shrimp (tail feathers left on)
1 cup diagonally thinly sliced scallions (green onions)
2 large plum tomatoes, seeded and cut into thin strips
1 small jalapeño pepper, seeded and thinly sliced
2 tablespoons freshly squeezed lime juice
½ teaspoon ground cinnamon
¼ teaspoon granulated sugar
1 tablespoon chopped fresh cilantro (Chinese parsley) *or* Italian (flat-leaf) parsley

1. In 9-inch nonstick skillet heat oil; add shrimp and scallions and cook over high heat, stirring frequently, until shrimp just turn pink, about 2 minutes.

2. Add remaining ingredients except cilantro and stir to combine; cook, stirring constantly, until flavors blend, about 2 minutes.

3. Sprinkle with cilantro.

APPROXIMATE TOTAL TIME: 15 MINUTES

MAKES 2 SERVINGS

Each serving provides: 1 Fat; 3 Proteins; 2¼ Vegetables; 3 Optional Calories
Per serving: 192 calories; 25 g protein; 7 g fat; 9 g carbohydrate; 102 mg calcium; 175 mg sodium; 173 mg cholesterol; 2 g dietary fiber

Open-Face Shrimp Melt

3 ounces shelled and deveined
  cooked small shrimp, cut
  lengthwise into halves
¼ cup finely chopped celery
2 tablespoons chopped scallion
  (green onion)
1 tablespoon plus 1 teaspoon
  reduced-calorie mayonnaise
1 tablespoon dry sherry
2 teaspoons lemon juice
1 teaspoon Dijon-style mustard
2 slices reduced-calorie wheat
  bread (40 calories per slice),
  lightly toasted
4 thin tomato slices
2 slices (¾ ounce each) reduced-
  fat Monterey Jack cheese

1. Preheat broiler. In small mixing bowl combine all ingredients except bread, tomato slices, and cheese; mix well.

2. Onto each slice of bread arrange 2 tomato slices and half of the shrimp mixture, then top with 1 cheese slice.

3. On nonstick baking sheet arrange sandwiches and broil 5 to 6 inches from heat source until cheese melts, about 1 minute.

APPROXIMATE TOTAL TIME: 15 MINUTES

MAKES 2 SERVINGS

Each serving provides: 1 Fat; 2½ Proteins; ¾ Vegetable; ½ Bread; 5 Optional Calories
Per serving: 192 calories; 17 g protein; 7 g fat; 13 g carbohydrate; 236 mg calcium; 492 mg sodium; 101 mg cholesterol; 1 g dietary fiber

Shrimp and Orzo Salad ▽F ▽S

¼ **pound shelled and deveined cooked small shrimp, cut lengthwise into halves**

1½ **ounces orzo (rice-shaped pasta), cooked according to package directions**

½ **cup thawed frozen whole-kernel corn**

¼ **cup diced red bell pepper**

2 **tablespoons chopped scallion (green onion)**

1 **tablespoon** *each* **chopped fresh dill, lemon juice, and red wine vinegar**

2 **teaspoons olive oil**

½ **teaspoon Dijon-style mustard**

⅛ **teaspoon pepper**

8 **lettuce leaves**

Use your microwave oven to cook the shrimp in minutes.

1. In medium mixing bowl combine first 5 ingredients; set aside.

2. In small bowl combine remaining ingredients except lettuce, mixing well. Pour over shrimp mixture and toss to coat.

3. To serve, line serving bowl with lettuce and top with shrimp mixture.

APPROXIMATE TOTAL TIME: 20 MINUTES

MAKES 2 SERVINGS

Each serving provides: 1 Fat; 2 Proteins; 1¼ Vegetables; 1½ Breads
Per serving: 226 calories; 16 g protein; 6 g fat; 28 g carbohydrate; 64 mg calcium; 172 mg sodium; 111 mg cholesterol; 2 g dietary fiber

Shrimp Salad Vinaigrette F S

1 *each* medium red and green bell pepper

2 teaspoons olive *or* vegetable oil

½ pound shelled and deveined shrimp (tail feathers left on)

2 small garlic cloves, minced

1 package (9 ounces) frozen quartered artichoke hearts, cooked according to package directions; drained and cooled

½ cup thinly sliced scallions (green onions)

2 tablespoons balsamic *or* red wine vinegar

1 tablespoon *each* chopped Italian (flat-leaf) parsley and fresh basil

4 lettuce leaves

This colorful dish can be served warm or eaten chilled.

1. Preheat broiler. On baking sheet lined with heavy-duty foil broil peppers 3 inches from heat source, turning frequently, until charred on all sides; let stand until cool enough to handle. Peel peppers; remove and discard stem ends and seeds. Cut peppers into strips.

2. In 9-inch nonstick skillet heat oil; add shrimp and garlic and cook over high heat, stirring frequently, until shrimp just turn pink, about 2 minutes. Add bell pepper strips and remaining ingredients except lettuce and cook, stirring occasionally, until thoroughly heated, about 3 minutes.

3. Line serving platter with lettuce and top with shrimp mixture.

APPROXIMATE TOTAL TIME: 40 MINUTES

MAKES 2 SERVINGS

Each serving provides: 1 Fat; 3 Proteins; 5 Vegetables
Per serving: 243 calories; 28 g protein; 7 g fat; 18 g carbohydrate; 132 mg calcium; 234 mg sodium; 173 mg cholesterol; 7 g dietary fiber

Shrimp Salad with Pineapple and Pecans ∇ⓢ

3 ounces shelled and deveined cooked shrimp, cut lengthwise into halves

½ cup *each* drained canned pineapple chunks (no sugar added) and snow peas (Chinese pea pods), stem ends and strings removed, blanched

½ ounce pecan halves, toasted

1 tablespoon plus 1½ teaspoons sliced scallion (green onion)

2 tablespoons *each* plain low-fat yogurt and sour cream

2 teaspoons *each* reduced-calorie mayonnaise and white wine vinegar

Dash *each* salt and pepper

Save time by cooking and shelling the shrimp the night before you plan to use them.

1. In medium mixing bowl combine shrimp, pineapple, snow peas, pecans, and scallion.

2. Using a wire whisk, in small mixing bowl beat together remaining ingredients; pour over shrimp mixture and toss to coat. Cover and refrigerate until ready to serve.

APPROXIMATE TOTAL TIME: 20 MINUTES

MAKES 2 SERVINGS

Each serving provides: 1 Fat; 2 Proteins; ½ Vegetable; ½ Fruit; 45 Optional Calories
Per serving: 197 calories; 12 g protein; 10 g fat; 16 g carbohydrate; 89 mg calcium; 219 mg sodium; 92 mg cholesterol; 2 g dietary fiber

Baked Fish in Cream Sauce ⬦S⬦

½ pound bluefish *or* red snapper
  fillet, cut in half
½ cup chopped onion
½ medium tomato, chopped
Dash *each* garlic powder and
  pepper
¼ cup low-fat milk (1% milk fat)
2 teaspoons reduced-calorie
  margarine (tub), melted and
  cooled
1 teaspoon cornstarch
1 tablespoon *each* chopped fresh
  basil and Italian (flat-leaf)
  parsley

1. Preheat oven to 400°F. Spray 9-inch pie plate with nonstick cooking spray. Arrange fish in plate and top with onion, tomato, garlic powder, and pepper.

2. In 1-cup liquid measure combine milk, margarine, and cornstarch, stirring to dissolve cornstarch; pour over fish. Bake until fish flakes easily when tested with a fork, 12 to 15 minutes.

3. To serve, carefully transfer each fillet to a serving plate; stir pan juices to thoroughly combine and pour half over each fillet. Sprinkle each portion with half of the basil and parsley.

APPROXIMATE TOTAL TIME: 25 MINUTES

MAKES 2 SERVINGS

Each serving provides: ½ Fat; 3 Proteins; 1 Vegetable; 20 Optional Calories
Per serving with bluefish: 197 calories; 25 g protein; 7 g fat; 7 g carbohydrate; 72 mg calcium; 128 mg sodium; 68 mg cholesterol; 1 g dietary fiber
With red snapper: 170 calories; 25 g protein; 4 g fat; 7 g carbohydrate; 101 mg calcium; 132 mg sodium; 43 mg cholesterol; 1 g dietary fiber

Broiled Fish with Stewed Tomatoes

½ pound bluefish *or* red snapper fillet, cut in half
1 tablespoon plus 1 teaspoon reduced-calorie margarine (tub), divided
⅛ teaspoon *each* garlic powder and pepper, divided
1 cup canned stewed tomatoes
1 tablespoon *each* finely chopped fresh basil and Italian (flat-leaf) parsley

1. Preheat broiler. Spray 9-inch flameproof pie plate with nonstick cooking spray. Arrange fish in plate and brush with half of the margarine; sprinkle with half of the garlic powder and pepper.

2. Broil for 5 minutes; carefully turn each fillet over. Brush with remaining margarine and sprinkle with remaining garlic powder and pepper. Spoon tomatoes around fillets and sprinkle with basil and parsley. Broil until fish flakes easily when tested with a fork, about 5 minutes.

3. To serve, carefully transfer each fillet to a serving plate; stir tomato mixture and spoon half over each fillet.

APPROXIMATE TOTAL TIME: 20 MINUTES

MAKES 2 SERVINGS

Each serving provides: 1 Fat; 3 Proteins; 1 Vegetable
Per serving with bluefish: 210 calories; 24 g protein; 9 g fat; 9 g carbohydrate; 65 mg calcium; 473 mg sodium; 67 mg cholesterol; 0.1 g dietary fiber (this figure does not include stewed tomatoes; nutrition analysis not available)
With red snapper: 183 calories; 25 g protein; 6 g fat; 9 g carbohydrate; 93 mg calcium; 477 mg sodium; 42 mg cholesterol; 0.1 g dietary fiber (this figure does not include stewed tomatoes; nutrition analysis not available)

Fillets with Peppers and Tomatoes � ⟨F⟩ ⟨S⟩

2 fish fillets (sole, flounder, *or* red snapper), ¼ pound each
2 tablespoons all-purpose flour
2 teaspoons olive *or* vegetable oil
½ cup *each* sliced onion and green bell pepper
1 garlic clove, minced
½ cup seeded and chopped drained canned Italian tomatoes
¼ cup dry white table wine
⅛ teaspoon pepper
Dash thyme leaves

1. On sheet of wax paper dredge fish in flour.

2. In 10-inch nonstick skillet heat oil; add fish and cook over medium-high heat until lightly browned and fish flakes easily when tested with a fork, 2 to 3 minutes on each side. Using a spatula, transfer fish to serving platter; keep warm.

3. In same skillet combine onion, bell pepper, and garlic; cook over medium-high heat, stirring frequently, until bell pepper is tender-crisp, 2 to 3 minutes. Stir in tomatoes, wine, pepper, and thyme. Reduce heat to low and cook, stirring occasionally, until mixture thickens, 5 to 6 minutes. Spoon over fish.

APPROXIMATE TOTAL TIME: 30 MINUTES

MAKES 2 SERVINGS

Each serving provides: 1 Fat; 3 Proteins; 1½ Vegetables; 55 Optional Calories
Per serving with sole or flounder: 226 calories; 24 g protein; 6 g fat; 14 g carbohydrate; 56 mg calcium; 193 mg sodium; 54 mg cholesterol; 2 g dietary fiber
With red snapper: 236 calories; 25 g protein; 6 g fat; 14 g carbohydrate; 71 mg calcium; 174 mg sodium; 42 mg cholesterol; 2 g dietary fiber

Golden Fish Meunière ⑤

1½ ounces (about ¼ cup)
   uncooked yellow cornmeal
¼ teaspoon grated lemon peel
2 sole *or* flounder fillets
   (¼ pound each)
1 tablespoon vegetable oil
¼ cup dry white table wine
2 tablespoons lemon juice
1 tablespoon chopped fresh
   parsley
1 teaspoon rinsed drained capers
1 tablespoon whipped butter

1. On sheet of wax paper combine cornmeal and lemon peel. Dredge fish in cornmeal mixture, coating both sides and using all of mixture.

2. In 10-inch nonstick skillet heat oil; add fish to skillet and cook until lightly browned and fish flakes easily when tested with a fork, 2 to 3 minutes on each side. Using a spatula, transfer fish to serving platter; keep warm.

3. In same skillet combine remaining ingredients except butter; cook until liquid is reduced by half, 1 to 2 minutes. Add butter and stir until melted; pour evenly over fish.

APPROXIMATE TOTAL TIME: 20 MINUTES

MAKES 2 SERVINGS

Each serving provides: 1½ Fats; 3 Proteins; 1 Bread; 50 Optional Calories
Per serving: 290 calories; 23 g protein; 11 g fat; 18 g carbohydrate; 30 mg calcium; 163 mg sodium; 62 mg cholesterol; 1 g dietary fiber (this figure does not include capers; nutrition analysis not available)

Sesame Flounder Fillets ⬦

⅓ cup plus 2 teaspoons plain dried bread crumbs

1 tablespoon sesame seed

1¾ teaspoons vegetable oil, divided

¼ teaspoon Chinese sesame oil

3 tablespoons low-fat buttermilk (1% milk fat)

1 teaspoon *each* reduced-sodium soy sauce and lemon juice

2 flounder fillets (¼ pound each)

1. Preheat broiler. In shallow mixing bowl combine bread crumbs, sesame seed, ¾ teaspoon vegetable oil, and the sesame oil; mix well until thoroughly combined. Set aside.

2. In shallow mixing bowl combine buttermilk, soy sauce, and lemon juice. Dip fillets in buttermilk mixture and dredge in crumb mixture, coating both sides and using all of the mixtures.

3. Arrange fillets on nonstick baking sheet. Drizzle each fillet with ¼ teaspoon vegetable oil. Broil 5 to 6 inches from heat source until lightly browned, 3 to 4 minutes.

4. Using spatula, carefully turn fillets over and drizzle each with ¼ teaspoon vegetable oil. Broil until fillets flake easily when tested with a fork, 3 to 4 minutes longer.

APPROXIMATE TOTAL TIME: 20 MINUTES

MAKES 2 SERVINGS

Each serving provides: 1 Fat; 3 Proteins; 1 Bread; 40 Optional Calories

Per serving: 254 calories; 25 g protein; 9 g fat; 16 g carbohydrate; 115 mg calcium; 355 mg sodium; 56 mg cholesterol; 1 g dietary fiber (this figure does not include sesame seed; nutrition analysis not available)

Sesame Monkfish

1 cup chopped onions
1 teaspoon vegetable oil
5 ounces monkfish fillet, cut into 6 equal strips
Dash *each* salt and pepper
1 tablespoon *each* tahini (sesame paste) and finely chopped fresh parsley
1 teaspoon sesame seed, toasted

1. In 1-quart microwavable casserole combine onions and oil and stir to coat. Cover and microwave on High (100%) for 2 minutes, until onions are soft.

2. Sprinkle fish with salt and pepper and arrange over onions. Spread tahini over fish and then sprinkle with parsley.

3. Cover and microwave on High for 3 minutes. Let stand for 1 minute, until fish flakes easily when tested with a fork.

4. Sprinkle with sesame seed.

APPROXIMATE TOTAL TIME: 15 MINUTES

MAKES 2 SERVINGS

Each serving provides: 1 Fat; 2½ Proteins; 1 Vegetable; 10 Optional Calories
Per serving: 155 calories; 13 g protein; 8 g fat; 8 g carbohydrate; 75 mg calcium; 90 mg sodium; 18 mg cholesterol; 2 g dietary fiber (this figure does not include sesame seed; nutrition analysis not available)

Salmon Chowder ▽ⓒ

1 tablespoon plus 1 teaspoon
  margarine
½ cup chopped onion
1 tablespoon all-purpose flour
1 cup *each* bottled clam juice,
  seeded and diced drained
  canned Italian tomatoes, and
  low-fat milk (1% milk fat)
6 ounces diced pared all-purpose
  potato
½ cup thawed frozen whole-
  kernel corn
1 tablespoon chopped fresh
  parsley
⅛ teaspoon *each* white pepper
  and thyme leaves
5 ounces salmon fillet, cut into
  ½-inch cubes

*A little fish goes a long way when
added to this hearty chowder.*

1. In 3-quart saucepan melt margarine; add onion and sauté over medium-high heat, stirring frequently, until onion is softened, 1 to 2 minutes. Sprinkle flour over onion and stir quickly to combine. Continuing to stir, add *1 cup water*, the clam juice, and tomatoes. Reduce heat to medium-low and cook until mixture thickens, about 5 minutes.

2. Add remaining ingredients except salmon and stir to combine; cook until potato is tender, about 10 minutes. Add salmon and cook until opaque, about 5 minutes longer.

APPROXIMATE TOTAL TIME: 30 MINUTES

MAKES 4 SERVINGS, ABOUT 1¼ CUPS EACH

Each serving provides: ¼ Milk; 1 Fat; 1 Protein; ¾ Vegetable; ¾ Bread; 25 Optional Calories
Per serving: 189 calories; 12 g protein; 7 g fat; 21 g carbohydrate; 115 mg calcium; 321 mg sodium; 22 mg cholesterol; 2 g dietary fiber

Grilled Salmon with Lime Butter

2 tablespoons freshly squeezed lime juice
2 teaspoons mashed pared gingerroot
2 salmon fillets (¼ pound each)
1 tablespoon whipped sweet butter, softened
2 teaspoons fresh grated lime peel
Garnish: lemon and lime slices

So easy to make, but a truly elegant recipe. Serve it on a special occasion.

1. In glass or stainless-steel shallow bowl combine lime juice and gingerroot; add salmon fillets and let stand at room temperature for 15 minutes, turning fillets over every 5 minutes.

2. In small bowl combine butter and lime peel; cover and refrigerate until ready to serve.

3. Preheat broiler. Spray nonstick baking sheet with nonstick cooking spray and arrange fillets on baking sheet. Broil until fish flakes easily when tested with a fork, about 2 minutes on each side.

4. To serve, on serving platter arrange salmon fillets; top each fillet with half of the lime butter and garnish with lemon and lime slices.

APPROXIMATE TOTAL TIME: 10 MINUTES (does not include marinating time)

MAKES 2 SERVINGS

Each serving provides: 3 Proteins; 25 Optional Calories
Per serving: 194 calories; 23 g protein; 10 g fat; 2 g carbohydrate; 19 mg calcium; 51 mg sodium; 70 mg cholesterol; dietary fiber data not available

Variation: Grilled Salmon with Lime Margarine — Substitute 1 tablespoon plus 1 teaspoon reduced-calorie margarine (tub) for the butter. In Serving Information add 1 Fat and omit Optional Calories.
Per serving: 201 calories; 23 g protein; 11 g fat; 2 g carbohydrate; 18 mg calcium; 130 mg sodium; 62 mg cholesterol; dietary fiber data not available

Salmon with Creamy Horseradish Sauce ⬇ⓢ

¼ cup dry white table wine
2 tablespoons chopped onion
1 tablespoon lemon juice
1 teaspoon peppercorns
2 salmon steaks (5 ounces each)
2 tablespoons sour cream
2 teaspoons prepared horseradish
1 teaspoon *each* all-purpose flour
   and chopped fresh mint
⅛ teaspoon white pepper

1. In 10-inch nonstick skillet combine ½ cup water, the wine, onion, lemon juice, and peppercorns; cover and cook over medium-high heat until mixture comes to a boil.

2. Reduce heat to medium-low; add salmon, cover, and simmer until salmon flakes easily when tested with a fork, 5 to 6 minutes (depending on thickness of salmon).

3. While salmon cooks, prepare horseradish mixture. In small mixing bowl combine sour cream, horseradish, flour, mint, and white pepper; stir to combine and set aside.

4. Transfer salmon to serving platter; keep warm.

5. Pour cooking liquid through sieve into bowl, discarding solids. Return to skillet and cook over medium-high heat until mixture comes to a boil; stir in horseradish mixture. Reduce heat to low and cook, stirring frequently, until mixture thickens, 2 to 3 minutes. Pour over salmon.

APPROXIMATE TOTAL TIME: 15 MINUTES

MAKES 2 SERVINGS

Each serving provides: 3 Proteins; 65 Optional Calories
Per serving: 267 calories; 29 g protein; 12 g fat; 4 g carbohydrate; 48 mg calcium; 79 mg sodium; 84 mg cholesterol; 0.5 g dietary fiber (this figure does not include horseradish; nutrition analysis not available)

Lite Sea Breeze

Cranberry Wheat Muffins
Oat-Raisin Pancakes with Sausage
Western Omelet

Mussels with
Pepper Vinaigrette
Clams Fra Diavolo
Corn with Basil Butter

Chicken Burgers
Orange-Poppy Cupcakes

Sole with Vegetable-Rice Stuffing ▽F ▽S

¼ cup *each* finely chopped celery, finely chopped onion, and shredded carrot
1 tablespoon plus 1 teaspoon reduced-calorie margarine (tub), divided
1 cup cooked regular long-grain rice
¼ cup plain low-fat yogurt
1 tablespoon fresh grated lemon peel
¼ teaspoon *each* thyme leaves and paprika
2 lemon *or* grey sole fillets (¼ pound each)
1 teaspoon all-purpose flour
½ cup bottled clam juice
1 tablespoon dry white table wine

If you are unable to purchase sole, you can substitute flounder fillets in this recipe.

1. In 1-quart microwavable casserole combine celery, onion, carrot, and 2 teaspoons margarine; microwave on High (100%) for 2 minutes until celery is soft, stirring once halfway through cooking.

2. In small mixing bowl combine half of the vegetable mixture, the rice, yogurt, lemon peel, thyme, and paprika; mix well.

3. Onto center of each fillet arrange an equal amount of the vegetable-rice mixture; roll fillets to enclose filling. Arrange fillets on microwavable plate.

4. Microwave on High for 6 minutes, rotating plate ½ turn every 2 minutes, until fish flakes easily when tested with a fork. Set aside and keep warm.

5. In small microwavable mixing bowl melt remaining margarine on High for 30 seconds; stir in flour. Microwave on High for 30 seconds. Stir in clam juice, wine, and reserved vegetable mixture and microwave on High for 2 minutes, stirring once halfway through cooking, until hot.

6. To serve, spoon clam juice mixture onto serving platter; arrange fillets on serving platter.

APPROXIMATE TOTAL TIME: 30 MINUTES

MAKES 2 SERVINGS

Each serving provides: ¼ Milk; 1 Fat; 3 Proteins; ¾ Vegetable; 1 Bread; 20 Optional Calories
Per serving: 287 calories; 26 g protein; 6 g fat; 30 g carbohydrate; 111 mg calcium; 341 mg sodium; 56 mg cholesterol; 1 g dietary fiber

Fiesta Swordfish

2 teaspoons olive *or* vegetable oil

½ cup sliced red onion

½ medium mild chili pepper, seeded and minced

½ small jalapeño pepper, seeded and minced

1 small garlic clove, minced

4 large plum tomatoes, blanched, peeled, seeded, and chopped

¼ cup bottled clam juice

2 tablespoons *each* chopped cilantro (Chinese parsley) *or* Italian (flat-leaf) parsley and half-and-half (blend of milk and cream)

½ pound boneless swordfish steak

3 tablespoons lime juice (no sugar added)

1. Preheat broiler. In 9-inch nonstick skillet heat oil; add onion, chili pepper, jalapeño pepper, and garlic and cook over medium-high heat, stirring occasionally, until peppers are tender-crisp, about 1 minute.

2. Add tomatoes and clam juice and stir to combine; bring mixture to a boil. Reduce heat to low and let simmer until mixture is slightly reduced, about 3 minutes.

3. Remove skillet from heat and stir in cilantro and half-and-half. Return to low heat and cook until thoroughly heated. Set aside and keep warm.

4. Spray nonstick baking sheet with nonstick cooking spray and arrange swordfish on baking sheet. Broil for 2 minutes, basting with 1 tablespoon plus 1½ teaspoons lime juice. Turn swordfish over, baste with remaining lime juice, and broil until fish flakes easily when tested with a fork, about 2 minutes longer.

5. To serve, spoon tomato mixture onto serving platter; top with swordfish.

APPROXIMATE TOTAL TIME: 25 MINUTES

MAKES 2 SERVINGS

Each serving provides: 1 Fat; 3 Proteins; 2¾ Vegetables; 30 Optional Calories
Per serving: 242 calories; 25 g protein; 11 g fat; 11 g carbohydrate; 49 mg calcium; 187 mg sodium; 50 mg cholesterol; 2 g dietary fiber

Swordfish Kabobs

2 tablespoons reduced-sodium
   soy sauce
2 teaspoons minced pared
   gingerroot
1 garlic clove, minced
7 ounces boneless swordfish
   steak, cut into ¾-inch cubes
½ cup cubed yellow bell pepper
   (1-inch cubes)
½ cup cubed zucchini
6 cherry tomatoes
4 medium mushrooms
½ teaspoon Chinese sesame oil

*For a change of pace, grill kabobs
on the barbecue grill and serve with
parslied rice.*

1. In medium glass or stainless-steel bowl combine first 3 ingredients; add fish and stir to coat. Cover and refrigerate for at least 20 minutes or up to 2 hours.

2. Using a slotted spoon, remove fish from marinade, reserving marinade. Onto each of two 12-inch wooden skewers thread half of the fish cubes, bell pepper, zucchini, cherry tomatoes, and mushrooms, alternating ingredients.

3. Arrange kabobs on 12-inch microwavable serving platter. Using a pastry brush, brush kabobs with reserved marinade. Cover and microwave on High (100%) for 4 minutes, rotating platter halfway through cooking. Let stand for 1 minute to complete cooking. Brush kabobs evenly with sesame oil.

APPROXIMATE TOTAL TIME: 20 MINUTES (does not include marinating time)

MAKES 2 SERVINGS

Each serving provides: ¼ Fat; 2½ Proteins; 2 Vegetables
Per serving: 165 calories; 22 g protein; 5 g fat; 7 g carbohydrate; 20 mg calcium; 695 mg sodium; 39 mg cholesterol; 1 g dietary fiber

Italian-Style Tuna ▽ⓒ ▽ⓢ

1 teaspoon olive oil
½ cup chopped onion
½ ounce pignolias (pine nuts)
1 anchovy fillet, rinsed and
  chopped
2 tablespoons dry white table
  wine
1 tablespoon *each* balsamic *or* red
  wine vinegar and rinsed
  drained capers
2 large plum tomatoes, blanched,
  peeled, seeded, and chopped
Dash *each* ground cinnamon and
  ground cloves
7 ounces boneless tuna steak
1 tablespoon chopped fresh
  Italian (flat-leaf) parsley

*This recipe uses tuna, but it's fresh
rather than canned.*

1. Preheat broiler. In 9-inch nonstick skillet heat oil; add onion, pignolias, and anchovy and cook over medium heat, stirring frequently, until onion is tender-crisp, about 3 minutes. Stir in wine and vinegar and bring mixture to a boil. Reduce heat to low; add capers, tomatoes, cinnamon, and cloves and stir to combine. Let simmer until flavors blend, about 5 minutes.

2. While tomato mixture is simmering broil tuna. Spray nonstick baking sheet with nonstick cooking spray and arrange tuna on baking sheet. Broil until fish flakes easily when tested with a fork, about 3 minutes on each side (depending on thickness of steak).

3. To serve, arrange tuna on serving platter; top with tomato mixture and sprinkle with parsley.

APPROXIMATE TOTAL TIME: 30 MINUTES

MAKES 2 SERVINGS

Each serving provides: 1 Fat; 3 Proteins; 1½ Vegetables; 15 Optional Calories
Per serving: 239 calories; 26 g protein; 11 g fat; 7 g carbohydrate; 25 mg calcium; 229 mg sodium; 39 mg cholesterol; 1 g dietary fiber (this figure does not include pignolias and capers; nutrition analyses not available)

Mexican Tuna Salad ⮟C ⮟S

4 ounces drained canned tuna
(packed in oil), flaked
½ medium tomato, finely
chopped
¼ cup *each* finely chopped red
onion and red *or* green bell
pepper
2 tablespoons plus 2 teaspoons
reduced-calorie mayonnaise
1 tablespoon *each* chopped
cilantro (Chinese parsley) *or*
Italian (flat-leaf) parsley and
lime juice (no sugar added)

*Serve this Mexican-style salad in a
taco with shredded lettuce and diced
tomato.*

1. In small mixing bowl combine all ingredients, mixing well.

APPROXIMATE TOTAL TIME: 10 MINUTES

MAKES 4 SERVINGS

Each serving provides: 1½ Fats; 1 Protein; ½ Vegetable
Per serving: 92 calories; 9 g protein; 5 g fat; 3 g carbohydrate; 8 mg calcium; 157 mg sodium; 8 mg cholesterol; 0.5 g dietary fiber

Olive-Tuna Salad ▽C

4 ounces drained canned tuna
   (packed in oil), flaked
¼ cup *each* finely chopped onion
   and finely chopped rinsed
   drained pimiento
6 large pimiento-stuffed green
   olives, finely chopped
2 tablespoons reduced-calorie
   mayonnaise
1 tablespoon lemon juice

1. In small mixing bowl combine all ingredients, mixing well.

APPROXIMATE TOTAL TIME: 10 MINUTES

MAKES 4 SERVINGS

Each serving provides: 1½ Fats; 1 Protein; ¼ Vegetable
Per serving: 87 calories; 8 g protein; 5 g fat; 2 g carbohydrate; 11 mg calcium; 294 mg sodium; 7 mg cholesterol; 0.3 g dietary fiber (this figure does not include pimiento; nutrition analysis not available)

Oriental Tuna Salad ▽c̄

4 ounces drained canned tuna
  (packed in oil), flaked
¼ cup *each* finely chopped
  scallions (green onions), celery,
  and drained canned bamboo
  shoots
2 tablespoons plus 2 teaspoons
  reduced-calorie mayonnaise
2 teaspoons reduced-sodium soy
  sauce
1 teaspoon *each* grated pared
  gingerroot and minced fresh
  garlic

*This zippy variation of tuna salad
also makes a fabulous sandwich
filling.*

1. In small mixing bowl combine all ingredients, mixing well.

APPROXIMATE TOTAL TIME: 10 MINUTES

MAKES 4 SERVINGS

Each serving provides: 1½ Fats; 1 Protein; ¼ Vegetable
Per serving: 91 calories; 9 g protein; 5 g fat; 2 g carbohydrate; 13 mg calcium; 283 mg sodium; 8 mg cholesterol;
0.3 g dietary fiber (this figure does not include bamboo
shoots; nutrition analysis not available)

Tuna-Rice Salad ▽C ▽F

1 tablespoon *each* sweet pickle
  relish and red wine vinegar
2 teaspoons vegetable oil
½ teaspoon Dijon-style mustard
1 cup cooked long-grain rice
2 ounces drained canned tuna
  (packed in water), flaked
¼ cup *each* diced green bell
  pepper, carrot, and cucumber
2 tablespoons diced drained
  pimiento

*This is a great way to use up leftover
cooked rice.*

1. In medium mixing bowl combine relish, vinegar, oil, and mustard, mixing well. Add remaining ingredients and toss to coat. Cover and refrigerate until flavors blend, at least 15 minutes.

APPROXIMATE TOTAL TIME: 15 MINUTES (does not include chilling time)

MAKES 2 SERVINGS

Each serving provides: 1 Fat; 1 Protein; ¾ Vegetable; 1 Bread; 15 Optional Calories
Per serving: 216 calories; 11 g protein; 5 g fat; 31 g carbohydrate; 22 mg calcium; 201 mg sodium; 12 mg cholesterol; 1 g dietary fiber (this figure does not include pimiento; nutrition analysis not available)

Pecan Trout

1 trout fillet (7 ounces)
1 tablespoon whole wheat *or* all-purpose flour
1 teaspoon *each* vegetable oil and margarine
½ ounce chopped pecans
¼ cup dry white table wine
1 tablespoon lemon juice
1 teaspoon chopped fresh parsley
½ teaspoon Worcestershire sauce

1. On sheet of wax paper dredge trout in flour, coating both sides.

2. In 10-inch nonstick skillet heat oil and margarine until margarine is melted; add trout and cook over medium heat until trout flakes easily when tested with a fork, 2 to 3 minutes on each side. Using a spatula, transfer trout to serving platter; keep warm.

3. To same skillet add pecans and cook over low heat, stirring frequently, until toasted, 1 to 2 minutes. Stir in remaining ingredients and cook until thoroughly heated, 1 to 2 minutes. Pour over trout.

APPROXIMATE TOTAL TIME: 15 MINUTES

MAKES 2 SERVINGS

Each serving provides: 1½ Fats; 3 Proteins; 40 Optional Calories
Per serving: 267 calories; 22 g protein; 16 g fat; 5 g carbohydrate; 52 mg calcium; 91 mg sodium; 58 mg cholesterol; 1 g dietary fiber

Poultry

Poultry continues to soar on the popularity charts because it's a source of low-fat protein for less money than most meats. These days turkey, as well as chicken, is available in easy-to-prepare parts, a boon for those who don't want to cope with a whole bird. Italian-style turkey sausage links become Skillet Sausages with Apple—an appetizing way to get in some of that fabled "apple a day." Our Creamy Chicken Fettuccine enables one chicken cutlet to stretch into two satisfying servings. For gourmet dining, try Braised Cornish Hen, prepared with a touch of dry sherry. You won't lay an egg with these dishes!

Chicken and Tomato Egg Drop Soup ▽C ▽F

2 cups tomato juice
¼ pound thinly sliced skinned and boned chicken breast
2 teaspoons reduced-sodium soy sauce
¼ cup *each* thawed frozen egg substitute and diagonally thinly sliced scallions (green onions)

————

Here's our variation of a familiar Chinese specialty.

1. In 1-quart microwavable casserole combine tomato juice, *1 cup water*, the chicken, and soy sauce and microwave on High (100%) for 4 minutes until chicken is no longer pink, stirring once halfway through cooking.

2. Remove casserole from oven and, stirring constantly, pour egg substitute into tomato juice mixture in a slow stream. Microwave on Medium (50%) for 1 minute. Stir in scallions.

APPROXIMATE TOTAL TIME: 10 MINUTES

MAKES 2 SERVINGS, ABOUT 1½ CUPS EACH

Each serving provides: 2 Proteins; 1¼ Vegetables
Per serving: 127 calories; 19 g protein; 1 g fat; 12 g carbohydrate; 50 mg calcium; 1,172 mg sodium; 33 mg cholesterol; 0.3 g dietary fiber

Hot and Spicy Chicken Soup ▽C ▽F

2 teaspoons vegetable oil
5 ounces thinly sliced chicken
cutlets
½ cup *each* sliced mushrooms,
onion, and Chinese chard (bok
choy)
½ medium mild *or* hot chili
pepper, seeded and thinly
sliced
1 small garlic clove, minced
Dash Chinese five-spice powder
1 cup canned ready-to-serve low-
sodium chicken broth
1 tablespoon *each* dry sherry and
reduced-sodium soy sauce
1 cup drained canned *or* thawed
frozen baby corn ears
½ cup *each* snow peas (Chinese
pea pods), stem ends and
strings removed; bean sprouts,
and julienne-cut (matchstick
pieces) red bell pepper
2 tablespoons thinly sliced
scallion (green onion), green
portion only

1. In 4-quart nonstick saucepan heat oil; add chicken and cook over high heat, stirring frequently, until browned, about 3 minutes.

2. Add mushrooms, onion, Chinese chard, chili pepper, garlic, and five-spice powder and cook, stirring frequently, until vegetables are tender-crisp, about 3 minutes.

3. Stir in broth, sherry, and soy sauce; bring mixture to a boil. Reduce heat to low; add remaining ingredients and stir to combine. Continue cooking until bell pepper is tender-crisp, about 2 minutes.

APPROXIMATE TOTAL TIME: 25 MINUTES

MAKES 2 SERVINGS, ABOUT 2½ CUPS EACH

Each serving provides: 1 Fat; 2 Proteins; 3¼ Vegetables; ½ Bread; 25 Optional Calories
Per serving: 255 calories; 25 g protein; 7 g fat; 22 g carbohydrate; 67 mg calcium; 410 mg sodium; 41 mg cholesterol; 6 g dietary fiber (this figure does not include Chinese chard; nutrition analysis not available)

Chicken Breasts Bonne Femme ▽F▽

2 chicken breasts (6 ounces
  each), skinned and cut into
  halves
1 tablespoon all-purpose flour
2 teaspoons olive *or* vegetable oil
1 cup *each* sliced onions and
  sliced shiitake *or* white
  mushrooms
¼ cup dry white table wine
6 ounces pared all-purpose
  potato, cut into quarters
1 packet instant chicken broth
  and seasoning mix
¼ teaspoon chopped fresh
  tarragon *or* ⅛ teaspoon
  tarragon leaves
⅛ teaspoon white pepper

*Our version of a classic French rec-
ipe is as fine as any you'll find in a
restaurant.*

1. On sheet of wax paper dredge chicken in flour,
coating all sides.

2. In 3-quart nonstick saucepan heat oil; add chicken
and cook over medium-high heat, turning occasionally, until browned on all sides, 3 to 4 minutes. Transfer chicken to plate and set aside.

3. In same saucepan combine onions and mushrooms and cook over medium-high heat, stirring frequently, until vegetables are softened, 1 to 2 minutes.
Continuing to stir, add *1½ cups water* and the wine.
Add remaining ingredients; return chicken to saucepan. Reduce heat to low, cover, and let simmer, stirring occasionally, until chicken and potato are tender,
about 20 minutes.

APPROXIMATE TOTAL TIME: 35 MINUTES

MAKES 2 SERVINGS

Each serving provides: 1 Fat; 3 Proteins; 2 Vegetables;
1 Bread; 45 Optional Calories
Per serving: 307 calories; 31 g protein; 6 g fat; 27 g carbohydrate; 45 mg calcium; 578 mg sodium; 66 mg cholesterol; 3 g dietary fiber

Chicken Burgers ▽F

5 ounces skinned and boned
  chicken, sliced
⅓ cup plus 2 teaspoons plain
  dried bread crumbs, divided
2 tablespoons minced onion
1 tablespoon freshly squeezed
  lemon juice
1 teaspoon prepared horseradish
½ teaspoon Worcestershire sauce
⅛ teaspoon white pepper
2 teaspoons vegetable oil
2 small pitas (1 ounce each);
  each cut in half horizontally
2 lettuce leaves
4 tomato slices
1 tablespoon reduced-calorie
  Russian dressing (25 calories
  per tablespoon)

1. In food processor process chicken, using on-off motion, until chicken is finely ground. Transfer to medium mixing bowl; add ¼ cup bread crumbs, the onion, lemon juice, horseradish, Worcestershire sauce, and pepper and mix well until thoroughly combined.

2. Shape chicken mixture into 2 equal patties. On sheet of wax paper coat patties evenly with remaining bread crumbs.

3. In 10-inch nonstick skillet heat oil; add chicken patties and cook over medium heat until cooked through and lightly browned, 2 to 3 minutes on each side.

4. Onto bottom half of each pita arrange 1 lettuce leaf; top with 1 chicken patty, 2 tomato slices, and 1½ teaspoons dressing. Top each sandwich with remaining pita half.

APPROXIMATE TOTAL TIME: 20 MINUTES

MAKES 2 SERVINGS

Each serving provides: 1 Fat; 2 Proteins; 1 Vegetable; 2 Breads; 15 Optional Calories
Per serving: 310 calories; 21 g protein; 8 g fat; 37 g carbohydrate; 50 mg calcium; 463 mg sodium; 51 mg cholesterol; 2 g dietary fiber (this figure does not include horseradish; nutrition analysis not available)

Chicken Cordon Bleu

2 thin chicken cutlets (3 ounces each)

2 slices *each* turkey-ham and reduced-fat Swiss cheese (½ ounce each)

1 tablespoon plus 2 teaspoons Dijon-style mustard, divided

1 teaspoon honey

⅓ cup plus 2 teaspoons plain dried bread crumbs

2 teaspoons vegetable oil

½ cup canned ready-to-serve low-sodium chicken broth

2 teaspoons all-purpose flour

1 tablespoon sour cream

1. Preheat oven to 375°F. Top each chicken cutlet with 1 slice turkey-ham and 1 slice cheese; starting from the narrow end, roll each cutlet jelly-roll fashion. Secure with toothpicks.

2. In small mixing bowl combine 1 tablespoon mustard and the honey; spread half of the mixture evenly over each chicken roll.

3. On sheet of wax paper arrange bread crumbs; turn chicken rolls in bread crumbs, coating all sides and using all of the bread crumbs. Arrange chicken rolls on nonstick baking sheet and drizzle each with 1 teaspoon oil. Bake until chicken is cooked through, 20 to 25 minutes.

4. While chicken is baking prepare sauce. In small saucepan combine broth and flour, stirring to dissolve flour. Cook over medium-high heat, stirring frequently, until mixture thickens, 3 to 4 minutes. Reduce heat to low and stir in sour cream and remaining mustard; cook, stirring occasionally, 3 to 4 minutes longer *(do not boil)*.

5. To serve, remove toothpicks and cut each chicken roll crosswise into 4 equal slices. Onto each of 2 serving plates pour half of the sauce and top with 4 chicken roll slices.

APPROXIMATE TOTAL TIME: 40 MINUTES (includes baking time)

MAKES 2 SERVINGS

Each serving provides: 1 Fat; 3 Proteins; 1 Bread; 60 Optional Calories
Per serving: 329 calories; 31 g protein; 12 g fat; 22 g carbohydrate; 218 mg calcium; 750 mg sodium; 63 mg cholesterol; 1 g dietary fiber

Chicken in Flavored Vinegar ⟨S⟩

2 teaspoons olive *or* vegetable oil
2 chicken cutlets (¼ pound each)
1 cup sliced onions
½ cup sliced celery
1 small garlic clove, minced
3 tablespoons raspberry,
 balsamic, *or* red wine vinegar
1 tablespoon sour cream
1 teaspoon *each* country Dijon-
 style mustard and tomato paste
2 large plum tomatoes, blanched,
 peeled, seeded, and finely
 chopped
1 tablespoon finely chopped fresh
 Italian (flat-leaf) parsley

We recommend raspberry or balsamic vinegar for this unusual dish.

1. In 9-inch nonstick skillet heat oil; add chicken and cook over high heat until golden, 3 to 4 minutes on each side. Transfer to plate; set aside.

2. In same skillet combine onions, celery, and garlic and cook over medium-high heat, stirring occasionally, until celery is tender-crisp, about 3 minutes. Stir in vinegar, sour cream, mustard, and tomato paste; cook over medium-high heat, stirring constantly, until mixture thickens, 2 to 3 minutes.

3. Stir in plum tomatoes and bring mixture to a boil. Reduce heat to low and return chicken to skillet; cover and cook until chicken is heated through, 3 to 4 minutes. Sprinkle with parsley.

APPROXIMATE TOTAL TIME: 30 MINUTES

MAKES 2 SERVINGS

Each serving provides: 1 Fat; 3 Proteins; 2½ Vegetables; 20 Optional Calories
Per serving: 232 calories; 28 g protein; 8 g fat; 11 g carbohydrate; 60 mg calcium; 207 mg sodium; 69 mg cholesterol; 3 g dietary fiber

Chicken-in-the-Rye ⬇ⓢ

2 tablespoons rye *or* all-purpose flour
½ teaspoon caraway seed, crushed
2 thin chicken cutlets (3 ounces each)
2 teaspoons vegetable oil
1 ounce diced fully cooked smoked ham
¼ cup chopped onion
1 teaspoon all-purpose flour
¼ cup canned ready-to-serve low-sodium chicken broth
½ teaspoon *each* Dijon-style mustard and chopped fresh dill
¼ cup plain low-fat yogurt
Garnish: dill sprigs

1. On sheet of wax paper combine rye flour and caraway seed. Dredge chicken in flour mixture, coating both sides, and set aside.

2. In 10-inch nonstick skillet heat oil; add chicken and cook over medium-high heat until cooked through, 3 to 4 minutes on each side. Remove from skillet; set aside and keep warm.

3. In same skillet combine ham and onion and cook over medium-high heat, stirring frequently, until onion is softened, 1 to 2 minutes. Sprinkle all-purpose flour over ham-onion mixture and stir quickly to combine; continuing to stir, add broth, mustard, and dill. Reduce heat to medium-low and cook, stirring frequently, until mixture thickens, 3 to 4 minutes. Stir in yogurt (*do not boil*).

4. To serve, place chicken on serving platter, top with ham-onion sauce, and garnish with dill sprigs.

APPROXIMATE TOTAL TIME: 25 MINUTES

MAKES 2 SERVINGS

Each serving provides: ¼ Milk; 1 Fat; 2½ Proteins; ¼ Vegetable; 45 Optional Calories
Per serving: 214 calories; 25 g protein; 7 g fat; 10 g carbohydrate; 74 mg calcium; 290 mg sodium; 59 mg cholesterol; 1 g dietary fiber (this figure does not include caraway seed; nutrition analysis not available)

Chicken 'n' Biscuits

¼ cup *each* chopped onion and celery
3 tablespoons whipped cream cheese
1 teaspoon cornstarch
½ packet (about ½ teaspoon) instant chicken broth and seasoning mix
3 ounces cooked, skinned, and boned chicken, cut into cubes
½ cup *each* frozen whole-kernel corn and finely diced red *or* green bell pepper
Dash crushed red pepper
2 ready-to-bake refrigerated buttermilk flaky biscuits (1 ounce each); cut in half horizontally and baked according to package directions

—

For variety, serve this creamy chicken-vegetable mixture over rice or noodles rather than biscuits.

1. Spray 1-quart saucepan with nonstick cooking spray and heat; add onion and celery and cook over medium-high heat, stirring frequently, until onion is translucent, about 1 minute.

2. In small mixing bowl combine ½ *cup water*, the cream cheese, cornstarch, and broth mix, stirring to dissolve cornstarch; add to onion-celery mixture. Reduce heat to medium and, using a wire whisk, cook, stirring, until mixture thickens slightly, 2 to 3 minutes.

3. Add remaining ingredients except biscuits to onion-celery mixture and cook, stirring frequently, until corn is heated through, about 5 minutes.

4. To serve, arrange biscuit halves on serving platter and top with chicken mixture.

APPROXIMATE TOTAL TIME: 25 MINUTES

MAKES 2 SERVINGS

Each serving provides: 1½ Proteins; 1 Vegetable; 1½ Breads; 60 Optional Calories
Per serving: 273 calories; 17 g protein; 12 g fat; 26 g carbohydrate; 30 mg calcium; 648 mg sodium; 52 mg cholesterol; 2 g dietary fiber (this figure does not include biscuits; nutrition analysis not available)

Chicken Pot Pie

2 teaspoons margarine
1 cup *each* sliced mushrooms and broccoli florets
½ cup *each* diced onion and sliced carrot
¼ pound cooked, skinned, and boned chicken, cubed
1 teaspoon all-purpose flour
½ cup canned ready-to-serve low-sodium chicken broth
1 cup skim *or* nonfat milk
1 egg white
⅓ cup plus 2 teaspoons buttermilk baking mix

Use leftover cooked chicken in this tasty pie.

1. In 9-inch nonstick skillet melt margarine; add vegetables and sauté over medium heat until carrot is tender-crisp, 2 to 3 minutes. Add chicken and stir to combine.

2. Sprinkle flour over vegetable-chicken mixture and stir quickly to combine; cook, stirring constantly, for 1 minute. Continuing to stir, gradually add broth; bring mixture to a boil. Reduce heat to low and let simmer until mixture thickens, about 5 minutes.

3. Preheat oven to 350°F. In small mixing bowl add milk and egg white to baking mix and stir until thoroughly combined.

4. Spray 8-inch pie plate with nonstick cooking spray; spoon vegetable-chicken mixture into plate. Stir baking mix mixture and spread evenly over vegetable-chicken mixture. Bake until topping is golden brown, about 15 minutes.

APPROXIMATE TOTAL TIME: 35 MINUTES (includes baking time)

MAKES 2 SERVINGS

Each serving provides: ½ Milk; 1 Fat; 2 Proteins; 3 Vegetables; 1 Bread; 45 Optional Calories
Per serving: 346 calories; 28 g protein; 12 g fat; 32 g carbohydrate; 239 mg calcium; 487 mg sodium; 53 mg cholesterol; 2 g dietary fiber (this figure does not include broccoli florets; nutrition analysis not available)

Chicken Saté ▽C ▽S

¼ cup plain low-fat yogurt
1 teaspoon *each* minced fresh
  garlic and pared gingerroot
¼ teaspoon curry powder
5 ounces skinned and boned
  chicken breast, cut into twelve
  ¾-inch cubes
1 tablespoon peanut butter
1 teaspoon *each* cornstarch,
  lemon juice, and reduced-
  sodium soy sauce

1. In small mixing bowl combine yogurt, garlic, gingerroot, and curry powder; add chicken and turn to coat. Cover and refrigerate at least 30 minutes or overnight.

2. Onto each of six 6-inch wooden skewers arrange 2 chicken cubes, reserving marinade. Arrange skewers like spokes of a wheel on microwavable plate; cover and microwave on High (100%) for 2 minutes, rotating plate ½ turn halfway through cooking. Let stand 1 minute until chicken is cooked through.

3. In small microwavable mixing bowl combine reserved marinade, the remaining ingredients, and *1 teaspoon water*, stirring to dissolve cornstarch. Microwave on Medium-High (70%) for 1 minute, stirring once halfway through cooking.

4. To serve, arrange skewers on serving platter with bowl of sauce for dipping.

APPROXIMATE TOTAL TIME: 15 MINUTES (does not include marinating time)

MAKES 2 SERVINGS

Each serving provides: ¼ Milk; ½ Fat; 2½ Proteins; 5 Optional Calories
Per serving: 155 calories; 20 g protein; 5 g fat; 6 g carbohydrate; 68 mg calcium; 205 mg sodium; 43 mg cholesterol; 1 g dietary fiber

Chicken with Artichoke Hearts ⬦S⬦

½ cup *each* julienne-cut (matchstick pieces) red bell pepper and thawed frozen artichoke hearts

1 garlic clove, minced

1 teaspoon vegetable oil

2 tablespoons dry white table wine

1 teaspoon cornstarch

¼ teaspoon Italian seasoning

7 ounces skinned and boned chicken breast, cut into ¼-inch-thick strips

6 large pitted black olives, cut into quarters

1 tablespoon rinsed drained capers

1. Spray 1-quart microwavable casserole with non-stick cooking spray; add pepper, artichoke hearts, garlic, and oil and stir to coat. Cover and microwave on High (100%) for 1 minute.

2. In small mixing bowl combine wine, cornstarch, and Italian seasoning, stirring to dissolve cornstarch; stir into pepper-artichoke heart mixture. Add chicken, olives, and capers and stir to combine.

3. Cover and microwave on Medium-High (70%) for 4 minutes, stirring once halfway through cooking. Let stand 1 minute until chicken is cooked through.

APPROXIMATE TOTAL TIME: 20 MINUTES

MAKES 2 SERVINGS

Each serving provides: 1 Fat; 2½ Proteins; 1 Vegetable; 20 Optional Calories

Per serving: 192 calories; 24 g protein; 6 g fat; 7 g carbohydrate; 38 mg calcium; 391 mg sodium; 58 mg cholesterol; 2 g dietary fiber (this figure does not include capers; nutrition analysis not available)

Chicken with Herb-Caper Sauce ⟨S⟩

1 tablespoon chopped fresh
   rosemary *or* ½ teaspoon
   rosemary leaves
1 tablespoon lemon juice
2 teaspoons olive *or* vegetable
   oil, divided
1 small garlic clove, mashed
½ pound thin chicken cutlets
1 cup quartered small mushrooms
¼ cup *each* dry white table wine
   and canned ready-to-serve low-
   sodium chicken broth
1 tablespoon rinsed drained
   capers
⅛ teaspoon poultry seasoning

This recipe requires a little time for marinating, but the flavor it adds is well worth it.

1. In shallow glass or stainless-steel bowl combine rosemary, lemon juice, 1 teaspoon oil, and the garlic, stirring well; add chicken and turn to coat. Let stand at room temperature for 15 minutes.

2. Spray 9-inch nonstick skillet with nonstick cooking spray; add remaining oil and heat. Add chicken, reserving marinade, and cook over high heat until golden, 3 to 4 minutes on each side. Transfer to plate; set aside.

3. In same skillet cook mushrooms over medium-high heat until browned, about 4 minutes. Stir in remaining ingredients and reserved marinade and bring mixture to a boil. Reduce heat to low and return chicken to skillet; cook until chicken is heated through, 2 to 3 minutes.

APPROXIMATE TOTAL TIME: 20 MINUTES (does not include marinating time)

MAKES 2 SERVINGS

Each serving provides: 1 Fat; 3 Proteins; 1 Vegetable; 30 Optional Calories
Per serving: 202 calories; 27 g protein; 6 g fat; 3 g carbohydrate; 24 mg calcium; 195 mg sodium; 66 mg cholesterol; 0.5 g dietary fiber (this figure does not include capers; nutrition analysis not available)

Creamy Chicken Fettuccine

1 teaspoon vegetable oil
1 chicken cutlet (3 ounces)
½ cup sliced shiitake *or* white
  mushrooms
1 garlic clove, minced
1 teaspoon all-purpose flour
½ cup canned ready-to-serve
  low-sodium chicken broth
¼ cup evaporated skimmed milk
2 tablespoons whipped cream
  cheese
¾ ounce grated Parmesan cheese
⅛ teaspoon white pepper
1½ cups cooked fettuccine (hot)

1. In 10-inch nonstick skillet heat oil; add chicken and cook over medium-high heat until tender, 2 to 3 minutes on each side.

2. Remove chicken from skillet and cut into ½-inch cubes; set aside.

3. In same skillet combine mushrooms and garlic and cook over medium-high heat, stirring occasionally, for 1 minute. Sprinkle with flour and stir quickly to combine; continuing to stir, add chicken broth and milk. Reduce heat to low and let simmer, stirring frequently, until mixture thickens, 2 to 3 minutes. Stir in cheeses and pepper; return chicken to skillet and cook, stirring frequently, until chicken is heated through, 2 to 3 minutes.

4. To serve, on serving platter arrange fettuccine; top with chicken mixture.

APPROXIMATE TOTAL TIME: 25 MINUTES

MAKES 2 SERVINGS

Each serving provides: ¼ Milk; ½ Fat; 1½ Proteins; ½ Vegetable; 1½ Breads; 50 Optional Calories
Per serving: 342 calories; 23 g protein; 11 g fat; 35 g carbohydrate; 266 mg calcium; 314 mg sodium; 81 mg cholesterol; 3 g dietary fiber

Microwave Brunswick Stew ▽F ▽S

1 cup canned Italian tomatoes (reserve liquid), seeded and diced

¼ cup *each* chopped onion, dry white table wine, and canned ready-to-serve low-sodium chicken broth

1 tablespoon *each* all-purpose flour and Worcestershire sauce

1 small ear fresh *or* thawed frozen corn on the cob (5 inches long), cut into 4 equal pieces

½ cup *each* frozen okra, sliced, and frozen green lima beans

¾ pound chicken breasts, skinned and cut into halves

▬

Corn on the cob makes an appearance in this satisfying stew.

1. In 3-quart microwavable casserole combine tomatoes with reserved liquid, onion, wine, broth, flour, and Worcestershire sauce, stirring to dissolve flour.

2. Add corn, okra, and lima beans; arrange chicken pieces over vegetables with meatier parts facing toward center of casserole.

3. Cover and microwave on High (100%) for 15 minutes, stirring once and rotating casserole ½ turn every 3 minutes.

APPROXIMATE TOTAL TIME: 25 MINUTES

MAKES 2 SERVINGS

Each serving provides: 3 Proteins; 1¾ Vegetables; 1 Bread; 45 Optional Calories
Per serving: 292 calories; 33 g protein; 3 g fat; 30 g carbohydrate; 104 mg calcium; 391 mg sodium; 66 mg cholesterol; 9 g dietary fiber

Oriental Chicken Salad with Peanuts ▽C

2 tablespoons reduced-sodium
  soy sauce
1 tablespoon creamy peanut
  butter
¼ teaspoon *each* minced pared
  gingerroot, minced garlic, and
  Chinese sesame oil
¾ teaspoon peanut oil
Dash ground red pepper
1 cup cooked thin spaghetti
3 ounces diced cooked chicken
½ cup rinsed drained bean
  sprouts
¼ cup sliced scallions (green
  onions)
½ ounce unsalted shelled roasted
  peanuts
1 cup shredded lettuce

*Using leftover cooked chicken and
cooked spaghetti will speed the preparation of this recipe.*

1. In blender combine soy sauce, *1 tablespoon water*, the peanut butter, gingerroot, garlic, oils, and pepper and process until thoroughly combined. Set aside.

2. In medium mixing bowl combine remaining ingredients except lettuce; add soy sauce mixture and toss to coat.

3. On serving platter arrange lettuce; top with spaghetti mixture.

APPROXIMATE TOTAL TIME: 15 MINUTES

MAKES 2 SERVINGS

Each serving provides: 1½ Fats; 2½ Proteins; 1¾ Vegetables; 1 Bread
Per serving: 295 calories; 21 g protein; 14 g fat; 24 g carbohydrate; 48 mg calcium; 680 mg sodium; 38 mg cholesterol; 3 g dietary fiber

Variation: Oriental Chicken Salad—Omit peanuts from recipe. In Serving Information decrease Fat to 1 and Proteins to 2.
Per serving: 252 calories; 19 g protein; 10 g fat; 22 g carbohydrate; 48 mg calcium; 680 mg sodium; 38 mg cholesterol; 2 g dietary fiber

Pacific Chicken ▽s

2 teaspoons olive *or* vegetable oil
7 ounces thin chicken cutlets
½ cup *each* quartered mushrooms
   and drained canned pineapple
   chunks (no sugar added)
1 tablespoon dark rum
¼ cup canned ready-to-serve
   low-sodium chicken broth
½ cup sliced scallions (green
   onions)
½ ounce macadamia nuts,
   chopped

Macadamia nuts, rum, and pineapple combine to give this dish a tropical flavor.

1. In 9-inch nonstick skillet heat oil; add chicken and cook over high heat until golden, 3 to 4 minutes on each side. Transfer to plate and keep warm.

2. In same skillet cook mushrooms over medium-high heat, stirring frequently, until browned, about 2 minutes. Add pineapple and stir to combine; stir in rum.

3. Stir in broth and bring mixture to a boil. Reduce heat to low; return chicken to skillet and turn to coat with mushroom-pineapple mixture. Stir in scallions and nuts and cook until thoroughly heated.

APPROXIMATE TOTAL TIME: 20 MINUTES

MAKES 2 SERVINGS

Each serving provides: 1 Fat; 3 Proteins; 1 Vegetable; ½ Fruit; 45 Optional Calories
Per serving: 267 calories; 25 g protein; 11 g fat; 13 g carbohydrate; 40 mg calcium; 74 mg sodium; 58 mg cholesterol; 1 g dietary fiber (this figure does not include macadamia nuts; nutrition analysis not available)

Spicy Oriental Chicken ▽F

2 tablespoons reduced-sodium
   soy sauce
1 tablespoon *each* dry sherry and
   honey
1 small garlic clove, minced
1 teaspoon minced pared
   gingerroot
Dash *each* Chinese five-spice
   powder and crushed red pepper
½ pound thinly sliced skinned
   and boned chicken breasts
1½ teaspoons peanut *or*
   vegetable oil
½ cup *each* diagonally sliced
   scallions (green onions), red
   bell pepper strips, and
   diagonally thinly sliced carrot
½ teaspoon Chinese sesame oil
1 teaspoon sesame seed, toasted

---

*Marinating the chicken for a short
time in a mixture of seasonings im-
parts added flavor.*

1. In shallow glass or stainless-steel mixing bowl combine soy sauce, sherry, honey, garlic, gingerroot, five-spice powder, and crushed red pepper; add chicken and turn to coat. Let stand for 15 minutes.

2. In 9-inch nonstick skillet heat peanut oil; add chicken, reserving marinade, and cook over high heat, stirring occasionally, until golden, 3 to 4 minutes. Push chicken to side of skillet and add scallions, bell pepper, and carrot. Cover and cook until carrot is tender, about 2 minutes.

3. Stir in reserved marinade and Chinese sesame oil and bring mixture to a boil; cook, stirring constantly, until liquid evaporates, 1 to 2 minutes. Sprinkle with sesame seed.

APPROXIMATE TOTAL TIME: 25 MINUTES (does not include marinating time)

MAKES 2 SERVINGS

Each serving provides: 1 Fat; 3 Proteins; 1½ Vegetables; 45 Optional Calories
Per serving: 252 calories; 28 g protein; 7 g fat; 17 g carbohydrate; 44 mg calcium; 687 mg sodium; 66 mg cholesterol; 2 g dietary fiber (this figure does not include sesame seed; nutrition analysis not available)

Sweet and Savory Chicken ▽F ▽S

2 chicken cutlets (¼ pound each)
2 teaspoons all-purpose flour
1 tablespoon plus 1 teaspoon
  reduced-calorie margarine (tub)
1 cup *each* sliced mushrooms and
  sliced thoroughly washed leeks
  (white portion and some
  green)
1 small garlic clove, minced
4 large plum tomatoes, blanched,
  peeled, seeded, and chopped
2 tablespoons *each* balsamic *or*
  red wine vinegar and dry white
  table wine
1 tablespoon *each* chopped fresh
  Italian (flat-leaf) parsley and
  honey

*Many of our recipes are flavored
with a small amount of wine. Make
sure the wine you use in cooking is
a wine that is good enough to drink.*

1. On sheet of wax paper dredge chicken in flour.

2. In 9-inch nonstick skillet melt margarine; add chicken and cook over high heat until golden, 3 to 4 minutes on each side. Transfer to plate; set aside.

3. In same skillet combine mushrooms, leeks, and garlic and sauté over medium-high heat until leeks are tender-crisp, about 2 minutes. Stir in remaining ingredients and bring mixture to a boil.

4. Reduce heat to low and return chicken to skillet; cover and let simmer until chicken is heated through, about 3 minutes.

APPROXIMATE TOTAL TIME: 30 MINUTES

MAKES 2 SERVINGS

Each serving provides: 1 Fat; 3 Proteins; 4 Vegetables; 55 Optional Calories
Per serving: 273 calories; 29 g protein; 6 g fat; 25 g carbohydrate; 58 mg calcium; 176 mg sodium; 66 mg cholesterol; 3 g dietary fiber

Franks and Beans Pizza ▽C

½ cup finely chopped onion
4 ounces (½ cup) canned baked
   beans (without meat)
1 large pita (2 ounces), toasted
3 ounces chicken frankfurters, cut
   into ½-inch-thick slices
¾ ounce reduced-fat Cheddar
   cheese, shredded

Pizza lovers will enjoy this recipe.

1. Preheat oven to 400°F. Spray small nonstick skillet with nonstick cooking spray and heat; add onion, cover, and cook over medium heat until translucent, about 2 minutes. Stir in beans; cover and cook until heated, about 3 minutes.

2. On baking sheet arrange pita; top with frankfurters and onion-bean mixture. Sprinkle with cheese. Bake until cheese is melted, 1 to 2 minutes.

3. To serve, cut into quarters.

APPROXIMATE TOTAL TIME: 15 MINUTES (includes baking time)

MAKES 2 SERVINGS

Each serving provides: 2 Proteins; ½ Vegetable; 1½ Breads; 25 Optional Calories
Per serving: 296 calories; 14 g protein; 11 g fat; 36 g carbohydrate; 177 mg calcium; 1,065 mg sodium; 50 mg cholesterol; 5 g dietary fiber

Braised Cornish Hen

1 Cornish hen (1 pound*), cut in half and skinned
1 tablespoon all-purpose flour
2 teaspoons olive *or* vegetable oil
1 cup *each* frozen pearl onions and sliced celery (1-inch pieces)
6 ounces baby carrots
¼ cup dry sherry
1 packet instant chicken broth and seasoning mix
2 teaspoons chopped fresh thyme *or* ½ teaspoon thyme leaves
⅛ teaspoon white pepper

1. On sheet of wax paper dredge hen halves in flour, coating all sides.

2. In 4-quart Dutch oven or saucepot heat oil; add hen halves and cook over medium-high heat until lightly browned, 2 to 3 minutes on each side. Transfer to plate and set aside.

3. In same pot combine onions, celery, and carrots and cook, over medium-high heat, stirring frequently, until onions are lightly browned, 2 to 3 minutes. Stir in *1 cup water*, the sherry, broth mix, and seasonings.

4. Return hen halves to pot. Reduce heat to low, partially cover, and let simmer, stirring occasionally, until hen halves are tender, 25 to 30 minutes.

* A 1-pound hen will yield about 6 ounces cooked poultry.

APPROXIMATE TOTAL TIME: 45 MINUTES

MAKES 2 SERVINGS

Each serving provides: 1 Fat; 3 Proteins; 4 Vegetables; 45 Optional Calories
Per serving: 347 calories; 28 g protein; 11 g fat; 26 g carbohydrate; 101 mg calcium; 663 mg sodium; 76 mg cholesterol; 4 g dietary fiber

Grilled Cornish Hen with Stuffing ⧖

1 Cornish hen (about 1 pound*), cut in half

2 tablespoons lemon juice

1 tablespoon plus 1 teaspoon reduced-calorie margarine (tub), divided

1 small Golden Delicious apple (about ¼ pound), cored and chopped

½ cup *each* chopped celery and onion

1 small garlic clove, minced

½ teaspoon poultry seasoning

1 cup canned ready-to-serve low-sodium chicken broth, divided

6 small canned chestnuts (no sugar added), chopped

½ ounce seasoned croutons

2 teaspoons *each* all-purpose flour and honey

1. Preheat broiler. Spray rack in broiling pan with nonstick cooking spray; set hen halves on rack, skin-side down. Broil 6 to 8 inches from heat source, basting with lemon juice and turning once, about 8 minutes on each side, or until thickest portion of hen is pierced with a knife and juices run clear.

2. While hen halves are broiling, prepare stuffing. In 9-inch nonstick skillet melt 2 teaspoons margarine; add apple, celery, onion, garlic, and poultry seasoning and sauté over medium-high heat until apple is tender-crisp, 3 to 4 minutes. Stir in ½ cup broth and bring mixture to a boil. Add chestnuts and croutons and cook, stirring constantly, until liquid has evaporated, about 2 minutes. Transfer to serving platter and keep warm.

3. In same skillet melt remaining margarine; add flour and stir quickly to combine; cook, stirring constantly, for 1 minute. Stir in remaining broth and the honey and cook, stirring constantly, until mixture thickens, about 4 minutes.

4. To serve, remove and discard skin from hen. Arrange hen halves on serving platter; top with sauce and serve with stuffing.

* A 1-pound hen will yield about 6 ounces cooked poultry.

APPROXIMATE TOTAL TIME: 30 MINUTES

MAKES 2 SERVINGS

Each serving provides: 1 Fat; 3 Proteins; 1 Vegetable; 1 Bread; ½ Fruit; 50 Optional Calories
Per serving: 345 calories; 28 g protein; 13 g fat; 30 g carbohydrate; 59 mg calcium; 313 mg sodium; 76 mg cholesterol; 2 g dietary fiber (this figure does not include chestnuts; nutrition analysis not available)

Roast Duck with Cherry Relish $\triangledown{C}$ $\triangledown{S}$

4 duck breasts (6 ounces each)
2 teaspoons olive *or* vegetable oil
1 cup *each* diced red bell peppers
and red onions
1 tablespoon *each* granulated
sugar and lemon juice
½ teaspoon cornstarch
48 large fresh *or* frozen pitted
cherries (no sugar added)

———

Duck breast is ready to serve in far less time than it would take to prepare a whole duck, but it is just as elegant.

1. Preheat oven to 375°F. Spray rack in roasting pan with nonstick cooking spray. Arrange duck breasts, skin-side up, on rack and roast until skin is crisp and browned, about 20 minutes.

2. While duck breasts are roasting prepare relish. In 1-quart saucepan heat oil; add peppers and onions and cook over medium heat, stirring occasionally, until softened, 2 to 3 minutes.

3. In 1-cup liquid measure combine ½ *cup water*, the sugar, lemon juice, and cornstarch, stirring to dissolve cornstarch. Stir into pepper-onion mixture and cook, stirring constantly, until mixture thickens. Reduce heat to low; add cherries and let simmer until thoroughly heated, about 5 minutes.

4. To serve, remove and discard skin from duck. Serve duck breasts topped with relish.

APPROXIMATE TOTAL TIME: 30 MINUTES (includes baking time)

MAKES 4 SERVINGS

Each serving provides: ½ Fat; 3 Proteins; 1 Vegetable; 1 Fruit; 15 Optional Calories
Per serving: 198 calories; 12 g protein; 8 g fat; 21 g carbohydrate; 29 mg calcium; 30 mg sodium; 38 mg cholesterol; 2 g dietary fiber

Tex-Mex Turkey Cutlets ⓢ

2 taco shells (1 ounce), made
  into crumbs
1 tablespoon uncooked yellow
  cornmeal
2 tablespoons low-fat buttermilk
  (1% milk fat)
1 teaspoon *each* chili powder and
  freshly squeezed lime juice
2 turkey cutlets (¼ pound each)
2 teaspoons vegetable oil
1 medium tomato, seeded and
  diced
½ cup mixed vegetable juice
2 tablespoons chopped scallion
  (green onion)
1 tablespoon seeded and minced
  mild chili pepper

1. On sheet of wax paper combine taco shell crumbs and cornmeal; set aside.

2. In small mixing bowl combine buttermilk, chili powder, and lime juice and stir to combine.

3. Dip turkey cutlets into buttermilk mixture and then dredge in cornmeal mixture, coating both sides and using all of the mixtures. Arrange cutlets on nonstick baking sheet; drizzle ½ teaspoon oil over each cutlet.

4. Broil 5 to 6 inches from heat source until lightly browned, 6 to 8 minutes. Turn cutlets over, drizzle each with ½ teaspoon oil, and continue broiling until cutlets are tender, about 5 minutes longer.

5. While cutlets are broiling prepare sauce. In small mixing bowl combine remaining ingredients.

6. To serve, transfer cutlets to serving platter and top with tomato mixture.

APPROXIMATE TOTAL TIME: 30 MINUTES

MAKES 2 SERVINGS

Each serving provides: 1 Fat; 3 Proteins; 1½ Vegetables; ¾ Bread; 5 Optional Calories
Per serving: 352 calories; 29 g protein; 12 g fat; 32 g carbohydrate; 51 mg calcium; 323 mg sodium; 71 mg cholesterol; 4 g dietary fiber

Turkey Cutlets Tonnato F S

2 thin turkey cutlets (3 ounces each)
2 teaspoons dry white table wine
Dash salt
1 ounce drained canned tuna (packed in water)
1 tablespoon plus 1 teaspoon *each* reduced-calorie mayonnaise and plain low-fat yogurt
2 teaspoons rinsed drained capers, divided
1 teaspoon lemon juice
Dash pepper

Our version of this classic dish tops turkey with a sauce that includes canned tuna.

1. Spray 1-quart microwavable casserole with non-stick cooking spray. Arrange turkey cutlets in casserole; pour in wine and sprinkle with salt. Cover and microwave on Medium-High (70%) for 1½ minutes. Let stand 1 minute to complete cooking. Transfer turkey to serving platter; cover and refrigerate until chilled, about 30 minutes.

2. In blender combine tuna and *1 tablespoon water* and process until pureed, about 1 minute. Add mayonnaise, yogurt, 1 teaspoon capers, the lemon juice, and pepper and process until pureed, about 1 minute. Pour over turkey and garnish with remaining capers.

APPROXIMATE TOTAL TIME: 10 MINUTES (does not include chilling time)

MAKES 2 SERVINGS

Each serving provides: 1 Fat; 2½ Proteins; 10 Optional Calories
Per serving: 152 calories; 25 g protein; 4 g fat; 2 g carbohydrate; 31 mg calcium; 308 mg sodium, 63 mg cholesterol; dietary fiber data not available

Turkey Paprika

2 teaspoons vegetable oil
2 thin turkey cutlets (¼ pound each)
½ cup sliced mushrooms
¼ cup chopped onion
1 tablespoon all-purpose flour
½ cup canned ready-to-serve low-sodium chicken broth
¼ cup plain low-fat yogurt
1 teaspoon *each* paprika and chopped fresh parsley
⅛ teaspoon white pepper
1 cup cooked wide noodles (hot)

1. In 10-inch nonstick skillet heat oil; add turkey cutlets and cook over medium-high heat, until tender, 2 to 3 minutes on each side. Transfer to plate and set aside.

2. In same skillet combine mushrooms and onion and cook, stirring occasionally, until mushrooms are softened, 1 to 2 minutes. Sprinkle flour over vegetables and stir quickly to combine; continuing to stir, add broth. Cook over medium heat, stirring frequently, until mixture thickens, about 5 minutes.

3. In small mixing bowl combine yogurt, paprika, parsley, and pepper; stir in 1 tablespoon broth from vegetable mixture. Stir yogurt-broth mixture into skillet; return cutlets to skillet. Cook until cutlets are heated through, 2 to 3 minutes *(do not boil)*.

4. To serve, on serving platter arrange noodles; top with turkey mixture.

APPROXIMATE TOTAL TIME: 25 MINUTES

MAKES 2 SERVINGS

Each serving provides: ¼ Milk; 1 Fat; 3 Proteins; ¾ Vegetable; 1 Bread; 25 Optional Calories
Per serving: 324 calories; 33 g protein; 9 g fat; 27 g carbohydrate; 83 mg calcium; 113 mg sodium; 97 mg cholesterol; 2 g dietary fiber

Turkey with Orange Sauce Ⓕ Ⓢ

½ pound skinned and boned
  turkey breast, thinly sliced
1 tablespoon all-purpose flour
1 tablespoon plus 1 teaspoon
  reduced-calorie margarine (tub)
½ cup *each* red bell pepper strips
  and sliced thoroughly washed
  leeks (white portion only)
½ cup *each* canned ready-to-
  serve low-sodium chicken
  broth and skim *or* nonfat milk
2 tablespoons orange zest*
2 teaspoons chopped fresh
  rosemary *or* ¼ teaspoon
  rosemary leaves
Dash white pepper

1. On sheet of wax paper dredge turkey in flour, coating all sides and reserving any remaining flour.

2. In 9-inch nonstick skillet melt margarine; add turkey and cook over medium heat until golden, 5 to 6 minutes on each side. Transfer to plate and set aside.

3. In same skillet combine bell pepper and leeks and cook over medium heat until bell pepper is tender-crisp, about 3 minutes. Sprinkle any remaining flour over pepper-leek mixture and stir quickly to combine; cook, stirring constantly, for 1 minute.

4. Remove skillet from heat and, continuing to stir, add remaining ingredients; return turkey to skillet. Cover and let simmer over low heat until turkey is heated through and sauce has thickened, about 5 minutes.

* The zest of the orange is the peel without any of the pith (white membrane). To remove zest from orange, use a zester or vegetable peeler; wrap orange in plastic wrap and refrigerate for use at another time.

APPROXIMATE TOTAL TIME: 30 MINUTES

MAKES 2 SERVINGS

Each serving provides: ¼ Milk; 1 Fat; 3 Proteins; 1 Vegetable; 25 Optional Calories
Per serving: 235 calories; 30 g protein; 6 g fat; 13 g carbohydrate; 118 mg calcium; 207 mg sodium; 72 mg cholesterol; 1 g dietary fiber

Grilled Turkey Sandwich ▽C ▽F

4 slices reduced-calorie wheat *or* white bread (40 calories per slice)

2 teaspoons *each* Dijon-style mustard and pickle relish

2 ounces thinly sliced roast turkey breast

¾ ounce reduced-fat Cheddar *or* Swiss cheese, shredded

¼ cup *each* skim *or* nonfat milk and thawed frozen egg substitute

⅛ teaspoon *each* garlic powder and onion powder

Dash pepper

1. Onto each slice of bread spread ½ teaspoon mustard and ½ teaspoon relish; top each of 2 bread slices with half the turkey, half the cheese, and the remaining bread slices, mustard-relish side down.

2. Using a wire whisk, in shallow small mixing bowl beat together remaining ingredients. Spray 10-inch nonstick skillet with nonstick cooking spray and heat over medium-high heat. Dip each sandwich in milk mixture, coating both sides and using all of mixture. Add sandwiches to skillet and cook for 1 minute on each side. Reduce heat to medium and cook until bread is golden, about 3 minutes longer on each side.

3. To serve, cut each sandwich in half.

APPROXIMATE TOTAL TIME: 15 MINUTES

MAKES 2 SERVINGS

Each serving provides: 2 Proteins; 1 Bread; 20 Optional Calories
Per serving with Cheddar cheese: 199 calories; 20 g protein; 3 g fat; 23 g carbohydrate; 192 mg calcium; 540 mg sodium; 28 mg cholesterol; dietary fiber data not available
With Swiss cheese: 199 calories; 21 g protein; 3 g fat; 23 g carbohydrate; 227 mg calcium; 482 mg sodium; 28 mg cholesterol; dietary fiber data not available

Sausage and Macaroni Casserole

½ pound sweet Italian-style
  turkey sausage links, cut into
  ½-inch-thick pieces
2 teaspoons olive *or* vegetable oil
1½ cups canned stewed tomatoes
1 cup cooked elbow macaroni
1 teaspoon ketchup
½ teaspoon *each* Dijon-style
  mustard and Worcestershire
  sauce

1. In 1-quart microwavable casserole combine sausage and oil; microwave on High (100%) for 5 minutes, stirring once halfway through cooking. Add remaining ingredients and stir to combine; microwave on High for 5 minutes, stirring once halfway through cooking.

APPROXIMATE TOTAL TIME: 15 MINUTES

MAKES 2 SERVINGS

Each serving provides: 1 Fat; 3 Proteins; 1½ Vegetables; 1 Bread; 3 Optional Calories
Per serving: 385 calories; 24 g protein; 18 g fat; 33 g carbohydrate; 85 mg calcium; 1,149 mg sodium; 69 mg cholesterol; 1 g dietary fiber (this figure does not include stewed tomatoes; nutrition analysis not available)

Savory Sausage Puddings ▽

5 ounces turkey sausage links,
  cut into 1-inch pieces
½ cup skim *or* nonfat milk
¼ cup thawed frozen egg
  substitute
3 tablespoons all-purpose flour
1 teaspoon vegetable oil
¼ teaspoon *each* onion powder
  and garlic powder
Dash pepper

1. Spray 1-quart microwavable casserole with nonstick cooking spray and arrange sausage in casserole. Cover and microwave on High (100%) for 2 minutes.

2. In blender combine remaining ingredients and process until thoroughly combined, about 1 minute.

3. Spray two 10-ounce custard cups with nonstick cooking spray and spoon half of the sausage into each cup. Pour half of the milk mixture into each cup. Cover each cup and microwave on Medium-High (70%) for 3½ minutes, rotating cups ½ turn after 2 minutes. Let stand 1 minute to complete cooking.

APPROXIMATE TOTAL TIME: 15 MINUTES

MAKES 2 SERVINGS

Each serving provides: ¼ Milk; ½ Fat; 2½ Proteins; ½ Bread
Per serving: 231 calories; 19 g protein; 11 g fat; 13 g carbohydrate; 103 mg calcium; 473 mg sodium; 47 mg cholesterol; 0.3 g dietary fiber

Skillet Sausages with Apple

1 teaspoon margarine
½ pound Italian-style turkey
   sausage links
1 cup sliced onions
½ cup sliced celery
1 small Red Delicious apple
   (about ¼ pound), cored
   and sliced
2 teaspoons all-purpose flour
¾ cup canned ready-to-serve
   low-sodium chicken broth
½ cup apple juice (no sugar
   added)
⅛ teaspoon *each* crushed
   rosemary leaves and pepper

1. In 10-inch nonstick skillet melt margarine; add sausages and sauté over medium-high heat, turning occasionally, until browned on all sides, 4 to 5 minutes.

2. Add onions, celery, and apple and sauté until vegetables are softened, 1 to 2 minutes. Sprinkle with flour and stir quickly to combine; continuing to stir, add remaining ingredients. Reduce heat to low and let simmer, stirring occasionally, until apple is tender, 10 to 15 minutes.

APPROXIMATE TOTAL TIME: 30 MINUTES

MAKES 2 SERVINGS

Each serving provides: ½ Fat; 3 Proteins; 1½ Vegetables; 1 Fruit; 25 Optional Calories
Per serving: 322 calories; 21 g protein; 16 g fat; 25 g carbohydrate; 58 mg calcium; 653 mg sodium; 69 mg cholesterol; 3 g dietary fiber

California Chicken Salad ⬇ⓢ

1 cup shredded lettuce
¼ pound cooked, skinned, and boned chicken, chilled and thinly sliced
½ small cantaloupe (about 1 pound), pared, seeded, and thinly sliced
¼ medium avocado (about 2 ounces), pared and thinly sliced
2 tablespoons *each* plain low-fat yogurt and mild chunky-style salsa
1 teaspoon *each* minced cilantro (Chinese parsley) *or* Italian (flat-leaf) parsley and lime juice (no sugar added)
Dash pepper

For a perfect summertime lunch, serve this salad with iced tea and warm rolls or biscuits.

1. Onto each of 2 individual plates arrange half of the lettuce; decoratively arrange half of the chicken, cantaloupe, and avocado over lettuce.

2. In small bowl combine remaining ingredients and stir to combine. Spoon over salad.

APPROXIMATE TOTAL TIME: 15 MINUTES

MAKES 2 SERVINGS

Each serving provides: 1 Fat; 2 Proteins; 1⅛ Vegetables; 1 Fruit; 10 Optional Calories
Per serving: 212 calories; 19 g protein; 9 g fat; 15 g carbohydrate; 70 mg calcium; 165 mg sodium; 51 mg cholesterol; 2 g dietary fiber

Chicken-Tahini Salad ⬩C⬩ ⬩S⬩

3 ounces cooked, skinned, and boned chicken, chilled and cut into strips
½ cup *each* diagonally thinly sliced scallions (green onions) and chopped red bell pepper
¼ cup plain low-fat yogurt
2 tablespoons tahini (sesame paste), stirred until smooth
1 tablespoon finely chopped cilantro (Chinese parsley) *or* Italian (flat-leaf) parsley
2 teaspoons lime juice (no sugar added)
1 small garlic clove, minced
Dash *each* ground red pepper and ground cumin
8 lettuce leaves, torn into pieces

This salad requires cooked, skinned, and boned chicken that has had time to chill. We suggest you cook it the night before and refrigerate overnight.

1. In small mixing bowl combine chicken, scallions, and bell pepper; set aside.

2. In small mixing bowl combine remaining ingredients except lettuce; pour over chicken mixture and toss to coat.

3. On serving platter arrange lettuce; top with chicken mixture.

APPROXIMATE TOTAL TIME: 10 MINUTES

MAKES 2 SERVINGS

Each serving provides: ¼ Milk; 1 Fat; 2½ Proteins; 2 Vegetables
Per serving: 209 calories; 17 g protein; 12 g fat; 10 g carbohydrate; 164 mg calcium; 80 mg sodium; 40 mg cholesterol; 3 g dietary fiber

"Fried" Chicken

⅓ cup plus 2 teaspoons low-fat
  buttermilk (1% milk fat)
1 pound 2 ounces chicken parts,
  skinned
1½ ounces cornflake crumbs
2 teaspoons sesame seed

*Cornflake crumbs provide the crispy
coating for the chicken in this recipe.
Prepare the crumbs by processing
the cereal in a blender or food processor or save time and purchase the
packaged crumbs.*

1. Preheat oven to 350°F. Pour buttermilk into shallow bowl; add chicken and turn to coat.

2. On paper plate combine cornflake crumbs and sesame seed; dredge chicken in crumb-seed mixture.

3. Arrange chicken on nonstick baking sheet and bake until chicken is browned and crispy, about 40 minutes.

APPROXIMATE TOTAL TIME: 50 MINUTES (includes baking time)

MAKES 2 SERVINGS

Each serving provides: 3 Proteins; 1 Bread; 40 Optional Calories
Per serving: 280 calories; 28 g protein; 8 g fat; 21 g carbohydrate; 96 mg calcium; 385 mg sodium; 78 mg cholesterol; 0.2 g dietary fiber (this figure does not include sesame seed; nutrition analysis not available)

Turkey, Bean, and Rice Salad ▽C

¼ pound ground turkey
2 teaspoons olive *or* vegetable oil
1 cup mild salsa
4 ounces rinsed drained canned black (turtle) beans
1 tablespoon lime juice (no sugar added)
1 cup cooked quick-cooking rice (hot)
2 cups torn lettuce leaves
¾ ounce reduced-fat Cheddar cheese, shredded

While this recipe is cooking in the microwave oven, have the rice cooking on the range.

1. In 1-quart microwavable casserole combine turkey and oil; microwave on High (100%) for 4 minutes, stirring once every 1½ minutes, until turkey is no longer pink. Stir in salsa, beans, and lime juice; microwave on Medium (50%) for 1 minute until thoroughly heated. Add rice and stir to combine.

2. To serve, on serving platter arrange lettuce; top with turkey mixture and sprinkle with cheese.

APPROXIMATE TOTAL TIME: 20 MINUTES

MAKES 2 SERVINGS

Each serving provides: 1 Fat; 2 Proteins; 3 Vegetables; 2 Breads
Per serving: 366 calories; 20 g protein; 13 g fat; 43 g carbohydrate; 182 mg calcium; 1,038 mg sodium (estimated); 46 mg cholesterol; 4 g dietary fiber

Turkey-Ham and Black-Eyed Pea Salad ⟨C⟩

¼ pound turkey-ham, diced
4 ounces rinsed drained canned
  black-eyed peas
½ cup *each* diced onion, diced
  celery, and shredded carrot
½ medium tomato, chopped
2 tablespoons finely chopped
  Italian (flat-leaf) parsley
1 tablespoon *each* olive oil, red
  wine vinegar, and lemon juice
1 small garlic clove, minced
¼ teaspoon granulated sugar
4 drops hot sauce
8 lettuce leaves

▬

If you are trying to incorporate legumes into your diet, this recipe offers a tasty opportunity.

1. In large mixing bowl combine turkey-ham, peas, onion, celery, carrot, tomato, and parsley.

2. In small mixing bowl combine remaining ingredients except lettuce; pour over turkey-ham mixture and toss to coat. Cover and refrigerate until ready to serve.

3. To serve, on serving platter arrange lettuce leaves; toss turkey-ham mixture and spoon onto lettuce leaves.

APPROXIMATE TOTAL TIME: 15 MINUTES (does not include chilling time)

MAKES 2 SERVINGS

Each serving provides: 1½ Fats; 2 Proteins; 3 Vegetables; 1 Bread; 3 Optional Calories
Per serving: 245 calories; 17 g protein; 10 g fat; 23 g carbohydrate; 86 mg calcium; 799 mg sodium (estimated); 0 mg cholesterol; 8 g dietary fiber

Meats

The good word about meats is *leaner*, thanks to improved methods of breeding and feeding livestock. Retail butchers are trimming more fat, and packaged ground meats are often labeled with the percent of fat content. (For the leanest products, select those that read "10% or less fat.") Our recipes take advantage of this health-conscious trend in exotic ways such as Thai-Marinated Steak. Citrus-rich orange juice delicately flavors Orange Veal Marsala and vitamin-packed vegetables add new appeal to favorite foods, as in Lamb with Pepper and Olives. Isn't it great to welcome these meats aboard the nutrition bandwagon?

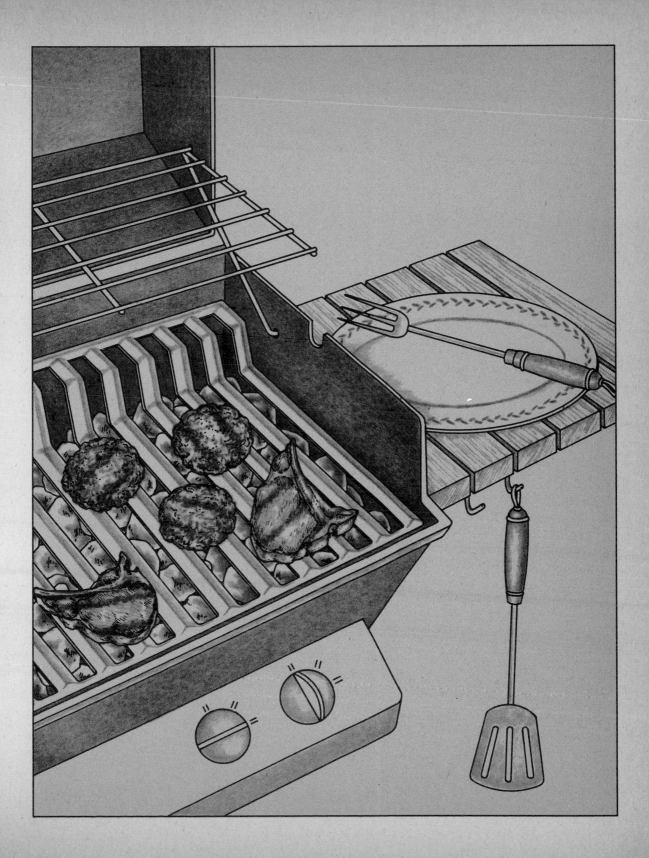

Beef 'n' Barley Stew ▽Ⓕ

1 tablespoon tomato paste
1 packet instant beef broth and seasoning mix
1½ ounces uncooked medium pearl barley
1 cup *each* frozen pearl onions and sliced carrots (1-inch pieces)
½ cup green beans, cut in half
1 tablespoon all-purpose flour
6 ounces cubed cooked top round steak (1-inch pieces)
¼ teaspoon *each* rosemary leaves and pepper

▬

Leftover steak can be used as the basis for this flavorful stew.

1. In shallow 1-quart microwavable casserole combine *1 cup water*, the tomato paste, and broth mix, stirring to dissolve tomato paste. Add barley and stir to combine; cover and microwave on High (100%) for 10 minutes, stirring every 2½ minutes.

2. Add onions, carrots, and green beans to barley mixture. Cover and microwave on High for 5 minutes, stirring once and rotating casserole ½ turn halfway through cooking.

3. In 1-cup liquid measure combine ¼ *cup water* and the flour, stirring to dissolve flour. Stir into barley-vegetable mixture. Cover and microwave on High for 5 minutes, until carrots are tender.

4. Add beef, rosemary, and pepper to barley-vegetable mixture and stir to combine. Cover and microwave on High for 2 minutes, until beef is heated through.

APPROXIMATE TOTAL TIME: 30 MINUTES

MAKES 2 SERVINGS

Each serving provides: 3 Proteins; 2½ Vegetables; 1 Bread; 25 Optional Calories
Per serving: 333 calories; 33 g protein; 6 g fat; 37 g carbohydrate; 75 mg calcium; 614 mg sodium; 71 mg cholesterol; 5 g dietary fiber

Beef 'n' Mushrooms on a Roll

2 teaspoons margarine
¾ cup chopped mushrooms
¼ cup diced onion
1 teaspoon all-purpose flour
¼ pound broiled lean ground
  beef
¼ cup *each* low-fat milk (1%
  milk fat) and canned ready-to-
  serve low-sodium chicken
  broth
2 teaspoons chopped fresh
  parsley
1 teaspoon Worcestershire sauce
1 whole wheat *or* white
  hamburger roll (2 ounces), split
  in half and toasted

*This tasty meat mixture can be
served over cooked rice, noodles, or
with a baked potato.*

1. In 10-inch nonstick skillet melt margarine; add mushrooms and onion and sauté over medium-high heat, until onion is softened, about 1 minute. Sprinkle with flour and stir quickly to combine; continuing to stir, cook 1 minute longer.

2. Add remaining ingredients except hamburger roll to mushroom-onion mixture and stir to combine. Reduce heat to medium and cook until mixture thickens slightly, about 3 minutes.

3. To serve, onto each half of roll spoon half of the beef-mushroom mixture.

APPROXIMATE TOTAL TIME: 15 MINUTES

MAKES 2 SERVINGS

Each serving provides: 1 Fat; 2 Proteins; 1 Vegetable; 1 Bread; 25 Optional Calories
Per serving: 295 calories; 19 g protein; 16 g fat; 19 g carbohydrate; 81 mg calcium; 289 mg sodium; 51 mg cholesterol; 3 g dietary fiber

California Burgers

5 ounces ground beef sirloin
1 slice (¾ ounce) reduced-fat
   Monterey Jack cheese,
   cut in half
2 kaiser rolls (1 ounce each);
   each cut in half horizontally
   and lightly toasted
2 lettuce leaves
2 tablespoons ketchup
4 tomato slices
4 slices avocado (½ ounce each),
   pared
¼ cup alfalfa sprouts
1 medium pickle, cut in half

For that great outdoor flavor, cook burgers on the barbecue grill.

1. Preheat broiler. Shape sirloin into 2 equal patties and arrange on rack in broiling pan; broil 5 inches from heat source until medium-rare, 2 to 3 minutes on each side, or until done to taste.

2. Top each burger with half of the cheese and broil until cheese melts, about 1 minute.

3. Onto bottom half of each roll arrange 1 lettuce leaf and 1 burger; then top each with 1 tablespoon ketchup, 2 tomato slices, 2 avocado slices, 2 tablespoons sprouts, and remaining half of roll. Serve each burger with pickle half.

APPROXIMATE TOTAL TIME: 20 MINUTES

MAKES 2 SERVINGS

Each serving provides: 1 Fat; 2½ Proteins; 2⅛ Vegetables; 1 Bread; 15 Optional Calories
Per serving: 303 calories; 24 g protein; 11 g fat; 26 g carbohydrate; 135 mg calcium; 884 mg sodium; 59 mg cholesterol; 2 g dietary fiber

Philly Burgers ▽Ⓕ

5 ounces ground beef sirloin
2 slices reduced-fat Cheddar
  cheese (½ ounce each)
1 teaspoon margarine
½ cup *each* sliced onion and
  green *or* red bell pepper
2 tablespoons sliced pepperoncini
  peppers (pickled hot peppers)
2 sandwich rolls (2 ounces each);
  each cut in half horizontally

1. Preheat broiler. Shape sirloin into 2 equal patties and arrange on rack in broiling pan; broil 5 inches from heat source until medium-rare, 2 to 3 minutes on each side, or until done to taste.

2. Top each burger with 1 slice of cheese and broil until cheese melts, about 1 minute.

3. While burgers are broiling prepare topping. In 9-inch nonstick skillet melt margarine; add onion and peppers and sauté until lightly browned, 2 to 3 minutes. Stir in ¼ *cup water* and continue cooking until water has evaporated, 1 to 2 minutes.

4. Onto bottom half of each roll arrange 1 burger; top each with half of the onion-pepper mixture and remaining half of roll.

APPROXIMATE TOTAL TIME: 20 MINUTES

MAKES 2 SERVINGS

Each serving provides: ½ Fat; 2½ Proteins; 1⅛ Vegetables; 2 Breads; 10 Optional Calories
Per serving: 379 calories; 27 g protein; 12 g fat; 39 g carbohydrate; 170 mg calcium; 628 mg sodium; 62 mg cholesterol; 2 g dietary fiber

Meatballs with Stewed Tomatoes

5 ounces ground beef

¼ cup *each* part-skim ricotta cheese and thawed frozen egg substitute

1 tablespoon *each* plain dried bread crumbs and chopped fresh basil

2 teaspoons grated Parmesan cheese

1 teaspoon chopped shallot *or* onion

2 cups canned stewed tomatoes

1. Preheat oven to 425°F. In medium mixing bowl thoroughly combine all ingredients except tomatoes. Shape mixture into 6 equal balls. Spray rack set on 8 × 8 × 2-inch baking pan with nonstick cooking spray and arrange meatballs on rack. Bake, turning once, until cooked through, about 20 minutes.

2. In 1-quart saucepan bring tomatoes to a boil. Reduce heat to low and, using the back of a fork, press tomatoes against side of pan, breaking into smaller pieces. Add meatballs to tomatoes and simmer until flavors blend, about 10 minutes.

APPROXIMATE TOTAL TIME: 40 MINUTES (includes baking time)

MAKES 2 SERVINGS

Each serving provides: 3 Proteins; 2 Vegetables; 25 Optional Calories

Per serving: 289 calories; 24 g protein; 13 g fat; 22 g carbohydrate; 221 mg calcium; 820 mg sodium; 69 mg cholesterol; 0.1 g dietary fiber (this figure does not include stewed tomatoes; nutrition analysis not available)

London Broil with Mixed Vegetables ▽ⓢ

15 ounces boneless top round
steak

¼ cup balsamic *or* red wine
vinegar

1 tablespoon plus 1 teaspoon
olive *or* vegetable oil

1 cup *each* sliced onions *or*
shallots, red bell pepper strips,
and sliced mushrooms

1 small garlic clove, minced

1 package (9 ounces) thawed
frozen artichoke hearts, cut
into halves

½ cup canned ready-to-serve
low-sodium chicken broth

2 tablespoons dry red table wine

1 teaspoon cornstarch

1 tablespoon *each* chopped fresh
mint and fresh basil *or* ½
teaspoon basil leaves

▬

*Marinate the steak while preparing
the remainder of this recipe, or marinate the steak overnight in the
refrigerator.*

1. In glass or stainless-steel bowl combine steak and vinegar, turning to coat; set aside.

2. In 10-inch nonstick skillet heat oil; add onions, pepper, mushrooms, and garlic and cook over medium-high heat, stirring occasionally, until pepper is tender-crisp, 3 to 4 minutes. Add artichokes and stir to combine. Reduce heat to medium, cover, and cook for about 5 minutes.

3. In 1-cup liquid measure combine broth, wine, and cornstarch, stirring to dissolve cornstarch; stir into skillet. Cook over low heat, stirring constantly, until mixture thickens slightly. Remove steak from marinade and set aside. Stir marinade, mint, and basil into vegetable mixture and cook, stirring constantly, until mixture comes to a boil, about 2 minutes. Set aside and keep warm.

4. Preheat broiler. Spray rack in broiling pan with nonstick cooking spray; arrange steak on rack and broil until browned and done to taste, 6 to 8 minutes on each side.

5. To serve, thinly slice steak diagonally across the grain and arrange on serving platter; top with vegetable mixture.

APPROXIMATE TOTAL TIME: 30 MINUTES (does not include marinating time)

MAKES 4 SERVINGS

Each serving provides: 1 Fat, 3 Proteins; 2½ Vegetables; 30 Optional Calories
Per serving: 273 calories; 30 g protein; 11 g fat; 12 g carbohydrate; 36 mg calcium; 91 mg sodium; 71 mg cholesterol; 4 g dietary fiber

Steak with Madeira-Mushroom Sauce ▽Ⓢ

½ pound boneless sirloin steak *or* boneless top round steak
2 teaspoons olive *or* vegetable oil
½ cup *each* sliced white mushrooms and shiitake mushrooms
2 teaspoons all-purpose flour
½ cup canned ready-to-serve low-sodium beef broth
¼ cup dry Madeira wine
Dash pepper

1. Preheat broiler. Arrange steak on rack in broiling pan and broil 5 to 6 inches from heat source, until medium-rare, 3 to 4 minutes on each side, or until done to taste.

2. In 10-inch nonstick skillet heat oil; add mushrooms and cook over medium-high heat, stirring frequently, until lightly browned, 1 to 2 minutes. Sprinkle with flour and stir quickly to combine. Continuing to stir, add remaining ingredients; cook, stirring frequently, until mixture thickens, 3 to 4 minutes.

3. To serve, thinly slice steak diagonally across the grain and arrange on serving platter; top with mushroom mixture.

APPROXIMATE TOTAL TIME: 20 MINUTES

MAKES 2 SERVINGS

Each serving provides: 1 Fat; 3 Proteins; 1 Vegetable; 45 Optional Calories
Per serving: 288 calories; 27 protein; 13 g fat; 8 g carbohydrate; 14 mg calcium; 61 mg sodium; 76 mg cholesterol; 1 g dietary fiber

Steak with Sauerbraten Sauce ⧖

½ pound boneless sirloin steak *or* boneless top round steak
1 teaspoon olive *or* vegetable oil
2 tablespoons finely chopped onion
¾ cup canned ready-to-serve low-sodium beef broth
2 tablespoons red wine vinegar
⅛ teaspoon ground nutmeg
3 whole cloves
3 gingersnap cookies (½ ounce), finely crushed

▬

Weather permitting, broil the steak on an outdoor grill.

1. Preheat broiler. On rack in broiling pan arrange steak and broil 5 to 6 inches from heat source until medium-rare, 4 to 5 minutes on each side, or until done to taste.

2. While steak is broiling prepare sauce. In 10-inch nonstick skillet heat oil; add onion and cook over medium-high heat, stirring frequently, until lightly browned, 1 to 2 minutes.

3. Add remaining ingredients except gingersnaps and cook until liquid is slightly reduced, 2 to 3 minutes. Remove and discard cloves. Add gingersnaps and stir to combine; cook 1 minute longer.

4. To serve, thinly slice steak diagonally across the grain and arrange on serving platter; top with gingersnap mixture.

APPROXIMATE TOTAL TIME: 20 MINUTES

MAKES 2 SERVINGS

Each serving provides: ½ Fat; 3 Proteins; ⅛ Vegetable; 55 Optional Calories
Per serving: 243 calories; 26 g protein; 11 g fat; 8 g carbohydrate; 18 mg calcium; 99 mg sodium; 78 mg cholesterol; 0.2 g dietary fiber (this figure does not include gingersnap cookies; nutrition analysis not available)

Thai-Marinated Steak

1 medium mild chili pepper, seeded and finely chopped

¼ cup *each* finely chopped scallions (green onions), finely chopped fresh cilantro (Chinese parsley) *or* Italian (flat-leaf) parsley, and reduced-sodium soy sauce

2 tablespoons freshly squeezed lime juice

2 garlic cloves, finely chopped

1 pound boneless sirloin steak *or* boneless top round steak

Garnish: 4 *each* lime slices, cut into halves, and cilantro (Chinese parsley) sprigs

Delicious when prepared on the barbecue grill.

1. In small mixing bowl combine all ingredients except steak and garnish and mix well.

2. In glass or stainless-steel mixing bowl arrange steak; add pepper mixture and turn to coat. Cover with plastic wrap and refrigerate overnight or at least 1 hour.

3. Preheat broiler. Transfer steak to rack in broiling pan, reserving marinade. Broil 5 to 6 inches from heat source, basting with marinade mixture until medium-rare, 3 to 4 minutes on each side, or until done to taste.

4. Thinly slice steak diagonally across the grain and arrange on plate; garnish each portion with a lime slice and cilantro sprig.

APPROXIMATE TOTAL TIME: 15 MINUTES (does not include marinating time)

MAKES 4 SERVINGS

Each serving provides: 3 Proteins; ¼ Vegetable
Per serving: 199 calories; 27 g protein; 8 g fat; 4 g carbohydrate; 22 mg calcium; 658 mg sodium; 76 mg cholesterol; 0.2 g dietary fiber

Lamb Chops with Fennel ⎔

2 rib *or* loin lamb chops
  (5 ounces each)
1½ teaspoons vegetable oil
1 cup *each* chopped onions and
  thinly sliced fennel
1 small garlic clove, minced
4 large plum tomatoes, blanched,
  peeled, seeded, and chopped
5 small Gaeta, Calamata, *or* black
  olives, pitted and finely
  chopped
1 tablespoon chopped Italian
  (flat-leaf) parsley
1 teaspoon Italian seasoning
Dash pepper

*The licorice taste of fennel adds a
unique flavor to this hearty dish.*

1. Preheat broiler. Spray rack in broiling pan with nonstick cooking spray; arrange chops on rack and broil 6 inches from heat source, until browned and done to taste, 4 to 5 minutes on each side.

2. While chops are broiling prepare fennel mixture. In 9-inch nonstick skillet heat oil; add onions, fennel, and garlic and cook over medium-high heat until fennel is tender-crisp, 3 to 4 minutes. Stir in remaining ingredients and bring to a boil. Reduce heat to low, cover, and let simmer until flavors blend, about 4 minutes.

3. To serve, on serving platter arrange fennel mixture; top with lamp chops.

APPROXIMATE TOTAL TIME: 30 MINUTES

MAKES 2 SERVINGS

Each serving provides: 1 Fat; 3 Proteins; 4 Vegetables
Per serving: 305 calories; 26 g protein; 16 g fat; 13 g carbohydrate; 80 mg calcium; 203 mg sodium; 77 mg cholesterol; 3 g dietary fiber

Lamb Chops with Vegetable Chutney ⬇ⓢ

1 teaspoon vegetable oil
½ cup *each* diced green bell
  pepper and onion
1½ teaspoons minced pared
  gingerroot
1 garlic clove, minced
4 large plum tomatoes, blanched,
  peeled, seeded, and chopped
2 tablespoons apple cider vinegar
1½ teaspoons firmly packed light
  or dark brown sugar
¼ teaspoon grated lemon peel
Dash *each* ground cinnamon,
  ground cloves, and powdered
  mustard
2 rib *or* loin lamb chops
  (5 ounces each)

1. In small saucepan heat oil; add pepper, onion, gingerroot, and garlic and cook over medium heat until pepper is tender, about 3 minutes.

2. Stir in remaining ingredients except lamb chops and bring to a boil. Reduce heat to low and let simmer, stirring occasionally, until liquid evaporates, about 15 minutes.

3. While vegetable-chutney mixture simmers broil lamb chops. Preheat broiler. Spray rack in broiling pan with nonstick cooking spray; arrange chops on rack and broil 6 inches from heat source, until browned and done to taste, 4 to 5 minutes on each side.

4. To serve, arrange chops on serving platter and top with vegetable-chutney mixture.

APPROXIMATE TOTAL TIME: 30 MINUTES

MAKES 2 SERVINGS

Each serving provides: ½ Fat; 3 Proteins; 3 Vegetables; 15 Optional Calories
Per serving: 278 calories; 25 g protein; 14 g fat; 14 g carbohydrate; 41 mg calcium; 84 mg sodium; 77 mg cholesterol; 2 g dietary fiber

Lamb with Pepper and Olives ⟨S⟩

1 medium yellow *or* red bell
  pepper
2 loin lamb chops (5 ounces
  each)
1 teaspoon olive *or* vegetable oil
1 garlic clove, minced
6 large Calamata *or* black olives,
  pitted and cut into halves
2 tablespoons dry sherry
1 tablespoon balsamic *or* red
  wine vinegar
¼ teaspoon rosemary leaves,
  crushed

1. Preheat broiler. On baking sheet lined with heavy-duty foil broil pepper 3 inches from heat source, turning frequently, until charred on all sides; let stand until cool enough to handle, 15 to 20 minutes.

2. Peel pepper; remove and discard stem ends and seeds. Cut pepper into thin strips and set aside.

3. On rack in broiling pan arrange lamb chops and broil 6 inches from heat source, until medium-rare, 3 to 4 minutes on each side, or until done to taste.

4. While lamb is broiling prepare pepper-olive mixture. In 9-inch nonstick skillet heat oil; add garlic and cook over medium-high heat until softened. Add pepper strips, olives, *2 tablespoons water*, the sherry, vinegar, and rosemary and stir to combine. Reduce heat to low and let simmer until reduced by half, about 5 minutes.

5. To serve, on serving platter arrange lamb chops and top with pepper-olive mixture.

APPROXIMATE TOTAL TIME: 35 MINUTES

MAKES 2 SERVINGS

Each serving provides: 1 Fat; 3 Proteins; 1 Vegetable; 15 Optional Calories
Per serving: 262 calories; 26 g protein; 13 g fat; 5 g carbohydrate; 37 mg calcium; 166 mg sodium; 81 mg cholesterol; 1 g dietary fiber

German-Style Pork Patties ⬡S

½ pound ground pork
⅓ cup plus 2 teaspoons plain dried bread crumbs, divided
¼ cup *each* rinsed and drained sauerkraut,* applesauce (no sugar added), and chopped onion
1 teaspoon caraway seed, crushed
½ cup canned ready-to-serve low-sodium chicken broth
1½ teaspoons Dijon-style mustard
1 teaspoon *each* cornstarch, prepared horseradish, and honey

1. Preheat broiler. In medium mixing bowl combine pork, all but 2 tablespoons of the bread crumbs, the sauerkraut, applesauce, onion, and caraway seed, mixing well. Shape mixture into 4 equal patties and arrange on rack in broiling pan.

2. Sprinkle 1 tablespoon of the remaining bread crumbs evenly over patties. Broil 5 inches from heat source, until patties are lightly browned, about 5 minutes.

3. Turn patties over; sprinkle with remaining bread crumbs. Broil until patties are cooked through, about 5 minutes longer.

4. While patties are broiling prepare sauce. In small saucepan combine remaining ingredients, stirring to dissolve cornstarch. Cook over medium heat, stirring frequently, until mixture thickens, 3 to 5 minutes.

5. To serve, on serving platter arrange patties and top with horseradish-honey mixture.

* Use the sauerkraut that is packaged in plastic bags and stored in the refrigerator section of the supermarket; it is usually crisper and less salty than the canned.

APPROXIMATE TOTAL TIME: 25 MINUTES

MAKES 2 SERVINGS

Each serving provides: 3 Proteins; ½ Vegetable; 1 Bread; ¼ Fruit; 35 Optional Calories
Per serving: 346 calories; 24 g protein; 16 g fat; 25 g carbohydrate; 47 mg calcium; 397 mg sodium; 84 mg cholesterol; 2 g dietary fiber (this figure does not include caraway seed and horseradish; nutrition analyses not available)

Pork Chops in Wine Sauce ⬦S⬦

2 pork loin chops (5 ounces each)
2 teaspoons olive *or* vegetable oil
**1 cup *each* chopped onions and
  quartered mushrooms**
½ cup chopped red bell pepper
1 small garlic clove, minced
¼ cup dry white table wine
½ teaspoon powdered mustard
**1 tablespoon rinsed drained
  capers**
1 teaspoon Italian seasoning
**2 large plum tomatoes, blanched,
  peeled, seeded, and finely
  chopped**

1. Preheat broiler. Arrange chops on rack and broil 6 inches from heat source, until browned and done to taste, 5 minutes on each side.

2. While chops are broiling prepare sauce. In 9-inch nonstick skillet heat oil; add onions, mushrooms, pepper, and garlic and cook over medium-high heat, stirring frequently, until pepper is tender-crisp, about 3 minutes.

3. In 1-cup liquid measure combine wine and mustard, stirring to combine; stir into skillet. Add capers and Italian seasoning; cook, stirring constantly, until mixture comes to a boil.

4. Reduce heat to low; stir in tomatoes. Add pork chops to skillet and turn to coat. Cover and let simmer until flavors blend, about 5 minutes.

APPROXIMATE TOTAL TIME: 30 MINUTES

MAKES 2 SERVINGS

Each serving provides: 1 Fat; 3 Proteins; 3½ Vegetables; 25 Optional Calories
Per serving: 315 calories; 30 g protein; 14 g fat; 12 g carbohydrate; 37 mg calcium; 194 mg sodium; 83 mg cholesterol; 3 g dietary fiber (this figure does not include capers; nutrition analysis not available)

Buttery Braised Scallops
Spinach Salad with Oysters
Grilled Salmon with Lime Butter

Spinach and Carrot
Chicken-in-the-Rye
Lemon Mousse (p. 154)

Oven-"Fried"
Potato Wedges
Bean Burritos
Two-Bean Chili
Savory Corn Fritters

Cherry-Vanilla "Ice Cream" Soda
Mocha Pudding Pie

Pork Chops with Raisin-Pignolia Sauce ▽ⓢ

**2 boneless pork loin chops
  (¼ pound each)**
1 teaspoon olive *or* vegetable oil
½ ounce pignolias (pine nuts)
**¼ cup sliced shallots *or* chopped
  onion**
1 teaspoon all-purpose flour
**½ cup canned ready-to-serve
  low-sodium chicken broth**
2 tablespoons dry vermouth
¼ cup golden raisins
**1 teaspoon chopped fresh
  rosemary *or* ¼ teaspoon
  rosemary leaves**

1. Preheat broiler. Spray rack in broiling pan with nonstick cooking spray; arrange chops on rack and broil 6 inches from heat source, until browned and done to taste, 4 to 5 minutes on each side.

2. While chops are broiling prepare sauce. In 9-inch nonstick skillet heat oil; add pignolias and shallots and cook over medium heat, stirring constantly, until pignolias are golden brown, about 2 minutes. Sprinkle with flour and stir quickly to combine; continuing to stir, cook 1 minute longer. Stir in broth and vermouth and bring mixture to a boil. Reduce heat to low; stir in raisins and rosemary and let simmer until flavors blend, 3 to 4 minutes.

3. To serve, arrange chops on serving platter and top with sauce.

APPROXIMATE TOTAL TIME: 25 MINUTES

MAKES 2 SERVINGS

Each serving provides: 1 Fat; 3 Proteins; ¼ Vegetable; 1 Fruit; 30 Optional Calories
Per serving: 358 calories; 31 g protein; 15 g fat; 22 g carbohydrate; 26 mg calcium; 86 mg sodium; 83 mg cholesterol; 1 g dietary fiber (this figure does not include pignolias; nutrition analysis not available)

Roast Pork with Raisin-Onion Sauce ▽F ▽S

½ pound pork tenderloin
½ teaspoon cracked pepper
1 teaspoon vegetable oil
¼ cup sliced onion
2 teaspoons all-purpose flour
½ cup canned ready-to-serve
   low-sodium chicken broth
¼ cup *each* dark raisins and port
wine

1. Preheat oven to 425°F. Rub all sides of pork with pepper and set on rack in roasting pan. Roast until pork is cooked through, 15 to 18 minutes.

2. While pork is roasting prepare raisin-onion mixture. In 6-inch nonstick skillet heat oil; add onion and cook over medium-high heat, stirring frequently, until softened, 1 to 2 minutes. Sprinkle with flour and stir quickly to combine; continuing to stir, add chicken broth, raisins, and wine.

3. Reduce heat to medium-low and cook, stirring occasionally, until mixture thickens, 8 to 10 minutes.

4. To serve, slice pork diagonally and arrange on serving platter; top with raisin-onion mixture.

APPROXIMATE TOTAL TIME: 30 MINUTES

MAKES 2 SERVINGS

Each serving provides: ½ Fat; 3 Proteins; ¼ Vegetable; 1 Fruit; 70 Optional Calories
Per serving: 287 calories; 26 g protein; 7 g fat; 22 g carbohydrate; 27 mg calcium; 76 mg sodium; 79 mg cholesterol; 1 g dietary fiber

Orange Veal Marsala ⬩F⬩ ⬩S⬩

½ pound veal scallops *or* thin veal cutlets
1 tablespoon plus 1 teaspoon all-purpose flour
1 teaspoon *each* margarine and olive oil
½ cup orange juice (no sugar added)
1 small orange (about 6 ounces), peeled and sectioned
¼ cup dry Marsala wine
1 tablespoon chopped fresh parsley
Dash pepper

If veal cutlets do not fit into your budget, chicken cutlets will work as well in this recipe.

1. On sheet of wax paper dredge veal in flour, coating both sides.

2. In 10-inch nonstick skillet heat margarine and oil until margarine is melted; add veal and cook over medium-high heat, until lightly browned, 4 to 5 minutes on each side. Transfer to plate and set aside.

3. In same skillet combine remaining ingredients and cook over high heat, until thoroughly heated, 3 to 5 minutes, scraping particles from bottom of pan.

4. Return veal to skillet and turn to coat with orange mixture; cook until veal is heated through, 1 to 2 minutes.

APPROXIMATE TOTAL TIME: 25 MINUTES

MAKES 2 SERVINGS

Each serving provides: 1 Fat; 3 Proteins; 1 Fruit; 45 Optional Calories
Per serving: 281 calories; 26 g protein; 6 g fat; 22 g carbohydrate; 45 mg calcium; 99 mg sodium; 89 mg cholesterol; 2 g dietary fiber

Veal Scaloppine with Sun-Dried Tomatoes ⛛F ⛛S

1 tablespoon plus 1½ teaspoons all-purpose flour

1 teaspoon Italian seasoning

½ pound veal scallops *or* thin veal cutlets, pounded to ⅛-inch thickness

2 teaspoons reduced-calorie margarine (tub)

1 teaspoon olive oil

2 small garlic cloves, minced

2 tablespoons dry white table wine

4 large plum tomatoes, blanched, peeled, seeded, and finely chopped

8 sun-dried tomato halves (not packed in oil), plumped, drained, and thinly sliced

1 tablespoon *each* chopped fresh basil and Italian (flat-leaf) parsley

1 teaspoon grated lemon peel

1. On sheet of wax paper combine flour and Italian seasoning; dredge veal in flour mixture, coating both sides.

2. In 10-inch nonstick skillet heat margarine and oil until margarine is melted; add veal and cook over medium-high heat until cooked through and lightly browned, about 2 minutes on each side. Transfer veal to serving platter and keep warm.

3. To same skillet add garlic and cook over medium heat until golden brown; stir in wine and bring to a boil. Stir in remaining ingredients and return to a boil. Reduce heat to low and let simmer until flavors blend, about 5 minutes. Spoon over veal.

APPROXIMATE TOTAL TIME: 25 MINUTES

MAKES 2 SERVINGS

Each serving provides: 1 Fat; 3 Proteins; 4 Vegetables; ¼ Bread; 15 Optional Calories
Per serving: 250 calories; 27 g protein; 7 g fat; 18 g carbohydrate; 46 mg calcium; 145 mg sodium; 89 mg cholesterol; 4 g dietary fiber

Variation: Veal Scaloppine with Tomatoes—Omit sun-dried tomatoes. In Serving Information decrease Vegetables to 2.
Per serving: 217 calories; 26 g protein; 7 g fat; 11 g carbohydrate; 34 mg calcium; 131 mg sodium; 89 mg cholesterol; 2 g dietary fiber

Marinated Veal Chops with Sage ⟨S⟩

¼ cup dry white table wine
1 tablespoon balsamic *or* red
   wine vinegar
2 garlic cloves, minced
4 to 5 fresh sage leaves, chopped
2 veal loin chops (5 ounces each)
2 teaspoons *each* olive *or*
   vegetable oil and all-purpose
   flour

1. In shallow glass or stainless-steel mixing bowl combine first 4 ingredients, mixing well; add veal and turn to coat. Cover with plastic wrap and refrigerate overnight or at least 30 minutes.

2. In 10-inch nonstick skillet heat oil; transfer chops to skillet, reserving marinade. Cook over medium heat until medium, or until done to taste, 3 to 4 minutes on each side. Transfer chops to plate and set aside.

3. Add flour to reserved marinade, stirring to dissolve flour. To same skillet add marinade-flour mixture and cook over high heat, stirring frequently, until mixture thickens, 2 to 3 minutes. Return chops to skillet, turn to coat with mixture, and cook until heated through, about 1 minute.

4. To serve, on serving platter arrange chops and top with sauce.

APPROXIMATE TOTAL TIME: 20 MINUTES (does not include marinating time)

MAKES 2 SERVINGS

Each serving provides: 1 Fat; 3 Proteins; 35 Optional Calories
Per serving: 224 calories; 23 g protein; 10 g fat; 4 g carbohydrate; 29 mg calcium; 84 mg sodium; 90 mg cholesterol; 0.1 g dietary fiber

Stuffed Veal Chops ⬦S⬦

3 tablespoons plain dried bread crumbs

5 small Calamata *or* black olives, pitted and chopped

2 sun-dried tomato halves (not packed in oil), finely chopped

1 tablespoon *each* chopped fresh parsley and grated Parmesan cheese

1½ teaspoons olive oil

1 small garlic clove, minced

2 veal loin *or* rib chops (5 ounces each)

1. In small mixing bowl combine all ingredients except veal; mix well until thoroughly combined. Set aside.

2. Preheat broiler. Using a sharp knife, cut along thick edge of each chop, making a pocket. Fill pocket of each chop with half of the bread crumb mixture.

3. Arrange chops on rack in broiling pan and broil 5 to 6 inches from heat source, until cooked through, 4 to 5 minutes on each side.

APPROXIMATE TOTAL TIME: 25 MINUTES

MAKES 2 SERVINGS

Each serving provides: 1 Fat; 3 Proteins; ½ Vegetable; ½ Bread; 15 Optional Calories
Per serving: 251 calories; 25 g protein; 12 g fat; 10 g carbohydrate; 79 mg calcium; 260 mg sodium; 93 mg cholesterol; 1 g dietary fiber

Veal Chops with Swiss Chard ▽Ⓢ

1 tablespoon plus 1½ teaspoons all-purpose flour
1 teaspoon Italian seasoning
2 veal top loin *or* loin chops (5 ounces each)
2 teaspoons reduced-calorie margarine (tub)
1 teaspoon olive *or* vegetable oil
½ cup *each* sliced onion and red bell pepper strips
1 small garlic clove, minced
4 cups thoroughly washed and drained Swiss chard,* shredded
2 tablespoons dry white table wine *or* dry vermouth

1. On sheet of wax paper combine flour and Italian seasoning; dredge chops in flour mixture, coating both sides.

2. In 10-inch nonstick skillet combine margarine and oil and heat until margarine is melted; add chops and cook over medium-high heat until done to taste, 2 to 3 minutes on each side. Transfer to serving platter; keep warm.

3. In same skillet combine onion, pepper, and garlic and cook over medium-high heat until tender-crisp, about 3 minutes. Reduce heat to low; add Swiss chard, cover, and cook until wilted, 3 to 4 minutes. Stir in wine and cook, stirring occasionally, for 2 minutes. Spoon Swiss chard mixture over chops.

* Four cups fresh Swiss chard yield about 1 cup cooked Swiss chard.

APPROXIMATE TOTAL TIME: 30 MINUTES

MAKES 2 SERVINGS

Each serving provides: 1 Fat; 3 Proteins; 2 Vegetables; ¼ Bread; 15 Optional Calories
Per serving with wine: 255 calories; 25 g protein; 11 g fat; 13 g carbohydrate; 70 mg calcium; 286 mg sodium; 90 mg cholesterol; 1 g dietary fiber (this figure does not include Swiss chard; nutrition analysis not available)
With vermouth: 260 calories; 25 g protein; 11 g fat; 13 g carbohydrate; 70 mg calcium; 286 mg sodium; 90 mg cholesterol; 1 g dietary fiber (this figure does not include Swiss chard; nutrition analysis not available)

Legumes

What a lot you get for your money with legumes! Low in both cost and fat, legumes (dry beans, lentils, and peas) are high in nutritional pluses such as B vitamins, potassium, and iron, as well as being a good source of protein and dietary fiber. Legumes are also convenient to stock up on, since they're available both canned and dried. The canned varieties make for easy dishes like Cuban Black Bean Salad, which takes a mere 15 minutes to prepare, or our economically meatless Two-Bean Chili. For an attention-getting combination, we've combined bulgur with chick-peas in Tabouleh with Chick-Peas. As a bonus, legumes are often interchangeable, so by varying the ingredients you get more mileage from the recipes.

Bean and Barley Soup �(C) �(F)

1½ ounces uncooked medium pearl barley

3 packets instant vegetable broth and seasoning mix

8 ounces rinsed drained canned pinto *or* pink beans

½ cup *each* diced onion, diced celery, diced carrot, and canned Italian tomatoes (reserve liquid), seeded and chopped

1 garlic clove, minced

1 tablespoon chopped fresh parsley

⅛ teaspoon *each* white pepper and thyme leaves

1. In 3-quart microwavable casserole combine *1 quart water*, the barley, and broth mix. Cover and microwave on High (100%) for 10 minutes, rotating casserole ½ turn halfway through cooking.

2. Add beans, onion, celery, carrot, tomatoes with reserved liquid, and garlic and stir to combine. Cover and microwave on High for 15 minutes, rotating casserole ½ turn halfway through cooking. Let soup stand 3 to 5 minutes, until barley is tender.

3. Stir in remaining ingredients.

APPROXIMATE TOTAL TIME: 40 MINUTES

MAKES 4 SERVINGS, ABOUT 1¼ CUPS EACH

Each serving provides: 1 Protein; 1 Vegetable; ½ Bread; 10 Optional Calories
Per serving: 133 calories; 7 g protein; 0.5 g fat; 26 g carbohydrate; 51 mg calcium; 834 mg sodium (estimated); 0 mg cholesterol; 5 g dietary fiber

Ranch Bean Soup with Sour Cream $\triangledown$C $\triangledown$F

1 teaspoon vegetable oil
¼ cup *each* chopped onion,
   chopped green bell pepper, and
   diced carrot
1 cup spicy mixed vegetable juice
6 ounces rinsed drained canned
   pink beans
½ cup drained canned Italian
   tomatoes
2 tablespoons *each* barbecue
   sauce and sour cream
2 corn tortillas (6-inch diameter
   each), lightly toasted, each cut
   into 6 wedges

1. In 3-quart nonstick saucepan heat oil; add onion, pepper, and carrot and cook over medium-high heat, stirring frequently, until onion is tender, 1 to 2 minutes.

2. Add *1 cup water*, the juice, beans, tomatoes, and barbecue sauce and stir to combine. Reduce heat to low and let simmer, stirring occasionally, until carrot is tender, 15 to 20 minutes.

3. To serve, ladle soup into 2 soup bowls and top each with 1 tablespoon sour cream; serve each portion with 6 tortilla wedges.

APPROXIMATE TOTAL TIME: 30 MINUTES

MAKES 2 SERVINGS, ABOUT 1½ CUPS EACH

Each serving provides: ½ Fat; 1½ Proteins; 1¾ Vegetables; 1 Bread; 50 Optional Calories
Per serving: 277 calories; 10 g protein; 7 g fat; 45 g carbohydrate; 134 mg calcium; 979 mg sodium (estimated); 6 mg cholesterol; 6 g dietary fiber

Variation: Ranch Bean Soup—Omit sour cream from recipe. In Serving Information decrease Optional Calories to 15.
Per serving: 246 calories; 10 g protein; 4 g fat; 44 g carbohydrate; 118 mg calcium; 972 mg sodium (estimated); 0 mg cholesterol; 6 g dietary fiber

Tuscan White Bean Soup ⬦C⬦ ⬦F⬦

½ cup chopped onion
2 teaspoons olive oil
2 garlic cloves, minced
3 tablespoons all-purpose flour
12 ounces rinsed drained canned
   white kidney (cannellini) beans
3 packets instant vegetable broth
   and seasoning mix
2 large plum tomatoes, blanched,
   peeled, seeded, and chopped
2 teaspoons *each* chopped fresh
   parsley and rosemary *or*
   ½ teaspoon rosemary leaves
⅛ teaspoon white pepper

*The Italian province of Tuscany
lends its name to this classic dish.*

1. In 3-quart microwavable casserole combine onion, oil, and garlic and stir to coat; microwave on High (100%) for 1 minute, stirring once halfway through cooking.

2. In medium mixing bowl combine *1 quart water* and the flour, stirring to dissolve flour; stir into onion mixture. Add beans and broth mix and stir to combine. Microwave on High for 10 minutes, stirring once halfway through cooking, until mixture thickens.

3. Using half of bean mixture, pour 1 cup into blender and process until pureed. Transfer pureed mixture to 1-quart bowl and repeat procedure with remaining bean mixture, 1 cup at a time. Pour pureed mixture back into casserole. Add tomatoes and stir to combine. Microwave on High for 5 minutes, until flavors blend.

4. Stir in remaining ingredients.

APPROXIMATE TOTAL TIME: 30 MINUTES

MAKES 4 SERVINGS, ABOUT 1¼ CUPS EACH

Each serving provides: ½ Fat; 1½ Proteins; ¾ Vegetable; ¼ Bread; 10 Optional Calories
Per serving: 158 calories; 9 g protein; 3 g fat; 26 g carbohydrate; 54 mg calcium; 869 mg sodium (estimated); 0 mg cholesterol; 4 g dietary fiber

Italian Chick-Pea Soup $\nabla^C \nabla^F$

½ cup *each* chopped onion, diced celery, and diced carrot
1 teaspoon olive *or* vegetable oil
1 large garlic clove, minced
1 cup *each* canned Italian tomatoes (reserve liquid), seeded and diced, and canned ready-to-serve low-sodium chicken broth
8 ounces rinsed drained canned chick-peas
1 tablespoon grated Parmesan cheese
1 tablespoon *each* chopped fresh parsley and chopped fresh basil *or* ½ teaspoon basil leaves
Dash pepper

1. In 3-quart microwavable casserole combine onion, celery, carrot, oil, and garlic and stir to coat. Microwave on High (100%) for 3 minutes, stirring once halfway through cooking, until onion is softened.

2. Add *1 cup water*, the tomatoes with reserved liquid, broth, and chick-peas to onion mixture and stir to combine; cover and microwave on High for 15 minutes, until carrot is tender.

3. Stir in remaining ingredients.

APPROXIMATE TOTAL TIME: 30 MINUTES

MAKES 2 SERVINGS, ABOUT 2 CUPS EACH

Each serving provides: ½ Fat; 2 Proteins; 2½ Vegetables; 35 Optional Calories
Per serving: 243 calories; 12 g protein; 7 g fat; 37 g carbohydrate; 148 mg calcium; 696 mg sodium (estimated); 2 mg cholesterol; 5 g dietary fiber

Bean Burritos

4 flour tortillas (6-inch diameter each)
1 teaspoon olive *or* vegetable oil
½ cup *each* finely chopped onion and green bell pepper
1 small garlic clove, minced
8 ounces rinsed drained canned pink *or* pinto beans
½ cup canned Italian tomatoes (reserve liquid), chopped
½ teaspoon finely chopped cilantro (Chinese parsley) *or* Italian (flat-leaf) parsley
Dash *each* chili powder and ground cumin
½ cup mild salsa

Here is a Mexican specialty that you can easily prepare at home.

1. Preheat oven to 375°F. Wrap each tortilla in foil and bake for 10 minutes.

2. In 9-inch nonstick skillet heat oil; add onion, pepper, and garlic and cook over medium-high heat, stirring occasionally, until vegetables are softened, about 2 minutes. Add beans, tomatoes with reserved liquid, cilantro, and seasonings and stir to combine. Reduce heat to low and cook, stirring occasionally, until moisture has evaporated, 3 to 4 minutes.

3. Remove tortillas from oven. Unwrap 1 tortilla and spread ¼ of bean mixture across tortilla; fold sides of tortilla over filling. Fold bottom of tortilla up over filling and roll to enclose filling. Place seam side down on serving plate. Repeat procedure using remaining bean mixture and tortillas, making 3 more burritos.

4. To serve, arrange burritos on serving platter and top with salsa.

APPROXIMATE TOTAL TIME: 25 MINUTES (includes baking time)

MAKES 2 SERVINGS, 2 BURRITOS EACH

Each serving provides: ½ Fat; 2 Proteins; 2 Vegetables; 2 Breads
Per serving: 338 calories; 13 g protein; 7 g fat; 59 g carbohydrate; 156 mg calcium; 1,124 mg sodium (estimated); 0 mg cholesterol; 8 g dietary fiber

Black Bean and Rice Bake �），）

2 cups cooked long-grain rice
8 ounces rinsed drained canned
   black (turtle) beans
1½ ounces reduced-fat Monterey
   Jack cheese, shredded
½ cup thawed frozen egg
   substitute
¼ cup *each* finely chopped red
   bell pepper and onion
1 tablespoon minced fresh
   cilantro (Chinese parsley) *or*
   Italian (flat-leaf) parsley
1 small garlic clove, minced
½ cup mild salsa

Rice and beans are a nutritious and delicious combination. This recipe provides a great opportunity for using up leftover rice.

1. Preheat oven to 350°F. In large mixing bowl combine all ingredients except salsa, mixing well. Spray 8 x 8 x 2-inch baking dish with nonstick cooking spray and spread bean-rice mixture in dish. Bake for 20 minutes (until golden and a knife, inserted in center, comes out dry).

2. To serve, cut into 4 equal portions and top each with ¼ of the salsa.

APPROXIMATE TOTAL TIME: 30 MINUTES (includes baking time)

MAKES 4 SERVINGS

Each serving provides: 2 Proteins; ½ Vegetable; 1 Bread
Per serving: 253 calories; 12 g protein; 2 g fat; 44 g carbohydrate; 142 mg calcium; 481 mg sodium (estimated); 8 mg cholesterol; 3 g dietary fiber

Serving Suggestion: Top each portion with 2 tablespoons plain low-fat yogurt. In Serving Information add ¼ Milk.
Per serving: 257 calories; 13 g protein; 3 g fat; 45 g carbohydrate; 155 mg calcium; 486 mg sodium (estimated); 8 mg cholesterol; 3 g dietary fiber

Haitian Black Beans ▽C ▽F

2 tablespoons *each* chopped
  onion, chopped seeded tomato,
  and chopped green bell pepper
1½ teaspoons chopped seeded
  mild chili pepper
½ teaspoon olive oil
4 ounces rinsed drained canned
  black (turtle) beans, divided
½ ounce diced boiled ham
Dash pepper
1 cup cooked long-grain rice
  (hot)

1. In shallow 1-quart microwavable casserole combine onion, tomato, bell pepper, chili pepper, and oil and stir to coat. Microwave on High (100%) for 1 minute, until onion is softened.

2. Using a fork, mash 2 ounces beans. Add mashed and whole beans, *⅓ cup water*, the ham, and pepper to onion mixture and stir to combine. Cover and microwave on High for 7 minutes, stirring once every 2 minutes, until flavors blend.

3. Serve over rice.

APPROXIMATE TOTAL TIME: 20 MINUTES

MAKES 2 SERVINGS

Each serving provides: ¼ Fat; 1¼ Proteins; ½ Vegetable; 1 Bread
Per serving: 204 calories; 8 g protein; 2 g fat; 38 g carbohydrate; 38 mg calcium; 278 mg sodium (estimated); 4 mg cholesterol; 3 g dietary fiber

Cannellini with Pasta and Vegetables ⬇C ⬇F ⬇S

2 teaspoons olive oil
½ cup *each* sliced red onion and red bell pepper (¼-inch wide strips)
1 cup cooked penne *or* ziti macaroni
8 ounces rinsed drained canned white kidney (cannellini) beans
1 tablespoon chopped fresh basil or ½ teaspoon basil leaves
½ teaspoon oregano leaves

While preparing the onion and bell pepper for this recipe you might want to slice more than you need and add it to a salad or sandwich.

1. In 9-inch nonstick skillet heat oil; add onion and pepper and cook over medium-high heat until tender-crisp, about 3 minutes.

2. Reduce heat to low; add remaining ingredients and stir to combine. Cook, stirring frequently, until thoroughly heated, about 5 minutes.

APPROXIMATE TOTAL TIME: 20 MINUTES

MAKES 2 SERVINGS

Each serving provides: 1 Fat; 2 Proteins; 1 Vegetable; 1 Bread
Per serving: 287 calories; 13 g protein; 6 g fat; 47 g carbohydrate; 84 mg calcium; 392 mg sodium (estimated); 0 mg cholesterol; 6 g dietary fiber

Maple Baked Beans ▽C ▽F

1 ounce diced fully-cooked
   smoked ham
¼ cup chopped onion
1 tablespoon maple syrup
2 teaspoons margarine, melted
1 teaspoon dark molasses
½ teaspoon powdered mustard
6 ounces rinsed drained canned
   small white beans

———

*The microwave oven bakes these
flavorful beans in minutes.*

1. In 2-cup microwavable casserole combine all ingredients except beans; mix well. Add beans and stir to combine. Cover and microwave on High (100%) for 5 minutes, rotating casserole ½ turn halfway through cooking, until heated through.

APPROXIMATE TOTAL TIME: 10 MINUTES

MAKES 2 SERVINGS

Each serving provides: 1 Fat; ½ Protein; ¼ Vegetable; 1½ Breads; 40 Optional Calories
Per serving: 189 calories; 9 g protein; 5 g fat; 28 g carbohydrate; 91 mg calcium; 540 mg sodium (estimated); 7 mg cholesterol; 3 g dietary fiber

Two-Bean Chili ▽ᶜ ▽ᶠ

2 teaspoons vegetable oil
½ cup *each* diced onion and
　green bell pepper
1 small garlic clove, minced
1 tablespoon all-purpose flour
1 cup canned Italian tomatoes
　(reserve liquid), seeded
　and diced
3 ounces *each* rinsed drained
　canned pink beans and rinsed
　drained canned black (turtle)
　beans
1 tablespoon chili powder
½ packet (about ½ teaspoon)
　instant vegetable broth and
　seasoning mix
Dash pepper
¾ ounce reduced-fat Monterey
　Jack *or* Cheddar cheese,
　shredded

1. In 3-quart nonstick saucepan heat oil; add onion, bell pepper, and garlic and cook over medium-high heat, stirring frequently, until onion is softened, 1 to 2 minutes.

2. Sprinkle flour over vegetables and stir quickly to combine; cook, stirring constantly, for 1 minute. Continuing to stir, add *2 cups water*, the tomatoes with reserved liquid, beans, chili powder, broth mix, and pepper.

3. Reduce heat to low, cover, and cook until mixture thickens, 15 to 20 minutes.

4. To serve, into each of 2 serving bowls spoon half of the chili; top each with half of the cheese.

APPROXIMATE TOTAL TIME: 30 MINUTES

MAKES 2 SERVINGS, ABOUT 1½ CUPS EACH

Each serving provides: 1 Fat; 2 Proteins; 2 Vegetables; 20 Optional Calories
Per serving with Monterey Jack cheese: 241 calories; 12 g protein; 8 g fat; 33 g carbohydrate; 185 mg calcium; 781 mg sodium (estimated); 8 mg cholesterol; 7 g dietary fiber
With Cheddar cheese: 245 calories; 12 g protein; 8 g fat; 33 g carbohydrate; 185 mg calcium; 788 mg sodium (estimated); 8 mg cholesterol; 7 g dietary fiber

Chick-Peas, Pasta, and Broccoli ▽C ▽F

2 tablespoons golden raisins
½ cup sliced onion
½ ounce pignolias (pine nuts)
2 teaspoons reduced-calorie margarine (tub)
1 small garlic clove, minced
1 tablespoon tomato paste
2 cups broccoli florets
1 cup cooked pasta twists
4 ounces rinsed drained canned chick-peas

1. In small mixing bowl combine raisins and ¼ cup water; set aside.

2. In 3-quart microwavable casserole combine onion, pignolias, margarine, and garlic; cover and microwave on High (100%) for 2 minutes.

3. Add tomato paste to raisin-water mixture and stir to combine; stir into onion mixture. Add broccoli florets and stir to combine. Cover and microwave on High for 5 minutes, stirring once halfway through cooking.

4. Add pasta and chick-peas and stir to combine. Cover and microwave on High for 3 minutes, until thoroughly heated.

APPROXIMATE TOTAL TIME: 20 MINUTES

MAKES 2 SERVINGS

Each serving provides: 1 Fat; 1½ Proteins; 2½ Vegetables; 1 Bread; ½ Fruit; 5 Optional Calories
Per serving: 305 calories; 14 g protein; 8 g fat; 51 g carbohydrate; 102 mg calcium; 333 mg sodium (estimated); 0 mg cholesterol; 4 g dietary fiber (this figure does not include pignolias and broccoli florets; nutrition analyses not available)

Braised Chestnuts and Lentils ▽ⓒ ▽ⓕ

2 teaspoons olive *or* vegetable oil
1 cup sliced mushrooms
¼ cup *each* sliced shallots *or*
   onion and diced red bell pepper
2 garlic cloves, minced
6 ounces rinsed drained canned
   lentils
6 small bottled chestnuts (packed
   without sugar),* chopped
2 tablespoons dry red table wine
½ packet (about ½ teaspoon)
   instant vegetable broth and
   seasoning mix

1. In 10-inch nonstick skillet heat oil; add mushrooms, shallots, pepper, and garlic and cook over medium-high heat, stirring frequently, until mushrooms are softened, 1 to 2 minutes.

2. Add lentils, chestnuts, *½ cup water*, the wine, and broth mix and stir to combine. Reduce heat to low and let simmer, stirring occasionally, until liquid is reduced by half, 4 to 5 minutes.

* Shelled roasted chestnuts may be substituted for the bottled chestnuts.

APPROXIMATE TOTAL TIME: 20 MINUTES

MAKES 2 SERVINGS

Each serving provides: 1 Fat; 1½ Proteins; 1½ Vegetables; ½ Bread; 15 Optional Calories
Per serving: 193 calories; 10 g protein; 5 g fat; 26 g carbohydrate; 36 mg calcium; 487 mg sodium (estimated); 0 mg cholesterol; 4 g dietary fiber (this figure does not include chestnuts; nutrition analysis not available)

Lentils and Spinach ♡ ♡

¼ cup chopped onion
2 garlic cloves, minced
1 teaspoon vegetable oil
½ cup thawed frozen chopped
   spinach
4 ounces rinsed drained canned
   lentils
1 teaspoon cornstarch, dissolved
   in ½ cup water
1 packet instant vegetable broth
   and seasoning mix

1. In shallow 1-quart microwavable casserole combine onion, garlic, and oil and stir to coat; microwave on High (100%) for 1 minute.

2. Add remaining ingredients to onion mixture and stir to combine. Cover and microwave on High for 4 minutes, stirring once halfway through cooking, until mixture thickens.

APPROXIMATE TOTAL TIME: 10 MINUTES

MAKES 2 SERVINGS

Each serving provides: ½ Fat; ¾ Vegetable; 1 Bread; 10 Optional Calories
Per serving: 117 calories; 8 g protein; 3 g fat; 17 g carbohydrate; 75 mg calcium; 620 mg sodium (estimated); 0 mg cholesterol; 4 g dietary fiber

Lentils 'n' Barley Sauté ▽C ▽F

1 teaspoon vegetable oil
1 cup sliced mushrooms
¼ cup *each* finely chopped carrot and scallions (green onions)
1 packet instant chicken broth and seasoning mix
¼ teaspoon *each* pepper and thyme leaves
1 cup cooked medium pearl barley
4 ounces rinsed drained canned lentils

1. In 10-inch nonstick skillet heat oil; add mushrooms, carrot, and scallions and cook over medium-high heat, stirring frequently, until mushrooms are softened, 1 to 2 minutes.

2. Add ¾ *cup water*, the broth mix, pepper, and thyme to mushroom mixture, stirring to dissolve broth mix. Reduce heat to low, cover, and cook until carrot is tender, 4 to 5 minutes.

3. Stir in barley and lentils and cook, uncovered, stirring occasionally, until liquid is absorbed, 2 to 3 minutes.

APPROXIMATE TOTAL TIME: 20 MINUTES

MAKES 2 SERVINGS

Each serving provides: ½ Fat; 1 Protein; 1½ Vegetables; 1 Bread; 5 Optional Calories
Per serving: 208 calories; 10 g protein; 3 g fat; 37 g carbohydrate; 33 mg calcium; 696 mg sodium (estimated); 0 mg cholesterol; 7 g dietary fiber

Lentil 'n' Macaroni Casserole �▽C ▽F

½ cup chopped onion
1 garlic clove, minced
1 teaspoon vegetable oil
6 ounces rinsed drained canned
   lentils
1 cup cooked elbow *or* small shell
   macaroni
½ cup tomato sauce
1 tablespoon chopped fresh
   Italian (flat-leaf) parsley
¼ teaspoon oregano leaves
Dash ground red pepper

1. In 1-quart microwavable casserole combine onion, garlic, and oil and stir to coat. Cover and microwave on Medium (50%) for 2 minutes, stirring once halfway through cooking, until onion is translucent.

2. Add remaining ingredients to onion-garlic mixture and stir to combine. Cover and microwave on High (100%) for 3 minutes, stirring once halfway through cooking, until thoroughly heated.

APPROXIMATE TOTAL TIME: 15 MINUTES

MAKES 2 SERVINGS

Each serving provides: ½ Fat; 1½ Proteins; 1 Vegetable; 1 Bread
Per serving: 226 calories; 11 g Protein; 3 g fat; 40 g carbohydrate; 42 mg calcium; 659 mg sodium (estimated); 0 mg cholesterol; 5 g dietary fiber

Creole Black-Eyed Peas ⍦ ⍦

2 teaspoons olive *or* vegetable oil
½ cup finely chopped onion
¼ cup *each* finely chopped carrot, celery, and red *or* green bell pepper
½ cup canned crushed tomatoes
1 bay leaf
¼ teaspoon powdered mustard
⅛ teaspoon *each* ground red pepper, ground ginger, and ground cumin
8 ounces rinsed drained canned black-eyed peas
1½ teaspoons finely chopped fresh Italian (flat-leaf) parsley

1. In 9-inch nonstick skillet heat oil; add onion, carrot, celery, and bell pepper and cook over medium-high heat, stirring occasionally, until tender-crisp, about 5 minutes.

2. Add tomatoes, bay leaf, mustard, pepper, ginger, and cumin to vegetable mixture; stir to combine and bring to a boil. Reduce heat to low; stir in peas and let simmer until peas are heated through, about 3 minutes. Remove and discard bay leaf. Sprinkle with parsley.

APPROXIMATE TOTAL TIME: 25 MINUTES

MAKES 2 SERVINGS

Each serving provides: 1 Fat; 2 Proteins; 1¾ Vegetables
Per serving: 208 calories; 10 g protein; 5 g fat; 31 g carbohydrate; 84 mg calcium; 504 mg sodium (estimated); 0 mg cholesterol; 12 g dietary fiber

Caponata with Chick-Peas

2 teaspoons olive *or* vegetable oil
I cup *each* cubed pared eggplant,
  diced red *or* yellow bell
  peppers, diced onions, diced
  celery, diced zucchini, and
  quartered mushrooms
½ ounce pignolias (pine nuts)
I small garlic clove, minced
I cup canned Italian tomatoes
  (reserve liquid), chopped
8 ounces rinsed drained canned
  chick-peas
3 *each* large pitted black and
  pimiento-stuffed green olives,
  sliced
I tablespoon rinsed drained
  capers
¾ ounce mozzarella cheese,
  shredded

*Pack this flavorful salad to take to
the office for lunch. Include I small
pita and a fruit and you're all set.*

1. In 10-inch nonstick skillet heat oil; add eggplant, peppers, onions, celery, zucchini, mushrooms, pignolias, and garlic and cook over medium-high heat, stirring frequently, until lightly browned, about 2 minutes.

2. Reduce heat to medium, cover, and cook until eggplant is tender, about 5 minutes. Add tomatoes with reserved liquid, chick-peas, olives, and capers and stir to combine. Cover and let simmer until thoroughly heated, about 8 minutes.

3. Transfer to serving bowl, cover, and refrigerate until chilled, about I hour. To serve, toss salad again and sprinkle with cheese.

APPROXIMATE TOTAL TIME: 30 MINUTES (does not include chilling time)

MAKES 4 SERVINGS

Each serving provides: I Fat; I½ Proteins; 3½ Vegetables
Per serving: 183 calories; 8 g protein; 8 g fat; 23 g carbohydrate; 105 mg calcium; 491 mg sodium (estimated); 4 mg cholesterol; 4 g dietary fiber (this figure does not include pignolias and capers; nutrition analyses not available)

Tofu, Tomato, and Onion Salad ▽c ▽s

6 ounces firm-style tofu, thinly
    sliced
1 medium tomato, thinly sliced
½ cup thinly sliced red onion
¼ cup fresh basil
1 tablespoon *each* olive oil and
    balsamic *or* red wine vinegar
1 teaspoon Italian seasoning

▬

*Tofu, also known as bean curd, is
available in the produce or refrigerator section of your supermarket.
Fresh tofu is packed in water in
small plastic containers. Once the
package is opened, change the water
daily.*

1. On serving platter decoratively arrange tofu, tomato, onion, and basil, overlapping edges slightly.

2. In small bowl combine remaining ingredients and
drizzle evenly over salad.

APPROXIMATE TOTAL TIME: 10 MINUTES

MAKES 2 SERVINGS

Each serving provides: 1½ Fats; 1½ Proteins; 1½
Vegetables
Per serving: 218 calories; 15 g protein; 14 g fat; 12 g
carbohydrate; 236 mg calcium; 27 mg sodium; 0 mg cholesterol; 1 g dietary fiber (this figure does not include tofu;
nutrition analysis not available)

Cajun Tofu ▽©

2 teaspoons vegetable oil
½ cup *each* diced onion and
   celery
1 garlic clove, minced
½ cup *each* diced green bell
   pepper, diced yellow squash,
   and tomato sauce
¼ cup dry red table wine
1 teaspoon Cajun seasoning
2 tablespoons Worcestershire
   sauce
1 teaspoon cornstarch
½ pound firm-style tofu, cut into
   1-inch cubes

1. In 10-inch nonstick skillet heat oil; add onion, celery, and garlic and cook over medium-high heat, stirring occasionally, until onion begins to soften, about 1 minute. Add pepper and squash and cook until tender-crisp, about 2 minutes.

2. Add tomato sauce, wine, and Cajun seasoning to vegetable mixture and stir to combine.

3. In small bowl combine Worcestershire sauce and cornstarch, stirring to dissolve cornstarch; stir into vegetable mixture. Add tofu and stir to combine; cook, stirring occasionally, until mixture thickens, about 3 minutes.

APPROXIMATE TOTAL TIME: 20 MINUTES

MAKES 2 SERVINGS

Each serving provides: 1 Fat; 2 Proteins; 2½ Vegetables; 30 Optional Calories
Per serving: 303 calories; 21 g protein; 15 g fat; 22 g carbohydrate; 275 mg calcium; 1,003 mg sodium; 0 mg cholesterol; 3 g dietary fiber (this figure does not include tofu; nutrition analysis not available)

Hot and Spicy Tofu with Pasta ▽©

1¾ teaspoons peanut *or* vegetable oil
½ cup *each* red bell pepper strips and sliced onion *or* scallions (green onions)
1 small garlic clove, minced
½ cup canned ready-to-serve low-sodium chicken broth
2 tablespoons reduced-sodium soy sauce
1 tablespoon dry sherry
1 teaspoon cornstarch
¼ teaspoon hot chili oil
½ pound firm-style tofu, cut into 1-inch cubes
1 cup cooked Japanese buckwheat pasta (soba) *or* thin egg noodles (hot)
1 tablespoon finely chopped cilantro (Chinese parsley) *or* Italian (flat-leaf) parsley

---

We recommend you prepare this dish using Japanese buckwheat pasta, known as soba. Look for it in your supermarket or in an Oriental specialty store. Thin egg noodles can be used as an alternative.

1. In 9-inch nonstick skillet heat peanut oil; add pepper, onion, and garlic and cook over medium-high heat, stirring occasionally, until tender-crisp, about 3 minutes.

2. In 1-cup liquid measure combine broth, soy sauce, sherry, cornstarch, and chili oil, stirring to dissolve cornstarch. Stir into vegetable mixture and cook, stirring constantly, until mixture comes to a boil. Reduce heat to low; add tofu, stir to combine, and cook until heated through, about 2 minutes.

3. To serve, on serving platter arrange pasta, top with vegetable-tofu mixture, and sprinkle with cilantro.

APPROXIMATE TOTAL TIME: 20 MINUTES

MAKES 2 SERVINGS

Each serving provides: 1 Fat; 2 Proteins; 1 Vegetable; 1 Bread; 20 Optional Calories
Per serving with pasta: 331 calories; 23 g protein; 15 g fat; 29 g carbohydrate; 258 mg calcium; 800 mg sodium; 0 mg cholesterol; 1 g dietary fiber (this figure does not include tofu and pasta; nutrition analyses not available)
With noodles: 366 calories; 24 g protein; 16 g fat; 33 g carbohydrate; 260 mg calcium; 637 mg sodium; 26 mg cholesterol; 3 g dietary fiber (this figure does not include tofu; nutrition analysis not available)

Tofu with Hoisin Sauce ▽© ▽⑤

½ cup *each* red bell pepper strips and sliced celery
1½ teaspoons vegetable oil
1 teaspoon minced pared gingerroot
1 small garlic clove, minced
2 tablespoons dry sherry
2 teaspoons hoisin sauce
1 teaspoon reduced-sodium soy sauce
½ teaspoon Chinese sesame oil
½ pound firm-style tofu, cut into cubes
½ cup sliced scallions (green onions), green portion only

1. In 1-quart microwavable casserole combine pepper, celery, oil, gingerroot, and garlic and stir to coat. Microwave on High (100%) for 2 minutes, stirring once halfway through cooking.

2. Add sherry, hoisin sauce, soy sauce, and sesame oil and stir to combine; microwave on High for 1 minute.

3. Add tofu and microwave on High for 1 minute; sprinkle with scallions.

APPROXIMATE TOTAL TIME: 15 MINUTES

MAKES 2 SERVINGS

Each serving provides: 1 Fat; 2 Proteins; 1½ Vegetables; 25 Optional Calories
Per serving: 256 calories; 19 g protein; 15 g fat; 13 g carbohydrate; 265 mg calcium; 316 mg sodium; 0 mg cholesterol; 1 g dietary fiber (this figure does not include tofu; nutrition analysis not available)

Bean and Tuna Salad ⌄C ⌄F

1¾ cups broccoli florets
¼ cup thinly sliced red bell
   pepper
4 ounces rinsed drained canned
   black (turtle) beans
1 ounce drained canned tuna
   (packed in water)
1 tablespoon red wine vinegar
2 teaspoons olive *or* vegetable oil
1 teaspoon *each* lemon juice and
   Dijon-style mustard

1. Fill bottom portion of microwavable steamer with *½ cup water*. Set steamer insert in place and fill with broccoli florets and pepper; cover and microwave on High (100%) for 4 minutes. Let stand 1 minute until vegetables are tender-crisp.

2. Transfer vegetables to 1-quart microwavable casserole; add beans and tuna and stir to combine. Cover and microwave on High for 1 minute.

3. Using a wire whisk, in small mixing bowl combine *1 tablespoon water*, the vinegar, oil, lemon juice, and mustard and beat until well combined; pour over vegetable-bean mixture.

APPROXIMATE TOTAL TIME: 15 MINUTES

MAKES 2 SERVINGS

Each serving provides: 1 Fat; 1½ Proteins; 2 Vegetables
Per serving: 165 calories; 12 g protein; 5 g fat; 20 g carbohydrate; 75 mg calcium; 344 mg sodium (estimated); 6 mg cholesterol; 3 g dietary fiber (this figure does not include broccoli florets; nutrition analysis not available)

Cuban Black Bean Salad ▽c ▽f

¼ cup orange juice (no sugar added)

2 tablespoons freshly squeezed lime juice

1 tablespoon *each* chopped fresh cilantro (Chinese parsley) *or* Italian (flat-leaf) parsley and red wine vinegar

1 teaspoon olive oil

¼ teaspoon granulated sugar

Dash pepper

6 ounces rinsed drained canned black (turtle) beans

½ cup cooked long-grain rice

¼ cup diagonally sliced scallions (green onions)

5 small pimiento-stuffed green olives, sliced

2 tablespoons chopped rinsed and drained pimiento

4 green leaf lettuce leaves

½ cup chicory (curly endive)

¼ medium avocado (about 2 ounces), pared and thinly sliced

1 small orange (about 6 ounces), peeled and sliced

Garnish: cilantro (Chinese parsley) *or* Italian (flat-leaf) parsley sprig

1. In 1-cup liquid measure combine orange juice, lime juice, cilantro, vinegar, oil, sugar, and pepper and stir to combine. Set aside.

2. In medium mixing bowl combine beans, rice, scallions, olives, and pimiento.

3. Around edge of serving platter arrange lettuce and chicory; spoon bean mixture onto center of platter and decoratively arrange avocado and orange slices around bean mixture. Pour dressing over entire salad. Garnish with cilantro sprig.

APPROXIMATE TOTAL TIME: 15 MINUTES

MAKES 2 SERVINGS

Each serving provides: 1¾ Fats; 1½ Proteins; 1¼ Vegetables; ½ Bread; ¾ Fruit; 3 Optional Calories
Per serving: 293 calories; 10 g protein; 7 g fat; 50 g carbohydrate; 143 mg calcium; 489 mg sodium (estimated); 0 mg cholesterol; 7 g dietary fiber (this figure does not include pimiento; nutrition analysis not available)

Greek-Style Chick-Pea Salad C F

1 tablespoon *each* chopped fresh
  dill, red wine vinegar, and
  freshly squeezed lemon juice
2 teaspoons olive oil
Dash white pepper
1 cup cooked long-grain rice,
  chilled
4 ounces rinsed drained canned
  chick-peas
¼ cup *each* seeded and diced
  tomato, diced green bell
  pepper, sliced scallions (green
  onions), and diced cucumber
2 tablespoons sliced radishes
8 lettuce leaves
¾ ounce feta cheese, cut into
  ¼-inch cubes

*This recipe provides a great way to
use leftover rice.*

1. In medium mixing bowl combine dill, *1 tablespoon
water*, the vinegar, lemon juice, oil, and pepper, stirring well.

2. Add remaining ingredients except lettuce and feta
cheese to dill mixture, tossing to coat.

3. Line serving bowl with lettuce; top with chick-pea
mixture and feta cheese.

APPROXIMATE TOTAL TIME: 20 MINUTES

MAKES 2 SERVINGS

Each serving provides: 1 Fat; 1½ Proteins; 2⅛ Vegetables;
1 Bread
Per serving: 272 calories; 8 g protein; 8 g fat; 42 g carbohydrate; 125 mg calcium; 322 mg sodium (estimated);
9 mg cholesterol; 3 g dietary fiber

Tabouleh with Chick-Peas ▽ᴄ ▽ꜰ

3 ounces uncooked bulgur
  (cracked wheat)
2 tablespoons freshly squeezed
  lemon juice
1 tablespoon chopped fresh mint
2 teaspoons olive oil
1 garlic clove, minced
½ cup pared and diced cucumber
4 ounces rinsed drained canned
  chick-peas
2 small plum tomatoes, diced
¼ cup sliced scallions (green
  onions)
Dash pepper
8 lettuce leaves

1. In medium mixing bowl pour 1½ cups water over bulgur and let stand until bulgur is slightly softened, about 20 minutes. Pour bulgur through fine sieve, discarding cooking liquid; set aside.

2. In medium mixing bowl combine lemon juice, 2 tablespoons water, the mint, oil, and garlic, stirring to combine. Add bulgur and remaining ingredients, except lettuce, and stir to coat.

3. Line serving bowl with lettuce and top with bulgur mixture. Cover and refrigerate until flavors blend, at least 15 minutes.

APPROXIMATE TOTAL TIME: 30 MINUTES (does not include chilling time)

MAKES 2 SERVINGS

Each serving provides: 1 Fat; 1 Protein; 2¼ Vegetables; 1½ Breads
Per serving: 288 calories; 9 g protein; 6 g fat; 51 g carbohydrate; 75 mg calcium; 205 mg sodium (estimated); 0 mg cholesterol; 10 g dietary fiber

Tofu and Vegetable Salad ▽Ⓒ ▽Ⓢ

1 medium tomato, blanched, peeled, and seeded
1 tablespoon rice vinegar
1½ teaspoons peanut *or* vegetable oil
1 teaspoon *each* reduced-sodium soy sauce and honey
½ teaspoon Chinese sesame oil
6 ounces firm-style tofu, cut into cubes
1 cup *each* sliced seeded pared cucumbers and julienne-cut (matchstick pieces) carrots
½ cup *each* julienne-cut (matchstick pieces) red bell pepper, sliced mushrooms, sliced scallions (green onions), and bean sprouts

---

Tofu takes on the flavor of the food around it. Combined with soy sauce, honey, Chinese sesame oil, and fresh vegetables, it becomes a tasty treat.

1. In blender combine tomato, vinegar, peanut oil, soy sauce, honey, and Chinese sesame oil and process until smooth.

2. In large mixing bowl combine remaining ingredients; add tomato mixture and toss to coat.

3. Cover and refrigerate until chilled, at least 30 minutes, or overnight. Toss again before serving.

APPROXIMATE TOTAL TIME: 15 MINUTES (does not include chilling time)

MAKES 2 SERVINGS

Each serving provides: 1 Fat; 1½ Proteins; 5 Vegetables; 10 Optional Calories
Per serving: 246 calories; 17 g protein; 12 g fat; 23 g carbohydrate; 227 mg calcium; 146 mg sodium; 0 mg cholesterol; 4 g dietary fiber (this figure does not include tofu; nutrition analysis not available)

Spicy Bean Patties

6 ounces rinsed drained canned white (cannellini) beans
1 cup cooked brown rice
¼ cup thawed frozen egg substitute
3 tablespoons plain dried bread crumbs
¼ teaspoon Mexican seasoning
Dash *each* ground red pepper and salt
¼ cup *each* diced red bell pepper and finely chopped scallions (green onions)
1 tablespoon finely chopped green chili pepper
1 small garlic clove, minced
2 teaspoons olive *or* vegetable oil

1. Preheat oven to 400°F. Using a fork, in medium mixing bowl mash beans; add rice, egg substitute, bread crumbs, Mexican seasoning, ground red pepper, and salt and stir to thoroughly combine; set aside.

2. Spray small nonstick skillet with nonstick cooking spray and heat; add bell pepper, scallions, chili pepper, and garlic and cook over medium heat, stirring frequently, until softened, about 1 minute. Add to bean mixture and stir to combine.

3. Shape bean mixture into 4 equal patties. Spray nonstick baking sheet with nonstick cooking spray and arrange patties on baking sheet. Brush each patty with ¼ teaspoon oil and bake for 15 minutes. Carefully turn each patty over and brush each with ¼ teaspoon oil. Bake 5 minutes longer.

APPROXIMATE TOTAL TIME: 30 MINUTES (includes baking time)

MAKES 2 SERVINGS, 2 PATTIES EACH

Each serving provides: 1 Fat; 2 Proteins; ½ Vegetable; 1½ Breads
Per serving: 302 calories; 13 g protein; 6 g fat; 49 g carbohydrate; 83 mg calcium; 540 mg sodium (estimated); 0.5 mg cholesterol; 6 g dietary fiber

Side Dishes

Nutrition won't get sidetracked when you serve our unusual side dishes, with complex carbohydrates playing a major role for those who want to lower their cholesterol and increase their intake of dietary fiber. Our dishes feature pasta and rice and, for a change of pace, barley, cornmeal, and couscous. Vegetables brighten meals in a colorful Confetti Sweet and Sour Slaw or turn into such sophisticated fare as Parmesan Broccoli in Wine. Pasta, once a dietary "no-no," is featured in such delightful dishes as Greek Pasta Salad and Parmesan Pasta Provençal. And roam the culinary globe with such nutrient-laden treats as Greek Eggplant Salad and Tropical Squash Rings prepared with rum. (Who says healthy eating can't be happy eating??)

Asparagus Vinaigrette ⧗C⧗ ⧗S⧗

18 asparagus spears
¼ cup canned ready-to-serve
   low-sodium chicken broth
2 tablespoons raspberry *or* rice
   vinegar
2 teaspoons olive oil
½ teaspoon grated orange peel
⅛ teaspoon pepper

This recipe is also delicious when served chilled. Simply refrigerate for 30 minutes or as long as overnight.

1. In 1-quart shallow microwavable casserole arrange asparagus spears; add broth. Cover and microwave on High (100%) for 2½ minutes, rotating casserole ½ turn after 1 minute.

2. Add remaining ingredients; cover and microwave on High for 30 seconds, until asparagus spears are tender-crisp.

APPROXIMATE TOTAL TIME: 10 MINUTES

MAKES 2 SERVINGS

Each serving provides: 1 Fat; 1½ Vegetables; 5 Optional Calories
Per serving: 76 calories; 4 g protein; 5 g fat; 6 g carbohydrate; 31 mg calcium; 12 mg sodium; 0 mg cholesterol; 1 g dietary fiber

Parmesan Broccoli in Wine ⟨C⟩

½ cup sliced onion
1½ teaspoons walnut *or* olive oil
1 small garlic clove, minced
2 cups broccoli florets
1 tablespoon *each* finely chopped Italian (flat-leaf) parsley and dry red table wine
3 large Calamata olives, pitted and chopped
2 teaspoons grated Parmesan cheese

1. In 1-quart microwavable casserole combine first 3 ingredients and stir to coat; microwave on High (100%) for 2 minutes.

2. Add broccoli and stir to combine; cover and microwave on High for 5 minutes, stirring once halfway through cooking.

3. Add remaining ingredients except cheese; stir to combine. Microwave, uncovered, on Medium (50%) for 1 minute, stirring once halfway through cooking.

4. Let stand for 1 minute for flavors to blend. Sprinkle with cheese.

APPROXIMATE TOTAL TIME: 15 MINUTES

MAKES 2 SERVINGS

Each serving provides: 1 Fat; 2½ Vegetables; 15 Optional Calories
Per serving: 113 calories; 6 g protein; 6 g fat; 11 g carbohydrate; 97 mg calcium; 205 mg sodium; 1 mg cholesterol; 1 g dietary fiber (this figure does not include broccoli florets; nutrition analysis not available)

Variation: Broccoli in Wine—Omit Parmesan cheese from recipe. In Serving Information decrease Optional Calories to 5.
Per serving: 105 calories; 5 g protein; 5 g fat; 11 g carbohydrate; 74 mg calcium; 174 mg sodium; 0 mg cholesterol; 1 g dietary fiber (this figure does not include broccoli florets; nutrition analysis not available)

Brussels Sprouts and Pasta Vinaigrette C F S

2 teaspoons olive *or* vegetable oil
½ cup *each* sliced mushrooms, sliced onion, and red bell pepper strips
1 small garlic clove, minced
2 cups brussels sprouts, trimmed, cooked, and cut into quarters
1 cup cooked spiral macaroni
1 slice crisp bacon, crumbled
1 tablespoon *each* chopped fresh parsley and balsamic *or* red wine vinegar
Dash pepper

Don't overcook the brussels sprouts or they will taste bitter.

1. In 10-inch nonstick skillet heat oil; add mushrooms, onion, bell pepper, and garlic and cook over medium heat until bell pepper is tender-crisp, about 3 minutes.

2. Add remaining ingredients and stir to combine; cook, stirring occasionally, until heated through, about 1 minute.

APPROXIMATE TOTAL TIME: 30 MINUTES

MAKES 2 SERVINGS

Each serving provides: 1 Fat; 3½ Vegetables; 1 Bread; 20 Optional Calories
Per serving: 201 calories; 7 g protein; 7 g fat; 30 g carbohydrate; 60 mg calcium; 76 mg sodium; 3 mg cholesterol; 8 g dietary fiber

Sweet and Sour Red Cabbage with Bacon ▽ⓒ ▽ⓢ

¼ cup chopped onion
1 teaspoon *each* olive *or*
  vegetable oil and margarine
1 tablespoon apple cider vinegar
2 teaspoons firmly packed dark
  brown sugar
3 cups shredded red cabbage
1 slice crisp bacon, crumbled
⅛ teaspoon pepper
Dash ground cloves

It takes no time at all to crisp the bacon in your microwave oven.

1. In 3-quart microwavable casserole combine onion, oil, and margarine and stir to coat; microwave on High (100%) for 1 minute, until onion is translucent.

2. Add *¼ cup water*, the vinegar, and sugar, stirring to dissolve sugar; add cabbage and stir to combine. Cover and microwave on High for 4 minutes, stirring every 2 minutes, until cabbage is tender-crisp.

3. Top cabbage mixture with bacon; cover and microwave on High for 1 minute. Add pepper and cloves and stir to combine.

APPROXIMATE TOTAL TIME: 20 MINUTES

MAKES 2 SERVINGS

Each serving provides: 1 Fat; 3¼ Vegetables; 40 Optional Calories
Per serving: 109 calories; 3 g protein; 6 g fat; 13 g carbohydrate; 65 mg calcium; 86 mg sodium; 3 mg cholesterol; 2 g dietary fiber

Variation: Sweet and Sour Red Cabbage—Omit bacon from recipe. In Serving Information decrease Optional Calories to 20.
Per serving: 91 calories; 2 g protein; 4 g fat; 13 g carbohydrate; 65 mg calcium; 36 mg sodium; 0 mg cholesterol; 2 g dietary fiber

Sweet and Sour Sauerkraut ▽C

1 cup chopped onions
1 teaspoon vegetable oil
1 cup rinsed drained sauerkraut*
¼ cup unfermented apple cider
½ teaspoon caraway seed

This pungent side dish is a wonderful accompaniment to pork or chicken.

1. In 1-quart microwavable casserole combine onions and oil and stir to coat; microwave on High (100%) for 2 minutes, stirring once halfway through cooking.

2. Add remaining ingredients and stir to combine. Microwave on Medium (50%) for 5 minutes, until flavors blend.

* Use the sauerkraut that is packaged in plastic bags and stored in the refrigerator section of the supermarket; it is usually crisper and less salty than the canned.

APPROXIMATE TOTAL TIME: 15 MINUTES

MAKES 2 SERVINGS

Each serving provides: ½ Fat; 2 Vegetables; ¼ Fruit; 5 Optional Calories
Per serving: 75 calories; 2 g protein; 3 g fat; 12 g carbohydrate; 38 mg calcium; 274 mg sodium; 0 mg cholesterol; 3 g dietary fiber (this figure does not include caraway seed; nutrition analysis not available)

Parmesan Braised Citrus Fennel ▽C ▽F

½ cup canned ready-to-serve
  low-sodium chicken broth
2 tablespoons lemon juice
2 teaspoons grated lemon peel
1 teaspoon *each* grated orange
  peel and chopped fresh parsley
1 garlic clove, minced
⅛ teaspoon pepper
3 cups thinly sliced fennel
2 teaspoons grated Parmesan
  cheese

1. In 10-inch nonstick skillet combine broth, lemon juice, lemon peel, orange peel, parsley, garlic, and pepper; cover and bring to a boil.

2. Add fennel and reduce heat to medium; cover and cook, stirring frequently, until fennel is tender-crisp, 3 to 4 minutes.

3. Transfer fennel mixture to serving bowl and sprinkle with cheese.

APPROXIMATE TOTAL TIME: 15 MINUTES

MAKES 2 SERVINGS

Each serving provides: 3 Vegetables; 20 Optional Calories
Per serving: 51 calories; 3 g protein; 1 g fat; 7 g carbohydrate; 112 mg calcium; 210 mg sodium; 1 mg cholesterol; 2 g dietary fiber

Variation: Braised Citrus Fennel—Omit Parmesan cheese from recipe. In Serving Information decrease Optional Calories to 10.
Per serving: 43 calories; 3 g protein; 1 g fat; 7 g carbohydrate; 89 mg calcium; 179 mg sodium; 0 mg cholesterol; 2 g dietary fiber

Creamy Dijon Green Beans $\triangledown$

2 teaspoons *each* reduced-calorie
  margarine (tub) and all-
  purpose flour
½ cup low-fat milk (1% milk fat)
2 tablespoons sour cream
2 teaspoons Dijon-style mustard
⅛ teaspoon white pepper
3 cups cooked green beans (hot)

1. In 1-quart saucepan melt margarine over medium-high heat; add flour and stir quickly to combine. Continuing to stir, gradually add milk. Reduce heat to low and cook, stirring frequently, until mixture thickens, 3 to 4 minutes. Stir in remaining ingredients except green beans.

2. In serving bowl arrange green beans; add sour cream mixture and stir to coat.

APPROXIMATE TOTAL TIME: 15 MINUTES

MAKES 2 SERVINGS

Each serving provides: ¼ Milk; ½ Fat; 3 Vegetables; 50 Optional Calories
Per serving: 154 calories; 6 g protein; 7 g fat; 21 g carbohydrate; 178 mg calcium; 234 mg sodium; 9 mg cholesterol; 3 g dietary fiber

Oven-"Fried" Onion Rings ▽C ▽S

2 cups thinly sliced onions
   (separated into rings)
2 teaspoons vegetable oil
¾ ounce (5 tablespoons)
   cornflake crumbs

Crunchy onion rings without deep-fat frying.

1. Preheat oven to 450°F. In medium mixing bowl combine onions and oil; stir to thoroughly coat. Add cornflake crumbs and toss to coat.

2. Spray nonstick baking sheet with nonstick cooking spray and spread onion mixture on sheet. Bake, turning frequently, until onion rings are crisp and browned, about 20 minutes.

APPROXIMATE TOTAL TIME: 30 MINUTES (includes baking time)

MAKES 2 SERVINGS

Each serving provides: 1 Fat; 2 Vegetables; ½ Bread
Per serving: 136 calories; 3 g protein; 5 g fat; 21 g carbohydrate; 40 mg calcium; 135 mg sodium; 0 mg cholesterol; 3 g dietary fiber

Braised Vegetable Medley ▽C ▽F ▽S

¼ cup dry white table wine
2 tablespoons *each* lemon juice
 and balsamic *or* red wine
 vinegar
2 garlic cloves
¼ teaspoon *each* mustard seed
 and fennel seed
1 teaspoon chopped fresh parsley
1 cup *each* sliced carrots and
 zucchini (1-inch-thick pieces),
 and quartered mushrooms
½ cup frozen pearl onions

1. In 10-inch nonstick skillet combine ¼ *cup water*, the wine, lemon juice, vinegar, garlic, mustard seed, fennel seed, and parsley; cover and cook over high heat until mixture comes to a boil. Boil for 2 minutes, until flavors blend.

2. Set sieve over small mixing bowl and pour wine mixture through sieve, reserving liquid and discarding solids. Return wine mixture to skillet.

3. Bring wine mixture to a boil; add carrots. Reduce heat to medium-low, cover, and cook until tender-crisp, 5 to 7 minutes. Add remaining ingredients, cover, and cook until vegetables are fork-tender, about 5 minutes.

APPROXIMATE TOTAL TIME: 25 MINUTES

MAKES 2 SERVINGS

Each serving provides: 3½ Vegetables; 25 Optional Calories
Per serving: 91 calories; 3 g protein; 1 g fat; 16 g carbohydrate; 59 mg calcium; 33 mg sodium; 0 mg cholesterol; 3 g dietary fiber

Barley Casserole ▽C ▽F ▽S

2 teaspoons sweet margarine
½ cup *each* diced onion and
   sliced shiitake *or* white
   mushrooms
1 small garlic clove, minced
2¼ ounces uncooked pearl barley
½ teaspoon Italian seasoning
Dash salt

1. In 1-quart microwavable casserole melt margarine on High (100%) for 30 seconds. Add onion, mushrooms, and garlic and stir to combine. Cover and microwave on High for 2 minutes, stirring once halfway through cooking, until onion is softened.

2. Add 1½ cups *water* and remaining ingredients. Cover and microwave on High for 25 minutes, until barley is tender and liquid is almost completely absorbed.

3. Let stand, covered, for 2 minutes, until all liquid is absorbed.

APPROXIMATE TOTAL TIME: 35 MINUTES

MAKES 2 SERVINGS

Each serving provides: 1 Fat; 1 Vegetable; 1½ Breads
Per serving: 167 calories; 4 g protein; 4 g fat; 29 g carbohydrate; 23 mg calcium; 75 mg sodium; 0 mg cholesterol; 6 g dietary fiber

Bacon-Flavored "Fried" Corn ⌄ᶜ ⌄ˢ

¼ cup *each* diced red bell pepper
and onion
2 teaspoons reduced-calorie
margarine (tub)
1 cup thawed frozen whole-
kernel corn
1 slice crisp bacon, crumbled
1 tablespoon half-and-half (blend
of milk and cream)
¼ teaspoon granulated sugar
Dash pepper

1. In 1-quart microwavable casserole combine bell pepper, onion, and margarine; microwave on High (100%) for 2 minutes, stirring once halfway through cooking.

2. Add remaining ingredients except pepper and stir to combine; microwave on High for 4 minutes, stirring once halfway through cooking.

3. Add pepper and stir.

APPROXIMATE TOTAL TIME: 10 MINUTES

MAKES 2 SERVINGS

Each serving provides: ½ Fat; ½ Vegetable; 1 Bread; 35 Optional Calories
Per serving: 129 calories; 4 g protein; 5 g fat; 20 g carbohydrate; 18 mg calcium; 97 mg sodium; 5 mg cholesterol; 2 g dietary fiber

Variation: "Fried" Corn—Omit bacon. In Serving Information decrease Optional Calories to 15.
Per serving: 111 calories; 3 g protein; 4 g fat; 20 g carbohydrate; 17 mg calcium; 46 mg sodium; 3 mg cholesterol; 2 g dietary fiber

Chinese Corn and Peppers $\boxed{C}$ $\boxed{F}$ $\boxed{S}$

½ cup *each* red bell pepper strips, green bell pepper strips, sliced onion, and quartered small mushrooms
¾ teaspoon vegetable oil
1 small garlic clove, minced
1 cup frozen *or* drained canned whole baby corn ears
1 tablespoon dry sherry
1½ teaspoons *each* rice vinegar and reduced-sodium soy sauce
¼ teaspoon *each* cornstarch and Chinese sesame oil

1. In 1-quart microwavable casserole combine peppers, onion, mushrooms, oil, and garlic; stir to coat. Cover and microwave on High (100%) for 4 minutes, stirring once halfway through cooking.

2. Add corn and stir to combine; cover and microwave on High for 1 minute.

3. In small bowl combine *1 tablespoon water* and the remaining ingredients, stirring to dissolve cornstarch. Add to vegetable mixture and stir to combine.

4. Microwave, uncovered, on High for 2 minutes, stirring once halfway through cooking.

APPROXIMATE TOTAL TIME: 15 MINUTES

MAKES 2 SERVINGS

Each serving provides: ½ Fat; 2 Vegetables; ½ Bread; 10 Optional Calories
Per serving: 116 calories; 5 g protein; 3 g fat; 16 g carbohydrate; 17 mg calcium; 174 mg sodium; 0 mg cholesterol; 5 g dietary fiber

Corn with Basil Butter ▽C ▽S

2 ears corn on the cob (each 10 inches long), with husks attached
1 tablespoon plus 1 teaspoon reduced-calorie margarine (tub)
1 tablespoon whipped butter, softened
¼ teaspoon grated orange peel
1 tablespoon chopped fresh basil

1. Set corn on floor of microwave oven and microwave on High (100%) for 5 minutes, turning corn over halfway through cooking, until corn is tender.

2. Using a fork, in small mixing bowl combine margarine, butter, and orange peel, mixing well; stir in basil.

3. To serve, pull back corn husks and remove corn silk. Brush each ear with half of the butter mixture.

APPROXIMATE TOTAL TIME: 10 MINUTES

MAKES 2 SERVINGS

Each serving provides: 1 Fat; 2 Breads; 25 Optional Calories
Per serving: 193 calories; 5 g protein; 9 g fat; 30 g carbohydrate; 16 mg calcium; 133 mg sodium; 8 mg cholesterol; 5 g dietary fiber

Corn with Chive "Cream" ▽C ▽S

2 small ears corn on the cob
   (each 5 inches long)
1 tablespoon plus 1 teaspoon
   reduced-calorie margarine
   (tub), melted
1 tablespoon *each* chopped fresh
   chives *or* chopped chives and
   sour cream
⅛ teaspoon pepper

1. In 1-quart shallow microwavable casserole arrange corn; add *¼ cup water*. Cover and microwave on High (100%) for 5 minutes, rotating casserole ½ turn halfway through cooking, until corn is tender.

2. In small mixing bowl combine remaining ingredients; stir to combine.

3. Remove corn from casserole, discarding cooking liquid. Serve each ear of corn with half of the chive mixture.

APPROXIMATE TOTAL TIME: 10 MINUTES

MAKES 2 SERVINGS

Each serving provides: 1 Fat; 1 Bread; 15 Optional Calories
Per serving: 116 calories; 3 g protein; 6 g fat; 15 g carbohydrate; 12 mg calcium; 95 mg sodium; 3 mg cholesterol; 3 g dietary fiber

Savory Corn Fritters

⊽F ⊽S

⅓ cup plus 2 teaspoons all-purpose flour
¼ teaspoon double-acting baking powder
1 egg
½ cup *each* thawed frozen whole-kernel corn and canned cream-style corn
2 tablespoons finely chopped red bell pepper
2 teaspoons vegetable oil, divided
½ medium red bell pepper, cut into rings
2 jalapeño peppers

1. On sheet of wax paper sift together flour and baking powder; set aside.

2. Using a fork, in small mixing bowl beat egg; stir in corns and chopped red bell pepper. Add flour mixture and stir until thoroughly combined.

3. In 10-inch nonstick skillet heat 1 teaspoon oil; using half of the batter, drop batter by tablespoonfuls into skillet, forming 4 fritters. Cook over medium heat until bottoms are lightly browned, 2 to 3 minutes; using pancake turner, turn fritters over and cook until other sides are browned, 2 to 3 minutes longer.

4. Transfer fritters to serving platter; keep warm. Repeat procedure with remaining oil and batter, making 4 more fritters. Garnish platter with red bell pepper rings and jalapeño peppers.

APPROXIMATE TOTAL TIME: 20 MINUTES

MAKES 4 SERVINGS, 2 FRITTERS EACH

Each serving provides: ½ Fat; ¼ Protein; ¼ Vegetable; 1 Bread
Per serving: 126 calories; 4 g protein; 4 g fat; 20 g carbohydrate; 23 mg calcium; 134 mg sodium; 53 mg cholesterol; 1 g dietary fiber

Polenta Toasts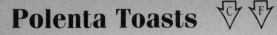

3 ounces uncooked instant polenta (quick-cooking yellow cornmeal)

3 ounces reduced-fat Cheddar cheese, shredded

Serve Polenta Toasts with salsa for dipping.

1. Preheat oven to 450°F. In 1-quart saucepan bring *3 cups water* to a full boil; stir in polenta and cook, stirring constantly, for 5 minutes.

2. Spray 15 × 10½ × 1-inch jelly-roll pan with nonstick cooking spray and spread polenta evenly in prepared pan; sprinkle with cheese. Bake until cheese is melted, about 20 minutes.

3. Let cool slightly. Cut polenta into 24 equal strips; transfer to wire rack and let cool.

APPROXIMATE TOTAL TIME: 30 MINUTES (includes baking time; does not include cooling time)

MAKES 4 SERVINGS, 6 TOASTS EACH

Each serving provides: 1 Protein; 1 Bread
Per serving: 145 calories; 8 g protein; 4 g fat; 17 g carbohydrate; 189 mg calcium; 151 mg sodium; 15 mg cholesterol; 1 g dietary fiber

Southwestern Polenta ⓒ ⓕ

1 teaspoon vegetable oil
¼ cup *each* chopped onion and
    diced red bell pepper
1 tablespoon seeded and finely
    diced jalapeño pepper
1 garlic clove, minced
⅛ teaspoon salt
2¼ ounces uncooked instant
    polenta (quick-cooking yellow
    cornmeal)
¾ ounce reduced-fat Monterey
    Jack *or* Cheddar cheese,
    shredded
1 teaspoon margarine
¼ cup mild salsa

Jalapeño pepper and salsa add spice to the mild flavor of polenta.

1. In 1½-quart nonstick saucepan heat oil; add onion, peppers, and garlic and cook over medium-high heat, stirring occasionally, until onion is softened, about 2 minutes.

2. Increase heat to high; add *1½ cups water* and the salt and bring mixture to a boil. Stirring constantly, add polenta in a thin steady stream; stir in cheese and margarine.

3. Reduce heat to medium and cook, stirring constantly, until mixture thickens, about 4 minutes.

4. Spray 7-inch pie plate with nonstick cooking spray; transfer polenta to pie plate. Let cool for 5 minutes.

5. To serve, top with salsa.

APPROXIMATE TOTAL TIME: 20 MINUTES

MAKES 2 SERVINGS

Each serving provides: 1 Fat; ½ Protein; ¾ Vegetable; 1½ Breads
Per serving with Monterey Jack cheese: 206 calories; 6 g protein; 7 g fat; 30 g carbohydrate; 106 mg calcium; 410 mg sodium; 8 mg cholesterol; 2 g dietary fiber
With Cheddar cheese: 210 calories; 6 g protein; 7 g fat; 30 g carbohydrate; 106 mg calcium; 418 mg sodium; 8 mg cholesterol; 2 g dietary fiber

Spicy Cornmeal Biscuits ▽

½ cup plus 1 tablespoon all-purpose flour
1½ ounces uncooked yellow cornmeal
2 ounces reduced-fat Cheddar cheese, shredded
½ teaspoon *each* baking soda and seeded and finely chopped jalapeño pepper
¾ cup low-fat buttermilk (1% milk fat)
2 tablespoons plus 2 teaspoons reduced-calorie margarine (tub), melted

1. Preheat oven to 450°F. In medium mixing bowl combine flour, cornmeal, cheese, baking soda, and pepper; set aside.

2. In small mixing bowl combine buttermilk and margarine; pour into flour mixture and stir to combine (mixture will be sticky).

3. Onto nonstick baking sheet drop batter by tablespoonfuls, making 8 biscuits. Bake in middle of center oven rack until biscuits are golden brown, about 15 minutes. Transfer to wire rack and let cool.

APPROXIMATE TOTAL TIME: 25 MINUTES (includes baking time)

MAKES 4 SERVINGS, 2 BISCUITS EACH

Each serving provides: 1 Fat; ½ Protein; 1¼ Breads; 30 Optional Calories
Per serving: 200 calories; 8 g protein; 7 g fat; 24 g carbohydrate; 182 mg calcium; 331 mg sodium; 12 mg cholesterol; 1 g dietary fiber

Southwestern Succotash ▽C ▽F ▽S

2 teaspoons reduced-calorie margarine (tub)
½ cup *each* julienne-cut (matchstick pieces) red bell pepper and diced zucchini
¼ cup finely chopped onion
½ medium mild chili pepper, seeded and minced
½ small garlic clove, minced
2 large plum tomatoes, blanched, peeled, seeded, and finely chopped
¾ cup drained canned whole yellow hominy
¼ cup *each* frozen green lima beans and canned ready-to-serve low-sodium chicken broth
Dash pepper

This version of succotash combines lima beans with hominy rather than corn kernels. Hominy is hulled dried corn kernels. Canned hominy has been reconstituted and cooked prior to canning.

1. In 9-inch nonstick skillet melt margarine; add bell pepper, zucchini, onion, chili pepper, and garlic and sauté over medium-high heat until tender-crisp, 2 to 3 minutes.

2. Add remaining ingredients and stir to combine; bring to a boil. Continue cooking, stirring frequently, until mixture is reduced by half, 6 to 8 minutes.

APPROXIMATE TOTAL TIME: 20 MINUTES

MAKES 2 SERVINGS

Each serving provides: ½ Fat; 2½ Vegetables; 1 Bread; 5 Optional Calories
Per serving: 117 calories; 4 g protein; 3 g fat; 20 g carbohydrate; 29 mg calcium; 191 mg sodium; 0 mg cholesterol; 6 g dietary fiber

Tex-Mex Posole ▽C

1 cup drained canned whole
   yellow hominy
¼ cup evaporated skimmed milk
2 tablespoons sour cream
1 teaspoon *each* margarine and
   olive *or* vegetable oil
¼ cup *each* chopped onion and
   green bell pepper
1 tablespoon crushed dried chili
   pepper
1 garlic clove, minced
½ cup canned Italian tomatoes
   (reserve liquid), seeded and
   diced
¾ ounce reduced-fat Monterey
   Jack cheese, shredded

▬

*In the Southwest, posole is another
word for hominy.*

1. In food processor combine hominy, milk, and sour cream and process, using on-off motion, until hominy is coarsely chopped; set aside.

2. In 9-inch nonstick skillet heat margarine and oil until margarine is melted; add onion, peppers, and garlic and sauté over medium-high heat until vegetables are softened, 1 to 2 minutes.

3. Add tomatoes with reserved liquid to onion-pepper mixture and stir to combine. Reduce heat to low and cook, stirring frequently, until flavors blend, 5 to 7 minutes.

4. Stir hominy mixture into tomato mixture and cook until heated through, about 5 minutes. Stir in cheese.

APPROXIMATE TOTAL TIME: 25 MINUTES

MAKES 2 SERVINGS

Each serving provides: ¼ Milk; 1 Fat; ½ Protein; 1 Vegetable; 1 Bread; 35 Optional Calories
Per serving: 219 calories; 9 g protein; 10 g fat; 25 g carbohydrate; 236 mg calcium; 555 mg sodium; 15 mg cholesterol; 4 g dietary fiber

Curried Couscous Pilaf ▽C ▽F ▽S

3 ounces uncooked couscous (dry precooked semolina)
1 tablespoon plus 1 teaspoon olive *or* vegetable oil
½ cup *each* shredded carrot, diced red *or* yellow bell pepper, and sliced scallions (green onions)
⅓ cup plus 2 teaspoons golden raisins
½ cup apple juice (no sugar added)
½ medium tomato, diced
1 teaspoon curry powder

1. In 1-quart saucepan bring *1½ cups water* to a full boil. Remove from heat and stir in couscous. Cover and let stand, stirring occasionally, until water is absorbed, about 5 minutes.

2. In 9-inch nonstick skillet heat oil; add carrot, pepper, and scallions and cook over medium heat, stirring occasionally, until carrot is tender, about 2 minutes. Stir in raisins and apple juice and bring mixture to a boil. Reduce heat to low; stir in tomato and curry powder and let simmer until flavors blend, about 2 minutes. Stir in couscous.

APPROXIMATE TOTAL TIME: 20 MINUTES

MAKES 4 SERVINGS

Each serving provides: 1 Fat; 1 Vegetable; ¾ Bread; 1 Fruit
Per serving: 184 calories; 4 g protein; 5 g fat; 34 g carbohydrate; 25 mg calcium; 13 mg sodium; 0 mg cholesterol; 2 g dietary fiber (this figure does not include couscous; nutrition analysis not available)

Hungarian Noodles

⅓ cup low-fat cottage cheese (2% milk fat)

¼ cup evaporated skimmed milk

2 tablespoons sour cream

1 teaspoon paprika

Dash white pepper

2 teaspoons margarine

¼ cup chopped onion

1 garlic clove, minced

1 tablespoon *each* Worcestershire sauce and all-purpose flour

1½ cups cooked medium noodles (hot)

1. In blender combine first 5 ingredients and process until smooth, scraping down sides of container as necessary; set aside.

2. In 1-quart nonstick saucepan melt margarine; add onion and garlic and sauté over medium-high heat until onion is softened, 1 to 2 minutes. Stir in Worcestershire sauce.

3. Sprinkle flour over onion mixture and stir quickly to combine; stir in cottage cheese mixture. Cook, stirring frequently, until mixture thickens, 4 to 5 minutes. Add noodles and stir to combine.

APPROXIMATE TOTAL TIME: 20 MINUTES

MAKES 2 SERVINGS

Each serving provides: ¼ Milk; 1 Fat; ½ Protein; ¼ Vegetable; 1½ Breads; 50 Optional Calories
Per serving: 275 calories; 13 g protein; 9 g fat; 35 g carbohydrate; 154 mg calcium; 326 mg sodium; 39 mg cholesterol; 1 g dietary fiber

Lemon-Poppy Seed Noodles

1 tablespoon *each* whipped
  butter and freshly squeezed
  lemon juice
1 teaspoon *each* poppy seed and
  margarine
½ teaspoon grated lemon peel
⅛ teaspoon white pepper
1 cup cooked noodles (hot)

A little butter adds a lot of flavor to this simple side dish.

1. In small nonstick saucepan combine all ingredients except noodles; cook over high heat until butter and margarine are melted, about 1 minute. Add noodles and stir to coat with butter mixture.

APPROXIMATE TOTAL TIME: 15 MINUTES

MAKES 2 SERVINGS

Each serving provides: ½ Fat; 1 Bread; 35 Optional Calories
Per serving: 135 calories; 3 g protein; 6 g fat; 16 g carbohydrate; 31 mg calcium; 53 mg sodium; 28 mg cholesterol; 1 g dietary fiber (this figure does not include poppy seed; nutrition analysis not available)

Thai Two-Noodle Stir-Fry ⌄C⌄ ⌄F⌄

2 cups boiling water
I ounce uncooked rice sticks (rice noodles)*
¼ cup canned ready-to-serve low-sodium chicken broth
I tablespoon *each* firmly packed dark brown sugar, reduced-sodium soy sauce, and freshly squeezed lime juice
1¾ teaspoons peanut oil
¼ teaspoon chili oil
¼ cup *each* thinly sliced red bell pepper and scallions (green onions)
I teaspoon crushed dried chili pepper
I garlic clove, minced
I cup *each* cooked thin noodles and bean sprouts

This recipe calls for rice sticks, a type of Chinese rice noodle. Look for it in the Oriental section of your supermarket.

1. In medium mixing bowl pour water over rice sticks and let stand for 10 minutes. Drain, discarding water, and set aside.

2. In 1-cup liquid measure combine broth, sugar, soy sauce, and lime juice, stirring to dissolve sugar; set aside.

3. In 10-inch nonstick skillet heat oils; add bell pepper, scallions, chili pepper, and garlic and cook over high heat, stirring frequently, until scallions are lightly browned, 1 to 2 minutes. Stir in broth mixture; add rice sticks, noodles, and sprouts and stir to combine. Cook, stirring frequently, until liquid is reduced by half, 3 to 5 minutes.

* One ounce uncooked rice sticks yields about ½ cup cooked.

APPROXIMATE TOTAL TIME: 30 MINUTES

MAKES 2 SERVINGS

Each serving provides: 1 Fat; 1½ Vegetables; 1½ Breads; 35 Optional Calories
Per serving: 240 calories; 6 g protein; 6 g fat; 41 g carbohydrate; 33 mg calcium; 316 mg sodium; 20 mg cholesterol; 2 g dietary fiber

Cuban Black Bean Salad

Microwave Brunswick Stew
Italian Seafood Stew
Beef 'n' Barley Stew
Oriental Hot Pot

Tropical Oatmeal Cookies
Spicy Deviled Eggs
Bibb and Grapefruit Salad
"Fried" Chicken

Blueberry-Oat Bran Loaf
Quick Rugalach (Raisin Crescents)
Iced Apple Turnovers

California Burgers
Thai Marinated Steak
Swordfish Kabobs

Parmesan Pasta Provençal ⩔C ⩔F

1 cup *each* diced eggplant and zucchini

2 teaspoons olive oil

1 large garlic clove, minced

2½ cups canned Italian tomatoes, divided

1 tablespoon chopped fresh basil *or* ½ teaspoon basil leaves

1½ cups cooked orecchiette pasta (saucer-shaped pasta) *or* small shell macaroni (hot)

1 tablespoon grated Parmesan cheese

▬

To speed preparation, cook the pasta on the range while the vegetables cook in the microwave oven.

1. In 3-quart microwavable casserole combine eggplant, zucchini, oil, and garlic and stir to coat. Microwave on High (100%) for 2 minutes, until softened.

2. In blender process 1½ cups tomatoes until smooth. Set sieve over eggplant mixture and press processed tomatoes through sieve into casserole, discarding solids.

3. Seed and dice remaining tomatoes; add to eggplant mixture and stir to combine. Add ¼ *cup water* and stir to combine.

4. Cover and microwave on High for 12 minutes, stirring once every 4 minutes, until mixture thickens. Stir in basil.

5. To serve, in serving bowl arrange pasta; top with eggplant mixture and sprinkle with cheese.

APPROXIMATE TOTAL TIME: 25 MINUTES

MAKES 2 SERVINGS

Each serving provides: 1 Fat; 4½ Vegetables; 1½ Breads; 15 Optional Calories
Per serving: 253 calories; 9 g protein; 7 g fat; 42 g carbohydrate; 157 mg calcium; 540 mg sodium; 2 mg cholesterol; 4 g dietary fiber

Variation: Pasta Provençal—Omit Parmesan cheese from recipe. In Serving Information omit Optional Calories.
Per serving: 241 calories; 8 g protein; 6 g fat; 42 g carbohydrate; 123 mg calcium; 494 mg sodium; 0 mg cholesterol; 4 g dietary fiber

Parmesan Pasta with Broccoli Rabe ∇ ∇ ∇

2 teaspoons olive oil
½ cup *each* diced red bell pepper,
    yellow bell pepper, and onion
1 small garlic clove, minced
4 cups thoroughly washed and
    trimmed broccoli rabe, chopped
1½ cups cooked elbow *or* small
    shell macaroni (hot)
2 teaspoons grated Parmesan
    cheese
Dash pepper

*Prepare the pasta for this dish while
the broccoli rabe is cooking.*

1. In 10-inch nonstick skillet heat oil; add bell peppers, onion, and garlic and cook over medium heat, stirring occasionally, until tender-crisp, about 2 minutes.

2. Add broccoli rabe and stir to combine. Reduce heat to low, partially cover, and cook until tender, about 10 minutes.

3. Add macaroni and stir to combine. Sprinkle with cheese and pepper.

APPROXIMATE TOTAL TIME: 25 MINUTES

MAKES 2 SERVINGS

Each serving provides: 1 Fat; 5½ Vegetables; 1½ Breads; 10 Optional Calories
Per serving: 229 calories; 10 g protein; 6 g fat; 37 g carbohydrate; 144 mg calcium; 103 mg sodium; 1 mg cholesterol; 7 g dietary fiber

Variation: Pasta with Broccoli Rabe—Omit Parmesan cheese. In Serving Information omit Optional Calories.
Per serving: 221 calories; 9 g protein; 6 g fat; 37 g carbohydrate; 121 mg calcium; 72 mg sodium; 0 mg cholesterol; 7 g dietary fiber

Pasta and Vegetable Toss ⬦C⬦ ⬦F⬦ ⬦S⬦

2 teaspoons olive *or* vegetable oil
1 cup *each* sliced onions,
    shredded zucchini, and
    shredded carrots
1 small garlic clove, minced
1½ cups cooked spiral macaroni
1 tablespoon chopped fresh
    Italian (flat-leaf) parsley
2 teaspoons balsamic *or* red wine
    vinegar

For an Italian-style topping sprinkle with grated Parmesan cheese before serving.

1. In 9-inch nonstick skillet heat oil; add onions, zucchini, carrots, and garlic and cook over medium heat, stirring occasionally, until onions are tender, about 5 minutes.

2. Add macaroni to skillet and stir to combine. Add parsley and vinegar and stir to combine. Reduce heat to low; cook, stirring frequently, until thoroughly heated, about 1 minute.

APPROXIMATE TOTAL TIME: 30 MINUTES

MAKES 2 SERVINGS

Each serving provides: 1 Fat; 3 Vegetables; 1½ Breads
Per serving: 219 calories; 6 g protein; 5 g fat; 38 g carbohydrate; 57 mg calcium; 25 mg sodium; 0 mg cholesterol; 5 g dietary fiber

Pasta-Stuffed Artichokes ⬦C⬦

2 artichokes (½ pound each)
½ lemon
2 teaspoons olive *or* vegetable
   oil, divided
½ cup sliced shiitake *or* white
   mushrooms
1 small garlic clove, minced
1 cup cooked thin spaghetti (hot)
¾ ounce grated Parmesan cheese
   (reserve 2 teaspoons)
1½ teaspoons *each* chopped fresh
   Italian (flat-leaf) parsley and
   balsamic *or* red wine vinegar
½ teaspoon grated lemon peel
Garnish: lemon wedges

1. Using large stainless-steel knife, cut off stem of each artichoke flush with base so that artichokes will stand upright; snap off any small or discolored leaves, at base. Using scissors, remove barbed tips of leaves, cutting about ½ inch off tip of each leaf.

2. In 2-quart saucepan add artichokes and lemon to *1 quart water.* Bring water to a full boil and cook until artichokes are tender, about 20 minutes. Drain and let cool.

3. While artichokes are cooking prepare filling. In 9-inch nonstick skillet heat 1 teaspoon oil; add mushrooms and garlic and cook over medium-high heat, stirring frequently, until mushrooms are tender, about 3 minutes. Add spaghetti, cheese, parsley, vinegar, remaining oil, and the lemon peel and stir to combine.

4. Using a spoon or fork, remove and discard center chokes from artichokes. Fill center of each artichoke with ½ of the spaghetti-mushroom mixture; sprinkle each with 1 teaspoon reserved cheese. Garnish with lemon wedges.

APPROXIMATE TOTAL TIME: 45 MINUTES

MAKES 2 SERVINGS, 1 ARTICHOKE EACH

Each serving provides: 1 Fat; ½ Protein; 1½ Vegetables; 1 Bread
Per serving: 240 calories; 11 g protein; 8 g fat; 32 g carbohydrate; 199 mg calcium; 273 mg sodium; 8 mg cholesterol; 6 g dietary fiber

Pasta with Broccoli ⓒ ⓢ

2 teaspoons olive oil
½ ounce pignolias (pine nuts)
2 garlic cloves, minced
1 cup broccoli florets
½ cup canned ready-to-serve
  low-sodium chicken broth
2 tablespoons dried currants
1½ cups cooked orecchiette
  (saucer-shaped pasta) *or* small
  shell macaroni (hot)

If you prefer, dark raisins may be used in place of currants in this recipe.

1. In 10-inch nonstick skillet heat oil; add pignolias and garlic and cook over medium-high heat, stirring frequently, until pignolias are lightly browned, 1 to 2 minutes.

2. Add broccoli, broth, and currants. Reduce heat to medium-low, cover, and cook until broccoli is tender, 4 to 5 minutes. Add pasta and stir to combine.

APPROXIMATE TOTAL TIME: 25 MINUTES

MAKES 2 SERVINGS

Each serving provides: 1½ Fats; ½ Protein; 1 Vegetable; 1½ Breads; ½ Fruit; 10 Optional Calories
Per serving: 251 calories; 9 g protein; 9 g fat; 37 g carbohydrate; 51 mg calcium; 31 mg sodium; 0 mg cholesterol; 1 g dietary fiber (this figure does not include pignolias and broccoli florets; nutrition analyses not available)

Pasta with Double Tomato Sauce ▽C ▽F ▽S

2 teaspoons olive *or* vegetable oil
½ cup finely chopped onion
1 small garlic clove, minced
6 large plum tomatoes, blanched, peeled, seeded, and chopped
6 sun-dried tomato halves (not packed in oil), chopped
½ cup low-fat milk (1% milk fat)
1 tablespoon chopped fresh Italian (flat-leaf) parsley
1½ cups cooked penne *or* ziti macaroni (hot)

▬

While preparing the tomato sauce, you can also be cooking the pasta.

1. In 9-inch nonstick skillet heat oil; add onion and garlic and cook over medium heat until softened, about 2 minutes. Stir in plum tomatoes and sun-dried tomatoes.

2. Reduce heat to low and gradually stir in milk; stir in parsley. Cook, stirring occasionally, for 5 minutes.

3. Add pasta to tomato mixture and stir to combine.

APPROXIMATE TOTAL TIME: 30 MINUTES

MAKES 2 SERVINGS

Each serving provides: ¼ Milk; 1 Fat; 5 Vegetables; 1½ Breads; 5 Optional Calories
Per serving: 251 calories; 9 g protein; 6 g fat; 43 g carbohydrate; 117 mg calcium; 56 mg sodium; 2 mg cholesterol; 6 g dietary fiber

Variation: Pasta with Tomato Sauce—Omit sun-dried tomatoes. In Serving Information decrease Vegetables to 3½.
Per serving: 226 calories; 7 g protein; 6 g fat; 37 g carbohydrate; 108 mg calcium; 45 mg sodium; 2 mg cholesterol; 4 g dietary fiber

Pasta with Swiss Chard and Cheese ▽c ▽f ▽s

2 teaspoons olive *or* vegetable oil
1 tablespoon chopped onion
2 small garlic cloves, minced
1 cup thoroughly washed and
  drained Swiss chard,* chopped
Dash *each* black pepper and
  crushed red pepper
¼ cup canned ready-to-serve
  low-sodium chicken broth
1½ cups cooked spaghetti *or*
  linguine (hot)
2 teaspoons grated Parmesan *or*
  Romano cheese

1. In 10-inch nonstick skillet heat oil; add onion and garlic and cook over medium-high heat, stirring frequently, until onion is translucent, about 1 minute. Add Swiss chard, black pepper, and red pepper. Reduce heat to medium and cook, stirring frequently, for 2 minutes.

2. Add broth and reduce heat to low; let simmer until Swiss chard is tender-crisp, about 8 minutes.

3. Add spaghetti and toss to combine. Sprinkle with cheese.

* One cup fresh Swiss chard yields about ¼ cup cooked Swiss chard.

APPROXIMATE TOTAL TIME: 20 MINUTES

MAKES 2 SERVINGS

Each serving provides: 1 Fat; ¼ Vegetable; 1½ Breads; 15 Optional Calories
Per serving with Parmesan cheese: 208 calories; 6 g protein; 6 g fat; 32 g carbohydrate; 45 mg calcium; 78 mg sodium; 1 mg cholesterol; 2 g dietary fiber (this figure does not include Swiss chard; nutrition analysis not available)
With Romano cheese: 207 calories; 6 g protein; 6 g fat; 32 g carbohydrate; 40 mg calcium; 67 mg sodium; 2 mg cholesterol; 2 g dietary fiber (this figure does not include Swiss chard; nutrition analysis not available)

Variation: Pasta with Swiss Chard—Omit cheese. In Serving Information decrease Optional Calories to 5.
Per serving: 200 calories; 6 g protein; 5 g fat; 32 g carbohydrate; 22 mg calcium; 47 mg sodium; 0 mg cholesterol; 2 g dietary fiber (this figure does not include Swiss chard; nutrition analysis not available)

Sicilian Pasta with Peas ⬡C ⬡F

¼ cup chopped onion
1 teaspoon olive oil
1 garlic clove, minced
2 cups canned Italian tomatoes, pureed
½ cup frozen tiny peas
1 cup cooked rotelle (spiral macaroni), hot
¼ cup part-skim ricotta cheese
1 tablespoon grated Parmesan cheese

1. In shallow 1-quart microwavable casserole combine first 3 ingredients, stirring to coat; microwave on High (100%) for 1 minute.

2. Set sieve over casserole and pour pureed tomatoes through sieve into casserole, discarding solids. Add peas and stir to combine. Cover with wax paper and microwave on High for 10 minutes, stirring once every 3 minutes.

3. To serve, in serving bowl combine pasta and half of the tomato mixture and stir to combine. Top with remaining tomato mixture, the ricotta cheese, and Parmesan cheese.

APPROXIMATE TOTAL TIME: 25 MINUTES

MAKES 2 SERVINGS

Each serving provides: ½ Fat; ½ Protein; 2¼ Vegetables; 1½ Breads; 15 Optional Calories
Per serving: 240 calories; 12 g protein; 6 g fat; 35 g carbohydrate; 202 mg calcium; 541 mg sodium; 12 mg cholesterol; 4 g dietary fiber

Spicy Country Pasta and Cheese ▽C ▽F

2 tablespoons chopped onion
2 garlic cloves, minced
1 teaspoon olive oil
1 cup shiitake *or* white
  mushrooms, sliced
1 cup canned Italian tomatoes
  (reserve liquid), seeded and
  chopped
5 small pitted black cured olives,
  cut into halves
⅛ teaspoon crushed red pepper
2 cups cooked penne *or* ziti
  macaroni (hot)
2 teaspoons grated Parmesan
  cheese
Garnish: fresh basil leaves

1. In 3-quart microwavable casserole combine onion, garlic, and oil and stir to coat. Microwave on High (100%) for 1 minute. Add mushrooms and tomatoes with reserved liquid and stir to combine. Cover and microwave on High for 7 minutes, stirring once every 3 minutes.

2. Add olives and pepper and stir until thoroughly combined.

3. To serve, in serving bowl arrange pasta; top with mushroom-tomato mixture and toss to combine. Sprinkle with Parmesan cheese and garnish with basil.

APPROXIMATE TOTAL TIME: 25 MINUTES

MAKES 2 SERVINGS

Each serving provides: ¾ Fat; 2⅛ Vegetables; 2 Breads; 10 Optional Calories
Per serving: 275 calories; 10 g protein; 5 g fat; 49 g carbohydrate; 81 mg calcium; 300 mg sodium; 1 mg cholesterol; 4 g dietary fiber

Variation: Spicy Country Pasta—Omit Parmesan cheese. In Serving Information omit Optional Calories.
Per serving: 267 calories; 9 g protein; 4 g fat; 49 g carbohydrate; 58 mg calcium; 269 mg sodium; 0 mg cholesterol; 4 g dietary fiber

Greek Pasta Salad ▽C

1½ teaspoons olive oil
2 garlic cloves, cut into halves
1½ cups cooked thin spaghetti
12 cherry tomatoes, cut into halves
10 small pitted black *or* Calamata olives, cut into halves
¾ ounce feta cheese, crumbled, divided
1 tablespoon chopped fresh mint
¼ teaspoon grated lemon peel
⅛ teaspoon pepper
Garnish: mint sprig

1. In small saucepan heat oil; add garlic and cook over medium heat, until lightly browned, 1 to 2 minutes. Remove and discard garlic, reserving oil.

2. In medium mixing bowl combine spaghetti, tomatoes, olives, ½ ounce feta cheese, the mint, lemon peel, and pepper; add heated oil and toss to coat.

3. To serve, transfer spaghetti mixture to serving bowl and sprinkle with remaining feta cheese; garnish with mint sprig.

APPROXIMATE TOTAL TIME: 20 MINUTES

MAKES 2 SERVINGS

Each serving provides: 1¼ Fats; ½ Protein; 1 Vegetable; 1½ Breads
Per serving: 221 calories; 6 g protein; 9 g fat; 29 g carbohydrate; 89 mg calcium; 241 mg sodium; 9 mg cholesterol; 2 g dietary fiber

Pasta Salad with Broccoli ▽C ▽F

2 tablespoons plain low-fat
  yogurt
1 tablespoon plus 1 teaspoon
  reduced-calorie mayonnaise
1 tablespoon pickle relish
2 teaspoons red wine vinegar
1 teaspoon finely chopped shallot
  or onion
1 cup cooked shell macaroni,
  chilled
½ cup broccoli florets, blanched
2 ounces rinsed drained canned
  chick-peas
¼ cup *each* diced tomato and red
  or green bell pepper

▬

*Prepare the pasta for this dish ahead
so it will have time to chill.*

1. Using a wire whisk, in medium mixing bowl blend together first 5 ingredients; add remaining ingredients and toss to coat.

2. Cover and refrigerate until ready to serve.

APPROXIMATE TOTAL TIME: 20 MINUTES

MAKES 2 SERVINGS

Each serving provides: 1 Fat; ½ Protein; 1 Vegetable; 1 Bread; 25 Optional Calories
Per serving: 178 calories; 7 g protein; 4 g fat; 30 g carbohydrate; 60 mg calcium; 247 mg sodium (estimated); 4 mg cholesterol; 2 g dietary fiber (this figure does not include broccoli florets; nutrition analysis not available)

Spring Peas and Carrots ▽C ▽F ▽S

2 cups sugar snap peas *or* snow peas (Chinese pea pods), stem ends and strings removed
1 cup thinly sliced carrots
½ cup apple juice (no sugar added)
2 teaspoons reduced-calorie margarine (tub)
Garnish: mint sprigs

This brightly colored side dish goes from the microwave oven to the dinner table in no time.

1. In 1-quart microwavable casserole combine first 3 ingredients. Cover and microwave on High (100%) for 5 minutes, until tender-crisp.

2. Add margarine and stir to combine; microwave, uncovered, on High for 3 minutes. Let stand 1 minute.

3. To serve, transfer to serving platter and garnish with mint sprigs.

APPROXIMATE TOTAL TIME: 20 MINUTES

MAKES 2 SERVINGS

Each serving provides: ½ Fat; 3 Vegetables; ½ Fruit
Per serving: 130 calories; 5 g protein; 2 g fat; 24 g carbohydrate; 82 mg calcium; 67 mg sodium; 0 mg cholesterol; 5 g dietary fiber

Caraway Potatoes

2 teaspoons margarine
2 teaspoons all-purpose flour,
  divided
¼ cup canned ready-to-serve
  low-sodium chicken broth
1 teaspoon chopped fresh parsley
½ teaspoon caraway seed
⅛ teaspoon salt
Dash pepper
9 ounces cooked red potatoes,
  quartered
¼ cup plain low-fat yogurt

In a hurry? Use your microwave oven to cook the potatoes for this recipe in minutes.

1. In 9-inch nonstick skillet melt margarine over medium heat; add 1 teaspoon flour and stir quickly to combine. Continuing to stir, gradually add broth and cook, stirring constantly, until mixture thickens, about 1 minute.

2. Add parsley, caraway seed, salt, and pepper and stir to combine. Reduce heat to low; add potatoes and cook, stirring frequently, until potatoes are heated through, 4 to 5 minutes.

3. In small bowl combine yogurt and remaining flour, stirring to dissolve flour; stir into skillet. Cook, stirring frequently, until mixture thickens, 3 to 4 minutes.

APPROXIMATE TOTAL TIME: 30 MINUTES

MAKES 2 SERVINGS

Each serving provides: ¼ Milk; 1 Fat; 1½ Breads; 20 Optional Calories
Per serving: 170 calories; 5 g protein; 5 g fat; 27 g carbohydrate; 60 mg calcium; 220 mg sodium; 2 mg cholesterol; 2 g dietary fiber (this figure does not include caraway seed; nutrition analysis not available)

Florentine Potatoes ▽C ▽F ▽S

9 ounces pared all-purpose
   potatoes, thinly sliced
½ cup chopped onion
1 tablespoon plus 1 teaspoon
   reduced-calorie margarine (tub)
1 small garlic clove, minced
½ cup thoroughly drained cooked
   spinach
¼ cup plain low-fat yogurt
¼ teaspoon ground nutmeg

1. In 1-quart microwavable casserole combine 2 *cups water* and the potatoes. Cover and microwave on High (100%) for 10 minutes, stirring once halfway through cooking, until potatoes are soft.

2. Drain potatoes; transfer to medium mixing bowl. Using a fork, mash potatoes; set aside.

3. In same casserole combine onion, margarine, and garlic; microwave on High, uncovered, for 1 minute, stirring once halfway through cooking. Add potatoes, spinach, yogurt, and nutmeg and stir to combine. Microwave on High for 1 minute, until heated through.

APPROXIMATE TOTAL TIME: 30 MINUTES

MAKES 2 SERVINGS

Each serving provides: ¼ Milk; 1 Fat; 1 Vegetable; 1½ Breads
Per serving: 179 calories; 6 g protein; 5 g fat; 30 g carbohydrate; 134 mg calcium; 140 mg sodium; 2 mg cholesterol; 4 g dietary fiber

Garlic 'n' Onion-Mashed Potatoes ▽C ▽F ▽S

9 ounces pared all-purpose
   potatoes, cubed
¼ cup diced onion
1½ garlic cloves, chopped
¼ cup evaporated skimmed milk
2 teaspoons margarine
Dash white pepper

1. In 2-quart saucepan bring *1½ quarts water* to a boil; add potatoes, onion, and garlic and cook until potatoes are fork-tender, 10 to 15 minutes.

2. While potatoes are cooking prepare milk mixture. In small nonstick saucepan combine milk, margarine, and pepper and cook over low heat until margarine is melted. Keep warm over low heat.

3. Pour potato-onion mixture through colander, discarding cooking liquid. Transfer potato-onion mixture to large mixing bowl. Using mixer on low speed, mash potato-onion mixture. Gradually increase speed to high; add milk mixture and continue beating until potatoes are light and fluffy.

APPROXIMATE TOTAL TIME: 25 MINUTES

MAKES 2 SERVINGS

Each serving provides: ¼ Milk; 1 Fat; ¼ Vegetable; 1½ Breads
Per serving: 170 calories; 5 g protein; 4 g fat; 29 g carbohydrate; 112 mg calcium; 90 mg sodium; 1 mg cholesterol; 2 g dietary fiber

Potato Crêpes ▽C ▽F ▽S

6 ounces pared baking potato,
   shredded
½ cup grated onion
3 egg whites
1 tablespoon all-purpose flour
Dash *each* white pepper and
   ground nutmeg
2 teaspoons vegetable oil, divided
12 asparagus spears, cooked
¾ ounce reduced-fat Swiss
   cheese, shredded
¼ cup plain low-fat yogurt

1. In medium mixing bowl combine potato, onion, egg whites, flour, pepper, and nutmeg; mix well.

2. Spray 9-inch nonstick skillet with nonstick cooking spray and heat; brush with ½ teaspoon oil. Pour ¼ of potato mixture into skillet and, using the back of a spoon, spread mixture over bottom of pan; cook over medium-high heat until bottom is browned, about 1 minute. Using a pancake turner, carefully turn crêpe over and cook over medium heat until other side is browned, about 1 minute longer.

3. Repeat procedure 3 more times, using remaining oil and potato mixture and making 3 more crêpes.

4. Preheat oven to 400°F. Onto center of each crêpe arrange 3 asparagus spears; fold sides of crêpes over to enclose asparagus.

5. In 8 x 8 x 2-inch baking dish arrange crêpes, seam-side down; sprinkle with cheese. Bake until asparagus are heated through, about 10 minutes.

6. Top each crêpe with 1 tablespoon yogurt.

APPROXIMATE TOTAL TIME: 40 MINUTES (includes baking time)

MAKES 2 SERVINGS, 2 CRÊPES EACH

Each serving provides: ¼ Milk; 1 Fat; 1 Protein; 1½ Vegetables; 1 Bread; 15 Optional Calories
Per serving: 233 calories; 16 g protein; 7 g fat; 27 g carbohydrate; 223 mg calcium; 127 mg sodium; 9 mg cholesterol; 3 g dietary fiber

Scalloped Potatoes and Leeks � C � F � S

9 ounces pared all-purpose
potatoes, thinly sliced
½ cup thoroughly washed sliced
leeks (white portion and
some green)
1½ ounces reduced-fat Swiss
cheese, shredded
⅛ teaspoon *each* salt and white
pepper
½ cup canned ready-to-serve
low-sodium chicken broth

1. Preheat oven to 400°F. Spray 9-inch pie plate with nonstick cooking spray and arrange half of the potato slices in plate. Top with half of the leeks, half of the cheese, the remaining potato slices, and the remaining leeks. Sprinkle with salt and pepper and then top with remaining cheese.

2. Pour broth evenly over cheese and bake until potatoes are fork-tender, 15 to 20 minutes.

APPROXIMATE TOTAL TIME: 30 MINUTES (includes baking time)

MAKES 2 SERVINGS

Each serving provides: 1 Protein; ½ Vegetable; 1½ Breads; 10 Optional Calories
Per serving: 193 calories; 12 g protein; 5 g fat; 28 g carbohydrate; 288 mg calcium; 199 mg sodium; 15 mg cholesterol; 2 g dietary fiber

Spicy Oven-"Fried" Potato Wedges ⩔C ⩔F ⩔S

¾ **pound baking potatoes, cut
into thin wedges**
2 **teaspoons vegetable oil**
¼ **teaspoon** *each* **onion powder,
garlic powder, ground red
pepper, and black pepper**

1. Preheat oven to 450°F. Spray nonstick baking sheet with nonstick cooking spray; arrange potatoes on sheet and drizzle with oil. Turn potatoes, coating well with oil.

2. Bake for 10 minutes; turn potatoes over and bake until edges are lightly browned, about 10 minutes longer.

3. Transfer potatoes to mixing bowl; sprinkle with spices and mix well.

APPROXIMATE TOTAL TIME: 25 MINUTES (includes baking time)

MAKES 4 SERVINGS

Each serving provides: ½ Fat; 1 Bread
Per serving: 85 calories; 2 g protein; 2 g fat; 14 g carbohydrate; 12 mg calcium; 6 mg sodium; 0 mg cholesterol; 2 g dietary fiber

Waldorf Potato Salad ▽C ▽F

1 small apple (about ¼ pound), cored and cubed
1 tablespoon lemon juice
9 ounces pared cooked all-purpose potatoes, cubed
¼ cup diced celery
2 tablespoons *each* diced onion and low-fat buttermilk (1% milk fat)
1 tablespoon *each* reduced-calorie mayonnaise and apple cider vinegar
¼ teaspoon granulated sugar
⅛ teaspoon salt
Dash white pepper
¼ ounce shelled walnuts, lightly toasted and chopped

1. In medium mixing bowl combine apple and lemon juice; stir to coat. Add potatoes, celery, and onion and stir to combine; set aside.

2. In small mixing bowl combine remaining ingredients except walnuts, stirring until thoroughly combined. Pour over apple-potato mixture and stir to coat. Cover and refrigerate until flavors blend, at least 30 minutes.

3. To serve, sprinkle salad with walnuts.

APPROXIMATE TOTAL TIME: 20 MINUTES (does not include chilling time)

MAKES 2 SERVINGS

Each serving provides: 1 Fat; ¼ Protein; ¼ Vegetable; 1½ Breads; ½ Fruit; 10 Optional Calories
Per serving: 200 calories; 4 g protein; 5 g fat; 38 g carbohydrate; 45 mg calcium; 232 mg sodium; 3 mg cholesterol; 4 g dietary fiber

Fruit-Spiced Rice ▽C ▽F ▽S

2 tablespoons whipped butter
⅛ teaspoon salt
4 ounces uncooked regular long-
  grain rice
3 large dried figs, diced
6 dried apricot halves, diced
¼ teaspoon ground cinnamon
⅛ teaspoon *each* ground
  cardamom and grated lemon
  peel

1. In 1-quart saucepan combine 1 ½ *cups water*, the butter, and salt and cook over high heat until mixture comes to a boil. Add rice and stir to combine. Reduce heat to low, cover, and let simmer until rice is tender and liquid is almost absorbed, about 15 minutes.

2. Add remaining ingredients and stir to combine. Cover and cook until liquid is fully absorbed and fruits are plumped, 2 to 3 minutes.

APPROXIMATE TOTAL TIME: 25 MINUTES

MAKES 4 SERVINGS

Each serving provides: 1 Bread; 1 Fruit; 25 Optional Calories
Per serving: 157 calories; 2 g protein; 3 g fat; 30 g carbohydrate; 21 mg calcium; 101 mg sodium; 8 mg cholesterol; 1 g dietary fiber

Green Onion Rice

1 cup thoroughly washed chopped leeks (white portion and some green)
2 teaspoons olive *or* vegetable oil
2 ounces uncooked regular long-grain rice
1½ cups canned ready-to-serve low-sodium chicken broth
½ cup diagonally sliced scallions (green onions)
2 tablespoons minced fresh chives *or* 1 tablespoon chopped chives

1. In 1-quart microwavable casserole combine leeks and oil and stir to coat; microwave on High (100%) for 4 minutes, stirring once halfway through cooking.

2. Stir in rice and broth; cover and microwave on High for 10 minutes, stirring every 4 minutes.

3. Add scallions and stir to combine; cover and microwave on High for 6 minutes until rice is tender.

4. Sprinkle with chives.

APPROXIMATE TOTAL TIME: 30 MINUTES

MAKES 2 SERVINGS

Each serving provides: 1 Fat; 1½ Vegetables; 1 Bread; 30 Optional Calories
Per serving: 204 calories; 5 g protein; 6 g fat; 33 g carbohydrate; 54 mg calcium; 53 mg sodium; 0 mg cholesterol; 2 g dietary fiber

Mushroom Risotto ▽C ▽F

¼ cup chopped onion
1 teaspoon olive oil
1 garlic clove, minced
3 ounces uncooked short-grain rice (arborio rice)
½ cup quartered mushrooms
2 sun-dried tomato halves (not packed in oil), chopped
1 packet instant vegetable broth and seasoning mix
1 tablespoon *each* grated Parmesan cheese and whipped butter
Garnish: rosemary sprig

▬

Arborio rice is a short-grained rice from Northern Italy that is traditionally used to prepare risotto.

1. In 1-quart microwavable casserole combine first 3 ingredients and stir to coat; microwave on High (100%) for 1 minute, until onion is softened. Stir in rice and microwave on High for 30 seconds.

2. Stir in 1¾ *cups water*, the mushrooms, tomato, and broth mix. Cover and microwave on High for 15 minutes, stirring every 2 minutes, until rice is tender and liquid is absorbed.

3. Add cheese and butter and stir to combine. Transfer to serving bowl and garnish with rosemary.

APPROXIMATE TOTAL TIME: 25 MINUTES

MAKES 2 SERVINGS

Each serving provides: ½ Fat; 1¼ Vegetables; 1½ Breads; 45 Optional Calories
Per serving: 239 calories; 6 g protein; 6 g fat; 39 g carbohydrate; 59 mg calcium; 465 mg sodium; 10 mg cholesterol; 2 g dietary fiber

Rice-Vermicelli Pilaf ▽C ▽F

1 teaspoon margarine
¾ ounce uncooked vermicelli (thin spaghetti), broken into ½-inch pieces
2 ounces uncooked regular long-grain rice
1 packet instant onion broth and seasoning mix
1 teaspoon chopped fresh mint
⅛ teaspoon white pepper

1. In 2-quart nonstick saucepan melt margarine; add vermicelli and cook over medium heat, stirring frequently, until vermicelli is lightly browned, 1 to 2 minutes. Add *1 cup water* and the remaining ingredients and stir to combine; cover and bring mixture to a boil.

2. Reduce heat to low, cover, and let simmer until rice is tender and liquid is absorbed, 10 to 15 minutes.

APPROXIMATE TOTAL TIME: 20 MINUTES

MAKES 2 SERVINGS

Each serving provides: ½ Fat; 1½ Breads; 5 Optional Calories
Per serving: 165 calories; 4 g protein; 2 g fat; 32 g carbohydrate; 11 mg calcium; 406 mg sodium; 0 mg cholesterol; 1 g dietary fiber

Rice with Sun-Dried Tomatoes ⟨C⟩ ⟨F⟩ ⟨S⟩

½ cup chopped onion
1 teaspoon vegetable oil
2 small garlic cloves, minced
4 sun-dried tomato halves (not packed in oil), diced
2 ounces uncooked regular long-grain rice
1 tablespoon chopped fresh parsley

1. In 1-quart microwavable casserole combine onion, oil, and garlic and stir to coat. Cover and microwave on High (100%) for 1 minute, until onion is softened.

2. Add tomatoes, rice, and 1¼ cups water. Cover and microwave on High for 20 minutes.

3. Let stand, covered, for 2 to 3 minutes, until liquid is absorbed. Stir in parsley.

APPROXIMATE TOTAL TIME: 30 MINUTES

MAKES 2 SERVINGS

Each serving provides: ½ Fat; 1½ Vegetables; 1 Bread
Per serving: 157 calories; 3 g protein; 3 g fat; 30 g carbohydrate; 30 mg calcium; 10 mg sodium; 0 mg cholesterol; 2 g dietary fiber

Variation: Rice with Tomatoes—Substitute ½ cup drained canned Italian tomatoes, seeded and chopped, for the sun-dried tomatoes. In Serving Information decrease Vegetables to 1.
Per serving: 153 calories; 3 g protein; 3 g fat; 29 g carbohydrate; 40 mg calcium; 101 mg sodium; 0 mg cholesterol; 1 g dietary fiber

Spinach and Cheddar Rice (C) (F) (S)

- **2 tablespoons chopped scallion (green onion)**
- **3 ounces uncooked regular long-grain rice**
- **2 teaspoons *each* reduced-calorie margarine (tub) and all-purpose flour**
- **½ cup low-fat milk (1% milk fat)**
- **¾ ounce sharp reduced-fat Cheddar cheese, shredded**
- **¼ cup thawed frozen chopped spinach**

1. In 1-quart saucepan combine *1¼ cups water* and the scallion; cover and cook over high heat until mixture comes to a boil. Stir in rice.

2. Reduce heat to low, re-cover, and let simmer until rice is tender and liquid is absorbed, about 15 minutes.

3. While rice is cooking prepare sauce. In small nonstick saucepan melt margarine over high heat. Sprinkle flour over margarine and stir quickly to combine; cook, stirring constantly, for 1 minute.

4. Stir in milk. Reduce heat to medium and cook, stirring frequently, until mixture thickens, about 5 minutes. Stir in cheese and cook until cheese melts.

5. Add spinach to rice mixture and stir to combine. Pour cheese mixture over spinach-rice mixture and stir to combine.

APPROXIMATE TOTAL TIME: 25 MINUTES

MAKES 2 SERVINGS

Each serving provides: ¼ Milk; ½ Fat; ½ Protein; ¼ Vegetable; 1½ Breads; 15 Optional Calories
Per serving: 248 calories; 9 g protein; 5 g fat; 41 g carbohydrate; 213 mg calcium; 168 mg sodium; 10 mg cholesterol; 1 g dietary fiber

Vegetable Risotto ⟨C⟩ ⟨F⟩

2 cups *each* sliced mushrooms and thoroughly washed chopped leeks (white portion only) *or* onions

1 cup chopped red bell peppers

1 tablespoon plus 1 teaspoon olive *or* vegetable oil

4 ounces uncooked short-grain rice (arborio rice)

2 packets instant chicken broth and seasoning mix, dissolved in 2 cups water

1 package (9 ounces) frozen artichoke hearts (halves *or* quarters)

2 tablespoons dry white table wine *or* dry vermouth

1 tablespoon chopped fresh Italian (flat-leaf) parsley

1 teaspoon oregano leaves

1. In 2-quart microwavable casserole combine mushrooms, leeks, peppers, and oil and stir to coat; microwave on High (100%) for 2 minutes, stirring once halfway through cooking, until peppers are tender.

2. Add rice and stir to combine; microwave on High for 1 minute. Stir in dissolved broth mix and microwave on High for 8 minutes, stirring every 2 minutes.

3. Add remaining ingredients; microwave on Medium (50%) for 4 minutes, stirring once halfway through cooking, until artichokes are heated through.

APPROXIMATE TOTAL TIME: 25 MINUTES

MAKES 4 SERVINGS

Each serving provides: 1 Fat; 3½ Vegetables; 1 Bread; 10 Optional Calories
Per serving with wine: 224 calories; 6 g protein; 5 g fat; 39 g carbohydrate; 61 mg calcium; 540 mg sodium; 0 mg cholesterol; 4 g dietary fiber
With vermouth: 227 calories; 6 g protein; 5 g fat; 39 g carbohydrate; 61 mg calcium; 540 mg sodium; 0 mg cholesterol; 4 g dietary fiber

Rum-Baked Plantain ▽C ▽F ▽S

6 ounces peeled plantain
2 tablespoons dark rum
1 tablespoon lemon juice
2 teaspoons margarine, melted
1 teaspoon firmly packed light
   brown sugar
¼ teaspoon ground cinnamon

1. Preheat oven to 425°F. Cut plantain in half cross-wise, then slice each half lengthwise into thin slices. Spray 10-inch flameproof pie pan or shallow 1-quart casserole with nonstick cooking spray; arrange plantain slices in a single layer in pan. Set aside.

2. In small bowl combine ¼ *cup water* and the remaining ingredients, stirring to combine; pour evenly over plantain slices. Cover and bake until plantain slices are fork-tender, about 15 minutes.

3. Turn oven control to broil. Remove cover and broil until plantain slices are lightly browned, 1 to 2 minutes.

APPROXIMATE TOTAL TIME: 25 MINUTES (includes baking time)

MAKES 2 SERVINGS

Each serving provides: 1 Fat; 1 Bread; 50 Optional Calories
Per serving: 181 calories; 1 g protein; 4 g fat; 30 g carbohydrate; 10 mg calcium; 51 mg sodium; 0 mg cholesterol; dietary fiber data not available

Tropical Squash Rings ⬨C ⬨F ⬨S

1 acorn squash (about 1 pound)*
½ cup canned crushed pineapple (no sugar added)
⅓ cup pineapple juice (no sugar added)
2 tablespoons dark rum
2 teaspoons margarine, melted
1 teaspoon *each* all-purpose flour and firmly packed light brown sugar
⅛ teaspoon ground nutmeg

1. Preheat oven to 375°F. Cut squash in half crosswise; remove and discard seeds. Cut each squash half crosswise into 2 slices.

2. Spray 9-inch pie plate with nonstick cooking spray and arrange squash slices in plate. Fill center of each squash slice with an equal amount of pineapple.

3. In 1-cup liquid measure combine remaining ingredients, stirring to dissolve flour. Pour mixture evenly over squash slices. Bake until squash slices are fork-tender, 20 to 25 minutes.

* A 1-pound squash yields about 6 ounces cooked squash.

APPROXIMATE TOTAL TIME: 30 MINUTES (includes baking time)

MAKES 4 SERVINGS

Each serving provides: ½ Fat; ½ Bread; ½ Fruit; 25 Optional Calories
Per serving: 102 calories; 1 g protein; 2 g fat; 18 g carbohydrate; 37 mg calcium; 26 mg sodium; 0 mg cholesterol; 3 g dietary fiber

Bibb and Grapefruit Salad ⛛C ⛛S

1½ cups torn Bibb lettuce leaves
1 medium pink grapefruit (about
  1 pound), peeled and sectioned
  (reserve juice)
2 tablespoons sliced scallion
  (green onion)
1 teaspoon *each* finely chopped
  cilantro (Chinese parsley) *or*
  Italian (flat-leaf) parsley,
  peanut oil, white wine vinegar,
  and Dijon-style mustard
Dash crushed red pepper

1. Line serving platter with lettuce; decoratively arrange grapefruit over lettuce and sprinkle with scallion.

2. Using a wire whisk, in small mixing bowl beat together reserved grapefruit juice, cilantro, oil, vinegar, mustard, and pepper. Pour over salad.

APPROXIMATE TOTAL TIME: 10 MINUTES

MAKES 2 SERVINGS

Each serving provides: ½ Fat; 1½ Vegetables; 1 Fruit
Per serving: 69 calories; 1 g protein; 3 g fat; 11 g carbohydrate; 46 mg calcium; 79 mg sodium; 0 mg cholesterol; 1 g dietary fiber

Carrot-Radish Salad ⓥⒸ ⓥⒻ

2 cups shredded carrots
½ cup sliced radishes
1 tablespoon plus 1½ teaspoons
   lime juice (no sugar added)
1 tablespoon *each* finely chopped
   cilantro *or* Italian (flat-leaf)
   parsley and reduced-sodium
   soy sauce
1½ teaspoons *each* seeded and
   finely chopped jalapeño *or* chili
   pepper and finely chopped
   pared gingerroot
1 teaspoon Chinese sesame oil
½ teaspoon honey

1. In medium glass or stainless-steel bowl combine all ingredients; stir to combine. Cover and refrigerate until flavors blend, 30 minutes or overnight.

2. Stir salad just before serving.

APPROXIMATE TOTAL TIME: 15 MINUTES (does not include chilling time)

MAKES 2 SERVINGS

Each serving provides: ½ Fat; 2½ Vegetables; 5 Optional Calories
Per serving: 87 calories; 2 g protein; 3 g fat; 16 g carbohydrate; 40 mg calcium; 348 mg sodium; 0 mg cholesterol; 4 g dietary fiber

Confetti Sweet and Sour Slaw ▽C ▽F ▽S

3 cups finely shredded red
cabbage
1 cup shredded carrots
¼ cup julienne-cut (matchstick
pieces) red *or* yellow bell
pepper
2 tablespoons *each* thinly sliced
onion and celery
2 tablespoons golden raisins,
plumped
2 teaspoons vegetable oil
¾ teaspoon *each* granulated
sugar, apple cider vinegar,
and honey
¼ teaspoon lemon juice
Dash pepper

*A food processor shreds the cabbage
and carrots for this recipe with ease.*

1. In large glass or stainless-steel bowl combine all ingredients; stir to combine. Cover and refrigerate until flavors blend, 30 minutes or overnight.

2. Stir salad just before serving.

APPROXIMATE TOTAL TIME: 20 MINUTES (does not include chilling time)

MAKES 2 SERVINGS

Each serving provides: 1 Fat; 4½ Vegetables; ½ Fruit; 15 Optional Calories
Per serving: 143 calories; 3 g protein; 5 g fat; 25 g carbohydrate; 80 mg calcium; 39 mg sodium; 0 mg cholesterol; 5 g dietary fiber

Cucumber-Corn Salad ▽c ▽f ▽s

¼ cup plain low-fat yogurt
1 tablespoon plus 1 teaspoon
   reduced-calorie mayonnaise
1 tablespoon lemon juice
1 teaspoon chopped fresh dill
¼ teaspoon granulated sugar
Dash pepper
2 cups thinly sliced cucumbers
½ cup thawed frozen whole-
   kernel corn
¼ cup *each* sliced scallions (green
   onions) and diced red bell
   pepper

1. In medium mixing bowl combine first 6 ingredients, stirring until combined. Add remaining ingredients, stirring to coat.

APPROXIMATE TOTAL TIME: 10 MINUTES

MAKES 2 SERVINGS

Each serving provides: ¼ Milk; 1 Fat; 2½ Vegetables; ½ Bread; 3 Optional Calories
Per serving: 105 calories; 4 g protein; 4 g fat; 17 g carbohydrate; 80 mg calcium; 101 mg sodium; 5 mg cholesterol; 3 g dietary fiber

Cucumber, Orange, and Fennel Salad ▽C ▽S

1 tablespoon raspberry *or* rice
  vinegar
2 teaspoons olive oil
⅛ teaspoon oregano leaves
Dash pepper
3 cups chicory leaves
1 small navel orange (about 6
  ounces), peeled and sectioned
1 cup thinly sliced cucumbers
½ cup thinly sliced fennel
2 tablespoons *each* sliced radishes
  and chopped scallion (green
  onion)

The fennel you use for this salad should be the tender inner stalks of the fennel bulb, rather than the tougher outer stalks.

1. In small bowl combine *2 tablespoons water*, the vinegar, oil, oregano, and pepper; mix well and set aside.

2. Line serving platter with chicory leaves; decoratively arrange orange sections, cucumbers, fennel, radishes, and scallion over chicory. Top with vinegar mixture.

APPROXIMATE TOTAL TIME: 10 MINUTES

MAKES 2 SERVINGS

Each serving provides: 1 Fat; 4¾ Vegetables; ½ Fruit
Per serving: 144 calories; 6 g protein; 5 g fat; 23 g carbohydrate; 321 mg calcium; 153 mg sodium; 0 mg cholesterol; 7 g dietary fiber

Fennel-Olive Salad ▽c

2 cups chopped fennel
3 large pimiento-stuffed green
  olives, sliced
1 tablespoon *each* finely chopped
  Italian (flat-leaf) parsley and
  balsamic *or* red wine vinegar
1½ teaspoons olive oil
1 teaspoon oregano leaves
1 small garlic clove, mashed
Dash pepper

The licorice flavor of fennel stands out in this attractive salad.

1. In medium glass or stainless-steel bowl combine all ingredients; stir to combine. Cover and refrigerate until flavors blend, 30 minutes or overnight.

2. Stir salad just before serving.

APPROXIMATE TOTAL TIME: 10 MINUTES (does not include chilling time)

MAKES 2 SERVINGS

Each serving provides: 1 Fat; 2 Vegetables
Per serving: 60 calories; 2 g protein; 4 g fat; 4 g carbohydrate; 73 mg calcium; 249 mg sodium; 0 mg cholesterol; 1 g dietary fiber

Greek Eggplant Salad ⟨C⟩ ⟨S⟩

1 small eggplant (about ¾ pound)
1 medium red bell pepper
1 medium tomato, seeded and diced
½ cup diced green bell pepper
¼ cup sliced scallions (green onions)
6 large pitted black olives, sliced
1 small garlic clove, minced
2 tablespoons red wine vinegar
1 tablespoon *each* lemon juice and olive oil
¼ teaspoon pepper
1½ ounces feta cheese, crumbled

1. Preheat broiler. On baking sheet lined with heavy-duty foil broil eggplant and red bell pepper 4 inches from heat source, turning frequently, until charred on all sides; let stand until cool enough to handle.

2. Over small bowl to catch juice, peel eggplant and red bell pepper; reserve juice. Remove and discard stem end and seeds from red bell pepper. Cut eggplant into ½-inch cubes and dice red bell pepper.

3. In medium mixing bowl combine eggplant, red bell pepper, tomato, green bell pepper, scallions, olives, and garlic; stir well to combine and set aside.

4. In small bowl combine 2 *tablespoons water*, the vinegar, lemon juice, oil, and pepper; pour over eggplant mixture and stir to coat. Cover and refrigerate until flavors blend, at least 1 hour or overnight.

5. Onto each of 4 salad plates arrange eggplant mixture and top each portion with an equal amount of cheese.

APPROXIMATE TOTAL TIME: 20 MINUTES (does not include chilling time)

MAKES 4 SERVINGS

Each serving provides: 1 Fat; ½ Protein; 2¼ Vegetables
Per serving: 104 calories; 3 g protein; 7 g fat; 9 g carbohydrate; 93 mg calcium; 172 mg sodium; 9 mg cholesterol; 2 g dietary fiber

Green Bean and Pasta Salad (C) (F) (S)

½ cup *each* thinly sliced onion and red bell pepper strips
2 teaspoons olive oil
1 small garlic clove, minced
2 cups sliced green beans (2-inch pieces), cooked (hot)
1 cup cooked small shell macaroni (hot)
1 tablespoon balsamic *or* red wine vinegar
1 tablespoon chopped fresh basil *or* ½ teaspoon basil leaves
1½ teaspoons chopped fresh Italian (flat-leaf) parsley
Dash pepper

While you prepare this recipe in your microwave oven, cook the macaroni on top of the range.

1. In 1-quart microwavable casserole combine onion, bell pepper, oil, and garlic and stir to coat; microwave on High (100%) for 3 minutes, until bell pepper is tender-crisp, stirring once halfway through cooking.

2. Add remaining ingredients and stir to combine. Serve immediately.

APPROXIMATE TOTAL TIME: 30 MINUTES

MAKES 2 SERVINGS

Each serving provides: 1 Fat; 3 Vegetables; 1 Bread
Per serving: 175 calories; 5 g protein; 5 g fat; 29 g carbohydrate; 69 mg calcium; 10 mg sodium; 0 mg cholesterol; 4 g dietary fiber

Spicy Southwestern Salad ⬇C ⬇F ⬇S

1 cup julienne-cut (matchstick pieces) yellow straightneck squash

½ cup julienne-cut (matchstick pieces) pared jicama

1 small apple (about ¼ pound), cored and cut into matchstick pieces

2 tablespoons sliced scallion (green onion)

8 lettuce leaves

¼ cup spicy mixed vegetable juice

1 tablespoon balsamic *or* red wine vinegar

1½ teaspoons *each* chopped fresh cilantro (Chinese parsley) and fresh parsley

1 teaspoon olive oil

1 garlic clove

1. In medium bowl combine first 4 ingredients; mix well. Line serving platter with lettuce leaves; top with squash mixture.

2. In blender combine remaining ingredients and process until smooth. Pour over salad.

APPROXIMATE TOTAL TIME: 20 MINUTES

MAKES 2 SERVINGS

Each serving provides: ½ Fat; 2¾ Vegetables; ½ Fruit
Per serving: 94 calories; 2 g protein; 3 g fat; 17 g carbohydrate; 60 mg calcium; 108 mg sodium; 0 mg cholesterol; 3 g dietary fiber

Desserts, Snacks, and Beverages

Cinderella's fairy godmother turned a pumpkin into a coach. Our culinary wand does even better, turning nutritious items into sweet-tooth delights. These treats avoid the hazards of empty calories, while providing the satisfied feeling that wards off a "poor me" detour into wrong foods. Sample the magical way oats become Tropical Oatmeal Cookies and low-fat yogurt turns into a luscious treat like Fruit and Nut Pinwheels. Our beverages help you keep your eye on the nutrition goal too. Toast your efforts with a Lite Sea Breeze, using low-calorie cranberry juice as a mixer. Like many of our recipes, it's a breeze to whip up—in a whirlwind five minutes!

Chocolate-Iced Sponge Cake ⑂Ⓢ

¾ cup cake flour
1 teaspoon double-acting
  baking powder
4 eggs (at room temperature)
⅓ cup granulated sugar
1 cup plain low-fat yogurt
1 envelope (four ½-cup servings)
  reduced-calorie chocolate
  instant pudding and pie filling
  mix

1. Preheat oven to 400°F. Spray a 15 x 10½ x 1-inch jelly-roll pan with nonstick cooking spray and line with sheet of parchment paper or wax paper; spray again with nonstick cooking spray and set aside.

2. On sheet of wax paper sift together flour and baking powder; set aside.

3. Using mixer on high speed, in large mixing bowl beat eggs, gradually adding sugar 1 tablespoon at a time, until double in volume; fold in flour mixture.

4. Spread batter evenly in paper-lined pan and bake in middle of center oven rack until golden, 5 to 8 minutes (top should spring back when touched lightly with finger). Remove to wire rack and let cool.

5. While cake cools, prepare icing. In blender combine yogurt and pudding mix and process until smooth.

6. Invert cake onto work surface; remove and discard paper. Cut cake crosswise into 4 equal pieces. Spread ¼ of the yogurt mixture over each portion of cake.

7. On serving platter arrange 1 cake layer, yogurt-mixture side up; repeat with remaining 3 layers.

APPROXIMATE TOTAL TIME: 25 MINUTES (includes baking time)

MAKES 8 SERVINGS

Each serving provides: ½ Milk; ½ Protein; ½ Bread; 40 Optional Calories
Per serving: 150 calories; 6 g protein; 3 g fat; 25 g carbohydrate; 94 mg calcium; 105 mg sodium; 108 mg cholesterol; 0.2 g dietary fiber

Orange-Poppy Cupcakes ⬡

1 cup plus 2 tablespoons cake flour

1½ teaspoons double-acting baking powder

2 tablespoons *each* poppy seed and grated orange peel

3 eggs

⅓ cup plus 2 teaspoons granulated sugar

¼ cup sweet margarine, melted, cooled

1 teaspoon confectioners' sugar

Cupcakes aren't just for children. These sophisticated cupcakes bake up fast and can be stored in the freezer for when you want a special treat.

1. Preheat oven to 350°F. Line twelve 2½-inch muffin-pan cups with paper baking cups; set aside.

2. In small mixing bowl sift together flour and baking powder; stir in poppy seed and orange peel and set aside.

3. Using mixer, in large mixing bowl beat together eggs and granulated sugar on medium speed until light and fluffy; add margarine and beat until combined. Stir in flour mixture until moistened.

4. Spoon an equal amount of batter into each lined cup (each will be about ¾ full).

5. Bake in middle of center oven rack for 15 to 20 minutes (until cupcakes are golden and a toothpick, inserted in center, comes out dry). Remove cupcakes to wire rack and let cool at least 10 minutes.

6. Sift confectioners' sugar evenly over cupcakes.

APPROXIMATE TOTAL TIME: 30 MINUTES (includes baking time; does not include cooling time)

MAKES 12 SERVINGS, 1 CUPCAKE EACH

Each serving provides: 1 Fat; ¼ Protein; ½ Bread; 40 Optional Calories
Per serving: 127 calories; 3 g protein; 6 g fat; 16 g carbohydrate; 58 mg calcium; 70 mg sodium; 53 mg cholesterol; 0.2 g dietary fiber (this figure does not include poppy seed; nutrition analysis not available)

Orange Sunshine Cakes △F △S

2¼ cups cake flour
1 teaspoon baking soda
¼ cup reduced-calorie margarine (tub)
2 tablespoons margarine
⅓ cup less 1 teaspoon granulated sugar
1 cup plain low-fat yogurt
2 eggs
1 tablespoon vanilla extract
¼ cup confectioners' sugar
½ teaspoon grated orange peel

1. Preheat oven to 375°F. On sheet of wax paper sift together flour and baking soda; set aside.

2. Using electric mixer on medium speed, in large mixing bowl beat margarines until combined; gradually add granulated sugar and continue beating until mixture is light and fluffy.

3. Add yogurt, eggs, and vanilla and beat 1 minute longer; add flour mixture and beat on low speed until thoroughly combined.

4. Spray twelve 2½-inch nonstick muffin-pan cups with nonstick cooking spray and fill each cup with an equal amount of batter (about 2 tablespoons). Bake in middle of center oven rack for 15 to 20 minutes (until cakes are golden, and a cake tester, inserted in center, comes out dry). Invert cakes onto wire rack and let cool.

5. In small mixing bowl combine confectioners' sugar, *1½ teaspoons water*, and the orange peel and stir until smooth. Drizzle an equal amount of icing over each cake.

APPROXIMATE TOTAL TIME: 30 MINUTES (includes baking time)

MAKES 12 SERVINGS

Each serving provides: 1 Fat; 1 Bread; 70 Optional Calories
Per serving: 172 calories; 4 g protein; 5 g fat; 27 g carbohydrate; 43 mg calcium; 155 mg sodium; 37 mg cholesterol; 0.4 g dietary fiber

Fruit and Nut Pinwheels ⊽C ⊽S

1½ cups plus 3 tablespoons all-purpose flour, divided
¼ teaspoon salt
⅓ cup reduced-calorie margarine (tub)
½ cup plain low-fat yogurt
Water
½ cup dark raisins, chopped
2 ounces sliced almonds
¼ cup reduced-calorie orange marmalade (16 calories per 2 teaspoons)
1 tablespoon plus 1 teaspoon honey

1. In medium mixing bowl combine 1½ cups flour and the salt; using pastry blender, cut in margarine until mixture resembles coarse meal. Add yogurt and mix thoroughly, adding water by teaspoonfuls, if necessary, to form a dough. Form dough into a ball; cover with plastic wrap and refrigerate for at least 1 hour.

2. In small mixing bowl combine raisins, almonds, and marmalade; stir to combine.

3. Preheat oven to 425°F. Using remaining flour to prevent dough from sticking to work surface, roll dough into a 12 x 9-inch rectangle about ⅛ inch thick. Spread raisin mixture over rectangle. Starting from one of the wide sides, roll dough jelly-roll fashion to enclose filling and press seam to seal.

4. Using a serrated knife, cut roll crosswise into 16 equal slices. Spray nonstick baking sheet with nonstick cooking spray and place slices cut-side down on sheet. Bake in middle of center oven rack until golden, about 18 minutes.

5. Immediately drizzle ¼ teaspoon honey over each pinwheel. Remove to wire rack and let cool.

APPROXIMATE TOTAL TIME: 30 MINUTES (includes baking time; does not include chilling time)

MAKES 8 SERVINGS, 2 PINWHEELS EACH

Each serving provides: 1½ Fats; ½ Protein; 1 Bread; ½ Fruit; 45 Optional Calories
Per serving: 230 calories; 5 g protein; 8 g fat; 36 g carbohydrate; 54 mg calcium; 159 mg sodium; 1 mg cholesterol; 2 g dietary fiber

Iced Apple Turnovers ▽Ⓒ ▽Ⓢ

1 pound Granny Smith apples,
   cored, pared, and finely
   chopped
1 tablespoon lemon juice
½ teaspoon *each* granulated
   sugar and ground cinnamon
1 refrigerated ready-to-bake
   9-inch pie crust
2 tablespoons confectioners'
   sugar
1 teaspoon grated orange peel

1. Preheat oven to 425°F. In 1-quart saucepan combine apples, lemon juice, granulated sugar, and cinnamon and cook over medium heat, stirring occasionally, until apples are very soft, about 5 minutes. Remove from heat; set aside.

2. On work surface roll pie crust into a 16 x 8-inch rectangle; cut rectangle into eight 4 x 4-inch squares. Spoon an equal amount of apple mixture onto center of each square. Fold square in half, forming a triangle. Using tines of fork, press edges to seal.

3. Arrange turnovers on nonstick baking sheet and bake in middle of center oven rack until golden brown, 8 to 10 minutes. Remove to wire rack and let cool.

4. While turnovers cool, prepare icing. In small bowl combine confectioners' sugar, orange peel, and *1 teaspoon water*, mixing to form icing; decoratively drizzle icing over turnovers.

APPROXIMATE TOTAL TIME: 30 MINUTES (includes baking time)

MAKES 8 SERVINGS, 1 TURNOVER EACH

Each serving provides: ½ Bread; ½ Fruit; 65 Optional Calories
Per serving: 157 calories; 1 g protein; 8 g fat; 22 g carbohydrate; 4 mg calcium; 155 mg sodium; 0 mg cholesterol; 1 g dietary fiber (this figure does not include pie crust; nutrition analysis not available)

Quick Rugalach (Raisin Crescents) ▽C ▽S

½ cup dark raisins
2 ounces shelled walnuts *or*
  blanched almonds
1 tablespoon granulated sugar
1 teaspoon ground cinnamon
1 refrigerated ready-to-bake
  9-inch pie crust
1 teaspoon confectioners' sugar

1. Preheat oven to 425°F. In food processor combine first 4 ingredients and, using on-off motion, process until nuts are finely chopped; set aside.

2. On work surface cut pie crust into 16 equal wedges. Spoon an equal amount of raisin-nut mixture evenly over each wedge; roll each wedge from curved end toward point. Place crescents on nonstick cookie sheet, point-side down, and shape each into a half moon.

3. Bake in middle of center oven rack until cookies are golden, 8 to 10 minutes. Transfer to wire rack and let cool.

4. Sift confectioners' sugar evenly over crescents.

APPROXIMATE TOTAL TIME: 30 MINUTES (includes baking time)

MAKES 8 SERVINGS, 2 RUGALACH EACH

Each serving provides: ½ Fat; ½ Protein; ½ Bread; ½ Fruit; 60 Optional Calories
Per serving with walnuts: 200 calories; 2 g protein; 12 g fat; 23 g carbohydrate; 15 mg calcium; 157 mg sodium; 0 mg cholesterol; 1 g dietary fiber (this figure does not include pie crust; nutrition analysis not available)
With almonds: 197 calories; 3 g protein; 11 g fat; 23 g carbohydrate; 25 mg calcium; 157 mg sodium; 0 mg cholesterol; 0.5 g dietary fiber (this figure does not include almonds and pie crust; nutrition analyses not available)

Orange-Poppy Seed Cookies ⱽⓒ ⱽⓢ

¼ cup reduced-calorie sweet
  margarine (tub)
3 tablespoons granulated sugar
1 tablespoon plus 1½ teaspoons
  poppy seed
1 teaspoon *each* grated orange
  peel and orange juice (no sugar
  added)
½ cup plus 1 tablespoon all-
  purpose flour
½ teaspoon double-acting baking
  powder

*Prepare the dough for these cookies
in advance and it can be refrigerated
overnight.*

1. Using mixer, in medium mixing bowl beat together margarine and sugar on medium speed until light and fluffy; add poppy seed, orange peel, and orange juice and stir to combine (mixture may appear curdled).

2. In small mixing bowl combine flour and baking powder and stir well to combine; add margarine mixture, 2 tablespoonfuls at a time, mixing well after each addition, until mixture forms smooth dough but is not sticky. Cover dough with plastic wrap and refrigerate at least 30 minutes.

3. Preheat oven to 375°F. Divide dough into 6 equal portions and, using hands, shape each portion into a ball; arrange balls on nonstick cookie sheet, leaving a space of about 1 inch between each. Using the tines of a fork, slightly press each cookie to flatten, then press down in opposite direction to create a checkerboard pattern.

4. Bake in middle of center oven rack until cookies are golden, 10 to 15 minutes. Transfer to wire rack and let cool.

APPROXIMATE TOTAL TIME: 25 MINUTES (includes baking time; does not include chilling time)

MAKES 6 SERVINGS, 1 COOKIE EACH

Each serving provides: 1 Fat; ½ Bread; 45 Optional Calories
Per serving: 113 calories; 2 g protein; 5 g fat; 16 g carbohydrate; 52 mg calcium; 36 mg sodium; 0 mg cholesterol; 0.3 g dietary fiber (this figure does not include poppy seed; nutrition analysis not available)

Tropical Oatmeal Cookies ▽C ▽S

6 ounces uncooked quick oats
¾ cup all-purpose flour
⅓ cup plus 2 teaspoons dark
  raisins
¼ cup granulated sugar
2 tablespoons shredded coconut
1 ounce chopped walnuts
½ teaspoon baking soda
⅓ cup plus 1 tablespoon plus
  1 teaspoon reduced-calorie
  sweet margarine (tub), melted,
  cooled
¼ cup thawed frozen egg
  substitute
1 teaspoon vanilla extract

1. Preheat oven to 375°F. In large mixing bowl combine first 7 ingredients; set aside.

2. In small mixing bowl combine remaining ingredients; add to oat mixture and stir to combine.

3. Using half of dough, drop dough by tablespoonfuls onto nonstick cookie sheet, forming 12 equal cookies and leaving a space of about 1 inch between each. Bake in middle of center oven rack until cookies are golden, 10 to 12 minutes. Transfer cookies to wire rack and let cool (cookies will harden as they cool).

4. Using a cooled cookie sheet, repeat procedure 1 more time, making 12 more cookies.

APPROXIMATE TOTAL TIME: 20 MINUTES (includes baking time)

MAKES 12 SERVINGS, 2 COOKIES EACH

Each serving provides: 1 Fat; ¼ Protein; 1 Bread; ¼ Fruit; 25 Optional Calories
Per serving: 163 calories; 4 g protein; 6 g fat; 24 g carbohydrate; 15 mg calcium; 44 mg sodium; 0 mg cholesterol; 2 g dietary fiber

Canadian Maple-Walnut Chiffon ⬇Ⓢ

1½ teaspoons unflavored gelatin
½ cup evaporated skimmed milk
2 eggs, separated
2 tablespoons maple syrup
1 teaspoon imitation maple extract
⅛ teaspoon cream of tartar
½ cup thawed frozen dairy whipped topping
1 ounce chopped walnuts (reserve 1 tablespoon plus 1 teaspoon for garnish)

1. In 1-quart saucepan sprinkle gelatin over milk and let stand 1 minute to soften; cook over low heat, stirring frequently, until gelatin is completely dissolved.

2. Using a wire whisk, in small mixing bowl lightly beat egg yolks; gradually beat in ¼ cup of the gelatin-milk mixture. Gradually stir egg yolk–milk mixture back into saucepan and cook, stirring constantly, until mixture thickens slightly, about 1 minute (do not boil).

3. Remove from heat; stir in maple syrup and extract. Pour egg yolk–milk mixture into large mixing bowl and set aside.

4. Using electric mixer on high speed, in medium mixing bowl beat egg whites until foamy; add cream of tartar and continue beating until whites are stiff but not dry.

5. Gently fold beaten whites into egg yolk–milk mixture; fold in whipped topping and walnuts.

6. Into each of four 6-ounce custard cups or dessert dishes spoon ¼ of chiffon. Top each portion with 1 teaspoon of the reserved walnuts. Cover and refrigerate until set, about 2 hours.

APPROXIMATE TOTAL TIME: 20 MINUTES (does not include chilling time)

MAKES 4 SERVINGS

Each serving provides: ¼ Milk; ½ Fat; 1 Protein; 55 Optional Calories
Per serving: 161 calories; 7 g protein; 9 g fat; 14 g carbohydrate; 122 mg calcium; 81 mg sodium; 108 mg cholesterol; 0.3 g dietary fiber

Lemon-Raspberry Cloud ▽C ▽F ▽S

¼ cup freshly squeezed lemon juice
2 tablespoons thawed frozen concentrated orange juice (no sugar added)
1 tablespoon granulated sugar
½ teaspoon grated lemon peel
1 teaspoon unflavored gelatin
½ cup thawed frozen dairy whipped topping
3 egg whites
¼ teaspoon cream of tartar
½ cup raspberries
Garnish: lemon zest*

1. In small nonstick saucepan combine lemon juice, ¼ *cup water*, the orange juice, sugar, and lemon peel; sprinkle gelatin over juice mixture and let stand 1 minute to soften. Stir mixture to combine; cook over low heat, stirring frequently, until gelatin is dissolved, 1 to 2 minutes.

2. Transfer mixture to large mixing bowl; stir in whipped topping and set aside.

3. Using mixer on high speed, in large mixing bowl beat egg whites until frothy; add cream of tartar and continue beating until whites are stiff but not dry. Gently fold egg whites into gelatin mixture until mixture is thoroughly combined.

4. Into each of four 6-ounce dessert dishes pour ¼ of gelatin mixture. Cover and refrigerate until firm, at least 1 hour (when gelatin mixture is chilled it will form 2 layers). Garnish each portion with 2 tablespoons raspberries and lemon zest.

* The zest of the lemon is the peel without any of the pith (white membrane). To remove zest from lemon, use a zester or vegetable peeler; wrap lemon in plastic wrap and refrigerate for use at another time.

APPROXIMATE TOTAL TIME: 15 MINUTES (does not include chilling time)

MAKES 4 SERVINGS

Each serving provides: ¼ Protein; ½ Fruit; 40 Optional Calories
Per serving: 76 calories; 4 g protein; 2 g fat; 12 g carbohydrate; 9 mg calcium; 52 mg sodium; 0 mg cholesterol; 1 g dietary fiber

Rum-Raisin Custard C F S

2 cups skim *or* nonfat milk
1 cup thawed frozen egg
   substitute
⅓ cup plus 2 teaspoons all-
   purpose flour
¼ cup granulated sugar
2 tablespoons dark rum
1 teaspoon vanilla extract
1 cup golden raisins
2 ounces sliced almonds

Custard can be refrigerated over-
night to chill.

1. Preheat oven to 375°F. In blender combine first 6 ingredients and process until smooth. Spray 9-inch pie plate with nonstick cooking spray and pour milk mixture into plate. Add raisins and stir to combine; sprinkle with almonds.

2. Bake for 25 minutes (until a knife, inserted in center, comes out dry). Transfer to wire rack and let cool. Refrigerate until ready to serve.

APPROXIMATE TOTAL TIME: 30 MINUTES (in-cludes baking time)

MAKES 8 SERVINGS

Each serving provides: ¼ Milk; ½ Fat; 1 Protein; ¼ Bread; 1 Fruit; 40 Optional Calories
Per serving: 186 calories; 7 g protein; 4 g fat; 30 g carbohydrate; 115 mg calcium; 75 mg sodium; 1 mg cholesterol; 1 g dietery fiber

Apple-Wheat Bread Pudding ⬇C ⬇F

1 cup low-fat milk (1% milk fat)
½ cup *each* thawed frozen egg
   substitute and applesauce (no
   sugar added)
⅓ cup instant nonfat dry milk
   powder
2 tablespoons granulated sugar
1 teaspoon vanilla extract
½ teaspoon ground cinnamon
4 slices reduced-calorie wheat
   bread (40 calories per slice),
   cut into cubes
1 small apple (about ¼ pound),
   cored, pared, and diced
¼ cup thawed frozen dairy
   whipped topping

---

*Old-fashioned bread pudding with
the nutrition of wheat bread.*

1. In medium mixing bowl beat together milk, egg substitute, applesauce, milk powder, sugar, vanilla, and cinnamon until thoroughly combined. Set aside.

2. Into each of four 10-ounce microwavable custard cups arrange ¼ of the bread cubes and apple. Pour ¼ of milk mixture into each custard cup, being sure to moisten bread cubes.

3. Cover cups; fill 4 x 10-inch microwavable baking dish with water to a depth of about 1 inch and set cups in dish. Microwave on Medium (50%) for 20 minutes, rotating dish ½ turn halfway through cooking (until a knife, inserted in center, comes out dry).

4. Remove cups from water bath; set cups on wire rack and let cool at least 5 minutes. Serve each pudding topped with 1 tablespoon whipped topping.

APPROXIMATE TOTAL TIME: 30 MINUTES (does not include cooling time)

MAKES 4 SERVINGS

Each serving provides: ½ Milk; ½ Protein; ½ Bread; ½ Fruit; 50 Optional Calories
Per serving: 169 calories; 9 g protein; 2 g fat; 30 g carbohydrate; 183 mg calcium; 215 mg sodium; 3 mg cholesterol; 1 g dietary fiber

Chunky Chocolate Pudding ▽C

2 cups skim *or* nonfat milk
1 envelope (four ½-cup servings)
reduced-calorie instant
chocolate pudding mix
1¼ ounces mini chocolate chips
1 ounce shelled walnuts, toasted
and chopped
¼ cup thawed frozen dairy
whipped topping
1 teaspoon chocolate syrup

1. Using milk, prepare pudding according to package directions. Cover and refrigerate until soft set, about 30 minutes.

2. Stir in chocolate chips and walnuts. Into each of four 6-ounce dessert dishes spoon ¼ of the pudding; top each with 1 tablespoon whipped topping and then drizzle ¼ teaspoon chocolate syrup over whipped topping. Refrigerate until ready to serve.

APPROXIMATE TOTAL TIME: 10 MINUTES (does not include chilling time)

MAKES 4 SERVINGS

Each serving provides: 1 Milk; ½ Fat; ½ Protein; 65 Optional Calories
Per serving: 183 calories; 6 g protein; 9 g fat; 22 g carbohydrate; 164 mg calcium; 321 mg sodium; 2 mg cholesterol; 0.3 g dietary fiber (this figure does not include pudding mix, chocolate, and syrup; nutrition analyses not available)

Double Chocolate-Nut Treat ▽C

2 cups skim *or* nonfat milk
1 envelope (four ½-cup servings) reduced-calorie instant chocolate pudding mix
½ cup thawed frozen dairy whipped topping
1 tablespoon chocolate syrup
1 ounce shelled almonds, toasted and chopped
2 maraschino cherries, cut into halves

1. Using milk, prepare pudding according to package directions. Into each of four 6-ounce dessert dishes spoon ¼ of the pudding; set aside.

2. In small mixing bowl combine whipped topping and syrup; stir to combine. Spread ¼ of whipped topping mixture over each portion of pudding.

3. Sprinkle each dessert with ¼ of the almonds and then top each with a cherry half. Cover and refrigerate at least 30 minutes.

APPROXIMATE TOTAL TIME: 15 MINUTES (does not include chilling time)

MAKES 4 SERVINGS

Each serving provides: 1 Milk; ½ Fat; ½ Protein; 45 Optional Calories
Per serving: 155 calories; 6 g protein; 6 g fat; 21 g carbohydrate; 174 mg calcium; 329 mg sodium; 2 mg cholesterol; 0.3 g dietary fiber (this figure does not include pudding mix and chocolate syrup; nutrition analyses not available)

Variation: Double Chocolate Treat—Omit almonds from recipe. In Serving Information omit ½ Protein and ½ Fat.
Per serving: 113 calories; 5 g protein; 3 g fat; 19 g carbohydrate; 156 mg calcium; 328 mg sodium; 2 mg cholesterol; dietary fiber data not available

Mocha Pudding Pie ▽C

12 graham crackers (2½-inch squares), made into crumbs
1 ounce ground walnuts
2 tablespoons margarine, softened
½ cup plain low-fat yogurt, divided
1 cup skim *or* nonfat milk, divided
2 teaspoons instant espresso coffee powder
1 envelope (four ½-cup servings) reduced-calorie chocolate instant pudding mix
½ cup thawed frozen dairy whipped topping
½ ounce semisweet chocolate, shaved
½ cup raspberries

1. In medium mixing bowl combine graham cracker crumbs and walnuts; with pastry blender, cut in margarine until mixture resembles coarse crumbs. Remove ¼ cup crumb mixture and set aside. Using a fork, add 2 tablespoons yogurt to crumb mixture in mixing bowl and mix thoroughly.

2. Using the back of a spoon, press crumb-yogurt mixture over bottom and up sides of 9-inch microwavable pie plate. Microwave on High (100%) for 4 minutes, rotating plate ½ turn halfway through cooking. Cover pie plate with foil and freeze until ready to fill.

3. In medium microwavable mixing bowl microwave 2 tablespoons milk on High for 15 seconds; add espresso and, using a wire whisk, stir to dissolve. Stir in remaining yogurt, then stir in remaining milk. Add pudding mix, stirring to dissolve.

4. Pour pudding mixture into cooled crust. Sprinkle reserved crumb mixture around edge of pudding mixture. Refrigerate for at least 1 hour.

5. To serve, cut pie into 8 equal wedges and set each wedge on a dessert plate. Top each portion with 1 tablespoon whipped topping and ⅛ of the chocolate shavings. Garnish each portion with 1 tablespoon raspberries.

APPROXIMATE TOTAL TIME: 25 MINUTES (does not include chilling time)

MAKES 8 SERVINGS

Each serving provides: ½ Milk; 1 Fat; ¼ Protein; ½ Bread; 30 Optional Calories
Per serving: 151 calories; 4 g protein; 8 g fat; 18 g carbohydrate; 77 mg calcium; 261 mg sodium; 1 mg cholesterol; 1 g dietary fiber (this figure does not include pudding mix and chocolate; nutrition analyses not available)

Mint Julep Sorbet ▽C ▽F ▽S

1½ cups packed fresh mint, divided (reserve 8 mint sprigs for garnish)
⅓ cup granulated sugar
2 tablespoons bourbon
1 teaspoon lemon juice

Celebrate the Kentucky Derby with Mint Julep Sorbet.

1. In 1-quart saucepan combine *2 cups water*, 1 cup mint, and the sugar. Cook over high heat, stirring occasionally, until mixture comes to a boil. Reduce heat to medium and continue to boil until mixture has a syrupy consistency, about 5 minutes.

2. Set sieve over 8 x 8 x 2-inch freezer-safe pan and pour mint mixture through sieve into pan, discarding solids. Set aside and let cool for 15 minutes.

3. Finely chop remaining mint and add to mint mixture; add bourbon and lemon juice and stir to combine. Cover and freeze until frozen, about 3 hours.

4. Into 8 dessert dishes scoop an equal amount of sorbet; garnish each portion with a mint sprig.

APPROXIMATE TOTAL TIME: 25 MINUTES (does not include freezing time)

MAKES 8 SERVINGS

Each serving provides: 50 Optional Calories
Per serving: 43 calories; 0.1 g protein; 0.1 g fat; 9 g carbohydrate; 7 mg calcium; 0.2 mg sodium; 0 mg cholesterol; dietary fiber data not available

Piña Colada Ice

12 ounces pineapple, pared and
 sliced, *or* 1 cup canned
 pineapple chunks (no sugar
 added)
1 medium banana (about
 6 ounces), peeled
1½ cups low-fat buttermilk
 (1% milk fat)
2 tablespoons light rum
1 tablespoon plus 1 teaspoon
 each granulated sugar and
 shredded coconut, toasted

1. In blender combine all ingredients except coconut
and process until smooth. Transfer to 1-quart freezer-
safe bowl; stir in coconut. Cover and freeze until solid,
about 3 hours.

**APPROXIMATE TOTAL TIME: 15 MINUTES (does
not include freezing time)**

MAKES 4 SERVINGS

Each serving provides: ¼ Milk; 1 Fruit; 70 Optional Calories
Per serving: 120 calories; 4 g protein; 2 g fat; 21 g carbohydrate; 111 mg calcium; 101 mg sodium; 4 mg cholesterol; 1 g dietary fiber

Calypso Plantain Dessert (C) (F) (S)

6 ounces peeled plantain, sliced crosswise
¼ cup *each* canned crushed pineapple (no sugar added) and orange juice (no sugar added)
1 teaspoon margarine, melted
½ teaspoon cornstarch
½ ounce finely chopped almonds
2 tablespoons shredded coconut
1 teaspoon firmly packed light brown sugar
½ cup plain low-fat yogurt

1. Preheat oven to 375°F. Spray 10-inch pie pan with nonstick cooking spray; arrange plantain slices in an even layer in bottom of pan. Spread pineapple evenly over plantain slices.

2. In 1-cup liquid measure combine orange juice, margarine, and cornstarch, stirring to dissolve cornstarch; pour evenly over pineapple.

3. In small mixing bowl combine almonds, coconut, and sugar and sprinkle evenly over pineapple. Bake until plantain is soft and coconut mixture is lightly browned, 15 to 20 minutes.

4. To serve, into each of two 6-ounce dessert dishes spoon half of the plantain mixture, then top each with ¼ cup yogurt. Drizzle pan juices over yogurt.

APPROXIMATE TOTAL TIME: 30 MINUTES (includes baking time)

MAKES 2 SERVINGS

Each serving provides: ½ Milk; 1 Fat; ½ Protein; 1 Bread; ½ Fruit; 45 Optional Calories
Per serving: 264 calories; 6 g protein; 8 g fat; 46 g carbohydrate; 136 mg calcium; 79 mg sodium; 3 mg cholesterol; 1 g dietary fiber (this figure does not include plantain; nutrition analysis not available)

Fig and Melon Compote ▽C ▽F ▽S

¼ cup freshly squeezed orange
   juice
2 tablespoons freshly squeezed
   lime juice
1 tablespoon chopped fresh mint
1 teaspoon honey
1 cup seeded and diced melon
   (cantaloupe *or* crenshaw)
1 large fresh fig (2 ounces), cut
   in half and sliced
Garnish: 2 mint sprigs

1. In medium mixing bowl combine first 4 ingredients, stirring to dissolve honey; add melon and fig and stir to coat. Cover and refrigerate until flavors blend, at least 30 minutes.

2. To serve, into each of two 6-ounce dessert dishes spoon half of the fruit mixture and garnish each portion with a mint sprig.

APPROXIMATE TOTAL TIME: 10 MINUTES (does not include chilling time)

MAKES 2 SERVINGS

Each serving provides: 1¼ Fruits; 10 Optional Calories
Per serving: 78 calories; 1 g protein; 0.4 g fat; 20 g carbohydrate; 25 mg calcium; 8 mg sodium; 0 mg cholesterol; 1 g dietary fiber (this figure does not include melon and fig; nutrition analyses not available)

Peaches and Kiwi in Champagne ⛛C ⛛F ⛛S

¾ pound peaches, pitted and thinly sliced
1 medium kiwi fruit (about ¼ pound), pared and sliced
¼ cup dry champagne
Garnish:
  2 mint sprigs
  1 tablespoon *each* julienne-cut (matchstick pieces) lime and orange zests*

This elegant dessert is completed in a mere 15 minutes and can be refrigerated overnight to chill.

1. In bowl combine all ingredients except garnish. Cover and refrigerate until chilled, at least 30 minutes.

2. Garnish with mint sprigs and zests before serving.

* The zest is the peel without any of the pith (white membrane). To remove zest from lime and orange, use a zester or vegetable peeler; wrap lime and orange in plastic wrap and refrigerate for use at another time.

APPROXIMATE TOTAL TIME: 15 MINUTES (does not include chilling time)

MAKES 2 SERVINGS

Each serving provides: 1½ Fruits; 25 Optional Calories
Per serving: 99 calories; 1 g protein; 0.3 g fat; 20 g carbohydrate; 19 mg calcium; 3 mg sodium; 0 mg cholesterol; 3 g dietary fiber

Cinnamon Crisp Tortillas ♥C ♥S

2 flour tortillas (6-inch diameter each)
2 teaspoons reduced-calorie margarine (tub), melted, divided
½ teaspoon *each* ground cinnamon, divided, and granulated sugar

---

Serve with fresh fruit for a satisfying snack.

1. Preheat broiler. Arrange tortillas on nonstick baking sheet and brush each tortilla with ¼ of the margarine and sprinkle with ¼ of the cinnamon. Broil 6 inches from heat source until margarine is bubbly, 1 to 2 minutes.

2. Combine remaining cinnamon with the sugar. Turn tortillas over; brush each with half of the remaining margarine and then sprinkle each with half of the cinnamon-sugar mixture. Broil until cinnamon-sugar mixture caramelizes, about 1 minute.

APPROXIMATE TOTAL TIME: 10 MINUTES

MAKES 2 SERVINGS, 1 TORTILLA EACH

Each serving provides: ½ Fat; 1 Bread; 5 Optional Calories
Per serving: 92 calories; 2 g protein; 4 g fat; 13 g carbohydrate; 47 mg calcium; 180 mg sodium; 0 mg cholesterol; 1 g dietary fiber

Garlic Bagel Chips $\vee_C$ $\vee_S$

4 small bagels (1 ounce each)
1 tablespoon plus 1 teaspoon
   olive oil, divided
¼ teaspoon *each* garlic powder
   and onion powder

1. Preheat oven to 275°F. Cut bagels horizontally into very thin slices and arrange in a single layer on a nonstick baking sheet. Using a pastry brush, lightly brush 2 teaspoons oil over tops of bagel slices.

2. In small mixing bowl combine garlic and onion powders and sprinkle half of the mixture evenly over bagel slices. Bake for 20 minutes.

3. Increase oven temperature to 425°F. Turn bagel slices over and repeat procedure using remaining oil and garlic-onion powder mixture. Bake until bagel slices are lightly browned, 5 to 10 minutes longer.

APPROXIMATE TOTAL TIME: 40 MINUTES (includes baking time)

MAKES 4 SERVINGS

Each serving provides: 1 Fat; 1 Bread
Per serving: 115 calories; 3 g protein; 5 g fat; 15 g carbohydrate; 11 mg calcium; 175 mg sodium; 0 mg cholesterol; 1 g dietary fiber

Cranberry Cooler ▽C ▽F ▽S

¾ **cup seltzer**
½ **cup dry white *or* rosé table wine**
⅓ **cup cranberry juice**
1 **teaspoon lemon juice**
6 **ice cubes**
2 **lemon slices**

1. In 2-cup pitcher or small mixing bowl combine all ingredients except ice and lemon slices; stir well.

2. Into each of two 8-ounce cocktail glasses place 3 ice cubes; add half of the juice mixture to each glass. Garnish each portion with a lemon slice.

APPROXIMATE TOTAL TIME: 5 MINUTES

MAKES 2 SERVINGS, ABOUT ¾ CUP EACH

Each serving provides: ½ Fruit; 50 Optional Calories
Per serving with white wine: 67 calories; 0.2 g protein; 0.1 g fat; 8 g carbohydrate; 15 mg calcium; 5 mg sodium; 0 mg cholesterol; dietary fiber data not available
With rosé wine: 69 calories; 0.3 g protein; 0.1 g fat; 8 g carbohydrate; 14 mg calcium; 5 mg sodium; 0 mg cholesterol; dietary fiber data not available

Lite Sea Breeze ▽C ▽F ▽S

2 cups low-calorie cranberry juice
2 tablespoons plus 2 teaspoons
  vodka *or* gin
12 ice cubes
Garnish:
  1 lemon slice, cut in half
  2 mint sprigs

1. In 3-cup pitcher or small mixing bowl combine juice and vodka.

2. Into each of two 12-ounce glasses place half of the ice cubes; add half of the juice mixture to each glass. Garnish each portion with ½ lemon slice and a mint sprig.

APPROXIMATE TOTAL TIME: 5 MINUTES

MAKES 2 SERVINGS, ABOUT 1 CUP EACH

Each serving provides: 1 Fruit; 50 Optional Calories
Per serving: 91 calories 0.2 g protein; trace fat; 13 g carbohydrate; 30 mg calcium; 8 mg sodium; 0 mg cholesterol; dietary fiber data not available

Cherry-Vanilla "Ice Cream" Soda ⛛C ⛛F ⛛S

1 packet reduced-calorie vanilla-
  flavored dairy drink mix
6 ice cubes
1 cup reduced-calorie black
  cherry soda (2 calories per
  6 fluid ounces)
½ cup vanilla ice milk
2 maraschino cherries

1. In blender combine ½ *cup cold water* and the drink mix and process on low speed until combined. Add ice cubes, 1 at a time, and process on high speed after each addition until mixture is thick and frothy.

2. Turn blender off; add soda. Process on low speed until thoroughly combined.

3. Into each of two 12-ounce glasses pour half of the drink mix–soda mixture; add ¼ cup ice milk to each glass. Top each with a cherry and serve immediately.

APPROXIMATE TOTAL TIME: 5 MINUTES

MAKES 2 SERVINGS

Each serving provides: ½ Milk; 70 Optional Calories
Per serving: 84 calories; 4 g protein; 1 g fat; 14 g carbohydrate; 119 mg calcium; 60 mg sodium; 0 mg cholesterol; dietary fiber data not available

MENU PLANNERS

—On a treasure hunt for new and exciting menu ideas?
—Too busy to plan menus?
—Looking for ways to combine some of our recipes into delicious meals?

If you answered yes to any or all of the above, you've turned to the right section! In the following pages, you'll discover 14 days of menu planners for Levels 1 and 2 and Level 3 of the Weight Watchers food plan. All of them include recipes from this book. As a plus, each of these meals can be prepared in *less than one hour*. So when you're trying to add the spice of variety to your meals, brighten your breakfast, lunch, and dinner by selecting one of our menus.

A few points to keep in mind:

- **Bold type** indicates that the item is a recipe from this book.
- Menus are based on *one* serving of each recipe.
- Weights indicated for poultry, meat, and fish are net cooked or drained weights without skin or bones.
- Canned fish on menus is packed in water.
- The menus were designed for women. Since the daily food requirements differ slightly for men and youths, the menus should be adjusted as follows:

Levels 1 and 2:

Men and Youths: Add 1 Fat, 2 Proteins, 2 Breads, and 1 Fruit.

Youths only: Add 1 Milk.

Level 3:

Men and Youths: Add 1 Fat, 2 Proteins, 2 Breads, and 2 Fruits.

Youths only: Add 2 Milks.

Keep in mind that these menus are a bonus to ward off monotony. However, they are not meant to be combined into a full week's menu, since they weren't designed to fit weekly Program requirements.

MENU 1—LEVELS 1 AND 2

BREAKFAST
½ cup Orange Sections
1 serving **Egg in a Nest** (page 49)
¾ cup Skim Milk
Coffee or Tea

LUNCH
Crunchy Tuna Pocket (1½ ounces tuna with 2 tablespoons chopped celery, 2 teaspoons reduced-
   calorie mayonnaise, 3 tomato slices, and ¼ cup alfalfa sprouts in 1 small whole wheat pita)
6 *each* Red Bell Pepper Strips and Cucumber Spears
Coffee, Tea, or Mineral Water

DINNER
1 serving **Creamy Chicken Fettuccine** (page 129)
6 Cooked Broccoli Spears
Carrot and Mushroom Salad (½ cup *each* sliced carrot and mushrooms with red wine vinegar and
   herbs on 4 lettuce leaves)
½ cup Reduced-Calorie Chocolate Pudding topped with 1 tablespoon Whipped Topping
Coffee or Tea

SNACK
1 small Apple; 1 cup Plain Popcorn

Floater: 1 Bread
Optional Calories: 63

MENU 1—LEVEL 3

BREAKFAST
½ cup Orange Sections
1 serving **Egg in a Nest** (page 49)
¾ cup Skim Milk
Coffee or Tea

LUNCH
Crunchy Tuna-Cheese Pocket (1 ½ ounces tuna with ¾-ounce slice American cheese, 2 tablespoons
    chopped celery, 2 teaspoons reduced-calorie mayonnaise, 3 tomato slices, and ¼ cup alfalfa
    sprouts in 1 small whole wheat pita)
6 *each* Red Bell Pepper Strips and Cucumber Spears
20 small Grapes
Coffee, Tea, or Mineral Water

DINNER
1 serving **Creamy Chicken Fettuccine** (page 129)
¾ ounce Breadsticks
6 Cooked Broccoli Spears
Carrot and Mushroom Salad (½ cup *each* sliced carrot and mushrooms with 1 teaspoon olive oil plus
    red wine vinegar and herbs on 4 lettuce leaves)
½ cup Reduced-Calorie Chocolate Pudding topped with 1 tablespoon Whipped Topping
Coffee or Tea

SNACK
1 small Apple; 1 cup Plain Popcorn

Floater: 1 Bread
Optional Calories: 63

MENU 2—LEVELS 1 AND 2

BREAKFAST
1 cup Strawberries
¾ ounce Cold Cereal
1 cup Skim Milk
Coffee or Tea

LUNCH
1 serving **Tuna-Rice Salad** (page 112)
½ cup *each* Sliced Yellow Squash and Cauliflower Florets
1 medium Peach
Coffee, Tea, or Mineral Water

DINNER
3 ounces Sliced Grilled Steak with ½ cup Cooked Sliced Onion
1 serving **Corn with Chive "Cream"** (page 222)
½ cup Cooked French-Style Green Beans
1½ cups Tossed Salad with 1 tablespoon Reduced-Calorie French Dressing
Iced Tea with Lemon Slice

SNACK
2 × 3-inch wedge Watermelon; 1 serving Reduced-Calorie Vanilla-Flavored Milk Beverage

Floater: 1 Fruit
Optional Calories: 40

BREAKFAST
I cup Strawberries
¾ ounce Cold Cereal
I cup Skim Milk
Coffee or Tea

LUNCH
I serving **Tuna-Rice Salad** (page 112)
½ cup *each* Sliced Yellow Squash and Cauliflower Florets
I medium Peach
Coffee, Tea, or Mineral Water

DINNER
4 ounces Sliced Grilled Steak with ½ cup Cooked Sliced Onion
I serving **Corn with Chive "Cream"** (page 222)
½ cup Cooked French-Style Green Beans
I ½ cups Tossed Salad with I ½ teaspoons French Dressing mixed with 2 teaspoons Lemon Juice and ¼ teaspoon Mustard
½ cup Fresh Fruit Salad with Mint Sprig
Iced Tea with Lemon Slice

SNACK
2 × 3-inch wedge Watermelon; 3 Graham Crackers; I serving Reduced-Calorie Vanilla-Flavored Milk Beverage

Floater: I Fruit
Optional Calories: 30

MENU 3—LEVELS 1 AND 2

BREAKFAST
1 serving **Cranberry-Wheat Muffins** (page 41)
2 teaspoons Reduced-Calorie Apricot Spread
1 serving Reduced-Calorie Hot Cocoa

LUNCH
Turkey-Tomato Sandwich (2 ounces sliced turkey with 3 tomato slices, ½ cup shredded lettuce, and
 1 teaspoon Dijon-style mustard on 2 slices reduced-calorie wheat bread)
6 Yellow Squash Sticks and ½ cup Broccoli Florets
1 small Orange
Coffee, Tea, or Mineral Water

DINNER
1 serving **Sesame Flounder Fillets** (page 100)
Maple Carrots (½ cup cooked carrot sticks with ½ teaspoon maple syrup)
Tomato—Red Onion Salad (6 tomato wedges with ½ cup sliced red onion, red wine vinegar, and
 2 teaspoons chopped fresh basil on 2 lettuce leaves)
Coffee or Tea

SNACK
Cherry-Vanilla Yogurt (6 large cherries, pitted and sliced, mixed with ½ cup plain low-fat yogurt and
 ¼ teaspoon vanilla extract)

Floater: 1 Protein
Optional Calories: 106

MENU 3—LEVEL 3

BREAKFAST
$\frac{1}{3}$ cup Pineapple Juice
1 serving **Cranberry-Wheat Muffins** (page 41)
2 teaspoons Reduced-Calorie Apricot Spread
1 serving Reduced-Calorie Hot Cocoa

LUNCH
Turkey-Tomato Sandwich (3 ounces sliced turkey with 3 tomato slices, $\frac{1}{2}$ cup shredded lettuce, and
    1 teaspoon Dijon-style mustard on 2 slices reduced-calorie wheat bread)
6 Yellow Squash Sticks and $\frac{1}{2}$ cup Broccoli Florets
1 small Orange
Coffee, Tea, or Mineral Water

DINNER
1 serving **Sesame Flounder Fillets** (page 100)
Mushroom Rice ($\frac{1}{2}$ cup cooked rice with $\frac{1}{4}$ cup cooked sliced mushrooms)
Maple Carrots ($\frac{1}{2}$ cup cooked carrot sticks with $\frac{1}{2}$ teaspoon maple syrup)
Tomato—Red Onion Salad (6 tomato wedges with $\frac{1}{2}$ cup sliced red onion and 1 teaspoon olive oil
    plus red wine vinegar and 2 teaspoons chopped fresh basil on 2 lettuce leaves)
2-inch wedge Honeydew Melon
Coffee or Tea

SNACK
Cherry-Vanilla Yogurt (6 large cherries, pitted and sliced, mixed with $\frac{1}{2}$ cup plain low-fat yogurt and
    $\frac{1}{4}$ teaspoon vanilla extract)

Floaters: 1 Protein; 1 Fruit
Optional Calories: 106

BREAKFAST
½ medium Banana, sliced
¾ ounce Cold Cereal
½ cup Skim Milk
Coffee or Tea

LUNCH
Shrimp-Pasta Salad (1½ ounces cooked tiny shrimp with 1 cup cooked elbow macaroni, 2 tablespoons chopped celery, and 2 teaspoons reduced-calorie mayonnaise)
6 *each* Carrot Sticks and Red Bell Pepper Strips
1 cup Strawberries
Coffee, Tea, or Mineral Water

DINNER
Tomato Juice Cocktail (1 cup tomato juice with 4 ice cubes, dash hot sauce, and celery stick stirrer)
1 serving **California Burgers** (page 157)
1 cup Cooked Green Beans
1½ cups Tossed Salad with 1 tablespoon Reduced-Calorie Italian Dressing
½ cup Reduced-Calorie Vanilla Pudding
Coffee or Tea

SNACK
1 serving **Cherry-Vanilla "Ice Cream" Soda** (page 297)

Floater: 1 Bread
Optional Calories: 91

MENU 4—LEVEL 3

BREAKFAST
½ medium Banana, sliced
¾ ounce Cold Cereal
½ cup Skim Milk
Coffee or Tea

LUNCH
Shrimp-Pasta Salad (2½ ounces cooked tiny shrimp with 1 cup cooked elbow macaroni, 2 tablespoons chopped celery, and 2 teaspoons reduced-calorie mayonnaise)
6 *each* Carrot Sticks and Red Bell Pepper Strips
1 cup Strawberries
Coffee, Tea, or Mineral Water

DINNER
Tomato Juice Cocktail (1 cup tomato juice with 4 ice cubes, dash hot sauce, and celery stick stirrer)
1 serving **California Burgers** (page 157)
1 cup Cooked Green Beans
1½ cups Tossed Salad with 1½ teaspoons Italian Dressing mixed with 2 teaspoons Red Wine
  Vinegar
Peach Pudding (½ cup reduced-calorie vanilla pudding mixed with ½ cup diced peach)
Coffee or Tea

SNACK
3 Graham Crackers; 1 serving **Cherry-Vanilla "Ice Cream" Soda** (page 297)

Floater: 1 Bread
Optional Calories: 85

MENU 5—LEVELS 1 AND 2

BREAKFAST
1 cup Honeydew Melon Balls
1 serving **German Egg Cakes** (page 56)
1 cup Skim Milk
Coffee or Tea

LUNCH
Ham 'n' Swiss on Rye (1½ ounces sliced baked Virginia ham with ¾ ounce sliced reduced-fat Swiss cheese, 2 lettuce leaves, 2 green bell pepper rings, and 2 teaspoons country Dijon-style mustard on 2 slices reduced-calorie rye bread)
6 *each* Carrot and Celery Sticks
Coffee, Tea, or Mineral Water

DINNER
1 serving **Tuscan White Bean Soup** (page 181)
Garlic Toast (1½-ounce slice Italian bread with 1 teaspoon reduced-calorie margarine and dash garlic powder, toasted)
Spinach-Mushroom Salad (1 cup torn spinach leaves with ½ cup sliced mushrooms, 3 cherry tomatoes, cut into halves, and 1 teaspoon olive oil plus balsamic vinegar and herbs)
"Jelly"-Topped Pear (1 canned pear half topped with 1 teaspoon reduced-calorie grape spread)
Coffee or Tea

SNACK
Apple-Yogurt Crunch (½ cup plain low-fat yogurt mixed with ¼ cup applesauce, 1 teaspoon wheat germ, and dash cinnamon)

Floaters: 1 Protein; ¼ Bread
Optional Calories: 73

MENU 5—LEVEL 3

BREAKFAST
1 cup Honeydew Melon Balls
1 serving **German Egg Cakes** (page 56)
1 cup Skim Milk
Coffee or Tea

LUNCH
Ham 'n' Swiss on Rye (2½ ounces sliced baked Virginia ham with ¾ ounce sliced reduced-fat Swiss
  cheese, 2 lettuce leaves, 2 green bell pepper rings, and 2 teaspoons country Dijon-style mustard on
  2 slices reduced-calorie rye bread)
6 *each* Carrot and Celery Sticks
Coffee, Tea, or Mineral Water

DINNER
1 serving **Tuscan White Bean Soup** (page 181)
Garlic Toast (1½-ounce slice Italian bread with 1 teaspoon reduced-calorie margarine and dash garlic
  powder, toasted)
Spinach-Mushroom Salad (1 cup torn spinach leaves with ½ cup sliced mushrooms, 3 cherry toma-
  toes, cut into halves, and 2 teaspoons olive oil plus balsamic vinegar and herbs)
"Jelly"-Topped Pear (2 canned pear halves topped with 2 teaspoons reduced-calorie grape spread)
Coffee or Tea

SNACK
Apple-Yogurt Crunch (½ cup plain low-fat yogurt mixed with ½ cup applesauce, 1 teaspoon wheat
  germ, and dash cinnamon); 2 cups Plain Popcorn

Floaters: 1 Protein; ¼ Bread
Optional Calories: 81

MENU 6—LEVELS 1 AND 2

BREAKFAST
½ cup Grapefruit Sections
1 Scrambled Egg
1 slice Reduced-Calorie Wheat Bread, toasted
2 teaspoons Reduced-Calorie Raspberry Spread
1 cup Skim Milk
Coffee or Tea

LUNCH
Tuna Salad Pita (1 ounce tuna with 1 tablespoon chopped celery, 1 teaspoon reduced-calorie mayonnaise, 3 tomato slices, and 2 red onion slices in 1 small pita)
½ cup Cauliflower Florets and 6 Zucchini Sticks
1 small Nectarine
Coffee, Tea, or Mineral Water

DINNER
1 serving **Braised Cornish Hen** (page 136)
1 serving **Rice-Vermicelli Pilaf** (page 255)
6 Cooked Asparagus Spears topped with Grated Lemon Peel
1½ cups Tossed Salad with 1 tablespoon Reduced-Calorie French Dressing
Rosé Wine Spritzer (¼ cup *each* rosé wine and club soda)

SNACK
1 serving Reduced-Calorie Chocolate-Flavored Milk Beverage

Floater: 1 Protein
Optional Calories: 126

MENU 6—LEVEL 3

BREAKFAST
½ cup Grapefruit Sections
1 Scrambled Egg
1 slice Reduced-Calorie Wheat Bread, toasted
2 teaspoons Reduced-Calorie Raspberry Spread
1 cup Skim Milk
Coffee or Tea

LUNCH
Tuna Salad Pita (2 ounces tuna with 1 tablespoon chopped celery, 1 teaspoon reduced-calorie mayonnaise, 3 tomato slices, and 2 red onion slices in 1 large pita)
½ cup Cauliflower Florets and 6 Zucchini Sticks
1 small Nectarine
Coffee, Tea, or Mineral Water

DINNER
1 serving **Braised Cornish Hen** (page 136)
1 serving **Rice-Vermicelli Pilaf** (page 255)
6 Cooked Asparagus Spears topped with Grated Lemon Peel
1½ cups Tossed Salad with 1½ teaspoons French Dressing mixed with 2 teaspoons Lemon Juice and ¼ teaspoon Mustard
Rosé Wine Spritzer (¼ cup *each* rosé wine and club soda)

SNACK
½ medium Banana; 1 serving Reduced-Calorie Chocolate-Flavored Milk Beverage

Floater: 1 Protein
Optional Calories: 116

BREAKFAST
1 cup Cantaloupe Chunks
½ cup Cooked Oatmeal sprinkled with dash Cinnamon
1 cup Skim Milk
Coffee or Tea

LUNCH
Turkey Sandwich (2 ounces sliced turkey with 2 lettuce leaves, ¼ cup alfalfa sprouts, and 1½ teaspoons reduced-calorie Thousand Island dressing on 2 slices reduced-calorie rye bread)
½ cup Broccoli Florets and 6 Red Bell Pepper Strips
Coffee, Tea, or Mineral Water

DINNER
1 serving **Pork Chops in Wine Sauce** (page 168)
½ cup Cooked Sliced Yellow Squash
Spinach Salad (1 cup torn spinach leaves with 4 tomato wedges, 2 tablespoons shredded carrot, and
1 tablespoon reduced-calorie Italian dressing)
Coffee or Tea

SNACK
Tropical Yogurt Treat (½ cup plain low-fat yogurt mixed with ½ cup canned crushed pineapple and
topped with 1 teaspoon shredded coconut); 1 serving **Garlic Bagel Chips** (page 294)

Floater: 1 Protein
Optional Calories: 56

MENU 7—LEVEL 3

BREAKFAST
1 cup Cantaloupe Chunks
1 cup Cooked Oatmeal sprinkled with dash Cinnamon
1 cup Skim Milk
Coffee or Tea

LUNCH
Turkey Sandwich (3 ounces sliced turkey with 2 lettuce leaves, ¼ cup alfalfa sprouts, and 1½ tea-
    spoons Thousand Island dressing on 2 slices reduced-calorie rye bread)
½ cup Broccoli Florets and 6 Red Bell Pepper Strips
1 small Pear
Coffee, Tea, or Mineral Water

DINNER
1 serving **Pork Chops in Wine Sauce** (page 168)
½ cup Cooked Sliced Yellow Squash
Spinach Salad (1 cup torn spinach leaves with 4 tomato wedges, 2 tablespoons shredded carrot, and
    1 tablespoon reduced-calorie Italian dressing)
Coffee or Tea

SNACK
Tropical Yogurt Treat (½ cup plain low-fat yogurt mixed with ½ cup canned crushed pineapple and
    topped with 1 teaspoon shredded coconut); 1 serving **Garlic Bagel Chips** (page 294)

Floater: 1 Protein
Optional Calories: 41

MENU 8—LEVELS 1 AND 2

BREAKFAST
½ medium Grapefruit sprinkled with ½ teaspoon Sugar
¾ ounce Reduced-Fat Swiss Cheese
½ English Muffin, toasted
1 teaspoon Reduced-Calorie Margarine
¾ cup Skim Milk
Coffee or Tea

LUNCH
Russian Roast Beef Sandwich (1 ounce sliced roast beef with ½ cup shredded lettuce and 1½ teaspoons Russian dressing on 2 slices reduced-calorie wheat bread)
6 Cucumber Spears and 3 Cherry Tomatoes
Coffee, Tea, or Mineral Water

DINNER
1 serving **Salmon with Creamy Horseradish Sauce** (page 104)
Yogurt-Chive Potato (3-ounce baked potato, split and topped with ½ cup plain low-fat yogurt mixed with 2 teaspoons chopped chives)
½ cup Cooked Sliced Carrots
Mushroom–Red Cabbage Salad (½ cup sliced mushrooms with ¼ cup shredded red cabbage and ½ teaspoon olive oil plus red wine vinegar and herbs)
Coffee or Tea

SNACK
1 serving **Piña Colada Ice** (page 289)

Floater: 1 Protein
Optional Calories: 145

MENU 8—LEVEL 3

BREAKFAST
½ medium Grapefruit sprinkled with ½ teaspoon Sugar
¾ ounce Reduced-Fat Swiss Cheese
1 English Muffin, split in half and toasted
2 teaspoons Reduced-Calorie Margarine
¾ cup Skim Milk
Coffee or Tea

LUNCH
Russian Roast Beef Sandwich (2 ounces sliced roast beef with ½ cup shredded lettuce and 1½ teaspoons Russian dressing on 2 slices reduced-calorie wheat bread)
6 Cucumber Spears and 3 Cherry Tomatoes
1 small Apple
Coffee, Tea, or Mineral Water

DINNER
1 serving **Salmon with Creamy Horseradish Sauce** (page 104)
Yogurt-Chive Potato (3-ounce baked potato, split and topped with ½ cup plain low-fat yogurt mixed
   with 2 teaspoons chopped chives)
½ cup Cooked Sliced Carrots
Mushroom—Red Cabbage Salad (½ cup sliced mushrooms with ¼ cup shredded red cabbage and
   1 teaspoon olive oil plus red wine vinegar and herbs)
Coffee or Tea

SNACK
1 serving **Piña Colada Ice** (page 289)

Floater: 1 Protein
Optional Calories: 145

MENU 9—LEVELS 1 AND 2

BREAKFAST
½ cup Orange Juice
1 Poached Egg on 1 slice Rye Bread, toasted
½ cup Skim Milk
Coffee or Tea

LUNCH
Ham Sandwich (1 ounce sliced boiled ham with 2 lettuce leaves, 3 tomato slices, and 2 teaspoons country Dijon-style mustard on 2 slices reduced-calorie wheat bread)
6 *each* Carrot and Celery Sticks
2 small Plums
Coffee, Tea, or Mineral Water

DINNER
1 serving **Puree of Green Bean Soup** (page 30)
1 serving **Chicken Burgers** (page 120)
Tomato-Cauliflower Salad (6 tomato slices with ½ cup cauliflower florets, 1 radish rose, and ½ teaspoon olive oil plus red wine vinegar and herbs on 1 cup torn lettuce leaves)
Coffee or Tea

SNACK
3 medium Apricots; 1 cup Skim Milk

Floaters: 1 Bread; 1 Fruit
Optional Calories: 35

MENU 9—LEVEL 3

BREAKFAST
½ cup Orange Juice
1 Poached Egg on 1 slice Rye Bread, toasted
½ cup Skim Milk
Coffee or Tea

LUNCH
Ham Sandwich (1 ounce sliced boiled ham with 2 lettuce leaves, 3 tomato slices, and 2 teaspoons
    country Dijon-style mustard on 2 slices reduced-calorie wheat bread)
6 *each* Carrot and Celery Sticks
2 small Plums
Coffee, Tea, or Mineral Water

DINNER
1 serving **Puree of Green Bean Soup** (page 30)
1 serving **Chicken Burgers** (page 120)
Tomato-Cauliflower Salad (6 tomato slices with 2 ounces rinsed drained canned chick-peas, ½ cup
    cauliflower florets, 1 radish rose, and 1½ teaspoons olive oil plus red wine vinegar and herbs on 1
    cup torn lettuce leaves)
½ cup Warm Applesauce with dash Cinnamon
Coffee or Tea

SNACK
3 medium Apricots; 3 Graham Crackers; 1 cup Skim Milk

Floaters: 1 Bread; 1 Fruit
Optional Calories: 35

MENU 10—LEVELS 1 AND 2

BRUNCH

Mock Mimosa (½ cup orange juice with ¼ cup club soda and a mint sprig)
1 serving **Basil-Vegetable Quiche** (page 53)
3 ounces Cooked Small Red Potatoes
1 teaspoon Reduced-Calorie Margarine
Artichoke Salad Vinaigrette (½ cup chilled cooked artichoke hearts with 3 cherry tomatoes, cut into halves, ¼ cup sliced mushrooms, ½ teaspoon olive oil plus balsamic vinegar and herbs on 4 lettuce leaves)
Cappuccino (½ cup *each* hot espresso and hot skim milk with 1 tablespoon whipped topping and dash cinnamon)

DINNER

1 serving **Italian Chick-Pea Soup** (page 182)
1-ounce slice Italian Bread
1 teaspoon Reduced-Calorie Margarine
1½ cups Tossed Salad with 1 tablespoon Reduced-Calorie Italian Dressing
1 cup Strawberries, sliced and topped with ½ cup Plain Low-Fat Yogurt
Coffee or Tea

SNACK

1 medium Peach; 3 Graham Crackers; ½ cup Skim Milk

Floater: 1 Fruit
Optional Calories: 54

MENU 10—LEVEL 3

BRUNCH

Mock Mimosa (½ cup orange juice with ¼ cup club soda and a mint sprig)
1 serving **Basil-Vegetable Quiche** (page 53)
3 ounces Cooked Small Red Potatoes
1 teaspoon Reduced-Calorie Margarine
Artichoke Salad Vinaigrette (½ cup chilled cooked artichoke hearts with 3 cherry tomatoes, cut into halves, ¼ cup sliced mushrooms, ½ teaspoon olive oil plus balsamic vinegar and herbs on 4 lettuce leaves)
2-inch wedge Honeydew
Cappuccino (½ cup *each* hot espresso and hot skim milk with 1 tablespoon whipped topping and dash cinnamon)

DINNER

1 serving **Italian Chick-Pea Soup** (page 182)
2-ounce slice Italian Bread
1 teaspoon Reduced-Calorie Margarine
1½ cups Tossed Salad with ¾ ounce Diced Mozzarella Cheese and 1½ teaspoons Italian Dressing mixed with 2 teaspoons Red Wine Vinegar
1 cup Strawberries, sliced and topped with ½ cup Plain Low-Fat Yogurt
Coffee or Tea

SNACK

1 medium Peach; 3 Graham Crackers; ½ cup Skim Milk

Floater: 1 Fruit
Optional Calories: 48

MENU 11—LEVELS 1 AND 2

BREAKFAST
Cinnamon-Raisin Oatmeal (½ cup cooked oatmeal with 1 tablespoon dark raisins and dash cinnamon)
1 cup Skim Milk
Coffee or Tea

LUNCH
1 cup Tomato Juice
Tuna Salad Sandwich (2 ounces tuna with 1 tablespoon chopped celery, 1 teaspoon reduced-calorie mayonnaise, 3 tomato slices, and 2 lettuce leaves on 2 slices reduced-calorie rye bread)
6 Red Bell Pepper Strips and ½ cup Broccoli Florets
Coffee, Tea, or Mineral Water

DINNER
1 serving **Orange Veal Marsala** (page 171)
½ cup Cooked Fettuccine Noodles sprinkled with 1 teaspoon Grated Parmesan Cheese
1 serving **Spring Peas and Carrots** (page 244)
Cucumber-Sprout Salad (½ cup cucumber slices with ¼ cup alfalfa sprouts and red wine vinegar and herbs on 1 cup shredded lettuce)
Coffee or Tea

SNACK
½ cup Reduced-Calorie Chocolate Pudding

Floater: 1 Protein
Optional Calories: 55

MENU 11—LEVEL 3

BREAKFAST
Cinnamon-Raisin Oatmeal (½ cup cooked oatmeal with 1 tablespoon dark raisins and dash cinnamon)
1 cup Skim Milk
Coffee or Tea

LUNCH
1 cup Tomato Juice
Tuna Salad Sandwich (3 ounces tuna with 1 tablespoon *each* chopped celery and reduced-calorie mayonnaise, 3 tomato slices, and 2 lettuce leaves on 2 slices reduced-calorie rye bread)
6 Red Bell Pepper Strips and ½ cup Broccoli Florets
20 small Grapes
Coffee, Tea, or Mineral Water

DINNER
1 serving **Orange Veal Marsala** (page 171)
1 cup Cooked Fettuccine Noodles sprinkled with 1 teaspoon Grated Parmesan Cheese
1 serving **Spring Peas and Carrots** (page 244)
Cucumber-Sprout Salad (½ cup cucumber slices with ¼ cup alfalfa sprouts and red wine vinegar and herbs on 1 cup shredded lettuce)
Coffee or Tea

SNACK
½ cup Reduced-Calorie Chocolate Pudding

Floater: 1 Protein
Optional Calories: 55

MENU 12—LEVELS 1 AND 2

BREAKFAST
½ cup Blueberries
¾ ounce Cold Cereal
¾ cup Skim Milk
Coffee or Tea

LUNCH
Egg Salad in a Pita (1 hard-cooked egg, chopped, with 2 tablespoons chopped celery, 2 teaspoons reduced-calorie mayonnaise, ½ teaspoon Dijon-style mustard, 3 tomato slices, and ½ cup shredded lettuce in 1 small whole wheat pita)
6 Carrot Sticks and ½ cup Cauliflower Florets
Coffee, Tea, or Mineral Water

DINNER
1 serving **Chicken-in-the-Rye** (page 123)
Mushroom Rice (½ cup cooked rice with ¼ cup cooked sliced mushrooms)
6 Cooked Broccoli Spears
Chick-Pea and Tomato Toss (1 cup torn lettuce with 1 ounce rinsed drained canned chick-peas, 4 tomato wedges, ¼ cup shredded carrot, and 1 tablespoon reduced-calorie Thousand Island dressing)
1 serving **Peaches and Kiwi in Champagne** (page 292)
Coffee or Tea

SNACK
1 cup Cantaloupe Chunks; 1 serving Reduced-Calorie Vanilla-Flavored Milk Beverage

Floaters: 1½ Fruits
Optional Calories: 100

MENU 12—LEVEL 3

BREAKFAST
½ cup Blueberries
¾ ounce Cold Cereal
½ cup Skim Milk
Coffee or Tea

LUNCH
Egg Salad in a Pita (1 hard-cooked egg, chopped, with 2 tablespoons chopped celery, 2 teaspoons
   reduced-calorie mayonnaise, ½ teaspoon Dijon-style mustard, 3 tomato slices, and ½ cup shredded
   lettuce in 1 small whole wheat pita)
6 Carrot Sticks and ½ cup Cauliflower Florets
12 large Cherries
Coffee, Tea, or Mineral Water

DINNER
1 serving **Chicken-in-the-Rye** (page 123)
Mushroom Rice (1 cup cooked rice with ¼ cup cooked sliced mushrooms)
Broccoli Melt (6 cooked broccoli spears topped with ¾ ounce reduced-fat Swiss cheese, melted)
Chick-Pea and Tomato Toss (1 cup torn lettuce with 1 ounce rinsed drained canned chick-peas,
   4 tomato wedges, ¼ cup shredded carrot, and 1½ teaspoons Thousand Island dressing mixed with
   2 tablespoons plain low-fat yogurt and dash garlic powder)
1 serving **Peaches and Kiwi in Champagne** (page 292)
Coffee or Tea

SNACK
1 cup Cantaloupe Chunks; 1 serving Reduced-Calorie Vanilla-Flavored Milk Beverage

Floaters: 1½ Fruits
Optional Calories: 70

MENU 13—LEVELS 1 AND 2

BREAKFAST
½ medium Banana, sliced
½ cup Cooked Cream of Wheat
1 cup Skim Milk
Coffee or Tea

LUNCH
Turkey and Swiss Cheese Sandwich (1 ounce sliced turkey with ¾ ounce sliced reduced-fat Swiss
  cheese, 2 lettuce leaves, and 2 teaspoons reduced-calorie mayonnaise on 2 slices pumpernickel
  bread)
6 *each* Celery Sticks and Cucumber Spears
Coffee, Tea, or Mineral Water

DINNER
1 serving **Fillets with Peppers and Tomatoes** (page 98)
1 serving **Parmesan Braised Citrus Fennel** (page 214)
1½ cups Tossed Salad with 1 tablespoon Reduced-Calorie French Dressing
Coffee or Tea

SNACK
½ cup Orange Sections; 1 serving Reduced-Calorie Hot Cocoa

Floater: 1 Protein
Optional Calories: 85

MENU 13—LEVEL 3

BREAKFAST
½ medium Banana, sliced
½ cup Cooked Cream of Wheat
1 cup Skim Milk
Coffee or Tea

LUNCH
Turkey and Swiss Cheese Sandwich (2 ounces sliced turkey with ¾ ounce sliced reduced-fat Swiss cheese, 2 lettuce leaves, and 2 teaspoons reduced-calorie mayonnaise on 2 slices pumpernickel bread)
6 *each* Celery Sticks and Cucumber Spears
Coffee, Tea, or Mineral Water

DINNER
1 serving **Fillets with Peppers and Tomatoes** (page 98)
3-ounce Baked Potato, split and topped with 1 teaspoon Margarine
1 serving **Parmesan Braised Citrus Fennel** (page 214)
1½ cups Tossed Salad with 1 tablespoon Reduced-Calorie French Dressing
2 slices Canned Pineapple
Coffee or Tea

SNACK
½ cup Orange Sections; 1 serving Reduced-Calorie Hot Cocoa

Floater: 1 Protein
Optional Calories: 85

MENU 14—LEVELS 1 AND 2

BREAKFAST
½ cup Grapefruit Juice
Pepper and "Egg" Scramble (¼ cup egg substitute scrambled with 2 tablespoons chopped green bell pepper)
½ English Muffin, toasted
1 teaspoon Reduced-Calorie Margarine
1 cup Skim Milk
Coffee or Tea

LUNCH
Tuna—Green Bean Salad (2 ounces tuna with 1 cup sliced chilled cooked green beans, 3 cherry tomatoes, cut into halves, and ½ teaspoon olive oil plus red wine vinegar and herbs)
¾ ounce Flatbreads
Coffee, Tea, or Mineral Water

DINNER
1 serving **Two-Bean Chili** (page 188)
2 Taco Shells, heated and broken into pieces
1½ cups Mixed Green Salad with 1 tablespoon Reduced-Calorie Buttermilk Dressing
1 serving **Fig and Melon Compote** (page 291)
Coffee or Tea

SNACK
½ cup Reduced-Calorie Chocolate Pudding

Floaters: 1 Protein; ¼ Fruit
Optional Calories: 60

MENU 14—LEVEL 3

BREAKFAST
½ cup Grapefruit Juice
Pepper and "Egg" Scramble (¼ cup egg substitute scrambled with 2 tablespoons chopped green bell pepper)
½ English Muffin, toasted
I teaspoon Reduced-Calorie Margarine
I cup Skim Milk
Coffee or Tea

LUNCH
Tuna—Green Bean Salad (3 ounces tuna with I cup sliced chilled cooked green beans, 3 cherry tomatoes, cut into halves, and 1½ teaspoons olive oil plus red wine vinegar and herbs)
¾ ounce Flatbreads
2 cups Plain Popcorn
Coffee, Tea, or Mineral Water

DINNER
I serving **Two-Bean Chili** (page 188)
2 Taco Shells, heated and broken into pieces
1½ cups Mixed Green Salad with I tablespoon Reduced-Calorie Buttermilk Dressing
I serving **Fig and Melon Compote** (page 291)
Coffee or Tea

SNACK
I small Pear; ½ cup Reduced-Calorie Chocolate Pudding

Floaters: I Protein; ¼ Fruit
Optional Calories: 60

Appendix

Glossary

Bake: To place food in a container and cook in an oven.

Baste: To moisten food while it cooks in order to add flavor and prevent the surface from drying out by coating with a liquid such as melted fat, a sauce, or meat drippings.

Beat: To make a mixture smooth by mixing ingredients vigorously with a spoon or electric mixer.

Blanch: To cook a food for a few minutes in boiling water to preserve the color, texture, or nutritional value or to loosen the skin from the food for easy removal.

Blend: To mix two or more ingredients thoroughly until smooth.

Boil: To cook in water or a liquid consisting mostly of water in which bubbles rise continually and break on the surface. A rolling boil is when the bubbles form rapidly.

Braise: To cook meat or poultry in a small amount of liquid in a covered container in the oven or over low heat on the range.

Broil: To cook by direct dry heat.

Brown: To cook a food usually in a small amount of fat on the range until the surface of the food changes color.

Chill: To refrigerate food or let it stand in ice or iced water until cold.

Chop: To cut into small pieces.

Combine: To mix together two or more ingredients.

Cool: To let a hot food come to room temperature.

Crimp: To press or pinch together.

Cube: To cut food into ½-inch squares.

Cut in: To distribute solid fat in flour or a flour mixture using a pastry blender until flour-coated fat particles resemble a coarse meal.

Dash: Less than ⅛ teaspoon of an ingredient.

Dice: To cut a food into small squares, less than ½ inch in size.

Dredge: To cover a food with flour or a fine crumb mixture.

Fold: To lightly combine ingredients using a rubber scraper and cutting vertically through the mixture and then sliding the spatula across the bottom of the bowl, turning mixtures over.

Fry: To cook uncovered in a small amount of fat.

Grate: To cut food into tiny particles using the small holes of a grater.

Grill: To cook over direct heat.

Julienne: To cut into slivers that resemble matchstick pieces.

Marinate: To let food stand in a mixture that will tenderize it or add flavor.

Mince: To cut or chop into very small pieces.

Mix: To combine ingredients so they are evenly distributed.

Pare: To cut off the outer covering of a food using a knife or vegetable peeler.

Peel: To remove the outer covering of a food using hands rather than a knife or vegetable peeler.

Pierce: A term applied to microwave cooking. To puncture a cover, thick skin, or membrane to allow steam to escape and prevent bursting.

Poach: To cook a food in a hot liquid.

Puree: To press food through a food mill or to process in a blender or food processor into a smooth, thick mixture.

Rearrange: A term applied to microwave cooking. To move food in its dish to another position for even cooking when the food cannot be stirred.

Reduce: To boil a liquid in an uncovered container until it evaporates, resulting in a specific consistency and flavor.

Roast: To cook meats on a rack, uncovered, in an oven.

Rotate: A term applied to microwave cooking. To turn a dish in a microwave oven one-quarter or one-half turn in order for the food to cook more evenly when it cannot be stirred.

Sauté: To brown or cook in a small amount of fat.

Shred: To cut food into long thin pieces using the large holes of a grater.

Simmer: To cook in liquid just below the boiling point.

Slice: To cut a food into thin flat pieces.

Soften: To let cold butter or margarine stand at room temperature until it has a softer consistency.

Standing time: A term applied to microwave cooking. A period of time, after microwaving, which allows foods to complete heating or cooking in the center or in the thicker areas, without overcooking on the thin areas or edges.

Steam: To cook food on a rack or in a colander in a covered pan over steaming hot water.

Stir: To use a utensil in a circular motion to combine portions of a food.

Strain: To separate solid food from liquid by pouring the mixture into a strainer or sieve.

Whip: To beat a mixture rapidly with a wire whisk or electric mixer to incorporate air and increase volume.

Pan Substitutions

It's best to use the pan size that's recommended in a recipe; however, if your kitchen isn't equipped with that particular pan, chances are a substitution will work just as well. The pan size is determined by the volume of food it holds. When substituting, use a pan as close to the recommended size as possible. Food cooked in too small a pan may boil over; food cooked in too large a pan may dry out or burn. To determine the dimensions of a baking pan, measure across the top, between the inside edges. To determine the volume, measure the amount of water the pan holds when completely filled.

When you use a pan that is a different size from the one recommended, it may be necessary to adjust the suggested cooking time. Depending on the size of the pan and the depth of the food in it, you may need to add or subtract 5 to 10 minutes. If you substitute glass or glass-ceramic for metal, the oven temperature should be reduced by 25°F.

The following chart provides some common pan substitutions.

Recommended Size	Approximate Volume	Possible Substitutions
8 × 1½-inch round baking pan	1½ quarts	10 × 6 × 2-inch baking dish 9 × 1½-inch round baking pan 8 × 4 × 2-inch loaf pan 9-inch pie plate
8 × 8 × 2-inch baking pan	2 quarts	11 × 7 × 1½-inch baking pan 12 × 7½ × 2-inch baking pan 9 × 5 × 3-inch loaf pan two 8 × 1½-inch round baking pans
13 × 9 × 2-inch baking pan	3 quarts	14 × 11 × 2-inch baking dish two 9 × 1½-inch round baking pans two 8 × 1½-inch round baking pans

Dry and Liquid Measure Equivalents

Teaspoons	Tablespoons	Cups	Fluid Ounces
3 teaspoons	1 tablespoon		½ fluid ounce
6 teaspoons	2 tablespoons	⅛ cup	1 fluid ounce
8 teaspoons	2 tablespoons plus 2 teaspoons	⅙ cup	
12 teaspoons	4 tablespoons	¼ cup	2 fluid ounces
15 teaspoons	5 tablespoons	⅓ cup less 1 teaspoon	
16 teaspoons	5 tablespoons plus 1 teaspoon	⅓ cup	
18 teaspoons	6 tablespoons	⅓ cup plus 2 teaspoons	3 fluid ounces
24 teaspoons	8 tablespoons	½ cup	4 fluid ounces
30 teaspoons	10 tablespoons	½ cup plus 2 tablespoons	5 fluid ounces
32 teaspoons	10 tablespoons plus 2 teaspoons	⅔ cup	
36 teaspoons	12 tablespoons	¾ cup	6 fluid ounces
42 teaspoons	14 tablespoons	1 cup less 2 tablespoons	7 fluid ounces
45 teaspoons	15 tablespoons	1 cup less 1 tablespoon	
48 teaspoons	16 tablespoons	1 cup	8 fluid ounces

Note: Measurement of less than ⅛ teaspoon is considered a dash or a pinch.

Metric Conversions

If you are converting the recipes in this book to metric measurements, use the following chart as a guide.

Volume

1/4 teaspoon	1 milliliter
1/2 teaspoon	2 milliliters
1 teaspoon	5 milliliters
1 tablespoon	15 milliliters
2 tablespoons	30 milliliters
3 tablespoons	45 milliliters
1/4 cup	50 milliliters
1/3 cup	75 milliliters
1/2 cup	125 milliliters
2/3 cup	150 milliliters
3/4 cup	175 milliliters
1 cup	250 milliliters
1 quart	1 liter

Weight

1 ounce	30 grams
1/4 pound	120 grams
1/2 pound	240 grams
3/4 pound	360 grams
1 pound	480 grams

Length

1 inch	25 millimeters
1 inch	2.5 centimeters

Oven Temperatures

250°F	120°C
275°F	140°C
300°F	150°C
325°F	160°C
350°F	180°C
375°F	190°C
400°F	200°C
425°F	220°C
450°F	230°C
475°F	250°C
500°F	260°C
525°F	270°C

Index

Cholesterol-Reduced Recipes Index

Index for Recipes with 30% or Less of Their Calories Coming from Fat

Sodium-Reduced Recipes Index